The Enduring Vision

The Enduring Vision

A HISTORY OF THE AMERICAN PEOPLE
Concise Second Edition

VOLUME 2: FROM 1865

Paul S. Boyer
University of Wisconsin, Madison

Clifford E. Clark, Jr.
Carleton College

Sandra McNair Hawley
San Jacinto College

Joseph F. Kett
University of Virginia

Neal Salisbury
Smith College

Harvard Sitkoff
University of New Hampshire

Nancy Woloch
Barnard College

D. C. Heath and Company
Lexington, Massachusetts   Toronto

Address editorial correspondence to:

D. C. Heath and Company
125 Spring Street
Lexington, MA 02173

Acquisitions Editor: James Miller
Developmental Editor: Sylvia Mallory
Production Editor: Jennifer Brett
Designer: Henry Rachlin
Photo Researcher: Martha Shethar
Art Editor: Gary Crespo
Production Coordinator: Chuck Dutton
Permissions Editor: Margaret Roll

Cover: *Council Grove* by E. L. Spybuck, courtesy of Elizabeth Waldo-Dentzel Collection,
   Multicultural Arts Studio, Northridge, CA.

Preface

The decision to write a concise edition of *The Enduring Vision* arose from the popularity of the full-length version and from the increasing demand for abridged editions of textbooks, which afford instructors more opportunity to assign readings beyond a text. In this concise edition we have preserved the uniquely successful features of the longer book while reducing the number of pages by about 40 percent. We extensively recast text to meet this goal, but we were careful to maintain the graceful and occasionally witty style that distinguishes the larger book.

This concise edition of *The Enduring Vision* interweaves traditional and more recent approaches to the study of history. In addition to political, diplomatic, and economic history, for example, the book examines and integrates social history, cultural history, the histories of the diverse peoples who make up our pluralistic society, and environmental history. We have maintained a balance that reflects the best of both the traditional and the new emphases in historical scholarship, a blend that will serve the modern student well. And we have taken the student to the very edge of the twenty-first century, with analysis of the end of the Cold War, the problems as well as the solutions that this momentous event has created, and the early initiatives of the Clinton administration.

We must stress that this concise version is *not The Enduring Vision Lite*. We have retained virtually all the information from the original text—all the major topics and issues. The result is a textbook suitable for any introductory United States history course at the freshman or sophomore level, whether in four-year colleges and universities or in two-year community and junior colleges.

This concise edition features a generous array of maps. Reproduced in two colors, they vividly establish the physical and spatial setting of American history, enabling the student to grasp both the immensity of the United States and of the North American continent and the complexities of Native American and European settlement of that continent. We chose photographs not only for their freshness and visual impact but also for their complementarity with the text. Clear, easily understood charts and other graphics round out the illustrations. Each chapter has an extensive chronology at the end to help the student to set events in historical context, and an extensive annotated bibliography of works for further reading or research.

A wide range of ancillaries to aid both instructor and student is available with *The Enduring Vision*, Concise Second Edition. They include the *Instructor's Guide with Test Item File*, the *Student Guide with Map Exercises*, and *ESATEST* computerized testing for Macintosh and IBM-compatible computers. The instructor may also opt to use some of the following additional supplements for the course and should contact a D. C. Heath sales representative for more information:

- *Getting the Most Out of Your U.S. History Course: The History Student's Vade Mecum*—a handy, concise student guide to getting the most out of the U.S. history survey course
- *Reading and Writing American History*, Volumes 1 and 2—a skills-based sourcebook for U.S. history students
- *The D. C. Heath U.S. History Transparency Set*, 1994 Update, Volumes 1 and 2

- *Enduring Voices Document Sets*, Volumes 1 and 2
- *Surveying the Land: Skills and Exercises in U.S. Historical Geography*, Volumes 1 and 2
- *An American Portfolio*—Videodisc for the U.S. history survey course
- *What Makes America Different?*—Videodisc featuring discussions among the authors of *The Enduring Vision*
- *Audiocassette* for the U.S. history survey course
- *The Enduring Vision*, Complete Version on CD-ROM—Integrates the full text of the Second Edition of *The Enduring Vision* with documents, images, video, animation, and various study aids

No project the magnitude of this book could reach fruition without the hard work and assistance of many individuals. I would like to thank all those who supported me and the project. In particular, my thanks go first to my mother and my daughter, who often gave up precious time together for reasons that they may not always have understood but always accepted; to James K. Semones, who showed me that it could be done; to James A. Hall, who made it possible for me to do it; and to James D. Heil, who made sure that it did get done and helped in innumerable ways. Thanks as well to Linda Whitfield, Neva Dare, and Dean A. Minix for their aid. Special thanks must also go to staff members at D. C. Heath who were unfailingly helpful: to James Miller, for shepherding the project; to Sylvia Mallory, for her brilliant editing; to Jennifer Brett, for her superb work; to Henry Rachlin, for his eye-appealing design; to Martha Shethar, for her excellent photo research; to Daphne Zervoglos, for all her support; and to D. C. Heath's outstanding sales and marketing staff.

In addition, we must thank all those who read early versions of the text and whose comments made it stronger, clearer, and more accurate. (We of course reserve to ourselves responsibility for errors that made it into print.) Those who reviewed the manuscript include William Anderson, Western Carolina University; Robert Becklund, College of Marin; Michael Bradley, Motlow State Community College; John Broesamle, California State University, Northridge; Kendrick Clements, University of South Carolina; John Coleman, Southeast Missouri State University; Thomas Deaton, Dalton College; Bruce Dierenfield, Canisius College; Stephen Gelber, Santa Clara University; George Gerdow, Northeastern Illinois University; Jon Gjerde, University of California, Berkeley; Gregory Goodwin, Bakersfield College; Albert Gunns, California State University, Long Beach; Jane Hunter, Lewis and Clark College; Judith Ishkanian, Santa Barbara City College; James Johnson, United States Military Academy; Armand La Potin, State University of New York, Oneonta; Kathy Long, Chattanooga State Technical Community College; Michael Magliari, California State University, Chico; David Moore, Golden West College; Margaret Morley, Northern Arizona University; Franklin Nickell, Southeast Missouri State University; Kenneth Noe, West Georgia College; Linda Papageorge, Kennesaw State College; Ross Peterson, Utah State University; Christopher Phillips, Emporia State University; Norman Raiford, Greenville Technical College; Richard Roberts, Weber State College; Philip Reed Rulon, Northern Arizona University; Lura Scales, Hinds Community College; Ronald Schaffer, California State University, Northridge; Gerald Schwartz, Western Carolina University; Gene Sessions, Weber State College; Frank J. Siltman, U.S. Military Academy; Barbara Tagger, Morehouse College; Michael Tate, University of Nebraska, Omaha; Stephen Ware, Louisiana Technological University; Alan Watson, University of North Carolina, Wilmington. We are most grateful to them all.

S. M. H.

Contents

19

The Transformation of Urban America

405

20

Daily Life, Popular Culture, and the Arts, 1860–1900

425

21

Politics and Expansion in an Industrializing Age

445

The Progressive Era

469

23

World War I

495

The 1920s

517

25

Crash, Depression, and
New Deal

539

26

American Life in a Decade of Crisis at Home and Abroad

561

27

Waging Global War, 1939–1945

581

28

Cold War America,
1945–1952

607

31

A Troubled Journey:
From Port Huron to Watergate

673

32

Turning Inward: Society and Politics from Ford to Reagan

697

33

The Cold War Ends

717

Maps

Charts, Graphs, and Tables

The Enduring Vision
Volume 2: From 1865

The Crises of Reconstruction, 1865—1877

When the Civil War ended, parts of the South resembled a wasteland. The landscape "looked for many miles like a broad black streak of ruin and desolation," wrote a Union general. Homes, crops, and railroads had been destroyed; farming and business had come to a standstill. Refugees, demobilized soldiers, and former slaves flooded the roads. The prevailing mood was as grim as the landscape. "The South lies prostrate—their foot is on us—there is no help," a Virginia woman lamented. That 200,000 Union troops occupied the former Confederacy contributed to the sense of despair.

After most wars, victors care little for the mood of the vanquished, but the Civil War was different. The Union had sought not merely victory but the return of national unity. The federal government faced unprecedented questions. How could the Union be restored and the South reintegrated? Who would control the process, Congress or the president? Should Confederate leaders be tried for treason? Most important, what would happen to the 3.5 million former slaves? The

(Right) Richmond in ruins, 1865

Reconstruction Politics
Reconstruction Governments
The Impact of Emancipation
New Concerns in the North
Reconstruction Abandoned

freedmen's future was *the* crucial postwar issue, for emancipation had set in motion the most profound upheaval in the nation's history. Slavery had been both a labor system and a means of racial control; it had determined the South's social, economic, and political structure. The end of the Civil War, in short, posed two huge challenges that had to be addressed simultaneously: readmitting the Confederate states to the Union and defining the status of free blacks in society.

From 1865 to 1877, the drama of Reconstruction—the restoration of the former Confederate states to the Union—unfolded in several theaters. In Washington, conflict between president and Congress led to stringent measures. In the South, Republicans temporarily took power, and far-reaching social and economic changes transformed the former Confederacy. Freed slaves wrestled with new identities and new problems. Meanwhile, the North hurtled headlong into an era of industrial expansion, labor unrest, and financial crises. By the mid-1870s, however, northern Republicans abandoned Reconstruction, and southern Democrats regained control of their states. Reconstruction collapsed in 1877, and the nature and causes of its failure have engaged historians ever since.

Reconstruction Politics

The end of the Civil War offered multiple possibilities for chaos and vengeance. The federal government could have imprisoned Confederate leaders; former rebel troops could have become guerrillas; slaves could have waged a racial war against their former masters. None of this happened. Instead, intense *political* conflict dominated the immediate postwar period. The political upheaval, sometimes attended by violence, produced new constitutional amendments, an impeachment crisis, and some of the most ambitious domestic legislation ever enacted by Congress, the Reconstruction Acts of 1867–1868. It culminated in something that few expected, the enfranchisement of black men.

In 1865 only a handful of Radical Republicans advocated black suffrage. Any plan to restore the

Union, Senator Thaddeus Stevens of Pennsylvania proclaimed, must "revolutionize Southern institutions, habits, and manners . ... or all our blood and treasure have been spent in vain." In the complex political battles of Reconstruction, the Radicals won broad support for their program, including black male enfranchisement. Just as the Civil War had led to emancipation, so Reconstruction led to black suffrage.

Lincoln's Plan

Conflict over Reconstruction began even before the war ended. In December 1863 President Lincoln issued the Proclamation of Amnesty and Reconstruction, which allowed southern states to form new governments if at least 10 percent of those who had voted in the 1860 elections swore an oath of allegiance to the Union and accepted emancipation. This plan excluded most Confederate officials and military officers, who would have had to apply for presidential pardons, as well as blacks, who had not voted in 1860. Lincoln hoped both to undermine the Confederacy and to build a southern Republican party.

Radical Republicans in Congress wanted a slower readmission process that would exclude even more ex-Confederates from political life. The Wade-Davis bill, passed by Congress in July 1864, provided that a military government would rule each former Confederate state and that at least half of the eligible voters would have to swear allegiance before they could choose a convention to repeal secession and abolish slavery. In addition, to qualify as a voter or a delegate, a southerner would have to take the "ironclad" oath, swearing that he had never voluntarily supported the Confederacy. The Wade-Davis bill would have delayed readmission of southern states almost indefinitely.

Lincoln pocket-vetoed* the Wade-Davis bill, and an impasse followed. Arkansas, Louisiana,

---

*Pocket-vetoed: failed to sign the bill within ten days of Congress's adjournment.

Tennessee, and parts of Virginia moved toward readmission under variants of Lincoln's plan, but Congress refused to seat their delegates. Lincoln hinted that he might be moving toward a more rigorous policy than his original one, a program that would include black suffrage. But his death foreclosed the possibility that he and Congress might draw closer to agreement, and Radicals now looked with hope to the new president, Andrew Johnson.

Presidential Reconstruction Under Johnson

At first glance, Andrew Johnson seemed a likely ally for the Radicals. The only southern senator to remain in Congress when his state seceded, Johnson had taken a strong anti-Confederate stance and had served as military governor of Tennessee for two years. Self-educated, an ardent Jacksonian, a foe of the planter class, a supporter of emancipation—Johnson carried impeccable credentials. However, as a lifelong Democrat, he had his own political agenda, sharply different from that of the Radicals.

In May 1865, with Congress out of session, Johnson shocked Republicans by announcing his own program to bring the southern states still without reconstruction governments back into the Union. Virtually all southerners who took an oath of allegiance would receive pardon and amnesty, and all their property except slaves would be restored to them. Confederate civil and military officers would still be disqualified, as would well-to-do former Confederates (anyone owning taxable property worth $20,000 or more). By purging the plantation aristocracy, Johnson claimed, he would aid "humble men, the peasantry and yeomen of the South, who have been decoyed . . . into rebellion." Oath takers could elect delegates to state conventions, which would call regular elections, proclaim secession illegal, repudiate debts incurred under the Confederacy, and ratify the Thirteenth Amendment, which abolished slavery.

This presidential Reconstruction took effect in the summer of 1865, with unforeseen results. Johnson handed out pardons liberally (some 13,000 of them) and dropped his plans for the punishment of treason. By the end of 1865, all seven states had created new civil governments that in effect restored the *status quo ante bellum*. Confederate officers and large planters resumed state offices, and former Confederate congressmen and generals won election to Congress. Because many of these new representatives were former Whigs who had not supported secession, southerners believed that they genuinely had elected "Union" men. Some states refused to repudiate their Confederate debts or to ratify the Thirteenth Amendment.

Most infuriating to the Radicals, every state passed a "black code" intended to ensure a landless, dependent black labor force—to "secure the services of the negroes, teach them their place," in the words of one Alabamian. These codes, which replaced earlier slave codes, guaranteed the freedmen some basic rights—marriage, ownership of property, the right to testify in court against other blacks—but also harshly restricted freedmen's behavior. Some states established segregation, and most prohibited racial intermarriage, jury service by blacks, and court testimony by blacks against whites. Most harmful, black codes included economic restrictions to prevent blacks from leaving the plantation, usually by establishing a system of labor contracts and then stipulating that anyone who had not signed a labor contract was a vagrant and thus subject to arrest.

These codes left freedmen no longer slaves but not really liberated. Although many of their provisions never actually took effect—for example, the Union army and the Freedmen's Bureau suspended the enforcement of the racially discriminatory laws—the black codes reflected white southern attitudes and showed what "home rule" would have been like without federal intervention.

When former abolitionists and Radical Republicans decried the black codes, Johnson defended them and his restoration program. Former Confederates should not become "a degraded and debased people," he said. To many northerners, both the black codes and the election of former Confederates to high office reeked of southern defiance. "What can be hatched from such an egg but another rebellion?" asked a Boston newspaper. When the

King Andrew

This Thomas Nast cartoon, published just before the 1866 congressional elections, conveyed Republican antipathy to Andrew Johnson. The president is depicted as an autocratic tyrant. Radical Republican Thaddeus Stevens, upper right, has his head on the block and is about to lose it. The Republic sits in chains.

Thirty-ninth Congress convened in December 1865, it refused to seat the southern delegates and prepared to dismantle the black codes and to lock ex-Confederates out of power.

Congress Versus Johnson

Southern blacks' status became the major issue in Congress. With Congress split into four blocs—Democrats, and radical, moderate, and conservative Republicans—a politically adroit president could have protected his program. Ineptly, Johnson alienated the moderates and pushed them into the Radicals' arms by vetoing some key moderate measures.

In late 1865 Congress voted to extend the life of the Freedmen's Bureau for three more years. Staffed mainly by army officers, the bureau provided relief, rations, and medical care; built schools for the former slaves; put them to work on abandoned or confiscated lands; and tried to protect their rights as laborers. To strengthen the bureau, Congress had voted to allow it to run special military courts that would settle labor disputes and invalidate labor contracts forced on blacks under the black codes. In February 1866 Johnson vetoed the bill; the Constitution, he declared, neither sanctioned military trials of civilians in peacetime nor supported a system to care for "indigent persons." Then in March 1866 Congress passed the Civil Rights Act of 1866, which made blacks U.S. citizens with the same civil rights as other citizens and authorized federal intervention to ensure blacks' rights in court. Johnson vetoed this measure also, arguing that it would "operate in favor of the colored and against the white race." In April Congress overrode his veto, and in July it enacted the Supplementary Freedmen's Bureau Act over another presidential veto.

These vetoes puzzled many Republicans, for the new laws did not undercut the basic structure of presidential Reconstruction. Although the vetoes gained support for Johnson among northern Democrats, they cost him dearly among moderate Republicans, who began to ally with the Radicals. Was Johnson a political incompetent, or was he merely trying, unsuccessfully, to forge a centrist coalition? Whatever the case, he drove moderate and Radical Republicans together toward their next step: the passage of a constitutional amendment to protect the new Civil Rights Act.

The Fourteenth Amendment

In April 1866 Congress adopted the Fourteenth Amendment, its most ambitious attempt to deal with the problems of Reconstruction and the freed slaves. In its first clause, the amendment proclaimed that all persons born or naturalized in the United States were citizens and that no state could abridge their rights without due process of law or deny them equal protection under the law. Second, the amendment guaranteed that if a state denied suffrage to any male citizen, its representation in Congress would be proportionally reduced. Third, it disqualified from state and national offices *all* prewar officeholders who had supported the Confederacy. Finally, it repudiated the Confederate debt and maintained the validity of the federal debt. In effect, the Fourteenth Amendment nullified the *Dred Scott* decision, threatened southern states that deprived black men of the right to vote, and invalidated most of the pardons that President Johnson had ladled out. Beyond demonstrating widespread receptivity to the Radicals' demands, including black male suffrage, the Fourteenth Amendment represented the first national effort to limit the states' control of civil and political rights.

Passage of the amendment created a firestorm. Abolitionists said that it did not go far enough to protect black voting rights, southerners blasted it as vengeful, and President Johnson denounced it. The president's unwillingness to compromise solidified the new alliance between moderate and Radical Republicans and transformed the congressional elections of 1866 into a referendum on the Fourteenth Amendment.

Over the summer Johnson set off on a whistle-stop train tour campaigning against the amendment. Humorless and defensive, the president made fresh enemies, however, and his hope collapsed of creating a new political party, the National Union party, opposed to the amendment. Meanwhile, the moderate and Radical Republicans defended the amendment, condemned President Johnson, and branded the Democratic party "a common sewer . . . into which is emptied every element of treason, North and South."

Republicans carried the congressional elections of 1866 in a landslide, winning nearly two-thirds of the House and three-fourths of the Senate. They had secured a mandate for the Fourteenth Amendment and their own Reconstruction program.

Congressional Reconstruction

The congressional debate over reconstructing the South began in December 1866 and lasted three months. Radical leaders, anxious to stifle a resurgence of Confederate power, called for black suffrage, federal support for public schools, the confiscation of Confederate estates, and an extended military occupation of the South. Moderate Republicans accepted part of this plan. The lawmakers debated every ramification of various legislative proposals, and in February 1867, after complex political maneuvers, Congress passed the Reconstruction Act of 1867. Johnson vetoed it, and on March 2 Congress passed the law over the veto. Three more Reconstruction acts, passed in 1867 and 1868 over presidential vetoes, refined and enforced the first act.

The Reconstruction Act of 1867 invalidated the state governments formed under the Lincoln and Johnson plans; only Tennessee, which already had ratified the Fourteenth Amendment and had been readmitted to the Union, escaped further Reconstruction. The new law divided the other ten former Confederate states into five military districts. It provided that voters—all black men, plus whites not disqualified by the Fourteenth Amendment—could elect delegates who would write a new state constitution granting black suffrage. After congressional approval of the state constitution, and after the state legislature's ratification of the Fourteenth Amendment, Congress would readmit the state into the Union. The enfranchisement of blacks and disfranchisement of so many ex-Confederates made the Reconstruction Act of 1867 far more radical than Johnson's program. Even then, however, it provided only temporary military rule, made no provisions to prosecute Confederate leaders for treason, and neither confiscated nor redistributed property.

Radical Republican leader Thaddeus Stevens had proposed confiscation of large Confederate estates to "humble the proud traitors" and to provide land for the former slaves. He hoped to create a new class of self-sufficient black yeomen farmers. Because political independence rested on economic independence, he contended, land grants would be

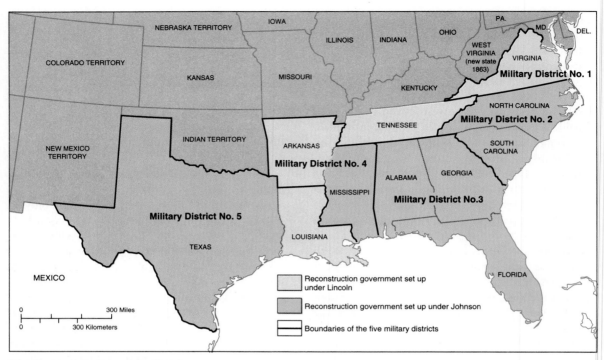

The Reconstruction of the South
*The Reconstruction Act of 1867 divided the former Confederate states, except Tennessee,
into five military districts and set forth the steps by which new state governments could
be created.*

far more valuable to African-Americans than the
vote. But moderate Republicans and others backed
away from Stevens's proposal. Tampering with
property rights in the South might well jeopardize
them in the North, they argued, and could endanger
the entire Reconstruction program. Thus Congress
rejected the most radical parts of the Radical Republican program.

Congressional Reconstruction took effect in
the spring of 1867, but Johnson impeded its implementation by replacing pro-Radical military officers
with conservative ones, since it could not be enforced without military power. Furious and more
suspicious than ever of the president, congressional
moderates and Radicals again joined forces to block
Johnson from further hampering Reconstruction.

The Impeachment Crisis

In March 1867, responding to Johnson's obstruc-
tionist tactics, Republicans in Congress passed two
laws to restrict presidential power. The Tenure of
Office Act prohibited the president from removing
civil officers without Senate consent. Its purpose
was to protect Secretary of War Stanton, a Radical
ally needed to enforce the Reconstruction acts. The
other law banned the president from issuing military
orders except through the commanding general,
Ulysses S. Grant, who could not be removed without the Senate's consent. Not satisfied with clipping
the president's wings, Radicals also began to look
for grounds for impeachment and conviction, to
remove all possible obstacles to Reconstruction.

Intense investigations by the House Judiciary Committee and private detectives turned up no impeachable offenses, but Johnson himself soon provided the charges that his opponents needed.

In August 1867 Johnson fired Stanton. The president's defiance of the Tenure of Office Act drove moderate Republicans back into alliance with the Radicals. The House approved eleven charges of impeachment, nine of them based on violation of the Tenure of Office Act and the others accusing Johnson of being "unmindful of the high duties of the office," of seeking to disgrace Congress, and of not enforcing the Reconstruction acts.

Johnson's trial by the Senate, which began in March 1868, riveted public attention for eleven weeks. Seven congressmen, including leading Radicals, served as prosecutors, or "managers." Johnson's lawyers maintained that he was merely seeking a court test of a law that he believed unconstitutional, the Tenure of Office Act, by violating it. They also contended that the law did not protect Stanton, because Lincoln, not Johnson, had appointed him. And they asserted that Johnson was guilty of no crime indictable in a regular court.

The congressional "managers" countered that impeachment was a political process, not a criminal trial, and that Johnson's "abuse of discretionary power" constituted an impeachable offense. Some Senate Republicans wavered, fearful that the removal of a president would destroy the balance of power within the federal government. They also were reluctant to see Benjamin Wade, a Radical Republican who was president pro tempore of the Senate, become president, as the Constitution then provided.

Intense pressure weighed on the wavering Republican senators. Ultimately, seven Republicans risked political suicide by voting with the Democrats against removal, and the Senate failed by one vote to convict Johnson. In so doing, the legislators set two critical precedents: in the future, a president would be impeached neither solely on political grounds nor because two-thirds of Congress disagreed with the chief executive. In the short term, nonetheless, the anti-Johnson forces achieved their goals, for Andrew Johnson had no future as president. Republicans in Congress could now pursue their last major Reconstruction objective: guaranteeing black male suffrage.

The Fifteenth Amendment

Black suffrage was the linchpin of congressional Reconstruction. Only with the support of black voters could Republicans secure control of the southern states. The Reconstruction Act of 1867 had forced southern states to enfranchise black men in order to reenter the Union, but most northern states still refused to grant suffrage to African-Americans. The Fifteenth Amendment, drawn up by Republicans and approved by Congress in 1869, aimed both to protect black suffrage in the South and to extend it to the northern and border states, on the assumption that newly enfranchised blacks gratefully would vote Republican. The amendment prohibited the denial of suffrage by the states to anyone on account of race, color, or previous condition of servitude.

Democrats opposed the amendment on the grounds that it violated states' rights, but they did not control enough states to prevent its ratification. However, to some southerners, the amendment's omissions made it acceptable; as a Richmond newspaper pointed out, it had "loopholes through which a coach and four horses can be driven." Indeed, the new amendment did not guarantee black officeholding, nor did it prohibit restrictions on suffrage such as property requirements and literacy tests, both of which might be used to deny blacks the vote.

The debate over black suffrage drew new participants into the fray. Women's rights advocates had tried to promote both black suffrage and woman suffrage, but Radical Republicans rejected any linkage between the two, preferring to concentrate on black suffrage. Supporters of women's rights were themselves divided. Frederick Douglass argued that black suffrage must receive priority. "If the elective franchise is not extended to the Negro, he is dead,"

The Reconstruction Amendments

Amendment and Date of Congressional Passage	Provisions	Ratification
Thirteenth (January 1865)	Prohibited slavery in the United States.	December 1865
Fourteenth (June 1866)	Defined citizenship to include all persons born or naturalized in the United States.	July 1868, after Congress made ratification a prerequisite for readmission of ex-Confederate states to the Union.
	Provided proportional loss of congressional representation for any state that denied suffrage to any of its male citizens.	
	Disqualified prewar officeholders who supported the Confederacy from state or national office.	
	Repudiated the Confederate debt.	
Fifteenth (February 1869)	Prohibited the denial of suffrage because of race, color, or previous condition of servitude.	March 1870; ratification required of Virginia, Texas, Mississippi, and Georgia for readmission to the Union.

explained Douglass. "Woman has a thousand ways by which she can attach herself to the ruling power of the land that we have not." Women's rights leaders Elizabeth Cady Stanton and Susan B. Anthony disagreed. If the Fifteenth Amendment did not include women, they emphasized, it would establish an "aristocracy of sex" and increase the disabilities under which women already labored. The argument fractured the old abolition–women's rights coalition and would lead to the development of an independent women's rights movement.

By the time the Fifteenth Amendment was ratified in 1870, Congress could look back on five years of momentous achievement. Three constitutional amendments had broadened the scope of democracy by abolishing slavery, affirming the rights of citizens, and prohibiting the denial of suffrage on the basis of race. Congress had readmitted the former Confederate states into the Union. At the same time, momentum had slowed at the federal level. In 1869 the center of action shifted to the South, where tumultuous change was under way.

Reconstruction Governments

During the years of presidential Reconstruction, 1865–1867, the southern states faced formidable tasks: creating new governments, reviving war-torn economies, and dealing with the impact of emancipation. Racial tensions flared as freedmen organized political meetings to protest ill treatment and demand equal rights, and deadly race riots erupted in major southern cities. In May 1866 white crowds attacked black veterans in Memphis and rampaged through black neighborhoods, killing forty-six people. Two months later, in New Orleans, whites assaulted black delegates on their way to a political meeting and left forty people dead.

Congressional Reconstruction, supervised by federal troops, began in the spring of 1867 with the dismantling of existing governments and the formation of new state governments dominated by Republicans. By 1868 most former Confederate states had rejoined the Union, and within two years the process was complete.

But Republican rule did not long endure in the South. Opposition from southern Democrats, the landowning elite, vigilantes, and most white voters proved insurmountable. Still, these Reconstruction governments were unique, because black men, including former slaves, participated in them. Slavery had ended in other societies, too, but only in the United States had freedmen gained democratic political rights.

A New Electorate

The Reconstruction laws of 1867–1868 transformed the southern electorate by temporarily disfranchising 15 percent of potential white voters and by enfranchising more than 700,000 freed slaves. Black voters outnumbered whites by 100,000 overall and held voting majorities in five states.

This new electorate provided a base for the Republican party, which had never existed in the South. To scornful Democrats, the Republicans comprised three types of scoundrels: northern "carpetbaggers" who had come south for wealth and power; southern scalawags, poor and ignorant, looking to profit from Republican rule; and hordes of uneducated freedmen, easily manipulated. In fact, the hastily assembled Republican party, crossing racial and class lines, constituted a loose coalition of diverse factions with often contradictory goals.

To northerners who moved south after the war, the former Confederacy was an undeveloped region, ripe with possibilities. The carpetbaggers included many former Union soldiers who hoped to buy land, open factories, build railroads, or simply enjoy the warmer climate. Wielding disproportionate political power—they held almost one in three state offices—carpetbaggers recruited black support through a patriotic society called the Union League, which urged African-Americans to vote and escorted them to the polls.

A handful of scalawags (white southerners who supported the Republicans) were old Whigs, but most were small farmers from the mountain regions of North Carolina, Georgia, Alabama, and Arkansas. Former Unionists who had owned no slaves and who felt no loyalty to the old plantation elite, they wanted to improve their economic position and cared little one way or the other about black suffrage. Scalawags held the most political offices during Reconstruction but proved the least stable element of the Republican coalition. Many drifted back into the Democratic fold.

Freedmen, the backbone of southern Republicanism, provided eight out of ten Republican votes. They sought land, education, civil rights, and political equality and remained loyal Republicans. "We know our friends," an elderly freedman said. Although Reconstruction governments depended on black votes, freedmen held at most one in five political offices and constituted a legislative majority only in South Carolina, whose population was more than 60 percent black. No African-Americans won the office of governor, and only two served in the U.S. Senate. A mere 6 percent of southern members of the House were black, and almost half came from South Carolina.

A significant status gap divided high-level black officials from black voters. Most freedmen cared mainly about their economic future, especially about acquiring land, whereas African-American officeholders concerned themselves far more with attaining equal rights. Still, both groups shared high expectations and prized enfranchisement. "We are not prepared for this suffrage," admitted a former slave. "But we can learn. Give a man tools and let him commence to use them and in time he will learn a trade. So it is with voting. . . . In time we shall learn to do our duty."

Republican Rule

Large numbers of blacks participated in American government for the first time in the state constitutional conventions of 1867–1868. The South Carolina convention had a black majority, and in Louisiana half the delegates were freedmen. In general, these conventions instituted democratic changes such as universal manhood suffrage and public-school systems but failed to provide either integrated schools or land reform. Wherever proposed, plans for the confiscation and redistribution of land failed.

Once civil power shifted to the new state governments, Republican administrations began ambitious public-works programs. They built roads and bridges, promoted railroad development, and funded institutions to care for orphans, the insane, and the disabled. Republican regimes also expanded state government and formed state militia in which blacks often were heavily represented. Finally, they created public-school systems, almost nonexistent in the antebellum South.

These reforms cost millions, and state debts and taxes skyrocketed. During the 1860s taxes rose 400 percent. Although northern tax rates still exceeded southern tax rates, southerners, particularly landowners, resented the new levies. In their view, Reconstruction strained the pocketbooks of the propertied in order to finance the vast expenditures of Republican legislatures, the "no property herd."

Opponents of Reconstruction viewed Republican rule as wasteful and corrupt, the "most stupendous system of organized robbery in history." Indeed, corruption did permeate some state governments, as in Louisiana and South Carolina. The main profiteers were government officials who accepted bribes and railroad promoters who doled them out. But neither group was exclusively Republican. In fact, corruption increasingly characterized government *nationally* in these years and was both more flagrant and more lucrative in the North. But such a comparison did little to quiet the critics of Republican rule.

Counterattacks

For ex-Confederates, black enfranchisement and the "horror of Negro domination" created nightmares. As soon as congressional Reconstruction began, it fell under attack. Democratic newspapers assailed delegates to the North Carolina constitutional convention as an "Ethiopian minstrelsy . . . baboons, monkeys, mules . . . and other jackasses." They demeaned Louisiana's constitution as "the work of ignorant Negroes cooperating with a gang of white adventurers."

But Democrats delayed any political mobilization until the readmission of the southern states was completed. Then they swung into action, often calling themselves Conservatives to attract former Whigs. At first, they pursued black votes, but when that initiative failed, they switched tactics. In every southern state, the Democrats contested elections, backed dissident Republican factions, elected some Democratic legislators, and lured scalawags away from the Republican party.

Vigilante efforts to reduce black votes bolstered Democratic campaigns to win white ones. Antagonism toward free blacks, long present in southern life, grew increasingly violent. As early as 1865, Freedmen's Bureau agents itemized a variety of outrages against blacks, including shooting, murder, rape, arson, and "severe and inhuman beating." White vigilante groups sprang up in all parts of the former Confederacy, but one organization became dominant. In the spring of 1866, six young Confederate war veterans in Tennessee formed a social club, the Ku Klux Klan, distinguished by elaborate rituals, hooded costumes, and secret passwords. New Klan dens spread rapidly. By the election of 1868, when black suffrage had become a reality, the Klan had become a terrorist movement directed against potential African-American voters.

The Klan sought to suppress black voting, to reestablish white supremacy, and to topple the Reconstruction governments. It targeted Union League officers, Freedmen's Bureau officials, white Republicans, black militia units, economically

The Ku Klux Klan *This cartoon of 1880 features Klan members preparing for terrorist activities. The Klan hoped to end Republican rule, to restore white supremacy, and to obliterate, in one southern editor's words, "the preposterous and wicked dogma of negro equality."*

successful blacks, and African-American voters. Some Democrats denounced Klan members as "cut-throats and riff-raff," but some prominent Confederate leaders, including General Nathan Bedford Forrest, were active Klansmen. Vigilantism united southern whites of different social classes and drew on the energy of many Confederate veterans.

Republican legislatures tried to outlaw vigilantism, but when state militia could not enforce the laws, state officials turned to the federal government for help. In response, between May 1870 and February 1871, Congress passed three Enforcement Acts, each progressively more stringent. The First Enforcement Act protected black voters. The Second Enforcement Act provided for federal supervision of southern elections, and the Third Enforcement Act (also known as the Ku Klux Klan Act) authorized the use of federal troops and the suspension of habeas corpus. Although thousands were arrested under the Enforcement Acts, most terrorists escaped conviction.

By 1872 the federal government had effectively suppressed the Klan, but vigilantism had served its purpose. Only a large military presence in the South could have protected black rights, but instead troop levels fell steadily. Congress allowed the Freedmen's Bureau to die in 1869, and the Enforcement Acts became dead letters. White southerners, a Georgia politician explained in 1871, could not discard "a feeling of bitterness, a feeling that the Negro is a sort of instinctual enemy of ours." The battle over Reconstruction was in essence a battle over the implications of emancipation, and it had begun as soon as the war had ended.

The Impact of Emancipation

"The master he says we are all free," a South Carolina slave declared in 1865. "But it don't mean we is white. And it don't mean we is equal." Yet despite the daunting handicaps they faced—illiteracy, lack of property, lack of skills—most former slaves found the exhilaration of freedom overwhelming. Emancipation had given them the right to their own labor and a sense of autonomy, and during Reconstruction they asserted their independence by casting off white control and shedding the vestiges of slavery.

Confronting Freedom

For the ex-slaves, mobility was often liberty's first fruit. Some left the slave quarters; others fled the plantation completely. "I have never in my life met with such ingratitude," a South Carolina mistress exclaimed when a former slave ran off.

Emancipation stirred waves of migration within the former Confederacy. Some slaves headed to the Deep South, where desperate planters would pay higher wages for labor, but more moved to towns and cities. Urban black populations doubled and tripled after emancipation. The desire to find lost family members drove some migrations. "They had a passion, not so much for wandering as for getting together," explained a Freedmen's Bureau official. Parents sought children who had been sold; husbands and wives who had been separated reunited; and families reclaimed children who were being raised in masters' homes. The Freedmen's Bureau helped former slaves to get information about missing relatives and to travel to find them, and bureau agents also tried to resolve entanglements over the multiple alliances of spouses who had been separated under slavery.

Not all efforts at reunion succeeded. Some fugitive slaves had died during the war or were untraceable. Other ex-slaves had formed new partnerships and could not revive old ones. But the success stories were poignant. "I's hunted an' hunted till I track you up here," one freedman told the wife whom he found twenty years after their separation by sale.

Once reunited, freed blacks quickly legalized unions formed under slavery, sometimes in mass ceremonies of up to seventy couples. Legal marriage

Richmond Street Scene
In this photograph taken after the Civil War, several woodcutters and passersby pose for the camera. Some of the individuals appear to be wearing old military clothing.

had a tangible impact on family life. In 1870 eight out of ten black families in the cotton-producing South were two-parent families, about the same proportion as white families. Men asserted themselves as household heads, and their wives and children often withdrew from the work force. Thus severe labor shortages followed immediately after the war, because women had made up half of all field workers. However, by Reconstruction's end, many black women had rejoined the work force out of economic necessity, either in the fields or working as cooks, laundresses, and domestic servants.

Black Institutions

The freed blacks' desire for independence also led to the growth of black churches. The African Methodist Episcopal Church, founded by Philadelphia blacks in the 1790s, gained thousands of new southern members. Negro Baptist churches, their roots often in plantation "praise meetings" organized by slaves, sprouted everywhere.

The influence of African-American churches extended far beyond religion. They provided relief, raised funds for schools, and supported Republican policies. Black ministers assumed leading political roles. Even after southern Democrats excluded most freedmen from political life at Reconstruction's end, ministers remained the main pillars of authority within black communities.

Schools, too, played a crucial role for freedmen as the ex-slaves sought literacy for themselves and above all for their children. At emancipation, African-Americans organized their own schools, which the Freedmen's Bureau soon supervised. Northern philanthropic organizations paid the wages of instructors, half of whom were women. In 1869 the bureau reported more than 4,000 black schools in the former Confederacy. Within three more years, each southern state had a public-school system, at least in principle, generally with separate schools for blacks and whites. The Freedmen's Bureau and others also helped to establish Howard, Atlanta, and Fisk universities in 1866–1867 and Hampton Institute in 1868. Nonetheless, black

education remained limited. Few rural blacks could reach the schools, and those who tried were sometimes the targets of vigilante attacks. Thus by the end of Reconstruction, more than 80 percent of the black population remained illiterate, although literacy was rising among children.

Not only school segregation but also other forms of racial separation were taken for granted. Whether by law or by custom, segregation continued on streetcars and trains as well as in churches, theaters, and restaurants. In 1875 Congress passed the Civil Rights Act, banning segregation except in schools, but in the 1883 *Civil Rights Cases*, the Supreme Court threw the law out. The Fourteenth Amendment did not prohibit discrimination by individuals, the Court ruled, only that perpetrated by the state.

White southerners adamantly rejected the prospect of racial integration, which they insisted would lead to racial amalgamation. "If we have social equality, we shall have intermarriage," contended one white southerner, "and if we have intermarriage, we shall degenerate." Urban blacks occasionally protested segregation, but most freed blacks were less interested in "social equality" than in African-American liberty and community. Moreover, the new black elite—teachers, ministers, and politicians—served African-American constituencies and thus had a vested interest in separate black institutions. Too, rural blacks had little desire to mix with whites; rather, they sought freedom from white control. Above all, they wanted to secure personal independence by acquiring land.

Land, Labor, and Sharecropping

"The sole ambition of the freedman," a New Englander wrote from South Carolina in 1865, "appears to be to become the owner of a little piece of land, there to erect a humble home, and to dwell in peace and security, at his own free will and pleasure." Indeed, to free blacks everywhere, "forty acres and a mule" promised emancipation from plantation labor, white domination, and cotton, the "slave crop." Landownership signified economic independence. "We want to be placed on land until we are able to buy it and make it our own," a black minister told General Sherman in Georgia during the war.

But the freedmen's visions of landownership failed to materialize, for large-scale land reform never occurred. Proposals to confiscate or to redistribute Confederate property failed. A few slaves did obtain land, either by pooling resources or through the Southern Homestead Act. In 1866 Congress passed this law, setting aside 44 million acres of land in five southern states for freedmen; but the land was poor, and few slaves had resources to survive until their first harvest. About 4,000 blacks claimed homesteads, though few could establish farms. By the end of Reconstruction, only a fraction of former slaves owned working farms. Without large-scale land reform, barriers to black landownership remained overwhelming.

Three obstacles impeded black landownership. Freedmen lacked capital to buy land or tools. Furthermore, white southerners generally opposed selling land to blacks. Most important, planters sought to preserve a cheap labor force and forged laws to ensure that black labor would remain available on the plantations.

The black codes written during presidential Reconstruction were designed to preserve a captive labor force. Under labor contracts in effect in 1865–1866, freedmen received wages, housing, food, and clothing in exchange for fieldwork. But cash was scarce, and wages often became a small share of the crop, typically one-eighth or less, to be divided among the entire work force. Freedmen's Bureau agents encouraged blacks to sign the contracts, seeing wage labor as a step toward economic independence. "You must begin at the bottom of the ladder and climb up," bureau head O. O. Howard told the freedmen.

Problems arose immediately. Freedmen disliked the new wage system, especially the use of gang labor, which resembled the work pattern under slavery. Moreover, postwar planters had to compete for labor even as many scorned black workers as lazy or inefficient. One landowner estimated that workers accomplished only "two-fifths of what they did under the old system." As productivity fell, so did land values. Plummeting cotton prices and poor harvests in 1866 and 1867 combined with these other factors to create an impasse: landowners lacked labor, and freedmen lacked land.

Southerners began experimenting with new labor schemes, including the division of plantations into small tenancies. Sharecropping was the most widespread arrangement. Under this system, landowners subdivided large plantations into farms of thirty to fifty acres and rented them to freedmen under annual leases for a share of the crop, usually half. Freedmen liked this decentralized system, which let them use the labor of family members and represented a step toward independence. A half-share of the crop far exceeded the fraction that they had received under the black codes. Planters benefited, too, for the leases gave them leverage over their tenants, and tenants shared the risk of poor harvests with them. Most important, planters retained control of their land. The most productive land thus remained in the hands of a small group of owners, and, in effect, sharecropping helped to preserve the planter elite.

Although the wage system continued on sugar and rice plantations, by 1870 the plantation tradition had yielded to sharecropping in the cotton South. A severe depression in 1873 drove many blacks and independent white farmers into sharecropping. By 1880 sharecroppers, white and black, farmed 80 percent of the land in cotton-producing states. In fact, white sharecroppers outnumbered black, although a higher proportion of southern blacks, almost 75 percent, were involved in the system. Changes in marketing and finance, meanwhile, made the sharecroppers' lot increasingly precarious.

Toward a Crop-Lien Economy

Before the Civil War, planters had depended on factors, or middlemen, who sold them supplies, extended credit, and marketed their crops through urban merchants. Because the high value of slave property had backed these long-distance credit arrangements, this system collapsed with the end of

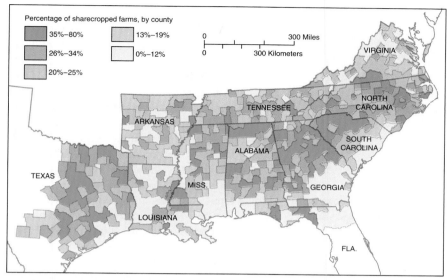

Southern Sharecropping, 1880

The depressed economy of the late 1870s caused poverty and debt, increased tenancy among white farmers, and forced many renters, black and white, into sharecropping. By 1880 the sharecropping system pervaded most southern counties, with highest concentrations in the cotton belt from South Carolina to eastern Texas.

SOURCE: U.S. Census Office, Tenth Census, 1880, *Report of the Production of Agriculture* (Washington, D.C.: Government Printing Office, 1883), Table 5.

slavery. The postwar South, with its hundreds of thousands of tenant farmers and sharecroppers, needed a local credit system.

Into this gap stepped rural merchants, who advanced supplies to tenants and sharecroppers on credit and sold their crops to wholesalers. Because renters had no property to serve as collateral, merchants secured their loans with a lien, or claim, on each farmer's next crop. Exorbitant interest rates, 50 percent or more, quickly forced many tenants and sharecroppers into a cycle of indebtedness. The sharecropper might well owe part of his crop to the landowner, and another part (the rest of his crop, or more) to the merchant. Illiterate tenants who could not keep track of their financial arrangements were at the mercy of sometimes unscrupulous merchants. "A man that didn't know how to count would

always lose," an Arkansas freedman explained. Once a tenant's real or alleged debts exceeded the value of his crop, he was tied to the land, to cotton, and to sharecropping.

By the end of Reconstruction, sharecropping and crop liens had bound the South to easily marketable cash crops such as cotton and prevented crop diversification. Soil depletion, land erosion, and outmoded equipment stranded capital-short planters in a cycle of poverty. Postwar changes in southern agriculture left the region with bleak economic prospects.

Trapped in perpetual debt, tenant farmers became the chief victims of the new agricultural order. Cotton remained the only survival route open to poor farmers, regardless of race, but low income from cotton locked them into sharecropping and crop liens. Black tenants, for whom neither landownership nor economic independence ever materialized, saw their political rights dwindle as rapidly as their hopes for economic freedom. When Reconstruction ended, neither state governments nor the national government offered them protection, for northern politicians were preoccupied with their own problems.

New Concerns in the North

The nomination of Ulysses S. Grant for president in 1868 launched a chaotic era in national politics. His eight years in office featured political scandals, a party revolt, a massive depression, and a steady retreat from Reconstruction. By the mid-1870s, northern voters cared more about economics, unemployment, labor unrest, and currency problems than the "southern question." Eager to end sectional conflict, Republicans turned their backs on the freedmen.

Grantism

Republicans had good reason to nominate General Grant. A war hero, he was endorsed by veterans and admired throughout the North and had come unscathed through the bitter feuds of Reconstruction politics. To oppose Grant, the Democrats nominated Horatio Seymour, arch-critic of the Lincoln administration and an opponent of Reconstruction and greenbacks. Grant ran on his personal popularity more than on issues. Although he carried all but eight states, the popular vote was close; newly enfranchised freedmen provided Grant's margin in the South. When he was inaugurated, Grant pledged to execute all the laws, whether he agreed with them or not, to support sound money, and to follow a humane policy toward the Indians.

Grant's presidential leadership proved as weak as his war leadership had been strong. He had little political skill; his cabinet appointments were at best mediocre, and a string of scandals plagued his administration. In 1869 financier Jay Gould and his partner Jim Fisk attempted to corner the gold market with the help of Grant's brother-in-law. When gold prices tumbled, investors were ruined, and Grant's reputation was tarnished. Near the end of Grant's first term, his vice president, Schuyler Colfax, got caught up in the Crédit Mobilier scandal, an elaborate scheme to skim off the profits of the Union Pacific Railroad. Then in 1875 Grant's personal secretary, Orville Babcock, was found guilty of accepting bribes from the "whiskey ring," distillers who preferred bribery to paying federal taxes. And in 1876 voters learned that Grant's secretary of war, William E. Belknap, had taken bribes to sell lucrative Indian trading posts in Oklahoma.

Although Grant was not personally involved in the scandals, he did little to restrain such activities, and "Grantism" came to stand for fraud, bribery, and corruption in office. Such evils, however, spread far beyond Washington. The New York City press in 1872 revealed that Democrat boss William M. Tweed led a ring that had looted the city treasury and collected some $200 million in kickbacks and bribes. When Mark Twain and coauthor Charles Dudley Warner published their scathing satire, The Gilded Age (1873), readers recognized the novel's speculators, self-promoters, and maniacal opportunists as familiar types in public life.

The Election of 1868				
Candidates	Parties	Electoral Vote	Popular Vote	Percentage of Popular Vote
ULYSSES S. GRANT	Republican	214	3,013,421	52.7
Horatio Seymour	Democratic	80	2,706,829	47.3

The Election of 1872				
Candidates	Parties	Electoral Vote	Popular Vote	Percentage of Popular Vote
ULYSSES S. GRANT	Republican	286	3,596,745	55.6
Horace Greeley*	Democratic		2,843,446	43.9

*Upon Greeley's death shortly after the election, the electors supporting him divided their votes among minor candidates.

Grant did enjoy some foreign-policy successes. His administration engineered the settlement of the *Alabama* claims with England; an international tribunal ordered Britain to pay $15.5 million to the United States in compensation for damage inflicted by Confederate-owned but British-built raiders. But the administration went astray when it tried to add nonadjacent territory to the Union. In 1867 the Johnson administration had purchased Alaska from Russia at the bargain price of $7.2 million. The purchase had rekindled expansionists' hope, and in 1870 Grant decided to annex the Caribbean island nation of Santo Domingo (the modern Dominican Republic). The president believed that annexation would promote Caribbean trade and provide a haven for persecuted southern blacks. Despite speculators' hopes for windfall profits, the Senate rejected the annexation treaty and further diminished Grant's reputation.

As the election of 1872 approached, dissident Republicans feared that "Grantism" would ruin the party. Former Radicals and other Republicans left out of Grant's "Great Barbecue" formed their own party, the Liberal Republicans.

The Liberals' Revolt

The Liberal Republican revolt split the Republican party and undermined Reconstruction. Liberals demanded civil-service reform to bring the "best men" into government. In the South they demanded an end to "bayonet rule" and argued that blacks, now enfranchised, could fend for themselves. Corruption in government posed a greater

threat than Confederate resurgence, the Liberals claimed, and they demanded that the "best men" in the South, ex-Confederates barred from holding office, be returned to government.

New York Tribune editor Horace Greeley, inconsistently supporting both a stringent Reconstruction policy and leniency toward the ex-Confederates, received the Liberal Republican nomination, and the Democrats endorsed Greeley as well. Republican reformers found themselves allied with the party that they had recently castigated as a "sewer" of treasonable sentiments.

Despite Greeley's arduous campaigning (he literally worked himself to death on the campaign trail and died a few weeks after the election), Grant carried 56 percent of the popular vote and won the electoral vote handily. But his victory had come at a high price: to nullify the Liberals' issues, "regular" Republicans passed an amnesty act allowing all but a few hundred ex-Confederates to resume office. And during Grant's second term, Republicans' desire to discard the "southern question" grew as a depression gripped the nation.

The Panic of 1873

The postwar years brought accelerated industrialization, rapid economic expansion, and frantic speculation as investors rushed to take advantage of seemingly unlimited opportunities. Railroads led the speculative boom. The transcontinental line reached completion in 1869 (see Chapter 17), and by 1873 almost 400 railroads crisscrossed the Northeast. But in addition to transforming the northern economy, the railroad boom led entrepreneurs to overspeculate, with drastic results.

In 1869 the Philadelphia banker Jay Cooke took over a new transcontinental line, the Northern Pacific. For four years Northern Pacific securities sold briskly, but in 1873 construction costs outran bond sales. In September, Cooke, his bank vaults stuffed with unsalable bonds, defaulted on his obligations. His bank, the largest in the nation, shut down. Then the stock market collapsed and smaller banks and other firms followed; and the Panic of 1873 plunged the nation into a devastating five-year depression. Thousands of businesses went bankrupt. By 1878 unemployment rose to more than 3 million. Labor protests mounted, and industrial violence spread (see Chapter 18). The depression of the 1870s demonstrated ruthlessly that conflicts born of industrialization had replaced sectional divisions.

The depression also fed a dispute over currency that had begun in 1865. During the Civil War, Americans had used greenbacks, a paper currency not backed by a specific weight in gold. "Sound-money" supporters demanded the withdrawal of greenbacks from circulation as a means of stabilizing the currency. Their opponents, "easy money" advocates such as farmers and manufacturers dependent on easy credit, wanted to expand the currency by issuing additional greenbacks. The deepening depression created even more demand for easy money, and the issue split both major parties.

Controversy over the type of currency was compounded by the question of how to repay the federal debt. In wartime the Union government had borrowed astronomical sums through the sale of war bonds. Bond holders wanted repayment in "coin," gold or silver, even though many of them had paid for the bonds in greenbacks. The Public Credit Act of 1869 promised payment in coin.

Senator John Sherman, the author of the Public Credit Act, put together a series of compromises to satisfy both "sound-money" and "easy-money" advocates. Sherman's measures, exchanging Civil War bonds for new ones payable over a longer period of time and defining "coin" as gold only, preserved the public credit, the currency, and Republican unity. His Specie Resumption Act of 1875 promised to put the nation back on the gold standard by 1879.

But Sherman's measures, however ingenious, did not placate the Democrats, who gained control of the House in 1875. Many Democrats, and a few Republicans, were "free-silver" advocates who wanted the silver dollar restored in order to expand the currency and end the depression. The Bland-Allison Act of 1878 partially restored silver coinage by requiring the government to buy and coin several million dollars' worth of silver each month. In 1876 other expansionists formed the Greenback party to keep the paper money in circulation for the sake of debtors, but they enjoyed little success. As the depression receded, the clamor for "easy money" subsided, only to return in the 1890s (see Chapter 21). Although it was never settled, the controversial "money question" diverted attention away from Reconstruction and thus contributed to its demise.

Reconstruction and the Constitution

During the 1870s the Supreme Court also played a role in weakening northern support for Reconstruction as new constitutional questions surfaced.

Would the Court support laws to protect freedmen's rights? The decision in *Ex Parte* Milligan (1866) had suggested not. In *Milligan*, the Court had ruled that a military commission could not try civilians in areas where civilian courts were functioning, thus dooming the special military courts that had been established to enforce the Supplementary Freedmen's Bureau Act. Would the Court sabotage the congressional Reconstruction plan? In 1869, in *Texas v. White*, the Court had let Reconstruction stand, ruling that Congress had the power to ensure each state a republican form of government and to recognize the legitimate government in any state.

However, during the 1870s the Supreme Court backed away from Reconstruction. The process began with the *Slaughterhouse* decision of 1873. In this case, the Court ruled that the Fourteenth Amendment protected the rights of *national* citizenship, such as the right to interstate travel, but that it did not protect the civil rights that individuals derived from *state* citizenship. The federal government, in short, did not have to safeguard such rights against violation by the states. The *Slaughterhouse* decision effectively gutted the Fourteenth Amendment, which was intended to secure freedmen's rights against state encroachment.

The Supreme Court retreated even further from Reconstruction in two cases involving the Enforcement Act of 1870. In *U.S.* v. *Reese* (1876), the Court threw out the indictment of Kentucky officials who had barred blacks from voting. The Fifteenth Amendment, the Court said, did not "confer the right of suffrage upon anyone"; it merely prohibited the hindrance of voting on the basis of race, color, or previous condition of servitude. Crucial sections of the Enforcement Act, the Court ruled, were invalid. Another decision that same year, *U.S.* v. *Cruikshank*, again weakened the Fourteenth Amendment. In the *Cruikshank* case, the Court ruled that the amendment barred *states,* but not *individuals,* from encroaching on individual rights. The decision threw out the indictments against white Louisianians charged with murdering more than thirty black militiamen who had surrendered after a battle with armed whites.

Continuing its retreat from Reconstruction, in 1883 the Supreme Court invalidated both the Civil Rights Act of 1875 and the Ku Klux Klan Act of 1871; later it would uphold segregation laws (see Chapter 21). Taken cumulatively, these decisions dismantled Republican Reconstruction and confirmed rising northern sentiment that Reconstruction's egalitarian goals were unenforceable.

Republicans in Retreat

The Republicans gradually disengaged from Reconstruction, beginning with the election of Grant as president in 1868. Grant, like most Americans,

hesitated to approve the use of federal authority in state or local affairs.

In the 1870s Republican idealism waned. Instead, commercial and industrial interests dominated both the Liberal and "regular" wings of the party, and few had any taste left for further sectional strife. When Democratic victories in the House of Representatives in 1874 showed that Reconstruction had become a political liability, the Republicans prepared to abandon it.

By 1875, moreover, the Radical Republicans had virtually disappeared. The Radical leaders Chase, Stevens, and Sumner had died, and others had grown tired of "waving the bloody shirt," or defaming Democratic opponents by reviving wartime animosity. Party leaders reported that voters were "sick of carpet-bag government" and tired of the "southern question" and the "Negro question." It seemed pointless to prop up southern Republican regimes that even President Grant found corrupt. Finally, Republicans generally agreed with southern Democrats that blacks were inferior. To insist on black equality, many party members believed, would be a thankless, divisive, and politically suicidal course that would quash any hope of reunion between North and South. The Republican retreat set the stage for Reconstruction's end in 1877.

Reconstruction Abandoned

"We are in a very hot political contest just now," a Mississippi planter wrote his daughter in 1875, "with a good prospect of turning out the carpetbag thieves by whom we have been robbed for the past six to ten years." Indeed, an angry white majority had led a Democratic resurgence throughout the South in the 1870s, and by the end of 1872, four ex-Confederate states already had returned the Democrats to power. By 1876 Republican rule survived in only three southern states. Democratic victories in state elections that year and political bargaining in Washington in 1877 ended what little remained of Reconstruction.

"Redeeming" the South

After 1872 the Republican collapse in the South accelerated. Congressional amnesty enabled virtually all ex-Confederate officials to regain office; divided Republicans lost their grip on the southern electorate; and attrition diminished Republican ranks. Carpetbaggers returned North or joined the Democrats, and scalawags deserted the Republicans in large numbers. Tired of northern interference and seeing the possibility of "home rule," scalawags decided that staying Republican meant going down with a sinking ship. Unable to win new white votes or retain the old ones, the fragile Republican coalition crumbled.

Meanwhile, the Democrats mobilized formerly apathetic white voters. Although still faction-ridden—businessmen who dreamed of an industrialized "New South" had little in common with the old planter elite, the so-called Bourbons—the Democrats shared one goal: kicking the Republicans out. The Democrats' tactics varied. In several Deep South states, Democrats resorted to violence. In Vicksburg in 1874, rampaging whites slaughtered about 300 blacks and terrorized thousands of potential voters. Vigilante groups in several southern states disrupted Republican meetings and threatened blacks who had registered to vote. "The Republicans are paralyzed through fear and will not act," the carpetbag governor of Mississippi wrote his wife. "Why should I fight a hopeless battle . . . when no possible good to the Negro or anybody else would result?"

Terrorism did not completely squelch black voting, but it deprived Republicans of enough black votes to win state elections. Throughout the South economic pressures reinforced intimidation; labor contracts included clauses barring attendance at political meetings, and planters threatened to evict sharecroppers who stepped out of line.

Redemption, the word that Democrats used to describe their return to power, introduced sweeping changes. States rewrote constitutions, cut expenses, lowered taxes, eliminated social programs, limited the rights of tenants and sharecroppers, and shaped laws to ensure a stable black labor force. Legislatures restored vagrancy laws, strengthened crop-lien statutes, and remade criminal law. New criminal

The Duration of Republican Rule in the Ex-Confederate States

Former Confederate States	Readmission to the Union Under Congressional Reconstruction	Democrats (Conservatives) Gain Control	Duration of Republican Rule
Alabama	June 25, 1868	November 14, 1874	6½ years
Arkansas	June 22, 1868	November 10, 1874	6½ years
Florida	June 25, 1868	January 2, 1877	8½ years
Georgia	July 15, 1870	November 1, 1871	1 year
Louisiana	June 25, 1868	January 2, 1877	8½ years
Mississippi	February 23, 1870	November 3, 1875	5½ years
North Carolina	June 25, 1868	November 3, 1870	2 years
South Carolina	June 25, 1868	November 12, 1876	8 years
Tennessee	July 24, 1866*	October 4, 1869	3 years
Texas	March 30, 1870	January 14, 1873	3 years
Virginia	January 26, 1870	October 5, 1869[†]	0 years

*Admitted before start of Congressional Reconstruction.
[†]Democrats gained control before readmission.

SOURCE: John Hope Franklin, *Reconstruction After the Civil War* (Chicago: University of Chicago Press, 1962), 231.

codes directed at blacks imposed severe penalties for what formerly were misdemeanors: stealing livestock or wrongly taking part of a crop became grand larceny, punishable by five years at hard labor. By Reconstruction's end, a large black convict work force had been leased out to private contractors.

Freedmen whose hopes had been raised by Republicans saw their prospects destroyed by the redeemers. The new laws, Tennessee blacks stated at an 1875 convention, imposed "a condition of servitude scarcely less degrading than that endured before the late civil war." In the late 1870s, an increasingly oppressive political climate gave rise to an "exodus" movement among African-Americans. Nearly 15,000 black "exodusters" from the Deep South moved to Kansas and set up homesteads. But scarce resources left most of the freed slaves stranded. Not until the twentieth century would the mass migration of southern blacks to the Midwest and North gain momentum.

The Election of 1876

By the autumn of 1876, with redemption almost complete, both parties moved to discard the animosity left by the war and Reconstruction. The Republicans nominated Rutherford B. Hayes, the governor of Ohio, for president. Popular with all factions and untainted by the Grant scandals, Hayes, a "moderate," favored "home rule" in the South and civil and political rights for all—clearly contradictory goals. The Democrats nominated Governor Samuel J. Tilden of New York, a political reformer known for his assaults on the Tweed Ring that had plundered New York City's treasury. Both candidates were fiscal conservatives, favored sound money, endorsed civil-service reform, and decried corruption.

Tilden won the popular vote by a small margin, but the Republicans challenged pro-Tilden electoral votes from South Carolina, Florida, and Louisiana. Giving those nineteen electoral votes to Hayes would make him the winner. For their part, the Democrats, requiring a single electoral vote to put Tilden in the White House, challenged one electoral vote from Oregon. But

Southern Republicans managed to throw out enough Democratic ballots in the contested states to proclaim Hayes the winner.

The nation now faced an unprecedented dilemma. Each party claimed victory, and each accused the other of fraud. In fact, both sets of southern votes were fraudulent: Republicans had discarded legitimate Democratic ballots, and Democrats illegally had prevented freedmen from voting. In January 1877 Congress created a special electoral commission to resolve the conflict. The commission originally consisted of seven Republicans, seven Democrats, and one independent, but when the independent resigned, a Republican replaced him. The commission gave the Republican Hayes the election by an 8–7 vote.

Congress now had to certify the new electoral vote. But the Democrats controlled the House, and some planned to forestall approval of the electoral vote. For many southern Democrats, regaining

The Disputed Election of 1876

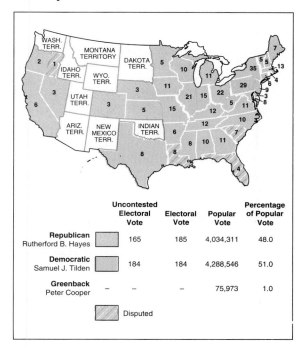

	Uncontested Electoral Vote	Electoral Vote	Popular Vote	Percentage of Popular Vote
Republican Rutherford B. Hayes	165	185	4,034,311	48.0
Democratic Samuel J. Tilden	184	184	4,288,546	51.0
Greenback Peter Cooper	–	–	75,973	1.0

Disputed

control of their states was far more important than electing a Republican president—*if* the new Republican administration would leave the South alone. For their part, Republican leaders were willing to bargain, for Hayes wanted not just victory but also southern approval. Informal negotiations followed, with both parties exchanging promises. Ohio Republicans and southern Democrats agreed that if Hayes won the election, he would remove federal troops from all southern states. Other negotiations led to the understanding that southerners would receive federal patronage, federal aid to railroads, and federal support for internal improvements. In turn, southerners promised to accept Hayes as president and to treat the freedmen fairly.

Congress thus ratified Hayes's election. Once in office, Hayes fulfilled many of the agreements made by his colleagues. Republican rule toppled in Louisiana, South Carolina, and Florida. But some of the bargains struck in the so-called Compromise of 1877 fell apart, particularly Democratic promises to treat the freedmen fairly and Hayes's pledges to ensure the freed slaves' rights. "When you turned us loose, you turned us loose to the sky, to the storm, to the whirlwind, and worst of all . . . to the wrath of our infuriated masters," Frederick Douglass had charged at the 1876 Republican convention. "The question now is, do you mean to make good to us the promises in your Constitution?" By 1877 the answer was clearly "No."

Conclusion

The end of Reconstruction benefited both major political parties. The "southern question" no longer burdened the Republicans. The Democrats, who had regained power in the ex-Confederate states, would remain entrenched there for almost a century. The postwar South was tied to sharecropping and economic backwardness as surely as it once had been tied to slavery; but "home rule" was firmly in place.

Reconstruction's end also signaled the triumph of nationalism and reconciliation. Battlefields became national parks. Jefferson Davis, who had served two years in prison but never had gone to trial, urged young men to "lay aside all rancor, all bitter sectional feeling." Americans increasingly dismissed Reconstruction as a fiasco, a tragic interlude of "radical rule" and "black reconstruction" fashioned by carpetbaggers, scalawags, and Radical Republicans.

Historians, too, still regard Reconstruction a failure, although for different reasons from those of Americans who lived through the era. Today scholars view Reconstruction as an unsuccessful democratic experiment that did not go far enough.

They cite two main failings. First, Congress did not promote land reform and thus left blacks propertyless, without the economic power to defend their rights. More important, the federal government did not back congressional Reconstruction militarily. Reconstruction's failure lay with the federal government's inability to fulfill its own goals and to create a biracial democracy in the South. Consequently, the nation's adjustment to emancipation would continue into the twentieth century.

The Reconstruction era left significant legacies, including the Fourteenth and Fifteenth amendments, monuments to Congress's democratic zeal in the 1860s. Above all, Reconstruction gave freedmen the opportunity to reconstitute their families, to form schools and churches, and to participate in government for the first time in U.S. history. However, in the 1880s the United States would consign Reconstruction to history and the freed slaves to their fate as Americans focused on their economic futures—on railroads, factories, and mills, and on the exploitation of their bountiful natural resources.

Chronology

1863 President Abraham Lincoln issues Proclamation of Amnesty and Reconstruction.

1864 Wade-Davis bill passed by Congress and pocket-vetoed by Lincoln.

1865 Freedmen's Bureau established.
Civil War ends.
Lincoln assassinated; Andrew Johnson becomes president.
Johnson issues Proclamation of Amnesty and Reconstruction.
Ex-Confederate states hold constitutional conventions (May–December).
Thirteenth Amendment added to the Constitution.
Presidential Reconstruction completed.

1866 Congress enacts the Civil Rights Act of 1866 and the Supplementary Freedmen's Bureau Act over Johnson's vetoes.
Ku Klux Klan founded in Tennessee.
Congress proposes the Fourteenth Amendment.
Race riots in southern cities.
Thirty-ninth Congress begins debates over Reconstruction policy.

1867 Reconstruction Act of 1867.
William Seward negotiates the purchase of Alaska.
Constitutional conventions meet in the ex-Confederate states.
Howard University founded.

1868 President Johnson is impeached, tried, and acquitted.
Fourteenth Amendment added to the Constitution.
Ulysses S. Grant elected president.

1869 Transcontinental railroad completed.

1870 Fifteenth Amendment added to the Constitution.
Enforcement Act of 1870.

1871 Second Enforcement Act.
Ku Klux Klan Act.

1872 Liberal Republican party formed.
Alabama claims settled.
Grant reelected president.

1873 Panic of 1873 begins (September–October), setting off a five-year depression.

1875 Civil Rights Act of 1875.
Specie Resumption Act.

1876 Disputed presidential election: Rutherford B. Hayes versus Samuel J. Tilden.

1877 Electoral commission decides election in favor of Hayes.
The last Republican-controlled governments overthrown in Florida, Louisiana, and South Carolina.

1879 "Exodus" movement spreads through several southern states.

FOR FURTHER READING

Eric Foner, *Reconstruction: America's Unfinished Revolution, 1863–1877* (1988). A thorough exploration of Reconstruction that draws on recent scholarship and stresses the centrality of the black experience.

John Hope Franklin, *Reconstruction After the Civil War* (1961). An overview that dismantles the traditional view of Reconstruction as a disastrous experiment in radical rule.

William Gillette, *Retreat from Reconstruction, 1869–1879* (1979). A survey of the era's national politics, indicting Republican policy makers for vacillation and lack of commitment to racial equality.

Leon Litwack, *Been in the Storm So Long: The Aftermath of Slavery* (1979). A comprehensive study of the black response to emancipation in 1865–1866.

Roger L. Ransom and Richard Sutch, *One Kind of Freedom: The Economic Consequences of Emancipation* (1977). Economic assessment of the impact of free black labor on the South and explanation of the rise of sharecropping and the crop-lien system.

Kenneth M. Stampp, *The Era of Reconstruction, 1865–1877* (1965). A classic revisionist interpretation of Reconstruction, focusing on the establishment and fall of Republican governments.

Joel Williamson, *The Negro in South Carolina During Reconstruction, 1861–1877* (1965). A pioneer study of black life and institutions after emancipation.

The Frontier West

*I*n the second half of the nineteenth century, Americans launched one of the greatest migrations in modern history, the exploration and development of half a continent. Optimistic, thirsting for fresh starts, they flooded westward seeking land and fortune.

Even before the Civil War, Americans had seen the trans-Mississippi West as a land of adventure, opportunity, and inexhaustible natural resources. Three hundred thousand Americans had poured into California during the Gold Rush in 1849 and 1850. Thousands of other midcentury pioneers had moved onto the fertile prairies of Iowa, Minnesota, Kansas, and Nebraska.

When the Civil War ended, the vision of the western frontier as a land of economic promise and limitless natural resources lured another generation west. Pushing aside the Native Americans, whose ancestors had inhabited the land for tens of thousands of years, settlers swarmed onto the rolling prairies of the Great Plains. They quickly filled the rich, rain-soaked farmlands of Wisconsin, Minnesota, Iowa, and eastern sections

(Right) Chief Joseph (1840?–1904) of the Nez Percés

Native Americans and the Frontier
Settling the West
Exploiting the West
The West of Life and Legend

of Kansas, Nebraska, and the Dakotas. A few continued westward onto the semiarid High Plains, hoping to make their fortunes in ranching and mining, and a handful trudged beyond them, through the Rocky Mountains and into the near-desert Great Basin of Nevada.

In viewing the West as a seedbed of economic opportunity, the migrants exploited its natural resources ruthlessly, in the process damaging the environment and destroying the Native Americans— and occasionally even themselves. Convinced of their cultural superiority, they saw nothing unjust in taking land from the resident Native Americans or Mexicans. Under the banner of progress, these new westerners stripped the landscape of trees, slaughtered millions of buffalo, skinned the mountainsides in search of minerals, and tore up the prairie sod to build farms.

Indian resistance, however, and the rugged Plains landscape slowed development and drove thousands away. This was stark, weather-beaten country, seared by hot winds in summer and lashed by blizzards in winter, and some could not take it. Still, by 1900 enough western development had occurred that the region required federal government support: military intervention, land subsidies, and financial aid to railroad builders. Investments by eastern bankers and foreign capitalists were also crucial to western growth. Yet the new westerners clung to their ideal of the self-reliant, independent individual who could overcome all obstacles. That ideal, often sorely tested, has survived to form the bedrock of western Americans' outlook even today.

Native Americans and the Frontier

The trans-Mississippi West was hardly empty before the newcomers arrived. About 360,000 Indians lived there, their cultures already shaped by European contact. Many pueblo dwellers, among them the Hopis and Zuñis of the Southwest, had reached accommodation with the Spanish-speaking *rancheros* (ranchers). Maintaining their traditional ways based on agriculture and sheepherding, the Indians traded mutton and produce for metal hoes, glass beads, knives, and guns. The fierce Apaches and Navajos, who raided pueblo dwellers and *rancheros* alike, also traded with Europeans for manufactured goods.

On the Great Plains, the acquisition of Spanish horses and British firearms had transformed the native peoples from walking nomads into the mounted warriors whom nineteenth-century pioneers encountered. Commercial and other contacts with the non-Indian world remained important to the Plains Indians as new settlers moved in. But beyond these generally positive exchanges, European contact disrupted Native American cultures. Smallpox, measles, and diphtheria, contracted from traders and settlers, ravaged tribes everywhere.

However, it was the physical disruption of Indian life on the Great Plains, home to nearly half the Native Americans of the West, that caught the public eye and weighed on the public conscience. The Americans who descended on the Plains after 1850 had little understanding of, and respect for, traditional "savage" ways. Consequently, the Plains Indians, defeated by the American military, forced onto reservations, and demoralized by disease, alcohol, and impoverishment, plunged along a downward spiral. By 1890 relocation to generally inadequate lands had become the fate of almost every Indian nation of the Great Plains. But from the wreckage of the Native Americans' traditional ways of life arose signs of a strong cultural response to conquest and forced modernization.

The Plains Indians

The Indians of the Great Plains inhabited two major subregions. Several large Siouan-speaking tribes, including the Sioux, Crows, and Assiniboins, dominated the northern Plains from the Dakotas and Montana southward to Nebraska. Mandans, Flatheads, Blackfeet, Cheyennes, and Arapahos also

Buffalo Head Trophies
To encourage buffalo hunting as a sport, railroads crossing the Great Plains had the animal heads mounted by their own taxidermists for display at ticket stations.

roamed the northern Plains. A few were allies, but most were bitter enemies constantly at war. The central and southern Plains were home to the agricultural "Five Civilized Tribes" driven there from the Southeast in the 1830s, to the partially settled Osages and Pawnees, and to the nomadic Comanches, Kiowas, southern Arapahos, and Kiowa Apaches.

Diversity characterized the Plains Indians and sometimes even flourished within divisions of the same tribe. The Dakota Sioux of Minnesota led a semisedentary life of agriculture, maple-sugar harvesting, and deer and bison hunting. In contrast, the Lakota Sioux roved the High Plains to the west, following the buffalo migrations. Nonetheless, life for all Plains Indians revolved around extended family ties and tribal cooperation. Within the Sioux nation, for example, families and clans joined forces to hunt and farm and reached decisions by consensus. Extended families formed small winter villages or larger summer encampments. Leaders relied on persuasion rather than authority; they governed by example, giving food and supplies to the needy and initiating projects in the hope that others would follow.

Religious and harvest celebrations provided the cement for life in Sioux villages and camps. Sioux religion was complex and very different from the Judeo-Christian tradition. Life consisted of a series of circles: family, band, tribe, and Sioux Nation. The Lakota Sioux also believed in plant and animal spirits, some more powerful than humans, whose help could be invoked in the Sun Dance. In this ceremony, young men would "sacrifice" themselves by suffering self-torture—stabbing their chests with skewers hung with buffalo skulls; hanging suspended from poles; or cutting pieces of their own flesh to place at the foot of the Sun Dance pole.

Many Plains tribes followed the buffalo migration. The huge herds, at their peak containing an estimated 32 million bison, served as an "ambulatory supermarket," for Indians used every part of the animal. They ate its meat, made clothing and shelter from its hides, fashioned its bones into tools, and burned dried buffalo dung ("chips") as fuel. They even used buffalo skulls for religious purposes, as in the Sun Dance.

By the 1870s the vogue among white Americans for wearing buffalo robes in carriages and sleighs, and a demand for buffalo hide for industrial belting, encouraged some Plains peoples to become professional hunters, with disastrous results. The Blackfeet, for example, began hunting for profit. At the height of the buffalo-hide trade between 1867 and 1873, a Blackfoot hunter could earn $2,000 a year, a small fortune for the time. Swept up in their new prosperity, the Blackfeet changed their traditional ways. Many men took additional wives to handle the task of tanning hides.

However, no sooner had the Indians become dependent on the buffalo trade than the great herds dwindled. Railroads hired hunters, usually whites, to slay bison with which to feed construction gangs. William F. "Buffalo Bill" Cody killed 4,300 buffalo in only eight months during 1867–1868 to provide food for Union Pacific crews. Eastern sport hunters and sightseers chartered trains to shoot animals for profit or adventure. Army commanders, seeing the destruction of the buffalo as a way to undermine the resistance of buffalo-dependent tribes, encouraged the slaughter. The resultant carnage was almost unbelievable. Between 1872 and 1875, non-Indian hunters killed 9 million buffalo, taking the skins but leaving the carcasses to rot. One railroad conductor recalled that a traveler "could have journeyed more than one hundred miles along the railroad right of way, without stepping off the carcass of a slaughtered bison." By the 1880s the relentless killing had reduced the herds to a few thousand animals, destroyed a way of life dependent on the buffalo, and cleared the path for farmers to settle former Indian hunting grounds.

The Transformation of Indian Life

Non-Indian hunters not only wiped out most of the buffalo but also encroached on the Plains Indians' lands. In the Minnesota Territory, for example, the Ojibwa Indians had controlled most of the land in the north as late as 1837, and Dakota Sioux dominated the south. Over the next thirty years, these tribes ceded 24 million acres to the federal government. Treaties established two large reservations within the Minnesota Territory and promised annual government support. However, federal authorities failed to give the Dakota Sioux their yearly payments on time and neglected to provide promised agricultural aid. Driven by hunger and anger at unfulfilled promises, the Sioux returned to their former hunting grounds in August 1862 and killed an estimated 700 white settlers. Reinforced by the U.S. Army, the settlers crushed the uprising in two weeks. Indian casualties far exceeded those of the settlers. Military officials then hanged 38 Indian leaders, jailed those considered dangerous, and exiled the rest to poor-quality reservations in the Dakotas and northeastern Nebraska. By 1866 the number of Sioux in Minnesota had plummeted from 7,000 to 374.

In the 1860s the federal government abandoned its previous policy of treating much of the West as a vast Indian reservation and created a system of smaller, separate tribal reservations on which the Native Americans were to be concentrated, by force if necessary. There, federal officials hoped, the Indians would abandon nomadism for a settled agricultural life. Some Indians, including southwestern Pueblos and the Crows of Montana, accepted this fate. Others, among them the Navajos of Arizona and New Mexico and the Dakota Sioux, initially opposed the new policy, but to no avail. However, the remaining Plains Indians, 100,000 strong, still possessed the will and power to resist. From the 1860s through the 1880s these tribes—the western Sioux, Cheyennes, Arapahos, Kiowas, Comanches, Nez Percés, Bannocks, and Apaches—faced the U.S. Army in a final battle for the West.

In this protracted, bitter conflict, both sides committed atrocities. Two examples illustrate the tragic pattern. In 1864 Cheyennes and Arapahos in southern Colorado, weary of fighting gold miners encroaching on their already-reduced lands, sued for peace and encamped by Sand Creek. Colorado militia attacked the camp, clubbing and slaughtering about 200 Indian men, women, and children even after the Indians had raised a white flag of surrender. "Kill and scalp all, big and little," shouted Colonel John M. Chivington, the militia leader, "nits make lice." Two years later, the Teton Sioux fought a ferocious war against U.S. cavalry to defend land along Wyoming's Powder River. Trying to stop construction of the Bozeman Trail, a road from Wyoming to the gold fields of Montana that intersected the native people's buffalo-hunting grounds, the Tetons, incensed, lured eighty soldiers out of their stockade and killed and mutilated them.

These massacres by both whites and Indians rekindled public debate over federal Indian policy. As western settlers pressed Congress to establish a strict reservation policy under army control instead of the present federal agents and local militia, critics urged a cessation of violence on both sides. In response, Congress in 1867 halted construction on the Bozeman Trail, sent a peace commission to end the fighting, and set aside two large districts where, it was hoped, the nomadic tribes would settle and become Christians. Behind the government's persuasion lay the threat of force. Native Americans who refused to "locate in [the] permanent abodes provided for them," warned the commissioner of Indian affairs, "would be subject wholly to the control and supervision of military authorities, [and] . . . treated as friendly or hostile as circumstances might justify."

At first the plan appeared to work. Representatives of 68,000 southern Plains Indians signed a treaty at Medicine Lodge Creek, Kansas, promising to live on reservations in present-day Oklahoma. The next year, scattered bands of Sioux, 54,000 in number, agreed to move to the Great Sioux Reserve in the western part of modern South Dakota in return for provisions. But Indian dissatisfaction with the treaties ran deep, and many refused to move to, or to remain on, the reservations. A Sioux chief explained, "We do not want to live like the white man. . . . The Great Spirit gave us hunting grounds, gave us the buffalo, the elk, the deer, and the antelope. Our fathers have taught us to hunt and live on the Plains, and we are contented."

In August 1868 war parties of defiant Cheyennes, Arapahos, and Sioux raided frontier settlements in Kansas and Colorado, burning homes and killing whites. In retaliation, army troops attacked any Indians who refused confinement, making little distinction between friendly Native Americans and those responsible for the violence. That autumn, a raiding party under the command of Lieutenant Colonel George Armstrong Custer attacked a sleeping Cheyenne village, killing more than 100 warriors, shooting more than 800 horses, and taking 53 women and children prisoner. Other Cheyennes and Arapahos were pursued, captured, and returned to reservations.

Spurred on by evangelical Christian reformers, Congress in 1869 established the Board of Indian Commissioners to mold reservation life along "desirable" lines. The board wanted to use the major Protestant denominations to break the Indians' nomadic tradition and to force them to remain on the reservations, where they would become Christian farmers. However, the new, inexperienced, church-appointed Indian agents encountered obstacles in trying to implement these policies. Lawrie Tatum, a pacifist Quaker, failed to persuade Comanches and Kiowas to cease raiding Texas settlements and to stay on their Oklahoma reservations. Kiowa chiefs Satanta and Big Tree insisted that they could be at peace with the federal government while remaining at war with Texas. Scheming by whites who fraudulently purchased reservation lands, and squabbling among the Protestant denominations, further undermined the new policy. By the 1880s the federal government, frustrated with the churches, ignored their nominations for Indian agents and made its own appointments.

Caught in an ambiguous and faltering policy, and infuriated by continuing non-Indian settlement of the Plains, Native Americans struck back. In 1874 a Kiowa, Comanche, and Cheyenne raid on the Adobe Walls trading post in the Texas panhandle ignited the Red River War. Regular army troops retaliated, destroying Indian supplies, slaughtering a hundred Cheyenne fugitives near the Sappa River in Kansas, and sending more than seventy "ringleaders" to military prison in Florida. Thus Native American independence on the southern Plains ended. In the Southwest, in what today are Arizona and New Mexico, Apaches under Geronimo fought a guerrilla war but were subdued by 1886.

Custer's Last Stand

Of all the acts of Indian resistance against the reservation policy, none aroused more passion or caused more bloodshed than the conflict between the western Sioux and the U.S. Army in the Dakotas, Montana, and Wyoming. Its roots went back to the Treaty of Fort Laramie (1868), which ended the Powder River War and set aside the Great Sioux Reserve "in perpetuity." But not all the Sioux had fought in the war or signed the treaty. For example, the highly respected Sitting Bull had kept his Hunkpapa Sioux out of the fighting. And western Sioux who had not signed the treaty, including the Oglala and Brulé Sioux, had no intention of moving to the reservation.

Skillfully playing off local officials against the federal government, the Oglala and Brulé bands in 1873 won permission to stay near the Indian agencies along the upper reaches of the White River in Nebraska, near their traditional hunting grounds. They enjoyed the best of both worlds, receiving government provisions but hunting on their customary range. To protect these hunting grounds, they raided white settlements, intimidated federal agents, and harassed miners, surveyors, and others who ventured onto their lands.

The Indian agents' inability to prevent the Sioux from entering and leaving the reservations at will, coupled with growing pressure from would-be colonists and developers, prompted the army to take action. In 1874 General William Tecumseh Sherman sent a force under George Armstrong Custer (now a colonel) into the Black Hills of South Dakota. Lean and mustachioed, with shoulder-length red-blond hair, Custer had been a celebrity since the Civil War. Now decked out in a fringed buckskin uniform and a crimson scarf, the ambitious Custer saw himself in the heroic mold of western adventurers Davy Crockett and Kit Carson.

Ostensibly, Colonel Custer was to find a location for a new fort and keep an eye on renegade Indians, but his real objective was to confirm rumors about gold deposits. While Custer's troops mapped the lush meadows and chose a site for the fort, two "practical miners" panned the streams. In a report telegraphed to the *New York World*, Custer described the region as excellent farm country and casually mentioned finding "gold among the roots of the grass." The resulting gold rush gave the army a new justification for proceeding against the Indians. Custer had in fact become part of an army plan to force concessions from the Sioux. In November 1875, after an attempt to purchase the Black Hills, President Ulysses S. Grant and his generals decided to remove all roadblocks to the entry of miners. As of January 31, 1876, Indians outside the reservations would be taken in by force.

When the Indians refused to return to the reservations, the army mobilized, with Custer in the thick of things. In June 1876 he led 600 troops of the Seventh Cavalry to the Little Bighorn River area of modern Montana, a hub of Indian resistance. On the morning of June 25, Custer, after dividing his forces and underestimating the number of Indians, recklessly led about 225 men against the Indian encampment of 1,500 to 5,000 warriors. Custer and the outnumbered cavalry were surrounded and wiped out.

"Custer's Last Stand" shocked Americans. Most agreed that the federal government must crush the Native American resistance. "It is inconsistent with our civilization and with common sense," trumpeted the *New York Herald*, "to allow the Indian to roam over a country as fine as that around the Black Hills, preventing its development in order that he may shoot game and scalp his neighbors. . . . This region must be taken from the Indian."

The Indians' unexpected coup at Little Bighorn made the army more cautious than before. Taking over the Sioux reservations, the military sent further expeditions into Montana, where troops harassed Sioux bands for the next five years to drive them back onto the reservations. The army attacked Indian camps in the dead of winter and destroyed all supplies. In 1881 lack of provisions forced Sitting Bull, a leader at Little Bighorn, to give up; for a time after his surrender, he suffered the ignominy of appearing as an attraction in Buffalo Bill's Wild West Show.

Similar tactics were used against Chief Joseph and the Nez Percés in Oregon and against the

Northern Cheyennes, who had been transported to Oklahoma after the Battle of Little Bighorn. In September 1878 the Northern Cheyennes' chief, Dull Knife, led 150 survivors north to join the Sioux. The army chased them down and imprisoned them at Fort Robinson, Nebraska. Denied the opportunity to stay on a reservation near their traditional lands, the Cheyennes refused to leave the fort, and the army then withheld all food, water, and fuel. In January 1879 a desperate Dull Knife and his followers shot the guards and broke for freedom. Soldiers gunned down half the Indians in the snow, including women, children, and Dull Knife himself. Although sporadic Indian resistance continued until the end of the century, such brutal tactics sapped the Indians' ability to resist.

"Saving" the Indians

Bloody massacres were not the United States' only answer to the "Indian problem." In 1879 army officer Richard H. Pratt founded the Carlisle Indian School in Pennsylvania to give Indians the skills and cultural attitudes necessary to succeed in American society. Pratt claimed to want to "kill the Indian and save the man." Uprooted from family and tribe, young Indians who attended Carlisle encountered teachers with no respect for traditional Indian culture. Reeducation represented as determined an assault on the Native American world as the slaughter of the buffalo, the seizure of hunting land, and military repression. And because it appealed to humanitarians' sincere concern for the Indians, it was more insidious.

Humanitarians, mainly well-educated easterners, felt outrage at bloody atrocities such as the Fort Robinson massacre and at the federal government's flagrant abuse of its Indian treaties. A lecture tour by Chief Standing Bear, whose peaceful Ponca tribe had been driven from land guaranteed by treaty, further aroused the reformers' indignation. Standing Bear's eloquence particularly affected Helen Hunt Jackson. In *A Century of Dishonor* (1881), Jackson, an easterner transplanted to Colorado, rallied public opinion against the government's record of broken treaties. "It makes little difference," she wrote,

". . . where one opens the record of the history of the Indians; every page and every year has its dark stain."

Well-intentioned humanitarians concluded that the best way to protect Indian interests lay in breaking up reservations, ending all recognition of the tribes, and propelling Native Americans into mainstream society. They would solve the "Indian problem" by eliminating Indians as a culturally distinct entity. They threw their support to the passage in 1887 of the Dawes Severalty Act.

The Dawes Act aimed at reforming the "weaknesses" of Indian life—the absence of private property, and the nomadic tradition—by forcing Indians

Major Indian–White Clashes in the West
Although they were never recognized as such in the popular press, the battles between Native Americans and the U.S. Army on the Great Plains amounted to a major undeclared war.

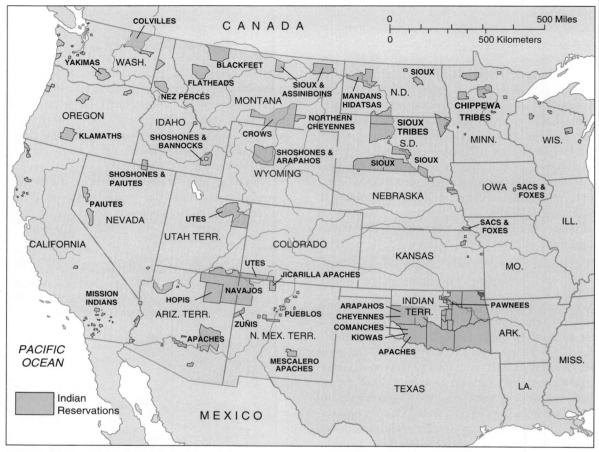

Western Indian Reservations, 1890

Native American reservations were almost invariably located on poor-quality lands. Consequently, when the Dawes Severalty Act broke up the reservations into 160-acre farming tracts, many of the semiarid divisions would not support cultivation.

to be farmers and landowners. The law emphasized severalty, the treatment of Indians as individuals instead of as members of tribes, and called for the breakup of reservations. Each head of an Indian family who accepted the law would receive 160 acres of land for farming or 320 acres for grazing. The government would carve this acreage from reservation lands and would sell off the remaining lands (often the richest). To prevent unscrupulous people from gaining control of parcels granted to individuals, the government would hold the property of each tribal member in trust for twenty-five years. The Dawes Act also made Indians U.S. citizens, with all the rights and responsibilities thereof, including the protection of federal laws and the requirement to pay taxes.

Western speculators who coveted reservation lands and military authorities who wanted to break up reservations lobbied heavily for the Dawes Act. But the bill's strongest support came from such "friends of the Indian" as Helen Hunt Jackson, who wanted to relieve the native peoples' suffering but who also believed in the innate superiority of white American culture. Convinced that citizenship would best protect the Indians, the reformers tried to "civilize" the Native Americans by weaning them from their traditional culture.

Few land allotments were made until the 1890s, but then the breakup of the reservations accelerated. Ultimately, the Dawes Act proved a boon not to Indians but to speculators, who obtained the best land. By 1934 total Indian acreage had declined by 65 percent, and much of what remained in Indian hands was too dry and gravelly for farming.

Some Native Americans who received land under the Dawes Act became large-scale farmers or ranchers, but countless others languished. Hunting restrictions prevented many from supplementing their land yields, and government support steadily increased Indian dependence on federal aid. Alcoholism, a continuing problem worsened by the easy availability of whiskey as a trade item and by boredom, became more prevalent as Native Americans struggled with the constraints of reservation life.

The Ghost Dance and the End of Indian Resistance on the Great Plains

In the late 1880s the Sioux grew desperate. The federal government had reduced their meat rations, and disease had killed a third of their cattle. They turned to Wovoka, a prophet popular among the Great Basin Indians of Nevada, who promised to restore the Sioux to their original dominance if they performed the Ghost Dance. In this ritual the dancers, wearing sacred Ghost Shirts decorated to ward off evil, moved in a circle, accelerating until they became dizzy and passed out. In their trance, they believed, they saw visions of the future. Some dancers claimed special powers to kill non-Indian settlers, and many believed that Ghost Shirts would protect them from harm.

Arapaho Women Performing the Ghost Dance

The dancers believed that, while under a dance-induced trance, their spirits would journey to the paradise promised by the prophet Wovoka.

In the fall of 1890, the spread of the Ghost Dance movement among the Sioux in the Dakota Territory alarmed military authorities. The local reservation agent, Major James McLaughlin, decided to arrest Chief Sitting Bull, whose cabin had become a rallying point for Ghost Dancers. On a freezing December morning, McLaughlin dispatched forty-two Indian policemen to take Sitting Bull into custody. As two policemen pulled the chief from his cabin, his bodyguard shot one of them and the policeman in turn shot Sitting Bull. Then, in the midst of bloody hand-to-hand fighting, Sitting Bull's horse began to perform tricks from its days in the Wild West show. The macabre scene terrified observers, who concluded that the dead chief's spirit had entered his horse.

Sitting Bull's violent death preceded by only two weeks one of the bloodiest episodes in the history of Plains Indian–white relations. On December 29, 1890, the Seventh Calvary began rounding up 350 starving Sioux at Wounded Knee, South Dakota. When several Indians refused to surrender, the soldiers retaliated with rapid-fire Hotchkiss cannons, and within a short time as many as 300 Indians, including infants, lay dead.

As the frozen corpses at Wounded Knee were dumped into mass graves, a generation of Indian-white conflict on the Great Plains shuddered to a close. Some Indians succeeded in adapting to non-Indian ways, but many were devastated at being forced to abandon their religious beliefs and a way of life rooted in hunting, cooperative living, and nomadism. Driven onto reservations, the Plains Indians became almost completely dependent as their cultural traditions, modes of survival, and social organization were crushed. By 1900 the Plains Indian population had shrunk from nearly 250,000 to just over 100,000. Nevertheless, after 1900 the population gradually rose. Against overwhelming odds, the pride, group memory, and cultural identity of the Plains Indians survived all efforts to trample them.

Unlike the nomadic western Sioux, the more settled Navajos of the Southwest adjusted to the reservation system and preserved traditional ways while incorporating elements of the new order. By 1900 the Navajos had tripled their reservation land, dramatically increased their numbers and their herds, and carved out for themselves a distinct place in Arizona and New Mexico.

By the end of the century, the U.S. government had forced extraordinary changes on Indians. In the name of civilization and progress, civic leaders mixed sincere (if misguided) benevolence, coercion wrapped in an aura of legality, and outbursts of naked violence. Some white Americans felt contempt and hatred toward the Indians, but others sought to uplift, educate, and Christianize them. Government officials and ordinary citizens were equally blind to any inherent value in Native American life and traditions, and both played their part in shattering a proud people and an ancient culture. The Indians' fate would weigh on the American conscience for generations.

Settling the West

The Native Americans' defeat opened the way for the settlement of a vast territory stretching from the prairie Plains to the Sierra Nevada and the Cascade Mountains. As railroad expansion lessened the time and hazards of the journey west, migration accelerated. In the next three decades, new settlers started up 2.5 million farms in the Dakotas, Kansas, and Nebraska. More land was parceled out into farms than in the previous 250 years of American history, and agricultural production doubled.

The First Transcontinental Railroad and the Movement West

On May 10, 1869, pealing church bells and booming cannons announced the completion of the first railroad spanning North America. At Promontory Point, Utah, beaming officials drove in a golden spike to link the Union Pacific and the Central Pacific tracks. With the new route's completion, the transcontinental journey shrank from several months to a single week.

The Pacific Railroad Act of 1862 had paved the way for railroad construction. Immigrant labor had done most of the backbreaking work of building the railroad. Chinese workers had blasted through solid rock in the Sierra Nevada, while Irish immigrants had dug their way across Nebraska and Wyoming.

Americans of many other backgrounds, including blacks and Mexican-Americans, had joined in.

The building and financing of the railroads had enormous consequences for the United States. The railroads acquired millions of acres of public land and became the largest landholders in the West under the Pacific Railroad Act. By 1893 many states also had deeded to the railroad companies huge

Transcontinental Railroads and Federal Land Grants, 1850–1900

Despite the laissez-faire ideology that argued against government interference in business, Congress heavily subsidized American railroads and gave them millions of acres of land. As illustrated in the box, belts of land were reserved on either side of a railroad's right of way. Until the railroad claimed the exact one-mile-square sections it chose to possess, all such sections within the belt remained closed to settlement.

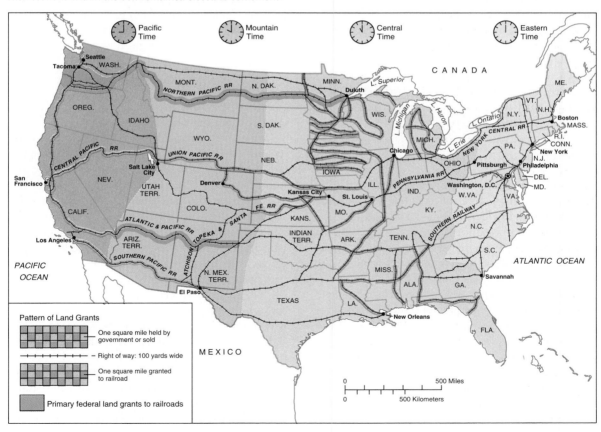

tracts of land, including one-quarter of Minnesota and Washington and one-fifth of the public lands in Wisconsin, North Dakota, and Montana. As landowners, the railroads shaped settlement of much of the West while reaping huge profits.

Between 1870 and 1900 railroads brought nearly 2.2 million immigrant settlers to the West. Entire villages of Germans and Eastern Europeans relocated. By 1905 the Santa Fe Railroad alone had brought 60,000 German-speaking Mennonites from the Ukraine to Kansas.

The railroads dictated settlement patterns. The coal and watering stations they set up along their lines became the nuclei for towns and later for cities. The street layouts and housing styles in the new communities, which rose up by the hundreds, were virtually identical from place to place, thanks to plans and materials furnished by the railroads. The railroads also influenced agriculture. To ensure quick payment of the money owed to them, railroads encouraged new immigrants to grow cash crops—wheat on the Plains, corn in Kansas and Iowa, cotton in Texas. These crops brought high revenues but left farmers dangerously vulnerable to fluctuating market prices.

Homesteaders on the Great Plains

Liberalized land laws also drew settlers west. The Homestead Act of 1862 offered 160 acres of free land to any individual who paid a $10 registration fee, lived on the land for five years, and cultivated and improved it. Because reaching the Great Plains was expensive, most settlers migrated from nearby states. In 1860 Kansas contained 31,000 settlers from Illinois but only 4,200 from New England. Many homesteaders had previously worked at other jobs; on the Dakota frontier, only one-third of the native-stock settlers had farmed before migrating.

The Homestead Act attracted immigrants from the British Isles and other areas of Europe where good-quality land was prohibitively expensive. Urged on by land promoters, waves of English, Irish, Germans, Swedes, Danes, Norwegians, and Czechs formed their own communities on the Great Plains.

Town names such as New Ulm, New Sweden, and New Prague testified to residents' origins. Within a generation, Minnesota's Red River valley boasted the largest Norwegian population outside Norway.

Although nearly 400,000 families claimed land under the Homestead Act between 1869 and 1900, the law did not function as its authors had intended. Speculators, railroads, and state governments acquired huge portions of land, and only one acre in every nine went to the pioneers for whom it was intended. In addition, the 160-acre limit specified by the Homestead Act was ample for farming the rich lands of Minnesota but not sufficient on the arid lands west of the hundredth meridian. Congress passed legislation to address this problem, but speculators, lumber companies, and ranchers abused the laws to amass large holdings. Even though families did not receive as much land as Congress had intended, federal laws kept alive the dream of the West as a place for new beginnings.

New Farms, New Markets

Railroad expansion and liberal land laws coincided with advances in farm mechanization and the development of improved strains of wheat and corn. Thanks to efficient steel plows, specially designed wheat planters, and improved threshers and windmills, the Great Plains farmer of the late nineteenth century harvested ten times more wheat than his counterpart of 1840. Barbed wire, patented in 1874, allowed farmers to keep roving livestock off their land and touched off violent conflict between farmers and ranchers. Generally, the farmers won, and the "open range" began to vanish.

The leap in wheat productivity was fueled by the spiraling growth of eastern urban populations, which increased 400 percent between 1870 and 1910. In turn, new milling techniques encouraged consumption by allowing the wheat's husk and bran to be culled out, producing a silky, better-tasting all-white flour. Minnesota's Washburn Mills (later called General Mills) used the new technology to market bread and cake flour nationally and around the world.

As farming entered a period of seemingly unparalleled prosperity, enthusiastic promoters claimed that anyone could make an easy living in the West. But few people fully understood the sacrifices and perils of agriculture. Land remained expensive, and the cost of horses, machinery, and seed could easily mount to more than $1,200, far more than the average industrial worker earned. Reliant on cash crops to pay off their mortgages, farmers depended on the railroads and were at the mercy of the international grain market's shifting currents.

Western grain growers lost their independence and became players in a world market economy. High demand could bring prosperity, but when overproduction pushed prices down, the heavily indebted farmer faced ruin. The emergence of a global grain trade also drove European peasants onto the Great Plains, where they, too, competed for land and markets. These stark realities forced many Plains farmers to abandon their illusions of independence and easy wealth.

On the western Plains, low rainfall, less than twenty inches a year, increased homesteaders' problems. Farmers compensated by "dry farming"—plowing deeply to stimulate the soil's capillary action, and harrowing lightly to raise a moisture-protective covering of dirt. They also diverted creeks for irrigation. But a drought that began in the 1870s, together with terrible grasshopper infestations and a national depression between 1873 and 1878, drove many to despair.

Building a Society and Achieving Statehood

Adapting to frontier life involved difficult psychological adjustments. Long hours of backbreaking work went into building a house, drilling a well, and plowing and planting fields. The severe conditions on the Kansas Plains prompted a transplanted Pennsylvanian to complain to his parents about the mosquitoes and bedbugs, but he warned them: "Don't publish my diary entire, . . . I don't care to let everybody know how I live, though it might deter some from coming who would otherwise throw away their money." Shining visions of the West as a new Eden dimmed. Blacks who migrated from the South to the Plains after the Civil War found that prejudice and racism compounded their difficulties.

Frontier life posed daunting obstacles for middle-class women settlers swept up in the romantic conventions of the day. The landscape enchanted many at first, and their letters home described the undulating plains as arrestingly beautiful. But soon "horrible tribes of mosquitoes," violent and extreme weather, isolation and loneliness, and the crude sod huts they called home made many miserable. In a typical reaction, a young bride burst into tears upon first seeing her new sod home, and told her husband that her father had better housing for his hogs.

Many people failed to adapt to their new environment, and the transiency rate on the frontier was high. Seventy-nine percent of the families in one typical Wisconsin county in 1880 had moved by 1895. The rigors of frontier life forced some out, and the hope of finding better land lured others westward. But those who "stuck it out" came to identify closely with the land. Wood-frame homes eventually replaced "soddies," and farm settlements blossomed into towns. Churches and Sunday schools became centers of social activity as well as worship. Farmers gathered for barn raisings and group threshings; families pooled their energies in quilting and husking bees. Cooperation was both a practical necessity and a form of insurance in a rugged environment where everyone was vulnerable to disaster. As settlements mushroomed into towns, their residents eagerly established libraries, lyceums, and Masonic lodges and other social clubs, in part to dispel the image of small towns as cultural backwaters. Larger communities built fashionable hotels and imported entertainers for their new "opera houses." Basically conservative, the new pioneers patterned their churches, schools, courts, and government after the ones they had left behind.

To achieve statehood, the residents of a territory had to petition Congress to pass an enabling act establishing the proposed state's boundaries and authorizing an election to select delegates for a state constitutional convention. Once a state constitution had been drawn up and ratified by popular vote, the territory applied to Congress for admission as a state. Under these procedures, Kansas entered the Union in 1861, followed by Nevada in 1864, Nebraska in 1867, and Colorado in 1876. Not until 1889 did North Dakota, South Dakota, Montana, and Washington become states. Wyoming and Idaho entered the Union the following year. Utah, its admission long delayed because of the Mormon practice of polygyny, finally outlawed plural marriages and entered in 1896. With Oklahoma's entry in 1907 and Arizona's and New Mexico's in 1912, the process of creating permanent political institutions along the frontier in the "lower forty-eight" states was complete.

Although conservative, several of the new state governments supported woman suffrage. Pioneer women battled for the vote, and between 1870 and 1910 seven western states held referenda on the issue. Success came first in the Wyoming Territory, where the legislature enfranchised women in 1869. By attracting the "gentler sex," who were outnumbered six to one, Wyoming lawmakers hoped to improve the territory's reputation as a haven of rowdy mining camps. Utah also supported woman suffrage, and Nebraska and Colorado permitted women to vote in school elections. Still, by 1910 only four states, Idaho, Wyoming, Utah, and Colorado, had granted women full voting rights.

The Grange

Plains farming remained risky. Between 1873 and 1877 terrible grasshopper infestations consumed half the midwestern wheat crop. After 1870 production rose and prices fell. Wheat tumbled from $2.95 a bushel in 1866 to $1.06 in 1880. Farmers who had borrowed to finance their homesteads and machinery went bankrupt or barely survived. In 1874 an elderly Minnesotan wrote, "We can see nothing but starvation in the future if relief does not come."

When relief did not come, farmers established their own cooperative ventures. In 1867, under the leadership of Oliver H. Kelley, a Department of Agriculture clerk, midwestern farmers formed the Grange, or "Patrons of Husbandry." The Grange offered education, emotional support, and fellowship; membership had climbed to more than 1.5 million by the early 1870s. The Grange maintained a library of information on planting and livestock and organized covered-dish dinners and songfests. Farmers isolated on remote farms could find "an opportunity for social, intellectual, and moral improvement."

At the heart of the Grange was farmers' concern over their economic plight. An 1874 circular defined its purpose: to help farmers to "buy less and produce more, in order to make our farms more self-sustaining." Grangers shared the old republican, Jeffersonian-Jacksonian belief that the bounty of the soil formed the basis of all honorable wealth and that the producers formed the true backbone of society. The Grangers wanted to restore self-sufficiency to family farms. The Grange negotiated discounts from farm-machinery dealers and established "cash-only" cooperative stores and grain elevators to eliminate the "middlemen"—bankers, grain brokers, and merchants who grew rich at the farmers' expense. And the Grangers attacked the railroads, which hurt farmers by giving discounts to large shippers, bribing state legislators for land grants, and charging higher rates for short runs than for long hauls. Although supposedly nonpolitical, midwestern Grangers lobbied state legislatures for laws setting maximum rates for freight shipments.

The railroads appealed these "Granger laws" to the Supreme Court. But in *Munn* v. *Illinois* (1877), the Court not only ruled against the railroads but also upheld an Illinois law fixing a maximum rate for grain storage. The case of *Wabash* v. *Illinois* (1886), however, later prohibited states from regulating *interstate* railroad rates. Then in 1887 Congress passed the Interstate Commerce Act, establishing a new agency, the Interstate Commerce Commission, to investigate and oversee railroad operations. The commission did little to curb the railroads, but it did establish the principle of federal regulation of interstate transportation.

Was the Grange correct in blaming greedy railroads and middlemen for farm problems? The answer is not simple. From 1873 to 1878, the entire economy was trapped in a depression that stung railroads and farmers alike. Although farm commodity prices fell between 1865 and 1900, so did prices on manufactured goods. Railroads could justify their stiff freight rates in part by the thin pattern of western settlement and the seasonality of grain shipments. Nonetheless, farmers and Grangers had reason to complain. Farmers had no control over the prices they received for their crops and were at the mercy of local merchants and farm-equipment dealers who held monopolies. Railroads sometimes transported wheat to only one mill or refused to stop at small towns. These policies struck farmers as arbitrary and left them feeling powerless.

Despite its gains, the Grange movement soon faltered. By 1878 intense railroad lobbying had won repeal of most state regulations. The cash-only cooperatives failed because few farmers had cash, and the Grange ideal of financial independence proved unrealistic. Under the conditions prevailing on the Plains after the Civil War, it was impossible to farm without borrowing money. Although the Grange movement had peaked by 1880, it laid the groundwork for an even more powerful wave of agrarian protest in the 1880s and 1890s (see Chapter 21).

The Southwestern Frontier

Until 1848, when the Treaty of Guadalupe-Hidalgo ceded an immense territory to the United States, Mexicans had controlled the Southwest. There they had built their own churches, maintained ranches, and traded with the Indians. Although the peace treaty pledged the United States to protect the liberty and property of Mexicans who remained on U.S. soil, over the next three decades, aggressive American ranchers and settlers forced the Spanish-speaking population off much of the land. Mexicans who stayed behind adapted to Anglo society with varying degrees of success.

In Texas, where the revolution against Mexico and later the Mexican War had left a legacy of bitterness and misunderstanding, Anglos frequently harassed Mexican-Americans and confiscated their lands. Border raids by Mexican bandits worsened the situation. Tensions peaked in 1859 when Juan Cortina, a Mexican rancher, led an attack on Brownsville, Texas, and freed all the prisoners in jail. Cortina slipped back and forth across the U.S.-Mexican border for years until the Mexican government, fearing an American invasion, imprisoned him in 1875.

Similar violence erupted in California in the 1850s and 1860s after a cycle of flood and drought ruined many large ranches owned by the *californios*, Spanish-speaking descendants of the original Spanish and Mexican settlers. The collapse of the ranch economy forced many *californios* to retreat into barrios—socially segregated urban neighborhoods. A rapid increase in Anglo migration left the Mexican-American minorities stranded within the cities, where they survived as low-paid day workers and kept a tenacious hold on their cultural traditions.

The adaptation of Spanish-speaking Americans to Anglo society unfolded more smoothly in Arizona and New Mexico, where the original Spanish settlement was sparse and where a small class of wealthy Mexican landowners dominated a poor, illiterate peasantry. As early as the 1820s, wealthy Mexicans in Arizona had sent their children to the United States for education and had formed trading and business partnerships with Americans. Perhaps the most successful was Estevan Ochoa, who began a freighting business in 1859 with an American partner and expanded it into a lucrative merchandising, mining, and sheep-raising operation. The achievements of Ochoa (who rose to become Tucson's mayor) and other Mexican businessmen helped to moderate Anglo antagonism toward the Mexican-American population.

But in the 1880s violence erupted between Mexican-American and Anglo ranchers in Arizona and New Mexico. Organized as *Las Gorras Blancas* (The White Caps) in 1888, Mexican-American ranchers attacked Anglo settlers who had fenced in parts of northern New Mexico that previously had been public grazing land. In the cities, Mexican-American businessmen commonly restricted their professional dealings to their own people, and the Spanish-speaking population as a whole became more impoverished. Even in Tucson, where the Mexican-American elite enjoyed considerable prosperity, 80 percent of Mexican-Americans in the

Wash Day
This photograph shows a Hispanic family in San Antonio doing washing chores, c. 1870.

work force were laborers by 1880, employed as butchers, barbers, cowboys, and railroad workers.

During the 1890s, a time of rising racism on the national level, violence and discrimination against the Southwest's Spanish-speaking citizens escalated. Riots occurred in the Texas communities of Beeville and Laredo in 1894 and 1899. Expressions of anti-Catholicism and verbal attacks on Mexican-Americans as violent and lazy increased among Anglos. Spanish-speaking citizens' battle for fair treatment and cultural respect would continue into the twentieth century.

Exploiting the West

From gold mines to cattle ranches to huge farms, the West appeared ripe with get-rich-quick opportunities between 1850 and 1890. Banner headlines across the country publicized bonanza after bonanza, building up the myth of the frontier as a place of boundless opportunity. In reality, the bonanzas set in motion a boom-and-bust economy in which a few

became fabulously rich, a lot lost their shirts, and most barely survived.

The Mining Frontier

Beginning with the California gold rush of 1849, mining booms consumed the west. The original California strike was followed by a gold strike in British Columbia in 1857. Then in 1858 prospector Henry Comstock stumbled on the rich Comstock Lode of gold and silver along Nevada's Carson River; and a few months later, gold and silver seekers found still more precious ore along Clear Creek, Colorado, near present-day Denver. By 1900 gold strikes dotted the map from Idaho, Montana, Wyoming, and South Dakota all the way north to the Alaskan Klondike. California yielded more than a billion dollars in gold; the Comstock Lode alone produced more than $300 million in gold and silver.

Early discoveries often consisted of "placer" gold, panned from riverbeds and streams. These finds reinforced the myth of the mining country as "a poor man's paradise." In 1860 almost one of every four Californians claimed mining as their occupation. Although a few prospectors mined huge fortunes, the majority remained poor. Most of the West's mining wealth fell into the hands of bankers and companies that could afford the huge amounts of capital necessary to tap the rich veins of gold and silver ore deep within the earth. Large mining companies, backed by eastern and British capital, soon took over the major discoveries. Henry Comstock sold one claim for $11,000 and another for two mules.

The great discoveries such as the Comstock Lode and the Clear Creek strike might not have brought wealth to many prospectors, but they did create boom towns. Virginia City, Nevada, was typical. A shantytown in 1859, it blossomed by 1873 into a metropolis of 20,000 residents. Males outnumbered females three to one. Among its buildings stood mansions, a six-story hotel, an opera house, 131 saloons, 4 banks, and uncounted brothels.

Word of new discoveries lured miners, ever anxious to get rich, to mining towns such as Virginia City. The chaotic rush to stake new claims led to widespread cheating and theft. When Virginia City's small, corrupt police force failed to maintain order, vigilantes took over the town, hanged two notorious outlaws, and forced others off the lode. Miners typically earned about $2,000 a year (teachers made $450 to $650), but meals and a room could cost between $480 and $720 annually in a boom town. Furthermore, mining was difficult and dangerous—more than 300 workers died in the Virginia City mines in less than twenty years. And

Chinese Immigrant Labor
These young Chinese workers at the Deadwood mines in the Dakota Territory served as a colorfully dressed hose squad.

when miners had exhausted the ore-bearing veins, they left for new territories. By 1900 Virginia City's population had shrunk to below 4,000.

Virginia City's boom-and-bust story was replayed again and again across the West between 1870 and 1900. Mark Twain captured the thrill of mining "stampedes" in his book *Roughing It* (1872). "Every few days," he wrote, "news would come of the discovery of a brand-new mining region; immediately the papers would teem with accounts of its richness, and away the surplus population would scamper to take possession. By the time I was fairly inoculated with the disease, 'Esmeralda' had just had a run and 'Humboldt' was beginning to shriek for attention. 'Humboldt! Humboldt!' was the new cry, and straightway Humboldt, the newest of the new, the richest of the rich, the most marvelous of the marvelous discoveries in silver-land, was occupying two columns of the public prints to 'Esmeralda's' one."

Most miners earned only enough to go elsewhere and try again, pursuing the elusive dream of riches across the West. The myth of the frontier exaggerated the opportunities of the mining West, but it contained just enough reality to sustain people's hopes.

Cowboys and the Cattle Frontier

Just as romanticized accounts of gold strikes fueled the feverish expansion of the mining frontier, romantic tales of hardy cowboys driving longhorns north from Texas helped to spark the transformation of the cattle industry in these same decades. Businessmen and railroad entrepreneurs promoted cattle herding as the new route to fame and fortune. The cowboy, once scorned as a ne'er-do-well and drifter, was glorified as a man of rough-hewn integrity and self-reliant strength who lived a life of adventurous simplicity on the Chisholm, Shawnee, and other fabled cattle trails of the Southwest.

In 1868 Joseph G. McCoy, a young cattle dealer from Illinois, combined organizational and promotional skills to make the cattle industry a new bonanza. McCoy had reaped substantial profits

trading livestock during the Civil War. He was well aware that attempts in the 1850s to drive longhorn cattle from south Texas grasslands northward to markets in Arkansas, Illinois, and Missouri had failed because of frequent Indian attacks and outbreaks of "Texas fever" that had killed thousands of cattle. But with the Plains Indians' relocation onto reservations and the railroads' extension into Kansas, McCoy saw a renewed potential in cattle shipping.

Having formed a partnership in 1867 with a company that shipped cattle to New Orleans and New York, McCoy went to Kansas to construct a new stockyard in Abilene. He overcame opposition by purchasing supplies from neighboring ranchers at high prices and reimbursing them for any stock that died of Texas fever. By guaranteeing to ship his steers by rail to hungry eastern markets, McCoy gained a five-dollar kickback on each cattle car. To make the overland drive from Texas easier, he helped to survey and shorten the Chisholm Trail. Finally, in a clever feat of showmanship, he organized the first Wild West show, sending four Texas cowboys to St. Louis and Chicago, where their roping and riding exhibitions attracted both exuberant crowds and eager buyers for the cattle he shipped. At the end of McCoy's first year in Abilene, 35,000 steers were trailed north and sold; the following year, the number more than doubled to 75,000.

The great cattle drives of the 1860s and 1870s became a bonanza for herd owners. Steers purchased in Texas for $9 a head sold for $28 in Abilene. A herd of 2,000 head could generate a tidy $30,000 profit. But cattlemen lived at the mercy of high interest rates and unstable markets. During the Panic of 1873, hundreds of cattle drovers fell into bankruptcy. At the same time, railroad promoters kept investors interested by shamelessly exaggerating the potential for profit.

Persuaded by these claims, miners, farmers, and others anxious to get rich quickly turned to ranching. Foreign investors sank huge sums into the cattle business. The English alone put $45 million into ranch companies in the 1870s and 1880s; by 1883 British companies owned or controlled nearly 20 million acres of western grazing land. American businesses dived in; during the 1880s twenty domestically owned companies, worth from $20,000 to $3 million, operated in Wyoming alone.

Little money found its way into the pockets of the cowboys themselves. Cowpunchers who drove herds 800 miles through dirt and dust from Texas to Kansas earned $30 a month, about the same as common laborers. Long hours, low pay, and hazardous work discouraged many older ranch hands from applying. Most cowboys were young men in their teens and twenties who worked for a year or two for quick money and then pursued different livelihoods.

One-fifth of trail riders were black or Mexican. Barred from many other trades, African-American cowboys enjoyed the freedom of life on the trail and distinguished themselves as shrewd and resourceful cowpunchers. One of the best-known black cowboys was Nat Love, the son of Tennessee slaves. By his own account, he was "wild, reckless, free" and "afraid of nothing." On July 4, 1876, with the Black Hills gold rush in full swing, Love delivered 3,000 head of cattle and then rode into Deadwood to celebrate. That same day, he won roping and shooting contests and a new title, Deadwood Dick. Close relationships sometimes developed between white and black cowboys. Charles Goodnight, a pioneer trailblazer, called the black cowboy Bose Ikard, a former slave, "my detective, banker, and everything else in Colorado, New Mexico, and the other wild country I was in."

At odds with the lonely, dirty, and often boring cowboy life were the exploits of the mythic frontier cowboy, glamorized by the eastern press as early as the 1870s. The image of the West as a lawless land where cowboys-turned-vigilantes battled brutish bandits fired easterners' imaginations. In 1877 Edward L. Wheeler wrote his first dime novel, *Deadwood Dick, The Prince of the Road: or, the Black Rider of the Black Hills.* Over the next eight years, Wheeler churned out thirty-three Deadwood Dick novels about the adventures of his muscular young hero, who turned his blazing six-shooters on ruthless ruffians and dishonest desperadoes. The fictional character had much in common with the real-life Deadwood Dick except that Wheeler, to appeal to his white readership, made Dick a white man. The vigilante justice and lynch law that reigned in these novels presented the western frontier as a throwback to a semilegendary earlier age in which honor had triumphed when the righteous took matters into their own hands.

The reality was much less picturesque. In Abilene, for example, a brief period of violence and turmoil ended when the town established a police force. City ordinances forbade carrying firearms and regulated saloons, gambling, and prostitution. James B. ("Wild Bill") Hickok served as town marshal in 1871, but his tenure was less eventful than legend has it. Dime novelists described him as "a veritable terror to bad men on the border," but Marshal Hickok killed just two men, one of them by mistake. "Cow towns" like Abilene, Wichita, and Dodge City did not have unusually high homicide rates.

More typical of western conflicts were the "range wars" that pitted ranchers, who thought that the open range existed for them, against farmers anxious to fence and plow it. Gaining the upper hand in state legislatures, farm interests tried to cripple the cattlemen with quarantine laws and inspection regulations. Ranchers retaliated against the spread of barbed-wire fence, first by cutting settlers' fences and then by buying and enclosing thousands of acres of their own. Small-scale shooting incidents broke out between farmers and cattle drivers and between rival cattlemen and sheep ranchers.

Peaking during 1880–1885, the bonanza produced more than 4.5 million head of cattle for eastern markets. However, as early as 1882 prices sagged and some ranchers fell into debt. In 1885 President Grover Cleveland, trying to improve federal observance of Indian treaties, ordered cattlemen to remove their stock from the Cheyenne-Arapaho reservation, and 200,000 more cattle crowded onto already overgrazed ranges. In 1885 and 1886 a devil's brew of winter blizzards, searing droughts, and Texas fever destroyed 90 percent of the cattle in some areas of open range and pushed thousands of ranchers into bankruptcy. Survivors had to irrigate and fence their land and raise their cattle on smaller ranches. The open range and the great cattle drives were finished.

Bonanza Farms on the Plains

The heady enthusiasm that permeated mining and ranching in the 1870s and 1880s also percolated into agriculture. A wheat boom in the Dakota Territory attracted large capital investments that produced the nation's first "agribusiness."

The boom began during the Panic of 1873, when bank failures caused Northern Pacific Railroad bond values to plummet, and the railroad exchanged land for the depreciated bonds. Speculators purchased more than 300,000 acres in the fertile Red River valley of North Dakota for between fifty cents and a dollar an acre. Singly or in groups, they established enormous factorylike farms run by hired managers, and they invested heavily in labor and equipment. The Cass-Cheney-Dalrymple farm near Fargo, North Dakota, for example, covered twenty-four square miles and hired fifty men to plow and an additional one hundred workers to harvest.

The publicity generated by the success of such large investors created an unprecedented wheat boom in the Red River valley. Banking syndicates and small farmers rushed to buy land, North Dakota's population tripled, and wheat production skyrocketed. But the profits soon evaporated, and by 1890 some Red River valley farmers were destitute. Overproduction, high investment costs, erratic rainfall, excessive reliance on one crop, and depressed international grain prices had all contributed to the boom's collapse. Large-scale farmers who had dreamed of getting rich felt lucky simply to survive. By 1889 Oliver Dalrymple, the "king" of the wheat growers, lamented that "it seems as if the time has come when there is no money in wheat raising."

The Oklahoma Land Rush

Meanwhile, would-be homesteaders greedily eyed the huge Indian Territory (modern Oklahoma).

Considering much of the land worthless, the federal government in the 1830s had reserved it for the Five Civilized Tribes. But to punish the tribes for supporting the Confederacy during the Civil War, the government had settled thousands of Indians from *other* tribes in the territory. In the 1880s land-hungry non-Indians argued that the Civilized Tribes' betrayal of the Union justified further confiscation of their land.

In 1889 Congress transferred 2 million acres of unassigned Oklahoma land to the federal public domain. At noon on April 22, 1889, thousands of men, women, and children in buggies and wagons stampeded onto the new lands to stake out homesteads. (Others, the so-called Sooners, had infiltrated the lands illegally and were already plowing fields.) Before nightfall, tent communities had risen at Oklahoma City and Guthrie, near the Santa Fe Railroad. Within two months, 6,000 claims had been filed. As the Dawes Severalty Act freed up additional land, new torrents of homesteaders poured into the territory.

The land rush demonstrated the continuing power of the frontier myth, which tied "free" land to the ideals of self-determination and individual opportunity. Most early Oklahoma homesteaders succeeded as farmers because ample rainfall and fertile soil yielded substantial crops. But within two generations, a combination of exploitive farming, poor land management, and drought would turn Oklahoma into the desolate center of the Dust Bowl.

The West of Life and Legend

In 1893, four years after the Oklahoma land rush, the young historian Frederick Jackson Turner delivered a lecture entitled "The Significance of the Frontier in American History." Turner declared that "the frontier has gone, and with its going has closed the first period of American history." Turner's remarks prompted historians to explore the effects of the frontier on U.S. history and helped to awaken broad popular interest in the frontier experience.

As the real West had developed, a parallel mythic West had taken root in the American imagination. Originally the product of nineteenth-century novels, songs, and paintings, the legend would be perpetuated by twentieth-century mass media. Its evolution is fascinating, and its influence far-reaching.

The American Adam and the Dime-Novel Hero

James Fenimore Cooper and other nineteenth-century writers presented the frontiersman as an American Adam—simple, virtuous, innocent, and untainted by a corrupt social order. Similarly, an early biographer of Kit Carson portrayed the mountain man as an antidote to refined society, a person of "genuine simplicity . . . truthfulness . . . [and] bravery." And in Mark Twain's *The Adventures of Huckleberry Finn* (1885), Huck heads west "because Aunt Sally she's going to adopt me and sivilize [*sic*] me, and I can't stand it." Themes of adventure, romance, contemplation, and escape from society and its pressures pervaded these works.

An alternative West emerged in the dime novels that blanketed the nation in the 1860s and 1870s. This West featured a frontiersman deeply immersed in society and its concerns. In a fictionalized biography of "Buffalo Bill" Cody, Edward Judson (who used the pen name Ned Buntline) made Cody a powerful force for justice and social order as he drives off treacherous Indians and rounds up horse thieves and cattle rustlers. So wildly popular was this new fictional frontiersman that the real Cody started his own Wild West show in 1883. In Chicago the spectacle attracted 42,000 people on the first day. They thrilled to steer roping and rodeo contests and even to the appearance of the great Sioux chief Sitting Bull, whose role was to stare malevolently at the crowd. Cody also presented mock "battles" between army scouts and Indians, morality dramas of good versus evil. The Wild West show thus reinforced the dime-novel image of the West as an arena of moral encounter where virtue always triumphed.

Revitalizing the Frontier Legend

Three notable members of the eastern establishment, historian and essayist Theodore Roosevelt, painter and sculptor Frederic Remington, and novelist Owen Wister, used both mythical Wests—the refuge from society, and the stage for moral conflict—in their work. In the 1880s all three spent much time in the West, and the experience intensely affected them. Feeling constrained by their genteel urban world, they went west for the physical challenges and moral simplicities of the dime novels. Each found what he sought.

The frontier that Roosevelt glorified in *The Winning of the West* (1889–1896) and other works, and that Remington portrayed in his art, was a stark physical and moral environment that tested true character. Viewing the West through the lens of Charles Darwin's evolutionary theory, which characterized life as a struggle that only the fittest and the best survived, Roosevelt and Remington exalted the disappearing frontier as the last outpost of an honest and true social order. This version of the frontier myth reached full flower, however, in Owen Wister's popular novel *The Virginian* (1902). In Wister's tale, the physical and social environment of the Great Plains produced individuals like his unnamed cowboy hero "the Virginian," an honest, strong, compassionate man, quick to help the weak and to fight the wicked. The Virginian is one of nature's aristocrats—ill educated and unsophisticated but upright, steady, and deeply moral. For Wister, and for Roosevelt and Remington, too, the cowboy was the Christian knight on the Great Plains, indifferent to material gain as he upheld virtue, pursued justice, and attacked evil.

Western myth was far removed from western realities. The mythical West ignored the hard physical labor of the cattle range and glossed over the ugly underside of frontier expansion—the brutalities of Indian warfare, the perils of commercial agriculture and cattle ranching, and the boom-and-bust mentality rooted in the selfish exploitation of natural resources. Further, the myth obscured the complex links between the settlement of the frontier and the emergence of the United States as a major industrial nation. Indeed, eastern and foreign capital bankrolled mining, ranching, and farming; technology underlay agricultural productivity; and without railroads, western expansion would have been unthinkable.

Beginning a Conservation Movement

Despite its one-sided, idealistic vision, Wister's celebration of the western experience reinforced a growing recognition that overeager entrepreneurs might well ruin the western landscape. Two important results of the western legend were surging public support for national parks and the beginning of an organized conservation movement.

The natural beauty of the landscape awed the explorers and mappers of the High Plains and Rocky Mountains. Major John Wesley Powell, who charted the Colorado River in 1869, wrote eloquently about the region's towering rock formations and thundering cataracts. Powell's *Report on the Lands of the Arid Regions of the United States* (1878) not only recognized the awesome beauty of the Colorado River basin but argued that settlers needed to adjust their expectations about the use of water in the dry western terrain.

At the same time that Powell was exploring the Grand Canyon, General Henry D. Washburn led a party to the Yellowstone River area of Wyoming and Montana. The explorers were stunned. "Amid the canyon and falls, the boiling springs and sulphur mountains, and, above all, the mud volcano and the geysers of the Yellowstone, your memory becomes filled and clogged with objects new in experience, wonderful in extent, and possessing unlimited grandeur and beauty," one member of the party later wrote. The Washburn explorers abandoned their plan to claim this area for the Northern Pacific Railroad and instead petitioned Congress to protect it from settlement, occupancy, and sale. In 1872 Congress created Yellowstone National Park to "provide for the preservation . . . of all time, mineral deposits, natural curiosities, or wonders within said park . . . in their natural condition."

These steps to conserve the West's natural resources reflected the beginnings of a changed awareness of the environment. George Perkins Marsh, a Vermont architect and politician, used his influential study *Man and Nature* (1864) to attack the view that nature existed to be conquered. He warned Americans to stop their destructive use of the land. "Man," he wrote, "is everywhere a disturbing agent. Wherever he plants his foot, the harmonies of nature are turned to discords."

Marsh's plea for conservation found its most eloquent support in the work of John Muir, a Scottish immigrant who had grown up in Wisconsin. Muir fell in love with the redwood forests of the Yosemite Valley, and for forty years he tramped the rugged mountains of the West. A romantic at heart, he struggled to experience the wilderness at its most elemental level. Once caught high in the Rockies during a summer storm, he climbed the tallest pine around and swayed back and forth in the raging wind. Muir became the late nineteenth century's most articulate publicist for wilderness protection. His campaign to preserve the wilderness contributed to the establishment of Yosemite National Park in 1890 and the creation two years later of the Sierra Club, committed to encouraging the enjoyment and protection of the wilderness in the mountain region of the Pacific coast.

The wilderness-protection movement reaffirmed the image of the West as a unique region whose magnificent landscape produced tough individuals of superior ability. Overlooking the senseless violence and ruthless exploitation of the land, writers, historians, and politicians kept alive the legend of the western frontier as a seedbed of American virtue.

Conclusion

The divergence between the mythic and the real West offers clues to the power and the importance of the myth. Ill at ease with changes produced by industrialization, urbanization, and immigration, countless Americans embraced the West as an uncomplicated Eden where flourished the social simplicity and moral clarity that for easterners were lost forever. Molded by writers, politicians, and artists, the myth captivated Americans. The more tenaciously they clung to the myth, the harder it became for them to understand, and adjust to, the transformations around them.

Of all those who tried to come to terms with the meaning of the West, Frederick Jackson Turner, who insisted that the frontier was the key to understanding American history, remains one of the most fascinating. "The expansion westward with its new opportunities, its continuous touch with the simplicity of primitive society," he argued, "furnish[es] the forces dominating [the] American character." The frontier experience, he continued, produced a practical, inventive, self-reliant people who valued individualism and freedom. As a description of social reality, Turner's analysis left much to be desired. But in his articulation and distillation of ideas about the West, Turner demonstrated the powerful hold of the frontier myth on the national imagination and became one of its most persuasive advocates.

The settlement of the West occupies two separate dimensions. First, it was a formidable episode in the social, economic, and political history of the United States. Second, it was a process that lived in the popular imagination long after the frontier had vanished, influencing Americans' ideas about society, government, and themselves.

Chronology

1849 California gold rush.

1858 Henry Comstock strikes gold in Nevada.
Gold discovered at Clear Creek, Colorado.

1862 Homestead Act.
Sioux War breaks out in Minnesota.

1864 Massacre of Cheyennes at Sand Creek, Colorado.
George Perkins Marsh, *Man and Nature*.

1867 Joseph McCoy organizes cattle drives to Abilene, Kansas.
The Grange (Patrons of Husbandry) founded.
New Indian policy of smaller reservations adopted.
Medicine Lodge Treaty.

1868 Fort Laramie Treaty.

1869 Board of Indian Commissioners established to reform Indian reservation life.

1872 Mark Twain, *Roughing It*.
Yellowstone National Park established.

1873 Panic allows speculators to purchase thousands of acres in the Red River valley of North Dakota cheaply.
Biggest strike on Nevada's Comstock Lode.

1874 Invention of barbed wire.
Gold discovered in the Black Hills of South Dakota.
Red River War pits the Kiowas, Comanches, and Cheyennes against the U.S. Army.
Grasshopper infestations ruin crops in Iowa and Kansas.

1876 Colorado admitted to the Union, gives women the right to vote in school elections.
Massacre of Colonel George Armstrong Custer and his troops at Little Bighorn.

1877 *Munn v. Illinois*.

1878 John Wesley Powell, *Report on the Lands of the Arid Regions of the United States*.

1879 Massacre of northern Cheyennes at Fort Robinson, Nebraska.

1881 Helen Hunt Jackson, *A Century of Dishonor*.

1883 William ("Buffalo Bill") Cody organizes Wild West show.

1886 Severe drought on the Plains destroys cattle and grain.
      Wabash v. *Illinois*.

1887 Dawes Severalty Act.

1888 *Las Gorras Blancas* (The White Caps) raid ranchers in northern New Mexico.

1889 Oklahoma Territory opened for settlement.

1889– Theodore Roosevelt, *The Winning of the West*.
1896

1890 Ghost Dance movement spreads to the Black Hills.
      Massacre of Teton Sioux at Wounded Knee, South Dakota.
      Yosemite National Park established.

1892 John Muir organizes the Sierra Club.

1893 Frederick Jackson Turner, "The Significance of the Frontier in American History."

1902 Owen Wister, *The Virginian*.

FOR FURTHER READING

Gilbert G. Fite, *The Farmers' Frontier, 1865–1900* (1966). A spirited introduction to farming on the Great Plains.

Peter Iverson, *The Navajos* (1990). A brief, insightful history of the culture and everyday life of the Navajos.

Patricia Nelson Limerick, *The Legacy of Conquest: The Unbroken Past of the American West* (1987). A critical assessment of the movement westward that critiques Turner's frontier thesis.

Sandra L. Myres, *Westering Women and the Frontier Experience, 1800–1915* (1982). An excellent brief survey of women's experiences on the frontier.

Richard Slotkin, *The Fatal Environment* (1985). A provocative exploration of the legend of the frontier and its relationship to Custer's last stand.

Duane A. Smith, *Mining America: The Industry and the Environment, 1800–1980* (1987). A thoughtful assessment of environmental damage caused by mining.

Richard White, *"It's Your Misfortune and None of My Own": A New History of the American West* (1991). A revisionist work depicting the nineteenth-century West as a meeting place and arena of conflict for many cultures.

The industrial transformation of the late nineteenth century both exhilarated and unsettled Americans. In thirty years (1870–1900), the United States became the world's leading industrial power, doubling its iron and textile production, quadrupling the number of workers in manufacturing, and increasing overall manufacturing output more than 600 percent. But while new technologies and new inventions made life vastly more comfortable and convenient, they also led to the victimization of laborers and deterioration of the environment.

Much of the rest of this book will examine the profound consequences of industrialization. First, we will examine how the transformation occurred and how it affected the people whose labor made it possible.

The Rise of Industrial America

(Right) Young water carriers at Homestead, Pennsylvania

The Character of Industrial Change
The New South
Industrial Work and the Work Force
Labor Unions and Industrial Conflict

The Character of Industrial Change

Four features marked the birth of industrial America: the rapid growth of technological innovation and of the factory system; ferocious competition and a tendency toward monopolistic consolidation; a relentless drop in prices; and high interest rates and tight credit as the growth of the money supply lagged behind productivity.

These factors were interrelated. Technological change increased productivity and catalyzed industrial expansion. It also let manufacturers cut costs and hire cheap unskilled or semiskilled labor. This cost cutting drove firms to undersell each other, pushing weak firms out of business and prompting stronger, more efficient, and more ruthless ones to consolidate. Until the mid-1890s, cost reduction, technology, and competition forced prices down. Farmers suffered from low commodity prices, and workers felt the sting of low wages, but both groups benefited as store-bought goods cheapened. Meanwhile, high interest rates and tight credit hurt farmers and small entrepreneurs. And the depressions of the 1870s and 1890s hit all Americans hard. Above all, business leaders' unflagging drive to maximize efficiency produced colossal fortunes for a handful even as it forced millions to live near the subsistence level.

The skyrocketing demand for consumer goods stimulated the production of "capital goods," machinery to boost farm and factory output. Railroads and corporations that manufactured capital goods, refined petroleum, and made steel propelled the economy forward.

A stunning expansion in the scale of industry reflected the magnitude of economic change. Until the 1870s Americans defined a company employing a hundred workers as a large business. By 1900, however, mammoth corporations dominated industry. Singer Sewing Machines employed more than 90,000 employees and sold 1.25 million sewing machines yearly. Similar marvels of production and size characterized railroads, meatpacking, steel, sugar,

Train Travel
Railroad companies established new standards for comfort, convenience, and speed. The Pullman Palace Car Company built special sleeping and dining cars that, according to one rider, made "traveling a pleasure and a recreation."

and oil. But nowhere was the aggressive competition that characterized the emergence of industrial America more intense than among the railroads, the symbol of industrial progress.

Railroad Innovations

By 1900, 193,000 miles of railroad track crisscrossed the United States—more than in all of Europe, including Russia. Connecting every state in the Union, the railroads opened an immense internal market and epitomized the new technological order. Railroad companies pioneered crucial aspects of large-scale corporate enterprise: issuing stock to meet capital needs, separating ownership from management, creating national distribution and marketing systems, diversifying production facilities, and forming new management structures.

Early railroad entrepreneurs faced huge financial problems. Buying land, laying track, building engines and cars, and erecting stations were horrendously expensive. The Pennsylvania Railroad, formed by the merger of seventy-three smaller lines in the 1850s, required $35 million in capitalization. Enormous subsidies from federal, state, and local governments helped to provide capital, but the large railroad companies also borrowed heavily by selling stocks and bonds. By 1900 the combined debt of all U.S. railroads stood at $5.1 billion, five times the federal debt.

Although stockholders owned the railroads, company officials directed day-to-day operations. Concerns about indebtedness and safety drove these managers to systematize operations nationally. Railroads relied on the telegraph to coordinate the complex flow of cars. By the end of the Civil War, the telegraph was the backbone of a network knitting together the entire nation. Using hierarchical structures and elaborate accounting systems that allowed tight control of expenditures, railroads could accurately predict profits on a daily basis. Such management innovations became models for other businesses seeking national markets.

Creativity, Cooperation, and Competition

The larger-than-life men who expanded the railroad industry in the 1870s and 1880s often seemed villainous; they were "robber barons" to their contemporaries. Jay Gould, the president of the Union Pacific, drew scorn as a "perfect eel" and "one of the most sinister figures that have ever flitted batlike across the vision of the American people." Recent historians have been kinder, viewing the great industrialists as a diverse group, some of them ironfisted pirates but others sophisticated businessmen of breathtaking originality and inventiveness.

The expansion and consolidation of railroading reflected both ingenuity and dishonesty. Although railroads had become the nation's major transportation system by the end of the Civil War, the industry was in chaos. Hundreds of small companies differed on everything from track width to engine size. By 1893 the small companies had been consolidated into major trunk lines.

Consolidation also meant standardization. In 1886 all railroads shifted to the new standard 4' 8½"–gauge track; they also adopted standard couplings, signals, and cooperative billing procedures that let one road ship cargo on several other lines. Perhaps the most symbolic example of standardization, and of the changes being wrought by industrialization, was the adoption of standard time zones in 1883. Many Americans felt far more comfortable with "God's time," based on the rising and setting of the sun, but the railroads certainly operated more efficiently on standard time.

The establishment of integrated transportation and communications networks cut both ways. Companies gained access to national markets, and consumers to goods produced in faraway factories. However, rancorous competition often saddled companies with massive debts and led to "watering" of stock, the issuing of stock certificates that far exceeded the company's assets. By 1885 one-third of the nation's railroad stock had been watered.

Entangled in heavy indebtedness, overextended systems, and crooked business practices, railroads fought each other recklessly for traffic. They cut rates for large shippers, offered special arrangements for handling bulk goods, dispensed free passes to influential politicians, and granted rebates and kickbacks to favored clients. The competition became so ferocious that railroads tried to curb it by establishing pools, agreements to divide traffic proportionately and to charge uniform rates. None of these tactics shored up the railroads' precarious finances, and some overbuilt lines careened into bankruptcy.

Caught in the middle of the railroads' tug-of-war, farmers and small businessmen turned to state governments for help. In the 1870s the Grange prompted many states to outlaw rate discrimination. In 1887 Congress passed the Interstate Commerce Act, which established the Interstate Commerce Commission (ICC) to oversee railroad practices and banned pooling, rebates, and other monopolistic activity. However, the Supreme Court ruled in favor of railroads over regulators until the Hepburn Act of 1906 strengthened the ICC by empowering it to set rates (see Chapter 22).

Vicious competition in the rail industry lessened only when the national depression that began in 1893 forced several roads into the hands of investment bankers. Supported by major investment houses in Boston, New York, and Philadelphia, J. Pierpont Morgan took over the weakened systems, reorganized them, refinanced their debts, and built intersystem alliances by purchasing blocks of stock in competing lines. By 1906, thanks to the bankers' centralized management, seven giant networks controlled two-thirds of the nation's track.

Railroad development thus reflected an enormous paradox. The massive trunk systems represented the largest business enterprise in the world, with the most advanced methods of accounting and organization. Their insatiable appetite for rails and engines stimulated the demand for steel and other products, and the transportation network they built opened up exciting possibilities for a truly national economy. But despite their power and innovations, railroads remained unstable. Cutthroat expansion inflated operating costs, reduced revenues, and made them vulnerable to economic downturns. In the depression of 1893, only intervention by investment bankers saved the industry from collapse.

Applying the Lessons of the Railroads to Steel

The career of Andrew Carnegie illustrates the link between railroad expansion and the growth of heavy industry. The diminutive Carnegie's salesmanship and managerial genius played a major role in his successful adaptation of railroad organization and finance to the steel industry.

Carnegie embodied the rags-to-riches dream. Born in Scotland, he immigrated to the United States in 1848 at age twelve. In his first job, bobbin boy in a textile mill, he earned $1.20 a week for sixty hours of work. In 1849 the ambitious youth became a Western Union messenger boy, and soon he was Pittsburgh's fastest telegrapher, "reading" the sound of the keys by ear. Decoding messages for the city's business leaders, Carnegie gained an insider's view of their operations.

In 1852 Tom Scott, superintendent of the Pennsylvania Railroad's western division, hired the seventeen-year-old Carnegie as his secretary and personal telegrapher. Carnegie quickly mastered the complex details of the most innovative business of the time. Seven years later, Scott became vice president of the Pennsylvania, and Carnegie took Scott's former job as head of the Pennsylvania's western division. In his six years as division chief, the daringly innovative Carnegie doubled the road's mileage and quadrupled its traffic. By 1868 his investments alone brought him nearly $60,000 a year, a substantial fortune.

Carnegie decided in the early 1870s to build his own steel mill, in part because of his connections with the railroad industry, the nation's largest purchaser of steel. His J. Edgar Thompson Mill incorporated the new Bessemer production technology, blasting air through molten iron to burn off carbon and other impurities. Carnegie also used the cost-analysis techniques pioneered by the railroads to cut production costs. His management philosophy was deceptively simple: "Watch the costs, and the profits will take care of themselves." He learned how to produce steel twenty dollars more cheaply than his competitors and how to parlay his railroad connections into huge orders.

Vertical integration—that is, controlling all aspects of manufacturing, from extracting raw materials to selling the finished product—enabled Carnegie to achieve even greater efficiency. From iron-ore fields to a huge sales force, Carnegie Steel controlled every phase of the industry. The shrewd selection of associates also aided Carnegie, particularly his partnership with Henry Clay Frick, who became chairman of Carnegie Steel in 1889. Under Frick's aggressive leadership, Carnegie Steel's profits rose each year, reaching $40 million in 1900. Carnegie Steel demonstrated how sophisticated technology and innovative management (combined with brutally low wages) could slash prices. By 1900 Carnegie was producing steel rails at $11.50 per ton, down from $65 per ton in the 1870s.

Frick's management of daily operations left Carnegie free to pursue philanthropy. Carnegie, who had decided that fortunes corrupted their possessors, established foundations and donated more than $300 million for libraries, universities, and international-peace causes. (He also knew that such actions would buttress his popularity.)

By 1900 Carnegie Steel, employing 20,000 people, had become the world's largest industrial corporation. But internal squabbling produced disgruntled subordinates, and a confrontation between Carnegie and Frick forced the latter out of the company. At the same time, rival firms, including Federal Steel, formed in 1898 by J. Pierpont Morgan, threatened Carnegie Steel's sales to the wire, nail, and pipe industries.

When Carnegie cunningly responded by announcing plans to produce seamless pipes by new and highly efficient techniques, his two largest competitors sought compromise and consolidation. Morgan asked Charles Schwab, the president of Carnegie Steel, to find out how much Carnegie wanted for his share of the company. Schwab tracked Carnegie to a golf course, and Carnegie informed Schwab that he would require nearly half a billion dollars. "Tell Carnegie I accept his price," Morgan responded; and United States Steel was born. Morgan combined the Carnegie companies with his own Federal Steel to create the first business capitalized at more than $1 billion. U.S. Steel, with its 200 member companies employing 168,000 people, marked a new scale in industrial enterprise.

Carnegie portrayed himself as a self-made man who rose through discipline, hard work, thrift, patience, and quick action in the face of opportunity. The reality was more complex. Carnegie had an uncanny ability to see the larger picture and to hire talented associates; he combined this gift with ingenuity in transferring techniques like cost accounting from railroads to steel, and he callously kept wages as low as possible. To a public little interested in details, Carnegie's success reaffirmed the possibilities of the American economic system and promised that anyone could rise from rags to riches.

Consolidating the Industrial Order

Between 1870 and 1900 rapacious competition also swept the oil, salt, sugar, tobacco, and meatpacking industries. Entrepreneurs responded by slashing costs, employing new technologies, and enlarging market shares. Ingenious new techniques of refrigerated shipping, for example, enabled Chicago meatpackers Philip Armour and Gustavus Swift to dominate eastern markets for meat.

Industrial Consolidation: Iron and Steel Firms, 1870 and 1900		
	1870	*1900*
No. of firms	808	669
No. of employees	78,000	272,000
Output (tons)	3,200,000	29,500,000
Capital invested	$121,000,000	$590,000,000

SOURCE: Robert L. Heilbroner and Aaron Singer, *The Economic Transformation of America: 1600 to Present*, 2d ed. (San Diego: Harcourt Brace Jovanovich, 1984), 92.

The evolution of the oil industry typified this process. After Edwin L. Drake drilled the first successful petroleum well in 1859 near Titusville in northwestern Pennsylvania, entry into the oil business came relatively easily. By the 1870s rickety drilling rigs, collection tanks, and ramshackle refineries littered the landscape near Pittsburgh and Cleveland, the sites of the first discoveries.

A young Cleveland merchant, John D. Rockefeller, gradually dominated in this new race for wealth. His methods reflected those of Carnegie: cost cutting and efficiency. After founding the Standard Oil Company in 1870, Rockefeller scrutinized the smallest detail of daily operations, insisting that one refinery manager find 750 missing barrel stoppers or that another reduce from 40 to 39 the number of drops of solder used to seal a kerosene can. He recognized that in a mass-production enterprise, small changes could save thousands of dollars. Rockefeller also stressed the importance of providing a reliable product and adopted the latest techniques to ensure the quality of his fuels and lubricants. In addition, he advertised heavily and made the red five-gallon can of Standard Oil kerosene instantly recognizable.

Like Carnegie, Rockefeller possessed an extraordinary ability to understand the workings of an entire industry. Seeing that the firm that controlled the shipment of oil could dominate the industry, Rockefeller purchased his own tanker cars. He wangled a 10 percent rebate from the railroads and a kickback on his competitors' shipments. When new technology made pipelines the most efficient method of transporting oil, Rockefeller established his own massive interregional pipeline network. And Rockefeller used aggression and deception to force out competitors. He priced his products below cost to strangle rivals and drove merchants who would not sell his products out of business. "The Standard Oil Company brooks no competition,"

Mergers in Mining and Manufacturing, 1895–1910

A wave of business mergers occurred after the Supreme Court's 1897 and 1898 rulings that any firms concluding price-fixing or market-allocating agreements violated the Sherman Anti-Trust Act. But the merger mania died down when business leaders quickly discovered that companies could remain profitable only through vertical integration.

a congressional investigating committee reported; " . . . its settled policy and firm determination is to crush out all who may be rash enough to enter the field against it." By 1879 Rockefeller controlled 90 percent of the nation's oil-refining capacity.

Convinced that competition wasted resources, Rockefeller established the Standard Oil Trust in 1882. Rockefeller and his associates persuaded stockholders of forty companies to exchange their stock for certificates of trust and then established a board of trustees to run all the companies. Within three years, the Standard Oil Trust had consolidated crude-oil buying throughout its member firms and cut the number of refineries by half. In this way Rockefeller went beyond Carnegie by integrating the petroleum industry both *vertically,* by controlling every function from production to local retailing, and *horizontally,* by merging competing companies into a single giant system. Consequently, Standard Oil grew into an industrial titan and spread to Asia, Africa, and South America. By 1890 Rockefeller's personal fortune had mushroomed to more than $800 million.

Success bred imitation, and trusts bloomed in the copper, sugar, whiskey, and lead industries. But rapacious tactics, monopolistic control, and sky-high earnings provoked a public outcry and led to investigations of the trusts' unscrupulous practices. In 1890 Congress, under the leadership of Ohio senator John Sherman, passed the Sherman Anti-Trust Act, outlawing trusts and any other contracts or combinations in restraint of trade and establishing both fines and jail time as penalties. However, the act never defined clearly either *trust* or *restraint of trade,* and the government prosecuted only a handful of cases before 1904. When Standard Oil was challenged in 1892, it simply reorganized as a holding company;* the nine trustees became the board of directors for Standard Oil (New Jersey), and profits soared.

Supreme Court decisions hamstrung antitrust efforts. In 1895, for example, the federal government brought suit against the sugar trust in *United States* v. *E. C. Knight Company,* arguing that the trust, which controlled more than 90 percent of all U.S. sugar refining, operated in restraint of trade. The Court, however, chose to define manufacturing as a local concern, not part of interstate commerce, and threw out the suit. Thus protected, corporate mergers and consolidations surged ahead. By 1900 mammoth firms controlled nearly 40 percent of all capital investment in manufacturing.

The Triumph of Technology

New technologies and machines offered another way in which to build profits, lower costs, and improve efficiency. They also created hungry markets for new products. After 1870 business corporations stepped up their research efforts and introduced a remarkable variety of new consumer goods.

The major inventions that stimulated industrial output and underlay mass production remained hidden from public view. Few Americans had heard of the Bessemer process for making steel or of the refrigerated railroad cars that allowed Swift to slaughter beef in Chicago and sell it fresh in New York City. But the public saw the *fruits* of technology—the sewing machine, the telephone, the light bulb, and other inventions that eased the drudgery of everyday life and reshaped social interactions. Mass-produced sewing machines replaced hand-sewn with factory-stitched clothing, relieved women of the tedium of hand-making the family apparel, and expanded personal wardrobes. Telephones not only transformed communications but also undermined the social conventions for polite behavior that had governed face-to-face or written exchanges. The light bulb made possible longer and more regular working hours. These wonders inspired optimism that technology would lead to the betterment of society.

Thomas A. Edison (1847–1931) epitomized the inventive impulse. Largely self-educated, Edison was a born salesman and self-promoter. Although he modestly stated that "genius is one percent inspiration and ninety-nine percent perspiration," he reveled in his own image as an inventing "wizard."

---

*Holding company: a corporation that owns a controlling share of the stock of one or more other firms

Thomas A. Edison (1847–1931)
This photograph shows a young Edison with his phonograph, in 1878. Between 1876 and 1882, Edison was granted more than 400 patents for inventions made at his laboratory at Menlo Park, New Jersey.

Like Carnegie, Edison envisioned a large, interconnected industrial system resting on a foundation of technological innovation.

In his early work, Edison concentrated on the telegraph; his first major invention was a stock-quotation printer. In 1876 his profits enabled him to establish an "invention factory" in Menlo Park, New Jersey, where he predicted "a minor invention every ten days, and a big one every six months."

When the advent of the telephone undercut the telegraph market, Edison turned his attention to the electric light. He realized that practical electrical lighting had to be part of a complete system—generators, voltage regulators, electric meters, insulated wiring—as well as cheap. In 1877, buoyed by the success of his invention of the phonograph,

Edison set out to develop a new filament for incandescent light bulbs. He perfected a process for generating electricity and discovered a carbon filament that would glow dependably in a vacuum. In 1882, backed by J. Pierpont Morgan, the Edison Illuminating Company opened a power plant in New York City's financial district, furnishing lighting for eighty-five buildings.

Others rushed into the electrical field. Most importantly, Edison competitor George Westinghouse developed an efficient system to deliver cheap high-voltage power through the use of alternating current. In the process, he stole many of Edison's ideas, and Edison angrily sued. Embittered by legal battles—defense of his patents cost him more than $2 million—Edison relinquished control of his enterprises in the late 1880s. In 1892 his company merged with a competitor to form the General Electric Company. Four years later, GE and Westinghouse agreed to exchange patents under a joint board. Such patent pooling agreements became another way in which to dominate markets.

Edison meanwhile continued to pump out invention after invention, including the mimeograph machine, the microphone, the motion-picture camera and film, and the storage battery. Over his long life, he patented 1,093 inventions and amassed an estate worth more than $6 million. Perhaps his greatest contribution was his Menlo Park laboratory, a model for industrial research, which demonstrated that the systematic use of science in support of industrial technology paid large dividends.

Mass Production, Mass Marketing

The technological and managerial innovations of Edison, Carnegie, and Rockefeller proved adaptable throughout U.S. industry, spurring marvels of production. When production outstripped demand, industries developed advertising and marketing techniques to whet the consumers' appetites and to differentiate the products.

The growth of the flour industry illustrates the spread of mass production and the emergence of new marketing concepts. In the 1870s adoption of advanced technology allowed companies to produce vast amounts of flour, more than they could sell. To solve this problem, companies developed product differentiation. Mills thought up new product lines such as cake flours and breakfast cereals and used hard-hitting advertising to sell them. Henry P. Crowell, for example, heavily promoted his new milled oat product under the easily remembered Quaker Oats brand name. The Pillsbury Company of Minneapolis touted "Pillsbury's Best" flour as "strongly recommended by Eminent authorities—Physicians and Chemists—as a powerful Brain-Muscle and Bone forming food, particularly adapted for Brain workers, growing children, and those suffering from digestive debility and disorders." Brand names, trademarks, guarantees, slogans, endorsements, and other gimmicks built product demand and consumer loyalty. Americans bought Ivory Soap because of the impressive pledge that it was "99 and 44/100s percent pure." The American Tobacco Company used trading cards, circulars, box-top premiums, prizes, and scientific endorsements to convert Americans to cigarette smoking and to its own products.

In the 1880s George Eastman invented a paper-based photographic film as an alternative to the bulky, fragile glass plates then in use. When professional photographers resisted the innovation, Eastman realized that "in order to make a large business we would have to reach the general public and create a new class of patrons." Mass-producing a cheap camera, the Kodak, and devising a catchy slogan ("You press the button, we do the rest"), Eastman introduced a system in which customers returned both the one-hundred-exposure film *and* the camera to his Rochester factory. For ten dollars, the company developed and printed the film, reloaded the camera, and returned everything to the customer. Eastman had revolutionized an industry and democratized a visual medium previously confined to a few.

Other companies with names well known today contributed to the production and marketing revolution—H. J. Heinz, Campbell Soup, Pabst Beer, and Borden Milk, to name a few. Benefiting from

savings made possible by new machinery, organizational efficiencies, high volume, and national distribution, such firms won a large share of the market with advertising that stressed their products' high quality and low cost.

Industrialization: Costs and Benefits

By 1900 an industrial economy dominated by a few mammoth firms had replaced the chaos of early competition among thousands of small companies. The industrial transformation begun by the railroads had spread throughout U.S. business. For those that fell behind in an unforgiving economic environment, the cost was measured in ruined fortunes, bankrupt companies, and shattered dreams. John D. Rockefeller summed up the prevailing atmosphere when he said that in the Standard Oil Trust he wanted "only the big ones, only those who have already proved they can do a big business. As for the others, unfortunately they will have to die."

The cost was high, too, for millions of workers. The new industrial order rested on the backs on laborers who received subsistence wages and could be fired at a moment's notice. Environmental devastation was part of the cost as well. Polluted rivers, smoky skies, and a landscape littered with reeking garbage and toxic by-products bore mute witness to the relentless drive for efficiency and profit.

But industrialization also brought social benefits: labor-saving products, lower prices for goods, and advances in transportation and communication. Benefits and liabilities seemed inextricably interconnected. The sewing machine, for example, created thousands of new jobs, made a wide variety of clothing available, and eased the lives of millions of housewives. However, it also encouraged greedy entrepreneurs to operate sweatshops in crowded tenements and unsafe lofts where immigrants toiled long hours for pitifully low wages.

Whatever the balance sheet of social gains and costs, one thing was clear: the United States had muscled its way onto the world stage as an industrial titan. In 1870 the United States turned out less than a quarter of the world's manufactured goods;

by 1900 it produced nearly a third. The ambition of countless inventors, financiers, managerial innovators, and marketing wizards had laid the groundwork for a new social and economic order.

The New South

The South entered the industrial era far more slowly than the North. Many factors hindered its progress: the Civil War's physical devastation, the relatively small number of towns and cities, lack of capital, illiteracy, northern control of financial markets and capital, and a low rate of technological innovation. The myth of the Lost Cause—the nostalgic portrayal of the antebellum South as traditional and unchanging—also impeded the region's economic growth.

Obstacles to Southern Economic Development

Much of the South's difficulty in industrializing stemmed from its lack of capital. The Civil War shattered the South's credit system and destroyed its assets. The fighting left cities burned, fields trampled, livestock slaughtered, and farms and plantations ruined. Banks failed in large numbers; by 1865 the South, with 25 percent of the nation's population, had only 2 percent of its banks.

Federal policies adopted during the war restricted the expansion of the southern banking system. Obtaining a national bank charter required $50,000 in capital, far beyond most southerners' postwar means. Federal laws also prohibited national banks' extension of mortgages on real estate, so even those with the necessary capital faced obstacles. Southern banks in effect were confined to cities and could lend only relatively small amounts.

Rural merchants, shopkeepers, and large landowners became bankers by default with the establishment of the crop-lien system (see Chapter 16). In exchange for the provision of seed and tools, they insisted that farmers specialize in cotton and tobacco, crops that initially brought high returns.

Prosperity did not follow, however. Instead, the shift from planting corn to raising cotton and tobacco made small southern farmers vulnerable to the fluctuations of commercial agriculture and reduced their self-sufficiency.

The South also remained the victim of federal policies designed to aid northern industry. High protective tariffs raised the price of imported machine technology; the retirement of federal greenbacks and the demonetization of silver (see Chapter 16) further limited capital; and discriminatory railroad freight rates hiked shipping prices.

The South's chronic shortage of funds affected the economy indirectly as well, by limiting resources available for education. Reconstruction had seen a modest expansion of public schooling for both whites and blacks, but many southern states refused to tax property for school support until 1889. Low school attendance limited the number of educated people available for technical positions in business and industry.

The myth of the Lost Cause further retarded economic progress. After the war, southern states often contributed the modest funds they had to veterans' pensions. This practice not only built a white patronage system for Confederate veterans and reinforced the myth of the Lost Cause, but also left little for economic and educational development.

The New South Creed and Southern Industrialization

In the 1870s, fearful that the South would become an economic backwater, some southern newspaper editors, planters, merchants, and industrialists championed "the New South creed" to encourage southern industrialization. Natural resources and cheap labor, they argued, made the South a natural site for industrial development. During the 1880s the movement to industrialize the South gained momentum. Southern states offered tax exemptions for new businesses, set up industrial and agricultural expositions, and leased convicts from state prisons to serve as cheap labor. Florida and Texas gave huge tracts of state land to railroads, and other states sold forest and mineral rights on 6 million acres of land to speculators. Between 1869 and 1899 lumber production increased 500 percent as the forests of Alabama and Louisiana were denuded. Southern iron and coal industries also expanded. Founded in 1871 in the heart of a region blessed with coal, limestone, and iron-ore deposits, Birmingham, Alabama, became a bustling city of noisy railroad yards and roaring blast furnaces. By 1900 it was the nation's largest pig-iron shipper.

Recruiting black workers, southern iron and steel mills contributed to the migration of African-Americans cityward. By 1900, 20 percent of the southern black population was urban. However, southern industry reflected the patterns of racism permeating other aspects of southern life. The burgeoning textile mills of the piedmont were lily-white; in the iron and steel industry, blacks composed 60 percent of the work force but had no chance of advancement. In a rare reversal of usual patterns, black workers in iron and steel on average earned more than white textile workers.

The Southern Mill Economy

The textile mills that mushroomed in the South in the 1880s took southern industrialization down a different path than that of the North and Midwest. The southern textile industry did not cluster in existing cities but sprang up in the countryside and often became a catalyst for the rise of new towns. Rural ways and values suffused the South's new industrial workplace.

The cotton-mill economy grew largely in the piedmont, a beautiful country of rolling hills and rushing rivers stretching from central Virginia to northern Georgia and Alabama. After the war most of the region's farmers had fallen into the crop-lien and sharecropping systems. But postwar railroad construction opened the piedmont to outside markets and sparked intense town building and textile-mill expansion. Between 1880 and 1900 track mileage in North Carolina grew more than 250 percent. Some 120 new mills were built in that state alone.

Textile Workers
Textile mills hired both adults and children. Here a man and two boys stand before the machines that they operated for sixty hours a week. Child laborers in the mills often went home so tired that they fell asleep before supper and could not be wakened until morning.

Merchants and newspaper editors hailed the prospect that cotton mills would lift the South out of poverty, and at first, sharecroppers and tenant farmers looked hopefully to the mills, which seemed to offer a way out of their misery. But appearances deceived. The cotton-mill promoters were the same men who had profited from the commercialization of southern agriculture and the rise of sharecropping and crop liens. They made low-skilled, low-paid workers the backbone of their operations.

Mill superintendents drew their workers from impoverished nearby farms and commonly hired entire families, usually poor whites. Although they promised that textile work would free these families from poverty, they shamelessly exploited them. By the 1880s, when mills earned 30 to 75 percent profit for their investors, mill workers twelve to eighteen years of age received seven to eleven cents an hour, half of comparable wages in New England.

The mill dominated the piedmont textile community. The mill operator built and owned workers' housing and the company store, supported the village church, financed the local elementary school, and pried into the mill hands' morals and behavior. Mill owners usually kept workers dependent and immobile by paying them only once a month, often in scrip—a certificate redeemable exclusively at the company store. Most families had to buy on credit during the month, overspent, and fell behind in their payments. As charges were deducted from the next month's paycheck, workers fell into a cycle of indebtedness indistinguishable from that of sharecroppers.

To help to make ends meet, mill workers kept their own gardens and raised chickens and an occasional cow or pig. Southern mill hands thus brought communal farm values into the mills and mill villages. Although they had to adapt to machine-paced work and earned barely enough to live on, the working poor in the mill districts eased the shift from rural to village-industrial life by clinging to a cooperative country ethic.

Southern textile mills, like their northern counterparts, exploited the cheap rural labor around them, settling transplanted farm people in paternalistic, company-run villages. The industry shot up 1,400 percent, and by 1920 the South was the nation's leading textile-mill center.

The Southern Industrial Lag

Still, in the South, industrialization was slower, slighter, and more dependent on outside forces than in the North, and the southern economy remained essentially colonial, subject to control by northern industries and financial syndicates. Except for the American Tobacco Company, southern industry was dominated by northern companies and bankers. For example, U.S. Steel controlled the foundries in Birmingham, and it forced southerners to pay higher prices for steel than northerners, even though southern production cost less.

Unfavorable federal banking regulations, scarce capital, staggering debt, and discriminatory business practices by northern-controlled enterprises hampered the South's economic development. Dragged down by a poorly educated and poorly trained population, both white and black, southern industry languished. Limited by outside forces, economic progress in the South occurred in its own distinctly regional way.

Industrial Work and the Work Force

Nationally, industrialization proceeded unevenly: during the late nineteenth century, most Americans still worked in small factories and locally run businesses. But as the century unfolded, more and more large factories appeared, with armies of skilled and semiskilled workers. Between 1860 and 1900 the number of industrial workers jumped from 885,000 to 3.2 million, and the trend toward large-scale production became unmistakable.

From Workshop to Factory

The changes that led to the factory economy involved a fundamental restructuring of work habits and a new emphasis on workplace discipline. The boot and shoe industry illustrates the impact of these changes. As late as the 1840s, shoemakers were the aristocrats of labor, working in small, independent shops where they set their own hours. A distinctive working-class culture evolved around them. Foreign-born English, German, and Irish shoe workers set up ethnic trade organizations; took time off for religious observances, funerals, and holidays; drank sociably on the job; and helped each other weather accidents or illness. Living in tenements within tight-knit ethnic neighborhoods, they developed strong ethnic and community pride.

As early as the 1850s, however, changes in the ready-made shoe industry affected the role and status of skilled labor. Management moved its growing production staffs into large buildings and broke the manufacturing process into a series of repetitive tasks. Skilled artisans now worked in teams, with each member responsible for a specific task. Workers lost the freedom to drink on the job or to take time off for special occasions. The working-class culture that had reinforced group solidarity appeared wasteful and inefficient to owners and foremen. Then in the 1880s, as shoe factories became larger and more mechanized, traditional skills vanished. Sophisticated machines allowed companies to replace skilled workers with low-paid, unskilled women and children. By 1890 unskilled women made up more than 35 percent of the work force in an industry that skilled men once dominated.

Skilled artisans in other trades also found their responsibilities changing. With the exception of crafts such as carpentry and bricklaying, artisans no longer participated in the production process *as a whole*. Rather, skilled workers performed numbingly repetitious, monotonous tasks. Factory work had become specialized, machine-paced, and deadeningly routine.

The Hardships of Industrial Labor

The expansion of the factory system created an unprecedented demand for unskilled labor. By the 1880s nearly one-third of the workers in the railroad and steel industries were common laborers. In the construction trades, the machine and tool industries, and garment manufacturing, industrialists used the contract system to hire unskilled laborers. Subcontractors hired, managed, and fired these common workers, who were taken on when needed and laid off in slack periods. The steel industry employed them to shovel ore, coal, and lime around the yards and to move ingots inside the mills. Foremen drove the gangs hard.

Unskilled workers drifted from city to city and from industry to industry. They earned about one-third the wages of skilled artisans. In the late 1870s, bricklayers earned $3.00 a day, but unskilled laborers a mere $1.30. Only southern mill workers, averaging $.84 a day, earned less.

Skilled and unskilled workers alike put in twelve-hour shifts, often under hazardous, unhealthful conditions. The alarming incidence of industrial accidents stemmed from workers' inexperience with the complicated, heavy machinery, and employers' unconcern for plant safety. One steelworker recalled that, on his first day at the mill, "I looked up and a big train carrying a big vessel with fire was making towards me. I stood numb, afraid to move, until a man came to me and led me out of the mill." The accident rate in steel mills was extremely high.

Children as young as eight worked in coal mines and cotton mills. Their attempts to play while on the job made them vulnerable to accidents. In cotton mills, when supervision was lax, child workers would grab the belts that powered the machines and see who could ride them farthest up toward the drive shaft in the ceiling before letting go and falling to the floor. In coal mines, children who worked as slate pickers sat in a cloud of black dust beneath the breakers that crushed coal, removing slate and other impurities. Black lung disease occurred commonly and often led to emphysema and tuberculosis. Cotton-mill workers, both children and adults, contracted brown lung, another crippling pulmonary disease, from breathing cotton dust.

For adult workers, the railroads presented the greatest peril. In 1889, the first year that reliable statistics were compiled, almost 2,000 railwaymen were killed on the job, and more than 20,000 were injured. Disabled workers and widows received minimal aid from employers. Until the 1890s the courts considered employer negligence one of the normal risks borne by the employee. Employers fought the adoption of safety and health standards on the grounds that the costs would be excessive. Workers joined fraternal organizations and ethnic clubs for sickness and accident benefits, but usually the amounts set aside were too low to give them much relief. When a worker was killed or maimed, the family depended on relatives or neighbors for help.

Immigrant Labor

Outside the South, factory owners turned to unskilled immigrants for the muscle needed in factories, mills, railroads, and heavy construction. In Philadelphia native-born Americans and recent German immigrants dominated the highly skilled metal-working trades, and Irish immigrants remained in unskilled occupations until the 1890s, when the "new immigrants" from southern and eastern Europe replaced them (see Chapter 19). On the West Coast, Chinese immigrants performed the dirtiest, most physically demanding jobs in mining, canning, and railroad construction.

Immigrants who lived frugally in a boardinghouse and worked an eighty-four-hour week could save fifteen dollars a month, far more than they could have earned in the old country. Intent on improving their economic standing, many immigrants readily accepted the exhausting work schedule and volunteered for overtime work. One worker summed up the typical routine: "A good job, save money, work all time, go home, sleep, no spend."

Rural peasants from southern and eastern Europe who immigrated after 1890 found abandoning their traditional work patterns and adjusting to factory schedules difficult. Changing daylight patterns shaped farm work, but the invariable speed of the machines dictated factory operations. When immigrant workers resisted the tempo of factory work, or drank on the job or took unexcused absences, employers enforced discipline. Some sponsored temperance societies and Sunday schools to teach punctuality and sobriety. Others published rule books outlining specific codes of behavior. When persuasion proved ineffective, employers cut wages and put workers on the piecework system, paying them only for items produced.

Workers sometimes fought attempts to tighten discipline by demanding a say in production quotas.

Seeking to re-create a village atmosphere, immigrant workers also often persuaded their employers to hire friends and relatives. Factory workers who came from farms where the entire family had toiled together sought to work with as many family members as possible.

In the face of immigrant labor's desire for a sociable, humane work environment, the proliferation of machines in factories kindled employer-employee tensions. When the factory owners' desire to increase output coincided with the immigrants' desire to maximize income, long hours at the machines were welcomed. But when employers cut wages or unreasonably accelerated the work schedule, unrest boiled to the surface.

Women and Work in Industrializing America

Between 1870 and 1900 the number of women working outside the home nearly tripled, and by the turn of the century, women made up 17 percent of the country's labor force. Many women workers abandoned domestic employment for better-paying, less demeaning jobs in the textile, food-processing, and garment industries.

Changes in agriculture prompted countless young farm women to seek employment in the industrial sector, and young immigrant women, too, worked in factories to increase their families' meager income. Factory owners welcomed young foreign-born women as a ready source of inexpensive unskilled labor; but because many of them would soon marry and leave the work force, employers treated them as temporary help. Young women in the clothing industry earned as little as five dollars for seventy hours of work but widely relished the independence of working. Although most of their income went to their parents, they delighted in having a little spending money.

When the typewriter and the telephone came into general use in the 1890s, office work became more specialized, and women with high-school educations moved into clerical and secretarial positions earlier filled by men. The clean, safe working conditions and relatively good pay attracted them; a first-rate typist could earn seven dollars a week. Even though women were excluded from managerial positions, office jobs carried higher prestige and offered steadier work than employment in factories or shops.

Nonetheless, women's work outside the home was seen as temporary. Society defined women's real achievement in terms of marriage and the family. A woman experienced vicarious satisfaction when her husband received a promotion or her son earned a raise. Few people imagined that women could attain national or even local prominence in the emerging corporate order.

Hard Work and the Gospel of Success

Influential opinion molders in these years preached that any man could achieve success in the new industrial era. In *Ragged Dick* (1867) and scores of later tales, minister-turned-novelist Horatio Alger recounted the adventures of poor but honest lads who rise through ambition, initiative, and self-discipline. Life is a struggle in Alger's America, but success comes from seizing the unexpected opportunities that fortune thrusts in one's path. In his widely read stories, shoeshine boys stop runaway horses or save children from drowning and are rewarded for their bravery by rich benefactors who give them a start in business. Andrew Carnegie served as proof that the United States remained the land of opportunity and "rags to riches."

But some disagreed. Mark Twain chided the public for naiveté and suggested that business success was more likely to come to those who lied and cheated. A New Yorker forced out of the carting business voiced his lament to Congress in 1883: "A man in the express business today owning one or two horses and a wagon cannot even eke out an existence. . . . The competition . . . from these monopolies . . . is too great. . . . I live in a tenement house, three stories up, where the water comes in through the roof, and I cannot better myself. My children will have to go to work before they are able to work. Why? Simply because this present sys-

tem . . . is all for the privileged classes, nothing for the man who produces the wealth."

Recent studies reveal that Carnegie was a rare exception. Ninety-five percent of industrial leaders had middle- and upper-class backgrounds. However, small companies provided opportunities for skilled immigrants and native-born working-class Americans to rise to the top. In Paterson, New Jersey, the most successful owners of small-to-medium-sized industrial companies between 1850 and 1880 had begun as workers, broadened their skills through apprenticeships, and then opened their own factories. Few reaped immense fortunes, but many attained substantial incomes.

Unskilled workers found far fewer opportunities for advancement. Many did move into semiskilled and even skilled positions that allowed them to increase their earnings and even to own a home. However, most immigrants, especially the Irish and Italians, progressed far more slowly than the sons of middle- and upper-class Americans who enjoyed educational advantages and family financial backing. Upward mobility for unskilled workers generally meant mobility *within* the working class. Immigrants who got ahead went from rags to respectability, not rags to riches.

Between 1860 and 1900 real wages rose 31 percent for unskilled workers and 74 percent for skilled workers. But high incidences of injury and unemployment kept unskilled immigrant workers in a precarious position. Even in a prosperous year such as 1890, one in every five workers was unemployed for at least a month. During the depressions of the 1870s and 1890s, wage cuts, extended layoffs, and unemployment pushed those at the base of the industrial work force to the brink of starvation.

The question of economic mobility in the late nineteenth century is complex. At the top, the rich amassed enormous fortunes; in 1890 a mere 10 percent of American families owned 73 percent of the national wealth. At the bottom, recent immigrants struggled to survive, with only 45 percent of U.S. industrial laborers taking in earnings above the $500 poverty line. Nevertheless, between these extremes, skilled immigrant workers and shopkeepers swelled the middle class. The standard of living rose for millions of Americans, although the gap between rich and poor remained an abyss.

Labor Unions and Industrial Conflict

Toiling long hours for low wages, often under dangerous conditions, some workers turned to labor unions. Unions, however, faced formidable obstacles. For one thing, employers could hire poor immigrants to work for lower wages than unionized help or to serve as strikebreakers. For another, ethnic and racial divisions hampered labor organization as immigrant workers, who tended to socialize and marry within their own tight groups, resisted appeals to unionize. In addition, not only did relatively prosperous skilled workers feel little in common with low-paid laborers, but workers (skilled and unskilled alike) in radically different work environments saw little reason for cooperation.

Two groups, the National Labor Union and the Knights of Labor, attempted to build mass labor movements but failed. The most successful late-nineteenth-century labor movement, the American Federation of Labor (AFL), was an amalgamation of powerful craft unions that represented only a fraction of the labor force. With unions so weak, labor unrest often led to unplanned wildcat walkouts that sometimes exploded into violence.

Organizing the Workers

The Civil War marked a watershed in the rise of organized labor. Small craft unions, with goals of fighting wage reductions and providing sickness benefits, had existed since the eighteenth century, but after the war labor leaders sought to increase union clout. To many, the answer lay in the formation of a single association that would transcend craft lines and draw a mass membership.

William H. Sylvis, elected president of the Iron Moulders' International Union in 1863, dreamed of creating such a super-union. Condemning "the monied aristocracy—proud, imperious and dishonest, . . . blasting and withering everything it [comes] in contact with," Sylvis quickly built his union from "a mere pygmy" to a membership of 8,500. In 1866 he called a convention that formed the National Labor Union (NLU). The new organization embraced an eight-hour workday, currency and banking reform, an end to convict labor, a federal department of labor, and restrictions on immigration, particularly of Chinese. Under Sylvis's leadership the NLU also endorsed the cause of working women and elected the head of a union of female laundry workers as one of its national officers. The NLU urged black workers to organize as well, although in racially separate unions.

After an iron founders' strike failed in the winter of 1866–1867, Sylvis concluded that national political reform held the key to labor's future. In 1868 a number of reformers, including woman-suffrage advocates Susan B. Anthony and Elizabeth Cady Stanton, attended the NLU convention. However, Sylvis's sudden death in 1869 shattered the NLU, which disintegrated by 1873.

The dream of a national labor movement lived on in a new organization, the Noble and Holy Order of the Knights of Labor. Founded in 1869 by Philadelphia tailors as a secret society modeled on the Masonic order (see Chapter 10), the Knights welcomed all wage earners; they excluded only bankers, physicians, lawyers, stockbrokers, professional gamblers, and liquor dealers. The Knights advocated equal pay for women, an end to child and convict labor, a graduated income tax, and cooperative employer-employee ownership of factories, mines, and other businesses.

At first the Knights grew slowly, in part because the Catholic church forbade Catholics to join. In the 1880s membership skyrocketed after the church lifted its prohibition and an Irish Catholic, Terence V. Powderly, became the Knights' head. The eloquent Powderly orchestrated successes in a series of labor clashes and brought in thousands of new members.

The Knights of Labor reflected its idealistic origins and Powderly's collaborative vision. Powderly

Ethnic and Racial Hatred
Conservative business owners used racist advertising such as this trade card stigmatizing Chinese laundry workers to promote their own products and to associate their company with patriotism.

condemned strikes as "a relic of barbarism" and organized producer and consumer cooperatives. He also advocated temperance and offered membership to both blacks and women. By 1886 women made up 10 percent of the Knights' membership.

Powderly and the Knights supported immigration restriction and a total ban on Chinese immigration. Union members feared that immigrants would steal jobs by working too cheaply. Westerners, especially Californians, saw the Chinese as a major threat. In 1877 a San Francisco demonstration for the eight-hour day turned into a riot that destroyed twenty-five Chinese laundries and terrorized the local Chinese population. Congress passed the Chinese Exclusion Act in 1882, placing a ten-year moratorium on Chinese immigration, but sporadic anti-Chinese violence continued.

Although inspired by Powderly's vision of a harmonious and cooperative future, most rank-and-file members cared more about immediate issues such as wage cuts, production speedups, and deteriorating working conditions. Most, moreover, rejected Powderly's anti-strike position. In 1883–1884 spontaneous local strikes led by Knights gained reluctant support from the national leadership. However, in 1885, when Jay Gould tried to drive the Knights out of his Wabash Railroad by firing active union members, Powderly recognized that the union's survival was at stake. He therefore authorized a strike against the Wabash and ordered Knights working for other lines to refuse to handle Wabash cars. With his railroad crippled, Gould halted his campaign against the Knights.

Membership soared; by 1886, 6,000 locals served more than 700,000 workers. That fall, the Knights entered politics, mounting campaigns in nearly 200 towns and cities, electing several mayors and judges, and helping a dozen congressmen to gain office. In state legislatures they secured passage of laws banning convict labor, and at the national level they lobbied successfully for legislation outlawing the importation of foreign contract labor. Conservatives warned darkly that the Knights could cripple the economy and take over the country.

In fact, the Knights' strength soon waned. Leaders lost control of the membership because of the union's explosive growth, and a series of failed (and unauthorized) strikes left members disillusioned. The national reaction to the Haymarket riot (see below) also contributed to the union's decline. By the late 1880s, the Knights of Labor was a shadow of its former self. But it had given major impetus to the labor movement and awakened a sense of group solidarity in hundreds of thousands of workers.

Even as the Knights became weaker, another labor organization, pursuing more immediate and practical goals, was growing strong. The skilled craft unions had long felt threatened by the Knights' broad base and emphasis on sweeping reform goals. In May 1886 the craft unions left the Knights to form the American Federation of Labor (AFL), which replaced the Knights' grand visions with practical tactics aimed at "bread-and-butter issues." "We have no ultimate ends," one skilled craft official commented; "we are going on from day to day. We fight only for immediate objectives."

Samuel Gompers, the English immigrant cigar maker who headed the AFL from its formation until his death in 1924, believed in "trade unionism, pure and simple." Having lost faith in utopian social reforms and catch-all labor organizations, he believed that "the poor, the hungry, have not the strength to engage in a conflict even when life is at stake." To stand up to corporations, Gompers argued, labor must harness the bargaining power of skilled workers, who were not easily replaced, and concentrate on practical goals of raising wages and reducing hours.

A master tactician, Gompers believed that large-scale industrial organization required comparable labor organization. At the same time, he knew that the individual skilled craft unions were committed to controlling their own affairs. To meet the challenge of persuading workers to join forces without violating their sense of craft autonomy, Gompers organized the AFL as a *federation* of trade unions, each retaining control of its own members but linked by an executive council to coordinate strategy. Focusing the federation's efforts on short-term improvements in wages and hours, Gompers sidestepped divisive political issues. The AFL advocated an eight-hour workday, employers' liability, and mine-safety laws. By 1904 the AFL had grown to more than 1.6 million members.

As a whole, although they held up ideals toward which workers might strive, late-nineteenth-century labor organizations remained weak. They enlisted less than 5 percent of the work force. Split between skilled artisans and common laborers, separated along ethnic and religious lines, and divided over tactics, the unions enjoyed only occasional success against the growing power of corporate enterprise. More often, they watched from the sidelines as unorganized workers launched sudden strikes that sometimes turned violent.

Strikes and Labor Violence

From 1881 to 1905, 7 million workers participated in some 37,000 strikes, some of which involved mobs, property damage, and looting. Shaken middle-class Americans feared that they were on the verge of a class war.

The Wall Street crash of 1873 triggered a major depression. Businesses collapsed, tramps roamed New York and Chicago streets, and labor unrest mounted. In 1877 a wildcat railroad strike turned deadly. Ignited by a wage reduction on the Baltimore and Ohio Railroad in July, the strike exploded up and down the rail lines and spread quickly from coast to coast. Rioters in Pittsburgh torched Union Depot and the Pennsylvania Railroad roundhouse. By the time newly inaugurated president Rutherford B. Hayes called out the troops and quelled the strike, nearly one hundred people had died and two-thirds of U.S. railroads stood idle.

The strike stunned middle-class America. Hysterical voices proclaimed that "if the club of the policeman, knocking out the brains of the rioter, will answer, then well and good, [but if not] then bullets and bayonets . . . constitute the one remedy." Employers exploited the public hysteria to crack down on labor. Many required workers to sign "yellow dog" contracts, in which they promised not to strike or join a union. Some hired Pinkerton agents to serve as a private police force, and, as in the 1877 rail strike, relied on the U.S. Army (or state militias) to suppress unrest.

The 1880s saw more strikes and violence. On May 1, 1886, 340,000 workers walked off their jobs to support the eight-hour workday. On May 3 Chicago police shot and killed four strikers at the McCormick Harvester plant. At a protest rally the next evening in the city's Haymarket Square, someone threw a bomb from a nearby building, killing or fatally wounding seven policemen. In turn, the police fired wildly into the crowd and slew four demonstrators. Business leaders and middle-class citizens lashed out at labor activists, particularly the Haymarket meeting sponsors, most of whom were associated with German anarchism. Eight were arrested. No evidence connected them directly to the bomb throwing, but all were convicted and four were executed; a fifth committed suicide in prison. Illinois governor John Altgeld pardoned the three survivors in 1893. As Americans became convinced that a deadly foreign conspiracy gripped the nation, animosity toward labor unions intensified.

Confrontations between business and labor continued into the 1890s. Federal troops were called out to crush strikes by Idaho silver miners and Carnegie steelworkers. The most systematic use of troops to smash unions came in 1894 in a strike against the Pullman Palace Car Company. George Pullman, a self-taught pioneer in the manufacture of elegant railroad sleeping and dining cars, had constructed a factory and a town called Pullman south of Chicago. The carefully planned community provided Pullman workers with brick houses, parks, playgrounds, a bank, a library, and even a sewage-treatment plant. However, Pullman policed workers' activities, banned saloons, and insisted that his properties turn a profit.

When the depression of 1893 hit, Pullman responded to declining orders by slashing wages. But he did not lower rents. Thousands of workers joined the newly formed American Railway Union and went on strike. They were led by a fiery young organizer, Eugene V. Debs, who vowed "to strip the mask of hypocrisy from the pretended philanthropist and show him to the world as an oppressor of labor." Union members working for other railroads refused to switch Pullman cars, paralyzing rail traffic in and out of Chicago and over the western half of the United States.

In response to the crisis, the General Managers' Association, composed of top railroad executives, decided to break the union. After importing strikebreakers, the organization asked U.S. attorney general Richard Olney, who sat on the board of directors of three major railroads, for a federal injunction against the strikers for allegedly refusing to move rail cars carrying U.S. mail. In fact, however, union members had volunteered to switch mail cars onto trains that did not carry Pullman cars; it was the railroads' managers who had delayed the mail by refusing to dispatch trains without the full complement of cars. Olney, supported by President Grover Cleveland, cited the Sherman Anti-Trust Act and secured an injunction against leaders of the American Railway Union for restraint of commerce. When the union refused to order its members back to work, Debs was arrested and federal troops poured in. During the ensuing rioting, 700 freight cars were burned, 13 people died, and 53 were wounded. The strike was crushed.

By exploiting the popular identification of strikers with anarchism and violence, corporate leaders hobbled organized labor's ability to bargain. When the Supreme Court upheld Debs's prison sentence and legalized the use of injunctions against labor unions (*In re Debs*, 1895), business gained a powerful new weapon against labor. Despite a series of attempts to build a strong working-class movement, turmoil sapped the vitality of organized labor and gave it a negative public image that it would not shed until the 1930s.

Social Thinkers Probe for Alternatives

The widespread industrial turmoil was particularly unsettling when juxtaposed with growing evidence of working-class destitution. A general public debate considered the social meaning of the new industrial order. At stake was a critical issue: should government become the mechanism for helping the poor and regulating big business?

Defenders of capitalism embraced a philosophy of laissez-faire ("hands-off"), insisting that government should never attempt to control business. They cited the argument of Scottish economist Adam Smith (1723–1790) that self-interest acted as an "invisible hand" in the marketplace, automatically balancing the supply of and demand for goods and services. In "The Gospel of Wealth," an influential essay published in 1889, Andrew Carnegie applied British scientist Charles Darwin's evolutionary theories to human society. "The law of competition," Carnegie wrote, "may be sometimes hard for the individual, [but] it is best for the race, because it insures the survival of the fittest in every department. We accept and welcome, therefore, . . . the concentration of business in the hands of a few; and law of competition between these, as being not only beneficial, but essential to the future progress of the race." Ignoring the contemporary scramble among businesses to eliminate competition and to form trusts, Carnegie praised unregulated competition as a source of positive long-term social benefits.

Yale professor William Graham Sumner shared Carnegie's Social Darwinism, as this conservative, laissez-faire outlook came to be known. Unchangeable laws controlled the social order, he contended; "a drunkard in the gutter is just where he ought to be. . . . The law of survival of the fittest was not made by man, and it cannot be abrogated by man. We can only, by interfering with it, produce the survival of the unfittest." Social theorists, sentimental humanitarians, and "labor fakers" intent on uplifting the poor and needy actually harmed the "forgotten man"—the hardworking individual whose taxes were expected to fund their do-good schemes. The state, declared Sumner, owed its citizens only law, order, and basic political rights.

Social Darwinism did not go unchallenged. In *Dynamic Sociology* (1883), geologist Lester Frank Ward argued that human will *could* circumvent the supposed "laws" of nature. Just as scientists had bred superior livestock, government experts could regulate big business, protect society's weaker members, and prevent the reckless exploitation of natural resources.

Henry George, a newspaper editor and economic theorist, proposed to solve the nation's uneven distribution of wealth through the "single tax." In *Progress and Poverty* (1879), he proposed that government tax the "unearned increment" that speculators reaped from rising land prices. These funds could then ameliorate the misery caused by industrialization. Americans could enjoy the benefits of socialism—a state-controlled economic system that distributed resources according to need—without abandoning capitalism.

Another newspaper editor, Edward Bellamy, turned to fiction to evoke visions of a harmonious industrialized society. In *Looking Backward* (1888), Bellamy's protagonist, Julian West, falls asleep in 1888 and awakens in 2000 to find a nation without poverty or strife, thanks to a centralized, state-run economy. Centralization and a new religion of solidarity have created a society in which everyone works for the common welfare. Bellamy's utopian novel resonated among middle-class Americans. Fearful of corporate power and working-class violence, they formed nearly 500 Nationalist clubs to implement Bellamy's scheme.

Ward, George, and Bellamy did not deny the industrial order's benefits; rather, envisioning a harmonious society whose members all worked together, they sought to humanize it. Marxist socialists advanced a different view. In *Das Kapital* (1867) and other works, German radical Karl Marx argued that the labor required to produce a commodity was the only true measure of that commodity's value. Profit made by a capitalist employer was "surplus value" appropriated from exploited workers. Competition among capitalists would increase, Marx predicted; wages would decline to starvation levels, and finally the impoverished working class would seize control of the state *and* the means of production and distribution. Class struggle would lead to a classless utopia in which the state would "wither away," and exploitation would end. But Marxism had little appeal in late-nineteenth-century America beyond a handful of mainly German-born immigrants. More alarming were the anarchists, mainly immigrants, who rejected Marxist discipline and preached the destruction of capitalism, the violent overthrow of the state, and the immediate introduction of a stateless utopia.

Conclusion

In the Republic's early years, Thomas Jefferson had warned of industrialization's threat to American virtue and democracy, even as Alexander Hamilton had promoted industrialization as essential to national prosperity and greatness. By 1900 Americans realized that both men had been right. Industrialization *had* catapulted the United States to world power, lowered the cost of goods, generated thousands of jobs, and made available a wide range of consumer products. But as Jefferson had foreseen, the cost was high. Savage competition, exploited workers, shady business practices, polluted landscapes, and the erosion of traditional skills had accompanied the rise of giant corporations. Labor violence, urban slums, and grinding poverty underlined the high cost.

Americans were uncertain about the new industrial order. Enjoying the higher standard of living that industrialization made possible, but fearing capitalist power and social chaos, they tried to keep the material benefits while alleviating the social harm. The Interstate Commerce Act, the Sherman Anti-Trust Act, and the vogue of Nationalist clubs testify to middle-class qualms. In the Progressive Era of the early twentieth century (see Chapter 22), Americans would redouble their efforts to create political and social solutions to the changes wrought by economic transformation.

Chronology

1837   Magnetic telegraph invented.

1859   First oil well drilled, in Titusville, Pennsylvania.

1866   National Labor Union founded.

1869   First transcontinental railroad completed.
Knights of Labor organized.

1870   Standard Oil Company established.

1873   Panic of 1873 triggers a depression lasting until 1879.

1876   Alexander Graham Bell invents and patents the telephone.
Thomas A. Edison opens research laboratory at Menlo Park, New Jersey.

1877   Edison invents the phonograph.
Railway workers stage the first nationwide strike.

1879   Henry George, *Progress and Poverty.*
Edison perfects the incandescent lamp.

1882   Standard Oil Trust established.
Edison opens the first electric power station on Pearl Street in New York City.
Chinese Exclusion Act.

1883   Railroads divide the country into time zones.
Lester Frank Ward, *Dynamic Sociology.*

1886   American Federation of Labor (AFL) formed.
Police and demonstrators clash at Haymarket Square in Chicago.

1887   Interstate Commerce Act establishes the Interstate Commerce Commission.

1888   Edward Bellamy, *Looking Backward.*

1889   Andrew Carnegie, "The Gospel of Wealth."

1890   Sherman Anti-Trust Act.

1892   Standard Oil of New Jersey and General Electric formed.
Steelworkers strike at Homestead, Pennsylvania.
Silver miners strike in Idaho.

1893   Panic of 1893 triggers a depression lasting until 1897.

1894   Pullman Palace Car workers strike, supported by the American Railway Union.

1901   J. Pierpont Morgan organizes United States Steel.

FOR FURTHER READING

Alfred D. Chandler, Jr., *The Visible Hand: The Managerial Revolution in American Business* (1977). A pathbreaking account of the innovative managerial changes in large-scale corporate enterprise.

Alice Kessler-Harris, *Out to Work: A History of Wage-Earning Women in the United States* (1982). An important survey of women's entry into the paid labor force and its impact on family roles, cultural attitudes, and class distinctions.

Martin V. Melosi, *Coping with Abundance: Energy and Environment in Industrial America* (1985). A valuable study of changing sources of energy and their impact on the environment.

David Montgomery, *The Fall of the House of Labor: The Workplace, the State, and American Labor Activism, 1865–1925* (1987). An insightful analysis of the transformation of industrial production and its impact on labor.

Stephen J. Ross, *Workers on the Edge: Work, Leisure, and Politics in Industrializing Cincinnati, 1788–1890* (1985). An important community study of the changing world of work and its impact on politics.

The Transformation of Urban America

$\mathcal{E}$xplosive growth transformed U.S. cities in the late nineteenth century. Between 1870 and 1900 New Orleans's population doubled, Buffalo's tripled, and Chicago's increased more than fivefold. By 1900 Philadelphia, New York City, and Chicago had each passed the 1-million-person mark, and 40 percent of all Americans lived in cities.

This spectacular urban growth, fueled by the influx of 11 million immigrants, created a dynamic environment for job development. Lured by the prospect of finding work, newcomers to America provided cheap labor for countless small businesses and industries. In turn, these developments made possible an unparalleled concentration of resources and markets that dramatically stimulated national economic expansion. Like the frontier, the city symbolized opportunity for all comers.

But the city's unprecedented size and diversity threatened traditional American expectations of community life and stability. A medley of immigrant groups contended with each other and with native-born Americans—for jobs, power, and influence. Rapid growth

(Right) Immigrant children, 1890 (detail); photograph by Jacob Riis

Urban Expansion
The Urban Challenge
Reshaping the Urban Environment

strained city services, generating terrible housing and sanitation problems.

Native-born American city dwellers found the noise, stench, and congestion disturbing. They worried about the newcomers' squalid tenements, fondness for drink, and strange social customs. Reformers who set out to "clean up" the cities aimed not only to improve the physical environment but to destroy the distinctive customs of the immigrant cultures. Resenting attacks on their way of life, the immigrants fought to protect their traditions. The late nineteenth century thus witnessed an intense struggle among diverse urban constituencies to control the city politically and to benefit from its economic and cultural potential.

Urban Expansion

Between 1840 and 1900 a critical need for factory sites, housing, and offices transformed the physical appearance of U.S. cities. Residential neighborhoods, parks, downtown business districts, and commercial and manufacturing areas blossomed. New transportation systems moved commuters on streetcars, trains, electric trolleys, and subway cars. Suburbs developed along railroad lines in the countryside, where land was cheap and the environment pleasant.

The New Urban World

The rapid growth of cities after the Civil War created a national urban network—a web of regional metropolises, specialized manufacturing cities, and smaller communities of varying size and function. Major cities such as New York, Boston, and San Francisco became regional centers providing manufacturing plants, banks, and financial services for the surrounding towns and countryside. In the 1850s Chicago emerged as the upper Midwest's center for shipping and marketing lumber, meat, and grain. Thirty years later, its factories employed

75,000 people, the largest industrial work force west of the Appalachians. Smaller cities specialized in particular products or processes: Holyoke, Massachusetts, in paper; Minneapolis, Minnesota, in milling and lumber; and Corning, New York, in glass.

Brisk expansion changed urban life forever. Small towns followed the seasonal rhythms of farming, but cities pulsed with people rushing to meet schedules and to beat deadlines. And whereas small-town residents knew their neighbors, city dwellers lived in a world of strangers. Time itself changed in the city as urbanites worked and played late into the night.

A Revolution in Transportation

Until the early nineteenth century, most cities were compact, densely settled communities of perhaps three square miles. Within these "walking" cities, rich and poor lived in close proximity. The advent of new transportation systems turned these cities inside out. The rich moved to the city's edge, and the poor relocated inward, crowding into abandoned mansions subdivided into apartments.

Early urban transportation networks consisting of horse-drawn coaches, which had appeared in the 1830s, yielded to larger "horsecars," horse-drawn streetcars. By the 1880s, 415 streetcar companies carried 188 million passengers a year over more than 6,000 miles of track, providing easy transportation between city dwellers' work and their homes. The horsecars, however, presented problems. Observers recoiled as they watched drivers whip horses straining to pull the crowded cars, or as they saw fallen animals destroyed where they lay. In New York alone, an estimated 15,000 horses died from overwork each year in the 1880s. In addition, horse droppings fouled city streets. In 1900 health officials in Rochester, New York, estimated that the city's 15,000 horses produced enough manure every year to fill a hole one acre in area and 175 feet deep, and to breed 16 billion flies.

Steam railroads were an obvious replacement. As early as 1849, fifty-nine commuter trains made the daily trip into Boston from as far as fifteen miles away. But because steam engines were not efficient for short runs, city officials began exploring more flexible alternatives such as cable cars and electric streetcars.

Chicago pioneered the most extensive cable-car system, which operated over eighty-six miles of track by 1887. More sanitary, better on hills, and quieter than horsecars, cable cars nonetheless had drawbacks, too, particularly high construction costs. Eventually, cable cars proved profitable only in hilly cities.

By the 1890s electric streetcars or trolleys had replaced horsecars and cable cars in most cities. In effect, trolley companies subsidized long-distance commuting by charging a fixed price per ride rather than by distance. Thus families could move farther and farther from city centers without increasing their transportation costs. Urban sprawl ensued. Many streetcar companies lost money in their operations because of low population densities along their lines but earned towering profits by buying and selling suburban land.

Radiating outward from the city center like the spokes of a wheel, streetcar lines revitalized cities by requiring crosstown commuters to pass through the downtown. The arrangement improved commercial opportunities in the central business district, and entrepreneurs hastened to capitalize on this potential. In 1874 John Wanamaker of Philadelphia turned an old downtown railroad freight depot into an elaborate department store. Merchants in other cities duplicated his success. The inexpensive convenience of traveling by trolley made shopping downtown a new form of recreation.

A Mobile Population

The expansion of streetcar systems and the completion of regional railroad networks dramatically increased residential instability as more and more people succumbed to the fever to move. People fled congested neighborhoods for outlying residential areas—now conveniently accessible by streetcar—to gain open space and fresh air. Fashionable homes sprouted on the city's periphery. The availability of larger houses at lower prices also lured people to the suburbs.

Movement *between* cities paralleled the frantic residential shifts *within* cities. Families commonly moved from city to city to boost their income or to improve their living conditions. Most cities, although growing in overall numbers, lost more than half their current inhabitants every decade. Historical demographers calculate that most U.S. cities experienced an astonishing turnover of three to four times their total population every ten years.

Contemporaries deplored the speed and scale of residential change. They viewed the migration of the middle and upper classes as a selfish attempt to escape responsibility for improving inner-city neighborhoods. Well-to-do city dwellers might be concerned about the poor, but they put the happiness, health, and safety of their own families first, moving to neighborhoods with better housing and an improved quality of life.

Thus mobility and change represented the norm in nineteenth-century urban society. New transportation systems permitted residential movement, and rich and poor alike freely changed residences and jobs in search of new paths to happiness and success. The city beckoned to the restless and ambitious.

Migrants and Immigrants

As the new industries concentrated in urban settings demanded thousands of new workers, the promise of good wages and plentiful jobs attracted many rural and small-town dwellers to the cities. So great was the migration from rural areas, especially in New England, that some farm communities vanished from the map.

Young women led the exodus. The growing commercialization and specialization of agriculture had turned much farm labor into male work. Mail-order sales of factory-made goods meanwhile reduced the need for women's work on subsistence tasks. So young farm women flocked to the cities, where they competed with immigrant, black, and city-born women for jobs.

From 1860 to 1890, the prospect of a better life also attracted nearly 10 million northern European immigrants to American cities, where they joined the more than 4 million who had settled there in the 1840s and 1850s. Their numbers included 3 million Germans, 2 million English, Scottish, and Welsh, and 1.5 million Irish. Moreover, by 1900 more than 800,000 French-Canadians had migrated southward to work in the New England mills, and nearly a million Scandinavians farmed the rich lands of Wisconsin and Minnesota. Then, in the three decades after 1890, more than 18 million "new immigrants" joined these "old immigrants." Predominantly peasants, they came from southern and eastern Europe.

The overwhelming majority of old and new immigrants settled in cities in the northeastern and north-central states. Dreams fired by exuberant letters from earlier immigrants, and by the extravagant claims of steamship lines seeking passengers, brought throngs of new arrivals in search of work and fresh beginnings. The numbers were staggering. In 1890 New York City contained twice as many Irish as Dublin, as many Germans as Hamburg, half as many Italians as Naples, and two-and-a-half times the Jewish population of Warsaw. Four out of five people in New York City were immigrants or the children of immigrants.

Overpopulation, crop failure, famine, and industrial depression had driven some of these immigrants from their homelands. However, many people, especially single young men, immigrated in the belief that the United States had a better future than their homeland. An eighteen-year-old Norwegian explained his decision: "My father is a schoolteacher and has, besides me, two younger sons, so that it often strains his resources to keep

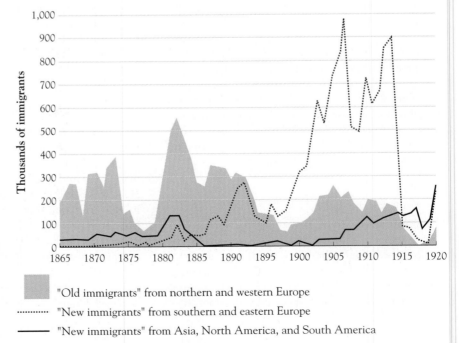

The Changing Face of U.S. Immigration, 1865–1920

Between 1865 and 1895, the majority of newcomers to America hailed from northern and western Europe. But the early twentieth century witnessed a surge of immigration from southern and eastern Europe.

"Old immigrants" from northern and western Europe

"New immigrants" from southern and eastern Europe

"New immigrants" from Asia, North America, and South America

Jakob Mithelstadt and Family, 1905
The Mithelstadts were Russian Germans who arrived in New York City on the S.S.
Pretoria. The poorest immigrants traveled in steerage, below-deck cargo areas that lacked
portholes and originally housed the cables to the ship's rudder.

us in school here. . . . I have come to feel that the most sensible thing I can do is to emigrate to America."

The transatlantic journey, cramped and often stormy, featured poor food, little privacy, and rudimentary sanitary facilities. Immigrants arrived tired, fearful, and in some cases very sick. Then customs officials examined them for physical handicaps and contagious diseases. After 1891 those with a "loathsome" infection such as leprosy or a sexually transmitted disease were deported. Immigrants who passed the physical examination then had their names recorded. If a customs official had difficulty pronouncing a foreign name, he Anglicized it. One German Jew became flustered when asked for his name and mumbled "Schoyn vergessen [I forget]." The inspector, who did not know Yiddish, wrote "Sean Ferguson."

In 1892 the U.S. government established a facility for admitting immigrants on Ellis Island in New York City's harbor. Here America's newest residents exchanged foreign currency for U.S. dollars, purchased railroad tickets, and arranged lodgings. Those who arrived with enough cash, including many Germans and Scandinavians, commonly traveled west to Chicago, Milwaukee, and the prairies beyond. But most of the Irish and Italians, largely from poor peasant backgrounds, stayed in eastern cities such as Boston, New York, and Philadelphia, where they filled the lowest-paying jobs. The Irish and Italians who did go west typically made the trip in stages, moving from job to job on the railroad and canal systems.

Adjusting to Urban Society

Immigrants tended to cluster together to ease the transition to life in a new society. In 1890 a reporter observed that if a map of New York City's streets were colored in by nationality, it "would show more stripes than on the skin of a zebra, and more colors than any rainbow."

Most newcomers preferred to live near others not merely of their own nationality but from their own region or village. New York's Lower East Side held not a single "Little Italy" but dozens of them, inhabited by Neapolitans and Calabrians at Mulberry Bend, Genoese on Baxter Street, northern Italians west of Broadway, and Tyrolese Italians on Sixty-ninth Street near the Hudson River.

Within these neighborhoods, immigrants endured incredibly crowded conditions. In New York City, where real-estate costs soared highest, landlords built virtually windowless five-story buildings on lots only twenty-five feet wide. In 1879 New York reformers secured passage of a law that forced landlords to construct buildings with central ten-foot-by-four-foot air shafts. Dubbed "dumbbell" tenements because of their shape, the buildings squeezed stairs, halls, and common bathrooms into the narrow central sections. By the 1890s a single New York block typically contained ten dumbbell tenements with between 2,000 and 4,000 immigrant residents. The worst conditions flourished in Manhattan, but in 1902 investigators in Buffalo, New York, found sixty Polish immigrants living in a single small row house.

Nonetheless, many immigrant families enjoyed richly textured lives. Ironically, it was the crowded conditions that fostered this richness. Within their tight ethnic neighborhoods, immigrants could speak their native language, purchase traditional foods, attend old-world church services, and celebrate the festivals that they had known in Europe. Despite attempts by well-intentioned reformers to change immigrants' habits and behaviors, many new Americans preserved their native language, dishes, and customs. Older immigrant women, confined to their tenement flats and immediate neighborhoods, often clung to traditional routines longer than their husbands and children, whose work and social activities increasingly drew them into the currents of city life. As immigrant children learned the English language and American ways in public schools, many began

to reject their parents' old-world accents, dress, and customs. For the second and third generation of immigrant families, the appeal of the ethnic neighborhoods faded.

Some immigrant groups adjusted more easily than others. Those with skilled trades and familiarity with Anglo-American customs had relatively few problems. Ethnic groups that formed a substantial percentage of a city's population also had a major advantage. The Irish of Boston, New York City, and Chicago, as well as the Germans of Milwaukee, dominated local government and church organizations and eased the path for their fellow immigrants.

The larger the immigrant group, the more effectively organized were its churches, newspapers, schools, banks, and benevolent associations. The New York Hebrew Free Loan Society (founded in 1892), one of numerous self-help organizations set up in this era, provided interest-free loans of up to $200 to Jewish immigrants who wanted to establish their own businesses. But the power of the larger immigrant groups sometimes made the adjustment to American society more difficult for members of the smaller groups. The English and Germans who dominated the building trades, for example, limited the numbers of Italians hired. In 1900 only 18 percent of New York's skilled brick masons were Italians, but 55 percent of its barbers and 97 percent of its poorly paid bootblacks were recent newcomers from Italy.

The smaller immigrant groups sometimes had trouble adjusting to American society, moreover, because many of their members did not intend to stay in the United States. Young Chinese and Italian males often immigrated to America to earn enough money to return home, where they hoped to buy land or to establish a business. They made little effort to learn English or to understand American customs. Of the Italians who migrated to New York before 1914, nearly 50 percent went back to Italy.

By 1900, whatever their degree of adaptation to the English language and U.S. culture, all immigrant groups faced increasing hostility from native-born Americans, who not only disliked the newcomers' social customs but also feared their growing influence.

Slums and Ghettos

Every major city had run-down, overcrowded slum neighborhoods, created when landlords subdivided old buildings and packed in too many residents. The poorer the renters, the worse the slums. Slums became ghettos when laws, prejudice, and community pressure prevented inhabitants from moving out. During the 1890s, Italians in New York City, blacks in Philadelphia and Chicago, Mexicans in Los Angeles, and Chinese in San Francisco increasingly became locked into ghettos. Italian immigrants in particular were pushed into substandard housing. Because so many young males intended to return to Italy, they took the cheapest available housing and endured filth and congestion in the belief that their stay was temporary.

To an urban reformer like Jacob Riis, the Italians themselves appeared to be the problem. Riis despised their custom of congregating in the streets to purchase food, chat with friends, or pass the time. In *How the Other Half Lives* (1890), he singled out a district called the Bend as the worst of New York City's slums and emphasized its Italian character. "Half of the people in 'the Bend' are christened Pasquale . . . ," he wrote. "When the police do not know the name of an escaped murderer, they guess at Pasquale and send the name out on an alarm; in nine cases out of ten it fits." Riis acknowledged the destructive effects of substandard housing, inadequate health care, and unsanitary conditions, as well as the social disruption of immigration, but still blamed the Italian residents for the crime, squalor, disease, and appallingly high infant death rate that plagued them. This tendency to fault the slum dwellers for their own plight, and to hold particular immigrant groups responsible for their living conditions, characterized even well-intentioned reformers and helped to shape, and to distort, middle-class perceptions of the immigrant city. Other cities also crumpled under the pressure of unremitting population growth. Social workers in Chicago deplored one slum's "filthy and rotten tenements, the dingy courts and tumble-down sheds, the foul stables and dilapidated outhouses, the broken sewer-pipes, the piles of garbage fairly alive with diseased odors, and the numbers of children filling every nook, working and playing in every room, eating and sleeping in every window-sill. . . ."

Epidemics of typhoid fever, smallpox, and diphtheria periodically ravaged the slums, and the slower killer tuberculosis claimed thousands of victims. Whooping cough, measles, and scarlet fever took a fearful toll among youth, and infant mortality was high. In 1900 one immigrant ward in Chicago saw 20 percent of all infants die in their first year.

Furthermore, tenements often bordered industrial districts, and so residents had to put up with the noise, pollution, and foul odors of tanneries, foundries, factories, and packing houses. Reliance on coal for steam engines and heating released vast quantities of soot and coal dust to drift over the slums. As smoke tinged the atmosphere hazy-gray, buildings took on a dingy, grimy patina.

The position of blacks was even worse than that of poor white immigrants. Trapped in segregated districts, and excluded from other areas by restrictive real-estate covenants, they had no way out of the ghetto. By the turn of the century, growing competition between immigrants and black migrants moving up from the South left African-Americans segregated in the poorest sections of northern cities, such as Chicago's "Black Belt" on the South Side and Cleveland's Central Avenue District. Intimidation as well as segregation plagued urban blacks. In the 1880s a black newspaper asserted that white police officers, especially the Irish, "delight in arresting every little colored boy they see on the street, who may be doing something not at all offensive, and allow the white boys to do what they please."

Rivalry over housing and jobs sometimes sparked racial violence. Usually, the victim of an attack was a lone individual; however, sometimes interracial clashes escalated into full-scale riots, as in New York City during the summer of 1900. The mêlée began when a young black man knifed and killed a plainclothes policeman who he believed was mishandling his wife. As news of the murder spread, lower Manhattan erupted in rage. "Men and women poured by the hundreds from the neighboring tenements," a local reporter wrote. "Negroes were set upon wherever they could be found and brutally beaten."

Fashionable Avenues and Suburbs

The same cities that harbored slums, suffering, and violence also boasted neighborhoods of dazzling opulence. The wealthy built monumental residences on exclusive thoroughfares just outside the downtown, among them Fifth Avenue in New York, Commonwealth Avenue in Boston, and Euclid Avenue in Cleveland. In Chicago, after a devastating fire in 1871, the elite moved south to Prairie Avenue around Eighteenth Street. Then, in the 1880s, with the extension of the street-railway system, well-to-do Chicagoans moved to Lake Shore Drive, the so-called Gold Coast on the near North Side. The gradual northward migration of Chicago's well-heeled citizens paralleled the expansion of immigrant neighborhoods on the South Side, where once-fashionable mansions, converted to cramped apartments, quickly filled with newcomers.

Middle-class city dwellers followed the wealthy, moving to new suburbs. In the 1890s Chicago developer Samuel Eberly Gross created entire low-cost subdivisions north and west of the city and advertised homes for as little as ten dollars a month. Lawyers, doctors, small businessmen, and other professionals moved farther out along the main thoroughfares served by the street railway, and purchased homes with large lots.

A pattern of informal residential segregation by income took shape in the cities and suburbs. Built for families of a particular income level, certain city neighborhoods and suburbs developed remarkably similar internal standards for lot size and house design. Commuters who rode the new street railways out from the city center could identify the changing neighborhoods along the way as readily as a geologist might distinguish different strata on a washed-out riverbank. And with the physical change in American cities came a new awareness of class and cultural disparities.

The Urban Challenge

Although middle- and upper-class Americans were abandoning their downtown residences in the 1880s and 1890s, the business and professional activities of merchants, journalists, manufacturers, lawyers, and others remained centered in the heart of the city. Growing evidence of social unrest, and especially the occasional strikes and riots that swept through the cities, deeply disturbed these old-stock citizens. Critics linked the disorder to the immigrant masses, who, they said, lacked self-discipline and moral conduct. The corruption-riddled political machines that dominated city government became a chief target of the critics.

Convinced that urgent steps must be taken to stem a rising tide of riot, robbery, and rotten government, concerned citizens waged a continuous battle to eradicate urban crime, to reform "boss" politics, and to assimilate immigrants into mainstream society. A powerful blend of altruism and self-interest motivated them.

Policing the City

In his novel *Ragged Dick* (1867), Horatio Alger detailed the scams and violence awaiting unwary newcomers to the city, perpetrated by dishonest shopkeepers, pickpockets, muggers, con artists, and Irish street gangs. Alger and other writers who associated crime with the growth of cities did not exaggerate. As Philadelphia's population tripled between 1850 and 1900, for example, so did its homicides. Concerned citizens worried publicly about easily available cheap handguns.

In the 1830s and 1840s, cities had established police forces to maintain law and order. Unlike their European counterparts, these regulatory agencies were civilian enterprises, separate from the military and controlled by local officials. Following New York's example, set in 1853, U.S. cities had outfitted their police officers with badges and uniforms and authorized them to carry clubs and revolvers. These police forces often had ill-defined responsibilities, ranging from maintaining order and preventing crime to cleaning streets, running lodging houses for the homeless, and supervising the sanitation of vegetable markets. The police made little headway in suppressing the rowdy street life, drinking, gambling, and prostitution that flourished in the immigrant working-class districts.

Middle-class civic leaders particularly deplored the neighborhood saloons, which provided a free lunch with a five-cent beer, meeting rooms, news of job openings, and, sometimes, gambling tables and prostitutes' services in back rooms. State legislatures, dominated by rural, native-born citizens who disapproved of the immigrants' drinking and gambling, regularly passed laws banning these practices, curtailing Sunday business operations, and regulating saloons.

Caught between moralistic state legislators and immigrant communities resentful of outside meddling, police tried to steer a middle course, tacitly allowing saloons to remain open on Sunday, for example, as long as their patrons behaved properly in public. Then in 1894 an investigation by a New York State legislator uncovered evidence that the New York City police not only were failing to suppress illegal activities but were actually licensing them. In return for payoffs, the police permitted gamblers, prostitutes, and saloonkeepers to operate more or less at will in poor neighborhoods where little organized opposition existed, provided that they remained discreet. Instead of fighting vice, the shocked legislator concluded, the police were conniving in it.

The complex relationship between the police and those whom they were supposed to be policing manifested itself in other ways. By the 1870s most police departments in major cities had squads of detectives who worked out of inner-city saloons. Often not easily distinguishable from the crooks and con men with whom they rubbed shoulders, these police detectives sometimes even functioned as go-betweens for thieves and robbery victims, returning stolen property in exchange for a reward. In some cities professional criminals reached an understanding with detectives and returned property stolen from citizens of high prestige and standing.

In late-nineteenth-century cities, reformers tried to make law enforcement more professional by appointing independent, nonpartisan boards of commissioners to hire and fire police officers. Pressured by such reformers as young Theodore Roosevelt, who headed New York's Board of Police Commissioners from 1895 to 1897, civic leaders gradually removed police departments from political patronage and adopted regular hiring procedures. But urban reformers had less success in legislating the stricter morality that rural legislators desired. Given the large immigrant populations within the cities, many police officers, especially those drawn from the immigrant ranks, remained sympathetic to the social customs of the ethnic groups among whom they circulated.

Governing the City

The competition for authority over the police reflected a deeper power struggle within urban politics. The demands placed on public utilities, rapid-transit systems, and fire and police departments forced cities to raise taxes, issue bonds, and create new municipal departments and positions. Large sums could be made by dominating any segment of this process, and state and local politicians fought for control of the city and the right to run these lucrative services. To complicate matters, city governments and state legislatures alike claimed jurisdiction over the urban environment. Ostensibly to curb governmental abuse, state legislatures altered city charters, bestowed special contracts and monopolies on railroad and utility magnates, and tried to minimize taxes by reducing the expenses of city government and limiting city services.

By midcentury, outside interference in local affairs had encouraged the rise of a new kind of professional politician, the "boss," who presided over the city's "machine," an unofficial political organization designed to keep a particular party or faction in office. Assisted by local ward or precinct "captains," the boss wielded enormous influence in city government. Often a former saloonkeeper or labor leader, the boss knew his constituents well. Cincinnati's George B. Cox was a typical boss, though more honest than many. The son of British immigrants, Cox worked his way up from newsboy and lookout for gamblers to saloon owner. Elected to Cincinnati's city council in 1879, Cox became head of the city's Republican machine, which swung elections to the GOP, controlled key public offices, and acted as a broker among competing corporate and political interests.

For better or worse, the political machine was America's unique contribution to the challenge of municipal government in an era of pell-mell urban growth. Typified by Tammany Hall, the Democratic organization that dominated New York politics from the 1830s to the 1930s, machines emerged in a host of cities during the late nineteenth century. Highly centralized, the machine consisted of loosely affiliated and largely autonomous organizations in the local wards, the city's smallest political divisions. Ward captains, also frequently saloonkeepers, got the people out to vote at election time in return for jobs, contracts, and political appointments from city hall.

Within its orbit, the machine ruled supreme. The politicians who ran it controlled the jobs of thousands of policemen, firemen, sanitation workers, and other city employees; they exerted enormous influence over courts, schools, hospitals, and other municipal agencies. Democratic in some cities, Republican in others, the machine hammered out compromises and resolved conflicts among competing urban interest groups.

The machine rewarded its friends and punished its enemies through its control of taxes, licenses, and inspections. It gave tax breaks to favored contractors and slipped them information about upcoming street and sewer projects. The ward captain doubled as a kind of welfare agent, helping the needy and protecting the troubled. He might intercede with a judge to secure clemency for a local boy caught running a gambling operation, dispense food

to a family when the breadwinner was sick or injured, or provide a city job for an immigrant. The machine helped to compensate for failings in the era's welfare system, but it entangled essential municipal functions and urban social services in a corrupt political system.

An effective precinct captain could work his way up from local to state or even national power. In Kansas City, Missouri, "Big Jim" Pendergast, an Irish hotelkeeper and saloonkeeper in an industrial ward, clawed his way to power in the 1890s by providing welfare services for his black, Italian, and Irish constituents. By controlling his ward's delegates to the city's Democratic conventions, he rose to city alderman. When opponents threatened to root out gambling interests associated with his saloon, Pendergast used his influence with the governor to engineer the appointment of a sympathetic police chief. By the turn of the century, Pendergast held near absolute sway in Kansas City politics and wielded considerable clout at the state level.

Cox, Pendergast, and other bosses transformed urban politics into a form of entrepreneurship. As ambitious and ruthless as any Rockefeller or Carnegie, they pioneered new forms of political and social organization. In some cases they also amassed vast fortunes. At times greedy and unscrupulous, they nevertheless responded to immigrant and working-class concerns in a society increasingly dominated by the middle and upper classes.

Under boss William Marcy Tweed, the Tammany Hall machine sank to new depths of corruption. Between 1869 and 1871, the machine dispensed 60,000 patronage positions and pumped up the city's debt by $70 million through graft and inflated contracts. The details of the Tweed ring's massive fraud were widely reported in newspapers and satirized in *Harper's Weekly* by cartoonist Thomas Nast. In one cartoon, Nast portrayed Tweed and his cronies as vultures picking at the city's bones. The caption read, "Let us prey." Tweed bellowed in fury. "I don't care a straw for your newspaper articles—my constituents don't know how to read," he told *Harper's;* "but they can't help seeing them damned pictures." Convicted of fraud and

"Let Us Prey," 1871
Cartoonist Thomas Nast hated William Marcy Tweed's ostentatious style. Pictured here as the chief vulture standing over the body of New York City, Boss Tweed wears an enormous diamond, a symbol of his insatiable greed.

extortion, Tweed was sentenced to jail in 1873, served two years, escaped to Spain, was caught, and died in jail in 1878.

Not all bosses were as crooked as Tweed. Boss Cox of Cincinnati, who maintained that he never had received an illegal payoff, gained the backing of local reformers by supporting voter-registration laws and placing police and fire departments under independent bipartisan boards. He also supported the construction of a new city waterworks and the improvement of parks and other recreation facilities. Although Cox's opponents doubted that his administration was as free of corruption as he claimed, they did not overthrow his machine until 1897.

Despite the stereotype of city bosses as crude and vulgar, not all bosses fit that mold. San Francisco boss Abraham Ruef graduated from the University of California at age eighteen with highest honors. Ed Flynn, the boss of the Bronx, New York, was a brilliant lawyer. Whatever their backgrounds, bosses represented a new political style that stressed grass-roots ties to the neighborhood and ward. They made sure that their constituents' concerns were heard, and displayed flexible, pragmatic, and opportunistic approaches to meeting the challenges of urban life.

Nevertheless, by the turn of the century, bosses faced well-organized assaults on their power, led by an urban elite seeking to restore "good government." In this atmosphere, the bosses increasingly forged alliances with civic organizations and reform leagues that paved the way for new sewer and transportation systems, expanded parklands, and improved public services—a record of considerable accomplishment, considering the magnitude of the problems created by urban growth.

Battling Poverty

From midcentury on, middle-class urban leaders sought alternative solutions to the rampant sickness and poverty around them. Prominent reformers, church officials, and settlement-house workers believed that cities were "putrefying" and that political bosses made matters worse.

Where the urban boss reacted to individual problems of poverty, charity workers eyed the destitute from a distance, often blaming them for their own problems. They therefore focused on the moral improvement of the poor and ignored the fact that immigrant attitudes toward drinking, work, and leisure differed drastically from their own. Consequently, humanitarian campaigns to help the poor turned into missions to Americanize the immigrants and to eliminate "offensive" and "self-destructive" customs.

Poverty-relief workers first targeted the young, whom many reformers considered the most malleable. Early Protestant social reformers started charitable societies to help transient youth and street waifs. In 1843 Robert M. Hartley, a former employee of the New York Temperance Society, founded the New York Association for Improving the Condition of the Poor. Convinced that slum children learned bad habits from their parents, Hartley organized a system of "home visitation" that sent volunteers into inner-city tenements to urge poor families to change their ways. The association also demanded pure-milk laws, public baths, and better housing.

The Young Men's Christian Association (YMCA), founded in England in 1841 and exported to America in 1851, focused on the dislocation and strain experienced by rural Americans who migrated to the cities in the post–Civil War years. The YMCA and later the YWCA (Young Women's Christian Association) provided decent housing and wholesome recreational facilities under close supervision and expelled members for drinking or other forbidden behavior.

Indeed, the departure of young people, especially farmers' daughters, from older rural areas had reached startling proportions. In one Vermont town, 73 percent of those aged five to fourteen in the 1880 census had left by 1900. The glamour and glitter of urban life dazzled the youthful rural migrants, who were drawn cityward mainly in search of economic opportunities. Far from home, with few friends and nowhere to stay, they easily fell victim to con artists. The YMCA and YWCA supplied these innocents safe temporary lodgings and reassuring reminders of home.

By 1900 more than 1,500 YMCAs acted as havens for nearly 250,000 men. But the YMCA and YWCA reached only a small portion of the young adult population. Their moralistic stance repelled some, and others preferred not to ask for help. Narrowly focused, the "Y" strategy could do little to relieve urban problems.

New Approaches to Social Work

The inability of relief organizations to cope with the explosive growth of the urban poor in the 1870s and 1880s convinced many middle-class Americans that urban poverty had reached epidemic proportions. In 1885 the Reverend Josiah Strong expressed this fear in his book *Our Country: Its Possible Future and Present Crisis*. Accusing cities of "multiplying and focalizing the elements of anarchy and destruction," Strong blamed immigration and Catholicism and pleaded for a cooperative Protestant effort to battle the dual plagues of intemperance and destitution.

Even before Strong mounted the battlements, reformers looked for new ways to combat urban poverty, especially among immigrants. Because needy families usually ignored idealistic appeals to change their ways, reformers developed coercive strategies. Only bold methods, they believed, could tear these unfortunates away from a way of life that bred dissipation and hardship.

One of the earliest and most effective agencies to combat poverty through tough-minded tactics was the Salvation Army. A church established along paramilitary lines in England in 1865 by Methodist minister "General" William Booth, the Salvation Army sent its uniformed volunteers to the United States in 1880 to provide food, shelter, and temporary employment for families. Known for its rousing music and attention-getting street meetings, the group ran soup kitchens and day nurseries and dispatched "slum brigades" to carry the message of morality to the immigrant poor. Funded by donations, the Salvation Army tried to aid—and to control—an urban population whose fondness for saloons, dance halls, and streetside entertainment threatened middle-class conceptions of a stable society. The organization's strategy was simple: attract the poor with marching bands and lively preaching; follow up with offers of food, assistance, and work; and then teach them the solid, middle-class virtues of temperance, hard work, and self-discipline.

New York's Charity Organization Society (COS), founded in 1882 by Josephine Shaw Lowell, implemented a similar approach, attempting to make the poor more honest and efficient. The society sent "friendly visitors" into the tenements to counsel families on how to improve their lives. Convinced that moral deficiencies lay at the root of poverty, and that the "promiscuous charity" of overlapping welfare agencies undermined the desire to work, the COS tried to foster self-sufficiency in its charges.

Critics justly accused the COS and similar groups of seeking more to control than to help the poor. More often than not, the friendly visitors wore cultural blinders, misunderstanding the real source of the difficulties faced by the poor and expecting to effect change by imposing middle-class standards. One journalist dismissed the typical friendly visitor as "235 pounds of Sunshine." Unable to see slum problems from the vantage point of the poor, the organizations ultimately failed to convert the poor to their own codes of morality and decorum.

The Moral-Purity Campaign

Unable to eradicate urban poverty and crime, reformers pushed for tougher measures against sin and immorality. In 1872 Anthony Comstock, a pious young dry-goods clerk, founded the New York Society for the Suppression of Vice and demanded that municipal authorities close down gambling and lottery operations and censor obscene publications. His purity crusade gained widespread support from civic leaders frustrated by the lack of progress in flushing away urban vice. Presbyterian minister Charles Parkhurst pursued the same goal by organizing the City Vigilance League in 1892 to attack the secret cooperation of New York authorities with gambling dens, saloons, and brothels. Parkhurst blamed the "slimy, oozy soil of Tammany Hall" and the New York City police for the city's rampant evil. In September 1894 a nonpartisan Committee of Seventy elected a new mayor who pressured city officials to enforce the laws against prostitution, gambling, and Sunday liquor sales.

The purity campaign, however, lasted scarcely three years. Irish and German neighborhoods rallied in defense of their cherished saloons. Individuals who had championed Parkhurst scoffed at his self-righteous and bombastic rhetoric and deserted his movement; the reform coalition fell apart. Tammany Hall regained its power in 1897 and installed a new police chief willing to regulate rather than to root out vice. New York's population was too large and its ethnic constituencies were too diverse for the middle and upper classes to curb all the illegal activities flourishing within the sprawling metropolis.

The Social Gospel

Meanwhile, in the 1870s and 1880s a handful of Protestant ministers explored radical alternatives for aiding impoverished city dwellers. Appalled by slum conditions, they argued that the rich and wellborn deserved part of the blame for poverty and thus had a responsibility to do something about it.

William S. Rainsford, the minister of New York City's St. George's Episcopal Church, pioneered the so-called institutional church movement, whereby large downtown churches in once elite districts now overrun by immigrants provided their new neighbors with social services as well as a place to worship. Supported by his wealthy church warden, J. Pierpont Morgan, Rainsford organized a boys' club, built recreational facilities on the Lower East Side, and established an industrial training program.

When his unorthodox approach provoked conservative wrath, Rainsford, unfazed, redoubled his criticism of complacent churchgoers' lack of concern. He argued that excessive drinking in immigrant wards did not stem from peoples' lack of willpower but was a by-product of the larger problem of the slums, where millions were trapped in desperate circumstances. Closing saloons on Sundays would accomplish far less than prosecuting the slum landlords and sweatshop owners who victimized the poor. In the end Rainsford's efforts fell short because of the magnitude of slum problems, but his sympathetic approach reflected an important dimension of a crusade by a group of late-nineteenth-century ministers to awaken American Protestants to the realities of the immigrant city.

Supporting that drive were the leaders of the Social Gospel movement, launched in the 1870s by the Congregational minister Washington Gladden of Columbus, Ohio. Dismayed by the way

Hull House Nursery
Explaining why she set up a nursery for children born into poverty, Jane Addams wrote that "this slaughter of the innocents, this infliction of suffering on the new-born, is so gratuitous and so unfair, that it is only a question of time until an outraged sense of justice shall be aroused on behalf of these children."

many middle-class churchgoers ignored the hardships of slum dwellers, Gladden insisted that true Christianity commits men and women to fight social injustice. If Gladden set the tone for the Social Gospel, Walter Rauschenbusch, a minister in New York City's notorious Hell's Kitchen neighborhood, articulated its philosophy. Strongly influenced by Henry George's and Edward Bellamy's criticism of laissez-faire ideology (see Chapter 18), Rauschenbusch sought to apply Jesus's teachings to society. A truly Christian society, he said, would unite all churches, reorganize the industrial system, and work for international peace.

The Social Gospel's fierce attacks on complacent Christian support of the status quo attracted only a handful of Protestants. Their earnest voices, however, blended with a growing chorus of critics bemoaning the nation's urban woes.

The Settlement-House Movement

By the 1880s many concerned citizens had become convinced that reform pressure applied from the top down, however well intentioned, was ineffective and wrongheaded. The passage of laws did not ensure obedience. A younger generation of charity workers, led by Jane Addams, developed a new weapon against destitution: the settlement house. Like the Social Gospelers, these reformers recognized that the hardships of slum life were often beyond individuals' control. Stressing the environmental causes of crime and poverty, settlement-house relief workers themselves moved into poor neighborhoods, where, in Addams's words, they could see firsthand "the struggle for existence, which is so much harsher among people near the edge of pauperism."

The Illinois-born Addams had graduated from Rockford College in 1882 and toured Europe a year later with her friend Ellen Gates Starr. Impressed by Toynbee Hall, a charity workers' residence deep in a London slum, the two women returned to Chicago and in 1889 purchased and repaired the dilapidated Charles J. Hull mansion, which they later opened as an experiment in the settlement-house approach. By living in Hull House and working in daily contact with poor immigrants, they hoped to provide a model creative outlet for college-trained women like themselves.

Drawing on the middle-class ideal of true womanhood as supportive and self-sacrificing, Addams turned Hull House into a social center for recent immigrants. She invited newly arrived Italian immigrants to plays; held classes in English, civics, cooking, and dressmaking; and encouraged them to preserve their traditional crafts. She also established a kindergarten, a laundry, an employment bureau, and a day nursery for working mothers. In the hope of upgrading filthy, overcrowded slum housing, Addams and her coworkers published systematic studies of city housing conditions and pressured politicians to enforce sanitary regulations.

By 1895 at least fifty settlement houses had opened around the nation. Their leaders trained a generation of young college students who later would serve as state and local government officials and would play an influential part in the regulatory movements of the Progressive Era (see Chapter 22). Through their sympathetic attitudes toward the immigrants and their systematic publication of data about slum conditions, settlement-house workers gave Americans new hope that the city's problems could be overcome.

Yet settlement houses enjoyed little success in their attempts to bridge the gap between rich and poor and to promote class cooperation and social harmony. They failed, moreover, to increase neighborhood immigrants' economic or political power. Limited by their own commitment to social order and class harmony, settlement-house advisers tended to overlook immigrant organizations and their leaders, and fell back on a tendency to impose their own middle-class taboos against drinking and gambling. "They're like the rest," complained one immigrant, "a bunch of people planning for us and deciding what is good for us without consulting us or taking us into their confidence."

Reshaping the Urban Environment

While reformers battled slum conditions and municipal corruption, landscape architects and city planners who shared their goal of an orderly urban society sought to reshape the urban masses by transforming their physical surroundings. Entire sections of America's metropolises were rebuilt in an attempt to clean up pollution and to restore beauty, dignity, and order to the urban environment.

To raise the level of urban and cultural awareness, these self-proclaimed saviors of America's cities established monumental public libraries, endowed art museums, constructed theaters and symphony halls, and expanded park and recreational facilities. At the same time, real-estate and business interests remodeled the city in their own way, erecting great towers of commerce and finance.

The motivations behind commercial construction were simple—profit and growth—but sponsors of the new urban landscape had more complex social objectives. They wanted both to make the city a more appealing place and to instill a sense of order that would tame and restrain the urban masses.

Parks and Public Spaces

Architects Andrew Jackson Downing and Frederick Law Olmsted were prominent in envisioning a new urban landscape. The ideal metropolis, they argued, should clearly differentiate shopping and housing areas from the industrial district. The city should have a compact commercial nucleus, but spacious parks and roadways should open up the landscape. Most important, public buildings and boulevards should be built on a grand scale, to inspire and awe ordinary citizens.

In 1858 Olmsted, one of the earliest and most successful promoters of this vision, had teamed up with English architect Calvert Vaux to develop the original plan for Central Park in New York City. They designed the park as a spacious, tranquil refuge, a sanctuary from the strains of urban life. After their success in New York, they designed major parks for Brooklyn, Chicago, Philadelphia, and Boston.

Boston's Back Bay

Olmsted and others who called for revitalizing the urban environment through planning and design took Boston's fashionable Back Bay district as their model. This area was a 450-acre tidal flat until 1857, when the state of Massachusetts began a massive engineering project to fill it in and to raise it twenty feet. For more than forty years, gravel trains ran around the clock from Needham, nine miles away, to the Back Bay. The state deeded some of the lots thus created to contractors as payment for the filling work, reserved others for educational and philanthropic organizations, and sold the rest as building lots. Each deed specified the height of the building, the distance it should be set back from the street, and the materials that could be used.

Engineers laid out Commonwealth Avenue, the Back Bay's main thoroughfare, along the lines of a French boulevard, with a formal central section graced by trees, stone benches, and statues. Elegant side streets branched off the avenue, with back alleys for deliveries. The uniform height of the district's five-story row houses established a line of vision that imparted formality and consistency.

Various cultural institutions reinforced the Back Bay's image as a center of civilization and refinement. In addition to the monumental Boston Public Library, the Back Bay eventually contained two colleges, two museums, five schools, and twelve churches. In the eyes of many social reformers and civic leaders, the Back Bay represented the classic example of the charming, cosmopolitan environment that city planning could create.

Rebuilding Chicago

In contrast to Boston, postwar Chicago was a planner's nightmare. Chicago was America's shock city, the extreme example of the kind of problems spawned by unregulated growth. Between 1850 and 1870, the city's population rose like a tidal wave, from 30,000 to 300,000, inundating neighborhoods and swamping city services. Although crisis rather than planning often dictated changes in the city, the sheer magnitude of the changes forced Chicagoans to accept innovations that others elsewhere later copied.

For example, the 1840s expansion had left residents with swampy, unpaved streets just above the water table. To remedy this soggy situation, the city council decided in 1855 that the streets' level must be raised, and so owners jacked up their buildings to meet the new grade level. In 1857 a British traveler noted in amazement that "the Briggs House, a gigantic hotel, five stories high, solid masonry, weighing 22,000 tons, was raised four and a half feet, and new foundations built below. The people were in it all the time, coming and going, eating and sleeping. . . ."

Chicago faced a new crisis in October 1871, when a fire razed nearly four square miles of the central city, devouring 61,000 buildings, gutting the commercial district, and leaving nearly 100,000 people homeless. The urgent need for downtown reconstruction gave Chicago architects, engineers, and civic leaders an unprecedented opportunity. In the next two decades, they cooperatively pioneered innovative methods for tall office building construction and created a new American building, the skyscraper.

The skyscraper depended on three technological innovations: fireproofing, the internal metal frame, and the elevator. Not until the 1880s did Chicago architects combine them into a distinctive commercial style. In view of the city's recent fire, officials insisted that all new structures be built of noncombustible materials. Stone was the obvious choice, but its great weight severely limited the size of buildings that could be erected on Chicago's marshy soil. Louis Sullivan and other architects developed a far lighter alternative—a central metal skeleton, fireproofed with fired-clay tile, to support the exterior walls. By placing the metal frame on an expanded foundation and installing motorized elevators, Chicago architects increased the city's building heights from four to twenty-two stories. Once Chicago skyscrapers demonstrated the technical feasibility and commercial advantages of constructing tall, metal-supported buildings on small, expensive urban lots, other American cities began to raise their skylines.

The dramatic rebuilding of the urban environment in Boston and Chicago encouraged business leaders and reformers in smaller cities. By the turn of the century, municipal art societies, park and outdoor-art associations, and civic-improvement leagues had sprung up around the country. Cities launched programs to replace muddy streets and unsightly billboards in downtown business districts with broad boulevards, sparkling fountains, and gleaming marble public buildings.

Known as the "city-beautiful movement," this crusade favored the interests of the rich and well-born, who took less interest in upgrading the slums than in making public buildings impressive and even monumental. They believed that attractive, imposing civic architecture would produce better citizens and reduce immorality and social disorder. In the early twentieth century, the city-beautiful impulse would evolve into a comprehensive city-planning movement (see Chapter 22) inspired by soaring visions of a transformed urban environment.

Toward a Metropolitan America

As city-beautiful advocates drafted plans for the urban future, harried city-hall bureaucrats, municipal administrators, and civic engineers wrestled with inadequate water supplies, antiquated sewer systems, and basic municipal services that lagged behind the pace of urban growth. To provide more efficient administration, new citywide agencies gradually took over matters once handled at the neighborhood and ward level. But while administration became centralized, urban power remained widely dispersed. Conflicts among different segments of the urban population—real-estate developers, businessmen, immigrants—ultimately encouraged compromise arrangements necessary for the smooth functioning of the entire city.

Around midcentury, city dwellers began to recognize that the deplorable quality of water and sewer systems threatened urban life. Even by the 1870s most urbanites still relied on private wells, outhouses, and cesspools; sewer systems were primitive and few. An engineer pungently described such systems as "reservoirs of liquid filth, ever oozing through the defective joints, and polluting the very earth upon which the city stands." Pouring its sewage directly into Lake Michigan, Chicago contributed to the frequent cholera, typhoid, and diphtheria epidemics that ravaged the city.

Early attempts to construct interconnected sewer systems fell victim to local politics. In Washington, D.C., contractors who had been hired for their political contacts produced lateral sewers that could not run uphill into the main trunk lines. In St. Louis and Cincinnati, politically motivated contracts resulted in inadequate systems that taxpayers had to replace within a decade, at an enormous expense.

Gradually and painfully, cities developed the centralized administrative structures that their size required. In 1889 Chicago officials persuaded the Illinois legislature to create a 185-square-mile sanitary district encompassing the city and its suburbs. By 1899 the city built the enormous Ship and Sanitary Canal, which reversed the flow of the Chicago River to carry the city's processed sewage downstate. By 1900 the establishment of water and sewer systems had cut mortality rates from typhoid fever nationwide by 65 percent.

The movement to centralize control over water and sewer facilities represented a broader process of physical and political consolidation in urban America. As cities grew, they added unincorporated surrounding land and absorbed adjacent municipalities, a development that allowed city governments to coordinate transportation, water, and sewer networks as well as to increase tax revenues. The largest such consolidation occurred in 1898, when Brooklyn, Queens, Staten Island, and the Bronx joined Manhattan to create the modern New York City. In the process, New York added nearly 2 million people to its population and ballooned from 44 to nearly 300 square miles.

Practically every U.S. city pushed out its boundaries in these years. Merchants saw annexation as a way to dilute the political power of immigrants who "stood in the way of progress," reformers hailed annexation as a step toward more professional city services, and real-estate promoters welcomed it as a means of securing municipal sewer and water systems that would increase the value of their holdings. Most middle-class suburbanites, eager for access to efficient city services, went along with the process. Not until the mid-twentieth century would suburban communities, valuing local autonomy and wary of urban tax rates and social problems, successfully fight off annexation.

Conclusion

The movement toward a metropolitan America culminated a long struggle to control the changing urban world after the Civil War. The expanding cities' size and diversity sometimes seemed overwhelming, while the battles for power and wealth raging in urban America proved at once exciting and disturbing.

The urban population grappled with the stresses of a social environment unfamiliar to many and undergoing tremendous flux. Middle- and upper-class urban residents were disturbed by the industrial city's massive physical problems—housing, sanitation, policing, schooling—and even more by the city's corrosive effect on traditional values and expectations. Migrants from America's farms and homogeneous small towns found themselves in an impersonal, fast-paced commercial world where antagonistic economic interests and ethnic and racial groups struggled for influence and power. Immigrants uprooted from centuries-old rhythms of peasant life or from the urban ghettos of eastern Europe had to adapt to the unremitting demands of industrial labor, to the mortal hazards and casual indignities of tenement life, and to the head-spinning diversity of the city. Remarkably impervious to the assaults of middle-class political opponents, to the pieties of would-be uplifters, or to the efforts of moral reformers to legislate behavior, immigrants rallied around the political boss. Of all the city's actors in these years, the boss learned best how to wield the levers of power in the new urban world.

Thus the post–Civil War city was a place of constant contention among wildly different groups. But from this boisterous conflict emerged the recognition that all city dwellers shared a basic interest in clean water, adequate sewers, garbage collection, and fire protection. Out of this realization blossomed a conception of what some have called the service city—a city that could efficiently meet the collective needs of its diverse inhabitants. By 1900 city bureaucracies had established responsibility for sanitation, transportation, street lighting, public health, parks, and police. Metropolitan America had taken shape.

Despite dark warnings of chaos and social upheaval, a remarkable degree of order and stability prevailed in the United States as the nineteenth century closed. Cities had evolved governmental forms sufficient to assure an adequate quality of life for all and to intervene when necessary to protect the welfare of the urban populace. This enlarged conception of government only slowly penetrated the arena of national politics, but the lessons so painfully learned in late-nineteenth-century cities would profoundly shape the progressive movement that lay ahead.

Chronology

1843 Robert M. Hartley founds the New York Association for Improving the Condition of the Poor.

1851 The American branch of the Young Men's Christian Association (YMCA) opens.

1853 Charles Loring Brace founds the New York Children's Aid Society.

1855 New York opens its Castle Garden immigrant center.

1857 Filling in of Boston's Back Bay begins.

1858 Frederick Law Olmsted and Calvert Vaux design Central Park.

1869 Boss William Marcy Tweed gains control of New York City's Tammany Hall political machine.

1871 The Great Chicago Fire.

1872 Anthony Comstock founds the New York Society for the Suppression of Vice and leads a "purity" campaign.

1874 John Wanamaker opens his Philadelphia department store.

1879 The New York "dumbbell" tenement law is passed.

1880 William Booth's followers establish an American branch of the Salvation Army.

1882 Josephine Shaw Lowell founds the New York Charity Organization Society (COS).

1888 First electric-trolley line, in Richmond, Virginia.

1889 Jane Addams and Ellen Gates Starr open Hull House.

1890 Jacob Riis, *How the Other Half Lives*.

1892 Immigrant-admitting station is opened on Ellis Island in the New York City harbor.
Reverend Charles Parkhurst organizes the City Vigilance League.
"Big Jim" Pendergast gains control of the Kansas City, Missouri, political machine.

1894 The Chicago Ship and Sanitary Canal is built.
Clarence Lexow's investigation of New York City reveals widespread police corruption.

1898 New York City consolidates five boroughs into Greater New York.

1900 Theodore Dreiser, *Sister Carrie*.

1907 Walter Rauschenbusch, *Christianity and the Social Crisis*.

1910 Jane Addams, *Twenty Years at Hull House*.

FOR FURTHER READING

Gunther Barth, *City People: The Rise of Modern City Culture in Nineteenth-Century America* (1980). A sprightly account of popular city culture from newspapers to ballparks.

Paul Boyer, *Urban Masses and Moral Order in America, 1820–1920* (1978). A richly detailed analysis of reformers' attempts to control city life.

William Cronon, *Nature's Metropolis: Chicago and the Great West* (1991). An innovative study of the linkages between urban growth and regional economic prosperity in the Midwest.

Allen F. Davis, *American Heroine: The Life and Legend of Jane Addams* (1973). A penetrating biography of a leader in the settlement-house movement.

Kenneth T. Jackson, *Crabgrass Frontier: The Suburbanization of the United States* (1985). A stimulating comparative study of city expansion and suburban development in Europe and America.

Martin V. Melosi, ed., *Pollution and Reform in American Cities, 1870–1930* (1980). A pioneering examination of the environmental impact of American industrial and urban growth.

Kathy Peiss, *Cheap Amusements: Working Women and Leisure in Turn-of-the-Century New York* (1986). A forceful and provocative analysis of immigrant women's lives.

Thomas L. Philpott, *The Slum and the Ghetto: Neighborhood Deterioration and Middle-Class Reform, Chicago, 1880–1930* (1978). An in-depth examination of the impact of ethnicity and race on one city.

Virginia Yans-McLaughlin, ed., *Immigration Reconsidered: History, Sociology, Politics* (1990). Provocative essays examining the American slave and immigrant experience within a global perspective.

Americans faced difficult adjustments as they shifted from a producer economy that valued hard work and thrift to a consumer economy stressing material possessions and leisure-time activities. A torrent of new products, including hot-air furnaces, indoor plumbing fixtures, sewing machines, and cast-iron kitchen ranges, poured out of U.S. factories, promising previously unimagined comforts and conveniences. But these advances were not equally available, and their great variety actually intensified class consciousness. The middle and upper classes, which included professionals and white-collar workers, increasingly defined their status in terms of material possessions, comfortable houses, education, genteel cultural standards, and leisure pursuits. In contrast, the larger proportion of farmers and working-class urbanites, paid low wages and frequently out of work, could pluck only small benefits from the economic cornucopia.

Although many people improved their economic position and social standing in these years, the gulf between the classes widened. The very rich lived in a world apart,

(Right) Victorian era family life; lithograph, 1885

Daily Life, Popular Culture, and the Arts, 1860—1900

Everyday Life in Flux
Middle-Class Society and Culture
Working-Class Leisure in the Immigrant City
Cultures in Conflict

the middle class embraced its own work code and life-style, and a vigorous working-class culture emerged in the heavily immigrant cities. Despite middle-class efforts to remake working-class ways, the mass lower-class culture ultimately proved most influential in shaping modern America.

Everyday Life in Flux

In the closing decades of the nineteenth century, industrialization not only introduced an unprecedented range of products but also created new jobs and destroyed old ones, in the process rearranging the occupational structure and altering income distribution. These changes, together with the expansion of white-collar occupations, elevated expectations for family life and fostered a growing class awareness.

Rising Standards of Living

After 1850 mechanization increased output, decreased prices, and encouraged the development of new products that revolutionized life for many Americans. The widespread use of sewing machines, for example, transformed the way people dressed. Before the Civil War, handmade shirts required 30,000 stitches, so most people wore hand-me-downs in simple designs. By the 1880s machine-sewn shirts took only two hours to complete and came in standard sizes and elaborate designs. Personal wardrobes for the middle and elite classes expanded dramatically. Clothes closets were now common household features, and dress became an important badge of social class. Immigrants and rural migrants rushed to buy cheap factory-made clothes and to shed their "greenhorn" or "hayseed" look.

Innovations in food technology changed eating habits. In 1878 physician John Harvey Kellogg marketed Granola, a wheat-oat-corn mixture advertised as healthier than the standard breakfast of sausage, eggs, and potatoes. In the next three decades,

Kellogg also would introduce wheat flakes, shredded wheat, and corn flakes. Competitors rushed in. Charles W. Post developed Grape Nuts Flakes and Postum, a breakfast drink made from bran, wheat, and molasses that was supposed to replace over-stimulating, unhealthful coffee. By the turn of the century, health-conscious middle- and upper-class Americans who could afford them had shifted to the new cereals and hot drinks.

Not all inventions lived up to their promoters' claims. Lydia Pinkham's vegetable extract "for all those painful Complaints and Weaknesses so common to our best female population" contained nearly 23 percent alcohol. Other tonics featured significant amounts of opium, and countless patent medicines that promised to cure everything from backache to deafness were totally ineffective. But a public that believed that material and physical improvements lay within everyone's reach eagerly snapped them up.

Nonetheless, industrialization was significantly improving the level of comfort and convenience for many American families. In 1870 most urban women, lacking a means of refrigeration, shopped daily, baked their own bread, and canned their own fruits and vegetables. They spent hours preparing food, doing laundry by hand, firing up smoky stoves and furnaces, and carrying "slop jars" to outdoor sewers or malodorous waste-collection tanks. By 1900, however, indoor plumbing, better stoves and furnaces, commercially prepared foods, and mechanical washing machines had eased domestic burdens. Urban middle- and upper-class families took for granted such innovations as central heating, electric lights, and telephone service. Ninety percent of urban families ate store-bought bread; two-thirds used commercial laundries. Iceboxes kept food fresh, and stores featured canned vegetables, pickles, and soups.

Bringing New Commodities to Rural and Small-Town America

As new products changed the lives of city dwellers, mail-order houses and chain stores expanded the horizons of rural and small-town America. Aaron

Montgomery Ward introduced the new products and conveniences to nonurban America. In the 1860s, as a traveling salesman, Ward recognized that rural Americans depended on local merchants selling limited goods at high prices. In 1872 he joined forces with the Grangers, who pledged to reduce farmers' costs by eliminating the middlemen, and he circulated a list of products for sale at a 40 percent discount. By 1884 Ward's catalog offered nearly 10,000 items to rural customers. Ward encountered competition from Richard Warren Sears, who in 1886 established a mail-order company (now Sears, Roebuck) that shipped farmers everything from tools to baby carriages. Sears built customer loyalty by guaranteeing low prices and publishing testimonials from satisfied patrons. The firm carried many products at different prices to suit all pocketbooks. Pump organs, for example, ranged from "Our AA Grade Home Favorite" at $64.95 to "Our Happy Home Organ, Grade B" at $22.00. Distributed to millions of rural families, the encyclopedic Sears and Ward's catalogs (available in German and Swedish as well as English) opened the door to a new world of consumer goods and educated their readers in middle-class taste.

Chain stores offered another way to bring low-priced mass-produced goods to consumers. In 1879 F. W. Woolworth, a farm boy from upstate New York, opened a "Five and Ten Cent Store" in Utica that sold merchandise such as crochet needles, safety pins, and harmonicas from a "five-cent counter." His stores multiplied rapidly. Together with the Great Atlantic and Pacific Tea Company, which consolidated several food stores into the "A&P" operation in 1859, Woolworth's pioneered national "chains" that stressed low prices and consumer savings.

By the 1890s a barrage of advertising presented daily choices about what to buy. More conscious than ever of the sparkling array of material options open to them, Americans had entered an era in which the goods and the services purchased dictated social position and status. Material possessions made possible new realms of comfort and convenience, but they also reinforced a pervasive sense of widening class differences.

A Shifting Class Structure

Patterns of consumption, culture, and everyday life are a reflection of a society's class structure, and in late-nineteenth-century America this structure underwent important modifications. Fundamental changes in the nature of work, in addition to shifts in residential location, massive immigration, and new patterns of consumption, redefined and sharpened the concept of social class. Life-style and self-identification joined income and occupation as determinants of social rank.

The working class felt these changes first and most keenly. In antebellum America the skilled artisans who had dominated the working class had shared a bond of common outlook and class identity with laborers. That bond began to dissolve in the mid-1870s as new production methods changed the work process and destroyed the jobs of skilled artisans. Unskilled immigrants who desperately needed work took the dangerous, low-paying jobs created in the steel mills and elsewhere. By the end of the century, skilled artisans looked down on these newcomers and identified themselves with the middle class.

As the working class fragmented, the middle class expanded. Demand for trained personnel increased in all sectors: growing municipal bureaucracies, school systems, businesses and corporations, and department stores, among others. These middle-class personnel worked in clean offices physically separated from the sooty factories and dirty mills that employed manual workers. Middle-class clerical and professional workers received fixed salaries considerably higher than the earnings of skilled artisans. Few skilled artisans took home more than $500 yearly, but clerks and bookkeepers were paid from $500 to $1,000, and other middle-class workers earned more than $1,000 a year.

Freed from worries about making ends meet, middle-class employees adopted long-term strategies for improving their income and maximizing their purchasing power. They devoted more resources to educating their children, buying expensive items on credit, and improving household comforts. A shorter workweek gave middle-class employees more time to spend with their families and greater

Telephone Operators, 1885

The anonymity of the new technology of the telephone sometimes led to flirtations between male callers and the young women who manually transferred calls. Mark Twain's narrator in A Connecticut Yankee in King Arthur's Court (1889) is so infatuated with telephone operators that he names his first child Hello Central.

opportunities for socializing and recreation than before.

The very wealthy flaunted their riches, honing public awareness of growing class divisions. The Carnegies, Morgans, and Rockefellers used their immense fortunes to build elaborate houses and country estates. Palatial houses offered the ultimate proof of success on the capitalist battlefield. Railroad financier Jay Gould built a Gothic castle of a home, with a 380-foot-long greenhouse filled with costly exotic plants. At resorts such as Newport, Rhode Island, the wealthy built stately mansions ("cottages"), kept stables of racehorses, and cruised on magnificent yachts.

Workplace restructuring, the expansion of the middle class, and the rise of enormous fortunes severely skewed income distribution. In 1896 a knowledgeable observer estimated that 5.5 million American families were working class, earning less than $500; 5.5 million were middle class, earning $500 to $5,000; and the remaining 1.5 million, composing 12 percent of the population, earned more than $5,000. This privileged 12 percent owned 86 percent of the nation's wealth. The middle class, 44 percent of the population, possessed 12.5 percent of the wealth, and the working class, the bottom 44 percent of the population, struggled to survive with a mere 1.5 percent of the wealth.

The Changing Family

This skewed distribution of resources had an important impact on family life. Income not only determined access to household technology and consumer goods but also affected family size, life expectancy, infant mortality, and relationships between parents and children.

Between 1860 and 1900 most Americans lived in nuclear families made up of parents and children. Boarders or servants might reside with them, but grandparents and other relatives typically did not. Families continued to become smaller as women bore fewer children. For white women, the number of live births fell from an average of 5.42 children in 1850 to 3.56 in 1900. At the same time, life expectancy rose from 38.4 years to 46.3 years for males and from 40.5 years to 48.3 years for females. The size of the typical nuclear family stabilized at five or six members.

Such statistics obscure important differences stemming from social class, race, and ethnicity. In 1900 a high infant mortality rate among black males dropped their average life expectancy at birth to 22.5 years, less than half that of white males. Farm and immigrant families continued to be large, typically with from six to eight children. Buffalo, New York, an industrial city with many immigrants, provides a striking confirmation of class differences. In 1900 the statistically average laborer's family had 5.7 children; a skilled worker's, 5.2; and a business owner's or manager's family, 3.5.

These statistics show how significantly middle- and upper-class families differed from working-class families. The correlation between income and family size indicates that the middle and upper classes practiced birth control, using either abstinence, contraception, or abortion. Women with small families had more free time, could give more attention to educating and training children, and enjoyed greater opportunities for leisure and recreation than those with many children.

Working-Class Family Life

Working-class families that lived just above or even below the poverty level relied on the labor of children and on a network of relatives who could pitch in when necessary. The poorer the family, the more it depended on the work of all its members.

In the postwar South, black families, with few possessions and little money, relied heavily on extended families—cousins, aunts, uncles, and other relatives—to help with child care, housing, and expenses. The members of this extended kinship network, which could include as many as 200 people, practiced a remarkable degree of cooperation. They reached decisions jointly, shared economic resources, provided emotional support, and strengthened mutual ties through visits, reunions, and membership in the same church.

Although often better off than their black counterparts, poor white families in the South and

Midwest also depended heavily on the efforts of all family members. The men and older boys worked in the fields, and farm wives and younger children ran the house and dairy, kept up the kitchen garden, sewed and mended clothes, knitted hats and gloves, churned butter, made soap, and trimmed the oil lamps that illuminated the home. When necessary, rural women and their daughters took over the duties normally performed by men. They built homes, plowed the fields, cared for the livestock, and pitched in at harvest time. Many farm families owed their survival to the hard work and resourcefulness of everyone involved.

The same was true for urban working-class families; the contributions of *all* family members often spelled the difference between survival and modest prosperity. The average urban family of five or six members in the 1890s needed $600 to $800 annually to live comfortably, more than the father's earnings alone could provide. To supplement their income, urban working-class families rented rooms to boarders, and the women commonly took in laundry. Urban working-class women who could not afford store-bought clothes sewed the family's wardrobe. If a husband became sick or lost his job, a wife might take a job in a garment factory alongside her elder daughters, who usually worked until they married. Immigrant children commonly went to work at the age of ten and turned over their earnings to their parents. Such responsibilities forced children to grow up quickly but also instilled a strong sense of family loyalty.

This cooperative family ethic was the key to improving working-class families' financial position. Pooling wages allowed families to set aside part of their income for monthly mortgage payments. Such thrift, and the availability of small, affordable houses, helped many families to purchase their own homes. Homeownership served as a kind of insurance; if the principal breadwinner fell sick or became unemployed, families could take in boarders or use the house as collateral on a loan. The cooperative family ethic enabled working-class Americans to survive and even to get ahead in the rapidly changing economy of the late nineteenth century. But it also accentuated the differences between poor families and their middle- and upper-class counterparts who managed comfortably on the salary of the main breadwinner alone.

Middle-Class Society and Culture

Spared the struggle for survival that confronted most Americans, the middle and upper classes faced a different challenge: explaining and rationalizing the material benefits of the emerging consumer society. To justify the achievements of society's wealthiest members, ministers, advice-book writers, and other commentators appealed to Victorian morality, a set of social ideas influential among the privileged classes of England and the United States during the reign (1837–1901) of Britain's Queen Victoria.

Proponents of Victorian morality argued that the success of the middle and upper classes rested on their superior talent, intelligence, morality, and self-control. Women were identified as the driving force for moral improvement. While men engaged in the world's work, women provided the gentle, elevating influence that would lead society in its upward march.

A network of institutions, from elegant department stores and hotels to elite colleges and universities, testified to the privileged position of the upper and middle classes.

Manners and Morals

The Victorian world view rested on several fundamental assumptions. Cautiously optimistic about human nature, the Victorian moral code held that only strenuous effort would bring progress. At its best, this code energized reform movements against suffering and injustice, including slavery; at its worst, this intense moralism could lead to an obsessive preoccupation with the details of personal behavior. Because more members of the elite and middle class believed that they had achieved their status through sobriety, industriousness, and self-restraint, they stressed these virtues. "Victorian morality" thus became synonymous with an intense suspicion of spontaneity and self-indulgence. Often violated in practice, this code was widely preached as the standard for society.

To their emphasis on sobriety and self-control, the champions of Victorian morality added the importance of "culture" (knowledge of the social graces, literature, the fine arts, and classical music) as an agency of social uplift. Prominent clergymen, among them Henry Ward Beecher of Brooklyn, urged cultural refinement. To further the cause, the elite founded, and the middle class supported, a series of cultural institutions including the Metropolitan Museum of Art in New York (1870) and the Museum of Fine Arts in Boston (1870).

At its pettiest, the middle-class focus on conduct degenerated into a preoccupation with manners and social rituals. Behavior as well as income defined social standing. Good manners, including a knowledge of proper etiquette in all social occasions, especially dining and entertaining, became a badge of status. Meals evolved into rituals that differentiated the social classes. They presented occasions for displaying the elaborate silver and china that middle- and upper-class families exclusively possessed, and they provided telltale clues to a family's level of refinement and sophistication.

The Victorian code, with its emphasis on morals, manners, and behavior, heightened the sense of class differences and created visible distinctions among social groups. Prominent Victorians might claim their sincere interest in helping others to improve themselves, but more often than not, their self-righteous, intensely moralistic outlook simply widened the gap already opened by income disparities.

The Cult of Domesticity

Victorian views on morality and culture, coupled with rising pressures on consumers to make decisions about a mountain of domestic products, had a subtle but important impact on middle-class expectations about woman's role within the home. From the 1840s onward, the home had been idealized as "the woman's sphere," a protected retreat where she could express her special maternal gifts, including a sensitivity toward children and an aptitude for religion. "The home is the wife's province," asserted one writer, "it is her natural field of labor."

Victorian advocates of the cult of domesticity added a new obligation for women: to foster an artistic environment that would nurture the family's cultural improvement. Houses became statements of cultural aspirations, and elaborately ornamented architectural styles gained popularity. Like intricate sculptures, these houses featured detailed wood ornamentation, windows of varying dimensions, and ornate chimneys. Women turned the front parlor into a treasure house whose furnishings and curios reflected family social standing and refinement. Souvenir spoons and other knickknacks demonstrated the household's cosmopolitanism. Excluded from the world of business and commerce, women directed their energy to transforming their homes into "a place of repose, a refuge from the excitement and distractions of outside . . . , provided with every attainable means of rest and recreation."

Not all middle-class women pursued this domestic ideal. For some, the drudgery of housework and of running the family overwhelmed any concern for artistic accomplishment. For others, the artistic ideal itself was not to their taste. In the 1880s and 1890s women increasingly sought other outlets for their creative energies.

Department Stores and Hotels

The idealistic, moralistic emphasis of Victorian social thought helped to justify the privileged status of the upper and middle classes. Nonetheless, the transition from the producer economy, with its emphasis on thrift and saving, to the consumer economy, with its stress on accumulating and displaying possessions, unsettled many Americans. In the 1880s and 1890s shrewd merchandisers dulled these pangs of guilt by emphasizing the high quality and low cost of their goods and by stressing that material possessions could promote artistic and cultural accomplishments. In response, Americans loosened their purse strings and began to enjoy prosperity, without inner reservations.

The department store played a key role in modifying attitudes toward consumption. In the final quarter of the nineteenth century, innovative entrepreneurs, among them Rowland Macy, John Wanamaker, and Marshall Field, made the giant department store an urban institution and transformed the shopping experience for their middle- and upper-class customers.

Department-store merchandising, with its diverse inventory and constant flow of new products, represented a radical departure from older general stores. Department-store magnates bought in large volume at low cost directly from manufacturers and sold every conceivable household item and article of clothing. The department store sold goods at fixed prices, allowed unconditional exchanges, and provided free delivery. Merchants such as Macy and Wanamaker overcame middle- and upper-class reluctance to spend by advertising products at "rock-bottom" prices and by waging price wars to validate their claims. End-of-season clearance sales at drastically marked-down prices prevented stock from piling up and attracted the thrifty.

Major downtown establishments tried to make shopping an adventure. The stores became more and more ornate, with stained-glass skylights, marble staircases, brilliant chandeliers, and plush carpets. When it opened in 1876, John Wanamaker's Grand Depot in Philadelphia boasted a gaslit "tent" where women could examine silk gowns under ballroom conditions. Marshall Field's Chicago emporium contained a stained-glass dome, blue English carpets, and rare walnut paneling.

Department stores lavished care and attention on shoppers, especially women. Richly decorated lounges, elegant restaurants serving modestly priced lunches, and glittering holiday decorations enticed visitors to linger and to buy on impulse. Sales clerks greeted customers at the door, answered questions, and made women feel at home. The large urban department store became a social club and home away from home for affluent women.

The stately metropolitan hotels that proliferated in the late nineteenth century provided further examples of high fashion and elite taste. New York's Waldorf Astoria, Chicago's Palmer House, and San Francisco's Palace became public shrines, epitomizing efficient organization and upper-class taste. Built in 1892 in the German Renaissance style, the Waldorf Astoria was a self-contained community with offices, restaurants, ballrooms, courtyards, and 500 guest rooms. Household reformers of the 1890s held up the highly organized restaurants and laundry systems of the big hotels as models for efficient cooperative-apartment complexes.

Whether one marveled at their efficiency or gazed in wonder at their gilt mirrors and plush carpets, the grand hotels set the pattern for luxury, convenience, and service. In a society that shunned aristocratic pretensions, hotels and department stores made luxury acceptable by clothing it in the guise of efficiency and good taste. They provided a setting where newly affluent members of society could indulge and pamper themselves, if only for a few minutes or a day.

The Transformation of Higher Education

At a time when relatively few Americans possessed even a high-school education, colleges and universities represented another stronghold of the business and professional elite and of the moderately well-to-do middle class. Wealthy capitalists gained stature and a measure of immortality by endowing colleges and universities. In 1885 Leland Stanford and his wife, Jane Lathrop Stanford, launched Stanford University with a bequest of $24 million; in 1891 John D. Rockefeller donated $34 million to the University of Chicago. Industrialists and businessmen dominated the boards of trustees of many educational institutions, and colleges were viewed as a training ground for future business and professional leaders.

The classroom played an important role in preparing students for later responsibilities, but so did social contacts and athletic activities, especially football. Invented by American students in 1869, football was an elite sport played by college teams. Players wore neither pads nor helmets, and in 1905 alone, eighteen students died of playing-field injuries.

Some college presidents dismissed football as a dangerous waste of time and money, but alumni and coaches credited the new sport with building character. Because Social Darwinism emphasized struggle, football seemed an ideal arena for improving the strength, courage, and self-discipline of youth. Some defenders of the sport insisted that football could substitute for the frontier experience in an increasingly urban society. By 1900 football had become a popular fall sport, stimulating alumni giving and building goodwill for those elite institutions that otherwise remained far outside the experience of the average American.

More than 150 new colleges and universities appeared between 1880 and 1900, and enrollments more than doubled, rising from 1.7 per cent of college-age youth in 1870 to 4 percent in 1900. A small but growing number of these newcomers to higher education were women. Wealthy capitalists financed some institutions, but public funds supported the state universities of the Midwest, and religious denominations continued to support many colleges.

Debates about what should be taught and how it should be taught swept through higher education, especially in science and medicine. Antebellum medical education had occupied less than a year of medical students' time, and most received their degrees without ever having visited a hospital or having seen a patient. The grim mortality rates of the Civil War, in which twice as many soldiers died from infections as from wounds, graphically illustrated the low state of medical education. In the 1880s and 1890s medical professors, many of whom had studied in France and Germany, began restructuring American medical education, insisting that students be trained in biology, chemistry, and physics. By 1900 the practice of medicine in America rested on a firm professional foundation. Similar reforms took place in the teaching of architecture, engineering, and law.

These changes were part of a larger transformation in higher education that produced a new institution, the research university. Unlike antebellum colleges, which taught little beyond classical languages, theology, logic, and mathematics, the new research universities offered courses in a wide variety of subjects, established professional schools, and encouraged faculty members to pursue basic research. For Andrew D. White, the first president of Cornell University (1869), the goal was to create a school "where any person can find instruction in any study." Cornell, the University of Wisconsin, Johns Hopkins, Harvard, and others laid the groundwork for the central role that U.S. universities would play in the intellectual, cultural, and scientific life of the twentieth century. However, higher education remained the privilege of a few as the nineteenth century ended; the age when college attendance would become the norm lay many years ahead.

Working-Class Leisure in the Immigrant City

In colonial America the subject of leisure time had generally arisen only when ministers condemned "idleness" as the first step toward sin. In the rural culture of the early nineteenth century, the unremitting routines of farm labor had left little time for relaxation. Family picnics, horse races, county fairs, revivals, and holidays such as the Fourth of July and Christmas had provided permissible diversion, but even in relaxation earlier generations had guarded against "laziness."

As immigration soared, urban populations shot up, and factories multiplied after the Civil War; however, new patterns of leisure and amusement emerged, especially among the urban working class. After long hours in factories and mills or behind department-store counters, working-class Americans craved relaxation and diversion. They thronged the streets, patronized saloons and dance halls, cheered at boxing matches and baseball games, and organized boisterous group picnics and holiday celebrations. Amusement parks, vaudeville theaters, sporting clubs, and racetracks provided further entertainment for workers, and mass leisure became a big business.

As factory labor grew impersonal, casual social interactions at the workplace virtually disappeared. Leisure time thus became especially important as an arena of freedom, spontaneity, and group solidarity where the time clock at least briefly vanished. Ironically, the same ethnic divisions that fragmented the labor movement in this era provided the foundation for a strong working-class culture beyond the factory gates.

The Streets, the Saloon, and the Boxing Match

Hours of tedious, highly disciplined, and physically exhausting labor left workers tired but thirsty for excitement and escape from their cramped living quarters. In 1889 a banner carried by a carpenters' union summed up their needs: "EIGHT HOURS FOR WORK, EIGHT HOURS FOR REST, AND EIGHT HOURS FOR WHAT WE WILL."

City streets provided some recreation. Relaxing after a day's work, shop girls and laborers clustered on busy corners, watching shouting pushcart peddlers and listening to organ grinders play familiar melodies. For a penny or a nickel, they could buy a bagel, a baked potato, or a soda. In the summer, when the heat and humidity within the tenements reached unbearable levels, the streets became the center of neighborhood life.

The streets beckoned to all, but some leisure institutions drew a male clientele. For example, in cities such as Baltimore, Milwaukee, and Cincinnati, with a strong German immigrant flavor, gymnastic clubs (*Turnvereine*) and singing societies (*Gesangvereine*) provided men with both companionship and the opportunity to perpetuate old-world traditions.

Saloons offered male companionship, conviviality, and five-cent beer, often with a free lunch thrown in. By 1900 New York City had an estimated 10,000 saloons. As gathering places in ethnic neighborhoods, saloons reinforced group identity and became centers for immigrant politics. Saloon-keepers often doubled as local ward bosses who performed small services for their patrons. With their rich mahogany bars, shiny brass rails, and elegant mirrors, saloons provided a taste of luxury for their factory-worker clientele.

What explains the saloons' popularity, and what was their impact? In the highly disciplined factories of the late nineteenth century, the old custom of taking a break from the job for a shared drink or for socializing had disappeared. A sharp distinction had emerged between the world of work and the world of leisure. The liveliness and sociability of saloon culture thus starkly contrasted with the socially isolating routines of factory labor. The saloon scene also clashed with the increasingly private and family-centered social life of the middle class. Indeed, saloons often served as bases for prostitution and criminal activity. Moreover, drinking too much at the saloon frequently led to family violence, and "treating"—buying drinks for friends—cut deeply into already meager paychecks.

For working-class males, bare-knuckles prize-fighting also became a popular amusement. Drawing heroes from society's poorer ranks, the boxing rings became an arena where lower-class men could assert their individuality and physical prowess. Blacks, Irish, and Germans formed their own "sporting clubs" and used athletics to bolster their self-confidence and to reaffirm their racial or ethnic identity.

Amateur boxing gained unexpected elite support in the 1880s and 1890s as an antidote to what some people considered a dangerous tendency toward decadence among privileged males. Theodore Roosevelt, a New York patrician and rising Republican, did much to make the sport respectable. The introduction of the Marquis of Queensbury code—a set of rules devised in England that required the use of gloves, outlawed wrestling holds, standardized the three-minute round, and changed the time required for a knockout from thirty seconds to ten—increased boxing's acceptability to the upper crust. Meanwhile, the sport, like other popular leisure-time diversions, was becoming professionalized.

The Rise of Professional Sports

As an English game called rounders, baseball had existed since the seventeenth century. If Americans did not create baseball, they nevertheless took this informal children's game and turned it into a major professional sport. In 1845 the New York Knicker-bockers, the first organized baseball team, was established. In the 1860s the rules were codified and the sport assumed its present form, featuring overhand pitching, fielders' gloves, nine-inning games, and bases spaced ninety feet apart. That same decade, promoters organized professional clubs and began to compete for players. In 1869 the Cincinnati Red Stockings, the first team to put its players under contract for the whole season, toured the country and ended the season with fifty-seven wins and no losses.

The National League was organized in 1876, and crowds of 10,000 to 12,000 turned out to watch the professional games. By the 1890s baseball was big business. Clubs scheduled doubleheaders, ran promotions like ladies' day, and made money by selling beer, peanuts, and hot dogs. The working class particularly took baseball to heart. The most profitable teams came from industrial cities with large working-class populations.

Newspapers thrived on baseball. Joseph Pulitzer introduced the first separate sports page when he bought the *New York World* in 1883, and baseball dominated the paper's sports reporting. Baseball, declared writer Mark Twain, had become "the very symbol . . . and visible expression of the drive and push and rush and struggle of the raging, tearing, booming nineteenth century."

Although no other organized sport attracted as large a following as baseball, horse racing and boxing also drew large crowds of spectators and received wide press coverage. But whereas races such as

World's Heavyweight Boxing Championship, 1892

In dethroning ring champion John L. Sullivan, "Gentleman Jim" Corbett demonstrated that speed and finesse were more than a match for brute strength.

Louisville's Kentucky Derby became social events for the rich, professional boxing aroused passionate devotion in the working class.

The hero of nineteenth-century professional sports was heavyweight fighter John L. Sullivan. Of Irish-immigrant stock, Sullivan began boxing in 1877 at age nineteen. With his massive physique, handlebar mustache, and arrogant swagger, Sullivan was enormously popular. Barnstorming across the country, he vanquished a succession of local strong men, invariably wearing his trademark green tights with an American flag wrapped around his middle.

Vaudeville, Amusement Parks, and Dance Halls

In contrast to the male preserve of saloons and prizefights, the world of vaudeville shows, amusement parks, and neighborhood dance halls welcomed all comers regardless of gender and proved particularly congenial to working-class women.

Vaudeville, with roots in antebellum minstrel shows, offered a succession of acts designed for mass appeal. The vaudeville show typically opened with an animal act or a dance number, followed by a musical interlude. Then came comic skits ridiculing the trials of urban life, satirizing police and municipal ineptitude, poking fun at the babel of accents in the immigrant city, and mining a rich vein of ethnic humor and stereotypes. After more musical numbers and acts by ventriloquists and magicians, the program ended with a "flash" finale featuring flying-trapeze artists or the like. By the 1880s vaudeville drew larger crowds than any other form of theater. It provided an evening of inexpensive, lighthearted entertainment and let immigrants laugh at their own experiences, as translated into slapstick and caricature.

While vaudeville offered psychological release from the stresses of working-class life, amusement parks provided physical escape. The fun houses, thrill rides, and games of New York's Coney Island, the prototype of urban amusement parks, sprawled along the Brooklyn waterfront. By 1900 as many as half a million people would throng the beach, the boardwalk, and the amusement parks on a summer Saturday. Young couples rode through the dark

Tunnel of Love, sped down the dizzying roller-coaster, and watched bellydancers in the sideshows, momentarily surrendering to the spirit of exuberant play and forgetting the restrictions and demands of the industrial world.

By the end of the nineteenth century, New York City had well over 300,000 female wage earners, most of them young, unmarried women. The amusement parks with their exhilarating rides and glittering dance pavilions, and the dance halls in the immigrant districts of most cities, exerted a powerful lure for them. There they could meet friends, spend time with young men beyond parents' watchful eyes, show off their new dresses, and try out the latest dance steps in a magical release from the drudgery of daily life.

Ragtime

Nothing more vividly illustrates the differences between the cultures of the middle class and the working class than the contrasting styles of popular music that each favored. While the middle class preferred hymns or songs with a moral message, the working class embraced ragtime, the product of African-American musicians in the saloons of the South.

Ragtime developed out of the rich tradition of songs through which black Americans had eased the burdens of their lives. Like spirituals, ragtime used syncopated rhythms and complex harmonies, but it blended them with marching-band musical structures to create a distinctive style. A favorite of "honky-tonk" piano players, ragtime was introduced to the broader public in the 1890s and became a national sensation. Its best-known composer, Scott Joplin, introduced his music at Chicago's Columbian Exposition in 1893. "Maple Leaf Rag," published in 1899, earned Joplin a national reputation.

Inventive, playful, and infectiously rhythmic, ragtime had an appealing originality. But part of its popularity also came from its origin in saloons and its association with blacks, whom white Victorians stereotyped as sexual and uninhibited. The "wild" and complex rhythms of ragtime supposedly

reflected a freer and more "natural" expression of love and affection. When genteel critics sneered, the new dance music became all the more attractive to the urban working class.

Ragtime's popularity proved a mixed blessing for blacks. It testified to the achievements of brilliant composers such as Joplin, helped to break down barriers in the music industry, and contributed to a spreading rebellion against Victorian repressiveness. At the same time, it confirmed white stereotypes of blacks as primitive and sensuous, a bias that underlay the racism of the period and helped to justify segregation and discrimination.

Cultures in Conflict

Class conflict and cultural unrest embroiled the United States in the late nineteenth century, even within the middle class. As 1900 dawned, ethical questions about Victorian morality and new cultural stirrings intensified. At the center of the cultural turbulence stood women, increasingly dissatisfied with the restrictive code of feminine propriety. The growth of women's clubs and women's colleges, and even the bicycle fad of the 1890s, all contributed to the emergence of the "new woman."

At the same time, a widening chasm divided the well-to-do from the mass of immigrant laborers. Perhaps in no period of American history have class conflicts been as open and raw. Nervously eying the noisy culture of city streets, saloons, boxing clubs, dance halls, and amusement parks, middle-class leaders perceived a massive, if unconscious, challenge to their own cultural and social standing. Some middle-class reformers promoted public schools as a means to impose middle-class values on the urban masses, and others battled urban "vice" and "immorality." The genteel mores of the middle class proved particularly vulnerable, so that by 1900 the Victorian social and moral ethos was crumbling.

The Genteel Tradition and Its Critics

In the 1870s and 1880s a group of upper-class writers and editors, led by Charles Eliot Norton of

Harvard and E. L. Godkin of *The Nation*, codified standards for writing and design and tried to create a coherent national artistic culture. Joining forces with allies in Boston and New York, these elites lobbied to "improve" American taste in interior furnishings, textiles, ceramics, wallpaper, and books.

The drive to improve the arts was prompted in part by the flood of cheap reproductions and sensationalistic novels that poured off the nation's presses after the Civil War. Despondent about what they termed a "chromo civilization" enamored of trashy books and garish color art prints, Norton, Godkin, and others lectured the middle class about the value of high culture and the insights to be gained from the arts. They also censored their own publications to remove all sexual allusions, vulgar slang, disrespectful treatment of Christianity, and unhappy endings.

Godkin and editors of other "quality" periodicals created an important forum for serious writers in *The Nation* and *The Atlantic Monthly*. Novelist Henry James, who published virtually all of his work in the *Atlantic*, reflected the views of this elite literary establishment. He wrote, "It is art that *makes* life, . . . and I know of no substitute whatever for [its] force and beauty." This art-for-art's-sake movement also influenced architects, jewelers, and interior decorators.

Although these genteel magazines provided an important forum for new authors, their editors' strident elitism and imperialistic desire to control national literary standards bred opposition. Samuel Langhorne Clemens, better known as Mark Twain, spoke for many young writers when he declared as early as 1869 that he was through with "literature and all that bosh." Attacking aristocratic literary conventions, Twain and others who shared his concerns worked to broaden literature's appeal to the general public.

These efforts by a younger generation of writers to chart new directions for American literature rested on sweeping changes within the publishing industry. New magazines such as *Ladies' Home Journal*, *Cosmopolitan*, and *McClure's* competed with the elite publications. The new magazines slashed their prices and tripled their circulation. Supported by advertising rather than subscriptions, they provided an outlet for younger authors who wanted to write about real people in everyday life.

Some of these writers were labeled regionalists because they captured the distinctive dialects and details of their featured locale, whether New England or the South. Others, among them William Dean Howells, focused on a truthful, if optimistic, depiction of the commonplace. Another group, called naturalists, stressed economic and psychological determinants and often examined the dark underside of life. In *Maggie: A Girl of the Streets* (1893), a bleak story of an innocent girl's exploitation and suicide in an urban slum, Stephen Crane wrote what is generally considered the first naturalist American novel. Labels aside, all these writers shared a skepticism toward literary conventions and an intense desire to understand the society around them.

The careers of Mark Twain and Theodore Dreiser highlight the changes in the publishing industry and the evolution of new forms of writing. Both were products of the Midwest, outsiders to the East Coast literary establishment—Twain from Missouri and Dreiser from Indiana. As young men, both worked as newspaper reporters and traveled widely. Both learned from direct experience about the greed, speculation, and fraud of the era.

Twain and Dreiser called on their own experiences to write about the human impact of the wrenching social changes that surrounded them: the flow of people to the expanding cities and the relentless scramble for power, wealth, and fame. In the *Adventures of Huckleberry Finn* (1884), Twain uses the river journey of two runaways, the rebellious Huck and the slave Jim, to explore the nature of contemporary American society by contrasting the idyllic life on the raft to the tawdry, fraudulent world of the small riverfront towns. Dreiser's *Sister Carrie* (1900) traces the journey of Carrie Meeber, an innocent and attractive girl, from her Wisconsin farm home to Chicago. Seduced by a traveling salesman, Carrie moves in with Hurstwood, the married proprietor of a fancy saloon. Driven by her desire for expensive department-store clothes and lavish entertainment, Carrie follows Hurstwood to New

Samuel Langhorne Clemens (Mark Twain) (1835–1910)

Before winning fame as a writer, the adventurous Twain worked as a printer; a river pilot on the Mississippi; a mining prospector in Carson City, Nevada; and a newspaper reporter.

York, abandons him when his money runs out, and pursues her own career in the theater.

Twain and Dreiser broke sharply with the genteel tradition's emphasis on manners and decorum. *Century* magazine readers complained that *Huckleberry Finn* was "destitute of a single redeeming quality." The publisher of *Sister Carrie* found the novel so repugnant that he printed only a thousand copies to fulfill his contract—and then stored them in a warehouse.

Similarly, growing numbers of scholars and critics challenged the elite's self-serving beliefs, including assumptions that moral worth and economic standing were closely linked and that the status quo

represented a social order decreed by God and nature alike. Economist Thorstein Veblen's *The Theory of the Leisure Class* (1899) caustically critiqued the life-style of the new capitalist elite. The product of a poor Norwegian farm community in Minnesota, Veblen looked at the captains of industry and their families with a jaundiced eye. He mercilessly documented their "conspicuous consumption" and lamented the widening economic gap between "those who worked without profit" and "those who profited without working."

Within the new discipline of sociology, Annie MacLean exposed the exploitation of department-store clerks, Walter Wyckoff uncovered the hand-to-mouth existence of unskilled laborers, and W. E. B. Du Bois documented the hardships of blacks in Philadelphia. The publication of these writings, coupled with the economic depression and seething labor agitation of the 1890s, made it increasingly difficult for turn-of-the-century middle-class Americans to accept the smug, self-satisfied belief in progress and genteel culture that had been a hallmark of the Victorian outlook.

Modernism in Architecture and Painting

The challenge to the genteel tradition also found support among architects and painters. Architects followed the lead of Louis Sullivan, who argued that a building's form should follow its function. In their view, banks, for example, should look like financial institutions, not Greek temples. Rejecting elite pretensions, architects looked to the future—to modernism, a quest for new modes of expression—for inspiration.

Frank Lloyd Wright's "prairie-school" houses, first built in the Chicago suburb of Oak Park in the 1890s, represented a typical modernist break with the past. Wright scorned the bulky Victorian house, with its wasted space and boxlike rooms; his designs, featuring broad, sheltering roofs and low silhouettes harmonious with the flat prairie landscape, used open, interconnecting rooms to create a sense of spaciousness.

Modernism's rejection of Victorian gentility influenced late-nineteenth-century painting as well. Winslow Homer's watercolors revealed nature as brutally tough and unsentimental; in his grim, elemental seascapes, lone men struggle against massive waves that threaten to overwhelm them. Thomas Eakins's canvases of swimmers, boxers, and rowers (such as his well-known *The Champion Single Sculls,* 1871) captured moments of vigorous physical exertion. Obsessed with making his paintings realistic, Eakins studied anatomy at a medical school, did photographic studies and dissection on cadavers in preparation for painting, and used nude models in his drawing classes.

The architects' and painters' revolt symptomized a larger shift in middle-class thought driven by the emergence of a complex social environment. As one minister observed in 1898, the transition from muscle to mechanical power had "separated, as by an impassable gulf, the simple, homespun, individualistic world of the . . . past, from the complex, closely associated life of the present." The increasingly evident gap between the quiet parlors and flickering kerosene lamps of small towns and life in the big, glittering cities of glass and iron made nineteenth-century Americans acutely aware of differences in wealth and upbringing.

Distrusting idealistic Victorian assumptions about social progress, the middle class nevertheless disagreed over how to replace them. Not until the progressive period would social reformers combine new expertise in social research with an enlarged conception of the federal government's regulatory power to break sharply with their Victorian predecessors' social outlook.

From Victorian Lady to New Woman

The role of middle-class women in the revolt against Victorian refinement was complex and ambiguous. Some women's dissatisfaction with the cult of domesticity did not necessarily lead to their open rebellion. Though chafing against the constraints of the genteel code and the assumption that they should limit their activities to the home, many women remained committed to playing a supportive role within the family. In fact, early advocates of a "widened sphere" for women often fused the traditional Victorian ideal of womanhood with a firm commitment to political action.

The career of temperance leader Frances Willard illustrates how the cult of domesticity could evolve into a broader view of women's social responsibilities. Willard believed that by nature women were compassionate, nurturing, and sensitive to others; she was equally convinced that drinking encouraged men to squander their earnings and profoundly threatened family life. In 1874 Willard resigned her positions as dean of women and professor of English at Northwestern University to devote her energies completely to the temperance cause. Five years later, she became president of the newly formed Woman's Christian Temperance Union (WCTU).

In 1880 Willard launched a crusade to win the franchise for women so that they could vote to outlaw liquor. Women's participation in politics, she argued, would help to protect the family and to improve public morality. Without challenging traditional Victorian views of women's proper role, Willard expanded the WCTU's activities to include welfare work, prison reform, labor arbitration, and public health. By 1890 the WCTU, with a membership of 150,000, had become the nation's first mass organization of women. Its members gained experience as lobbyists, organizers, and lecturers, undercutting the assumption of "separate spheres."

An expanding network of women's clubs offered another means by which middle- and upper-class women could hone their skills in civic affairs, public speaking, and intellectual analysis. Club women became involved in social-welfare projects, public-library expansion, and tenement reform. By 1892 the General Federation of Women's Clubs boasted 495 affiliates and 100,000 members.

College education also expanded women's roles. Coeducational colleges and universities in the Midwest enrolled increasing numbers of women, and private universities admitted women to affiliated but separate institutions such as Barnard

(1889) and Radcliffe (1894). Between 1880 and 1900 the percentage of colleges admitting women jumped from 30 percent to 71 percent; by the turn of the century, women constituted more than one-third of the total college-student population.

Although the earliest women's colleges had been founded to reinforce prevailing concepts of femininity, participation in college organizations, athletics, and dramatics enabled female students to learn traditionally "masculine" strategies for gaining power. The generation of women educated at female institutions in the late nineteenth century developed the self-confidence to break with the Victorian ideal of passive womanhood and to compete on an equal basis with men by displaying strength, aggressiveness, and intelligence, popularly considered male attributes.

A bicycling vogue that swept urban America at the end of the century further loosened Victorian constraints on women. Fearful of waning vitality, middle- and upper-class Americans sought new means of improving their vigor, ranging from health products such as cod-liver oil and sarsaparilla to enthusiastic participation in basketball. Bicycling, which could be enjoyed individually or in groups, quickly became the most popular sport with those who wished to combine exercise with recreation. The advent in the 1880s of smaller wheels, ball-bearing axles, and air-filled tires helped to make bicycling a national craze, so that by the 1890s more than a million Americans owned bicycles.

Bicycling especially appealed to young women uncomfortable with restrictive Victorian ideas, which included the views that proper young ladies must never sweat, the female body must be fully covered at all times, and physical exertion should take place in private. Pedaling along without corsets or padded clothing, the woman bicyclist implicitly broke with genteel conventions.

Changing attitudes about femininity also found expression in shifting ideas about marriage. Charlotte Perkins Gilman, a suffrage advocate and speaker for women's rights, asserted that women would make an effective contribution to society only when they won economic independence from men through work outside the home. The climbing divorce rate between 1880 and 1900 testified to women's changing relationship to men; in 1880 one in twenty-one marriages ended in divorce, but by 1900 the rate had shot up to one in twelve. Women who sued for divorce increasingly cited their husbands' failure to act responsibly and to respect their autonomy. Accepting such arguments, courts frequently awarded wives alimony, a monetary settlement payable by ex-husbands to support their former spouses.

Contemporary assessments of these changes differed widely. Riding a bicycle, demanding the vote, and "wearin' clothes that no lady shud wear," wrote humorist Peter Finley Dunne, "Molly Donahue have up an' become a new woman!" A Chicago newspaperman satirized the new woman of the 1890s as a "fast girl": shallow, superficial, and heedless of social conventions. A more sympathetic male observer, illustrator Charles Dana Gibson, captured the popular image of this new woman with his folio of "Gibson girls," who exuded independence and freedom. Playing tennis or riding her bicycle, Gibson's tanned, vigorous young woman enjoyed the healthy outdoor life and active participation in the community.

Women writers generally welcomed the new female commitment to self-sufficiency and independence. Mary Wilkins Freeman's short stories, for example, compare women's expanding role to the frontier ideal of freedom. Her characters fight for their beliefs without concern for society's reaction. Feminist Kate Chopin pushed the debate to the extreme by having the married heroine of her 1899 novel *The Awakening* violate social conventions by falling in love with another man and then taking her life when his ideas about women prove as narrow and traditional as those of her husband.

Nonetheless, attitudes changed slowly. The enlarged concept of women's role in society had its greatest influence on middle-class women who enjoyed the privilege of higher education, possessed some leisure time, and could hope for success in the limited range of occupations open to them. Increasing numbers of young female college graduates postponed marriage to pursue careers in journalism, education, social work, and other fields. For shop girls who worked sixty hours a week to make ends meet, such opportunities were a distant fantasy. Although many women sought more independence and control over their own lives, most still viewed the home as their primary responsibility.

Public Education as an Arena of Class Conflict

Controversy over the scope and function of public education engaged Americans of all socioeconomic levels and highlighted class and cultural divisions in late-nineteenth-century society. Viewing public

San Diego, California, Schoolhouse, c. 1890
The stained-glass windows, elaborate bell tower, and ornate entranceway of this San Diego school testified to the community's pride in and commitment to public education.

schools as an instrument for indoctrinating and controlling the lower ranks, middle-class educators and civic leaders campaigned to expand and centralize public schooling. These would-be reformers' efforts aroused opposition from ethnic and religious groups whose outlook and interests differed sharply from theirs.

Thanks to the crusade for universal public education started by Horace Mann, most states had public-school systems by the Civil War. More than half the nation's children received some formal education, but most attended only a few years, and few went to high school. In the 1870s middle-class activists, concerned that many Americans lacked sufficient knowledge to participate wisely in public affairs or to function effectively in the labor force, worked to raise the overall educational level and to increase the number of years spent in school.

One such reformer was William Torrey Harris, a Victorian moralist who viewed public schools as a "great instrument to lift all classes of people into . . . civilized life." Harris urged teachers to instill in students a sense of order, decorum, self-discipline, and civic loyalty. Believing that modern industrial society depended on citizens' conforming to the time-tables of factory and train, he envisioned schools as models of punctuality and scheduling: "The pupil must have his lesson ready at the appointed time, must rise at the tap of the bell, move to the line, return; in short, go through all the evolutions with equal precision."

To achieve these goals, reform-minded educators such as Harris wrested control of schools from neighborhood leaders and ward politicians by stressing punctuality and order, compulsory-attendance laws, and a tenure system to insulate teachers from political favoritism and parental pressure. By 1900 thirty-one states required all children from eight to fourteen years of age to attend school. But the steamroller methods by Harris and others to systematize public education prompted protests. New York pediatrician Joseph Mayer Rice, after interviewing 1,200 teachers, lashed out at the schools' singsong memorization and prisonlike discipline. In city after city he discovered teachers who drilled students mercilessly and were more concerned about their posture than their learning.

But Rice overlooked real advances; for example, the national illiteracy rate dropped from 17 percent in 1880 to 13 percent by 1900, despite the influx of immigrants. He was on target, however, in assailing many teachers' rigid emphasis on silence, docility, and unquestioning obedience to rules. When a Chicago school inspector found a thirteen-year-old boy huddled in the basement of a stockyard building and ordered him back to school, the weeping boy blurted, "They hits ye if yer don't learn, and they hits ye if ye whisper, and they hits ye if ye have string in yer pocket, and they hits ye if yer seat squeaks, and they hits ye if ye don't stand up in time, and they hits ye if ye late, and they hits ye if ye ferget the page."

By the 1880s several different groups were opposing the centralized urban public-school bureaucracies. Working-class families who depended on their children's meager wages for survival, for example, resisted attempts to force their sons and daughters to attend school past the elementary grades. Although some immigrant families sacrificed to give their children an education, many withdrew their offspring from school as soon as they had learned the rudiments of reading and writing, and sent them to work. Catholic immigrants, moreover, objected to the public schools' overwhelmingly Protestant orientation. The Catholic church thus established separate parochial systems, and it rejected federal aid to public schools as a ploy to "gradually extinguish Catholicity in this country, and to form one homogeneous American people after the New England Evangelical type." At the other end of the social scale from working-class immigrants, upper-class parents, especially in the Northeast, commonly did not wish to send their children to the immigrant-thronged public schools. Many therefore enrolled their children in private seminaries and academies. Shielding their privileged students from the temptations of urban life while preparing them to go on to college, these institutions reinforced the elite belief that higher education should be the preserve of the well-to-do.

The proliferation of private and parochial schools, along with controversies over compulsory education, public funding, and classroom decorum, reveals the extent to which public education had become entangled in ethnic and class differences. Unlike Germany and Japan, which standardized and centralized their national educational systems in the nineteenth century, the United States created a diverse system of locally run public and private institutions that allowed each segment of society some influence over its schools. Amid the disputes, school enrollments expanded dramatically. In 1870 fewer than 72,000 students attended the nation's 1,026 high schools. By 1900 the number of high schools had jumped to more than 5,000, and the number of students to more than 500,000.

The Middle-Class Assault on Working-Class Culture

On many fronts well-to-do Americans tried to impose their values on the urban working class and to restrain what they deemed improper or immoral behavior. Charity workers preached middle-class values, antivice societies battled against "indecent" books and stage shows, and other reformers waged war on gambling, prizefighting, Sunday baseball, and Fourth of July celebrations featuring greased-pig races and other "brutish" diversions lubricated with ample kegs of beer. Middle-class uplifters also denounced dance halls and amusement parks. One reformer who visited a dance hall reported with alarm that "most of the younger couples were hugging and kissing, [and] there was a general mingling of men and women at the different tables." Even public parks became arenas of conflict. The elite favored large, impeccably groomed parks that would serve as models of gentility and propriety, while working people fought for neighborhood parks where they could picnic, play ball, drink beer, and temporarily escape from their tenement apartments.

No reform attracted more middle-class support than the assault on that bastion of male working-class culture, the saloon. The WCTU, the Anti-Saloon League (1893), and the powerful Methodist

Board of Temperance and Morals led the charge. One popular strategy was to close saloons through "local-option" referenda, and in many industrial cities bitter local-option battles pitted the immigrants against the well-to-do.

Although alcohol abuse remained a serious problem, the antisaloon campaign also represented a head-on clash between the customs and values of different social classes and ethnic groups. As the editor of an immigrant newspaper observed cynically during a local-option struggle, many solid citizens who would vote to close the saloons themselves had cellars well stocked with liquor.

Conclusion

Despite the sense of assured superiority that the elite brought to the cultural wars of the late nineteenth century, the culture of the immigrant working classes proved more durable than elite culture. Shabby vaudeville houses became the nation's first movie theaters, ragtime gave rise to jazz, and primitive pleasure parks such as Coney Island paved the way for multimillion-dollar amusement complexes like Disneyland. The early professional baseball teams and professional prizefighters anticipated the TV-based professional sports industry of our own day. In short, the raffish, disreputable, raucous, and frequently denounced working-class culture of the late-nineteenth-century immigrant city formed nothing less than the fertile seedbed of twentieth-century mass culture.

Chronology

1865   Vassar College founded.

1869   Cornell University founded.
First intercollegiate football game.
The Great Atlantic & Pacific Tea Company (A&P) organizes a chain of food stores.

1871   Thomas Eakins, *The Champion Single Sculls*.

1875   Smith College founded.
Frances Willard joins the Woman's Christian Temperance Union.

1876   National League of baseball players organized.

1879   F. W. Woolworth opens his "Five and Ten Cent Store" in Utica, New York.

1884   Mark Twain, *Adventures of Huckleberry Finn*.
Bryn Mawr College founded.

1885   Stanford University founded.

1886   Richard Warren Sears starts Sears, Roebuck.

1889   Columbia University adds Barnard College as a coordinate institution for women.

1891   University of Chicago founded.

1892   Joseph Mayer Rice writes his exposé of public education in *Forum* magazine.
General Federation of Women's Clubs organized.

1893   Stephen Crane, *Maggie: A Girl of the Streets*.

1895   Coney Island amusement parks open in Brooklyn.

1899   Scott Joplin, "Maple Leaf Rag."
Kate Chopin, *The Awakening*.

1900   Theodore Dreiser, *Sister Carrie*.

FOR FURTHER READING

Clifford E. Clark, Jr., *The American Family Home, 1800–1960* (1986). An overview of the changing relationship between middle-class families and their homes.

Perry Duis, *The Saloon: Public Drinking in Chicago and Boston, 1880–1920* (1983). A colorful analysis of the economic and social functions of the saloon.

S. J. Kleinberg, *The Shadow of the Mills: Working-Class Families in Pittsburgh, 1870–1907* (1989). A compelling study of working-class everyday life.

Sheila M. Rothman, *Woman's Proper Place: A History of Changing Ideals and Practices, 1870 to the Present* (1978). A perceptive conceptualization of the shifting attitudes toward women's proper role in society.

Thomas J. Schlereth, *Victorian America: Transformations in Everday Life, 1876–1915* (1992). The fascinating story of daily life in the Victorian years told through an examination of material culture.

Susan Strasser, *Satisfaction Guaranteed: The Making of the American Mass Market* (1989). A probing inquiry into the brand-name, mass-marketed products that created the modern consumer culture.

Olivier Zunz, *Making America Corporate, 1870–1920* (1990). A pioneering exploration of corporate capitalism's impact on the creation of a consumer culture.

*L*ate-nineteenth-century politics was an exuberant affair. Elections attracted enormous interest, and voters participated in record numbers. Songs, parades, banners, and buttons transformed presidential campaigns into countrywide festivals.

Beneath the hoopla, serious national issues were at stake: tariff rates, veterans' pensions, railroad development, and monetary policy. Political feelings also ran high over local issues. Religious, ethnic, and cultural differences among voters shaped big-city and state politics.

But while industrialization and urbanization were transforming the nation, politicians seemed unable or unwilling to deal with the social consequences. The federal government's lack of engagement arose in part from the deeply entrenched tradition of localism in American public life and in part because the business leaders who dominated national politics generally opposed government intervention in the economy. These same capitalists welcomed government economic policies such as tariffs and railroad subsidies, but otherwise their motto was "Hands off."

(Right) Lynn, Massachusetts, shoe worker, 1895

Politics and Expansion in an Industrializing Age

Party Rivalries, Agrarian Stirrings, and Civil-Service Reform

Politics of Privilege, Politics of Exclusion

The 1890s: Politics in a Depression Decade

The Watershed Election of 1896

Expansionist Stirrings and War with Spain

Deepening Imperialist Ventures: The Philippines, China, and Panama

The government thus sidestepped social problems that in retrospect seem of central importance, even though officials spent an amazing amount of time passing out government jobs through a spoils system so notorious that a demand for civil-service reform swept the nation. Owing to government inaction, major groups became either political outcasts or political victims. Natural catastrophes and economic grievances ignited a grass-roots movement among aggrieved farmers in the 1880s, while an avowedly racist society disfranchised, exploited, segregated, and even terrorized southern blacks.

In the 1890s agrarian discontent led to the rise of the Populist party, which proposed far-reaching government programs to remedy economic and social problems. After the devastating Depression of 1893, voters in 1896 would choose for the first time in years between candidates with radically different political and economic philosophies.

As the century ended, returning prosperity silenced domestic protest and fueled territorial expansionism. Glowing with jingoistic fervor, millions cheered as the United States defeated Spain and acquired Caribbean and Pacific lands, setting the stage for expansion in Latin America and confrontation in Asia.

Party Rivalries, Agrarian Stirrings, and Civil-Service Reform

Geography, ethnic loyalties, sectional conflict, and state and local alignments shaped politics in the 1870s and 1880s. Two issues dominated national politics: the nature and size of the money supply, and the staffing of the government bureaucracy.

Patterns of Party Strength

Although American voters elected only one Democratic president, Grover Cleveland (on two separate occasions), between 1857 and 1912, presidential elections were often extremely close. In 1876 and again in 1888, the defeated Democrat received more popular votes than the victorious Republican. The two parties, moreover, often shared control of Congress in these years.

The Democrats' strength rested on three bases: the South, southern parts of border states such as Ohio, Indiana, and Illinois, and large northern cities. The bedrock of Republican strength was rural and small-town New England, Pennsylvania, and the upper Midwest; Republicans also received a substantial urban vote from businessmen and white-collar workers. But these broad geographic concentrations of party strength masked a far more complex reality. Family traditions, ethnic ties, religious affiliations, and other issues often determined how an individual voted. Nor did economic standing absolutely determine party affiliation.

With the two parties so evenly matched, "swing states" where elections could go either way—Connecticut, New York, New Jersey, Indiana, and Illinois—held the balance of power. By no coincidence, most presidential and vice-presidential candidates came from those states.

Voter participation ran high, although women were excluded from casting ballots and blacks increasingly were disfranchised. Participation among northern voters reached 80 percent or more and could rise to 95 percent in hard-fought state or local elections. Because only men could vote in most states, political parties functioned as male social organizations. Woman suffrage aroused resistance in part because it threatened the political subculture that offered men so many material and emotional rewards.

The Stakes of Politics

Late-nineteenth-century electoral campaigns centered on three issues that large numbers of voters considered important: the tariff, the nation's currency supply, and veterans' benefits. Import duties had a direct impact on entire regions, and government policies affecting the money supply and veterans' pensions similarly concerned millions of Americans directly.

Immigrant Entrepreneurs
This 1888 photograph of the staff of William C. Raue's house- and sign-painting business in Watertown, Wisconsin (a center of German immigrant culture), captures the expansive spirit of the 1880s—an exuberance reflected in the era's politics.

Elections frequently involved emotional side issues as Republicans "waved the bloody shirt," reminding voters of the Civil War, and as southerners made crude racist appeals to white voters. However, presidential candidates rarely confronted the problems created by industrialization. Except for the Interstate Commerce Act of 1887 and the Sherman Anti-Trust Act of 1890, Washington seemed caught in a time warp as society plunged into the modern era.

Several factors account for this neglect. For one thing, a series of lackluster men occupied a much diminished presidential office, and so political initiative rested with the legislative branch. But among those in Congress, party discipline had broken down, and members displayed little concern for large national issues. Jealously guarding their political turf, they were more competent to win elections than to govern. The doctrine of laissez-faire, which emphasized that the federal government should promote economic development but not regulate the industries that it subsidized, was widely preached.

When people wanted help from government, they turned to state or local authorities. On the Great Plains, angry farmers demanded that their state legislatures regulate railroad rates, while in the cities, immigrants depended variously on machine bosses and reformers, who contended among themselves for political power.

Moreover, state and local governments fought furiously with each other for control. States often held iron sway over cities; when Chicago wanted to issue permits to street popcorn vendors, the Illinois legislature had to pass a special act. To complicate matters, rural legislators had disproportionate influence. In Connecticut, villages of a few hundred people had the same voting strength as such cities as Hartford and Bridgeport.

Also on the local level, grass-roots rivalries pitted ethnic and social groups against one another. In New York City, immigrant Catholics and native-born Protestants locked horns over tax support to parochial schools. In 1889 native-born Republican legislators in Wisconsin passed a law requiring all children to attend English-language schools, a direct attack on parochial schools that held classes in German, Swedish, or Norwegian. And electoral skirmishes often centered on cultural differences, notably the perennial Protestant attempt to force prohibition on Irish whiskey drinkers, German beer drinkers, and Italian wine drinkers.

Thus Gilded Age politics formed an intricate mosaic of individuals, groups, and political parties pursuing varied interests in city halls, statehouses, and Washington, D.C. But despite all the furious activity, the political system lagged behind in addressing the social problems of an increasingly urban and industrial nation.

Hayes in the White House

In this era of locally based politics and a diminished presidency, the state leaders who controlled both major parties almost invariably chose appealing but pliable men as presidential candidates.

Rutherford B. Hayes (1877–1881) embodied this narrow view of the office. Hayes had won admiration as an honest Ohio governor, and his major presidential achievement was restoration of respect for the office after the Grant scandals. The benevolent, bearded Hayes brought dignity and decorum to the White House. His wife, Lucy, a highly intelligent, college-educated woman of great moral earnestness, actively supported the Woman's Christian Temperance Union (WCTU), and Hayes banished alcohol from the White House. After one presidential dinner, the secretary of state grumbled, "It was a brilliant affair. The water flowed like champagne."

Greenbacks and Silver

Meanwhile, a political issue surfaced in the 1870s that would agitate American politics for decades: how to create a money supply adequate for a diverse and growing economy. The chaotic antebellum system, featuring the circulation of currency from 1,600 state banks, had to be reformed. Many believed that the only trustworthy money was gold, silver, or certificates exchangeable for these scarce metals. All antebellum *federal* currency, about $228 million, consisted of gold or silver coins or U.S. Treasury notes redeemable in gold or silver.

There were other issues. Bankers, business leaders, and politicians believed that economic stability required a strictly limited currency supply, which would drive interest rates up and prices down. Debtors and manufacturers, however, wanted to expand the money supply, a policy that would help them to pay off their debts and would force up falling farm prices.

After the Civil War, these complex issues swirled around a specific question: should the wartime greenbacks still in circulation be retained or eliminated? The hard times associated with the Panic of 1873 (see Chapter 16) made this dispute even more bitter.

The money question entered electoral politics in the mid-1870s with the formation of the Greenback party, which called for an expanded money supply to benefit workers and farmers. In the 1878 midterm elections, Greenback candidates received more than a million votes and won fourteen seats in Congress.

As prosperity returned, the Greenback party declined, but the money issue did not disappear. An even longer-lasting controversy surged over the coinage of silver. In the Coinage Act of 1873, Congress instructed the U.S. mint to cease making silver coins, thus "demonetizing" silver. When discoveries in Nevada sharply increased the silver supply, the same coalition that had supported the Greenback party turned to silver with equal ardor, demanding that the government resume purchasing and coining silver.

In 1878 the passage of the Bland-Allison Act gave silver forces a partial victory. It required the treasury to purchase and mint $2 million to $4 million a month in silver. However, the conservative-controlled treasury sabotaged the law by purchasing the minimum amount and refusing to circulate the silver coins it minted.

Frustrated silver advocates tried a new approach in the Sherman Silver Purchase Act of 1890. This measure instructed the treasury to buy 4.5 million ounces of silver a month, almost exactly the amount produced by the nation's silver mines, and to issue treasury notes, redeemable in gold or silver, equivalent to the cost of the purchases. The money supply increased slightly, but as silver prices fell, the government paid less each month for its purchases and thus issued fewer treasury notes. The tangled controversy went on.

The Spoils System

Since Andrew Jackson's time, successful politicians had rewarded supporters and contributors with positions ranging from cabinet posts to post-office and customs-service jobs. Defenders called the system rotation in office and claimed that it was a democratic way of filling government positions. Critics, however, dubbed it the spoils system after the old expression "To the victor belong the spoils." Too often, the new officeholders were ill prepared or just incompetent, and even the well qualified often had to continue making campaign contributions to their patrons to keep their jobs.

In the 1870s the battle over patronage split the Republican party between rival factions, the Stalwarts and the Half-Breeds. The two differed primarily over who would control the party machinery and patronage. The vain Senator Roscoe Conkling of New York, who had gained control of his state's patronage in President Grant's day, led the Stalwarts, and Senator James G. Blaine of Maine led the Half-Breeds.

For years, a small but influential group of reformers had campaigned for a merit-based civil service. Well bred, well educated, and well heeled, these reformers little understood the immigrants for whom the public payroll could be a ticket out of poverty. They called for a civil service of "gentlemen . . . who need nothing and want nothing from government except the satisfaction of using their talents." In fact, as the government's functions grew more complex, a professional civil service became necessary.

In 1881 advocates of professionalism founded the National Civil Service Reform League; among its chief members were Senator Carl Schurz of Missouri, editor E. L. Godkin, and social-welfare advocate Josephine Shaw Lowell. Civil-service reformers displayed an almost religious fervor: "I have spent my life in fighting the spoils system," gasped one on his deathbed.

Cautiously embracing the civil-service cause, President Hayes in 1877 launched an investigation of the corrupt New York City customs office and demanded the resignations of two officials with strong ties to Conkling. When they refused Hayes's order, the president suspended them.

Civil-Service Reform

In 1880 a deadlocked Republican presidential convention turned to dark-horse candidate James A. Garfield of Ohio. Because Garfield had ties to the Half-Breeds, a Stalwart vice-presidential candidate was nominated, Chester A. Arthur—one of the two Conkling loyalists fired by Hayes. Garfield was healthy, so putting the unqualified Arthur on the ticket seemed safe.

Running against both Democratic and Greenback candidates, Garfield won the 1880 election by a razor-thin margin of under 40,000 votes. Conkling, to protest Garfield's appointment of several of his foes to government posts, resigned from the Senate, confident that the New York legislature would reelect him and thus strengthen his political power. To his surprise, the legislature elected another senator and ended Conkling's political career.

The Election of 1880				
Candidates	Parties	Electoral Vote	Popular Vote	Percentage of Popular Vote
JAMES A. GARFIELD	Republican	214	4,453,295	48.5
Winfield S. Hancock	Democratic	155	4,414,082	48.1
James B. Weaver	Greenback-Labor		308,578	3.4

Civil-service reformers sought more than the defeat of one spoilsman; they wanted a civil-service law. A tragic event helped them to realize their wish. On July 2, 1881, Charles J. Guiteau, a drifter, shot President Garfield in the delusion that the Stalwarts would reward him, Guiteau, with a job. Garfield eventually died, and Chester A. Arthur, the very symbol of the corrupt patronage system, became president. Guiteau was tried and hanged for assassinating the president.

Painting Garfield as a martyr to the spoils system, civil-service reformers in 1883 pushed through Congress the Pendleton Civil Service Act, drafted by the Civil Service Reform League. It established a civil-service commission to set up standards of merit for federal jobs and to prepare competitive examinations. Initially, the Pendleton Act covered only 12 percent of federal employees, but it was gradually expanded. The creation of a professional civil service marked an important step in the process by which the federal government gradually caught up with the transformation of America.

By becoming a mediocre president, Chester A. Arthur pleasantly surprised those who expected him to be an unmitigated disaster. He supported civil-service reform, but his easygoing nature made him a caretaker president at most. In 1882 frustrated voters gave Democrats an overwhelming majority in the House of Representatives, and in 1884 they put a Democrat, Grover Cleveland, in the White House for the first time since 1856.

Politics of Privilege, Politics of Exclusion

Grover Cleveland challenged powerful interests by calling for cuts in the tariff and veterans' pensions. After Cleveland served a single term (1885–1889), one of the most corrupt elections in American history put Republican Benjamin Harrison (1889–1893) in the White House—and restored big business and the veterans' lobby to the driver's seat. Simultaneously, debt-ridden farmers mounted a spirited protest movement. And in the South, the white majority used the machinery of politics to strip black citizens of their basic rights.

The Election of 1884: Cleveland Victorious

James G. Blaine, the Republican nominee in 1884, typified younger Republicans eager to build a truly national party that would promote economic development. But he carried a load of political baggage, including a series of damning letters that appeared to offer political favors in exchange for railroad stock and carried the unforgettable tag line "Burn this letter."

Sensing Blaine's vulnerability, the Democrats nominated Grover Cleveland of New York, who had enjoyed a meteoric career—first as Buffalo's mayor and then as New York's governor—as a reformer and opponent of bosses and spoilsmen. Cleveland's bulldog demeanor mirrored his determined independence.

Confronted with the sharp contrast between the soiled Blaine and the seemingly spotless Cleveland, Republican reformers bolted to Cleveland. However, early in the campaign, Republicans made the shocking charge that as a young man, Cleveland had fathered an illegitimate child. Cleveland immediately admitted the damaging accusation, but Republicans exploited the issue, chanting "Ma, Ma, where's my pa?" Defiant Democrats responded, "He's gone to the White House, ha, ha, ha!"

Shortly before the election, a prominent New York Protestant clergyman denounced the Democrats as the party of "Rum, Romanism, and Rebellion." But immigrants and southerners who had contemplated sitting out the election rallied to Cleveland, and he carried New York, the key to electoral victory.

Cleveland's First Term

The corpulent Cleveland settled comfortably into the shadowy role expected of Gilded Age presidents. From youth, he had embraced Jacksonian

The Election of 1884				
Candidates	Parties	Electoral Vote	Popular Vote	Percentage of Popular Vote
GROVER CLEVELAND	Democratic	219	4,879,507	48.5
James G. Blaine	Republican	182	4,850,293	48.2
Benjamin F. Butler	Greenback-Labor		175,370	1.8
John P. St. John	Prohibition		150,369	1.5

laissez-faire, the belief that progress and prosperity depended on government's not meddling in the economy. However, by the 1880s laissez-faire had become the rallying cry of an entrenched business elite staunchly opposed to public regulation of corporate America.

Enmeshed in the political views of his youth, Cleveland displayed little understanding of the United States' industrial transformation and warned people not to expect the government to bail them out of their troubles. But one issue did catch his attention: the tariff. A tangle of conflicting economic and political interests had wrapped themselves around this issue, particularly the question of which imports should be taxed and how high the duties should be. For example, producers of coal and other commodities wanted protective tariffs, as did many manufacturers. But other manufacturers sought low tariffs on commodities they needed, while farmers attacked *all* tariffs for inflating the price of farm equipment and endangering markets for U.S. farm products.

Business-oriented Republicans generally favored tariffs; Democrats, with their agrarian base, tended to oppose them. For his part, Cleveland supported tariff reform largely because the high protective tariffs of the era were creating huge federal-budget surpluses. To spend the surpluses, legislators devised expensive federally funded projects ("pork-barrel" projects) to benefit their home districts. The president believed that the system promoted corruption.

In 1887 Cleveland devoted his annual message to Congress to the tariff. He argued that lower tariffs

not only would cut the federal surplus but also would reduce prices and slow the development of trusts. Although politicians paid little attention, corporate leaders equated talk of lower tariffs with a direct assault on business prosperity.

Cleveland stirred up another hornet's nest by opposing the routine payment of veterans' disability pensions. Fraudulent claims proliferated in this era; one veteran collected a disability pension for poor eyesight caused, he said, by wartime diarrhea. Cleveland personally investigated these claims and rejected many. He also vetoed a bill that would have pensioned all disabled veterans, whether or not the disabilities were war related, and their dependents. The pension roll should be an honor roll, he stressed, not a refuge for frauds.

The Election of 1888

By 1888 some influential groups had concluded that Cleveland must go. Republican kingmakers nominated Benjamin Harrison, a corporation lawyer and former senator of such personal coldness that some ridiculed him as the human iceberg. Harrison's managers capitalized on the fact that he was the grandson of William Henry Harrison, dubbing him Young Tippecanoe. Instead of sending the candidate around the country, they brought delegations to his Indiana home, where he read flowery speeches appealing to their interests and vanity.

The Republicans focused on the tariff. They portrayed Cleveland as an advocate of "free trade"—the elimination of all tariffs—and warned

The Election of 1888

Candidates	Parties	Electoral Vote	Popular Vote	Percentage of Popular Vote
BENJAMIN HARRISON	Republican	233	5,477,129	47.9
Grover Cleveland	Democratic	168	5,537,857	48.6
Clinton B. Fisk	Prohibition		249,506	2.2
Anson J. Streeter	Union Labor		146,935	1.3

that only a high tariff could ensure business prosperity, decent wages, and a healthy home market for the farmer. Worried business leaders provided $4 million in campaign contributions, which purchased advertising and votes.

In the end, Cleveland received almost 100,000 more votes than Harrison but lost New York, Indiana, and the electoral vote. President-elect Harrison piously told his campaign chairman, Matthew Quay, that Providence had helped the Republican cause. "Providence hadn't a damn thing to do with it," Quay snorted; Harrison would never know "how close a number of men . . . approach[ed] the gates of the penitentiary to make him president."

Once in office, Harrison rewarded his supporters. He appointed a former Grand Army of the Republic commander to the position of commissioner of pensions. "God help the surplus!" exulted the new commissioner, who then swelled the roll of pensioners from 676,000 to nearly a million. So freely was money appropriated for pensions and pork-barrel projects that the Republican-dominated Congress of 1890 became known as the Billion-Dollar Congress. In 1890 the triumphant Republicans also passed the McKinley Tariff, which pushed rates to an all-time high.

Rarely has the federal government been so subservient to entrenched economic interests, so saturated in the native-born Protestant outlook, and so out of touch with the plight of the disadvantaged as during the 1880s. But discontent was intensifying. In 1890 voters ousted the Republicans and put Democrats in control of the House of Representatives. This outcome reflected not only a stinging rebuke of the Billion-Dollar Congress and the business-ruled Harrison administration but also immigrant resentment at native-born Protestant attempts to "uplift" newcomers by force of law. Above all, the 1890 election awakened the nation to a tide of political activism engulfing the agrarian South and West.

Turmoil in Rural America

Millions of farmers felt abandoned by the political process in the late nineteenth century. Agricultural productivity had grown, but many farmers, especially in the South and Midwest, faced a demoralizing cycle of falling prices, scarce money, and debt. In the Cotton South, the crop-lien system had entrapped many small planters in endless debt, forcing them into tenancy or sharecropping. On the Great Plains, wheat farmers faced equally perplexing problems. Plunging into debt to buy land at high interest rates, many owed the bank, the farm-implement dealer, the grain-elevator operator, and the railroad. The Greenback and Grange movements had collapsed.

Out of the despair emerged the alliance movement. This outburst of agrarian protest began in the 1870s when Texas farmers gathered to discuss their problems, and it spread eastward. Like Grangers, alliance members initially advocated farmers' cooperatives to purchase equipment and supplies and to market their cotton. And, as had the Grange cooperatives, these generally failed for lack of capital.

In 1887 a farsighted Texan, Charles W. Macune, assumed leadership of the alliance movement. By 1889 Macune had merged several regional groups into the National Farmers' Alliance and Industrial Union, or the Southern Alliance. A parallel organization of black farmers emerged, the National Colored Farmers' Alliance. By 1890 the Southern Alliance boasted 3 million members, and its black counterpart another 1.2 million. Alliance members generally comprised the poorest farmers, growers dependent on a single crop, and geographically isolated farmers. Gathering for picnics and rallies, hard-hit farm families realized the political potential of their collective undertaking. As a member wrote in 1889, "Reform never begins with the leaders, it comes from the people." Southern Alliance leaders Tom Watson of Georgia and Leonidas Polk of North Carolina even urged black and white farmers to act together on their common problems. For a while, this message of racial cooperation in the name of reform carried promise.

At the same time, alliance fever was also burning across the Great Plains, where alliances had sprung up in Kansas, Nebraska, Iowa, and Minnesota in the drought-plagued years 1880 and 1881. In 1886–1887 the alliance spirit was rekindled on the plains when killing winter blizzards gave way to severe drought. For the next decade, only two wheat crops were worth harvesting. Searing winds shriveled the half-ripe grain, and chinch bugs gnawed away the rest. Making matters worse, world grain prices fell.

Innumerable midwestern families packed up and returned East. "In God we trusted, in Kansas we busted," some scrawled on their wagons. Western Kansas lost 50 percent of its population between 1888 and 1892. But others hung on, and the organization that is usually called the Northwestern Alliance, including all the Great Plains states, grew rapidly, although it never approached the Southern Alliance in total size.

One of the best-known midwestern alliance leaders was the fiery Wichita lawyer Mary E. Lease. When she advised Kansans to "raise less corn and more hell," a conservative newspaper sneered,

"[Kansas] has started to raise hell, as Mrs. Lease advised, and [the state] seems to have an overproduction. But that doesn't matter. Kansas never did believe in diversified crops."

From this scalding rhetoric and feverish activity came a political agenda. In 1889 the Southern and Northwestern alliances arranged a loose merger and supported candidates who agreed with them. Among their goals were tariff reduction, a graduated income tax, public ownership of railroads, federal funding for irrigation research, a prohibition on landownership by aliens, and "the free and unlimited coinage of silver."

The 1890 elections illuminated the depth of agrarian discontent. Alliance-backed candidates won four governorships and controlled eleven legislatures. Three alliance-backed senators and fifty congressmen went to Washington in 1890 as angry winds from the hinterland buffeted the political system.

Northwestern Alliance leaders favored a third party, and by 1892 many Southern Alliance officials had reluctantly come around to their position. In February 1892 the top alliance leaders organized the People's Party of the United States—a name quickly shortened to the Populist party. At their convention that August, 1,300 cheering delegates nominated for the presidency Iowan James B. Weaver, a Union general in the Civil War and a former Greenback candidate.

The Populist platform contained the goals announced by the alliance leaders in 1889 and added a call for the direct popular election of senators and other electoral reforms. Minnesota Populist Ignatius Donnelly's ringing preamble pronounced the nation "on the verge of moral, political, and material ruin" and proclaimed, "We seek to restore the government of the Republic to the hands of 'the plain people' with which class it originated."

African-Americans After Reconstruction

The end of Reconstruction in 1877 and the restoration of power to southern white elites spelled bad news for the nation's blacks, most of whom still lived in the South. Southern white opinion sought an end to "Negro rule" and tried to suppress the black vote. Initially, whites relied on intimidation, terror, and fraud to limit black voting rights, but in 1890 Mississippi amended its state constitution to exclude most African-American voters, and other southern states followed suit.

The Fifteenth Amendment (1870) had guaranteed all male citizens' right to vote, so *indirect* means such as literacy tests, poll taxes, and property requirements were used to disfranchise blacks. To ensure that these measures excluded *only* blacks, whites employed such devices as the grandfather clause, which exempted from these electoral requirements anyone whose ancestor had voted in 1860. Black disfranchisement proceeded erratically, but by the early twentieth century it was effectively complete.

Disfranchisement was the keystone of an arch of white supremacy that stretched across the South. In a movement culminating early in the twentieth century, state after state also passed laws strictly segregating many realms of life by race (see Chapter 22). Black caterers, barbers, contractors, bricklayers, carpenters, and other artisans lost their white customers. And blacks sent to prison—sometimes for minor offenses—got caught up in the convict-lease system, which allowed cotton planters and others to "lease" prison gangs and to put them to work under degraded conditions.

The ultimate enforcer of white supremacy was the lynch rope. Through the 1880s and 1890s, an average of one hundred blacks were lynched annually in the United States, mainly in the South. Rumors and unsubstantiated accusations of blacks' rape of white women frequently unleashed this mob violence. ("Attempted rape" could mean a wide range of behavior unacceptable to whites.) The lynch mob exerted social control, terrorizing blacks and demonstrating whites' absolute power. By no coincidence, lynching reached its highest point in 1892 as many poor African-Americans joined the agrarian protest and rallied to the Populist party banner.

The relationship between southern agrarian protest and white racism was complex. Some Populists, among them Georgia's Tom Watson, tried to build a genuinely interracial movement and denounced both lynching and the convict-lease system. When a black Populist leader pursued by a lynch mob took refuge in his house during the 1892 campaign, Watson summoned 2,000 armed white Populists to defend him. But most white Populists, encouraged by such rabble-rousers as "Pitchfork Ben" Tillman of South Carolina, held fast to racism; Watson complained that most poor whites "would joyously hug the chains of . . . wretchedness rather than do any experimenting on [the race] question."

The white ruling elite, eager to drive a wedge in the farm-protest movement, worked to inflame lower-class white racism. Addressing an alliance meeting in 1889, an Atlanta editor warned against division among white southerners; the South's only hope, he said, was "the clear and unmistakable domination of the white race." On balance, the rise of southern agrarian protest deepened racial hatred and worsened blacks' situation.

While southern blacks suffered racist oppression, the federal government did nothing. In 1877 President Hayes noted that black rights were being destroyed; however, like most northern politicians, he paid lip service to egalitarian principles and failed to apply them to blacks.

The Supreme Court similarly abandoned African-Americans to their fates. The Court ripped gaping holes into the Fourteenth Amendment and the Civil Rights Act of 1875 (see Chapter 16). In the *Civil Rights Cases* (1883), the Court threw out the Civil Rights Act of 1875 on the grounds that the Fourteenth Amendment prevented governments, but not individuals, from infringing on civil rights. In *Plessy* v. *Ferguson* (1896), the Court upheld a Louisiana law requiring segregated railroad cars. Racial segregation was legal, the justices ruled, provided that equal facilities were made available to each race.

With the Supreme Court's blessing, the South also segregated its public schools, ignoring the caveat that separate facilities must be equal. White children studied in nicer buildings, used newer equipment, and were taught by better-paid teachers than black children. Not until 1954 would the Court abandon the "separate but equal" doctrine. Rounding out their dismal record, the justices in 1898 upheld the poll tax and literacy tests by which Mississippi and other states had disfranchised blacks.

Few northerners protested the indignities that underlay the South's white-supremacist society. Until the North condemned lynching, declared aged abolitionist Frederick Douglass in 1892, "it will remain equally involved with the South in this common crime." The restoration of sectional harmony came at a high price: northern acquiescence in the utter debasement of a people whose freedom had cost the lives of thousands of northern men.

African-Americans responded in various ways to their plight. The best-known black southerner of the period, Booker T. Washington, counseled patience, accommodation, and the acquisition of skills. Black churches provided emotional support, as did black fraternal lodges. And a handful of blacks established banks and successful businesses such as insurance companies and barber shops.

Meanwhile, voices of black protest never wholly died out. Frederick Douglass urged blacks to press on for full equality; he proclaimed, "[Those] who would be free, themselves must strike the first blow." But for some blacks, the solution was to leave the South. In 1879 several thousand moved to Kansas (see Chapter 16), and 10,000 migrated to Chicago between 1870 and 1890. Blacks who went north, however, discovered that they had not left racism behind, for public opinion sanctioned many forms of de facto discrimination in the North. Northern black laborers encountered widespread prejudice. Although the Knights of Labor had welcomed blacks and counted 60,000 black members in its heyday, the AFL looked the other way as its member craft unions excluded African-Americans.

The rise of the "solid South," firmly established on racist foundations, had profound implications for American politics. For one thing, it made a mockery of the two-party system; for nearly a century, the only important election in most southern states was the Democratic primary. Furthermore, the large bloc of southern Democrats in Congress accumulated seniority and power, exerting a potent influence on public policy. Finally, the solid South wielded enormous clout in the Democratic party; no national candidate unacceptable to the South stood a chance.

Above all, the rigid caste system of the post-Reconstruction South molded the consciousness of those caught up in it, black and white alike. Describing her girlhood in the turn-of-the-century South, white novelist Lillian Smith wrote, "From the day I was born, I began to learn my lessons. . . . I learned it is possible to be a Christian and a white southerner simultaneously; to be a gentlewoman and an arrogant callous creature at the same moment; to pray at night and ride a Jim Crow car the next morning; . . . to glow when the word *democracy* was used, and to practice slavery from morning to night."

The 1890s: Politics in a Depression Decade

The 1890s was one of the most unsettled decades in American history. Grover Cleveland, reelected president in 1892, had to cope with a business panic, a crisis of confidence in the government's fiscal stability, and a depression. Bloody labor strikes and, as we have seen, the emergence of the Populist party added to the presidential predicament.

1892: Cleveland Revisited

The year 1892 provided evidence of growing discontent. The Populist platform, adopted in July, angrily catalogued agrarian demands. The deaths of thirteen men in a gun battle between strikers and strikebreakers at the Homestead steel mill and the use of federal troops against silver-mine strikers in the Idaho panhandle seemed to justify the Populists' warning of a nation verging on class warfare.

The Election of 1892

Candidates	Parties	Electoral Vote	Popular Vote	Percentage of Popular Vote
GROVER CLEVELAND	Democratic	277	5,555,426	46.1
Benjamin Harrison	Republican	145	5,182,690	43.0
James B. Weaver	People's	22	1,029,846	8.5
John Bidwell	Prohibition		264,133	2.2

Both major parties reacted cautiously in the 1892 campaign for the White House. The election was a replay of 1888, Harrison versus Cleveland, but this time Cleveland won by more than 360,000 votes, a decisive margin in an age of close elections. The Populists' strength proved spotty. Their presidential candidate, James B. Weaver, got more than a million votes, 8.5 percent of the total, and the Populists elected five senators, ten congressmen, and three governors. But the party made no dent in New England or the urban East, and little in the Midwest.

In the South, racism, Democratic loyalty, distaste for the former Union general Weaver, and widespread intimidation and voter fraud kept the Populist tally under 25 percent. The party's failure killed the prospects for interracial agrarian reform. After 1892 southern politicians seeking to appeal to poor whites stayed within the Democratic fold and laced their populism with virulent racism.

The Panic of 1893

No sooner did Cleveland take office than he confronted the worst crisis to face any president since the Civil War: an economic collapse that began in the railroad industry but quickly spread. Railroads had led in the awesome industrial growth of the 1880s, unleashing both investment and speculation. In the early 1890s railroad growth slowed, affecting other industries, especially iron and steel. The bubble burst in 1893.

The first hint of trouble came in the February failure of the Philadelphia and Reading Railroad.

The bankruptcy occurred at a delicate moment of weakened confidence in the government's ability to redeem paper money for gold on demand. Specifically, economic problems in London in 1890 had forced British investors to unload millions of dollars of American stocks; $68 million in U.S. gold reserves flowed across the Atlantic to Britain. But at the same time, the largesse of the "Billion-Dollar Congress" had substantially reduced the federal surplus, while the Sherman Silver Purchase Act was straining the gold reserve. Finally, the election of the Democrat Cleveland further eroded confidence in the dollar; although the president endorsed the gold standard, his party harbored many advocates of inflationary policies. From January 1892 to March 1893 (the month Cleveland was inaugurated), the gold reserve fell from $192 million to $100 million. Those who believed that the gold standard offered the only sure evidence of financial stability were alarmed.

With the collapse of the Philadelphia and Reading, fear fed on itself as panicky investors converted their stock holdings to gold. Stock prices plunged, the gold reserve plummeted, and by the end of the year 74 railroads, 600 banks, and 15,000 businesses had failed. Four years of hard times would follow the Panic of 1893.

The Depression of 1893–1897

The crisis worsened in 1894. By June nearly 200 railroads had failed, and by 1897 a third of the nation's railroad mileage was in bankruptcy. The railroad boom had been the key to the prosperity of the 1880s, and the railroad collapse of the 1890s brought on a full-scale depression.

In human terms, the depression took a heavy toll. Industrial unemployment ranged from 20 to 25 percent. One-fifth of factory workers had no money to buy food or to heat their homes, and jobless men tramped the streets looking for work. Unusually harsh winters in 1893 and 1894 aggravated the misery. People were starving to death in New York City as a wealthy New Yorker named Bradley Martin threw a costume ball that cost hundreds of thousands of dollars. So grotesquely out of place was the extravagant party in a prostrate city that public outrage drove Martin and his family abroad.

In rural America, already hard hit by declining agricultural prices, the depression turned trouble into ruin. Farm prices dropped by more than 20 percent: corn plummeted from $.50 to $.21 a bushel, and wheat from $.84 to $.51.

Protest swelled among desperate Americans. The populist movement grew stronger. In Massillon, Ohio, self-taught monetary "expert" Jacob Coxey concluded that the answer to unemployment was a $500 million public-works program funded with paper money not backed by gold. Coxey organized a march on Washington in March 1894 to lobby for his scheme. Thousands joined him en route, and several hundred reached Washington in late April. Police arrested Coxey and other leaders for trespassing on Capitol grounds, and his "army" broke up. Though radical in the 1890s, Coxey's proposals anticipated programs that the government would adopt during the depression of the 1930s.

As disquiet intensified, fear and anger clutched middle-class Americans. A church magazine demanded that troops put a "pitiless stop" to all violent outbreaks of unrest. To some, a bloody upheaval seemed imminent.

Defending the Gold Standard

In the face of the mass turmoil, Cleveland retreated into a laissez-faire fortress. He insisted that boom-and-bust economic cycles were inevitable and that government could only ride out the storm. More-over, not understanding the depression's complex causes, Cleveland focused on a single peripheral issue, the gold standard. In August 1893 he persuaded a special session of Congress to repeal the Sherman Silver Purchase Act, which he blamed for the dwindling gold reserve.

But the gold drain continued and the depression deepened. In early 1895, with the gold reserve down to $41 million, Cleveland turned to Wall Street. Bankers J. P. Morgan and August Belmont agreed to lend the government $62 million in exchange for discounted U.S. bonds. The government then purchased 3.5 million ounces of gold, stemming the drain on the reserve, and Morgan and Belmont resold their bonds for a substantial profit. Cleveland had saved the gold standard, but at a high price. His deal with Morgan and Belmont, and the handsome profits they made, seemed to show more concern for moneyed men than for the average American and confirmed agrarian radicals' suspicions of an unholy alliance between Washington and Wall Street.

The failure of politics in the early 1890s did not stop at the presidency; Congress did no better. Despite Cleveland's insistence on tariff reform, the Wilson-Gorman Tariff of 1894 made so many concessions to special interests that a disgusted president allowed it to become law without his signature.

One feature of the Wilson-Gorman Tariff suggested an enlarging vision of government's role in an age of towering fortunes: an income tax of 2 percent on all income over $4,000 (roughly $40,000 in present-day purchasing power). But in 1895 the Supreme Court declared the tax unconstitutional on the grounds that the Constitution forbade the direct federal taxation of individuals. Thus whether one looked at the executive, the legislature, or the judiciary, the paralysis of government in the face of economic tribulation seemed complete.

Cleveland's policies also split the Democratic party. The rift decisively affected the elections of 1894 and 1896 and led to a major political realignment as the century ended.

Laissez-faire ideology suffered a grievous setback in the 1890s as depression-worn Americans adopted a broader conception of government's proper role in dealing with large-scale economic and social problems. The people concluded that a stronger, more active presidency was essential in this new industrial era. The depression was thus memorable not only for the suffering it caused but also for the lessons it taught.

The Watershed Election of 1896

Republican gains in the 1894 midterm elections revealed popular revulsion against Cleveland and the Democrats, whom Americans widely blamed for the hard times. In the 1896 presidential election, the monetary question became the overriding symbolic issue. Conservatives clung to the gold standard, but advocates of "free silver" triumphed at the Democratic convention when a young silver advocate, William Jennings Bryan, secured the nomination. However, his opponent, William McKinley, won the election, and his triumph laid the groundwork for a major political realignment.

1894: Repudiation of Cleveland

The midterm election of 1894 spelled Democratic disaster. The blizzard of protest votes, said one, left the party "buried under the drift a thousand feet deep." Republicans, aided by votes from immigrants battered by the depression, gained control of Congress and several key states. Populist candidates won nearly 1.5 million votes, 40 percent over their 1892 total. Most Populist gains came in the South. The party's leaders looked forward to 1896.

The Silver Issue

As serious economic divisions split Americans in the mid-1890s, a Supreme Court justice described the conflict as "a war of the poor against the rich: a war constantly growing in intensity and bitterness." It was a war of words, fought largely over a symbolic issue: free silver.

By clinging to the gold standard, Cleveland forced his opponents into an exaggerated obsession with silver. The genuine issues dividing rich and poor, creditor and debtor, and farmer and city

"Dubious"

A Republican poster called voters' attention to poverty-stricken nations that had a silver coinage, implying that the United States would sink to the same level if it adopted Bryan's panacea.

dweller disappeared in murky debates over the two semimythic metals. Conservatives warned of nightmarish dangers in abandoning the gold standard, and agrarian radicals extolled silver as a universal cure-all. Both sides had a point. Gold advocates recognized the potential disaster of uncontrolled inflation if paper money rested only on the government's ability to run printing presses. Silver advocates knew from personal experience how tight-money, high-interest policies depressed prices and devastated farmers.

Silver Advocates Capture the Democratic Party

At the 1896 Democratic convention in Chicago, outnumbered Cleveland supporters protested in vain as western and southern delegates adopted a platform demanding the free and unlimited coinage of silver—in effect, repudiating the Cleveland administration. An ardent advocate of the silver cause captured the party's nomination: William Jennings Bryan of Nebraska. Only thirty-six, the young lawyer had already served two terms in Congress.

Bryan brought mighty oratorical talents to politics. In Chicago, during the debate over the platform, his booming voice carried his rousing words to the highest galleries of the convention hall. Praising farmers as the nation's bedrock, Bryan roared to the cheering delegates, "You shall not press down upon the brow of labor this crown of thorns, you shall not crucify mankind upon a cross of gold." The speech passed into political legend.

The silverites' capture of the Democratic party left the Populists with a dilemma. Free silver was only one reform of many that they advocated. If they jumped aboard the Bryan bandwagon, they would abandon their own program. But a separate Populist ticket would siphon votes from Bryan and guarantee a Republican victory. Reluctantly, the Populists endorsed Bryan. Meanwhile, the Republicans nominated former Ohio governor William McKinley on a platform endorsing the high protective tariff and the gold standard.

1896: McKinley Triumphant

Bryan did his best to sustain the momentum of the Chicago convention, crisscrossing the country by train to deliver his free-silver campaign speech. One skeptic jeered that Bryan was well nicknamed the "Boy Wonder of the River Platte": his mouth was just as wide and his mind just as shallow.

Mark Hanna, a Cleveland industrialist, managed the Republican McKinley's campaign. Recognizing that the dignified, somewhat aloof McKinley could not match Bryan's popular touch—one wit noted that McKinley always seemed to be "determinedly looking for his pedestal"—Hanna built the campaign around posters and pamphlets that warned of the dangers of free silver, caricatured Bryan as a radical, and portrayed McKinley and the gold standard as twin pillars of prosperity.

Drawing on a war chest possibly as large as $7 million, Hanna spent lavishly. J. P. Morgan and John D. Rockefeller together contributed $500,000 to the McKinley campaign, more than Bryan's total

The Election of 1896

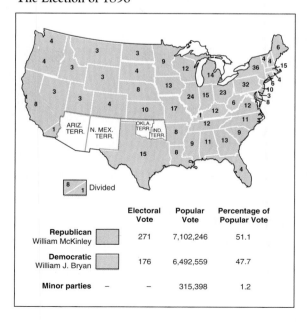

	Electoral Vote	Popular Vote	Percentage of Popular Vote
Republican William McKinley	271	7,102,246	51.1
Democratic William J. Bryan	176	6,492,559	47.7
Minor parties	–	315,398	1.2

The Election of 1900				
Candidates	Parties	Electoral Vote	Popular Vote	Percentage of Popular Vote
WILLIAM McKINLEY	Republican	292	7,218,491	51.7
William Jennings Bryan	Democratic; Populist	155	6,356,734	45.5
John C. Wooley	Prohibition		208,914	1.5

campaign contributions. McKinley himself stayed home in Canton, Ohio, emerging occasionally to read speeches from his porch to a stream of visiting delegations.

On election day, 1896, McKinley swamped Bryan by more than 600,000 votes; the Democrats carried only the South, the Great Plains, and the Rocky Mountains. In nominating Bryan, the Democrats had selected a candidate with little appeal for factory workers, the urban middle class, or immigrants.

The McKinley administration translated its conservative platform into law. The Dingley Tariff (1897) pushed rates to all-time highs, and the Currency Act of 1900 committed the United States to the gold standard. Because of returning prosperity, rising farm prices, and the discovery of gold in Alaska, these measures roused little opposition, and McKinley easily defeated Bryan again in 1900.

The elections of 1894 and 1896 produced a Republican majority that, except for Woodrow Wilson's presidency (1913–1921), would dominate national politics until the election of Franklin D. Roosevelt in 1932. Populism collapsed, but a new reform movement, progressivism, was picking up momentum and adopting many of its ideas.

Expansionist Stirrings and War with Spain

In the final decades of the nineteenth century, politicians, statesmen, editorialists, and Fourth of July orators insisted that national greatness required America to join Europe in the imperialist theater. Fanned by sensationalistic newspaper coverage of Cuba's struggle for independence from Spain, public enthusiasm for international assertiveness sparked a war between the United States and Spain in 1898.

Roots of Expansionist Sentiment

Since the time of the first English settlements along the Atlantic seaboard, newcomers to America had been expansionist. The Louisiana Purchase testified to that fervor, as did the Manifest Destiny of the 1840s that had led to war with Mexico and propelled America to the Pacific. Civil war and industrialization had temporarily damped expansionism, but it revived strongly after 1880 as the conviction grew that the United States had a global destiny.

European and Japanese imperialism intensified this expansionist sentiment. Great Britain, France, Belgium, Germany, Italy, and Japan were all collecting colonies from North Africa to remote Pacific islands, and many Americans concluded that true national greatness demanded an empire. Furthermore, continued prosperity as well as national pride dictated overseas markets, many felt. In 1890 the secretary of state noted that national productivity was outrunning "the demands of the home market" and insisted that American business look abroad.

Other voices joined in the expansionist chorus. Proponents of a strong navy contributed to the expansionist mood. In *The Influence of Sea Power upon History* (1890), Alfred Thayer Mahan equated sea power with national greatness and urged a rapid U.S. naval buildup. To do so required the

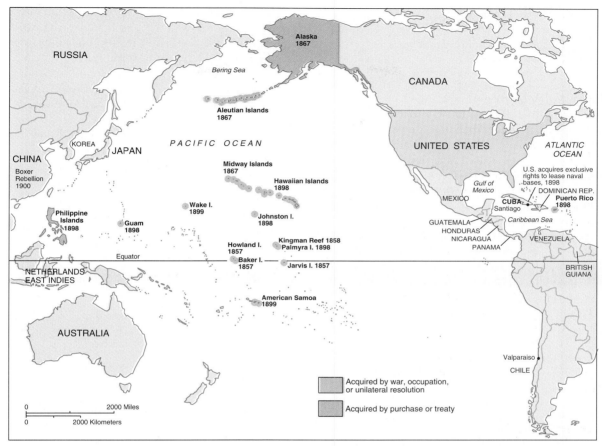

RUSSIA

Alaska
1867

Bering Sea

CANADA

Aleutian Islands
1867

KOREA JAPAN

PACIFIC OCEAN

UNITED STATES

*ATLANTIC
OCEAN*

CHINA
Boxer
Rebellion
1900

Midway Islands
1867

Hawaiian Islands
1898

U.S. acquires exclusive
rights to lease naval
bases, 1898

Gulf of
Mexico

DOMINICAN REP.

MEXICO

CUBA Puerto Rico
Santiago 1898

Wake I.
1899

Philippine
Islands
1898

Guam
1898

Johnston I.
1898

GUATEMALA
HONDURAS
NICARAGUA
PANAMA

Caribbean Sea

VENEZUELA

Howland I.
1857

Kingman Reef 1858
Palmyra I. 1898

Equator

Baker I.
1857

Jarvis I. 1857

BRITISH
GUIANA

NETHERLANDS
EAST INDIES

American Samoa
1899

AUSTRALIA

Valparaiso

CHILE

Acquired by war, occupation,
or unilateral resolution

Acquired by purchase or treaty

0	2000 Miles
0	2000 Kilometers

U.S. Territorial Expansion in the Late Nineteenth Century
*The major period of U.S. territorial expansion abroad came in a short burst of activity in
the late 1890s, when newspapers and some politicians beat the drums for empire.*

acquisition of territory overseas for bases. Some religious leaders talked of America's divine mission to spread Christianity, an argument with racist tinges. One minister averred that "God is training the Anglo-Saxon race for its mission"—a mission of bringing Christianity and civilization to the world's "weaker races." Theodore Roosevelt, Henry Cabot Lodge, and diplomat John Hay led a group of Republican expansionists who tirelessly preached imperial greatness and military might. "I should welcome almost any war," Roosevelt declared, "for I

think this country needs one." A series of diplomatic skirmishes in the mid-1890s revealed the newly assertive American mood and paved the way for the war that Roosevelt desired.

In the mid-1880s, quarrels between the United States and Great Britain had flared over fishing rights in the North Atlantic and North Pacific, reawakening latent anti-British feelings and the old dream of acquiring Canada. A poem published in the *Detroit News* provided a new nickname for expansionists—jingoists:

We do not want to fight,
But, by jingo, if we do,
We'll scoop in all the fishing grounds
And the whole dominion too!

In 1898 a compromise settled the fishing-rights dispute, but by then attention had shifted to Latin America. In 1891 tensions had flared between the United States and Chile after a mob in Valparaiso killed two American soldiers and injured seventeen others on shore leave. War fever subsided after Chile apologized and paid an indemnity of $75,000.

In 1895 another conflict erupted between the United States and Great Britain, this time over the boundary of British Guiana. Secretary of State Richard Olney sent the British a stern memorandum reminding them of the Monroe Doctrine, and the British condescendingly responded that this revered idea had no standing under law. Many Americans seriously contemplated war with Great Britain until the British agreed to accept the findings of a special arbitration commission.

Pacific Expansion

Even the far-off Pacific felt the stirrings of American expansionism. In the Samoan Islands, the U.S. Navy sought the port of Pago Pago as a refueling station. In March 1889 the United States narrowly avoided a naval clash with Germany over the islands when a timely hurricane intervened. Ultimately, America established a three-way protectorate over the islands with Germany and Great Britain.

The Hawaiian Islands also beckoned U.S. imperialists. American missionaries and merchants had been active in the islands since the end of the eighteenth century. American-owned sugar plantations dominated the Hawaiian economy. Under an 1887 treaty, the United States built a naval base at Pearl Harbor, near Honolulu. Then in 1891, angered by American economic domination, islanders welcomed Liliuokalani to the Hawaiian throne. Strong-willed and hostile toward Americans, she became queen amidst a crisis set off by a U.S. decision in 1890 to tax Hawaiian sugar. Hawaiian sugar

prices plunged 40 percent as a result. Facing ruin, the planters deposed the queen in January 1893, proclaimed the independent Republic of Hawaii, and requested U.S. annexation.

Cleveland was skeptical about annexation and grew more so when an emissary whom he sent to Hawaii cast doubt on whether the Hawaiians desired annexation. Such scruples infuriated expansionists. "In ordering Old Glory pulled down at Honolulu, President Cleveland turned back the hand on the dial of civilization," a New York newspaper fulminated. "Queen Lil" made matters difficult for her American supporters by declaring that if restored to power, she would behead the coup leaders.

When McKinley succeeded Cleveland, the annexation of Hawaii moved rapidly forward, and in 1898 Congress proclaimed Hawaii an American territory. Sixty-one years later, it joined the Union as the fiftieth state.

Crisis over Cuba

By 1898 American attention shifted to Cuba, where a rebellion against Spanish rule had erupted in 1895. American businessmen had $50 million invested in the island and annually imported $100 million in sugar and other products from Cuba. Revolutionary turmoil would jeopardize these interests. Neither the Cleveland nor the McKinley administration supported the rebellion.

But the rebels won widespread popular backing from Americans, support that increased with revelations of the cruelty inflicted on the Cuban people by the Spanish commander, Valeriano Weyler. Under Weyler's "reconcentration" policy, the civilian population was herded into camps in order to isolate the rebels. Brutality, malnutrition, and disease turned the concentration camps into death camps; perhaps 200,000 Cubans died there.

Fueling American anger were sensational stories published by two New York newspapers, William Randolph Hearst's *Journal* and Joseph Pulitzer's *World*, which were embroiled in a circulation war. The Cuban tragedy was ready-made for Hearst's and Pulitzer's lurid reporting. Daily headlines blared the latest developments, and feature stories detailed "Butcher" Weyler's atrocities.

In 1897 a liberal Spanish government made significant concessions, and a peaceful solution to the Cuban crisis seemed near. But Hearst and Pulitzer continued to inflame public opinion. On February 8, 1898, Hearst's *Journal* published a private letter from a Spanish diplomat describing McKinley as "weak" and "a bidder for the admiration of the crowd." Many Americans would have agreed, but they resented hearing it from a Spanish diplomat.

Irritation turned to outrage on February 15, 1898, when an explosion rocked the battleship *Maine* in Havana harbor, killing 226 American crewmen. Newspaper headlines blazed with accusations of Spanish perfidy. In fact, a 1976 investigation confirmed what experts had thought even in 1898: that an internal explosion in the ammunition storage area had destroyed the battleship. In 1898, however, few Americans wanted to see the tragedy as accidental.

President McKinley still hung back from war, but he was not prepared to risk his popularity by resisting an aroused public. With further Spanish concessions futile, on April 11 McKinley sent a war message to Congress, and legislators passed a joint

Major Battles in the Spanish-American War

The Spanish-American War was a short, sharp, one-sided encounter between the oldest European empire in the New World and the youngest power on the global stage. The conflict itself involved only a few limited U.S. engagements with outmatched Spanish forces in Cuba and the Philippines. The subsequent U.S. campaign to suppress an independence movement in the Philippines, however, proved long and costly.

resolution recognizing Cuba's independence and authorizing force to expel the Spanish. An amendment introduced by Senator Henry M. Teller of Colorado declared that the United States had no desire for "sovereignty, jurisdiction, or control" in Cuba.

The Spanish-American War

The conflict with Spain lasted three months. Action began on May 1, 1898, when a U.S. fleet under Admiral George Dewey steamed into Manila Bay in the Philippines and destroyed or captured all ten Spanish ships anchored there, at the cost of one American and 381 Spanish lives. In mid-August U.S. troops occupied the capital, Manila.

In Cuba the war's only significant land engagement took place on July 1, when American troops seized two strongly defended Spanish garrisons on El Caney Hill and San Juan Hill overlooking the Spanish military stronghold of Santiago de Cuba. Leading the volunteer "Rough Riders" at San Juan Hill was Theodore Roosevelt, getting his taste of war—and abundant publicity—at last. Two days later, the Spanish fleet, which had been blockaded by the Americans at Santiago de Cuba, made a gallant but doomed break for the open sea. American ships sank the seven ancient vessels, killing 474 Spaniards and ending 400 years of Spanish empire in America.

John Hay thought that it had all been "a splendid little war," but careful examination showed how terribly ill prepared the American forces had been. They went into battle in the tropical midsummer wearing heavy wool uniforms, received abysmal medical care, and died in droves from yellow fever and malaria. The United States lost more than 5,000 men in Cuba, only 379 of them in combat.

Negotiations in Paris followed a July 17 armistice. On December 10, 1898, the United States and Spain signed the Treaty of Paris. Spain recognized Cuba's independence and, after much pressure and a payment of $20 million, ceded the Philippines, Puerto Rico, and Guam to the United States. Americans possessed an island empire stretching from the Caribbean to the Pacific.

Deepening Imperialist Ventures: The Philippines, China, and Panama

The Spanish-American War opened a period of intensified world involvement for the United States. In the Philippines, America fought a brutal four-year war to suppress a Filipino struggle for independence. In China, Washington sought an "open door" for U.S. trade, and in Latin America, President Theodore Roosevelt used dubious methods to clear the way for an American-controlled canal across the Isthmus of Panama.

The Platt Amendment

American troops remained in Cuba after the withdrawal of the Spanish, despite the Teller Amendment. Although the soldiers, commanded by General Leonard Wood, accomplished much in public health, education, and sanitation, they did little for Cuban independence.

The troops withdrew after four years, under terms that severely compromised Cuban sovereignty. An amendment to the 1901 army appropriations bill offered by Senator Orville Platt of Connecticut authorized the U.S. withdrawal only after Cuba accepted severe restrictions on treaty making and borrowing. The United States reserved the right to intervene in Cuba when it saw fit and to maintain a naval base there. The Cuban government accepted the Platt Amendment, which remained in force until 1934. The United States reoccupied Cuba in 1906–1909 and again in 1912 and established a large naval base at Guantanamo Bay. By 1920 U.S. investments in Cuba soared from $50 million to $500 million.

Guerrilla War in the Philippines

When the Spanish-American War began, few Americans knew what or where the Philippine Islands were. President McKinley confessed that "I could not have told where those darn islands were within 2,000 miles." In fact, those 7,000 islands lay

U.S. Soldiers Question Filipino Women
The United States' military repression of the Filipino independence movement brought much suffering to the civilian population. As many as 200,000 people died of disease, malnutrition, and other wartime hazards.

in the South China Sea, and American business saw them as a stepping-stone to the rich China market. McKinley, as always reflecting public opinion, soon convinced himself that the United States must help "our little brown brothers" in the islands, who, he believed, were unfit to govern themselves and could not be left to predatory German or Japanese imperialists. America's mission, according to the president, was "to educate the Filipinos, and to uplift and civilize and Christianize them, and by God's grace do the very best we could by them." (McKinley ignored the fact that after 400 years of Spanish rule, most Filipinos were already Roman Catholics.) McKinley instructed the American peace negotiators in Paris to acquire the islands.

Ruling the Philippines proved difficult. Filipinos longed for independence, and in 1896 young Emilio Aguinaldo had organized a movement to drive out the Spanish. In the summer of 1898, with arms supplied by Admiral Dewey, Aguinaldo's forces captured most of Luzon, the Philippines' main island. In June, Aguinaldo proclaimed Filipino independence and drafted a democratic constitution. After the U.S. Senate ratified the Treaty of Paris in February 1899, fighting broke out between the American army and Aguinaldo's forces, who felt betrayed.

It took the United States four years to crush the Filipino independence movement, which waged a guerrilla war against the U.S. forces. More than 125,000 Americans troops ultimately served in the Philippine jungles. American casualties—4,000 troops died—were ten times greater than in the entire Spanish-American War. As many as 20,000 Filipino independence fighters perished, and untold tens of thousands of civilians died when the Americans implemented the same sort of reconcentration policy that they had denounced in Cuba. In 1902 a Senate committee investigating the war heard sobering testimony from U.S. soldiers about the execution of prisoners, the torture of suspects, and the burning of Filipino villages. The humanitarian mood of 1898, when Americans had rushed to save Cuba from the Spanish, seemed remote indeed.

In 1902 Congress passed the Philippine Government Act, providing that a presidentially appointed governor would rule the islands and that a Filipino assembly would be elected. The law also promised eventual self-government. But the Philippines would not become independent until July 4, 1946.

Critics of Empire

Influential critics lashed out against American imperialism. William Jennings Bryan, editor E. L. Godkin, settlement-house founder Jane Addams, and novelist Mark Twain led the outcry, and steel king Andrew Carnegie contributed thousands of dollars. In November 1899 these critics of empire formed the Anti-Imperialist League.

The United States' takeover of foreign territories and subjugation of other peoples, the anti-imperialists believed, violated the sacred principles of human equality and self-government on which the nation had been founded. The United States has "puked up our ancient national heritage" and "turned pirate," fumed Harvard philosopher William James. Another anti-imperialist leader wrote, "Dewey took Manila with the loss of one man—and all of our institutions." Twain suggested a new design for the American flag, with black replacing the white stripes and with a skull-and-crossbones superseding the field of stars. Other anti-imperialists feared that prolonged contact with "our little brown brothers" might "mongrelize" the "American race."

In February 1899 the Senate ratified the expansionist peace treaty with Spain by only one vote, but Bryan's crushing defeat in 1900 seemed to validate McKinley's expansionist policies. Nevertheless, the anti-imperialists for the most part had upheld an older and finer vision of America than that evoked by the jingoistic rhetoric and military posturing that surrounded them.

The Open Door Notes and the Boxer Uprising

As the Philippine war dragged on, Americans shifted their focus to China. The depression of 1893–1897 had heightened interest in foreign markets, and China was especially inviting. Opportunities for trade and investment seemed limitless in a land of 400 million potential customers. The tottering Manchu Dynasty, near collapse, could neither keep out nor limit foreign trade.

China's weakness had drawn other imperialists—including Russia, Germany, and Great Britain—who had won major concessions of land and trading rights. In September 1899, fearful of being shut out of China, Secretary of State John Hay sent notes to the imperialist powers in China requesting that they open the ports within their spheres of influence to all comers and not grant special privileges to traders of their own nations. Although the six imperialist nations returned noncommittal answers, Hay

blithely announced that they had accepted the principle of an "Open Door" to American business.

The Open Door notes illuminate how commercial considerations influenced U.S. foreign policy. They reflected a quest for what has been called informal empire in contrast to the formal acquisition of overseas territories. In this kind of economic expansionism, the government played a subordinate and supporting role to private enterprise in a kind of laissez-faire imperialism.

In 1899, even as the Open Door notes were circulating, Chinese anger at foreign exploitation exploded. Urged on by an aged Manchu Dynasty empress, a fanatical secret society, the Harmonious Righteous Fists ("Boxers" to Westerners) rampaged across China, killing thousands of foreigners and Chinese Christians. In June 1900 the Boxers occupied Beijing (Peking), China's capital, and besieged the district housing the foreign legations. In August 1900 an international army, including 2,500 U.S. troops, marched on Beijing, drove back the Boxers, rescued the occupants of the besieged legations, and sacked the city.

The failed uprising nearly toppled the Manchu Dynasty, an outcome that would have opened the way for the total partitioning of China among the imperialists. To prevent this development, Hay issued a second series of Open Door notes, reaffirming the principle of open trade in China for all nations and announcing U.S. support for China's territorial and administrative integrity. In the 1930s, when Japanese expansionism would threaten China, this Open Door policy would mold America's response.

Building the Panama Canal

The final episode in this expansionist cycle was the construction of the Panama Canal. Dreams of a canal across the ribbon of land linking North and South America dated back to the early Spanish conquest. Yellow fever and mismanagement brought a French company's late-nineteenth-century attempt to build a canal to disaster and left a half-completed waterway. To recoup some of its

$400-million-dollar loss, the company offered to sell its assets, including a concession from Colombia, which then controlled the isthmus, for $109 million.

Americans considered alternative routes, including a canal across Nicaragua, but in 1901 the French lowered the asking price to $40 million. President Theodore Roosevelt pressed the offer, but in 1902 the Colombian government refused to ratify the Hay-Herrán agreement, which would have turned the French concession over to the United States. Furious, Roosevelt privately denounced the Colombians as "greedy little anthropoids."

Roosevelt found a willing collaborator in Philippe Bunau-Varilla, an official of the French company. To prevent the loss of $40 million to his firm, Bunau-Varilla organized a "revolution" in Panama, then still a Colombian province. Working from a room at the Waldorf-Astoria Hotel in New York City, Bunau-Varilla wrote a declaration of independence and constitution. On November 3, 1903, the "revolution" erupted on schedule, with a U.S. warship anchored offshore as a warning to Colombia not to intervene. In short order, Bunau-Varilla proclaimed himself ambassador to Washington, gained American recognition of the newly hatched nation, and signed a treaty granting the United States a ten-mile-wide strip of land across Panama "in perpetuity" in return for $10 million and an annual payment of $250,000. Roosevelt later summarized the episode: "I took the Canal Zone, and let Congress debate, and while the debate goes on, the canal does also."

Before completing the canal, the United States first had to conquer yellow fever. After Dr. Walter Reed recognized the mosquito as its carrier, the U.S. Army carried out a prodigious drainage project that eradicated the disease-bearing pest. Construction began in 1906, and in August 1914 the first ship passed through the canal. The Atlantic and Pacific coasts were linked by a short sea route just in time for World War I.

A technical wonder, the canal also symbolized an arrogant American imperialism. For decades, the rancor generated by Roosevelt's high-handed actions, combined with other cases of U.S. interventionism, shadowed U.S.–Latin American relations.

Conclusion

The opening of the Panama Canal concluded thirty years of expansionism that trumpeted the United States' debut on the world stage. Left unanswered at the time was the question of how a government designed for a small agrarian nation could meet the needs of an industrialized land of immigrant cities. Clearly, limited laissez-faire government was not the solution.

In the 1890s agrarian discontent underscored major problems and gave rise to the Populist party, which challenged laissez-faire assumptions and demanded that the government play an assertive role in solving social and economic problems. Although the party faded, its ideas became the basis for the progressive movement, to which we now turn.

Chronology

1873	Panic of 1873.
	Coinage Act demonetizes silver.
1877	Rutherford B. Hayes becomes president.
1878	Bland-Allison Act requires U.S. Treasury to purchase silver.
1880	James Garfield elected president.
1881	Assassination of Garfield; Chester A. Arthur becomes president.
1883	Pendleton Civil Service Act.
1884	Grover Cleveland elected president.
1887	Cleveland urges tariff reform and vetoes veterans' pension bill.
1888	Benjamin Harrison elected president.
1889	United States, Great Britain, and Germany establish protectorate over Samoan Islands.
1890	Sherman Silver Purchase Act.
	Sherman Anti-Trust Act.
	McKinley Tariff pushes tariffs to all-time high.
1891	Crisis between United States and Chile over attack on U.S. sailors.
1892	Cleveland elected to second term as president.
1893	Panic of 1893; depression of 1893–1897 begins.
	Drain of treasury's gold reserve.
	Repeal of Sherman Silver Purchase Act.
	Overthrow of Queen Liliuokalani of Hawaii.
1894	"Coxey's Army" marches on Washington.
	Pullman strike.
	Wilson-Gorman Tariff.

1895	Supreme Court declares federal income tax unconstitutional.
	Banker's loans end drain on gold reserve.
	United States intervenes in Venezuela–Great Britain boundary dispute.
1896	Free-silver forces capture Democratic party and nominate William Jennings Bryan.
	William McKinley elected president.
1898	Spanish-American War.
1898–1902	United States suppresses guerrilla uprising in Philippines.
1899	First United States Open Door notes on China.
	United States helps put down Boxer uprising.
1900	Currency Act officially places United States on gold standard.
	Second Open Door notes on China.
	McKinley reelected.
1901	Platt Amendment retains U.S. role in Cuba.
	Assassination of McKinley; Theodore Roosevelt becomes president.
1902	Philippine Government Act.
1903	Hay-Herrán agreement rejected by Colombia.
	"Revolution" in Panama organized by Philippe Bunau-Varilla.
	Hay-Bunau-Varilla Treaty.
1914	Completion of Panama Canal.

FOR FURTHER READING

Robert L. Beisner, *From the Old Diplomacy to the New, 1865–1900*, 2d ed. (1986). A valuable study tracing the roots of expansionism.

Sean Dennis Cashman, *America in the Gilded Age: From the Death of Lincoln to the Rise of Theodore Roosevelt* (1984). A good synthesis.

Carl N. Degler, *The Age of the Economic Revolution, 1876–1900*, 2d ed. (1977). A readable overview, especially good on the economic context of Gilded Age politics.

John Garraty, *The New Commonwealth, 1877–1890* (1968). Well-written account focusing on the basic transformations of the period.

Lawrence Goodwyn, *The Populist Moment: A Short History of the Agrarian Revolt in America* (1978). A carefully researched interpretive account focusing on the political culture of the alliance movement.

Morton Keller, *Affairs of State: Public Life in Late Nineteenth-Century America* (1977). An excellent account of politics and government.

Walter LaFeber, *New Empire: American Expansionism, 1860–1898* (1963). A basic and influential study.

Industrialization brought benefits as well as problems to the United States. For the millions of immigrants working in unsafe factories and residing in unhealthful slums, life was a cycle of poverty, exhausting labor, and early death. But at the same time, corporations grew powerful, the new middle class of white-collar workers consolidated its position, and women demanded full participation in the political process. From this volatile milieu pulsed a current of reform that became the progressive movement, the response to the changes that transformed the United States between the Civil War and the twentieth century as Americans grappled with the new world of corporations, factories, cities, and immigrants.

The progressives were the first group of American reformers to view the government as an ally in the cause of reform. Neither glorifying the individual nor withdrawing from society as earlier reformers had done, they saw organizations and social engagement as essential to reform.

(Right) Boy working in a Lowell, Massachusetts, mill, c. 1920

The Progressive Era

A Changing American Society and Economy

The Progressive Movement Takes Shape

Progressivism and Social Control:
The Movement's Coercive Dimension

Blacks and Women Organize

National Progressivism—Phase I:
Roosevelt and Taft

National Progressivism—Phase II:
Woodrow Wilson

Progressivism emerged first at the state and local levels, generated by groups as different as women's clubs and political radicals. At the national level, these reform impulses coalesced into a single movement that turned Washington into a hotbed of activism. By 1917, when reform gave way to war, progressivism had fundamentally altered U.S. government and society. This chapter will examine first the social changes that spawned progressivism and then the movement itself.

A Changing American Society and Economy

Urban growth and corporate consolidation brought dramatic changes to the United States in the early twentieth century. Farm-born Americans streaming into cities met a swirling tide of immigrants. During this era of booming prosperity, new forms of business organization transformed American capitalism. Some benefited, but millions of industrial workers faced long hours, low wages, dangerous working conditions, and pressures for ever greater output. They organized to improve their lot through the labor union and the ballot box.

Immigrant Masses and a New Urban Middle Class

Through all the turbulence of the early twentieth century, people continued to flock to the cities. By 1920 the urban population had passed the 50 percent mark, sixty-eight American cities had more than 100,000 residents, and New York City alone had grown by 2.2 million since 1900. Millions of the new urbanites had come from small-town and rural America. However, immigration still provided the greatest source of urban growth; more than 17 million people entered the United States between 1900 and 1917, and most of them became city dwellers.

As in the 1890s, the immigrant stream flowed primarily from southern and eastern Europe, but 200,000 Japanese, 40,000 Chinese, and thousands

San Francisco's Chinatown
A turn-of-the-century street peddler offers toys. The immigrant tide into the nation's cities in the progressive years forever changed society, politics, and culture.

of Mexicans joined them. Although most came of economic necessity, revolution propelled many Mexicans northward, and religious persecution triggered the immigration of millions of eastern European Jews. By 1913 New York City's Lower East Side had a Jewish population of 1.4 million.

City life remained harsh. Urban governments' ability to provide decent schools and parks, safe water, sewers, garbage collection, and fire protection lagged behind the pace of growth. Death rates in the immigrant wards reached twice the national average, reflecting shockingly bad conditions.

Meanwhile, the urban middle class expanded rapidly. From 1900 to 1920, the white-collar work force jumped from 5.1 million to 10.5 million, twice the growth rate for the work force as a whole. This new middle class included such diverse groups as skilled engineers, technicians, bureaucrats, businessmen, lawyers, physicians, and teachers. Ambitious, well educated, and valuing self-discipline and social

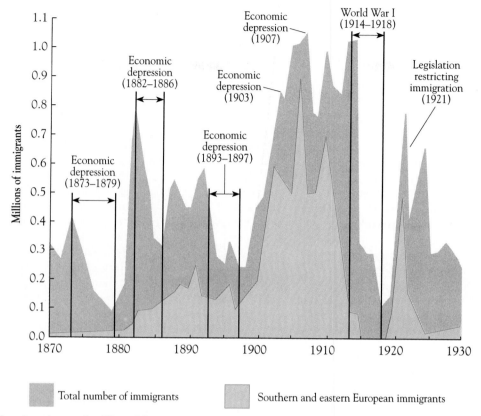

Immigration to the United States, 1870–1930

With the end of the depression of the 1890s, immigrants from southern and eastern Europe poured into America's cities, spurring an immigration-restriction movement, urban moral-control campaigns, and efforts to improve the physical and social conditions of immigrant life.

SOURCES: *Statistical History of the United States from Colonial Times to the Present* (Stamford, Conn.: Fairfield Publishers, 1965); and report presented by Senator William P. Dillingham, Senate document 742, 61st Congress, 3rd session, December 5, 1910: Abstracts of Reports to the Immigration Commission.

stability, they were eager to make their influence felt.

The city posed both opportunity and frustration for middle-class women. Some became public-school teachers, secretaries, librarians, and telephone operators, pushing the number of women in white-collar jobs from 949,000 in 1900 to 3.4 million in 1920. More and more women earned college

degrees, and women made up 40 percent of the college population in 1910. But married urban middle-class women, hedged in by the demands of home and children and the ideology of domesticity, typically faced isolation and limited opportunity. The divorce rate crept up from one in twelve marriages in 1900 to one in nine by 1920. Many middle-class women who were mired in domestic routines joined white-collar and college-educated women in a resurgent women's movement.

Black Americans in a Racist Age

In 1900 more than two-thirds of the nation's 10 million blacks lived in the South as sharecroppers and tenant farmers. By 1910 the cotton boll weevil and ruinous floods had driven 20 percent of these southern blacks into cities. Urban black men took jobs in factories, mines, docks, and railroads or became carpenters or bricklayers, while African-American women became domestic servants, seamstresses, and laundry or tobacco workers. By 1910, 54 percent of America's black women worked.

"Jim Crow"—legally enforced racism—peaked in the early twentieth century. Segregation separated black from from white in most public areas, including streetcars, trains, schools, parks, and even cemeteries. Until the Supreme Court outlawed it in 1917, a number of southern cities had legally imposed residential segregation. In some courts, black and white witnesses even took the oath on separate Bibles. Trapped on a treadmill of poverty, poor education, and discrimination, and prevented from voting, southern blacks faced formidable obstacles.

Northern blacks, just over a million in number, encountered similar conditions. Racism had deepened after 1890 as depression and immigration heightened social tensions. Segregation, although not legally imposed, existed everywhere, supported by social pressure and occasional violence. Blacks lived in run-down "colored districts," attended dilapidated schools, and took the low-paying jobs. Although African-Americans voted, their allegiance to the Republican party gave them little influence. Even the newest mass medium, the movies, reinforced racism. D. W. Griffith's 1915 classic film *The Birth of a Nation* glorified the Ku Klux Klan and vilified and ridiculed blacks.

Smoldering racism occasionally ignited. In an antiblack riot in Atlanta in 1906, four African-Americans were murdered, many blacks' homes were burned, and the president of a black theological seminary was severely beaten by a white police officer. Lynchings had peaked in the late nineteenth century, but from 1900 to 1920 an average of about seventy-five lynchings occurred yearly. The victims were usually black men accused of murder, rape, or some other crime. Lynchings could involve incredible sadism, with large crowds attending to watch the victim's mutilation before he was killed.

In the face of adversity, blacks developed self-reliance and a strong support network. Their unique culture remained vigorous. Black religious life, centered in the African Methodist Episcopal church, provided a bulwark of support for many. Black colleges and universities, among them Fisk in Nashville and Howard in Washington, D.C., survived against heavy odds. The urban African-American community included black-owned insurance companies and banks and boasted a small elite of entrepreneurs, teachers, ministers, and lawyers. Blacks also rose socially through sports, among them Texan Jack Johnson, who won the heavyweight boxing championship in 1908.

New black musical idioms emerged. In addition to ragtime, the blues, rooted in the mournful chants of sharecroppers, gained recognition with the songs of W. C. Handy, including the classic "St. Louis Blues" (1914). Jazz gained popularity as well. Originating in New Orleans with the band of Buddy Bolden in the 1890s, jazz moved north to Chicago and other cities during World War I, eventually winning recognition as the United States' greatest musical achievement.

Corporate Boardrooms and Factory Floors

The process of consolidation that had produced Carnegie Steel and Standard Oil accelerated in the early twentieth century, with an average of 260 companies annually absorbed in mergers. Following the Carnegie Steel pattern, J. P. Morgan in 1902 consolidated six competing companies into the International Harvester Company, which controlled 85 percent of the farm-implement business. In 1908 William C. Durant founded the General Motors Company, which, backed financially by the Du

Pont Corporation, bought up automobile manufacturers ranging from the inexpensive Chevrolet to the luxury Cadillac.

Many workers benefited from the prevailing good times. Industrial workers' average real (adjusted for inflation) wages had risen from $532 in the late nineteenth century to $687 by 1915. But even with the dollar's buying power much higher than today—a loaf of bread cost a mere seven cents—such pay barely supported a family and left no cushion for emergencies.

To make ends meet, entire immigrant families went to work. Two-thirds of immigrant girls had entered the labor force in the early 1900s, working in factories, as domestics, and in laundries and bakeries. Although the figures are imprecise, by 1910 the nonfarm labor force included at least 1.6 million children aged ten to fifteen. One investigator found a girl of five working at night in a South Carolina textile mill.

For all laborers, the hours were long and the hazards great. In 1900 the average worker toiled 9½ hours a day; some southern textile mill workers put in 12- and 13-hour days. Few employers accepted responsibility for work-related accidents or injuries, and vacations and retirement benefits were rare. Generally, American capitalism extracted the maximum of labor from its work force and gave a bare minimum in return. Efficiency experts such as Frederick W. Taylor dreamed of making human workers as rational and predictable as machines.

Workers Organize; Socialism Advances

As workers continued to organize, the American Federation of Labor (AFL) grew from half a million members in 1897 to 4 million by 1920—but this was only 20 percent of the nonfarm labor force. With thousands of immigrants competing for jobs, union activities could be risky; bosses could easily fire an "agitator" and hire a newcomer. Judicial hostility also plagued the labor movement. In the 1908 *Danbury Hatters* case, a unanimous Supreme Court ruled that boycotts in support of strikes violated the Sherman Anti-Trust Act.

The AFL's strength continued to rest in the skilled trades, not in factory and mill work. Yet few unions tried to reach the unskilled laborers at the lowest end of the scale. In 1900 immigrants in New York organized the International Ladies' Garment Workers Union (ILGWU), which conducted successful strikes in 1909 and 1911.

The Industrial Workers of the World (IWW), or Wobblies, founded in Chicago in 1905 and led by William D. "Big Bill" Haywood, also targeted the most exploited workers. Never large, and torn by dissent, the IWW peaked at around 30,000 members, mainly western miners, lumbermen, fruit pickers, and itinerant laborers. Its greatest success came in 1912, when it won a rancorous textile strike in Lawrence, Massachusetts. The victory owed much to Elizabeth Gurley Flynn, a fervent Irish-American orator, and Margaret Sanger, the leader of the birth-control movement, who publicized the cause by sending strikers' children to New York sympathizers for temporary care.

The IWW preached revolution. In 1908 it proclaimed, "The struggle must go on until the workers of the world . . . take possession of the earth and the machinery of production, and abolish the wage system." The Wobblies had a reputation, much exaggerated, for violence and sabotage, and they faced unremitting harassment through arrests and prosecution by government officials. By 1920 the IWW's strength was broken.

Others appalled by capitalism's human toll turned to socialism. Socialists advocated an end to capitalism and demanded public ownership of factories, utilities, railroads, and communications systems. But American workers generally rejected the revolutionary ideology of German social theorist Karl Marx in favor of democratic socialism achieved at the ballot box. In 1900 democratic socialists formed the Socialist Party of America (SPA). Eugene V. Debs, the Indiana labor leader converted to socialism during his imprisonment after the Pullman strike, became the SPA's most popular spokesman and its candidate for president five times between 1900 and 1920. The pinnacle of socialist strength came in 1912, when the SPA counted

118,000 members, Debs received over 900,000 votes for president, and the Socialists elected a congressman along with hundreds of municipal officials.

The upsurge in Socialist votes was only one sign of rising discontent with politics-as-usual. As the problems created by industrialism became obvious, the demand that government do something grew insistent.

The Progressive Movement Takes Shape

As the twentieth century began, intellectuals increasingly challenged the ideological foundations of a business-oriented social order, and writers publicized industrialization's human toll. Reformers sought to make government more democratic, to eradicate unhealthful and dangerous conditions in cities and factories, and to curb corporate power. Overwhelmed by the diversity of these reform efforts and awed at the political energies they unleashed, Americans grouped them under a single label: the progressive movement.

Progressivism: An Overview

Progressivism was a political response to industrialization and its social results: immigration, urban growth, the concentration of corporate power, and the widening of class divisions. Unlike populism, born of agrarian unrest, progressivism found its strength in the cities. And the progressives were *reformers*, not radicals or revolutionaries. They wanted to remedy the evils spawned by unregulated capitalism, not to destroy the system.

Progressivism never became a cohesive movement with a unified program; it remained a diverse array of reform activities that sometimes overlapped and sometimes sharply diverged. Many reformers insisted that the preservation of democracy required stricter regulation of business; others, emphasizing humanitarian themes, called for legislation to protect workers and the urban poor. Still others concentrated on reforming the structure of government, especially at the municipal level. And some, seeing immigration, urban immorality, and social disorder as the central problems, advocated social-control strategies such as immigration restriction and the abolition of prostitution and saloons.

The progressives themselves were a diverse lot, aligned in coalitions that shifted from issue to issue. At the center of the movement stood the native-born Protestant middle class. However, the urban-immigrant political machines provided critical support on issues affecting factory workers and slum conditions, and even corporate leaders at times helped to devise business-regulation measures, especially when pressures for such regulation became irresistible.

Public-citizen groups such as the American League for Civic Improvement provided the first impetus for reform. In an era of organizations, the roots of progressivism not surprisingly came from this organizational impulse. All the major progressive reforms, from woman suffrage and the abolition of child labor to prohibition, drew strength from such organizations.

Closely related to this organizational impulse was the progressive emphasis on a "scientific" approach to social problems. Scientific and technological expertise had shaped the industrial revolution, and progressives believed that such expertise would solve the social problems that industrialism had left in its wake. Progressives marshaled social research, expert opinion, and statistical data to support their causes.

Some historians, stressing the technological and managerial aspects of progressivism, portray the movement as an example of an organizing stage through which all modernizing societies pass. This is a useful interpretation, but one must remember that "progressivism" did not unfold automatically, independently of human will. Earnest and energetic leaders, journalists, ministers, and organizers all made a difference. Human drive and emotion propelled the movement forward. Progressivism, then, is not an impersonal historical abstraction but a useful term for the activities and concerns of thousands of individual Americans in the early twentieth century.

Intellectuals Lay the Groundwork

Building on the work of Lester Ward, Edward Bellamy, and the Social Gospel leaders, brilliant turn-of-the-century thinkers helped to reorient American social thought and laid the ideological foundation for progressivism.

William Graham Sumner and other Social Darwinists had argued that "survival of the fittest" justified unrestrained economic competition. Ward had begun the intellectual attack against these ideas, and the assault intensified in the opening years of the new century. Scholars in many disciplines produced work skeptical of the established order and implicitly supporting far-reaching changes.

Thorstein Veblen, a Norwegian-American, was prominent among the reshapers of economic thought. In *The Theory of the Leisure Class* (1899), he assailed the values and life-styles of the Gilded Age elite, and their "conspicuous consumption." In later writings he argued that engineers, molded by the stern discipline of the machine, were better fitted to lead society than was the business class. Veblen epitomized the admiration of efficiency, science, and technical expertise that lay at the heart of the progressive impulse.

Historians also contributed to the new currents of thought that fed into progressivism. In "The Significance of the Frontier in American History" (see Chapter 17), Frederick Jackson Turner argued that the social and political experience of generations of western pioneers constituted the central dynamic of American history. Equally influential in this historical revisionism were Mary Ritter Beard and her husband, Charles A. Beard. In such books as *Woman's Work in Municipalities* (1915) and *A Short History of the American Labor Movement* (1920), Mary Beard spotlighted groups ignored by traditional historians. In *An Economic Interpretation of the Constitution* (1913), Charles A. Beard gave ammunition to the progressive critics of big business by arguing that the Constitution makers of 1787 had served the interests of the moneyed class of their day.

Harvard philosopher William James also contributed to this intellectual reconstruction in his seminal work *Pragmatism* (1907), which argued that truth emerges neither from universal laws nor abstract theories but from experience. Truth is what *works*. James's emphasis on the fluidity of knowledge and the importance of practical action contributed to the progressive model of skepticism toward established ideologies. Reformer Jane Addams, James believed, exemplified his pragmatic philosophy. While others theorize about reality, he wrote to her, "you *inhabit* reality." In *Democracy and Social Ethics* (1902), Addams rejected individualistic morality and called for a new social ideology rooted in awareness of modern society's complex interdependence.

More than anyone else, Herbert Croly embodied the progressive faith in the power of ideas to transform society. In his masterpiece, *The Promise of American Life* (1909), Croly called for an activist federal government that would serve *all* citizens, not just the capitalist class. To build public support for such a transformed conception of government, Croly argued, socially engaged intellectuals must play a key role.

New Ideas About Education and the Law

With public-school enrollment leaping from 7 million children in 1870 to more than 23 million by 1920, progressive intellectuals realized that schools could be a powerful engine of social change. Chief among educational reformers was the philosopher John Dewey, who insisted that the intelligent application of the scientific method to social problems could build a just and harmonious society. Viewing intelligence above all as an instrument of social action, he called his philosophy Instrumentalism.

Public schools could lead to significant reform if they embraced the new ethic of social interdependence, Dewey maintained. Banishing bolted-down chairs and desks from the model school that he started at the University of Chicago in 1896, he encouraged children to move around the room, to ask questions, and to interact with each other as well as with the teacher. In *Democracy and Education* (1916), Dewey argued that schools must embody the values of democracy and cooperation through their methods and curriculum. In the ideal school, children would work together in a harmonious process of intellectual inquiry and social growth.

This mood of civic idealism spread across colleges and universities as well. No longer could the university be a "home of useless and harmless recluses," one university president emphasized; it must dedicate itself to the public good. Princeton's president Woodrow Wilson summed up the new spirit in his 1902 inaugural address, "Princeton for the Nation's Service."

Even the natural sciences felt the pull of social activism. A Massachusetts Institute of Technology chemist, Ellen Richards, applied chemistry to the issues of nutrition, food adulteration, and public hygiene. Statisticians used their skills to study labor conditions, epidemic diseases, and urban housing density.

New ideas influenced the legal profession as well. Instead of citing ancient precedent, according to Oliver Wendell Holmes, Jr., in his influential *The Common Law* (1881), jurists must recognize that law evolves as society changes. "The life of the law has not been logic; it has been experience," he argued. Appointed to the Supreme Court in 1902 as the Progressive Era began, Holmes wrote eloquent dissents from the conservative majority, establishing the framework for a more flexible view.

Novelists and Journalists Spread the Word

As intellectuals chipped away at laissez-faire ideology and laid the foundations for a new social ethic, novelists and journalists helped to transform progressivism into a national movement by revealing to middle-class readers the seamy details of corporate wrongdoing and the harsh realities of slum and factory life. Henry Demarest Lloyd's *Wealth and Commonwealth* (1894), a biting exposé of the Standard Oil Company, was a pathbreaking early work. Novelists followed with compelling indictments of corporate greed and heedless urban growth. In *The Octopus* (1901), Frank Norris portrayed the struggle

between wheat growers and railroad owners. David Graham Phillips's *Susan Lenox: Her Fall and Rise* (1917) explored links between slum life, political corruption, and prostitution. Theodore Dreiser's *The Financier* (1912) portrayed a hard-driving business tycoon devoid of social consciousness.

Mass-circulation magazines such as *McClure's*, *Cosmopolitan*, and *Everybody's* published expansive articles exposing political corruption and corporate wrongdoing. President Theodore Roosevelt, thinking some of these articles too one-sided, christened their authors "muckrakers" after a character in John Bunyan's *Pilgrim's Progress* who spends all his time raking up filth. The name became a badge of honor. The muckrakers' stark prose emphasized facts rather than abstractions. For example, in a 1903 series on working women, Maria Van Vorst offered a gripping account of a shoe factory where women's fingernails literally rotted off because the female employees had to immerse their hands in caustic dyes.

The muckrakers touched a nerve. *McClure's* circulation soared to 750,000 and *Cosmopolitan's* to more than a million during their heyday in 1901–1903. Many magazine exposés appeared in book form, including Lincoln Steffens's *The Shame of the Cities* (1904), Ida Tarbell's damning *History of the Standard Oil Company* (1904), and David Graham Phillips's *Treason of the Senate* (1906). In 1914 Herbert Croly founded *The New Republic* magazine, which provided a forum for reformist intellectuals.

Reforming the Political Process

The progressive movement had begun in the 1890s in well-to-do city neighborhoods as the urban elite and middle classes crusaded against political bosses. A succession of anti-Tammany reform waves set off by Protestant clergy had swept New York City. In Detroit, the reform administration of Mayor Hazen Pingree (1890–1897) had brought honesty to city hall, lowered transit fares, and made the tax structure more equitable. The shrewd Pingree once slapped a health quarantine on a brothel where a local business leader was paying a visit, and refused to let the man leave until he promised to drop his opposition to Pingree's reforms.

The municipal-reform impulse strengthened after 1900. In 1907 San Francisco newspaper editor Fremont Older crusaded against the city's notoriously corrupt boss, Mayor Abe Reuf. Attorney Hiram Johnson, who took over the prosecution of the Reuf machine when the original prosecutor was gunned down in court, obtained a conviction of Mayor Reuf and his cronies. Sternly self-righteous, Johnson embodied the reform fervor of the day—one observer called him "a volcano in perpetual eruption"—and he rode the Reuf case to the California governorship and the United States Senate. In Toledo, Ohio, a colorful eccentric named Samuel M. "Golden Rule" Jones led the reform crusade. A self-made businessman converted to the Social Gospel, Jones introduced profit sharing in his factory; as mayor, he established playgrounds, free kindergartens, lodging houses for tramps, and an open-air church for all faiths.

As the urban reform movement matured, it systematically attacked the roots of urban misgovernment, including the uncontrolled private monopolies that provided such basic services as water, gas, electricity, and public transportation. Reformers passed laws regulating the rates that utilities could charge, taxing them more equitably, and curbing their political influence. Reformers also advocated, and sometimes achieved, the public ownership of utilities.

Reflecting the progressive enthusiasm for expertise and efficiency, some reformers advocated *structural* changes in city government. They wanted to replace mayors and aldermen elected on a ward-by-ward basis with professional managers and administrators chosen in citywide elections. Supposedly above politics, these experts were expected to run the city like an efficient business.

Virtually all elements of the urban population participated in reform. The native-born middle class provided the initial impetus for urban beautification and political reform. Business leaders often

supported city-manager systems and citywide elections—structural changes that diminished the power of the ward bosses and increased that of the corporate elite. On matters of practical concern such as municipal services, immigrants and even political bosses supported the new urban-reform movement.

Municipal reform soon expanded to electoral reform at the state level. By 1910 all states had instituted secret ballots, making it much harder than before to rig elections. Another widely adopted Progressive Era reform was the direct primary, in which party members rather than leaders selected nominees for public office. And some western states inaugurated electoral reforms known as initiative, referendum, and recall, by which voters could, respectively, enact laws directly, decide whether to accept or reject a law, and kick public officials out of office. The culmination of this flurry of electoral reforms came in 1913 with the ratification of the Seventeenth Amendment to the Constitution, which shifted the election of U.S. senators from state legislatures to the voters at large.

These electoral changes produced mixed results. They were meant to democratize voting, but party leaders and organized interest groups learned to manipulate the new electoral machinery. Ironically, the new procedures appear primarily to have weakened party loyalties and reduced voter interest. Overall voter-participation rates declined steeply in the early twentieth century, but political activity by organized groups increased.

Reforming Society and City

If issues of municipal government, utility regulation, and electoral reform represented the brain of progressivism, the impetus to improve conditions in factories, mills, and slums represented its heart. By 1907 thirty states had abolished child labor. A 1903 Oregon law limited women in industry to a ten-hour workday. Other reforms concentrated on industrial safety, welfare programs, and disability benefits for workers injured on the job.

Political bosses in cities with heavy immigrant populations supported such legislation. State senator Robert F. Wagner, a leader of New York City's Tammany Hall machine, headed the New York State Factory Investigating Committee. Thanks to this committee's efforts, New York enacted fifty-six worker-protection laws, tightening factory-safety standards, permitting pregnancy leaves, and requiring chairs with backs for garment workers. By 1914 twenty-five states had passed laws making employers liable for job-related injuries or deaths.

City reformers worked for practical goals such as better garbage collection and street cleaning, milk inspection, public-health programs, and housing codes. Urban-beautification advocates campaigned for new parks, boulevards, and streetlights and against billboards, smoky factories, and unsightly overhead wires. Daniel Burnham, the developer of innovative city plans for San Francisco and Cleveland, recognized that such blueprints had to be bold and comprehensive in order to capture the public imagination. His proposed plan for Chicago incorporated a completely new layout that would make the city both efficient and aesthetically harmonious. In Burnham's vision, Chicago's focal point would be a new civic center containing a majestic city hall and a vast plaza. Many features of his plan eventually became reality as Chicago spent more than $300 million on urban-development projects between 1910 and 1920. Other urban beautifiers of the Progressive Era shared Burnham's belief that broad boulevards, imposing squares, and monumental civic buildings would restore public pride in metropolitan America.

Corporate Regulation

Progressives also believed that big business was out of control. Few wanted to destroy the giant corporations, but many became convinced that these enterprises that had benefited so enormously from the government's economic policies should be subject to government supervision. One state after another enacted legislation regulating railroads, mines, mills, telephone companies, and other businesses. Public-health officials, factory investigators, and other regulators monitored corporate America as never before.

Under Governor Robert La Follette (1901–1906), Wisconsin exemplified this process. A former Republican member of Congress, "Fighting Bob" was elected governor as an independent in 1900. Soon he was transforming state government just as reform mayors had transformed municipal government. Challenging the business interests long dominant in Wisconsin politics, the La Follette administration adopted the direct-primary system, set up a commission to regulate railroads operating within the state, increased corporate taxes, and passed a law limiting campaign spending.

Regulating national corporations at the municipal and state levels posed obvious problems. Once progressivism reached into national politics, however, the regulatory impulse, rooted in grass-roots activism, moved to the center of the reform agenda.

Progressivism and Social Control: The Movement's Coercive Dimension

Progressives believed that they could restore order to urban-industrial society through research, legislation, and enlightened social tinkering. This outlook gave progressivism a repressive and strongly moralistic edge; whereas some progressives focused on such issues as child labor and corporate regulation, others became obsessed with personal behavior and sought to impose morality by law.

Moral Control in the Cities

Quaint as they seem today, early movies, some of them featuring sexuality, struck many middle-class Americans as dangerously immoral. The shabbiness of the immigrant-district five-cent movie halls, called nickelodeons, intensified such feelings. But a New York garment worker who lived with her Italian immigrant parents recalled, "The one place I was allowed to go by myself was the movies. My parents wouldn't let me go anywhere else, even when I

Old-Time Movies

Early moviegoers were greeted by humorous lantern slides attempting to instill good behavior.

was twenty-four." This freedom from moral oversight was precisely what worried progressives. Warning of "nickel madness," they demanded film censorship. Several states did establish censorship boards, and Chicago empowered its police chief to ban movies that he considered immoral.

Targeting prostitution, too, the moral reformers, in true progressive fashion, investigated and quantified "the social evil." The American Social Hygiene Association (1914), financed by John D. Rockefeller, sponsored medical research on sexually transmitted diseases, underwrote "vice investigations" in various cities, and drafted model municipal statutes against prostitution. Soon a "white slave" hysteria gripped the country. Sensationalizing books, articles, and films warned that innocent farm girls were being kidnapped and forced into a life of sin in the city. The Mann Act (1910) made it a federal crime to transport a woman across a state line "for immoral purposes." Amid much fanfare, the red-light districts of New Orleans, Chicago, and other cities were shut down or forced to operate more discreetly.

The progressive moral-control movement reached its zenith with the prohibition crusade.

Temperance had long loomed large on the American reform agenda, but during the Progressive Era reformers' energies shifted to the legal abolition of alcoholic beverages.

The Anti-Saloon League (ASL), founded in 1895, was a typical progressive organization, with full-time professionals staffing a national office and Protestant ministers serving on a network of state committees. ASL presses produced tons of propaganda documenting the role of alcohol and the saloon in health problems, family disorder, political corruption, and workplace inefficiency and championing nationwide prohibition as a legislative cure-all. Supported by the Woman's Christian Temperance Union and influential church agencies, the ASL crusade led to the passage (1918) and ratification (1919) of the Eighteenth Amendment, outlawing the manufacture, sale, and transport of alcoholic beverages (see Chapter 23).

Immigration Restriction and Eugenics

The obvious answer to the threats posed by the immigrant city, some reformers concluded, lay in excluding immigrants. Many, though not all, progressives supported immigration restriction. Those who did documented their case with a flourish of scientific expertise. In 1911 a congressional commission produced a statistical study "proving" the new immigrants' innate degeneracy. In 1914 the progressive sociologist Edward A. Ross described recent immigrants as "hirsute, low-browed, big-faced persons of obviously low mentality." In 1896, 1913, and 1915, Congress passed literacy-test bills aimed at slowing immigration, but they fell victim to veto by a succession of presidents. In 1917, however, such a bill became law over President Wilson's veto. This, too, was part of progressivism's ambiguous legacy.

The most sinister perversion of "science" in the Progressive Era was the eugenics movement. Eugenics is the control of reproduction to alter the characteristics of a plant or animal species. Some American eugenicists believed that controlled breeding could also improve society. In 1904 the Carnegie Foundation funded a research center to study heredity and genetic manipulation. Its director, zoologist Charles B. Davenport, was a racist, an anti-Semite, and an advocate of immigration restriction. Yet inspired by Davenport and other eugenicists, some states legalized the forced sterilization of criminals, sex offenders, and the mentally deficient. A 1927 Supreme Court case upheld such laws.

This ugly underside of early-twentieth-century thought was plainly revealed in Madison Grant's *The Passing of the Great Race* (1916). In many ways Grant, a patrician supporter of numerous civic causes, represented the best in progressivism. In *The Passing*, however, he stirred together a rancid brew of pseudoscientific data and spewed out a vicious diatribe against Jews, blacks, and southern and eastern Europeans. Grant called for absolute racial segregation, immigration restriction, and the forced sterilization of "unfit" groups, including "worthless race types." He chillingly previewed the ideas that Adolf Hitler would one day bring to fruition.

Racism and Progressivism

As Grant's work suggests, racism rose to a high pitch during the Progressive Era. Taken as a whole, the progressive movement did little as blacks were lynched, disfranchised, and discriminated against. For many progressives, blacks represented a source of social menace to be studied, controlled, and kept out of public life.

In the South, progressives often led the movement for black disfranchisement and segregation. Numerous southern politicians backed a variety of progressive reforms while simultaneously pursuing viciously antiblack policies. In Washington, D.C., racism pervaded the administration of Woodrow Wilson (1913–1921). The southern-born Wilson displayed a patronizing attitude toward blacks and acquiesced as southerners in his cabinet and in Congress imposed rigid segregation on all levels of the government.

But some progressives spoke up eloquently for immigrants and blacks. Settlement-house worker Mary White Ovington helped to found the National Association for the Advancement of Colored People and wrote *Half a Man* (1911), a study of the effects of racial prejudice on New York City's blacks. Progressive social thought nevertheless included some disturbing ingredients—an assurance of moral and intellectual superiority, an exaggerated confidence in the social application of science, a readiness to use state power to coerce individual behavior—that all too readily could turn repressive and destructive.

Blacks and Women Organize

The early twentieth century was a time of intense organizational activity and intellectual ferment for blacks and women, especially those of the urban middle class. Both groups had ample cause for dissatisfaction, and among both, movements flowered to address those grievances.

Controversy in Black America

The nation's foremost black leader from the 1890s until his death in 1915 was Booker T. Washington. Born into slavery in Virginia in 1856, the son of a slave woman and her white master, Washington enrolled at a freedman's school in Hampton, Virginia, in 1872. In 1881 he organized a state vocational school in Tuskegee, Alabama, that became Tuskegee University.

Washington attained prominence in 1895 when he gave an address in Atlanta insisting that the first task of African-Americans must be that of acquiring vocational skills. Once blacks proved their economic value, he predicted, racism would ebb; meanwhile, they must accept their lot. Although Washington's "Atlanta Compromise" publicly urged accommodation to a racist society, he secretly contributed to organizations fighting racial discrimination.

Much admired by white America, Washington traveled and lectured widely. His autobiography, *Up from Slavery* (1901), recounted his rise from poverty through honesty, hard work, and the help of kindly patrons—familiar themes to a generation of white readers reared on Horatio Alger. But blacks were divided over Washington's program. Although many southern blacks revered Washington, some northern blacks challenged his dominance. With racism escalating and blacks' status declining, Washington's philosophy of accommodation and his optimistic predictions seemed unrealistic to critics, one of whom wrote in 1902 that Washington's acceptance of black disfranchisement struck "a fatal blow . . . to the Negro's political rights and liberty."

Washington's most powerful challenge came from W. E. B. Du Bois (1868–1963). A cultivated scholar, Du Bois set forth his differences with Washington in *The Souls of Black Folk* (1903). Rejecting Washington's call for patience and the cultivation of manual skills, Du Bois demanded full access for blacks to the same educational advantages and intellectual opportunities open to whites. Blacks must struggle ceaselessly against all forms of racial discrimination, he argued. In his assertiveness and militance, Du Bois set the direction of black activism in the new century.

The Founding of the NAACP

In the 1890s the Afro-American Council served as a forum for blacks who favored vigorous resistance to racism, but when Booker T. Washington gained control of the organization, his opponents turned elsewhere. In 1905, under Du Bois's leadership, these challengers met at Niagara Falls, and for the next few years participants in the "Niagara Movement" convened annually.

A small group of white reformers also rejected Washington's cautiousness, including newspaper publisher Oswald Garrison Villard, the grandson of abolitionist William Lloyd Garrison. In 1909 Villard and his allies, including Mary White Ovington, joined with Du Bois and other blacks from the Niagara Movement to form the National Association for the Advancement of Colored People (NAACP). Rejecting Washington's accommodationist policy, the NAACP called for full political equality for African-Americans and an end to racial discrimination. Attracting the urban black middle class, the NAACP by 1914 had 6,000 members.

Revival of the Woman-Suffrage Movement

As late as 1910, women could vote in only four sparsely populated western states: Wyoming, Utah, Colorado, and Idaho. Six states voted down referenda on woman suffrage after 1896, but onrushing social and ideological currents infused the suffrage movement with new vitality after 1900. Middle-class women found it absurd that they could not vote, particularly because recently arrived (and often uneducated) immigrant men could. A vigorous suffrage movement in Great Britain therefore reverberated on this side of the Atlantic. Women's leadership in the larger progressive movement, moreover, powerfully boosted the cause.

The renewal of the women's movement began at the grass roots. In big cities such as New York and Chicago, suffragists used street meetings and parades to gain publicity. A new generation of leaders, drawing on the rhetoric of progressive reform, translated this energy into a revitalized national movement. Under Carrie Chapman Catt, who succeeded Susan B. Anthony as president of the National American Woman Suffrage Association (NAWSA) in 1900, the movement adopted the so-called Winning Plan: grass-roots organization with centralized coordination.

Following a strategy devised in NAWSA's executive office, women nationwide lobbied legislators, distributed literature, conducted referenda, and organized marches and rallies. State after state fell into the suffrage column. A key victory came in 1917 when New York State voters approved a woman-suffrage referendum. Although a few black and immigrant women participated at the local level, NAWSA's membership remained largely white, native born, and middle class.

Not all suffragists accepted Catt's strategy. Alice Paul, who admired the militancy of British suffragists while a student in Great Britain, became a leading dissenter. Ambitious for leadership and

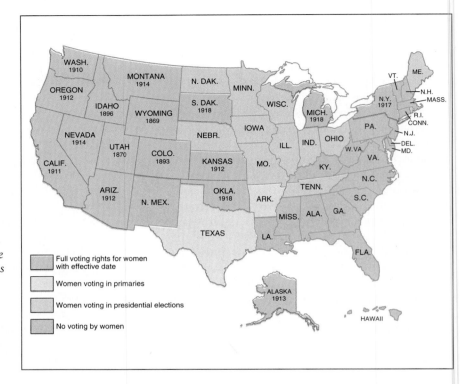

Woman Suffrage Before the Nineteenth Amendment

Beginning with Wyoming in 1869, woman suffrage made steady gains in western states before 1920. In the East key breakthroughs came in New York (1917) and Michigan (1918). The South remained an anti-woman-suffrage bastion throughout the period.

impatient with NAWSA's state-by-state approach, Paul in 1913 founded the Congressional Union, later renamed the Woman's party, to bring direct pressure on the federal government to enact a woman-suffrage amendment. Insisting that the party in power—the Democrats under President Woodrow Wilson—must be held accountable for the continued denial of votes to women, Paul and her followers picketed the White House around the clock in the wartime year 1917. Several demonstrators were arrested, jailed, and, when they went on a hunger strike, force-fed.

Thanks in part to women's active participation in the war effort (see Chapter 23), the tide turned. The Nineteenth Amendment, granting women the vote, passed Congress in 1919 and was ratified by August 1920. That November, seventy-two years after the first American women's rights convention

(at Seneca Falls, New York, in 1848), women all across America at last went to the polls.

Breaking Out of the "Woman's Sphere"

The suffrage movement did not exhaust American women's talents or organizational energies. Organizations such as the General Federation of Women's Clubs and the National Association of Colored Women grew briskly in the early twentieth century. Women's club members, settlement-house leaders, and individual female activists joined in various campaigns: to bring playgrounds and day nurseries to the slums, to abolish child labor, to improve conditions for women workers, and to ban unsafe foods and quack remedies.

Entrenched cultural assumptions about "woman's sphere" crumbled as women became active on many fronts. Katherine Bement Davis served as the innovative superintendent of a woman's reformatory before becoming New York City's commissioner of corrections. Anarchist Emma Goldman crisscrossed the country delivering riveting lectures on politics, feminism, and modern drama while coediting a radical monthly, *Mother Earth*. And in 1914 Margaret Sanger began a campaign for birth control, a term that she coined. A nurse and radical feminist, Sanger had witnessed the tragedy of unwanted pregnancies among slum women. In 1916 she opened the nation's first birth-control clinic, in Brooklyn, New York.

Leading feminist intellectual Charlotte Perkins Gilman, in her book *Women and Economics* (1898), traced the history of sexual discrimination, explored the cultural process of gender stereotyping, and linked the legal, political, and social subordination of women to their economic dependence on men. Gilman argued that confining women to the domestic sphere was outdated. She advocated women's economic independence through equality in the workplace and state-run day-care centers.

Two women especially typified the varied roles of women in progressive reform: Alice Hamilton and Florence Kelley. A bacteriologist and professor at Northwestern University, Hamilton was a close associate of Jane Addams at Hull House. In 1910, combining her scientific expertise with her social-welfare advocacy, Hamilton conducted a pathbreaking study of lead poisoning in industry. Appointed an investigator for the U.S. Bureau of Labor in 1911, she became an expert on, and tireless campaigner against, work-related health hazards.

In 1893 the investigations by Florence Kelley of conditions in factories and tenement workhouses helped to secure passage of an Illinois law prohibiting child labor and limiting working hours for women. In 1899 she became general secretary of the National Consumers' League, which lobbied for improved factory conditions. Kelley angrily asked, "Why are seals, bears, reindeer, fish, wild game in the national parks, buffalo, [and] migratory birds all found suitable for federal protection, but not

Birth-Control Pioneer Margaret Sanger (1883–1966)
One of eleven children, Sanger saw her exhausted mother die at age forty-nine. Sanger's National Birth Control League was the forerunner of the Planned Parenthood Federation of America.

children?" Her efforts did much to awaken Americans to the evils of child labor.

National Progressivism—Phase I: Roosevelt and Taft

By 1905 localized reform movements coalesced into a national effort. Symbolically, in 1906 Robert La

Follette became a United States senator. He arrived in Washington as progressivism found its first national leader, Theodore Roosevelt.

Bombastic, self-righteous, and jingoistic—but also brilliant, politically masterful, and endlessly interesting—Roosevelt, "TR," became president in 1901. He made the White House a volcano of political activism. Skillfully orchestrating public opinion, the popular young president pursued his goals: labor mediation, consumer protection, conservation, business virtue, and activism abroad. TR's hand-picked successor, William Howard Taft, lacked his master's political genius, however, and sniping among former allies marred his term.

Roosevelt's Path to the White House

On September 6, 1901, in Buffalo, an anarchist shot then-president William McKinley. At first McKinley's survival seemed certain, so Vice President Theodore Roosevelt proceeded with a hiking trip into the Adirondack Mountains. Then an urgent message about McKinley's worsening condition propelled Roosevelt out of the mountains on a breakneck journey by horse and wagon, and by train to Buffalo. On September 14 the forty-two-year-old Roosevelt took the presidential oath.

Reflecting the view of many politicians, Republican kingmaker Mark Hanna exclaimed, "My God, that damned cowboy in the White House!" Although Roosevelt was in fact the son of an aristocratic New York family, his emphasis on vigor and physical fitness reflected his love of the West. After a sickly childhood, Roosevelt used a body-building program and active summers in Wyoming to develop a strong physique. Later, two years on a Dakota ranch helped him to struggle past grief over his young wife's death in 1884 and nurtured the physical and mental toughness that he would later extol as "the strenuous life."

Plunging into politics when most of his social class considered it unbefitting gentlemen, Roosevelt held various posts in New York State before leading the Rough Riders in Cuba. He was elected New York's governor in 1898. Republican bosses, unsettled by this human dynamo, shunted him off to the limbo of the vice presidency in 1900. Angry at the maneuver, Roosevelt sputtered, "I would a great deal rather be anything, say a history professor, than Vice President."

Unexpectedly thrust into the White House, TR energized the presidency. "While President I have been President emphatically . . . ," he boasted; "I believe in a strong executive." Roosevelt enjoyed public life and loved the limelight. As a relative wryly observed, he wanted to be the bride at every wedding and the corpse at every funeral. Americans were fascinated by their rambunctious young president, with his toothy grin, machine-gun speech, and passion for the outdoors. After Teddy Roosevelt, the presidency was never quite the same. He enlarged the office in ways that permanently affected the balance of power within American government.

Roosevelt the Labor Mediator

The new president's political skills were quickly tested. In May 1902 the United Mine Workers Union (UMW) called a strike to gain higher wages, shorter hours, and recognition as a union. The mine owners refused to talk to UMW leaders. After five months, with coal reserves dwindling, TR summoned the deadlocked parties to the White House. Threatening to take over the mines, he won their reluctant acceptance of an arbitration commission to settle the dispute. In 1903 the commission granted miners a 10 percent wage hike and reduced their workday to nine hours.

TR approached such labor disputes very differently from his predecessors, who had called out federal troops to break strikes. He defended labor's right to organize, and when a well-known mine owner sanctimoniously claimed that miners' welfare could safely be left to "the Christian men to whom God in his infinite wisdom has given control of the property interests of the country," Roosevelt bristled at such "arrogant stupidity."

Trustbusting and Corporate Regulation

With his privileged social background, TR neither feared nor much respected the capitalists who had clawed their way to the top in Gilded Age America. Conservative at heart, he had no desire to abolish big corporations, but he embraced the progressive philosophy that corporate behavior must be carefully regulated. A strict moralist, he believed that corporations, like individuals, must meet a high standard of virtue.

As a political realist, Roosevelt recognized that many politicians did not share his views. Roosevelt's presidency was a story of continuing tension between his aristocratic conservatism, his gradual identification with progressive ideas, his moralism, and his recognition of the realities in capitalist America. The first test soon came.

The formation in 1901 of the United States Steel Company, the nation's first billion-dollar corporation, deepened public uneasiness over business consolidation. Dashing to the head of the parade, TR used his first State of the Union message to advocate "trustbusting," the break-up of business monopolies. In February 1902 Roosevelt's attorney general filed suit against the Northern Securities Company, a mammoth holding company formed to control railroading in the Northwest. To Roosevelt, the company clearly violated the Sherman Anti-Trust Act. He called for a "square deal" for all Americans and denounced special treatment for powerful capitalists. "We don't wish to destroy corporations," he insisted, "but we do wish to make them serve the public good." In 1904, by a 5–4 vote, the Supreme Court ordered the Northern Securities Company dissolved.

The Roosevelt administration sued forty-three other companies for violating the antitrust law. In two key cases in 1911, the Court ordered the breakup of the Standard Oil Company, the grand-daddy of all trusts, and the reorganization of the American Tobacco Company to make it less monopolistic.

As the 1904 presidential election approached, Roosevelt made peace with the Republicans' big-business wing. When the convention that unanimously nominated Roosevelt adopted a conservative, probusiness platform, $2 million in corporate campaign contributions poured in. The conservative-dominated Democrats meanwhile rejected William Jennings Bryan, nominated New York judge Alton B. Parker, and wrote a platform firmly embracing the gold standard.

Easily defeating Parker, Roosevelt turned to one of his major goals: railroad regulation. He saw regulation rather than trustbusting as the most promising long-term role for government and viewed antitrust suits as a means of compelling corporations to accept regulation. His work for passage of the Hepburn Act (1906) reflected this shift in outlook. The Hepburn Act tightened railroad regulation by empowering the Interstate Commerce Commission to set maximum railroad rates and to examine railroads' financial records. It also required standardized bookkeeping to make such inspection easy, and it curtailed the distribution of free passes. Although the measure did not entirely satisfy some reformers, it significantly increased government's ability to regulate the railroads.

Consumer Protection and Racial Issues

No progressive reform aroused a more visceral response than the fight against unsafe and falsely

The Election of 1904

Candidates	Parties	Electoral Vote	Popular Vote	Percentage of Popular Vote
THEODORE ROOSEVELT	Republican	336	7,628,461	57.4
Alton B. Parker	Democratic	140	5,084,223	37.6
Eugene V. Debs	Socialist		402,283	3.0
Silas C. Swallow	Prohibition		258,536	1.9

labeled food, drugs, and medicine. Upton Sinclair's *The Jungle* (1906) turned Americans' stomachs by describing the foul conditions under which their sausages and cold cuts were produced. In a vivid passage, Sinclair wrote, "It was too dark in these [packing-house] storage places to see well, but a man could run his hand over these piles of meat and sweep off handfuls of dried dung of rats. These rats were nuisances, and the packers would put poisoned bread out for them, they would die, and then rats, bread, and meat would go into the hoppers together." A socialist, Sinclair had intended his book to publicize the exploitation of immigrant workers, but most readers focused on the unsanitary packinghouse conditions he described. "I aimed at the nation's heart, but hit it in the stomach," he lamented.

Other muckrakers exposed useless, sometimes dangerous, patent medicines. Many popular nostrums, including children's medicines, contained cocaine, opium, and alcohol. "Colden's Liquid Beef Tonic," for example, "recommended for treatment of the alcohol habit," itself contained 26.5 percent alcohol. Peddlers of these potions claimed that they could cure cancer, grow hair, and restore sexual potency.

Ever sensitive to the public mood, Roosevelt strongly endorsed the Pure Food and Drug Act and the Meat Inspection Act, both passed in 1906. The former outlawed the sale of adulterated food and drugs and required the accurate labeling of ingredients; the latter imposed strict sanitary requirements for meatpackers, set up a quality-rating system, and created a program of federal meat inspection.

On racial matters, Roosevelt's record was marginally better than that of many other politicians in this racist age. On the positive side, he appointed an African-American as the head of the Charleston customhouse and closed a Mississippi post office rather than yield to racist demands that he dismiss the black postmistress. In a gesture of symbolic import, he met with Booker T. Washington at the White House. The worst blot on his record came in 1906, when he summarily discharged an entire regiment of black army troops charged with rioting in Brownsville, Texas.

The Conservation Movement

By 1900 decades of urban-industrial growth and western expansion had taken a heavy toll on the land. In the West, controversy over land use spilled into the political arena as mining and timber interests, farmers, ranchers, sheep growers, city officials, and preservationists advanced competing claims.

Western business interests and boosters preached the maximum exploitation of the region's resources, but the Sierra Club and other wilderness-protection groups sought to preserve large wild areas for their pristine beauty. After Congress in 1891 authorized the president to designate public lands as forest reserves, presidents Harrison and Cleveland set aside 35 million acres.

A wilderness vogue swept the United States in the early twentieth century. From their congested cities and clanging factories, Americans looked to the wilderness, with its unspoiled lakes, virgin forests, and inspiring vistas, for tranquillity and spiritual solace. Popular writers evoked the tang of the campfire and the lure of the primitive, and the Boy Scouts (1910) and Girl Scouts (1912) gave city children a taste of the outdoors.

The zest for wilderness colored the politics of the era. Resource-management issues pitted state and local authorities against the federal government. Local politicians, echoing their region's business groups, charged that mushy-headed preservationists were setting aside so much wilderness land that western economic development was suffering.

Between the wilderness enthusiasts and the proponents of unrestrained development stood a growing cadre of government professionals who saw the public domain as a resource to be managed scientifically. This characteristically progressive view found its ablest advocate in Gifford Pinchot. Named head of the new U.S. Forest Service in 1895, Pinchot campaigned for conservation—the planned, regulated use of forests for various public and commercial purposes.

Wilderness advocates saw Pinchot's Forest Service as a safeguard against mindless exploitation but

**Theodore Roosevelt
(1858–1919) and John
Muir (1838–1914) at
Yosemite**
*The conservation-minded
politician and naturalist-
conservationist pose on the
rim of Yosemite Valley.*

worried that commercial development would ruin unspoiled nature and erase its intangible benefits. A Sierra Club member wrote, "It is true that trees are for human use. But there are aesthetic uses as well as commercial ones—uses for the spiritual wealth of us all, as well as for the material wealth of some." But the professional conservationists dismissed such wilderness advocates as sentimental amateurs.

By temperament, President Roosevelt was a preservationist, a champion of wilderness and wildlife preservation. "When I hear of the destruction of a species," he wrote, "I feel just as if all the works of some greater writer had perished." However, Roosevelt the politician understood the conservationists' call for the planned development of natural resources. In this spirit he supported the National Reclamation Act of 1902, which earmarked the proceeds of public-land sales for water management in the Southwest and established the Reclamation Service to plan specific irrigation projects. Roosevelt also backed Pinchot's program of multi-use land management and set aside more than 200 million acres of public land as national forests, mineral reserves, and potential water-power sites. But because of opposition in the West, Congress in 1907 rescinded the president's power to create national forests in six timber-rich states. Roosevelt signed the bill—only, however, after designating twenty-one new national forests totaling 16 million acres in those six states.

Preservationists won important victories in this era. Initiatives by private citizens saved a large grove of California's giant redwoods and a lovely stretch of the Maine coastline. By 1916 thirteen national parks had been created, but without central management. That year, Congress established the National Park Service to oversee what one writer termed the nation's "crown jewels."

Environmental health hazards aroused concern as well. With factories pumping pollutants into the air and dumping poisons into rivers, urban reformers fought for restrictive legislation. Roosevelt was sympathetic, especially when a power plant spewing black smoke near the White House drove him to threaten legal action.

The Progressive Era saw environmental issues draw intense national concern for the first time. Roosevelt played a crucial part in the process; along with millions of acres of national forest, he created fifty-three wildlife reserves and five new national parks. Equally important, Roosevelt kept environmental concerns in the public mind. Declaring conservation the United States' "most vital internal question," he gave priority to an issue that would reverberate through the rest of the century.

Taft in the White House

Roosevelt had pledged not to run in 1908, and to the disappointment of millions, he kept his promise. The Republicans' most conservative wing regained control. Although they nominated Roosevelt's choice, William Howard Taft, for president, they selected a conservative vice-presidential candidate and drafted an extremely conservative platform.

On the Democratic side, the defeat of the conservative Alton B. Parker had opened the door for a last hurrah by William Jennings Bryan. Nominating him, the Democrats adopted a platform calling for a lower tariff, denouncing trusts, and embracing labor. Unlike its predecessors, Bryan's 1908 campaign aroused neither horror nor passionate support, and Taft coasted to victory.

Taft differed markedly from Roosevelt. Whereas TR kept in fighting trim, Taft was grossly overweight. TR had sparred in a boxing ring that he had set up in the White House; Taft played golf. TR loved dramatic public donnybrooks against the forces of evil and greed, but Taft had little use for political conflict. Above all, TR loved being president, while Taft's happiest days would come later, as chief justice of the Supreme Court.

Pledged to carry on TR's program, Taft supported the Mann-Elkins Act (1910), which strengthened the Interstate Commerce Commission and extended its authority to include telephone and telegraph companies. The Taft White House filed more antitrust suits than the Roosevelt administration had, but its lack of fanfare left most people considering TR the quintessential "trustbuster."

A Divided Republican Party

During the Roosevelt administration, a small group of reform-minded Republican legislators, nicknamed the Insurgents, had challenged their party's

The Election of 1908				
Candidates	Parties	Electoral Vote	Popular Vote	Percentage of Popular Vote
WILLIAM H. TAFT	Republican	321	7,675,320	51.6
William Jennings Bryan	Democratic	162	6,412,294	43.1
Eugene V. Debs	Socialist		420,793	2.8
Eugene W. Chafin	Prohibition		253,840	1.7

congressional leadership. Counting senators La Follette of Wisconsin and Albert Beveridge of Indiana and congressman George Norris of Nebraska among their members, the Insurgents turned against President Taft in 1909 after a tariff struggle.

Taft had originally believed that the tariff should be lowered, but in 1909 he signed the high Payne-Aldrich Tariff, praising it as "the best tariff bill that the Republican party ever passed." The battle lines between conservative and progressive Republicans were drawn.

A major Insurgent target was Speaker of the House Joseph G. Cannon of Illinois, whose benevolent nickname, Uncle Joe, belied his reactionary ideas and ruthless politics. With near-absolute power, Cannon prevented most reform bills from reaching a vote. In March 1910 Republican Insurgents joined with Democrats to curtail Cannon's power sharply. This Insurgent victory represented a slap at Taft, who supported Cannon.

Relations between Taft and Roosevelt eroded in 1909–1910 as TR's Washington allies sent him stormy letters about Taft's lack of reform zeal. The so-called Ballinger-Pinchot affair brought matters to a head. Richard A. Ballinger, Taft's secretary of the interior, was a conservative western lawyer who believed in the private development of natural resources. Ballinger approved the sale of several million acres of public land in Alaska to some Seattle businessmen, who promptly sold it to a banking consortium that included J. P. Morgan, the very symbol of the money power. A low-level Interior official protested and was dismissed, and when Gifford Pinchot of the Forestry Service criticized Ballinger in congressional testimony he, too, was fired. TR's supporters seethed.

When Roosevelt returned to the United States from an African safari in June 1910, Pinchot, not Taft, met the boat. TR came out with guns blazing in the midterm 1910 elections, supporting the Insurgents and defining a program called the New Nationalism that would make the federal government a powerful reform instrument. He appealed for expanded federal regulation of business, censured

judges who struck down progressive laws, and endorsed the idea of reversing judicial rulings by popular vote.

Democrats captured the House of Representatives in 1910, and a coalition of Democrats and Insurgents controlled the Senate. As fervor for reform rose, Roosevelt sounded more and more like a presidential candidate. Meanwhile, a new challenger for national leadership of the progressive movement was emerging from the ranks of the Democrats. He was Woodrow Wilson.

National Progressivism—Phase II: Woodrow Wilson

Defeating two other reform candidates in the presidential election of 1912, Woodrow Wilson played a pivotal role as Congress enacted an imposing array of reform measures.

The Four-Way Election of 1912

In February 1912 Roosevelt announced that he would seek the Republican nomination. With Taft showing no intention of withdrawing, the stage was set for a Republican battle royal. Roosevelt won virtually all the state primaries and conventions in which he challenged Taft, but Taft controlled the party machinery. When the Republican convention that June disqualified many of Roosevelt's hard-won delegates, TR's outraged supporters stalked out. They reassembled in August to form a third party, the Progressive party.

Declaring himself "stripped to the buff and ready for the fight," Roosevelt proclaimed that he felt "as fit as a bull moose," thus giving his party the nickname the Bull Moose party. The euphoric delegates nominated TR by acclamation and endorsed virtually every reform cause of the day.

Meanwhile, the new political spirit had infused the Democratic party and produced reform administrations at state and local levels. In New Jersey, voters elected a political novice, Woodrow Wilson, as governor in 1910. A "Wilson for President" movement had gained momentum in 1911–1912, and by the time the Democrats convened in late June 1912, the Wilson boom proved irresistible.

The Republican Taft essentially gave up. Eugene V. Debs ran on the Socialist platform, demanding an end to capitalism, and Roosevelt and Wilson vied for the moderate reform vote. TR preached his New Nationalism: governmental regulation of big business in the public interest. Wilson called for a "New Freedom," evoking an earlier era of small entrepreneurs and free competition. Government should encourage competition, he proclaimed, not regulate business enterprise. "The history of liberty is the history of the limitation of government power, not the increase of it," he insisted. The divided Republicans proved no match for the united Democrats. Although Roosevelt won 4 million popular votes and eighty-eight electoral votes, Wilson prevailed with 6.3 million votes, and the Democrats took both houses of Congress.

The Election of 1912

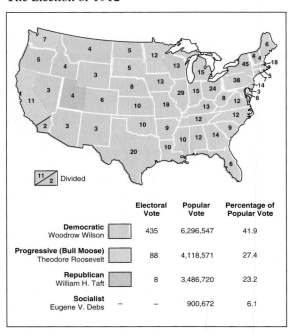

	Electoral Vote	Popular Vote	Percentage of Popular Vote
Democratic Woodrow Wilson	435	6,296,547	41.9
Progressive (Bull Moose) Theodore Roosevelt	88	4,118,571	27.4
Republican William H. Taft	8	3,486,720	23.2
Socialist Eugene V. Debs	–	900,672	6.1

The 1912 election solidly identified the triumphant Democrats with reform, launching a tradition on which Franklin D. Roosevelt would build in the 1930s. The breakaway Bull Moose movement simultaneously demonstrated the support for reform among grass-roots Republicans and left the Republican party in the grip of its most conservative elements.

Woodrow Wilson: The Scholar as President

The son, grandson, and nephew of Presbyterian ministers, Wilson grew up in southern towns during and after the Civil War in a churchly atmosphere that shaped his oratory and moral outlook. He had graduated from Princeton, earned a Ph.D. in political science from Johns Hopkins University, taught at Princeton, and become president there in 1902. Admired for his educational ideas, Wilson gradually lost support at Princeton because of his unwillingness to compromise and left the academic world for the political arena in 1910. Two years later, he was president of the United States.

Wilson displayed the same strengths and weaknesses at the national level that he had at Princeton. An eloquent orator, he could galvanize listeners with his idealism, but he could as easily alienate them with a righteousness that allowed no compromise. However, when he chose, Wilson could be a master of statesmanship and compromise. During Wilson's eight years as president, all these facets of his complex personality would come into play.

Tariff and Banking Reform

The first item on Wilson's agenda was tariff reform. When a low-tariff bill bogged down in the Senate, Wilson demonstrated his talent for dramatic leadership by shining the spotlight on tariff lobbyists and on individual senators' interests in maintaining a high tariff. In the aftermath of this publicity, the Senate passed a bill slashing tariff rates even more than the House had earlier. The Underwood-Simmons Tariff reduced rates an average of 15 percent and imposed an income tax, recently authorized by the Sixteenth Amendment (1913).

In June 1913, with the tariff battle raging, Wilson called for banking and currency reform. A consensus existed about the need for a strong central bank; the question was whether it should be privately or publicly controlled. Wilson finally sided with the progressives, insisting on public control. He played a critical part in the complex bargaining process that led to the Federal Reserve Act of 1913, his greatest legislative achievement.

The act created a network of twelve regional Federal Reserve banks under mixed public and private control. Each regional bank could issue currency to private banks in its district. Overall control of the system rested in the hands of the heads of the regional banks and the Washington-based Federal Reserve Board. Although its power was diffuse at first, the Federal Reserve grew after the 1930s into a strong institution capable of directing the nation's monetary policy.

Corporate Regulation

Wilson and his congressional allies turned next to that quintessential progressive cause, business regulation. President Wilson, more sympathetic than candidate Wilson to regulation, shepherded two important regulatory measures through Congress.

The Federal Trade Commission Act (1914) reflected an administrative approach by creating a "watchdog" agency, the Federal Trade Commission (FTC), with power to investigate suspected violations, to require regular reports from corporations, and to issue "cease and desist" orders against unfair methods. The Clayton Antitrust Act (1914) amplified the Sherman Anti-Trust Act by spelling out a series of illegal practices such as selling at a loss to monopolize a market. With the added clout of the Clayton Act, the Wilson administration filed antitrust suits against close to a hundred corporations.

Labor Legislation and Farm Aid

Sympathetic to labor, Wilson supported the American Federation of Labor, defended workers' right to organize, and endorsed a Clayton Act clause that exempted strikes, boycotts, and peaceful picketing from "restraint of trade." In 1916 he helped to push three important worker-protection laws through Congress: the Keating-Owen Act, barring from interstate commerce products manufactured by child labor (later declared unconstitutional); the Adamson Act, establishing an eight-hour workday for interstate railway workers; and the Workmen's Compensation Act, providing accident and injury protection to federal workers.

Wilson also championed the Federal Farm Loan Act and the Federal Warehouse Act (1916), which allowed farmers to secure long-term, low-interest loans using land or crops as security. The Federal Highway Act (1916) matched federal funds with state appropriations for highway construction, benefiting the new automobile industry as well as farmers plagued by bad roads.

Progressivism and the Constitution

The conservative, probusiness federal courts' tilt moderated as the Progressive Era ran its course. In 1908 the Supreme Court revealed the changing judicial climate when, in *Muller* v. *Oregon*, it upheld an Oregon law setting maximum working hours for women laundry workers at ten hours. To defend the constitutionality of the Oregon law, Boston attorney Louis Brandeis had offered economic, medical, and sociological evidence of the harmful effects of long hours on women workers. The Court's acceptance of the "Brandeis brief" marked a breakthrough in making the nation's legal system responsive to new social realities.

Progressivism also produced four constitutional amendments. The Sixteenth (ratified in 1913) granted Congress the authority to tax income; the Seventeenth (1913) mandated the direct election of U.S. senators; the Eighteenth (1919) established prohibition; and the Nineteenth (1920) granted women the vote. This array of amendments demonstrated how profoundly progressivism had resculpted the political landscape.

1916: Wilson Edges Out Hughes

In 1916 Wilson easily won renomination for the presidency. The Republicans nominated Charles

Evans Hughes, Supreme Court justice and former New York governor. With the Republicans more or less reunited, the election was extremely close. Wilson won the popular vote by more than 500,000, but the electoral-college outcome remained in doubt for weeks as the California tally seesawed back and forth. Ultimately, Wilson carried the state by under 4,000 votes, and with it, the election.

The Election of 1916

Candidates	Parties	Electoral Vote	Popular Vote	Percentage of Popular Vote
WOODROW WILSON	Democratic	277	9,127,695	49.4
Charles E. Hughes	Republican	254	8,533,507	46.2
A. L. Benson	Socialist		585,113	3.2
J. Frank Hanly	Prohibition		220,506	1.2

Conclusion

After the flurry of worker-protection legislation in the fall of 1916, the progressive movement lost momentum as the nation's attention turned to war. Yet progressivism left a remarkable legacy in specific laws and in a changed view of government. By 1916 most Americans agreed that it was proper and necessary for the government to play a central social and economic role. Progressivism had expanded the meaning of democracy and challenged the cynical view that government was nothing more than a tool of the economic elite. Progressives enlarged the government not for its own sake but because they realized that in an era of gargantuan industries, sprawling cities, and concentrated corporate power, the government's role had to grow in order to serve the public interest, give people a decent life, and protect vulnerable members of society.

Progressive ideals often faltered in practice, however. Corporations proved remarkably adroit at manipulating the new regulatory state, and bureaucratic routine frequently gutted programs rooted in moral indignation and a vision of social justice. Unquestionably, too, progressivism had its repressive, illiberal, and coercive elements; on questions of racial justice, it chalked up a miserable record.

Nonetheless, the Progressive Era shines as a time when American politics began to confront the social upheavals wrought by industrialization. Americans learned to think of their government as an arena of possibility where they could address public issues and social problems. Twenty years later, another great reform movement, the New Deal, would draw heavily on progressivism's legacy.

Chronology

1895	Anti-Saloon League founded. Booker T. Washington's "Atlanta Compromise" address.
1898	Charlotte Perkins Gilman, *Women and Economics*.
1899	Thorstein Veblen, *The Theory of the Leisure Class*.
1900	International Ladies' Garment Workers' Union (ILGWU) founded. Socialist Party of America organized. Theodore Dreiser, *Sister Carrie*. Carrie Chapman Catt becomes president of the National American Woman Suffrage Association (NAWSA).
1901	Assassination of McKinley; Theodore Roosevelt becomes president.
1902	Roosevelt mediates coal strike. Jane Addams, *Democracy and Social Ethics*.
1903	W. E. B. Du Bois, *The Souls of Black Folk*.
1904	Roosevelt elected president. *Northern Securities* case. Lincoln Steffens, *The Shame of the Cities*. Ida Tarbell, *History of the Standard Oil Company*
1905	Industrial Workers of the World (IWW) organized. Niagara Movement established.
1906	Hepburn Act. Upton Sinclair, *The Jungle*. Pure Food and Drug Act. Meat Inspection Act.
1907	Walter Rauschenbusch, *Christianity and the Social Crisis*. William James, *Pragmatism*.
1908	*Muller* v. *Oregon*. William Howard Taft elected president.

1909	Payne-Aldrich Tariff. Ballinger-Pinchot controversy. National Association for the Advancement of Colored People (NAACP) founded. Herbert Croly, *The Promise of American Life*.
1910	Mann Act.
1911	Supreme Court orders dissolution of Standard Oil Company.
1912	Progressive (Bull Moose) party founded. Woodrow Wilson elected president.
1913	Underwood-Simmons Tariff. Federal Reserve Act. Sixteenth Amendment added to the Constitution. Seventeenth Amendment added to the Constitution Thirty thousand march for woman suffrage in New York City.
1914	Federal Trade Commission Act. Clayton Antitrust Act.
1915	D. W. Griffith, *The Birth of a Nation*.
1916	Federal Farm Loan Act. Keating-Owen Act. Workmen's Compensation Act. Wilson reelected. John Dewey, *Democracy and Education*. Margaret Sanger opens nation's first birth-control clinic in Brooklyn, New York. National Park Service created.
1919	Eighteenth Amendment added to the Constitution.
1920	Nineteenth Amendment added to the Constitution.

FOR FURTHER READING

John D. Buenker, John C. Burnham, and Robert M. Crunden, *Progressivism* (1977). A still useful overview and survey of scholarship, stressing the movement's diversity.

John W. Chambers II, *The Tyranny of Change: America in the Progressive Era, 1900–1917* (1980). An interpretive work emphasizing the progressives' belief in intervention in the social and economic realms.

Gabriel Kolko, *The Triumph of Conservatism: A Reinterpretation of American History, 1900–1916* (1963). A seminal though controversial study that sees large corporate interests as underlying most progressive reforms.

Arthur S. Link and Richard L. McCormick, *Progressivism* (1983). Lucid, sensible unraveling of progressivism's diverse strands and comprehensive discussion of current interpretations.

Robert Wiebe, *The Search for Order, 1877–1920* (1967). A highly influential study treating progressivism as the response of a new middle class and professional groups to late-nineteenth-century urban-industrial changes.

Somber, trembling with emotion, President Woodrow Wilson asked Congress for a declaration of war against Germany on the evening of April 2, 1917. Applause and shouts greeted his statement that the world must be made "safe for democracy," and many members of Congress waved silk American Flags. When the speech ended, Senator Henry Cabot Lodge of Massachusetts, a fierce Wilson opponent, rushed forward to shake his hand. "Mr. President," said Lodge, "you have expressed in the loftiest manner the sentiments of the American people." But Wilson remained solemn. "Think what it was they were applauding," he mused to an aide; "my message today was a message of death for our young men. How strange it seems to applaud that."

Wilson delivered this message of death reluctantly, after months of trying to keep the United States out of the European war. Elected in a gale of reformist enthusiasm, Wilson was caught up in—and ultimately consumed by—the struggle engulfing Europe. He now brought to a series of foreign crises the same self-assured moralism that he had long applied to domestic issues.

(Right) Patriotic songsheet, World War I era

World War I

Defining America's World Role

War in Europe

Mobilizing at Home, Fighting in France

Promoting the War and Suppressing Dissent

Economic and Social Trends in Wartime America

Joyous Armistice, Bitter Aftermath

Even before the United States slipped into the European war, an assertive foreign policy had shaped American relations with the rest of the world as presidents Roosevelt and Taft both pursued an activist course in Asia and Latin America. Roosevelt's balance-of-power chess game, Taft's concentration on business opportunities, and Wilson's moralism illustrate the diverse, sometimes contradictory motives that underlay America's expanding global influence.

Defining America's World Role

The United States' growing determination to assert its might, to protect and extend American business interests, and to impose its own standards of good government throughout the world led to continued American involvement in Asia and Latin America as the twentieth century unfolded.

The Roosevelt Corollary in Latin America and the Balance of Power in Asia

Theodore Roosevelt, president from 1901 to 1909, believed that the United States must strengthen its world role, protect U.S. interests in Latin America, and preserve the balance of power in Asia. In 1904, when several European nations threatened to invade the Dominican Republic, a small Caribbean island nation that had defaulted on its debts, Roosevelt concluded that American interests were in jeopardy. He feared that the Europeans would turn debt collecting into permanent occupation. If any big power were to intervene in the region, he felt, it should be the United States. In December 1904 Roosevelt declared that "chronic wrongdoing" by any Latin American nation would justify intervention by the United States, acting as an international policeman.

This pronouncement became known as the Roosevelt Corollary to the Monroe Doctrine. (The original "doctrine," issued in 1823, had warned

European powers against meddling in Latin America.) The Roosevelt Corollary announced that, in some circumstances, the United States had the *right* to intrude. Suiting actions to words, the United States ran the Dominican Republic's customs service for two years and took over the management of its foreign debt.

On the other side of the world, meanwhile, the imperial rivalries that swirled over China continued unabated, catapulting Roosevelt into the role of peacemaker. In 1900 Russia tried to take advantage of the chaos unleashed by the Boxer uprising (see Chapter 21) by sending troops to occupy Manchuria, China's northeastern province. In February 1904 the Japanese, who had their own plans for Manchuria, launched a surprise attack on Russian forces at Port Arthur, Manchuria. In the Russo-Japanese War that followed, Japan dominated Russia.

Russian expansionism dismayed Roosevelt, but so did the possibility of a total Japanese victory—and disruption of the balance of power that TR considered essential to Asian peace and to the maintenance of America's role in the Philippines. In June 1905 he therefore invited Japan and Russia to a peace conference in Portsmouth, New Hampshire, and in early September the two exhausted foes signed a peace treaty. Russia recognized Japan's rule in Korea and made other territorial concessions. From then on, curbing Japanese expansionism became the United States' chief goal in Asia.

American relations with Japan deteriorated in 1906 when the San Francisco school board ordered Asian children to attend segregated schools. Roosevelt persuaded the board to reverse its decision, however, and in 1907 his administration tried to head off future problems by negotiating a "gentleman's agreement" by which Japan pledged to stop the Japanese emigration to the United States. But racist attitudes along the Pacific coast continued to poison U.S.-Japan relations, particularly after 1913, when the California legislature prohibited Japanese aliens from owning land. A 1922 Supreme Court decision (*Ozawa v. U.S.*) preventing Japanese from becoming naturalized citizens intensified U.S.-Japanese friction.

As Californians worried about the "yellow peril," Japanese journalists watching America's growing military strength wrote of a "white peril." In 1907 Roosevelt ordered a flotilla of sixteen gleaming white battleships to steam on a "training operation" to Japan and then around the world. The 1908 visit of the "Great White Fleet" to Japan underscored the United States' growing naval might—and led to huge increases in Japan's naval building program.

Dollar Diplomacy in China and Nicaragua

The foreign policy of William Howard Taft, Roosevelt's successor, focused mainly on advancing American commercial interests; critics called it dollar diplomacy. After a futile attempt to involve American bankers in Manchurian railroad building demonstrated the shortcomings of the Open Door policy, Woodrow Wilson, after he took presidential office in 1913, shelved dollar diplomacy.

Closer to home, in Nicaragua, dollar diplomacy seemed more successful. In 1911 a U.S.-supported revolution in Nicaragua brought to power Adolfo Díaz, an officer of an American-owned Nicaraguan mining property. U.S. bankers loaned the Díaz government $15 million in exchange for control of the Nicaraguan national bank, the customs service, and the national railroad. A revolt against Díaz in 1912 triggered action under the Roosevelt Corollary: Taft sent in 2,500 marines to protect the American investment. Except for a brief interval, U.S. marines remained in Managua, Nicaragua's capital, until 1933.

Wilson and Latin America

In 1913 the Democrat Wilson repudiated his Republican predecessors' expansionism and pledged that the United States would "never again seek one additional foot of territory by conquest." Nevertheless, Wilson, too, became deeply entangled in Latin America. In 1915, after bloody upheavals in Haiti and the Dominican Republic, Wilson ordered in the marines. A Haitian constitution favorable to American commercial interests was ratified in 1918 by a vote of 69,377 to 355—in a marine-supervised election—and marines brutally suppressed Haitian resistance to American rule. They remained in the Dominican Republic until 1924 and in Haiti until 1934.

From 1913 to 1914, Wilson's major foreign-policy preoccupation was Mexico, a nation divided between a tiny elite of wealthy landowners and a mass of poor peasants. In a particularly turbulent era for Mexico, Wilson tried to promote good government in Mexico City, to protect the large U.S. capital investments in the country, and ultimately to safeguard U.S. citizens traveling in Mexico or living along its border.

In 1911 rebels led by democratic reformer Francisco Madero had overthrown the autocratic Mexican president, Porfirio Díaz. Forty thousand Americans had settled in Mexico under Díaz, and $2 billion in U.S. investments had flowed into the country. Early in 1913, Mexican troops loyal to General Victoriano Huerta ousted and murdered Madero.

Wilson reversed the long-standing American policy of recognizing governments that held power regardless of how they had come to power. "I will not recognize a government of butchers," he declared, refusing to deal with Huerta. He authorized arms sales to Venustiano Carranza, a Huerta foe, and blockaded Vera Cruz to prevent weapons from reaching Huerta. "I am going to teach the South American republics to elect good men," Wilson asserted. In April 1914 American troops occupied Vera Cruz and began fighting Mexican forces. Sixty-five Americans and 500 Mexicans were killed or wounded. Bowing to U.S. might, Huerta abdicated, Carranza took power, and American troops withdrew.

But the turmoil continued. In January 1916 a bandit chieftain in northern Mexico, Pancho Villa, murdered sixteen American mining engineers and then crossed the border, burned Columbus, New Mexico, and killed nineteen of its inhabitants. Sharing the public's outrage, Wilson sent into Mexico a punitive expedition that eventually totaled 12,000 U.S. troops. When Villa brazenly staged another raid across the Rio Grande into Texas, Wilson ordered 150,000 National Guardsmen into duty along the border.

Early in 1917, with the United States teetering on the brink of the European war, Wilson withdrew the army from Mexico. When Carranza was formally elected president later that year, Wilson extended U.S. recognition. Mexico adopted a new constitution that sharply curtailed the freewheeling operations of American capitalists by centralizing control of oil and mineral resources and imposed strict regulations on foreign investors.

Although comparatively minor, these episodes in Latin America and Asia revealed American foreign-policy goals in this era. The United States searched for a world order on U.S. terms—an international system founded on the uniquely American blend of liberalism, democracy, open trade, and capitalism. Washington planners envisioned a harmonious, stable global order of democratic societies that would welcome both American political values and American corporate expansion.

These episodes also foreshadowed the future. The maneuvering between the United States and Japan reflected a growing clash of interests, compounded by racism, that would lead to the exclusion of Japanese immigrants in 1924 and culminate in war with Japan in 1941. The revolutionary and nationalistic energies stirring in Latin America portended developments that would explosively transform its politics half a century later. But of more immediate concern, the vision of a world order based on U.S. ideals would soon find expression in Woodrow Wilson's response to the crisis in Europe.

War in Europe

When war came to Europe in August 1914, most Americans wanted to remain aloof. For nearly three years, the United States did stay neutral, but then public opinion began to shift. Emotional ties to Britain and France, economic considerations, the vision of a world remade in America's image, and German violations of neutral rights, as defined by President Wilson, combined by April 1917 to draw the United States into the maelstrom.

The Coming of War

With minor exceptions, until the early twentieth century, Europe had remained at peace after the conclusion of the Napoleonic Wars in 1815. Problems lurked beneath this serene surface, however. In 1914 a complex network of alliances bound European nations together, even as forces of nationalism threatened to tear some of them apart.

The slow-motion collapse in the 1870s of the ancient Ottoman Empire, centered in Turkey, had created such newly independent Balkan nations as Romania, Bulgaria, and Serbia (later a part of Yugoslavia) and presented opportunities for great-power meddling. Nationalism reached a fever pitch in Serbia, which dreamed of absorbing other South Slavic peoples. Russia, the largest Slavic nation, supported the Serbian dream. Meanwhile, the Austro-Hungarian Empire, itself menaced, saw opportunities for expansion as the Ottoman Empire receded. In 1908 Austria-Hungary annexed Bosnia-Herzogovina, a Slavic land wedged between Austria-Hungary and Serbia. The Russians were alarmed, and the Serbs furious.

Moreover, Germany, under the leadership of Kaiser Wilhelm II, was in an expansionist mood. Many Germans believed that their nation, united only since 1871, was lagging in the quest for national greatness and empire. Expansion, modernization, and military power became the order of the day in Berlin, the German Empire's capital.

Ordinary Europeans experienced a vague restlessness as the twentieth century opened. Life seemed soft, boring, and stale. Like Theodore Roosevelt on the eve of the Spanish-American War, some Europeans openly speculated that a war would strengthen national character and add excitement to a languid age.

In mid-1914, this volatile mixture exploded. In June a terrorist with close links to Serbia gunned down the heir to the Austrian throne and his wife as they rode through the Bosnian capital, Sarajevo. Austria delivered a harsh ultimatum to Serbia and five days later, after an "unacceptable" Serbian response, declared war on its Balkan neighbor. The intricate machinery of the alliance system rumbled into action. Linked to Serbia by a secret treaty, Russia mobilized for war. Germany declared war on Russia and on Russia's ally, France. Great Britain, linked by treaty to France, declared war on Germany. Thus a lone assassin plunged Europe into a war that altered history.

The American People's Initial Responses

President Wilson immediately proclaimed U.S. neutrality and exhorted the nation to be neutral "in thought as well as in action." Most Americans, grateful that the Atlantic Ocean lay between them and the battlefields, supported Wilson's position. As a popular song said, "I Didn't Raise My Boy to Be a Soldier."

Although most Americans shared Wilson's desire to stay out of the war, remaining neutral in thought proved difficult. Not only economic ties but also a common language, ancestry, and culture linked many Americans to Britain by strong emotional bonds. Still, not all Americans shared these ties. Because millions were of German origin, many sided with Germany. Irish-Americans, raised for generations on "twisting the [British] lion's tail," had little sympathy for Britain.

The Perils of Neutrality

By 1917 the American commitment to neutrality had been transformed into strong popular support for war. What caused this turnabout?

First, Wilson's vision of a world order built on American political and economic values conflicted with his commitment to neutrality. The international system that he favored, based on liberalism, democracy, and capitalistic enterprise, could never

exist in a world dominated by imperial Germany. Wilson also believed that only U.S. leadership could ensure the achievement of this vision, and unless America helped to fight the war, America could not shape the peace.

This global vision influenced Wilson's approach to the first and perhaps most important problem confronting the United States: the question of neutral rights on the high seas. Within days of the war's outbreak, Britain had intercepted American merchant ships bound for Germany. In November 1914 Britain provoked more Wilsonian protests by declaring the North Sea a war zone and planting it with explosive mines, and in March 1915 Britain blockaded all German ports. U.S. denunciations had no effect, for Britain had resolved to exploit its naval advantage no matter how it alienated American public opinion.

Ultimately, however, it was German violations of American ideas of neutrality that drew the United States into the war. Determined to take advantage of a new and deadly weapon, the submarine, Germany in February 1915 designated the waters around the British Isles as a war zone and warned off all ships, including those of Americans. Wilson again protested, warning that Germany would be held to "strict accountability" for the loss of American ships or lives.

Developments in May 1915 underscored the problems of neutrality. Germany placed announcements in U.S. newspapers advising against travel on British or French vessels. Six days later, on May 7, a U-boat sank the British liner *Lusitania*, with a loss of 1,198 lives, including 128 Americans. In increasingly strong notes to the German government, Wilson demanded specific pledges that Germany would stop its unrestricted submarine warfare. Nonetheless, he also insisted that America could use persuasion rather than force to press the belligerents to recognize neutral rights.

The *Lusitania* disaster exposed deep divisions in U.S. public opinion. Many Americans concluded that war was inevitable. Theodore Roosevelt, strongly pro-British, condemned Wilson for "abject cowardice and weakness." The National Security League, a lobby of bankers and industrialists, led a

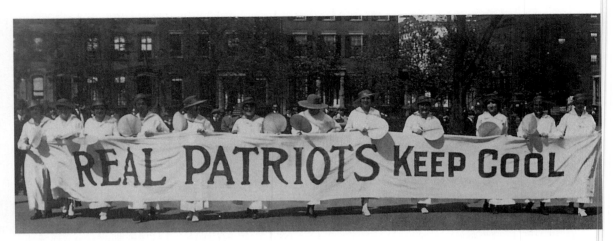

Woman's Peace Party Parade
With fans to symbolize their point, these marchers urged President Wilson to continue the search for peace despite German provocations on the high seas.

"preparedness" movement, stirring up patriotism and promoting an arms buildup and military training. By the fall of 1915, Wilson himself called for a military buildup. Many others, however, including pacifists, German-Americans, and those who had taken Wilson's speeches seriously, deplored the drift toward war. Leading feminists and social-justice reformers warned that the war spirit was eroding humanitarian values central to reform. As early as August 1914, 1,500 black-clad women marched down New York's Fifth Avenue protesting the war. In 1915 Jane Addams, Carrie Chapman Catt, and other feminists formed the Woman's Peace party, and later that year they and others sailed to Sweden on a ship chartered by industrialist Henry Ford in an attempt to mediate the war and bring peace before Christmas.

Wilson's firm but restrained policy seemed to work. In August 1915, when a U-boat violated orders and sank the *Arabic*, a British liner, with the loss of two American lives, Germany pledged that such an incident would not happen again. But in March 1916 it did, as a German sub sank a French vessel, *Sussex*, and injured several Americans. Wilson threatened to break diplomatic relations, a first

step toward war, and Berlin pledged not to attack merchant vessels without warning. The crisis over neutral rights eased temporarily.

Corporate boardrooms as well as the high seas proved an arena for quarrels over neutral rights. Early in the war, American bankers trying to lend money to the belligerents were told that such loans were "inconsistent with the true spirit of neutrality." The policy did not last. In August 1915 Wilson's cabinet began to warn that only substantial loans to Great Britain could prevent "a serious financial situation" in the United States. Wilson finally permitted the Morgan bank to lend $500 million to the British and French governments. By April 1917 U.S. banks had lent $2.3 billion to the Allies (Great Britain, France, Russia, and Italy) and only $27 million to the Central Powers (Germany and Austria-Hungary). Trade with the Allies had consequently soared as commerce with the Central Powers plummeted, and the Allies' economic dependence on America increased. Although the United States remained neutral, Wilson had taken full advantage of the Allies' credit needs to strengthen the nation's commercial and financial position in the world economy.

Stalemate in the Trenches

While Americans focused on neutral rights, the land war in Europe degenerated into a costly stalemate. After Germany's initial offensive drive stalled, the two sides dug in, forming a line of trenches that snaked across France from the English Channel to the Swiss border. For more than three years, this line remained essentially unchanged. A German offensive in 1916 near the French town of Verdun alone cost hundreds of thousands of casualties but did little to break the stalemate. The war in the trenches was nightmarish, a ghastly inferno of mud, lice, rats, artillery bursts, poison gas, and sudden, random death.

Determined to win the propaganda war, Britain bombarded the United States with posters and articles portraying alleged German atrocities, such as the impaling of babies on bayonets. German propaganda proved relatively ineffective.

The United States Enters the War

As the war had dragged on, German military leaders pushed for greater and greater use of the submarine. Although such stepped-up German aggression would almost certainly pull the United States into the war, American entry would have no significance, they said—"zero, zero, zero," according to one German naval officer. The generals prevailed. On January 9, 1917, the German government decided to return to the policy of unlimited U-boat attacks.

Events now rushed forward. Three days after Germany's formal announcement of the resumption of unrestricted submarine warfare, Wilson broke diplomatic relations. Five American ships fell victim to German torpedoes in February and March. And on February 24, the United States' discovery of the so-called Zimmermann telegram enormously widened the rift between the two nations. Attempting to create problems on the American side of the Atlantic, German foreign secretary Alfred Zimmermann had cabled the German ambassador in Mexico to propose a military alliance of Germany,

Mexico, and Japan, with Mexico promised the return of its "lost" territories of Texas, Arizona, and New Mexico. Publication of the telegram raised a furor in the United States.

Finally, on April 2, Wilson went before Congress to call for a declaration of war. By wide margins, both the Senate and the House voted for war. Three key factors—German attacks on American shipping, U.S. investment in the Allied cause, and American cultural links to the Allies, especially England—had converged to draw the United States into war.

Mobilizing at Home, Fighting in France

World War I would leave the United States with relatively few scars. At war for only nineteen months, the nation took comparatively light casualties—112,000 of the 7.5 million dead—and the American homeland remained untouched. Still, the war constituted a major turning point. It changed the lives of almost all Americans, transformed the nation's government and economy, and thrust the United States into the arena of global politics.

Raising an Army

A woefully unprepared American military faced war in April 1917. The regular army of 120,000 enlisted men had virtually no combat experience. An aging officer corps was dozing away the years until retirement. There was enough ammunition for only two days of fighting, and the War Department was a snakepit of jealous bureaucrats.

Raising an army and imposing order on the War Department posed a daunting challenge. Wilson's secretary of war, Newton D. Baker, performed brilliantly on the first task, skillfully implementing the Selective Service Act passed in May 1917. Baker cleverly made the first draft registration day a "festival and patriotic occasion." Thanks to a carefully orchestrated public-relations campaign and local civilian draft boards' deft handling of the draft, 24 million men registered by November 1918, of whom nearly 3 million were drafted. In addition, following a precedent-breaking decision by the secretary of the navy, 11,000 women served in the navy during the war, and several hundred in the marines. Although not assigned to combat, they performed crucial support functions as nurses, clerical workers, and telephone operators.

Army chief of staff General Peyton C. Marsh worked the same wonders in organizing and galvanizing the War Department that Baker had with the draft. In the military training camps, young men from all over the United States got their first taste of a soldier's discipline, and often their first experience of the world beyond their hometown.

Organizing the Economy for War

The coming of the war in 1917 brought not only military mobilization but also unprecedented government oversight of civilian life. Under the war emergency, the government quickly assumed greater control of the economy.

The War Industries Board (WIB) was established in 1917 to coordinate military purchasing, to fight waste, and to ensure that the military received the weapons, equipment, and supplies it needed. Especially under the wealthy Wall Street speculator Bernard Baruch, whom Wilson appointed to run the WIB in March 1918, the agency exercised enormous control over the industrial sector. In addition to allocating raw materials, the board established production priorities and introduced all kinds of efficiencies. To save steel, rubber, and other scarce commodities, competing companies coordinated their production processes. The standardization of bicycle manufacturing, for example, saved 2,000 tons of steel. Daylight savings time was instituted as a wartime conservation measure. Benjamin Franklin originally had proposed the idea of adjusting clocks to take advantage of long summer daylight hours, but it took the war emergency to bring the measure about.

Baruch's counterpart on the agricultural front was Herbert Hoover, the head of the Food Administration. A mining engineer who had amassed a fortune in Asia, Hoover oversaw the production and distribution of foodstuffs—especially wheat, meat, and sugar—to assure adequate supplies for the army and the food-short Allies. A master of persuasion, Hoover organized a public-relations campaign to convince Americans that they should conserve food. Bombarded with such slogans as "Serve Beans by All Means" and "Don't Let Your Horse Be More Patriotic Than You Are—Eat a Dish of Oatmeal," Americans observed "meatless days" and "wheatless days."

The War Industries Board and the Food Administration represented only the tip of the regulatory iceberg. Nearly 5,000 government agencies supervised home-front activities during the war. When a massive railroad tie-up during the snowy winter of 1917–1918 impeded the flow of supplies to Europe, the government took over and transformed the 3,000 competing companies into an efficient national transportation system.

In place of trustbusting, moreover, the government actively encouraged industrial cooperation. In 1917 major corporate mergers soared to nearly 200, more than twice the annual average for the immediate prewar years.

This colossal regulatory apparatus fell apart when the war ended, but its influence lingered. The old laissez-faire suspicion of government, already eroded, suffered further blows in 1917–1918. In the 1930s, when the nation faced a different kind of crisis, the government activism of World War I would be remembered.

With the AEF in France

About 2 million American soldiers went to France in 1917–1918 as members of the American Expeditionary Force (AEF) under General John J. Pershing. A West Point graduate and commander of the 1916 expedition against Pancho Villa, Pershing was an iron-willed officer with a ramrod bearing, steely eyes, and trim mustache. For most men of the AEF, the war at first seemed a great adventure. After traveling to France on crowded freighters or even captured German liners, they piled aboard freight cars marked "HOMMES 40, CHEVAUX 8" (40 men, 8

The United States on the Western Front, 1918

American troops first saw action in the campaign to throw back Germany's spring 1918 offensive in the Somme and Aisne-Marne sectors. The next heavy American engagement came that autumn as part of the Allies' Meuse-Argonne offensive that ended the war.

horses) on their way to the front. Once there, they marched, trained, became acquainted with the French—and waited.

Aerial dogfights between German and Allied reconnaissance planes offered spectacular sideshows. The most famous World War I ace, Germany's Manfred von Richthofen, the "Red Baron," shot down eighty Allied aircraft before his luck ran out in April 1918. Although Secretary of War Baker was "thoroughly fascinated" by the recently invented airplane's possibilities and pressed Congress to appropriate large sums for aircraft construction, only thirty-seven planes were built.

The war would be won or lost on land and sea, however, and when the United States entered,

Allied prospects looked bleak. German submarines took a horrendous toll on Allied shipping: 600,000 tons in March 1917, 900,000 tons in April. A failed French offensive in the spring led to an army mutiny, and an almost equally disastrous British-French offensive in November cost 400,000 casualties to gain four miles.

To make matters worse, Russia left the war in 1917. The all-out effort dictated by the massive war had undermined Russia's already toppling tsarist government, and in March 1917 the imperial government had collapsed. A provisional liberal government attempted to continue the war. Marxist revolutionaries under Vladimir Ilyich Lenin, however, capitalized on the provisional government's instability. On November 6, 1917, Lenin and Leon Trotsky led an armed coup that overthrew the provisional government, and began a civil war for the entire Russian empire. In March 1918 Lenin's bolshevik government signed a separate armistice with Germany, which freed thousands of German troops for transfer to the Western Front in France.

In these desperate circumstances, French and British commanders wanted to incorporate AEF troops into Allied units already at the front. But Pershing insisted that the AEF be "distinct and separate," in part because he scorned the defensive mentality of the Allied commanders and in part because separate combat would strengthen the United States' voice at the peace table.

American forces saw their first real combat in March 1918, when a German offensive threatened France's English Channel ports. The Allies created a unified command under French general Ferdinand Foch, and American troops were thrown into the fighting around Amiens and Armentières that stemmed the German advance. In May 1918 Germany launched the second phase of its spring offensive. By the end of the month, the Germans had broken through the Allied lines and had secured a nearly open road to Paris, only fifty miles away. At this critical moment, Americans spearheaded the forces that finally stopped the German advance at the town of Château-Thierry and nearby Belleau Wood. And 85,000 American troops helped to staunch the final German offensive of the war, a thrust at the ancient cathedral city of Rheims. This Allied victory marked the crucial turning point of the war. Germany's desperate attempt to take the offensive had failed. Now it was the Allies' turn.

Turning the Tide

On July 18, 1918, the Allies launched their counteroffensive. Of the 1 million American soldiers on French soil, 270,000 participated in a successful drive to push the Germans back.

In September Pershing took his first independent command and assembled nearly 500,000 American and 100,000 French troops to implement his strategy of hard-hitting offense. An American

Life at the Front
A battle-weary infantry corporal during the Argonne Forest campaign. Wrote Florence Bullard, working as a volunteer behind the lines, "I have had to write many sad letters to . . . mothers. I wonder if it will ever end."

wrote in his diary, "It was zero hour and in one instant the entire front as far as the eye could reach in either direction was a sheet of flame, while the heavy artillery made the earth quake."

The war's last great battle began on September 26 as 1.2 million Americans joined the struggle to drive the Germans from the Meuse River and the dense Argonne Forest north of Verdun. Poison gas hung in the air, and bloated rats scurried through the mud, feasting on human remains, as the offensive pressed forward over land devastated by four years of trench warfare. Theodore Roosevelt's "great adventure" seemed remote indeed in the Meuse-Argonne campaign. Death came in many forms, and without ceremony. Bodies, packs, rifles, photos, and letters from home sank into the all-consuming mud as more than 26,000 Americans died in the battle and thousands more perished in an influenza epidemic that would take 20 million lives worldwide. By early November the Allied counteroffensive had succeeded, but at terrible cost.

Blacks in the AEF

More than 260,000 blacks volunteered or were drafted in World War I, and 50,000 went to France. Racism pervaded the military as it did American society itself.

One racist senator from Mississippi, warning that the sight of "arrogant, strutting" black soldiers would trigger race riots in the United States, had urged that blacks not be drafted. Tensions reached the breaking point in Houston in August 1917, when some black members of the Twenty-fourth Infantry, endlessly goaded by local whites, seized weapons from the armory and killed seventeen whites. After a hasty trial with no opportunity for an appeal, thirteen black soldiers were hanged, and forty-one went to jail for life.

In France, blacks worked mainly as messboys (mealtime aides), laborers, and stevedores (ship-cargo handlers). Four black infantry regiments served with distinction under French command. One entire regiment, the 369th, was honored with the French Croix de Guerre, and several hundred individual black soldiers received French decorations for bravery. Most French people, military and civilian alike, at least superficially treated whites and blacks the same. For black members of the AEF, this eye-opening experience would remain with them when they returned home.

Promoting the War and Suppressing Dissent

Patriotic fervor pervaded American society in 1917–1918, in part the result of an elaborate government campaign to whip up enthusiasm for the war. In its wake came stifling intellectual conformity and intolerance for dissent. Government authorities and private vigilante groups hounded and arrested socialists, pacifists, and other dissidents and in the process trampled the basic constitutional rights of thousands.

Advertising the War

For President Wilson, the war at home was no less important than the war abroad. "It is not an army we must shape and train for war, it is a nation," he declared. Wilson knew that millions of Americans opposed the war. They represented diverse viewpoints but collectively they posed a formidable obstacle to the president's dream of rallying the nation behind his crusade for a new world order.

Trying initially to overcome domestic opposition by voluntary means, the Wilson administration called upon the new professions of advertising and public relations. Treasury Secretary William Gibbs McAdoo set the patriotic tone, raising enormous sums to defray the expense of the war. Including loans to the Allies, World War I cost the United States $35.5 billion. Almost two-thirds of this amount ($21 billion) came from government bond sales, called Liberty Loan drives, organized by McAdoo.

McAdoo surrounded the Liberty Loan campaigns with great ballyhoo. Posters exhorted citizens to "FIGHT OR BUY BONDS." Parades, rallies, and appearances by movie stars all aided the cause. An undercurrent of coercion also contributed to heavy sales; McAdoo declared that "only a friend of Germany" would refuse to buy bonds.

Stiff taxes supplied the other one-third of the war's funding. Taking advantage of its new power to tax incomes granted by the Sixteenth Amendment (ratified in 1913), Congress imposed wartime income taxes that rose to 63 percent at the top level.

George Creel, a progressive reformer and journalist, headed Washington's most effective wartime propaganda agency, the Committee on Public Information (CPI). Established in April 1917, ostensibly to combat rumors by providing authoritative information, the Creel committee became a propaganda agency that communicated the government's official version of reality and discredited those who questioned it. Posters, news releases, advertisements, and movies all trumpeted the government's sanitized version of events. The CPI poured foreign-language publications into the cities to ensure the loyalty of recent immigrants. Creel also organized the "four minute men": a network of 75,000 speakers throughout the nation who gave patriotic talks to audiences of all kinds. Creel calculated that this small army of propagandists delivered 7.5 million speeches to listeners totaling 314 million.

Intellectuals, Cultural Leaders, and Reformers Present Arms

The nation's teachers, writers, religious leaders, and magazine editors overwhelmingly supported the war. These custodians of culture viewed the conflict as a struggle to defend threatened values and standards. Historians contrasted Germany's malignant power and glorification of brute force with the Allies' loftier, more civilized ideals. Alan Seeger, a young Harvard graduate who volunteered to fight for France in 1916, wrote highly popular poems romanticizing the war. An artillery barrage became "the magnificent orchestra of war." The "sense of being the instrument of Destiny," wrote Seeger, represented the "supreme experience" of combat. He was killed in action in 1916.

Progressives hoped that the wartime climate of heightened government activism and sacrifice for the common good would encourage further reforms. Some of George Creel's most effective coworkers on the Committee for Public Information were former muckrakers. Herbert Croly, Walter Lippmann, and other progressive intellectuals associated with the *New Republic* zealously supported the war.

Prominent among these scholarly and journalistic champions of the war was John Dewey, who had particular influence with the reform-minded younger generation. In *New Republic* articles in 1917–1918, Dewey condemned the war's opponents. Socially engaged intellectuals, he wrote, must accept reality as they found it and shape it toward positive social goals, not stand aside in self-righteous indignation. The war presented exciting "social possibilities" for the advance of society at home and abroad. Domestically, the wartime growth of government power could be channeled to reform purposes once peace returned. Internationally, America's entry would transform a crude imperialistic clash into a worldwide democratic crusade, Dewey argued.

Wartime Intolerance and Hysteria

Responding to this drumfire of propaganda, some Americans became almost hysterical in their hatred of all things German, their hostility to aliens and dissenters, and their strident patriotism. Isolated actions by German saboteurs, including the blowing-up of a New Jersey munitions dump, fanned the antiforeign flames. In Collinsville, Illinois, a mob of 500 lynched a young German-born man in April 1918. When a jury exonerated the mob leaders, a jury member shouted, "Nobody can say we aren't loyal now."

German books vanished from libraries, towns with German names changed them, and "liberty sandwich" and "liberty cabbage" replaced "hamburgers" and "sauerkraut" on restaurant menus. Popular evangelist Billy Sunday proclaimed, "If you turn hell upside down you will find 'Made in Germany' stamped on the bottom." Leopold Stokowski, the conductor of the Philadelphia Orchestra, dropped German opera and songs from the repertoire but asked President Wilson's permission to retain Bach, Beethoven, Mozart, and Brahms.

The zealots of ideological conformity fell with special ferocity on war critics and radicals. A mob hauled a Cincinnati pacifist minister to a woods and whipped him. Theodore Roosevelt, never the voice of moderation, branded antiwar senator Robert La Follette "an unhung traitor." In Bisbee, Arizona, a vigilante mob forced 1,200 miners who belonged to the IWW onto a freight train and shipped them into the New Mexico desert without food, water, or shelter.

Opponents of the War

Despite the overheated conformist climate, a few Americans refused to support the war. Some were German-Americans with ties to the land of their forebears, and some others belonged to historically pacifist churches. Sixty-five thousand men registered as conscientious objectors, and 21,000 of them were drafted. The army assigned most of these to "noncombatant" duty on military bases.

Jane Addams, a founder of the Woman's Peace party in 1915, remained a pacifist throughout the war. She did, however, lecture for the Food Administration's Speakers Bureau because she saw increased food production as a means of aiding the war's innocent victims.

Socialist party leaders, including Eugene V. Debs, opposed the war on political grounds. They viewed it as a capitalist contest for world markets, with the soldiers on both sides mere cannon fodder. The U.S. declaration of war, they insisted, mainly reflected Wall Street's desire to protect its loans to England and France.

The war's most incisive critic was Randolph Bourne, a young journalist. Although Bourne much admired John Dewey, he rejected his hero's prowar position. Like moths near a flame, Bourne said, intellectuals were mesmerized by the lure of being near the center of action and power. He dismissed as a self-serving delusion the belief that liberal reformers could direct the war to their own purposes. War took on its own terrible momentum, he wrote, and could no more be controlled by intellectuals than a rogue elephant crashing through the bush. Ultimately, Dewey, Lippmann, and other prowar intellectuals agreed with Bourne. By 1919 Dewey had concedeed that the war, far from promoting liberalism, had unleashed the most reactionary and intolerant forces in the nation.

Suppressing Dissent by Law

Wartime intolerance also found expression in federal laws and in the actions of top government officials. The Espionage Act of June 1917 prescribed heavy fines and long prison sentences for a variety of loosely defined antiwar activities. The Sedition Amendment to the Espionage Act (May 1918) imposed heavy penalties on anyone convicted of using "disloyal, profane, scurrilous, or abusive language" about the government, the Constitution, the flag, or the military.

Wilson's reactionary attorney general, Thomas W. Gregory, freely employed these measures to stamp out dissent. Opponents of the war should expect no mercy "from an outraged people and an avenging government," he said. Under this sweeping legislation and sweeping state laws, hundreds of pacifists, socialists, and war opponents found themselves imprisoned. Kate Richards O'Hare, a midwestern socialist organizer, spent more than a year in prison for allegedly telling an audience that "the women of the United States are nothing more than brood sows, to raise children to get into the army and be made into fertilizer." Eugene V. Debs was sentenced to ten years in a federal penitentiary for a speech discussing the economic causes of the war.

The Espionage Act also authorized the postmaster general to bar suspect materials from the mail—a provision enthusiastically enforced by Wilson's postmaster general, Albert S. Burleson, a radical-hating superpatriot. In January 1919 Congressman-elect Victor Berger received a twenty-year prison sentence (later set aside by the Supreme Court) and was denied his seat in the House for publishing antiwar articles in his socialist newspaper, the *Milwaukee Leader*.

A few citizens protested. Muckraking novelist Upton Sinclair wrote to President Wilson to deplore that a man of Burleson's "pitiful and childish ignorance" should wield such power. Wilson did little to restrain either his postmaster general or his attorney general. Nor did the Supreme Court. In three 1919 decisions, the Court upheld Espionage Act convictions of people who had spoken out against the war. It also upheld Debs's conviction. Although the war was over, a vindictive Wilson refused to commute Debs's sentence. (President Warren Harding would at last release the ill and aging

Debs in December 1921, but the government would not restore his rights as a U.S. citizen.)

Thus wartime idealism and high resolve deteriorated into fearful suspicion, narrow ideological conformity, and the persecution of those who failed to meet the zealots' notion of "100 percent Americanism." The effects of this ugly wartime climate would linger long after the armistice.

Economic and Social Trends in Wartime America

All wars usher in unanticipated economic and social changes, and World War I was no exception. The war affected the lives of millions of industrial workers (including large numbers of blacks and women) and farmers. The wartime mood also gave a significant boost to the moral-reform movement.

Boom Times in Industry and Agriculture

For all its horrendous human toll, World War I brought glowing prosperity to the American economy. Factory production climbed about 35 percent from 1914 to 1918, and the civilian work force grew by 1.3 million from 1916 to 1918. Wages rose, but prices soared. The real wages of unskilled workers climbed by nearly 20 percent from 1914 to 1918.

A no-strike rule prevailed in American industry during the war. Samuel Gompers of the American Federation of Labor ordered workers to stay on the job for the duration. Union membership increased from 2.7 million in 1916 to more than 5 million by 1920. The National War Labor Board guaranteed workers' rights to organize and bargain collectively. It also pressured war plants to introduce the eight-hour workday, which by the war's end had become the standard in U.S. industry.

American agriculture prospered during the war years. With European farm production disrupted, U.S. agricultural prices more than doubled from 1913 to 1918. Cotton jumped from $.12 to $.29 per pound by 1918, and corn from $.70 to $1.52 a bushel. At the same time, farmers' real income rose significantly. But in the long run, this agricultural boom proved a mixed blessing. Farmers had borrowed heavily to expand their production, and when the artificially high wartime prices collapsed, they found themselves in a credit squeeze. During an ensuing, long agricultural depression in the 1920s and 1930s, farmers would look back to the war years as their last time of real prosperity.

Social disruption as well as prosperity came of the boom. The job seekers streaming into urban industrial centers strained housing, schools, and municipal services. Changes in social behavior occurred, taking many forms. The consumption of cigarettes shot up by 350 percent, to 48 billion a year. Automobile production quadrupled, reaching 1.8 million in 1917. With more cars on the road, American life began to change.

Blacks Migrate Northward

The war sharply accelerated blacks' migration to northern cities. An estimated half-million blacks left the South during the war. Chicago's African-American population swelled from 44,000 in 1910 to 110,000 in 1920, and Cleveland's from 8,000 to 34,000.

Economic opportunity drew them north. When the war sharply reduced immigration from Europe, American industry recruited black workers to take up the slack. The economic inducements found a ready response. To the black sharecropper mired in poverty and confronting blatant racism, the prospect of a salary of three dollars a day, in a region where racism seemed less intense, appeared a heaven-sent opportunity. One black, newly settled near Chicago, wrote his southern relatives, "Nothing here but money, and it is not hard to get." By 1920, 1.5 million American blacks were working in northern factories or other urban-based jobs.

Once the initial elation faded, black migrants often found they had traded one set of problems for another. White workers resented the competition, and white homeowners reacted in fear and hostility as crowded black neighborhoods spilled over into surrounding areas. Bloody violence broke out on

July 2, 1917, in East St. Louis, Illinois, home to 10,000 blacks recently arrived from the South. In a well-coordinated action, a white mob torched black homes and then shot the residents as they fled. At least thirty-nine African-Americans were killed. A few weeks later, the newly founded National Association for the Advancement of Colored People (NAACP) organized a silent march down New York's Fifth Avenue to protest racial violence. Despite this and other demonstrations, racial enmity in northern cities did not end with the signing of the armistice.

Women and the War

From one perspective, World War I seems a supremely male experience. Male politicians and statesmen made the decisions that led to war. Male generals issued the orders that sent untold thousands of other men to their death in battle. Yet any event as vast as war touches all of society. The war affected women differently than men, but it affected them profoundly.

Women activists hoped that the war would lead to equality and greater opportunity for women. One author offered a feminist variation of Woodrow Wilson's theme: women should energetically support the war, she said, in order to win a role in shaping the peace.

For a bright, brief moment, the war promised dramatic gains for women. Thousands of women served in the military and in volunteer agencies, and about 1 million women worked in industry in 1917–1918. The woman-suffrage movement sped toward victory in 1917–1918 on a tide of wartime idealism. "The services of women during the supreme crisis have been of the most signal usefulness and distinction," wrote President Wilson; "it is high time that part of our debt should be acknowledged." By overwhelming margins, Congress passed a woman-suffrage amendment to the Constitution in 1919. This Nineteenth Amendment was ratified in 1920.

But hopes that the war would permanently improve women's status proved unfounded. Relatively few women actually *entered* the work force for the first time in 1917–1918; most simply moved from poorly paying jobs to better-paying positions. And even those in better-paying jobs generally earned less than the men whom they replaced. As soon as the war ended, moreover, women lost their jobs to make room for the returning troops. The New York labor federation stated, "The same patriotism which induced women to enter industry during the war should induce them to vacate their positions after the war."

Despite the short-lived spurt in employment during the war, the percentage of working women declined slightly from 1910 to 1920. As industrial researcher Mary Van Kleeck wrote, when "the immediate dangers" ended, traditional male attitudes "came to life once more." The dark underside of the war spirit—prejudice, intolerance, conformism—demonstrated remarkable tenacity in peace; positive effects such as the beginning of gender equality in the workplace were more fleeting.

Moral Reform in Wartime

The war worked wonders for the prohibition movement. Nineteen states had gone dry by 1917, and the war decisively boosted the cause. Prohibitionists pointed out that most of the nation's biggest breweries bore such German names as Pabst, Schlitz, and Anheuser-Busch. Beer, they hinted, was part of a German plot to undermine the United States' moral fiber and fighting qualities. Furthermore, the use of grain to manufacture whiskey and gin seemed unpatriotic. The Eighteenth Amendment, which banned the manufacture, transportation, and sale of alcoholic beverages, passed in December 1917. It drew wide support as a war measure.

The war also strengthened the antiprostitution movement and encouraged strict sexual morality. The War Department closed all brothels near military bases, and Congress appropriated $4 million to combat prostitution and sexually transmitted disease on the home front. Among the red-light districts closed on military orders was New Orleans's famed Storyville. Many jazz musicians who had been performing in Storyville's brothels and clubs moved up the Mississippi, carrying their music to

Memphis, St. Louis, and Chicago. Thus, ironically, the moral reformism of World War I contributed to the diffusion of jazz northward.

Joyous Armistice, Bitter Aftermath

In November 1918 the war that had battered Europe for more than four years ground to a halt. Woodrow Wilson took the lead at the peace conference, but he failed in his cherished objective of securing American membership in the League of Nations. At home, racism and intolerance worsened. In the election of 1920, Americans repudiated Wilsonianism and sent conservative Republican Warren G. Harding to the White House.

Wilson's Fourteen Points

President Wilson planned to put a "Made in America" stamp on the peace. American involvement, he believed, could transform a sordid power conflict into something higher and finer—a struggle for a new, more democratic world order.

As the nation had mobilized in 1917, Wilson had striven to translate his vision into specific war aims. The need had grown urgent after Lenin's bolsheviks seized power in Russia late in 1917 and published many of the self-serving secret treaties signed by the European powers before 1914.

In his Fourteen Points speech to Congress in January 1918, Wilson summed up U.S. war aims. Eight points dealt with territorial settlement in postwar Europe, underscoring Wilson's belief in self-determination and autonomy for peoples formerly ruled by the Austro-Hungarian or the Ottoman Empire. A ninth point insisted that colonial disputes be resolved in the interests of the colonial peoples as well as of the European powers. The remaining five points revealed Wilson's larger vision: a world of free navigation, lowered trade barriers, reduced armaments, openly negotiated treaties, and "a general association of nations" to ensure peace and resolve conflicts by negotiation. The Fourteen Points

helped to solidify U.S. support for the war, especially among liberals. Such generous and high-minded goals proved that the nation had gone to war for noble objectives. Whether Wilson could achieve his goals remained to be seen.

Armistice

With the failure of Germany's spring 1918 offensive, and with Allied advances in the Meuse-Argonne and elsewhere, German military leaders acknowledged the inevitable. In early October they proposed to Wilson an armistice based on the Fourteen Points. The British and French hesitated, but in early November they agreed to peace on the basis of the Fourteen Points. Meanwhile, political turmoil in Berlin led to the abdication of Kaiser Wilhelm II and the proclamation of a German republic.

As dawn broke over the Forest of Compiègne on November 11, 1918, Marshal Foch and his German counterparts, seated in Foch's private railroad car, signed the armistice. Word spread swiftly: hostilities would cease at 11:00 A.M. As the booming guns fell silent, French, British, American, and German men cautiously approached each other. Rockets burst over the front that night in celebration. Back home, cheering throngs filled the streets. "Everything for which America has fought has been accomplished," Wilson's armistice message hopefully stated.

The Versailles Peace Conference

The challenge of forging a peace treaty remained. Wilson opted personally to lead the U.S. delegation to the peace conference. This decision was probably a mistake, for Wilson's oratorical skills outstripped his talent for negotiation and compromise. The president compounded his mistake by selecting only one Republican peace commissioner, an elderly diplomat. In the November 1918 congressional elections, Republicans gained control of both houses of Congress, an ominous sign for Wilson.

Wilson received a hero's welcome in Europe. Shouts of "Voodrow Veelson" rang out in Paris as

Woodrow Wilson in Paris, December 1918
Citizens of the victorious Allied nations greeted Wilson deliriously, but back home the Republicans had gained control of both houses of Congress, and the political climate would soon turn sharply hostile.

Wilson and the French president headed a parade up the Champs-Elysées, the city's elegant ceremonial boulevard. When Wilson reached Britain, children spread flowers in his path, and in Italy an exuberant official compared his visit to the Second Coming of Jesus Christ.

The exhilaration evaporated when the peace conference began on January 18, 1919, at the palace of Versailles near Paris. A Council of Four, comprising the Allied heads of state, dominated the proceedings: Wilson; Italy's Vittorio Orlando; the aged and cynical Georges Clemenceau of France, determined to avenge Germany's humiliating defeat of France in 1871; and David Lloyd George of Great Britain, of whom Wilson said, "He is slippery as an eel, and I never know when to count on him."

These European leaders represented bitter, vindictive nations that had suffered horrendously in the war. Their objectives bore little relationship to Wilson's vision of a liberal peace. As Clemenceau remarked, "God gave us the Ten Commandments and we broke them. Mr. Wilson has given us the Fourteen Points. We shall see." The squabbling among the Allies became intense.

Mirroring this poisonous political climate, the peace treaty signed by a sullen German delegation on June 28, 1919, was harshly punitive. Germany was disarmed, stripped of its colonies, forced to admit sole blame for the war, and saddled with unspecified but potentially enormous reparation payments. In all, Germany lost one-tenth of its population and one-eighth of its territory.

Wilson's idealism influenced some of the treaty's provisions. Germany's former colonies, as well as those of Turkey in the Middle East, went to various Allies under a trusteeship system by which they eventually, in theory, would become independent. The treaty recognized the independence of Poland; the Baltic states of Estonia, Latvia, and Lithuania, which Germany had seized from bolshevik Russia; and two new nations, Czechoslovakia and Yugoslavia, carved from the former Austro-Hungarian and Ottoman empires.

On balance, the Versailles treaty was a disaster. Its provisions awakened festering resentment in Germany. Its framers, moreover, failed to come to terms with revolutionary Russia. Even as the treaty makers devised territorial settlements in eastern Europe that were designed to keep Russia as weak as possible, the Allies found themselves embroiled in the Russian civil war.

Indeed, in August 1918 a fourteen-nation Allied force had landed in Russian ports in Europe and Asia. The troops soon began assisting the counter-revolutionaries (including both democrats and tsarists) fighting to overthrow Lenin. Wilson approved of American participation. He had welcomed the liberal revolution of March 1917 but viewed Lenin's seizure of power in November 1917 as a betrayal of the Allied cause and of his hopes for a liberal Russian future.

Before leaving Versailles, the Allied leaders agreed to support a Russian military leader, Admiral Aleksandr Kolchak, who was waging an ultimately unsuccessful campaign against the bolsheviks. Wilson refused to recognize Lenin's communist government; not until 1933 would the United States open formal diplomatic relations with the Soviet Union.

The Fight over the League of Nations

In the summer of 1919, drained by months of bargaining and dismayed by the treaty's vindictive features, Wilson increasingly focused on his one shining achievement at Versailles: the League of Nations. The League, whose charter, or "covenant," was written into the treaty itself, represented the highest embodiment of Wilson's vision of a liberal, harmonious, and rational world order. As he wrote an adviser, "That instrument will work wonders, bring the blessing of peace, and then when the war psychosis has abated, it will not be difficult to settle all the disputes that baffle us now."

But within a few months, Wilson's dream lay shattered. Warning signs appeared as early as February 1919, when several leading Republicans, including Senate Majority Leader Henry Cabot Lodge, expressed serious doubts about the League. Wilson told them defiantly, "You cannot dissect the Covenant from the treaty without destroying the whole vital structure."

When Wilson returned to the United States in June 1919 and submitted the Versailles treaty to the Senate for ratification, Lodge bottled it up for weeks in the Foreign Relations Committee. Convinced that he could rally popular opinion, Wilson began a speaking tour in early September. He covered more than 9,000 miles and gave 37 speeches in 22 days. Large, friendly crowds cheered Wilson's ideal of a world free of war.

But the grueling trip took a terrible toll. On September 25, outside Pueblo, Colorado, Wilson collapsed. Rushed back to Washington, he suffered a major stroke on October 2. Despite a partial recovery, he spent most of the rest of his term in bed or in a wheelchair, a reclusive invalid, his mind clouded, his fragile emotions betraying him into vengeful actions and petulant outbursts. Wilson's strong-willed second wife, Edith Galt, played an important but not entirely constructive role during these difficult months. Fiercely guarding her husband, she and his doctor concealed his condition, controlled his access to information, and decided who could see him and who could not.

The final act of the League drama played itself out. Senators split into three camps: Democrats who supported the Covenant without changes; Republican "Irreconcilables" who opposed the League completely; and Republican "Reservationists," led by Lodge, who demanded significant modifications before they would accept the Covenant. Article 10 of the Covenant, pledging each member nation to preserve the political independence and territorial integrity of all members, concerned the Reservationists. They felt that it infringed on America's freedom of action in foreign affairs and on Congress's right to declare war.

Had Wilson compromised, the Senate would have ratified the treaty and the United States would have joined the League. But the president dug in his heels as his physical and emotional condition aggravated his tendency toward rigidity. He lashed out against the reservations demanded by the Republicans as "a knife thrust at the heart of the treaty." The American people, moreover, did not rise up in support of the League. The wartime reactionary mood persisted: political idealism did not rule the day now that the war was over. In November 1919 and again in March 1920, Irreconcilables and Democrats obeying Wilson's orders voted against the treaty that included Lodge's reservations. A president elected amid high popular enthusiasm in 1912, applauded when he called for war in 1917, and adulated when he arrived in Europe in 1918, lay isolated and sick, his political leadership repudiated. What should have been Wilson's supreme triumph turned to ashes in his grasp.

Racism and Red Scare

The wartime spirit of "100 percent Americanism" left an acrid aftertaste as 1919–1920 saw racial violence and fresh antiradical hysteria. Lynch mobs murdered seventy-six African-Americans in 1919, including ten military veterans, several still in uniform. The bloodiest disorder occurred in 1919 in Chicago, where an influx of southern blacks had intensified tensions. On a hot July afternoon, whites at a Lake Michigan beach threw stones at a black youth swimming offshore. He sank and drowned. A thirteen-day reign of terror followed as white and black marauders roamed the streets, randomly attacked innocent victims, and torched buildings. The violence left 15 whites and 23 blacks dead and more than 500 injured.

Wartime antiradical panic, reinforced by the fear and hatred of bolshevism, crested in the Red Scare of 1919–1920. Such emotions deepened as a rash of strikes broke out, representing an accumulation of grievances. When Seattle's labor unions organized an orderly general work stoppage early in 1919, the mayor accused the strikers of trying to "duplicate the anarchy of Russia" and called for federal troops. In April mail bombs were sent to various public officials. One blew off the hands of a senator's maid, and another damaged the U.S. attorney general's home.

The mounting frenzy over supposed radicals took political form. In November 1919 the House of Representatives refused to seat Milwaukee socialist Victor Berger. The New York legislature expelled several socialist members. The Justice Department established a countersubversive division under young J. Edgar Hoover, the future head of the Federal Bureau of Investigation, who arrested hundreds of suspected communists and aliens. In December 1919, 249 Russian-born aliens were deported.

On January 20, 1920, the Justice Department coordinated federal marshals and local police in raids on the homes of suspected radicals and the headquarters of radical organizations. Without bothering about search or arrest warrants, authorities arrested more than 4,000 people and ransacked homes and offices. These lightning raids grossly violated civil rights and simple decency. Marshals barged into one woman's bedroom to arrest her. In Lynn, Massachusetts, police arrested thirty-nine men and women meeting to discuss forming a cooperative bakery. The rabidly antiradical and

politically ambitious attorney general, A. Mitchell Palmer, coordinated these "Red raids." Palmer had succumbed to the anticommunist hysteria of the early postwar period. He direfully described a "blaze of revolution . . . sweeping over every American institution of law and order . . . crawling into the sacred corners of American homes . . . burning up the foundations of society." The more outrageous manifestations of the Red Scare subsided as Palmer's irrational predictions failed to materialize. When a bomb exploded in New York City's financial district in September 1920, killing thirty-eight people, most Americans concluded that it was the work of an isolated fanatic, rather than evidence of an approaching revolution.

The Election of 1920

In this disturbing climate, the nation prepared for the election of 1920. The Democrats, meeting in San Francisco, half-heartedly endorsed Wilson's League position and nominated James M. Cox, the progressive governor of Ohio. They chose as Cox's running mate the young assistant secretary of the navy, Franklin D. Roosevelt, who possessed a potent political name. The confident Republicans turned to Senator Warren G. Harding of Ohio, an amiable politician with few discernable qualifications beyond a lack of enemies. One Republican politician observed, "There ain't any first raters this year. . . . We got a lot of second raters, and Harding is the best of the second raters." For vice president they chose Governor Calvin Coolidge of Massachusetts.

Wilson declared the election a "solemn referendum" on the League, but the nation was spiritually spent, both by the war and by the emotional rollercoaster ride from lofty idealism to cynical disillusionment on which Wilson had taken it. Sensing the popular longing for calm, Harding promised a return to "normalcy." There would be no more idealistic crusades, no more cavalcades of reforms.

Harding and Coolidge piled up a landslide, winning 16 million votes to the Democrats' 9 million. Nearly a million voters defiantly cast their ballots for Socialist Eugene V. Debs, serving time in an Atlanta penitentiary.

The election dashed all hope for American entry into the League of Nations. Harding announced that the question of U.S. membership in the League was "dead." Two decades of reform at home and idealism abroad thus came to an abrupt, embittered end.

The Election of 1920

Candidates	Parties	Electoral Vote	Popular Vote	Percentage of Popular Vote
WARREN G. HARDING	Republican	404	16,143,407	60.4
James M. Cox	Democratic	127	9,130,328	34.2
Eugene V. Debs	Socialist		919,799	3.4
P. P. Christensen	Farmer-Labor		265,411	1.0

Conclusion

By conservative estimate, the First World War cost 10 million dead and 20 million wounded worldwide. Included in this staggering toll were 112,000 Americans—49,000 killed in combat, the rest dead of influenza and other diseases.

The war's social, political, economic, and technological impact extended far beyond the battlefield. Many of the technologies of slaughter that would dominate in the rest of the century emerged: torpedoes, bombs, toxic gases, and deadly efficient machine guns. In the United States, the wartime spirit aided some progressive goals—woman suffrage, prohibition, government regulation—but ultimately undermined the progressive movement's commitment to social justice and its humanitarian concern for the underdog. When Americans repudiated Wilsonian idealism after the war, they also rejected reform. Internationally, the conflict propelled the United States to the center of world politics and left the nation's businesses and financial institutions poised for global expansion.

Some of these changes endured; others were fleeting. Their cumulative effect was profound. The United States that celebrated the armistice in November 1918 was a very different society from the one that Wilson had summoned to war only nineteen months earlier.

Chronology

1905 President Theodore Roosevelt mediates the end of the Russo-Japanese War.

1906 San Francisco ends segregation of Asian schoolchildren.

1907 Roosevelt sends the "Great White Fleet" around the world.

1912 U.S. Marines occupy Nicaragua.

1914 U.S. troops occupy Vera Cruz, Mexico.
Archduke Franz Ferdinand of Austria assassinated.
World War I begins.
Wilson protests British interception of U.S. merchant ships.

1915 U.S. Marines occupy Haiti and the Dominican Republic.
Woman's Peace party organized.
British liner *Lusitania* sunk by German U-boat.
U.S. "preparedness" movement begins.
Germany restricts U-boat campaign.
Wilson permits U.S. bank loans to Allies.

1916 U.S. punitive expedition invades Mexico, seeking Pancho Villa.
After *Sussex* sinking, Germany pledges not to attack merchant ships without warning.
Wilson reelected as president.

1917 U.S. troops withdraw from Mexico.
Germany resumes unrestricted U-boat warfare; United States breaks diplomatic relations.
United States enters the war.
Selective Service Act sets up national draft.
War Industries Board, Committee on Public Information, and Food Administration created.
Espionage Act passed.
NAACP march in New York City.
Bolsheviks grab power in Russia; Russia leaves the war.
U.S. government seizes the nation's railroads.

1918 Wilson outlines Fourteen Points for peace.
Sedition Amendment to Espionage Act.
American Expeditionary Force (AEF) helps stop Germans at Château-Thierry and Belleau Wood, closes St. Mihiel salient, and plays key role in the Meuse-Argonne campaign.
Armistice signed (November 11).

1919 Eighteenth Amendment added to the Constitution.
Peace treaty, including League of Nations covenant, signed at Versailles.
Racial violence in Chicago.
Wilson suffers paralyzing stroke.
Versailles treaty, with League covenant, rejected by Senate.

1920 "Red raids" organized by Justice Department.
Nineteenth Amendment added to the Constitution.
Warren G. Harding elected president.

FOR FURTHER READING

John M. Blum, *Woodrow Wilson and the Politics of Morality* (1956). Illuminating interpretive biography emphasizing Wilson's self-destructive personality traits.

Robert H. Ferrell, *Woodrow Wilson and World War I, 1917–1921* (1985). A vigorously written critical synthesis; especially good on the peace negotiations.

Frank Freidel, *Over There: The Story of America's First Great Overseas Crusade* (1964). Excellent, readable overview of the AEF experience based on soldiers' diaries and reminiscences.

David M. Kennedy, *Over Here: The First World War and American Society* (1980). Deeply researched interpretive study of the home front during the war.

Ernest R. May, *The World War and American Isolation, 1914–1917* (1966). Standard account of the steps from neutrality to intervention, stressing the role of Germany's shifting U-boat policies.

Arno Mayer, *Politics and Diplomacy of Peacemaking: Containment and Counterrevolution* (1967). Analysis of the making of the Versailles treaty.

Chapter
24

The 1920s

To many observers, F. Scott and Zelda Fitzgerald symbolized the rich possibilities of the United States in the 1920s. They had it all: he was a talented and extravagantly handsome novelist; she, a breathtakingly beautiful and madcap companion. They danced their way through the decade on the front pages of the nation's newspapers, and the less daring gasped at the recklessness with which they consumed life. Fittingly, Scott Fitzgerald coined the term *Jazz Age* to describe the new America of flivvers and flappers, flag-pole sitters, and get-rich-quick schemes. However, by the mid-1930s the Fitzgeralds' shocking decline made them seem still a metaphor again, this time a metaphor for American problems. Zelda had drifted far out of touch with reality and spent most of the last half of her life in asylums; Scott, in the grip of alcoholism, squandered his prodigious talent on Hollywood scripts that he despised. Their heady rise and sickening fall paralleled the 1920s in all too many ways.

In the 1920s the nation's industrial machinery poured out a torrent of automobiles, electrical appliances, and other consumer goods. These new products brought prosperity

A New Economic Order
Republicans in Power
Mass Society, Mass Culture
Cultural Ferment and Creativity
A Society in Conflict
Hoover at the Helm

(Right) Life *cover, 1926, by John Held jr.*

to the national economy and far-reaching changes to daily life. The prosperity proved fragile; the changes did not. Economic transformations led to marked shifts in diet, dress, housekeeping, travel, entertainment, and thought.

Following several decades of immigration and urban growth, social tensions remained acute. As Republican presidents espoused conservative political and cultural values, conflicts ripped at the fabric of society. But this same ferment stimulated creativity in literature and the arts. When the decade ended, Americans summed up these turbulent and change-filled years in a phrase: the Roaring Twenties.

A New Economic Order

With consumer products aplenty, sophisticated advertising, and innovative forms of corporate organization, the economy raced forward in the 1920s, but not everyone benefited. Some key industries declined, workers lost jobs as factories automated, and farmers relapsed into chronic economic problems. Still, the overall picture seemed rosy, and most Americans celebrated the nation's thriving business culture.

A Decade of Prosperity

The war-induced boom continued until late 1920, when demobilization disrupted the economy. As the government canceled contracts and as veterans swamped labor markets, a recession struck. Business slowed, bankruptcies increased, and unemployment jumped. Recovery came in 1922, and, for the next few years, the economy grew spectacularly. Unemployment dropped as low as 3 percent, prices held steady, and gross national product climbed from $70 billion in 1922 to nearly $100 billion in 1929. By mid-decade the 1920–1922 recession seemed only a minor setback.

Electricity powered the general prosperity. Factories had started to electrify late in the nineteenth century, and by now the construction of hydroelectric generating plants had brought the age of electricity to urban households as well. By the mid-1920s, with more than 60 percent of the nation's homes wired for electricity, a wondrous array of electrical appliances—refrigerators, ranges, washing machines, vacuum cleaners, fans, razors, and mixers—stood gleaming in the stores. Their manufacture provided a potent economic stimulus.

The era's business boom also rested on the automobile. Passenger-car registrations bounded from 8 million in 1920 to more than 23 million in 1930. Ford's Model T led the market until mid-decade, when General Motors Corporation (GM) spurted ahead by touting a range of colors (the Model T came only in black) and improved passenger comfort. Particularly popular was GM's lowest-price car, named for automotive designer Louis Chevrolet. In response, in 1927 Ford introduced the stylish Model A in a spectrum of colors. By the end of the decade, the automobile industry accounted for 9 percent of all wages in manufacturing and had stimulated such related industries as rubber, gasoline and petroleum, advertising, and highway construction.

American capitalism remained vigorously expansionist. Ford, GM, General Electric, and other large corporations invested heavily in production facilities abroad. Other U.S. firms acquired foreign processing facilities or sources of raw materials. Swift and Armour built meatpacking plants in Argentina; Anaconda Copper acquired Chile's biggest copper mine; and the mammoth United Fruit Company established processing factories throughout Latin America. By 1930 U.S. private investment abroad totaled more than $15 billion.

New Modes of Producing, Managing, and Selling

In the 1920s assembly-line mass production boosted the per capita output of industrial workers by 40 percent. At the sprawling Ford plants near Detroit, workers stood in one place and performed simple, repetitive tasks as an endless chain conveyed the

A Standard Oil Station in New Jersey, 1927
While the woman driver chats with friends on a rainy day, the attendant manually pumps the gasoline into the tank.

partly assembled vehicles past them. The technique quickly spread, and *Fordism* became a worldwide synonym for American industrial prowess.

Corporate consolidation continued. By 1930 more than 1,000 companies a year disappeared through merger. Corporate giants dominated major industries: Ford, GM, and Chrysler in automobiles; General Electric and Westinghouse in electricity; U.S. Steel in the steel industry. Consolidation reached epidemic proportions in public utilities. Samuel Insull of the Chicago Edison Company built an empire of local power companies that by 1929 had assets of $3.5 billion. At the decade's end, 100 corporations controlled nearly half the nation's business activity.

Merger mania was one expression of the search for a more integrated corporate order adapted for the new economic era. Where there were no mergers, companies that made the same product often cooperated on such matters as pricing, product specifications, and division of markets.

Streamlined operations resulted in a more bureaucratic management structure within individual businesses. Like the federal government, corporations nationalized their management in the twenties, establishing specialized divisions for product development, market research, economic forecasting, and employee relations. Professionals trained in management oversaw the day-to-day operations within this new corporate structure.

Wage policies also began to change. Some business leaders argued that employers should not necessarily pay the lowest wages possible; higher wages, they suggested, would generate higher productivity. Henry Ford led the way in 1914 by paying his workers an unprecedented five dollars a day, and other companies followed his lead in the 1920s.

In addition, new systems for distributing goods emerged. Automobiles now reached consumers through vast dealer networks; nearly 10,000 Ford dealerships had sprung up by 1926. A rapidly expanding network of chain stores accounted for about a quarter of all retail sales by 1930. Family-run roadside diners and tourist cabins prospered because of the spread of the automobile, but other small, locally owned businesses faded under relentless pressure from the chains. The A&P grocery chain expanded from 5,000 stores in 1922 to 17,500 in 1928. Installment buying represented another important mass-marketing innovation. By 1929, 75 percent of automobiles were bought on credit.

Above all, the 1920s business boom bobbed along on a sea of advertising. In 1919 corporations spent an estimated $1.8 billion promoting their wares. The advertising industry employed 600,000 people. Radio, the newest of the mass media, relied entirely on advertising for its income.

Advertisers used celebrity endorsements ("Nine out of ten screen stars care for their skin with Lux toilet soap"), promises of social success, and threats of social embarrassment. Beneath a picture of a pretty but obviously unhappy young woman, a 1923 Listerine mouthwash ad proclaimed,

> She was a beautiful girl and talented too. She had the advantages of education and better clothes than most girls of her set. She possessed that culture and poise that travel brings. Yet in the one pursuit that stands foremost in the mind of every girl and woman—marriage—she was a failure.

The young woman's problem was *halitosis*, a hitherto little-known term for bad breath. The remedy, of course, was Listerine, and lots of it.

Beyond touting specific products, advertisers redefined popular aspirations by offering a seductive vision of a new era of consumption. Ads for automobiles, cigarettes, electrical conveniences, clothing, and home furnishings created a fantasy world of elegance, grace, and boundless pleasure.

Business influence saturated life in the 1920s. A 1921 article summed up the prevailing mood: "Among the nations of the earth today America stands for one idea: Business. . . . Thru business, properly conceived, managed, and conducted, the human race is finally to be redeemed." Americans venerated the magnates of business and the new world of material progress they had created. In *The Man Nobody Knows* (1925), ad man Bruce Barton, the son of a Protestant minister, described Jesus Christ as a managerial genius who "picked up twelve men from the bottom ranks of business and forged them into an organization that conquered the world." Observed sociologists Robert and Helen Lynd: "More and more of the activities of life are coming to be strained through the bars of the dollar sign."

Women in the New Economic Era

Automobiles, electrical appliances, and other technological wonders profoundly affected women's lives. In the decade's ubiquitous advertising, glamorous women smiled behind the steering wheel and happily operated electric appliances. Housework became an exciting technological challenge. As one ad said, "Men are judged successful according to their power to delegate work. Similarly the wise woman delegates to electricity all that electricity can do."

In the workplace, the assembly line, offering less physically demanding work, should in theory have increased job opportunities for women. In fact, however, the assembly-line work force remained largely male. Although the number of women holding jobs increased by more than 2 million in the twenties, the *proportion* of women working outside the home remained unchanged, at 24 percent.

Wage discrimination continued. In 1929 a male trimmer in the meatpacking industry earned fifty-two cents an hour; a female trimmer, thirty-seven cents an hour. Reflecting the widespread view that women worked only until marriage, employers relegated most female employees to low-paying piece-rate jobs.

Business bureaucratization increased female employment opportunities. By 1930, 2 million women worked as secretaries, typists, and filing clerks. Few became managers, however. In the professions, women worked in the limited spheres of nursing, librarianship, social work, and public-school teaching. As medical schools imposed a ceiling of 5 percent on female admissions, the number of women physicians declined.

Organized Labor in a Business Age

The labor movement faced tough sledding in the twenties. Several factors led to dwindling union membership, from 5 million in 1920 to 3.4 million in 1929. Overall wage rates crept upward in the 1920s. In the steel industry, for example, real hourly wages rose about 17 percent from 1923 to 1929. Despite continuing workplace inequities, employees' fatter pay envelopes helped to undermine the union movement. Changes in the industrial process also played a role. The trade unions' traditional strength lay in established industries such as printing, railroading, and construction. This craft-based pattern of union organization was ill suited to the new mass-production industries.

Management hostility further weakened organized labor. Sometimes this antagonism took physical form, as when Henry Ford hired thugs and spies to intimidate would-be organizers. Typically, however, the anti-union campaign was subtler. Manufacturers' associations renamed the non-union shop the "open shop" and praised it as the "American Plan" of labor relations. Some companies sponsored their own "unions" and provided cafeterias, better rest rooms, and recreational facilities. Certain big corporations sold company stock to their workers at special prices.

Some corporate leaders heralded this new approach to labor relations as evidence of heightened ethical awareness in American business. General Electric's head insisted that workers' well-being stood second only to productivity in GE's hierarchy of values. Welfare capitalism, as this corporate paternalism was called, was intended to prevent the formation of independent unions.

Blacks' membership in unions remained low. Although the American Federation of Labor (AFL) officially prohibited racial discrimination, the independent unions composing the AFL discriminated against African-Americans in many ways. Some had constitutional clauses limiting membership to whites; others followed a de facto exclusionary policy. Corporations' hiring of blacks as strikebreakers further increased organized labor's hostility toward them.

Blacks, women, Mexican-Americans, and recent immigrants clustered at the bottom of the wage scale. Black workers entering the industrial labor force, last hired and first fired, typically performed the most menial jobs. Amid the general prosperity, wages for unskilled workers barely budged.

Agriculture: The Economy's Ailing Sector

The 1920s brought hard times for farmers. Dwindling military purchases and the revival of European agriculture sent prices plummeting 50 percent and more. In the period 1919–1921 total farm income fell from $10 billion to $4 billion. Increased production lowered prices even more, and farmers who had borrowed heavily to boost their harvests during the war found themselves unable to pay off loans and mortgages.

Farm groups turned to Washington for help. They asked for a price-support plan under which the government would purchase the surplus of six commodities—cotton, corn, rice, hogs, tobacco, and wheat—at a guaranteed high price and sell them on the world market. A tax, ultimately to be borne by consumers in the form of higher food costs, would make up the price differential. This plan, introduced in 1924 as the McNary-Haugen bill, passed Congress in 1927, only to be vetoed by President Calvin Coolidge. Repassed in 1928, the bill died after another executive veto.

Republicans in Power

Politics in the 1920s reflected the decade's business orientation. Republicans controlled Congress and supplied three presidents who mirrored the prevailing corporate outlook. In this atmosphere, former progressives and feminists faced difficult times.

Scandals and Silences: The Harding and Coolidge Years

In the 1920s the Republicans relied on a base of northern farmers, corporate leaders, small business-people, and skilled workers. The Democrats' base remained the white South and the urban political machines.

The conservatives who controlled the 1920 Republican convention selected Senator Warren G. Harding of Ohio as their nominee. A former newspaper editor and a genial backslapper, Harding enjoyed good liquor, good stories, poker with his cronies, and furtive encounters with his mistress. Yet this amiable second-rater won the presidency in a landslide (see Chapter 23). Harding's ordinariness appealed to war-weary voters longing for stability. Compared to Wilson's lofty sermons, his vacuous oratory had a soothing appeal.

Realizing his lack of qualifications, Harding compensated by making some notable appointments: Henry A. Wallace, the respected editor of a farm periodical, became secretary of agriculture; Charles Evans Hughes, a former New York governor and presidential candidate, was named secretary of state; and Andrew Mellon, a Pittsburgh banker and financier, served as treasury secretary. Wartime food administrator Herbert Hoover dominated the cabinet as secretary of commerce. Unfortunately, Harding made some disastrous appointments as well, including Harry Daugherty, his political manager, as attorney general; Albert B. Fall, New Mexico senator, as secretary of the interior; and Charles Forbes, a wartime draft dodger, as director of the Veterans' Bureau. These men draped the Harding years in an aura of back-room sleaze reminiscent of the Grant administration.

By 1922 Washington rumor hinted at criminal activity in high places. Dismayed, Harding confessed, "I have no trouble with my enemies. . . . But . . . my goddamn friends . . . , they're the ones that keep me walking the floor nights." In 1923, returning from an Alaskan cruise, Harding suffered a heart attack and died in San Francisco.

In 1924 a Senate investigation exposed the full scope of the scandals. Charles Forbes, convicted of stealing Veterans' Bureau funds, evaded prison by fleeing abroad. The bureau's general counsel committed suicide, as did an associate of Attorney General Daugherty who had been accused of influence peddling. Daugherty himself, forced from office in 1924, escaped conviction in two criminal trials. The seamiest scandal involved Interior Secretary Fall, who went to jail for secretly leasing government oil reserves in Elk Hills, California, and Teapot Dome, Wyoming, to two oilmen while accepting "loans" from them totaling $400,000. "Teapot Dome" became shorthand, like "Watergate" in the 1970s, for an entire presidential legacy of scandal.

Vice President Calvin Coolidge learned of Harding's death while visiting his family in New Hampshire. His father, a local magistrate, administered the presidential oath by lantern light. Coolidge brought a distinctly different style to the White House. His determined silence contrasted with Harding's chattiness. Once, as he left California, a radio reporter asked for a parting message to the people of the state. "Good-bye," Coolidge responded. Other than in style, however, Coolidge's advent meant little change. Tariff rates reached all-time highs, income taxes for the rich fell, and the Supreme Court overturned several progressive measures. Coolidge rejected a request for aid from Mississippi flood victims with the reminder that government had no duty to protect citizens "against the hazards of the elements."

In vetoing the McNary-Haugen farm bill, Coolidge warned against the "tyranny of bureaucratic regulation and control" and denounced the bill for benefiting farmers at the expense of "the general public welfare." Although his party had long championed high tariffs and other measures of benefit to business, Coolidge chafed when farmers pursued the same kind of special-interest politics.

Foreign Policy in an Isolationist Age

International relations produced President Harding's most notable achievement, the Washington Naval Arms Conference. To head off an expensive international naval-arms race, Harding called for a conference. When the delegates of various nations met in October 1921, Secretary of State Hughes startled them by proposing the destruction of ships to achieve an agreed-upon ratio of craft among the world's naval powers. Consequently, in February 1924 five nations—Great Britain, the United States, Japan, France, and Italy—signed a treaty

The Election of 1924				
Candidates	*Parties*	*Electoral Vote*	*Popular Vote*	*Percentage of Popular Vote*
CALVIN COOLIDGE	Republican	382	15,718,211	54.0
John W. Davis	Democratic	136	8,385,283	28.8
Robert M. La Follette	Progressive	13	4,831,289	16.6

pledging to reduce battleship tonnage and to observe a ten-year moratorium on battleship construction. The United States and Japan also agreed to respect each other's territorial holdings in the Pacific. Although the treaty did not prevent war, it represented a pioneering arms-control effort.

America otherwise followed an isolationist foreign policy in the 1920s, joining neither the League of Nations nor the Court of International Justice (the World Court). Symbolic gestures replaced genuine engagement. For example, in 1928 the United States and France cosponsored the Kellogg-Briand Pact renouncing aggression and calling for the outlawing of war. Lacking enforcement mechanisms, the high-sounding document did nothing to prevent the militarism that would plunge the world into war a decade later.

U.S. insistence on the full repayment of wartime debts generated ill will among former allies. In 1922 a Senate commission calculated the total bill, including interest, at $22 billion. As the German economy collapsed under the weight of reparations payments, and as other European economies foundered, America scaled down its demands, but high U.S. tariffs prevented foreign powers from earning the dollars needed to pay their debts.

Progressive Stirrings, Democratic Divisions

In Congress the progressive spirit had survived. Senator George Norris of Nebraska blocked the Coolidge administration from selling a federal hydroelectric facility at Muscle Shoals, Alabama, to Henry Ford for a fraction of its value. Congress's creation of the Federal Radio Commission (1927) extended to the fledgling broadcasting industry the progressive principle of goverment regulation of business activity.

In 1922 labor and farm groups formed the Conference for Progressive Political Action (CPPA), and in 1924 the CPPA revived the Progressive party. It adopted a prolabor, profarmer platform calling for government ownership of railroads and water-power resources and nominated Senator Robert La Follette for president.

Split between urban and rural wings, the Democratic party held its 1924 convention in New York. The extent of the division became evident when a resolution condemning the Ku Klux Klan failed by one vote. Rural Democrats supported William Gibbs McAdoo, Wilson's treasury secretary; urban Democrats backed Governor Alfred E. Smith of New York, an Irish Roman Catholic. Ballot after ballot left both candidates short of the two-thirds majority necessary for nomination. Humorist Will Rogers observed, "This thing has got to end. New York invited you folks here as guests, not to live." After 102 ballots, exhausted delegates turned to a compromise candidate, John W. Davis.

On the Republican side, Coolidge easily won renomination. The GOP platform praised high tariffs, urged tax and spending cuts, and applauded the Washington Naval Arms Conference. With the economy humming and the opposition divided, Coolidge cruised to victory with about 16 million votes. Davis trailed with 8 million votes, and La Follette collected a little under 5 million.

Women and Politics in the 1920s: A Dream Deferred

Suffragists' belief that votes for women would transform politics died quickly after the war. Women did achieve notable gains: states passed laws permitting them to serve on juries and to hold public office, the League of Women Voters emerged, and the Sheppard-Towner Act of 1921 appropriated $1.2 million for rural prenatal and baby-care centers. Beyond these advances, however, the Nineteenth Amendment had little political impact. With the vote attained, women scattered to all points on the political spectrum, and many withdrew from politics completely.

As the women's movement splintered, it lost focus. Drawing mainly middle-class and professional women, the League of Women Voters abandoned reform activism for the study of civic issues. Some feminists worked for peace: Carrie Chapman Catt founded the National Conference on the Cause and Cure of War, and Jane Addams supported the Women's International League for Peace and Freedom. Meanwhile, Alice Paul and her National Woman's party campaigned for an equal-rights amendment to the Constitution, but many feminists condemned her position. Such an amendment might benefit professional women, they charged, but could harm female factory workers by abolishing protective legislation. The proposed amendment got nowhere.

Underlying the disarray in women's ranks were the conservative political atmosphere and materialistic mass culture of the 1920s. Right-wing groups accused Jane Addams and other women's rights leaders of communist sympathies. Young women, bombarded by advertising that defined liberation in terms of life-style and the purchase of goods, found civic idealism embarrassingly passé.

In this milieu, reforms achieved by organized women's groups often proved short-lived. The women's movement suffered serious setbacks when the Supreme Court struck down child-labor laws (1922) and women's protective laws (1923). A child-labor constitutional amendment squeezed through Congress in 1924 but won ratification in only a few states. The Sheppard-Towner program of rural prenatal and baby care ended in 1929.

Mass Society, Mass Culture

The automobiles, electrical appliances, and other manufactures that roared off the assembly lines in the 1920s heralded a new social and cultural era. These products utterly changed Americans' lives. The standardized mass production that spawned them, moreover, proved as adaptable to ideas as to roadsters and refrigerators.

A Nation of Cities, Consumer Goods, and Automobiles

The 1920 census showed that, for the first time, America's urban population outnumbered its rural dwellers. The tally recorded a dozen cities of more than 600,000. Blacks constituted a major part of the movement to the cities. By 1930 more than 40 percent of the nation's 12 million blacks lived in cities, notably Chicago, Detroit, New York, and other northern and western metropolitan centers.

City growth reshaped American culture. The nation became increasingly urbanized "in the cast of its mind, in its ideals, and in its folkways," as one historian has written. The forces that molded culture—radio, the movies, corporations, advertising agencies, mass magazines—operated from cities. Even when they nostalgically evoked rural values, they did so from big-city editorial offices and radio studios. The new consumer goods, particularly electrical appliances, had the most dramatic impact in the cities. (Most rural dwellers lacked electricity.)

These innovations reduced the hours and sheer physical effort of housework. In 1925, nearly 75 percent of working women surveyed said that they spent less time on housework than their mothers had. Vacuum cleaners supplanted brooms and carpet beaters, firing up wood stoves became a memory, and store-bought clothes replaced handmade apparel. Electricity altered the ritual of doing laundry and preparing food as well. Urban wives who had relied on commercial laundries began doing their own wash with the advent of the electric washing machine and iron. Cooking and eating patterns shifted. The rise of the supermarket made sharp inroads on the practice of canning. Commercially baked bread replaced home-baked bread. Refrigeration, supermarkets, and motor transport made fresh fruits and vegetables available year-round and lead to significant improvement in the national diet.

The automobile, however, had the greatest social and cultural impact. Urban planners worriedly discussed traffic jams, parking problems, and the mounting accident rate (more than 26,000 Americans died in traffic accidents in 1924). Like electrical appliances, automobiles reached into the lives of ordinary Americans. Family vacations and long drives in the country became popular. The automobile diminished the isolation of rural life and gave farm dwellers easier access to the city for shopping and entertainment.

Family cohesion suffered from the new mobility. Young people welcomed the freedom from parental oversight that the car offered. On a whim, they could drive to a dance in a distant city. Complained one father, "It's getting so a fellow has to make a date with his family to see them."

The automobile's impact on individuality was similarly mixed. Car owners could travel where they wished, when they wished, freed from fixed routes and schedules. But the automobile also accelerated the standardization of American life. Millions chugged around in identical black vehicles. The one-room schoolhouse was abandoned as buses carried children to consolidated schools. Neighborhood shops and markets declined as people drove to chain stores. The automobile age brought the first suburban department stores, the first shopping center (in Kansas City), and the first fast-food chain (A & W Root Beer).

Yet even at $300 or $400, the automobile remained too expensive for the poor. The "automobile suburbs" that sprang up beyond the streetcar lines attracted the prosperous, but the urban poor, including the growing black population, remained behind.

At the same time, the automobile's farm cousin, the tractor, transformed agriculture. The horse and mule population declined in the 1920s, while the number of tractors grew to 920,000. As more and more farmers went into debt to buy mechanized equipment, the agricultural crisis worsened.

Soaring Energy Consumption and a Threatened Environment

The proliferation of automobiles and electrically driven products had important implications for the environment and natural resources. Power consumption surged from 57 million kilowatt hours in 1920 to 188 million by 1929. To produce this power, generating plants consumed 42 million tons of coal, 10 million barrels of oil, and 112 million cubic feet of natural gas in 1929.

The automobiles clogging the nation's highways represented tons of steel and had an insatiable appetite for fuel. In 1916 U.S. refineries produced less than 50 million barrels of gasoline. In 1929 they refined 435 million barrels, using more than a billion barrels of crude oil.

The zooming demand for gasoline triggered feverish activity in the oilfields of Texas, Oklahoma, California, and elsewhere. Major oil companies such as Standard, Texaco, Gulf, and Atlantic solidified their dominance of the industry. Domestic oil production rose by 250 percent, and annual oil imports crept up to 76 million barrels.

Intense competition for oil bred massive waste. Natural gas, considered almost worthless, was burned off. The Bureau of Mines calculated that through the 1920s, more than a billion cubic feet of natural gas went up in smoke *every day* in America's oil fields. The heedless consumption of nonrenewable fossil fuels, which would reach massive proportions after World War II, had begun.

The environment suffered in less obvious ways, too. Power plants, steel mills, and automobile engines spewed tons of pollutants into the atmosphere. As ribbons of asphalt and cement snaked across the land, gas stations, billboards, restaurants, and tourist cabins followed. The wilderness that nineteenth-century Americans had so cherished came under heavy siege.

Isolated voices protested. The Sierra Club and the Audubon Society worked to preserve wilderness and wildlife. Aldo Leopold of the U.S. Forest Service warned that for too long, "a stump was our symbol of progress." Americans accustomed to a seemingly boundless wilderness "are *unconscious* of what the disappearance of wild places would mean." Wilderness preservation demanded not just sentimental pronouncements, Leopold stressed, but careful planning and political savvy. But few listened. To most Americans of the day, energy resources appeared limitless. Pollution and a vanishing wilderness seemed small prices to pay for the benefits of the electric motor and the internal-combustion engine.

Routinized Work, Mass-Produced Pleasure

Assembly-line techniques—repetitive, unvaried, and requiring little individual initiative—affected workers' views of themselves and their jobs. Factory managers even discouraged communication among workers: laughing or talking could divert them from their task. Ford employees learned to whisper without moving their lips and adopted a fixed, impassive mask. And as work became more routine, its psychic rewards diminished. The assembly line offered few skills to take pride in, no specialized knowledge, no prospect of advancement. Leisure-time activities grew more important as workers sought in their free hours the fulfillment that their jobs did not provide.

Amusement itself became standardized. The mass production of culture dated to the penny press and dime novel of the 1830s, but the process accelerated in the twenties. Mass-circulation magazines flourished. By 1922 ten American magazines boasted circulations of more than 2.5 million each. The *Saturday Evening Post*, with its bucolic Norman Rockwell covers and fiction featuring small-town life, specialized in prepackaged nostalgia. In 1921 DeWitt and Lila Wallace founded *Reader's Digest*, which condensed articles originally published elsewhere. The *Digest* served up traditionalist, probusiness views in simple prose. Pitched to the mass market, it represented the journalistic counterpart

of the A&P. Bookselling also saw major changes as publishers began marketing their products through department stores and mail-order organizations such as the Book-of-the-Month Club (1924) and the Literary Guild (1926).

Radios and movies standardized culture even more dramatically. The radio era began on November 2, 1920, when station KDKA in Pittsburgh broadcast the news of Warren Harding's election. In 1922, 500 new stations went on the air, and by 1927 radio sales approached 7 million sets.

In 1926 three corporations—General Electric, Westinghouse, and the Radio Corporation of America—formed the first radio network, the National Broadcasting Company (NBC). The Columbia Broadcasting System (CBS) followed in 1927, and the networks soon ruled radio broadcasting. Elaborate research on audience preferences dictated programming. From Maine to California, Americans laughed at the same jokes, hummed the same tunes, and absorbed the same commercials. New York's WEAF broadcast the first commercially sponsored program in 1922, and the commercialization of radio proceeded rapidly. The first network comedy show, the popular (and racist) "Amos 'n' Andy" (1928), brought millions in sales to its sponsor, Pepsodent toothpaste.

The motion-picture business evolved similarly. Movies, having expanded from the immigrant slums into elegant uptown theaters with names like "Majestic," "Ritz," and "Palace," attracted audiences from all social levels. After Al Jolson's *The Jazz Singer* (1927) introduced sound, movies became even more popular and spawned a new generation of screen idols, including the western hero Gary Cooper and the aloof Scandinavian beauty Greta Garbo. Another enduring favorite, Mickey Mouse, debuted in 1928. By 1930 weekly movie attendance neared 80 million.

Movies transported their viewers to worlds far removed from reality. One movie ad succinctly promised "all the adventure, all the romance, all the excitement you lack in your daily life." The mass-produced fantasies shaped popular behavior and values, especially among the impressionable young. In the words of novelist John Dos Passos, Hollywood offered "a great bargain sale of five-and-ten-cent lusts and dreams."

Fads, Celebrities, and Heroes

In this era, when news could reach every corner of the nation in seconds, fads and media-promoted events preoccupied Americans. In 1921 Atlantic City promoted itself with a new bathing-beauty competition, the Miss America Pageant. In 1922 millions played mah-jongg, a game of Chinese origin, and in 1924 a crossword-puzzle craze consumed the country.

Larger-than-life celebrities emerged in professional sports: Babe Ruth of the New York Yankees; Ty Cobb of the Detroit Tigers; Gertrude Ederle, the first woman to swim the English Channel; Jack Dempsey and Gene Tunney, whose two heavy-weight title fights drew more than 200,000 spectators and millions of radio listeners. When Tunney won the 1927 bout thanks to a famous "long count" by a referee, five radio listeners dropped dead of heart attacks.

The idolization of celebrities illuminates the anxieties and hopes of ordinary Americans in these years. The young woman trying to define her role in a period of confusing social change could find an ideal in beauty pageants. For the man whose sense of mastery had been shaken by developments from feminism to Fordism, cheering himself hoarse for a towering hero like Dempsey or Ruth could momentarily restore a feeling of personal worth and self-confidence.

Charles Lindbergh, "Lucky Lindy," the young pilot who made the first nonstop flight across the Atlantic, illustrates the hero worship of the times. Lindbergh had been a stunt flyer and airmail pilot before he competed for a $25,000 prize offered for the first nonstop New York–Paris flight. Lindbergh's daring flight on May 20–21, 1927, in his silver-winged *Spirit of St. Louis* captured the popular imagination. From the moment he touched down in Paris, the glare of media attention enveloped him. Back home in America, radio, newspapers, magazines, and movie newsreels provided saturation coverage. The "Lone Eagle" handled his celebrity with

Charles A. Lindbergh (1902–1974) Begins His Epic Flight, May 20, 1927
Lindbergh's achievement helped reassure Americans that the lone individual could still make a mark in an age of mass production and mass culture.

dignity, proving an authentic hero in an age of scandals and scams. Many Americans saw his flight as evidence that the individual still counted in an era of standardization and mechanization. To conservatives, Lindbergh's solid virtues proved that the old verities survived in a time of moral disarray.

Clearly, the new mass media had mixed social effects. The technologies of mass communication promoted cultural standardization and a uniformity of thought that stifled local and regional diversity. But radio, the movies, and the mass magazines also helped to forge a national culture and introduced millions of Americans to fresh viewpoints and new behaviors. Mass media hammered home a powerful message: personal horizons need no longer be limited by one's immediate environment. The spread of mass culture in the 1920s opened up a large world for ordinary Americans. If that world was often vacuous and tawdry, it was also sometimes exciting and stimulating.

Cultural Ferment and Creativity

Ferment and creativity also characterized culture of the 1920s. Writers, artists, musicians, and scientists compiled a record of remarkable achievement. Blacks asserted their pride through the cultural flowering known as the Harlem Renaissance. Pulsing through the decade were the rhythms of jazz, the African-American musical idiom that was winning wild popularity.

The Jazz Age and the Postwar Crisis of Values

The war and its disillusioned aftermath brought to full boil the simmering cultural restlessness of the prewar years. The postwar crisis of values took many forms. The younger generation, especially college students, boisterously assailed older conventions of behavior. Taking advantage of prosperity and the mobility afforded by the automobile, they threw noisy parties, consumed bootleg liquor, flocked to jazz clubs, and danced the Charleston.

They also discussed sex freely and sometimes indulged openly in premarital sexual experimentation. Wrote novelist F. Scott Fitzgerald, "None of the Victorian mothers had any idea how casually their daughters were accustomed to be kissed." The ideas of Sigmund Freud, the Viennese physician whose studies of human sexuality first appeared in the 1890s, enjoyed a popular vogue in the 1920s, often in grossly oversimplified form.

But hard evidence for the "sexual revolution" of the 1920s remains skimpy. Premarital sexual activity may have increased, but it was still widely disapproved of by the young as well as their elders. Courtship patterns did change, however. In earlier periods "courting" implied a serious intention of marriage. In the 1920s the informal ritual of "dating" emerged, allowing young people to test compatibility and to gain confidence in dealing with the opposite sex without necessarily contemplating marriage.

The double standard, holding women to a stricter code of sexual conduct than men, remained in force. Young men could boast of their sexual activity, but "fast" women might be ostracized. The male's traditional role in initiating sexual activity also survived. Nonetheless, the 1920s did see some liberation for women. Female sexuality was acknowledged more openly. Skirts grew shorter, makeup (once the badge of the prostitute) appeared, and petticoats and constricting corsets disappeared. A trim, almost boyish figure replaced the Gibson girl as the ideal beauty. Thousands of young women began smoking cigarettes in defiance of convention.

Moral guardians protested these changes. A Methodist bishop denounced the new dances that brought "the bodies of men and women in unusual relation to each other." In 1925, when the president of the women's college Bryn Mawr permitted students to smoke, others were outraged.

The flapper—a sophisticated, fashionable, pleasure-mad young woman—summed up the "flaming youth" of the twenties. The creation of magazine illustrator John Held, Jr., the flapper symbolized an elaborate complex of cultural values. Her bobbed hair, defiant cigarette, dangling beads, heavy makeup, and shockingly short skirt epitomized the rebelliousness that composed at least a part of the youth culture of the twenties.

Like the flapper, the Jazz Age itself—the "Roaring Twenties"—was partially a mass-media and novelistic creation. F. Scott Fitzgerald's romanticized interpretation of the affluent postwar young, *This Side of Paradise* (1920), spawned many imitators. Fitzgerald himself was only twenty-four when his novel of the "lost generation" appeared. With his sculpted good looks, wavy blond hair, and striking green eyes, he both wrote about and personified the Jazz Age. Flush with royalties, he and his wife, Zelda, partied away the early twenties in New York, Paris, and the French Mediterranean. A moralist at heart, Fitzgerald both admired and

Miss America Competitors, 1926
Their dimpled knees looking like so many baby faces, contestants pose for a publicity shot in front of the Golden State, a popular train of the day, as two male onlookers form their judgments.

deplored his Jazz Age contemporaries. His finest novel, *The Great Gatsby* (1925), captured not only the gilded existence of the superrich and social climbers of the 1920s but also the cold-hearted self-ishness and romantic illusions that ruled their lives.

As a description of the 1920s, the "Jazz Age" label must be used carefully. The upheaval in manners and morals was limited to a narrow social stratum. Old values did not vanish entirely in a haze of alcoholic parties, suggestive dances, and backseat sex. Millions of Americans adhered to traditional ways and traditional standards. Millions more—farmers, blacks, industrial workers, recent immigrants—found economic survival more important than the latest dance craze or the newest flapper fads and fashions.

Other American Writers of the Twenties

Like Fitzgerald, many other young writers found the cultural turbulence of the 1920s stimulating. They forged a remarkable body of work equally hostile to the moralistic pieties of the old order and the business pieties of the new.

Sinclair Lewis's novels skewered postwar America. In *Main Street* (1920) Lewis caustically depicted the cultural barrenness and smug self-satisfaction of a fictional midwestern farm town. In *Babbitt* (1922) he wielded his satirical scalpel to dissect George F. Babbitt, a middle-aged real-estate agent trapped in stifling middle-class conformity, one of the most memorable figures of American literature.

The scorn for middle-class America that dripped from Lewis's pen found a journalistic outlet in the work of H. L. Mencken, a Baltimore newspaperman who founded and became coeditor of *The American Mercury* (1924), the Bible of the decade's alienated intellectuals. A penetrating stylist, Mencken ridiculed small-town Americans, Protestant fundamentalists, the middle class (which he labeled the Booboisie), and mainstream America generally. His withering essays on Wilson, Harding, Coolidge, and Bryan are classics of American political satire.

Some young American writers spent the 1920s abroad, often in France. Even before the war, T. S. Eliot, Ezra Pound, and Gertrude Stein had become expatriates, and after the armistice others joined them. The most famous expatriate, Ernest Hemingway, had been a reporter before serving as a Red Cross volunteer in Italy during the war. Seriously wounded, he settled in Paris in 1921 and began to write. In *The Sun Also Rises* (1926), he evoked the experiences of a group of young Americans and British, shattered by the war, as they drifted around Spain. Even writers who stayed at home underwent a kind of spiritual expatriation, distancing themselves from the dominant business culture. The novels of Willa Cather, for example, implicitly repudiated modern mass society by evoking alternatives ranging from early New Mexico (*Death Comes for the Archbishop*, 1927) to seventeenth-century Quebec (*Shadows on the Rock*, 1931).

World War I represented a seminal experience for this generation of writers. The best war novel, Hemingway's *A Farewell to Arms* (1929), powerfully depicted the war's futility and leaders' inflated rhetoric and captured the disillusionment of the author's generation. Hemingway and his counterparts gagged at Wilsonian rhetoric, village narrowness, and chamber-of-commerce cant, yet they remained committed to American ideals. A desire to create an authentic national culture inspired their literary efforts, just as it had earlier inspired Hawthorne, Melville, and Whitman.

Achievements in Architecture, Painting, and Music

The creative energies of the 1920s found other outlets. A burst of architectural activity, for example, transformed the skylines of larger cities. Chaotically electric, this architecture displayed enormous vitality. By the end of the decade, the United States boasted 377 buildings more than 70 stories tall.

Artists turned to America itself for inspiration—whether the real nation around them or the country that they held in memory. Painter Thomas Hart Benton evoked a half-mythic land of cowboys, pioneers, and riverboat gamblers, while Edward Hopper starkly sketched a nation of faded small towns and lonely cities. Charles DeMuth painted boldly geometric grain elevators, factories, and urban scenes; Georgia O'Keeffe's early paintings evoked the congestion and excitement of Manhattan; and Charles Sheeler recorded a dramatic series of photographs of Ford's River Rouge plant near Detroit.

Musical performers and composers contributed to the creativity of this extraordinary decade, drawing on the cultural resources they knew best. Composer Aaron Copland tapped into folk-music traditions, and other composers evoked the new urban-industrial America. Frederick Converse's 1927 tone poem about the automobile, "Flivver Ten Million," featured "Dawn in Detroit," "May Night by the Roadside," and "The Collision."

Above all, American music in the 1920s meant jazz. The Original Dixieland Jazz Band—five white musicians imitating the black jazz bands of New Orleans—debuted in New York in January 1917, and a jazz vogue was soon under way. But the white bands that introduced jazz drained it of much of its energy. Paul Whiteman, the most popular white band leader of the decade, offered watered-down "jazz" versions of standard tunes and light classical works. Of the white composers who wrote in jazz idiom, George Gershwin, with *Rhapsody in Blue* (1924) and *An American in Paris* (1928), was the most original.

Meanwhile, African-American musicians were replenishing the creative springs of authentic jazz. Guitar picker Huddie Ledbetter (nicknamed Leadbelly) performed his field shouts and raw songs before appreciative black audiences in the South. Singers including Bessie Smith and Gertrude ("Ma") Rainey drew packed audiences on Chicago's South Side and sold thousands of records. Trumpeter Louis ("Satchmo") Armstrong and band leader Fletcher Henderson did some of their most creative work in the 1920s, and the enormously talented black pianist, composer, and band leader Duke Ellington performed to packed audiences at Harlem's Cotton Club.

Creativity in Black America

The growing concentration of blacks in New York led to a cultural flowering known as the Harlem Renaissance, which was above all a literary movement. Gifted young black writers published an outpouring of novels, poems, and short stories exploring the African-American experience. Among the best were Langston Hughes's *The Weary Blues* (1926); Claude McKay's *Home to Harlem* (1928); Nella Larsen's *Quicksand* (1928), on the problems of young black women; and Jean Toomer's *Cane* (1923), an imaginative evocation of a black northerner's first encounter with the rural black South. The Harlem Renaissance gained national visibility with the publication of *The New Negro* (1925), an anthology edited by Howard University professor Alain Locke. The NAACP's *The Crisis* provided a forum for black writers.

Despite its vitality, the Harlem Renaissance faced serious obstacles, mirroring the problems of black society at large. The small black middle class and elite could provide little support, and the movement thus depended on whites' patronage. Although alienated white intellectuals and rebellious Jazz Age youth idealized black performers, artists, and writers for their Africanness and their supposed sensuality and "primitive" energy, they ignored the ghetto's complex social problems. (Ironically, Harlem's jazz clubs excluded black customers.) Langston Hughes's rich white patron supported him generously as long as his poems evoked the "African Soul," but dropped him angrily when he began to write about black working people.

Similar biases plagued white artists' and writers' treatment of black themes. Eugene O'Neill's play *The Emperor Jones* (1920) and Marc Connelly's folk drama *The Green Pastures* (1920) drew upon the black experience in artistically creative ways but perpetuated racial stereotypes. *Hallelujah* (1929), the first all-black movie, sentimentalized cotton-plantation life and presented the urban black world as a whirl of gambling, drinking, sex, and violence.

Although the Harlem Renaissance produced work of lasting significance, the movement proved fragile. With the stock-market plunge of 1929, the Harlem "vogue" ended abruptly.

Advances in Science and Medicine

The scientific developments of the 1920s would reverberate for decades. The first long-range television transmission, from New York to Washington, occurred in 1927. Arthur H. Compton won a Nobel Prize for his studies on X rays, and Ernest O. Lawrence laid the theoretical groundwork for the construction of the first cyclotron, a high-energy-particle accelerator vital in nuclear-physics research. Physicist Robert Goddard studied rocketry and in 1926 launched the first successful liquid-fuel rocket. His predictions of lunar landings and deep-space exploration, ridiculed at the time, proved prophetic.

The 1920s saw important gains in medical research as well. Harvey Cushing made dramatic advances in neurosurgery, and chemist Harry Steenbock discovered how to create Vitamin D in milk by bombarding it with ultraviolet rays. New discoveries in the treatment of diphtheria, whooping cough, measles, and influenza helped to significantly lengthen life expectancy.

A few observers sensed that a new era of scientific advance was dawning. In 1925 Harvard philosopher Alfred North Whitehead underscored science's growing power. "Individually powerless," White had concluded, scientists were "ultimately the rulers of the world." To many, the prospect of such power was simply part of the array of disorienting social changes that made the 1920s unusually stressful and conflict-ridden.

A Society in Conflict

Indeed, American society endured deep strains in the 1920s. Immigration, dizzying technological advances, urban growth, and Darwinian theory had shattered the cultural homogeneity of an earlier day. Rural Americans uneasily surveyed the mushrooming cities; native-born Protestants apprehensively eyed the swelling ranks of Catholics and Jews; and upholders of traditional standards viewed the revolution in manners and morals with dismay.

Immigration Restriction

Fed by wartime superpatriotism, the long-standing impulse to turn America into a nation of like-minded, culturally identical people culminated in the National Origins Act of 1924. This restrictive measure placed a ceiling of 164,000 on annual immigration and, more important, limited the number of people from any nation to 2 percent of the total number of that "national origin" living in the United States in 1890. Because the great influx of southern and eastern Europeans had occurred after 1890, the act virtually ended immigration from those areas. Calvin Coolidge observed when he signed the law: "America must be kept American." The law also excluded Asians entirely, deeply insulting the Chinese and Japanese.

In 1929 Congress made 1920 the base year for determining "national origins," but even this slightly liberalized formula kept the quota for Poland at 6,500; for Italy, 5,800; and for Russia, 2,700. This quota system, which survived into the 1960s, represented the most enduring counterattack of rural, native-born America against the immigrant cities.

Most proponents of restriction regarded Asia and southern and eastern Europe as sources of "undesirables," and the laws reflected this bias. No restrictions, however, were placed on immigration from the Western Hemisphere, and consequently immigration from French Canada and Latin America soared during the 1920s. By 1930 at least 2 million Mexican-born people lived in the United States. California's Mexican-American population quadrupled, from 90,000 to nearly 360,000, in the decade. Many of these newcomers became migratory workers in large-scale agribusiness.

The Ku Klux Klan

Nativism erupted viciously in the revived Ku Klux Klan. The original Klan had faded in the 1870s, but

A Ku Klux Klan Ceremony on Long Island in the Early 1920s
The baby has been outfitted with its own white hood and robe. During its brief heyday after World War I, the revived Klan won many adherents all over the country to its message of white supremacy, moral purity, and 100 percent Americanism.

in November 1915 a group of hooded men met at Stone Mountain, Georgia, to revive it.

In 1920 two Atlanta public-relations specialists propelled the Klan into a national organization by stressing nativism and white supremacy. A recruitment campaign promised money to everyone within an elaborate sales web. The enterprising Atlantans held the exclusive rights to sell everything from Klan robes and masks to the genuine Chattahoochee River water used in initiation rites. This elaborate scam succeeded beyond anyone's wildest dreams. By the mid-1920s, estimates of membership in the Klan and its auxiliary, Women of the Klan, ranged from 2 million to 5 million. The revived Klan, its targets not only blacks but Catholics, Jews, and immigrants, thrived in the Midwest and Far West as well as the South. Most of its members came from blue-collar ranks.

During its brief heyday, the Klan exercised real political power in many areas. In Oklahoma the Klan-controlled legislature impeached and removed an anti-Klan governor. The Klan elected a governor in Oregon and pushed through legislation (later overturned by the Supreme Court) requiring all the state's children to attend public schools.

Klan bigotry varied from region to region. In the South the antiblack theme loomed large, but Klaverns in the North and West more often targeted Catholics and Jews. In the Southwest the Klan focused on violators of prohibition and traditional morality, including adulterers and men who did not support their families.

The Klan filled important needs for its members. Although riddled with corruption at the top, the organization consisted primarily of ordinary people, not criminals or fanatics. The Klan's promise to restore the nation to an imagined purity—ethnic, moral, and religious—appealed powerfully to ill-educated, deeply religious, and economically marginal Americans disoriented by rapid social and moral change. Klan membership, moreover, bestowed a sense of importance and group cohesion on people who doubted their own worth. The Klan's rituals, ceremonials, and burning crosses lit up drab lives. One member wrote, "Who can look upon a multitude of white-robed Klansmen without thinking . . . of that throng of white-robed saints in the Glory Land?" But while the individual Klansman may seem more pitiful than sinister, the movement as a whole was violent. Klan members used intimidation, threats, beatings, and even murder in their quest for a "purified" America.

In March 1925 Indiana's politically influential Grand Dragon, David Stephenson, pressed bootleg liquor on a young secretary, forced her on a Pullman train, and raped her. When she later swallowed poison, Stephenson and his henchmen refused to call a physician. The woman died, and the Grand Dragon went to jail for first-degree manslaughter. From prison he revealed details of pervasive political corruption in Indiana. Its high moral pretensions shredded, the Klan faded rapidly but did not die. After World War II it would again surface as a malignant influence in American life.

The Garvey Movement

Among African-Americans, the decade's social strains ignited a different kind of mass movement. Blacks' widespread escape from southern rural poverty and racism led only to northern ghetto poverty similarly exacerbated by racism. Many poor urban blacks turned for relief to the spellbinding orator Marcus Garvey and his Universal Negro Improvement Association (UNIA). Garvey glorified all things black, urged black economic cooperation, and founded a chain of UNIA grocery stores and other businesses. He called on the world's blacks to return to "Motherland Africa" and establish a nation "strong enough to lend protection to the members of our race scattered all over the world." An estimated 80,000 blacks joined the UNIA, and thousands more felt the lure of Garvey's hypnotic oratory, the uplift of rousing UNIA parades, and the seduction of Garvey's dream of a mass return to Africa.

In 1923, however, a federal court convicted Garvey of fraud in connection with his Black Star Steamship Company. After two years' imprisonment, he was deported to Jamaica. Without its charismatic leader, the UNIA collapsed. But as the first mass movement in black America, it revealed the discontent seething in the ghettos and the potential for large-scale activism. "In a world where black is despised," wrote an African-American newspaper reporter upon Garvey's deportation, "he taught them that black is beautiful."

Fundamentalism and the Scopes Trial

In the half-century before 1920, American Protestantism had been severely tried. The prestige of science had increased steadily, challenging religion's cultural standing. Scholars had dissected the Bible's historical origins; psychologists had explained the religious impulse in terms of human emotional needs. Meanwhile, Catholic and Jewish immigrants had poured in.

Liberal Protestants responded by accepting the findings of science and emphasizing social service to the immigrants. But a powerful reaction, fundamentalism, was building. Named after *The Fundamentals,* a series of pamphlets published from 1909 to 1914, Protestant fundamentalism insisted on the divine inspiration of every word in the Bible, on the Genesis version of Creation, and on the virgin birth and resurrection of Jesus.

In the early 1920s fundamentalists took aim at the theory of evolution. Charles Darwin's ideas seemed to them a blatant rejection of biblical truth. In 1921–1922 fundamentalist legislators introduced bills to prohibit the teaching of evolution in twenty states' public schools, and several southern states enacted such legislation. Fundamentalism's best-known champion, aging politician William Jennings Bryan, vigorously endorsed the anti-evolution cause.

In 1925, when the Tennessee legislature outlawed the teaching of evolution in public schools, the American Civil Liberties Union (ACLU) volunteered to defend any teacher willing to challenge the law. A young high-school biology teacher in Dayton, Tennessee, John T. Scopes, accepted the offer. Scopes read a description of Darwin's theory to his class and was duly arrested.

Famed criminal lawyer Clarence Darrow headed the ACLU team of lawyers, and William Jennings Bryan enthusiastically assisted the prosecution. Journalists poured into Dayton, and radio stations broadcast the proceedings live. The Scopes "monkey trial" became an overnight sensation.

The trial's symbolic climax came when Darrow cross-examined Bryan on his religious beliefs and scientific knowledge. As Bryan insisted on the literal accuracy of the Bible, his ignorance of vast realms of human knowledge became painfully clear. Darrow succeeded in humiliating Bryan and ridiculing his ideas. The local jury found Scopes guilty, but the larger verdict, the one that really counted, differed. The Dayton trial marked a decisive setback for fundamentalism.

After the trial, fundamentalism diminished in mainstream Protestantism, but new denominations and "full gospel" churches carried on the cause. Evangelist Aimee Semple McPherson regularly filled the 5,200 seats of her Angelus Temple in Los Angeles and reached thousands more by radio. Her followers embraced the beautiful, white-gowned McPherson's fundamentalist theology while reveling in her mastery of mass entertainment. In many ways she anticipated the television evangelists of a later day. When she died in 1944, her International Church of the Foursquare Gospel had more than 600 branches. Clearly, although fundamentalism had suffered a severe blow at Dayton, Tennessee, it was far from dead.

The Sacco-Vanzetti Case

The Sacco and Vanzetti case represented another battle in the cultural wars of the 1920s. On April 15, 1920, robbers shot and killed the paymaster and guard of a shoe factory in South Braintree, Massachusetts, and stole nearly $18,000. Three weeks later, two Italian immigrants, Nicola Sacco and Bartolomeo Vanzetti, were arrested and charged with the murders. They were found guilty in 1921.

Bare facts cannot convey the texture of the case or the emotions it aroused. Sacco and Vanzetti were avowed anarchists, and from the beginning the prosecution harped on their radicalism. The judge, a conservative Republican, was openly hostile to the defendants, whom he privately called "those anarchist bastards." The Sacco-Vanzetti case in fact mirrored the larger divisions in society. Nativists dwelled on the defendants' immigrant origins, conservatives insisted that the alien anarchists must die, and prominent liberals rallied behind them.

In 1927 a commission appointed by the Massachusetts governor to review the case upheld the guilty verdict. Sacco and Vanzetti were executed in the electric chair. But whether they committed the murders remains uncertain. The original case against them was circumstantial and far from airtight. Recent findings, including ballistics tests on Sacco's gun, suggest that at least Sacco may have been guilty. But the poisonous political climate that tainted the trial remains indisputable, as does the case's importance in exposing divisions in American society.

Prohibition

A controversy over the attempt to rid America of alcoholic beverages deepened these social fissures. Prohibition was simultaneously a way to deal with the serious social problems associated with alcohol abuse and a sign of native-born Americans' struggle to maintain cultural and political dominance over the immigrant cities. Both components of the anti-alcohol crusade loomed large in the 1920s.

When the Eighteenth Amendment took effect in January 1920, prohibitionists rejoiced. Their cause had triumphed. Saloons closed; liquor advertising stopped; arrests for drunkenness dwindled. But by the end of the decade, prohibition was discredited, and in 1933 it ended. What went wrong? Essentially, the prohibition debacle illustrates the virtual impossibility, in a democracy, of enforcing rules of behavior with which a significant portion of the population disagrees.

From the beginning, enforcement of the Volstead Act, the 1919 law that established the Prohibition Bureau within the Treasury Department, was underbudgeted and largely ineffective, especially in strongly antiprohibition states. New York, for example, repealed its prohibition-enforcement law in 1923. Would-be drinkers grew bold as enforcement faltered. For young people already rebelling against traditional standards, alcohol's illegality added to its appeal. Every city boasted speakeasies where customers could buy drinks, and rumrunners routinely smuggled in liquor. Many people even concocted their own home brew. By 1929 alcohol consumption had risen to 70 percent of the prewar level.

Organized crime entered the liquor business, facilitating drinkers' efforts to circumvent the law. In Chicago rival gangs engaged in bloody wars to control the liquor business; the 1920s saw 550 gangland killings. By 1929 Chicago mob king Al Capone controlled a network of speakeasies with annual profits of $60 million. Chicago's heavily publicized crime wave appeared dramatic proof of prohibition's failure. A reform designed to produce a more orderly, law-abiding America seemed to be having the opposite effect.

Prohibition became still another battleground in the decade's cultural wars. The "drys"—usually native-born Protestants—praised prohibition as a necessary and legitimate reform. The "wets"—liberals, alienated intellectuals, Jazz Age rebels, urban immigrants—condemned it as moralistic meddling. Prohibition figured prominently in the 1928 presidential campaign. Democratic candidate Al Smith made no secret of his support for repeal of the Eighteenth Amendment. Republican Herbert Hoover praised prohibition as "a great social and economic experiment, noble in motive and far-reaching in purpose." In 1931 a presidential commission acknowledged the breakdown of prohibition but urged its retention. Nevertheless, in 1933 prohibition ended with the Eighteenth Amendment's repeal. By then the nation had other worries.

Hoover at the Helm

Herbert Hoover, overwhelmingly elected president in 1928, seemed ideal to sustain the nation's booming prosperity. He brought a distinctive social and political philosophy that reflected his background in engineering.

The Election of 1928

The presidential candidates of 1928, Al Smith and Herbert Hoover, personified opposite ends of the political and social spectrum. Both self-made men, they were "as far apart as Pilsner and Coca-Cola," as H. L. Mencken cracked.

Four-term governor of New York, Smith easily sewed up the Democratic nomination. A Catholic and a "wet," his brown derby perpetually askew, Smith exuded the flavor of immigrant New York. Originally a machine politician, he represented progressivism's urban-immigrant component, championing social welfare and civil rights. Herbert Hoover won the Republican nomination with equal ease. Conservative party leaders, however, remained suspicious of this intelligent but aloof progressive who had never run for public office and had spent most of his pre-1920 adult life overseas. An Iowan, orphaned early in life, Hoover had put himself through Stanford University and made a fortune as a mining engineer in China and Australia. His service as wartime food administrator saved millions of lives in Europe and earned him a place in the Harding and Coolidge cabinets.

Eschewing the handshaking and baby kissing of the campaign trail, Hoover delivered laboriously composed radio speeches in a boring monotone, so dully that people overlooked the originality of his ideas. Smith campaigned spiritedly throughout the country—a strategy that may have harmed him, for his big-city wisecracking and accent repelled many Americans west of the Hudson.

Smith's Catholicism figured importantly in the campaign as he faced a backlash of prejudice. Although Hoover urged tolerance, and Smith denied any conflict between his Catholic faith and the duties of the presidency, many Protestants, especially

rural southerners and urban fundamentalists, found the issue of Smith's religion vital. But prosperity, not religion, was the decisive campaign issue. Republicans took credit for the booming economy and warned that Smith would create "soup kitchens instead of busy factories." Hoover predicted "the final triumph over poverty."

Hoover won in a landslide victory, making deep inroads in the Democratic "solid South." Smith carried a meager 87 electoral votes to Hoover's 444. But beneath Hoover's victory lay evidence of an emerging political realignment. Smith did well in the midwestern farm belt among financially strapped Republicans and in northern cities, where first- and second-generation Catholic and Jewish immigrants voted Democratic in record numbers. In 1924 the nation's twelve largest cities had all gone Republican; in 1928 Smith carried all twelve. If prosperity should end, these signs suggested, the Republican party would face trouble.

Herbert Hoover's Social Thought

Americans looked hopefully to their new president, the Great Engineer. Hoover had a notable record of achievement and a well-developed social philosophy, expounded in his book *American Individualism* (1922). Although his own life followed the classic rags-to-riches formula, Hoover based his social outlook on his Quakerism, humanitarian activities, and engineering experience.

Like Theodore Roosevelt, Hoover believed that cutthroat competition was anachronistic. Rational economic development demanded corporate cooperation in marketing, wage policy, raw-material allocation, and product standardization. The economy should operate like a smoothly functioning machine. Capitalism, Hoover argued further, had social obligations. He welcomed the growth of welfare capitalism. But above all, Hoover believed in voluntarism. The cooperative, socially responsive economic order that he envisioned would arise through the voluntary action of capitalist leaders, not through government coercion or power struggles pitting labor against management.

The Election of 1928

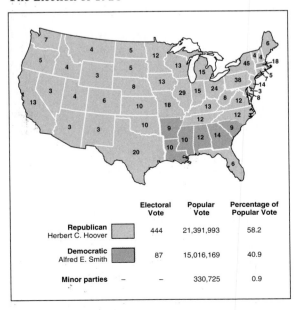

		Electoral Vote	Popular Vote	Percentage of Popular Vote
Republican Herbert C. Hoover		444	21,391,993	58.2
Democratic Alfred E. Smith		87	15,016,169	40.9
Minor parties		–	–	330,725	0.9

As secretary of commerce, Hoover had reorganized the Commerce Department along rational lines, making it a model for private industry, and tried to accelerate the trend toward corporate consolidation and cooperation. He had convened more than 250 conferences at which business leaders discussed unemployment, pricing, labor-management relations, and the virtues of trade associations. He urged higher wages to increase consumer purchasing power and in 1923 persuaded the steel industry to adopt an eight-hour workday in the name of efficiency.

But Hoover's ideas had limits. He displayed more interest in cooperation among capitalists than among consumers or workers, and he greatly over-estimated the role of philanthropic considerations in business decision making. His unqualified opposition to direct government economic intervention would bring him grief later in his administration, when such intervention became urgently necessary.

Applying his ideology to specific issues, Hoover compiled an impressive record early in his administration. He created commissions to study public-policy issues, gathered data for policy makers' guidance, and established the Federal Farm Board to cope with farmers' problems. Indeed, as the summer of 1929 turned to autumn, the Hoover administration seemed off to a promising start. But ominous long-term economic trends were converging toward a crisis that would overwhelm and destroy the methodical Hoover's presidency.

Conclusion

Memorable events bracket the 1920s: World War I at the beginning, a catastrophic stock-market crash at the end. Americans of the era had to cope with massive technological and social change, adapting themselves to a mass-production, mass-consumption, mass-culture metropolitan world that had seemingly emerged overnight.

The most interesting responses to these broad changes unfolded outside politics. The stresses and disorientation that produced bitter social conflict also made the 1920s one of the most creative decades in American cultural and intellectual history. Champions of prohibition and fundamentalism, the Ku Klux Klan, rebellious youth, urban blacks who cheered Marcus Garvey, and the novelists and poets who revitalized American literature were all trying to make sense of an unfamiliar, often threatening social order. The twenties saw political failure and reactionary social movements, but the decade also generated positive and lasting achievements.

Chronology

1915	Modern Ku Klux Klan founded.
1919	Volstead Act.
1920– 1921	Sharp postwar recession; agricultural prices plummet.
1920	Warren G. Harding elected president. Eighteenth Amendment takes effect. F. Scott Fitzgerald, *This Side of Paradise*. Sinclair Lewis, *Main Street*.
1921	Recovery from recession; economic boom begins; agriculture remains depressed. Sheppard-Towner Act. National Woman's party founded by Alice Paul.
1921– 1922	Washington Naval Arms Conference.
1922	Supreme Court declares child-labor laws unconstitutional.

Herbert Hoover, *American Individualism*.
Sinclair Lewis, *Babbitt*.

1923   Harding dies; Calvin Coolidge becomes president.
Supreme Court strikes down minimum-wage laws
for women.
Jean Toomer, *Cane*.

1924   Teapot Dome scandals investigated.
National Origins Act.
Calvin Coolidge elected president.
McNary-Haugen farm bill introduced.

1925   Scopes trial.
Ku Klux Klan scandal in Indiana.
Alain Locke, *The New Negro*.
F. Scott Fitzgerald, *The Great Gatsby*.

1926   Ernest Hemingway, *The Sun Also Rises*.
Langston Hughes, *The Weary Blues*.

1927   *The Jazz Singer*, first sound movie.
Coolidge vetoes the McNary-Haugen bill.
Willa Cather, *Death Comes for the Archbishop*.
Execution of Sacco and Vanzetti.
Charles A. Lindbergh's transatlantic flight.

1928   Kellogg-Briand Pact.
Herbert Hoover elected president.

1929   Sheppard-Towner program terminated.
Hallelujah, first all-black movie.
Ernest Hemingway, *A Farewell to Arms*.

FOR FURTHER READING

Charles C. Alexander, *Here the Country Lies: Nationalism and the Arts in Twentieth Century America* (1980). A useful revisionist study whose chapters on the 1920s stress the decade's positive achievements.

Loren Baritz, ed., *The Culture of the Twenties* (1970). A rich collection of primary documents with an introductory essay stressing the conflict between "provincial" and "metropolitan" values.

John Braeman, Robert Bremner, and David Brody, eds., *Change and Continuity in Twentieth Century America: The 1920s* (1968). Interpretive essays offering fresh insights on the political, economic, and social history of the decade.

Paul Carter, *The Twenties in America* (1968) and *Another Part of the Twenties* (1977). Two essays offering refreshingly personal interpretive judgments.

Ellis W. Hawley, *The Great War and the Search for a Modern Order* (1979). An economic study that traces the emergence (and collapse in 1929) of the first mass-consumption society.

John D. Hicks, *Republican Ascendancy, 1921–1933* (1960). The best comprehensive survey of the decade's national politics.

William E. Leuchtenberg, *The Perils of Prosperity, 1914–1932* (1970). A cogent examination, rejecting popular stereotypes of the serious thinkers and mass culture of the twenties.

George Soule, *Prosperity Decade: From War to Depression* (1947). A highly valuable economic history.

Crash, Depression, and New Deal

*I*n 1929 a stock-market collapse triggered the worst depression in American history. Crippled by his belief that voluntarism held the key to relieving individual suffering and that the economy would heal itself, President Herbert Hoover wrestled ineffectively with the crisis.

Franklin D. Roosevelt, who succeeded Hoover in 1933, dominated American politics until his death in 1945. As president, the forceful, ebullient Roosevelt not only directed American efforts to overcome the depression but also, as commander in chief during World War II, led the global struggle against Germany, Italy, and Japan.

This chapter focuses on the Great Depression and the New Deal, Roosevelt's economic and social programs to promote national recovery. A dizzying array of approaches, laws, and agencies characterized the New Deal, but certain patterns do emerge. From 1933 to 1935, the first phase of the New Deal emphasized relief and recovery. While Roosevelt urged unity, his administration and a heavily Democratic Congress battled massive unemployment, business stagnation, and agricultural distress. Around 1935, responding to a

(Right) President Franklin D. Roosevelt in a familiar setting

Crash and Depression
The New Deal Takes Shape
The New Deal Changes Course
The New Deal Draws to a Close

political challenge on the Left and buoyed by a ringing endorsement in the 1934 midterm election, the New Deal shifted to a more reformist course. The so-called Second New Deal (1935–1938) stressed business regulation as well as social programs and tax policies benefiting working people, small farmers, and others at the low end of the economic scale. Arguments still roil about specific New Deal programs and even its general merits, but no one disputes that the New Deal marked a watershed in twentieth-century American history.

The laws and agencies that made up the New Deal represented a complex amalgam of approaches influenced by political crosscurrents and countless individuals. But in the public mind, the New Deal meant Roosevelt. Loved by some almost as a member of the family, and reviled by others as a demagogue and an opportunist, Roosevelt is recognized today as a consummate politician whose administration set the national political agenda for a generation.

Crash and Depression

Like a joyride that ends in screeching tires and crunching metal, the prosperity of the 1920s crashed in October 1929 with the stock-market collapse. The ensuing depression reached into every household in the land. President Hoover's commitment to private initiative and his horror of governmental coercion handcuffed him. In November 1932 a disillusioned nation gave an overwhelming electoral mandate to the Democratic party and Franklin D. Roosevelt.

Black Thursday

Stock prices had climbed through the 1920s as investors responded to growing prosperity and increasing productivity. Beginning in 1928, optimism turned into frenzy as speculators plunged into the market. Stock prices floated into what one contemporary called "the blue and cloudless empyrean."

Stock speculation seemed the perfect form of gambling for an egalitarian society: everybody won.

In 1925 the market value of all stocks stood at $27 billion; by October 1929 it hit $87 billion. Nine million Americans "played the market," often with borrowed funds. Optimistic pronouncements drew people in. "Everybody Ought to Be Rich," proclaimed a *Ladies' Home Journal* article. Stockbrokers loaned speculators up to 75 percent of a stock's purchase price, and credit buying became the rule. Brokers' loans reached $6 billion by the summer of 1929. Easy-credit policies on the part of the Federal Reserve Board, along with Treasury Secretary Andrew Mellon's pressure for tax cuts, increased the money available for speculation.

With corporations hungry for their share of speculators' money, new securities "were manufactured almost like cakes of soap," in one historian's words, simply because money could be made from their sale. Brokerage agents grew rich peddling American Can, Studebaker, Houston Oil, and Westinghouse. Totally unregulated "investment trusts," akin to today's mutual funds, offered novices the benefit of the supposedly superior wisdom of seasoned investors. This speculative frenzy ignored hard economic realities. It rested on a precarious prosperity. Agriculture, mining, and textiles remained depressed, and automobile production slowed in the late 1920s. In 1928–1929 construction declined by 25 percent.

In July 1928 the Federal Reserve Board tried to dampen speculation by increasing interest rates, and early in 1929 it warned member banks not to lend money for stock-market speculation. But speculators paid up to 20 percent interest, and major banks and large corporations poured millions into the money market—somewhat like dumping gasoline onto a fire.

On October 24, 1929—"Black Thursday"—the collapse began. As prices plummeted, traders panicked. Some stocks found no buyers at all. Mounted police broke up crowds milling outside the New York Stock Exchange, while speculators huddled around ticker-tape machines "like friends around the bedside of a stricken friend," according to the *New York Times*. At midday a group of powerful bankers temporarily stopped the hemorrhage by issuing a reassuring statement and ostentatiously buying $30 million worth of major stocks. After a weak rally on Friday, prices continued to fall. The climax came on Tuesday, October 29, when a record 16 million stocks changed hands in frantic trading, most at inconceivably low prices. In the ensuing weeks, feeble upswings in stock prices alternated with further plunges.

On Black Thursday President Hoover issued the first of a series of optimistic pronouncements. "The fundamental business of the country . . . is on a sound and prosperous basis," he asserted. He was wrong. By mid-November stocks had lost $30 billion in value. The stock-market crash revealed the depth of other economic problems underlying the glittering prosperity of the 1920s.

Onset of the Depression

Despite confident predictions that business activity would quickly revive, the economy went into a prolonged tailspin that locked the country in a profound depression. Although it bottomed out in 1933, its effects lingered through the decade.

What caused the depression? Structural weaknesses in the American economy played a major role. Rises in productivity led not to higher wages but to high corporate profits. Between 1920 and 1929 the well-to-do increased their share of American income from 22 percent to 26 percent and spent much of that income on luxuries—discretionary spending that halted abruptly in 1929. The 40 percent of Americans at the lowest end of the economic scale received only 12 percent of the national income by 1929. At the same time, overproduction became a problem, in part because those at the lower end could not afford to buy goods, and consequently the summer of 1929 saw severe cutbacks in the output of durable commodities such as automobiles, tires, and homes. The decline in farm prices represented another weak spot. And some economists argue that major industries, such as railroads, steel, textiles, and mining, were lagging technologically and could not attract sufficient investment to stimulate the economy.

Other economists focus on the collapse of the banking system. The Federal Reserve System, they charge, failed to assure an adequate money supply to enable the economy to bounce back from the crash. In fact, the money supply did shrink by some 38 percent, but whether the Fed can be faulted is still hotly debated.

All analysts emphasize that the U.S. depression was part of a global economic crisis. Enfeebled by the devastation of World War I, massive debt payments, and a huge trade imbalance with the United States, European economies crashed in 1931. Austria's biggest bank failed in May; Germany imposed currency controls in July; Great Britain abandoned the gold standard in September. This larger crisis worsened an already bad American situation.

Statistics tell the bleak story of depression America. The gross national product slumped from $104 billion in 1929 to $59 billion in 1932. Farm prices, already low, fell nearly 60 percent from 1929 to 1932. Wheat prices plunged from $1.04 a bushel to $.51. Railroad corporations controlling one-third of the nation's track fell into bankruptcy. The banking system neared collapse as 5,500 banks closed their doors by early 1933. Unemployment soared from 3 percent in 1929 to 25 percent in 1933; 13 million Americans had no jobs, and many who worked faced cuts in wages and hours. These statistics translated into idled factories, bankrupted farms, closed banks, and hopelessness etched on the faces of the jobless as they waited in breadlines and trudged the streets looking for work.

The Depression's Human Toll

Most of the unemployed supported families, and so we must multiply the unemployment figures several times over to calculate the magnitude of human distress. The epidemic of bank closings deprived millions of their savings and even their pensions.

Jobless Men Along the Chicago & Northwestern Tracks near De Kalb, Illinois
A local artist painted this haunting scene from a 1930s photograph.

Blacks, Mexican-Americans, sharecroppers, and other groups endured particular hardships (see Chapter 26). Thousands of rural families lost their homes. In 1933 alone more than 5 percent of the nation's farms underwent mortgage foreclosures or forced sales because of tax delinquency.

For the children of the depression, poor diet and inadequate medical and dental care laid the groundwork for long-term health problems. Malnutrition, rickets, pellagra, and other diet-related ailments increased alarmingly. By early 1933, as local school boards shortened the school year and even closed schools, more than 300,000 children were out of school.

Newspapers conveyed the human dimensions of the crisis by focusing on dramatic vignettes. The *New York Times* described "Hoover Valley"—a section of Central Park where jobless men built makeshift shelters of boxes and packing crates. In Washington State, reporters wrote of a rash of forest fires set by men hoping to earn a few dollars as fire fighters. Some gave up. The suicide rate climbed 30 percent from 1928 to 1932. In Youngstown, Ohio, a jobless father of ten jumped to his death as authorities prepared to evict his family from their home. Although extreme, such stories portrayed the terrible social costs of the nation's worst depression.

Hoover's Response

Historically, Americans had equated economic depressions with acts of nature—one simply had to ride out the storm. Although his conservative cabinet members held this view, Hoover disagreed.

Drawing on the legacy of progressive reform and his own experiences as food administrator during World War I, he responded to the crisis with energy and determination. But his course reflected his ideological commitment to localism and private initiative. He told an Iowa farm audience, "Every time we find solutions outside of government, we have not only strengthened character, but we have preserved our sense of real self-government."

Business leaders whom Hoover summoned to the White House pledged to maintain wages and employment. Seeing unemployment as a local issue, Hoover called on municipal and state governments to create public-works projects. In October 1930 he established the Emergency Committee for Employment to coordinate voluntary relief agencies, and in 1931 he persuaded the nation's largest bankers to establish the National Credit Corporation to lend smaller banks money for business loans. The crisis only intensified, however. As early as November 1930, voters rendered a harsh verdict on Hoover's policies: Republicans lost not only eight Senate seats but control of the House of Representatives as well.

Hoover's strategy failed dismally. Unemployment mounted, and in 1931 U.S. Steel, General Motors, and other large corporations broke their pledges and announced large wage cuts. Public charities and local welfare agencies faltered. In Philadelphia, joblessness rose to 300,000. The city cut relief payments to $4.23 per family per week and in June 1932 suspended them entirely.

By 1932, with an election looming and the voluntarist approached discredited, Hoover endorsed an unprecedented federal response. In January Congress provided $2 billion in funding to a new agency, the Reconstruction Finance Corporation (RFC), to make loans to major economic institutions such as banks, railroads, and insurance companies. In February Hoover signed the Glass-Steagall Act, allocating $750 million of the government's gold reserves for loans to private businesses. In July he signed legislation authorizing the RFC to give $2 billion to state and local governments for public-works programs. But Hoover gained little political benefit. He supported the RFC reluctantly and signed the $2 billion public-works bill grudgingly.

Hoover blamed the depression on global forces and argued that only international measures would help. He advocated a one-year moratorium on war-debt and reparations repayments, a sensible plan but one that seemed irrelevant to Americans. In 1931, dreading an unbalanced budget, Hoover called for a tax increase, thereby further alienating voters.

The man once portrayed as a masterful manager and humane philanthropist was now portrayed as bumbling and hard-hearted. Unable to concede error, Hoover told an aide, "No president must ever admit that he has been wrong." He even continued to support the increasingly unpopular, and unsuccessful, prohibition acts. A presidency launched auspiciously in 1929 was ending in failure.

Mounting Discontent and Protest

A dark mood spread over the nation. Midwestern farmers organized the Farmers' Holiday Association to force prices up by withholding grain and livestock from the market, and dairy farmers dumped thousands of gallons of milk. But World War I veterans mounted the most alarming protest. In 1924 Congress had voted a veterans' bonus to be paid twenty years later. In 1931 Congress received a proposal to pay the bonus immediately, and in June 1932, 10,000 veterans, many jobless, descended on Washington to lobby for its passage. When Congress rejected the proposal in mid-June, several thousand "bonus marchers" and their families stayed on. They organized protest parades and built a makeshift settlement of tents and packing crates—one of many ironically named "Hoovervilles"—on Anacostia Flats in southeastern Washington, D.C.

Hoover, afraid that the bonus marchers were the forerunners of revolution, ordered them confined to Anacostia Flats. Army Chief of Staff General Douglas MacArthur decided to break up the settlement. On July 28 a thousand armed soldiers, equipped with tear gas, tanks, and machine guns, drove the veterans from their encampment and burned it to the ground. For many Americans, the image of armed troops using force against peaceful veterans symbolized the Hoover administration's insensitivity to human suffering.

The Election of 1932

Herbert Hoover ran unopposed for the 1932 Republican nomination. Smelling defeat, delegates to the Republican convention gloomily adopted a platform praising Hoover's antidepression measures.

The Democrats, in contrast, scented victory. They drafted a platform to heal the divisions that had weakened the party in the 1920s and to appeal to urban immigrants, farmers, and fiscal conservatives. Delegates gave New York's governor, Franklin D. Roosevelt, the two-thirds majority he needed for nomination. Breaking precedent, FDR accepted the nomination in person, promising "a new deal for the American people."

The Election of 1932

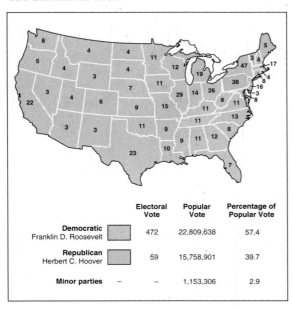

		Electoral Vote	Popular Vote	Percentage of Popular Vote
Democratic Franklin D. Roosevelt		472	22,809,638	57.4
Republican Herbert C. Hoover		59	15,758,901	39.7
Minor parties		–	1,153,306	2.9

Roosevelt's campaign provided no clear sense of the direction in which he would lead the country. He called for "bold, persistent experimentation" and promised more attention to "the forgotten man at the bottom of the economic pyramid" but also attacked Hoover's "reckless" spending.

If his campaign lacked specifics, Roosevelt himself exuded confidence. Above all, he was not Hoover! On November 8 FDR and his running mate, John Nance Garner of Texas, received nearly 23 million votes, almost half again as many as the Republicans. Both houses of Congress went heavily Democratic. After twelve years of Republican rule, the Democrats were back in charge.

The New Deal Takes Shape

The Roosevelt years began with feverish activity as FDR proposed a staggering array of emergency measures and as Congress passed most by wide margins. A strategy emerged from the welter of bills: *industrial recovery* through business-government cooperation and federal spending; *agricultural recovery* through subsidized crop reductions; and *short-term emergency relief for the jobless*, provided by the federal government if necessary. Presiding over this bustle was a smiling FDR, cigarette holder jauntily tilted upward, a symbol of confidence and renewed hope for millions.

New Beginnings

Shortly before FDR's inauguration, Congress passed the Twentieth Amendment, ending the nation's thirteen-year flirtation with prohibition. Supporters argued that repeal would stimulate economic recovery by producing a tax bonanza on the sale of alcoholic beverages. It would be a new beginning, they asserted.

Roosevelt's inaugural address also set an optimistic tone. The new president dedicated his administration to helping people to weather the crisis. "The only thing we have to fear is fear itself," he reassured an anxious population. Americans responded with a surge of support. Within a few days, half a million approving letters deluged the White House.

In many ways, FDR seemed an unlikely figure to rally Americans in the depression. Like his distant cousin Theodore Roosevelt, FDR was a member of the social elite. His Dutch-immigrant ancestors had been merchants and landed aristocrats for three centuries, and his Groton-Harvard-Columbia background found little resonance with the average American. However, a battle against polio that left him unable to walk but strong in spirit had prepared FDR for struggling against adversity and for feeling empathy with other people. As governor of New York when the depression struck, he had proposed such innovative measures as unemployment insurance, emergency relief, and a public-works program.

Roosevelt entered the White House sensitive to the public mood and determined to restore the nation to economic health within the framework of capitalism and democracy. But he had no detailed agenda for achieving these goals. Not interested in theory, FDR encouraged competing proposals, compromised (or papered over) differences, and then threw his weight behind measures that he could sell to Congress and the people.

In New York Roosevelt had built up a circle of advisers, "the brain trust," many of them from universities. FDR sought a wide range of opinions, and his brain trust included both very conservative and very liberal viewpoints. Consequently, Roosevelt's New Deal reflected many ideological and political orientations.

Eleanor Roosevelt played a key White House role. Niece to Theodore Roosevelt, the president's wife had a keen social conscience and a background in Progressive Era settlement-house work. She influenced FDR's ideas by exposing him to reformers, social workers, and advocates of minority rights. She traveled ceaselessly and served as the eyes, ears, and sometimes the conscience for her wheelchair-bound husband.

Roosevelt's top political adviser, James Aloysius Farley, became postmaster general but spent more time on politics than on postage. He distributed patronage jobs, managed FDR's 1932 and 1936 campaigns, and smoothed White House relations with state and local Democrats. Bored by the substantive issues of the New Deal, Farley had a master's sense of the treacherous currents of presidential politics.

Roosevelt's cabinet reflected the diversity of the New Deal. Secretary of Labor Frances Perkins, the first woman cabinet member in U.S. history, had served as state industrial commissioner during FDR's years as governor of New York. Interior Secretary Harold Ickes was a prickly but able Republican progressive. Secretary of Agriculture Henry A. Wallace excelled as an agricultural economist and farm-policy theorist. Secretary of the Treasury Henry Morgenthau, a fiscal conservative, was prepared to tolerate unbalanced budgets if necessary to finance New Deal programs.

A host of other newcomers poured into Washington in 1933—former progressive reformers, settlement-house workers, political scientists, economics professors, bright young lawyers. They energized the capital, drafting bills, competing for the president's attention, and debating strategies of reform and recovery. From this pressure-cooker environment emerged a flood of laws, programs, and agencies encompassed within a single, catch-all label: the New Deal.

The Hundred Days

Between March 9 and June 16, 1933, the "Hundred Days," Congress enacted more than a dozen major bills. It was a period of remarkable legislative productivity. Rooted in the Progressive Era, these measures sharply expanded federal involvement in the national economy.

The banking crisis was FDR's most immediate challenge. On March 5 he ordered all banks to close for four days. At the end of this "bank holiday," the Emergency Banking Act, which had sailed through Congress, permitted healthy banks to reopen with a

Major Measures Enacted During the "Hundred Days" (March 9–June 16, 1933)	
March 9	Emergency Banking Relief Act
20	Economy Act
31	Unemployment Relief Act (Civilian Conservation Corps)
May 12	Agricultural Adjustment Act
12	Federal Emergency Relief Act
18	Tennessee Valley Authority
27	Federal Securities Act
June 13	Home Owners' Refinancing Act
16	Farm Credit Act
16	Banking Act of 1933 (Federal Deposit Insurance Corporation)
16	National Industrial Recovery Act (National Recovery Administration; Public Works Administration)

Treasury Department license, provided for the orderly management of failed banks, and enlarged the government's regulatory power. In the first of a series of "fireside chats" broadcast by radio, FDR assured Americans that they could again entrust their money to banks. In June Congress created the Federal Deposit Insurance Corporation (FDIC) to insure all bank deposits up to $5,000.

To keep the budget-balancing pledges made in the Democratic platform, FDR proposed, and Congress passed, an economy measure cutting federal salaries, slashing veterans' pensions and benefits, and otherwise trimming spending. Other New Deal measures were more experimental. On March 31 Congress created the Civilian Conservation Corps (CCC) to employ jobless youths for reforestation, park maintenance, and erosion control. By 1935 half a million young men—no women were included—earned $35 a month plus room and board in CCC camps from Maine to California. Two federal agencies addressed the heartbreak of foreclosure. The Home Owners Loan Corporation (HOLC) helped people to refinance home mortgages, and the Farm Credit Administration did the same for farmers.

The most comprehensive relief measure of the early New Deal, the Federal Emergency Relief Act of May 1933, provided $500 million to fill the empty relief coffers of states and cities. To run this program, Roosevelt appointed Harry Hopkins, a former social worker who emerged as one of the New Deal's most powerful figures. In his first two hours on the job, working from a makeshift desk in a hallway, Hopkins distributed $5 million.

The Tennessee Valley Authority (TVA), also created in May, sought to revitalize the entire Tennessee River valley, one of the nation's poorest regions. The TVA built a hydroelectric network that supplied cheap power to seven states while developing a flood-control system, recreational facilities, and a soil-conservation program. TVA became one of the New Deal's most successful ventures and continues to operate even today.

The two most important measures of the Hundred Days, the Agricultural Adjustment Act and the National Industrial Recovery Act, addressed economic revival. The Agricultural Adjustment Act sought to raise crop prices by reducing production. The objective was to blunt farmers' natural instinct to increase their production as prices fell, a process that drove prices still lower. In the summer of 1933, the government paid southern cotton planters to plow under much of their crop and midwestern farmers to slaughter 6 million piglets. The killing of pigs at a time when many people were going hungry became a public-relations debacle that the New Deal never fully lived down.

In May 1933 the Agricultural Adjustment Administration (AAA) began paying commodity producers to take acreage out of production. Food processors paid a tax that supported the program, and in turn they passed the cost on to consumers in the form of higher food prices. Parity—the restoration of farmers' purchasing power to its 1909–1914 level—was the AAA's goal.

Passed in June 1933, The National Industrial Recovery Act (NIRA), tried to kindle a spirit of cooperation and shared purpose. Along the lines of the trade associations that President Hoover had promoted, representatives of major industries, granted immunity from antitrust prosecution, drafted codes of "fair competition" for their industries. They set production limits, prescribed wages and working conditions, and forbade price cutting and unfair competitive practices. To administer the codes, the National Recovery Administration (NRA) came into being.

The NRA aimed to foster recovery by breaking the cycle of wage cuts, falling prices, and layoffs. Social reformers, however, had further goals. Under pressure from Labor Secretary Perkins, the NRA's textile-industry code banned child labor. And Senator Robert Wagner of New York pushed through Section 7a of the NIRA, affirming workers' rights to organize and to bargain collectively.

Hugh Johnson, the NRA's head, had served with the War Industries Board in 1917–1918 and combined that experience with energy and a knack for publicity. He organized a national campaign to persuade consumers to buy only from companies that subscribed to the NRA code. The campaign's ubiquitous symbol, the blue eagle, and its slogan, "We Do Our Part," adorned billboards, magazine advertisements, and storefronts.

The NIRA appropriated $3.3 billion for a public-works program to employ the jobless and to pump money into the economy. Headed by Secretary of the Interior Harold Ickes, the Public Works Administration (PWA) spent more than $4 billion on 34,000 projects, many involving the construction of dams, bridges, and public buildings.

The NRA philosophy echoed Hoover's theme of government-business cooperation. FDR included corporations as key players in the "all-American team" fighting the depression. Although the NRA codes, once signed by the president, had the force of law, Washington relied on voluntary compliance. Caught up in the spirit of national unity, most business leaders cooperated—initially.

Moreover, the probusiness Reconstruction Finance Corporation remained active. FDR appointed as RFC chairman Jesse H. Jones, a millionaire Houston banker. Under Jones, the RFC loaned billions of dollars to banks, insurance companies, and railroads. Jones also extended loans for new business ventures and thus made the RFC a potent financial instrument serving corporate America.

A few early New Deal measures anticipated a more adversarial approach to business—a theme that would soon grow. The 1929 crash had produced a bitter reaction against business executives. A Senate investigation of Wall Street in 1932–1934 discovered that not one of the twenty partners of the giant Morgan Bank had paid a penny of income tax in 1931 or 1932. People jeered when the president of the New York Stock Exchange told a Senate committee considering regulatory legislation, "You gentlemen are making a big mistake. The Exchange is a perfect institution."

Reflecting this public mood, Congress in May 1933 passed the Federal Securities Act, regulating the sale of stocks. It required corporate executives to give the Federal Trade Commission full information on all stock offerings and made them personally liable for any misrepresentation of securities issued by their companies. In 1934 Congress sharply curbed the purchase of stock on credit, which had contributed to the 1929 debacle, and created the powerful Securities and Exchange Commission (SEC) to oversee the stock market.

When Congress adjourned on June 16, 1933, the Hundred Days ended. For many Americans, this burst of legislative activity symbolized the dynamism, as well as the confusion, of the Roosevelt years. The Hundred Days spawned a galaxy of "alphabet soup" agencies whose initials few could keep straight. How all these new programs and agencies would work remained to be seen.

The NRA Bogs Down

Although the economy improved for a short period in the summer of 1933, recovery proved elusive. Economic indicators remained bleak through 1934, and problems and controversy plagued the New Deal.

Hugh Johnson's hard-driving, hard-drinking ways created problems for the NRA, but its difficulties went deeper. As the crisis-induced national unity of early 1933 faded, corporate America grew unhappy with NRA regulation. Small business objected that the codes favored large business. Republicans and conservative jurists attacked the NRA as unconstitutional. The agency itself bogged down in drafting trivial codes. The trade associations that wrote and supervised the codes used them to restrict competition and maintain high prices, not to stimulate economic expansion.

Beset by problems and failing its essential aim, the NRA sank of its own weight. Johnson left in 1934, and in May 1935 the Supreme Court unanimously declared the NRA unconstitutional. The Court ruled that the act gave the president regulatory powers that belonged to Congress and that the NRA tried to regulate *intrastate* commerce, violating the *interstate* commerce clause. As an economic-recovery measure, the NRA had failed.

Troubled Agriculture

The AAA also generated controversy. Drought as well as New Deal policies combined to reduce production and drive up prices. From 1933 to 1937, total farm income increased 50 percent. But the AAA often harmed rather than helped tenants and sharecroppers. Landowners banked crop-reduction checks, removed the acreage from production, and left the sharecroppers to shift for themselves.

Some victims of this process resisted. In 1934 the interracial Southern Tenant Farmers' Union, led by the Socialist party, emerged in Arkansas. An elderly black sharecropper told the organizing meeting, "The same chain that holds my people holds your people too. . . . The landlord is always betwixt us, beatin' us and starvin' us and makin' us fight each other. There ain't but one way . . . that's for us to get together and stay together." Landowners struck back with a campaign of terror, chasing down union organizers as their ancestors had hunted runaway slaves.

In the mid-1930s nature itself conspired against farmers as drought turned the Great Plains into a dust bowl. In Oklahoma the temperatures rose above 100 degrees for thirty-six days in a row in the summer of 1934. Under a searing sun and rainless sky, dust storms rolled across the plains from the Dakotas to Texas. The choking, wind-driven clouds penetrated the tiniest cracks, covering furniture, clothing, and skin with fine dust. Drifting eastward, the clouds obscured the sky over Cleveland, dropped red snow in New England, and even sifted yellow dust into the White House.

Battered farmers of the South and Great Plains abandoned the land in droves. Some migrated to the cities; others packed their few belongings into old cars and headed west to become migrant workers in California and Arizona. The hardships of these "Okies" (who actually came from many states, not just Oklahoma) symbolized the suffering and disruption of the 1930s.

In 1933–1935 debate raged within the New Deal between those who wanted to restore prosperity to agriculture as a whole and those who urged special attention to the nation's poorest farmers. Although FDR at first took the more conservative view, the advocates of a farm policy reflecting broader social objectives scored significant legislative victories in the later New Deal (see below).

Controversy over Relief Strategy

Intense discussion focused on the issue of aid for the unemployed. Impatient with slow, inefficient state and local agencies, relief administrator Harry Hopkins had convinced FDR by November 1933 that only direct federal relief could prevent mass suffering that winter. FDR put Hopkins in charge of a temporary public-works agency, the Civil Works Administration (CWA). Through the winter, the CWA expended nearly a billion dollars on short-term work projects for the unemployed.

When spring came, FDR abolished the CWA. No one would starve in warm weather, he believed. FDR shared with his conservative critics a horror of creating a permanent underclass dependent on welfare payments. But continuing mass unemployment, and local agencies' inability to cope with the challenge, made further federal relief inevitable.

Hopkins's growing influence sharpened the behind-the-scenes struggle between him and Harold Ickes to control federal relief policy. The supercautious Ickes went over every PWA proposal with a fine-tooth comb, leaving billions in relief dollars stalled in the pipeline. The impatient Hopkins sought above all to put people to work and to get money circulating. To him, even make-work projects such as raking leaves had merit if they provided jobs. In the unemployment crisis, Hopkins, not Ickes, became the chief architect of federal relief policy.

The New Deal in Midstream: Popularity and Problems

Despite the New Deal's brave beginnings, the depression continued as 1934 ended. Major problems gripped the NRA, conflict flared over farm policy, and the need for federal relief spending appeared to expand rather than taper off.

But the New Deal remained highly popular, reflecting both its achievements and FDR's political skills. Roosevelt commanded the public stage and marshaled support for his programs with seemingly perpetual buoyancy, self-assurance, and good humor. Although many staunchly Republican newspaper publishers remained hostile, FDR enjoyed excellent relations with the working press, and reporters painted an overwhelmingly favorable portrait of his administration.

FDR savored public appearances and took naturally to radio. He viewed the radio audience not as an anonymous mass but as three or four listeners in a living room. In his fireside chats he patiently described his goals. To many, he seemed a family intimate. Roosevelt's easy mastery of radio provided a model for his successors in the television era.

The midterm election of November 1934 ratified the popular verdict on the New Deal as the Democrats increased their majorities in the House and Senate. Kansas journalist William Allen White observed of FDR that "he's been all but crowned by the people." Although some viewed the New Deal as complete, a different mood prevailed in Congress and the White House. As the 1934 election returns rolled in, Harry Hopkins turned to a group of New Deal friends and declared, "Boys, this is our hour!" A new surge of activism, rivaling the Hundred Days, lay ahead.

The New Deal Changes Course

As the economy slowly sprang back, national unity waned. Conservatives criticized the New Deal for going too far, and radicals attacked it for not going far enough. FDR shelved the unity theme, veered leftward, and took up the cause of the underdog. Buoyed by the 1934 election and eying the 1936 presidential race, FDR in 1935 pushed through a bundle of reform measures known as the Second New Deal. In 1936 his landslide reelection victory cemented a new Democratic coalition that would long remain a potent political force.

Challenges from Right and Left

Although the early New Deal was hardly radical, some conservative business leaders saw it as a mortal threat to capitalism. In 1934 several top corporate leaders, joined by disgruntled Democrats, formed the American Liberty League, dedicated to the proposition that the New Deal restricted individual freedom and pointed the way to socialism. The U.S. Chamber of Commerce blasted the New Deal, and anti-Roosevelt jokes circulated among the rich, many of whom denounced FDR as a traitor to his class.

Stronger challenges came from spokespersons for those in the lower ranks who demanded radical social and economic changes. Father Charles Coughlin, a Detroit priest and radio spellbinder, won an audience of 40 million with his potent brew of economics, politics, and piety. An early New Deal supporter, Coughlin by 1935 was condemning FDR as a "great betrayer and liar," indulging in anti-Semitism, and peddling such panaceas as the nationalization of banks. Coughlin's radio followers, organized as the National Union of Social Justice, drawn mainly from the urban lower-middle class, threatened FDR's 1936 electoral hopes.

Millions of older Americans rallied to California physician Francis E. Townsend, who proposed that the government pay $200 monthly to retired citizens over sixty, stipulating that they spend the money within thirty days. This plan would thereby help elderly Americans and stimulate the economy, Townsend argued, and would open up jobs by encouraging early retirement. Although the scheme would have quickly bankrupted the nation, many older citizens embraced it.

Huey Long, a flamboyant political hell-raiser from Louisiana, became FDR's wiliest rival. A country lawyer who had won the state's governorship in 1928, Long ruled Louisiana as his personal fiefdom while building highways, schools, and public housing. He roared into Washington as a senator in 1932 and preached his "Share Our Wealth" program: a 100 percent tax on annual incomes exceeding $1 million and appropriation of fortunes over $5 million. Long proposed to give every American family a comfortable income, a house, a car, old-age benefits, and educational opportunities.

"Every man a king," proclaimed Long. His baiting of the rich appealed to Americans who resented gaping disparities of wealth. He fleetingly endorsed the New Deal, but his book *My First Days in the White House* (1935) showed clearly that the presidential bug had bitten him. By 1935 Long boasted 7.5 million supporters. When an assassin's bullet cut him down that September, Gerald L. K. Smith, even more demagogic, took over Share Our Wealth.

Adding to Roosevelt's worries, economic recovery remained elusive. By 1934 national income stood 25 percent above 1933 levels but still far below 1929 figures. Millions, jobless for three or four years, were deeply demoralized. In 1934 frustration erupted in nearly 2,000 strikes, from New York taxi drivers to San Francisco dock workers. Ultimately, however, Roosevelt regained the political high ground in 1935 with an impressive new series of legislative initiatives—the Second New Deal.

The Second New Deal: Expanding Federal Relief

In his January 1935 State of the Union address, FDR called for broad social reforms. His program contained six central elements: enlarged federal relief, assistance to the rural poor, support for organized labor, social-welfare benefits for older Americans and other disadvantaged groups, stricter business regulation, and heavier taxes on the well-to-do.

With unemployment still high, Congress in April 1935 passed the Emergency Relief Appropriation Act, granting FDR $5 billion to spend more or less as he wished. He swiftly established the Works Progress Administration (WPA) under Harry Hopkins. The WPA funneled relief directly to individuals. FDR's horror of "the dole," however, led him to insist that the WPA provide work, not handouts. In its eight-year life, the WPA put more than 8 million Americans to work, injected $11 billion into the economy, and completed a mind-boggling number of projects: 650,000 miles of roads built or improved; 124,000 bridges constructed or repaired; 125,000 schools, hospitals, and other public buildings erected.

The WPA also assisted writers, performers, and artists. The Federal Writers' Project employed out-of-work authors to produce state guides and histories of ethnic and immigrant groups. In Massachusetts, WPA workers transcribed hundreds of pages of handwritten legal documents from the witchcraft episode of 1692. In the South they collected the reminiscences of aged ex-slaves. The Federal Theatre Project (FTP) put unemployed actors to work across the nation. Touring FTP drama companies gave millions of small-town audiences their first taste of live theater. Artists working for the Federal Art Project designed posters, taught classes, and decorated post offices and courthouses with murals. These arts agencies helped thousands of creative people to survive the depression and enlivened a dismal decade.

Other New Deal agencies also distributed relief funds. The National Youth Administration provided part-time work for more than 2 million high-school and college youths. Harold Ickes's Public Works Administration picked up steam, employing thousands of workers on construction projects, that included the Lincoln Tunnel in New York and the Grand Coulee Dam in Washington State.

But monumental relief spending generated monumental budget deficits. The national debt skyrocketed from $21 billion in 1933 to $43 billion in 1940. British economic theorist John Maynard Keynes argued that the economy needed such debt. Reversing the conventional budget-balancing wisdom, Keynes prescribed deficit spending as the key to recovery. On FDR's part, although the president never explicitly embraced Keynesianism, he tolerated deficit spending as the price of New Deal goals, not as an economic strategy valuable in itself.

The Second New Deal: Turning Leftward

Roosevelt's legislative proposals of 1935 revealed a pronounced turn to the left. In 1933, heartened by a spirit of national unity, FDR had played down class differences, stressed the common goal of recovery, and attempted an unprecedented degree of centralized economic planning. But by 1935 the political struggles inevitable in a democracy of conflicting social classes and diverse interests were reviving. The Second New Deal therefore abandoned the effort to devise programs with universal appeal.

Roosevelt now offered a program openly geared to the needs of the poor, the disadvantaged, and the laboring masses.

Social-justice advocates, including Secretary of Labor Frances Perkins, helped to shape this program. So did hard-headed political calculation. Indeed, Roosevelt's advisers feared that Coughlin, Long, and Townsend could siphon off enough votes to deny Roosevelt reelection. This concern shone through in FDR's 1935 political agenda.

The New Deal's leftward turn became evident in agricultural policy as the plight of sharecroppers, tenants, migrants, and other poor farmers attracted fresh attention. The Resettlement Administration, created in May 1935, made loans to help small farmers to buy their own farms and to enable sharecroppers and tenants to resettle on productive acreage. Although the agency achieved less than was hoped and lasted only two years, it kept the difficulties of tenants and sharecroppers alive as issues of government concern. In addition, the Rural Electrification Administration (REA), also established in the spring of 1935, made low-interest loans to utility companies and farmers' cooperatives to extend electricity to the 90 percent of rural America

---

Major Later New Deal Legislation (November 1933–1938)

1933 (Nov.)	Civil Works Administration	**1935**	Emergency Relief Appropriations Act (Works Progress Administration)
1934	Civil Works Emergency Relief Act		National Labor Relations Act (Wagner Act)
	Home Owners' Loan Act		Revenue Act of 1935
	Securities Exchange Act (Securities and Exchange Commission)		Social Security Act
	Communications Act (Federal Communications Commission)		Public Utilities Holding Company Act
	Federal Farm Bankruptcy Act		Banking Act of 1935
	National Housing Act (Federal Housing Administration)		Resettlement Administration
			Rural Electrification Act
		1937	National Housing Act of 1937
			Bankhead-Jones Farm Tenancy Act
		1938	Fair Labor Standards Act
			Agricultural Adjustment Act of 1938

that lacked it. By 1941, 40 percent of American farms enjoyed electricity.

In January 1936 the Supreme Court dealt a setback to the New Deal's agricultural-recovery program, declaring the Agricultural Adjustment Act unconstitutional. To replace the AAA, Congress passed the Soil Conservation and Domestic Allotment Act, which paid farmers to cut production of soil-depleting crops such as wheat and cotton (the major surplus commodities) and to plant soil-conserving grasses and legumes instead. When agricultural prices remained depressed, Congress passed another major farm law in 1938 (see below).

Organized labor won an important victory in the Second New Deal, thanks to the efforts of New York senator Robert Wagner. Although Roosevelt originally opposed a prolabor law as contrary to the early New Deal's national-unity theme, Wagner patiently built congressional support for his bill. In May 1935, when the Supreme Court ruled the NIRA unconstitutional, including Section 7a, protecting union members' rights, FDR announced his support for a labor law.

The result, the National Labor Relations Act of July 1935, guaranteed collective-bargaining rights, permitted closed shops, and outlawed such management practices as spying on unions and blacklisting labor "agitators." The law created the National Labor Relations Board (NLRB) to supervise shop elections and to deal with labor-law violations. The legislation, called the Wagner Act after its chief supporter, stimulated a wave of unionization (see Chapter 26).

Of all the Second New Deal measures, the Social Security Act of 1935 had extraordinary long-term significance. Drafted by a committee chaired by Frances Perkins, this measure combined ideas of Progressive Era reformers and the example of social-welfare programs in England and Germany. It established a mixed federal-state system of old-age pensions for workers, survivors' benefits for victims of industrial accidents, unemployment insurance, and aid for dependent mothers and children, the blind, and the crippled. Taxes, paid in part by

employers and in part by wages withheld from workers' paychecks, funded pensions and survivors' benefits. In the short run, payroll withholding withdrew money from circulation and contributed to a steep recession in 1937. But it made sense politically, because workers would fight the repeal of a social-security plan to which they had contributed. As FDR noted, "With those taxes in there, no damned politician can ever scrap my social security program."

The Social Security Act set benefit payments at low levels, contained no provision for health insurance, and excluded millions of farmers, domestic workers, and self-employed Americans. However, it established the principle of federal responsibility for social welfare and created the framework for a future welfare system.

The Second New Deal's more radical thrust resulted in two business regulatory measures in 1935. The Banking Act strengthened the Federal Reserve Board's control over the national banking system and money supply. The Public Utilities Holding Company Act regulated the interstate transmission of electricity and restricted gas and electric companies to one geographic region, dealing a mortal blow to the speculative public-utility empires of the 1920s.

Finally, the Revenue Act of 1935 raised personal taxes at upper income levels, increased corporate taxes, and boosted levies on gifts and estates. Although this tax law had numerous loopholes and was not quite the "soak the rich" measure that some believed, it expressed the class-conscious mood of the Second New Deal.

By September 1935 the Second New Deal was complete. Laws had been enacted to promote the interests of the jobless, the elderly, the rural poor, and blue-collar workers; to regulate major business enterprises more closely than before; and to hike taxes on the wealthy. Without fully embracing the radical prescriptions of Coughlin, Townsend, or Long, FDR directed his program to the fears and inequities on which these critics had thrived. Nonetheless, FDR remained a firm supporter of the capitalist system. In his view, the New Deal had

The Election of 1936				
Candidates	Parties	Electoral Vote	Popular Vote	Percentage of Popular Vote
FRANKLIN D. ROOSEVELT	Democratic	523	27,752,869	60.8
Alfred M. Landon	Republican	8	16,674,665	36.5
William Lemke	Union		882,479	1.9

saved capitalism by reforming its excesses and addressing its less desirable social consequences.

The Election of 1936: The New Deal at High Tide

With the Second New Deal in place and unemployment declining, FDR faced the 1936 election confidently. "There's one issue in this campaign," he told an aide; "it's myself, and people must be either for me or against me."

A number of FDR's Republican foes lambasted Roosevelt's alleged dictatorial ambitions and charged that soon workers would have to wear metal dog tags engraved with their social-security numbers. The Republican party nominated progressive governor Alfred Landon of Kansas. A fiscal conservative who nevertheless believed that government must respond to social issues, Landon proved an inept campaigner.

FDR struck back against his challengers with typical zest. Only the forces of "selfishness and greed" opposed him, he told an election-eve rally in New York; "never before in history have these forces been so united against one candidate as they stand today. They are united in their hatred for me—and I welcome their hatred."

In the most crushing electoral victory since 1820, FDR carried every state but Maine and Vermont. FDR swamped Landon by a popular-vote margin of 11 million, and the Democrats increased their already-large majorities in the Senate and the House. The 1936 election underscored the message of 1932: Republican dominance was over. The Roosevelt landslide buried minor-party opponents as well. The Socialist candidate received fewer than 200,000 votes, and the Communist party candidate only 80,000. Congressman William Lemke, the candidate of the Coughlin, Townsend, and Share Our Wealth enthusiasts who had appeared so formidable in 1935, polled fewer than 900,000 votes.

The New Democratic Coalition

From 1860 to 1930, the Democrats had counted on three bases of support: the white South, parts of the West, and urban machines such as Tammany Hall. FDR retained these centers of strength but pushed far beyond them to forge a new Democratic majority. Five partially overlapping groups constituted the foundation of this new coalition: farmers, urban immigrants, unionized industrial workers, northern blacks, and women.

Midwestern farmers, longtime Republicans, found the New Deal's agricultural program congenial and widely switched to Roosevelt. For example, in 1936 FDR decisively carried Iowa, where Democratic candidates had been lucky to garner a mere 20 percent of the vote in the 1920s.

Urban voters, many of them immigrants or immigrants' children, followed the same pattern. In 1936 FDR carried the nation's twelve largest cities. New Deal relief programs aided the urban masses, and FDR wooed them persuasively. Further solidifying his urban base, FDR appointed many representatives of urban-immigrant groups, including unprecedented numbers of Catholics and Jews, to high New Deal positions.

Organized labor also joined the New Deal coalition. The unions pumped money into Roosevelt's reelection campaigns (although not nearly as much as big business gave to the Republicans), and rank-and-file union members voted overwhelmingly for FDR. Despite his early foot-dragging on the Wagner bill, FDR's reputation as a "friend of labor" proved unassailable. By 1936 administration ties to organized labor did provoke a strong anti–New Deal mood in business circles. But FDR won some business support, particularly from officials of corporations that were aided by his programs—companies that provided equipment for TVA and PWA hydroelectric projects, for example—and from exporters profiting from the New Deal's aggressive free-trade policies.

Among African-Americans, although most southern blacks remained disfranchised, the swelling black population of northern cities had become an influential force in electoral politics. As late as 1932, two-thirds of northern blacks had voted for the Republican Hoover. One black editor, annoyed by this enduring Republican allegiance, had advised his readers to "turn Lincoln's picture to the wall. That debt has been paid in full." With the advent of the New Deal, a historic shift occurred. In 1934 Chicago's black voters had signaled the new order by electing a Democrat over a popular Republican congressman. In 1936 northern blacks voted in record numbers, and 76 percent cast their ballots for FDR. In Harlem, Roosevelt amassed 81 percent of the vote.

Many factors played a part in blacks' turnaround. First, as employees last hired and first fired, African-Americans had higher jobless rates than the general work force, but unemployed blacks in the urban North benefited heavily from New Deal relief programs. Second, many blacks saw the New Deal as a force for racial justice, even though the record does not fully bear this perception out. Indeed, racially discriminatory clauses in some NRA codes led black activists to dismiss the agency as "Negroes Ruined Again," and other New Deal agencies tolerated racism. Roosevelt kept aloof from an NAACP campaign to make lynching a federal crime. In 1935 and 1938 he remained passive as antilynching bills were narrowly defeated in Congress.

Otherwise, however, the New Deal modestly advanced the black cause. Assuring a black student audience in Washington, D.C., that there would be "no . . . forgotten races" in his administration, FDR supported those seeking to eradicate racism from New Deal agencies. He appointed more than a hundred African-Americans to policy-level positions. The highest-ranking black appointee, educator Mary McLeod Bethune, the daughter of ex-slaves, became director of minority affairs in the National Youth Administration. The influential Bethune led the "black cabinet" that served as a link between the New Deal and African-American organizations. In addition, the "Roosevelt Supreme Court" that took shape after 1936 made important antidiscrimination rulings on voting rights, wage discrimination, jury selection, and real-estate transactions.

Thanks in large part to Eleanor Roosevelt, the New Deal also supported racial justice in symbolic ways. In 1938 Jim Crow statutes stipulated segregated seating at a Birmingham, Alabama, meeting of the interracial Southern Conference for Human Welfare. Mrs. Roosevelt pointedly placed her chair in the area between the white and black delegates. In 1939, when the Daughters of the American Revolution barred a performance by black contralto Marian Anderson in Washington's Constitution Hall, Mrs. Roosevelt resigned from the organization, and New Deal officials arranged for an Easter Sunday concert by Anderson on the Lincoln Memorial steps.

The Roosevelt administration also worked strenuously to attract women voters. Molly Dewson led the effort as head of the Democratic party's women's division. In 1936 she mobilized 15,000 women who went door-to-door distributing 80 million flyers describing New Deal programs.

Dewson, who believed that women had a special interest in issues relating to the home, stressed how social security, the National Youth

Administration, federal school-lunch programs, and other New Deal initiatives strengthened the family. She did not push a specifically feminist agenda or women's rights legislation. New Deal programs of economic recovery and social welfare, in her view, offered the best promise of advancement for both men and women. Dewson did, however, advocate the appointment of women to federal policy-level positions and knew which strings to pull to place women in key New Deal posts. FDR appointed the first woman cabinet member, the first woman ambassador, and more female federal judges than any predecessor. The 1936 Democratic platform committee reflected a fifty-fifty gender balance.

Despite the visibility of a few blacks and women in New Deal circles, advancing the interests of these groups was not high on FDR's agenda. Racism and sexism had long pervaded American society, and Roosevelt's administration, preoccupied with the economic crisis, did little to change the situation.

The New Deal and the Environment

FDR's commitment to conservation ran deep. As early as 1910, he had chaired the Fish and Game Committee of the New York State senate, trying to regulate tree cutting that threatened wildlife. Of all the New Deal agencies, moreover, the Civilian Conservation Corps lay closest to his heart. He valued its conservation role as much as its depression-fighting function. Under his prodding, the CCC thinned forests, built hiking trails and fire-lookout towers, and planted hundreds of thousands of trees.

Soil conservation became an urgent New Deal priority. The terrible Great Plains dust storms of 1933–1935 resulted not only from drought but also from overgrazing and unwise farming practices. Less dramatic than the dust bowl but no less damaging was soil erosion. By the 1930s erosion had destroyed 9 million acres of farmland, and 80 million acres more lay jeopardized.

Under Hugh Bennett, "the father of soil conservation," the Soil Conservation Service of the Department of Agriculture established demonstration projects and research stations across the nation. Farmers learned the value of contour plowing, terracing, crop rotation, and cultivating grasses that strengthen the soil. The Taylor Grazing Act of 1934 restricted the grazing on public lands that had compounded the problem of erosion.

The Tennessee Valley Authority had an important environmental component: controlling the devastating floods that worsened soil erosion. TVA planners dreamed of harnessing the region's natural resources to serve its people—the goal of earlier conservationists, among them Gifford Pinchot. Although it fell short of this vision, the TVA became a model for similar multipurpose watershed projects in the United States and abroad.

During the 1930s, too, New Deal planners continued the national-park movement, creating Olympic National Park in Washington, Shenandoah National Park in Virginia, and Kings Canyon National Park in California. Wildlife preservation also gained ground. By 1940 the government had set aside 7.5 million acres for some 160 new wildlife refuges. In 1935 Robert Marshall of the U.S. Forest Service helped to form the Wilderness Society to lobby for the cause. Wilderness, said the society, was not "a luxury or plaything" but "a human need." Under pressure from wilderness advocates, Congress designated a large portion of Kings Canyon National Park a wilderness area.

The wilderness and wildlife movements brought together an unusual coalition: New Deal planners; men and women who cherished the wilderness on aesthetic and philosophical grounds; and corporations, particularly firearms companies, financially interested in preserving wildlife for hunters. The National Wildlife Federation (1935) was largely funded by the gun industry.

From a contemporary perspective, the New Deal's environmental record reveals gaps and blind spots. Matters of great concern today—atmospheric pollution, dwindling fossil fuels, pesticide hazards, and the pressures of an ever-growing population on limited global resources—received little attention.

Nor did all New Dealers agree on environmental matters. Disagreements erupted between wilderness advocates and officials of the National Park Service and the CCC who were intent on opening the national parks to the most visitors possible. Nevertheless, the New Deal focused attention on conserving nature to a degree that had not been true for twenty years and would not again be true for a generation.

The New Deal Draws to a Close

After his enormous victory in the 1936 election, Roosevelt launched an ill-conceived attack on the Supreme Court that weakened him politically. In the wake of this fight, he confronted a newly energized conservative opposition that helped to end the New Deal. But the legacy of the New Deal remained; in the span of a few years, it had rewritten the national political agenda.

FDR and the Supreme Court

Early in 1937, fresh from his second electoral triumph, FDR went after the one branch of government that had seemed immune to the New Deal, the Supreme Court. The Court comprised nine elderly men, one of whom had served since 1910; another, since 1914. Among these nine jurists, there were four archconservative justices who despised the New Deal. Joined by moderates, they had invalidated the NRA, the AAA, and progressive state laws and appeared determined to "tie Uncle Sam up in a hard knot," as liberal justice Harlan Stone observed. Roosevelt feared that key measures of the Second New Deal would meet a similar fate. Indeed, some lawyers were so sure that the Social Security Act would be found unconstitutional that they advised their clients to ignore it.

In February 1937 FDR put his political prestige on the line by proposing a sweeping court-reform bill that would have allowed the president to appoint an additional Supreme Court member for each justice over seventy, up to a total of six.

Roosevelt insisted that this proposal reflected his concern for the heavy workload of aging justices, but his political motivation escaped no one.

FDR erroneously believed that his personal popularity would translate into support for his plan. Congress and the public, however, greeted it with skepticism that became disapproval. The size of the Supreme Court (unspecified in the Constitution) had been changed several times in the Republic's early years, but over the ensuing decades the membership of nine had taken on an almost sacred quality. Livid conservatives lashed out at the president's "court-packing" scheme. Some feared a Rooseveltian grab for power in the wake of his electoral triumph; others resented the disingenuous way in which FDR presented the plan. Even some staunch New Dealers abandoned the president on this issue. FDR pushed his court-reform bill for several months, but in July he gave up the fight. For one of the rare times in his presidency, he had suffered an embarrassing defeat.

But in fact, the Supreme Court had yielded to Roosevelt's pressure. One of the most conservative justices retired in May 1937, and others announced plans to step down. In April and May the Court upheld several key New Deal measures, including the Wagner Act and a state minimum-wage law. This shift away from anti–New Deal rulings may have been FDR's goal all along. From 1937 to 1939, FDR appointed four new members to the Court—Hugo Black, Stanley F. Reed, Felix Frankfurter, and William O. Douglas—laying the groundwork for a liberal majority that would endure long after the 1930s.

The Roosevelt Recession

As the Supreme Court fight ended, FDR confronted a far more serious problem: the economy plunged ominously in August 1937. Industrial production slumped to 1934 levels. Steel output sank from 80 percent to 19 percent of capacity. The jobless toll soared to 11 million in early 1938, encompassing more than 20 percent of the work force.

Capturing the Migrant Experience
This family of Texas tenant farmers in a California migrant-labor camp was photographed in 1935 by Dorothea Lange, one of the gifted photographers who compiled a memorable visual record of the depression's human toll for the Farm Security Administration.

What caused this relapse? Federal policies that steeply reduced consumer income played a role. The new social-security program's payroll taxes withdrew some $2 billion from circulation. Concerned about mounting deficits, FDR had seized upon signs of recovery to terminate the PWA and to cut the WPA and other relief programs sharply. These economies reduced the federal deficit but contributed to the 1937–1938 downturn. So, too, did a drastic contraction of the money supply by the Federal Reserve Board.

Echoing Hoover, FDR assured his cabinet, "Everything will work out all right if we just sit tight and keep quiet." However, Keynesian New Dealers recruited Harry Hopkins to warn the president of fierce political backlash should breadlines and soup kitchens continue. Only a renewal of massive relief, Hopkins insisted, would offer hope, and so in April 1938 FDR authorized heavy new spending. The WPA money machine clanked into action; the PWA received a new lease on life. By the end of 1938, unemployment had declined and industrial output had risen.

The End of the New Deal

Distracted by the Supreme Court fight, the 1937–1938 recession, and a menacing world situation (see Chapter 26), FDR offered relatively few reform initiatives in his second term. Congress, however, enacted several significant measures. The Bankhead-Jones Farm Tenancy Act of 1937 created the Farm Security Administration (FSA) to replace the short-lived Resettlement Administration. The FSA made low-interest loans that enabled tenant farmers and sharecroppers to buy their own family-size farms. Although the FSA did little to help the poorest tenants and sharecroppers, who were considered bad credit risks, it loaned more than $1 billion by the end of 1941. Thousands of families became new farm owners.

The FSA also established camps offering clean, sanitary shelter and medical services to migrant farm workers, many of whom had lived under wretched, unhealthful conditions. In its most innovative program, the FSA commissioned talented photographers to preserve the lives of tenants, migrants, and dust bowl families on film. They collected a haunting album of stark images.

Other late New Deal measures set precedents. The National Housing Act (1937) appropriated $500 million for urban-slum clearance and public housing. The Fair Labor Standards Act of 1938 banned child labor and established a national minimum wage of forty cents an hour and a maximum workweek of forty hours. Humanitarianism mingled with northern legislators' desire to undermine the competitive edge of the South—its low wage scales—in securing passage of this law.

The Agricultural Adjustment Act of 1938 set up procedures for limiting the production of basic commodities such as cotton, wheat, corn, and tobacco. It also created a mechanism by which the government, in years of big harvests and low prices, would make loans to farmers and store their surplus crops in government warehouses. (These payments came directly from the federal treasury rather than a processors' tax, a feature that had caused the Agricultural Adjustment Act of 1933 to be declared unconstitutional.) In years of poor harvests and higher prices, farmers could repay their loans and market their commodities at a profit. These provisions helped to stabilize farm prices and established the framework of federal agricultural policy for decades to come.

The later 1930s also witnessed a leap in union membership (see Chapter 26). This labor activism, stimulated in part by Section 7a of the NIRA and by the Wagner Act, demonstrated the New Deal's continuing role in transforming the social contours of American life.

Despite such achievements, the New Deal clearly lost momentum after 1935, in part because of the growing strength of an anti–New Deal congressional coalition of Republicans and conservative southern Democrats. After the Supreme Court fight, the opposition became more outspoken. In 1937, with nerves rubbed raw by the Court fight,

Congress rejected FDR's proposal to reorganize the executive branch by regrouping existing agencies, bureaus, and commissions into twelve superdepartments under the president's direct authority. Although the plan made administrative sense, FDR's critics claimed that it would create a virtual White House dictatorship. The conservative coalition also slashed relief appropriations, launched an investigation of the NLRB, cut corporate taxes, and killed the Federal Theatre Project. Suspecting that FDR used WPA staff members for political purposes, conservatives in 1939 passed the Hatch Act, forbidding federal workers from participating in electoral campaigns. The Fair Labor Standards Act of 1938, moreover, made its way through Congress only after intense White House lobbying and watering down by conservatives. Harry Hopkins noted that as economic recovery proceeded, Congress and the public seemed "bored with the poor, the unemployed, the insecure."

Attempts by FDR to stem the anti–New Deal tide in 1938's midterm election notwithstanding, the Republicans gained heavily in the House and Senate and added thirteen governorships. Roosevelt had campaigned against several prominent anti–New Deal Democratic senators in 1938, but the major targets of his attempted purge all won handily.

Focusing mainly on unsettling foreign developments in his January 1939 State of the Union message, FDR proposed no new domestic measures and spoke of the need to "preserve our reforms." The New Deal was over.

Conclusion

The New Deal compiled a stunning record. Not all of its programs succeeded, nor did it achieve full economic recovery, but the New Deal nonetheless represents a watershed in U.S. history. The Roosevelt administration assumed that government was responsible for promoting economic prosperity and the well-being of all citizens. Social security, the Wagner Act, and the Fair Labor Standards Act defined the basic outline of the modern activist welfare state.

From the 1860s through the 1920s, the business class had dominated Washington. The New Deal eroded corporate sway over government: it acted as a broker for *all* organized interest groups— business, agriculture, labor, and other sectors. Although the unorganized, including sharecroppers and tenants, had little influence, government gradually grew more responsive to their interests.

New Dealers, unlike progressives, sought not to purify the nation but to solve practical problems of business stagnation, unemployment, and the maldistribution of economic resources. New Dealers' *style*, too, differed radically from that of progressives. As historian William E. Leuchtenberg has written, "If the archetypal progressive was Jane Addams singing 'Onward Christian Soldiers,' the representative New Dealer was Harry Hopkins betting on the horses at Laurel Race Track."

The New Deal vastly enlarged presidential power and prestige. Indeed, Roosevelt so commanded politics that Americans began to expect their president to formulate "programs" and to shape public debate. These developments forever altered the balance of power between the White House and Congress.

Any evaluation of the New Deal must come to grips with Franklin D. Roosevelt. Neither a saint nor a superman, he could be devious, as in the Supreme Court fight, and his administrative skills left much to be desired. But his strengths far outweighed his liabilities. He adopted an open, experimental approach in grappling with national problems. Above all, Roosevelt's infectious optimism renewed the confidence of a demoralized people. "We Americans of today . . . ," he said in 1939, "are characters in the living book of democracy. But we are also its author. It falls upon us now to say whether the chapters that are to come will tell a story of retreat or a story of continued advance."

Chronology

1929 Stock-market crash; onset of depression.

1931 Farmers' Holiday Association.

1932 Reconstruction Finance Corporation.
Glass-Steagall Act.
Veterans' bonus march.
Franklin D. Roosevelt elected president.

1933 Repeal of Eighteenth Amendment (Prohibition).
Federal Deposit Insurance Corporation created.
Emergency Banking Act.
Civilian Conservation Corps (CCC).
Federal Emergency Relief Act (FERA).
Tennessee Valley Authority (TVA).
Agricultural Adjustment Administration (AAA).
National Recovery Administration (NRA).
Public Works Administration (PWA).
Civil Works Administration (CWA).

1934 Securities and Exchange Commission (SEC).
Civil Works Emergency Relief Act.

1935 Supreme Court declares NRA unconstitutional.
Emergency Relief Appropriation Act.
Works Progress Administration (WPA).
National Youth Administration.
Resettlement Administration.

Rural Electrification Administration (REA).
National Labor Relations Act (Wagner Act).
Social Security Act.
Banking Act.
NAACP campaign for federal antilynching law.
Huey Long assassinated.

1936   Supreme Court declares AAA unconstitutional.
Soil Conservation and Domestic Allotment Act.
Roosevelt wins landslide reelection victory.

1937   Roosevelt's "court-packing" plan defeated.
Farm Security Administration (FSA).

1937–   The "Roosevelt recession."
1938

1938   Fair Labor Standards Act.
Agricultural Adjustment Act of 1938.

1939   Hatch Act.
Marian Anderson concert at Lincoln Memorial.

FOR FURTHER READING

Paul Conkin, *The New Deal,* 2d ed. (1975). A concise, balanced overview.

Steve Fraser and Gary Gerstle, eds., *The Rise and Fall of the New Deal Order, 1930–1980* (1989). Incisive critical essays on the New Deal's long-term legacy.

John Kenneth Galbraith, *The Great Crash, 1929* (1988). A lively account by a leading economist.

Otis L. Graham, Jr., ed., *The New Deal: The Critical Issues* (1971). Thoughtful interpretive essays on key themes.

William E. Leuchtenberg, *Franklin D. Roosevelt and the New Deal* (1983). A comprehensive, readable overview, rich in illuminating detail.

Albert U. Romasco, *The Politics of Recovery: Roosevelt's New Deal* (1983). A study particularly useful for the New Deal's policies toward business.

Harvard Sitkoff, *A New Deal for Blacks* (1978). An exploration of the Roosevelt administration's policies toward African-Americans.

Studs Terkel, *Hard Times* (1970). Oral-history interviews that poignantly convey the depression's human toll.

Susan Ware, *Beyond Suffrage: Women and the New Deal* (1981). A study of the network of women who held high office in the New Deal.

The Great Depression crashed down on America, bringing economic, social, and emotional havoc. To comprehend the depression, one must look beyond Wall Street and Washington to auto plants, harvest fields, artists' studios, and ordinary people's homes. One must consider the situation abroad as well, for in these economically cataclysmic years, brutal and militaristic dictators seized control of other powerful nations, raising the specter of war.

American Life in a Decade of Crisis at Home and Abroad

The American People in the Depression Decade

The American Cultural Scene in the Thirties

The United States in a Menacing World

(Right) Striking Chevrolet workers in St. Louis holding an impromptu dance, 1937

The American People in the Depression Decade

For millions of industrial workers, the New Deal created a favorable climate for unionization. But union growth did not come easily, and workers often had to fight for the right to organize. Although some female and minority workers shared in the benefits of unionization, for others, the depression worsened a difficult situation. Indeed, the 1930s saw a backlash against working women and feminist goals, and the circumstances of blacks and Hispanic-Americans grew even more desperate.

Native Americans became the objects of well-meaning but sometimes misguided attention. And the depression profoundly affected the most basic social group of all, the family. But while many families experienced disruption and conflict, others drew together in the face of adversity.

The Plight of the People

The depression exacted an enormous toll in human suffering. Unemployment never fell below about 14 percent, and for much of the decade it ran considerably higher. (In the 1960s the government defined 5 percent unemployment as the maximum tolerable level.) As late as 1939, 9 million men and women remained jobless. Bankruptcies, foreclosures, and abandoned farms multiplied. A quarter of all farm families had to accept public or private assistance during the 1930s.

In some cities the jobless rate far exceeded the national average. In 1932, for example, Toledo's unemployment rate stood at an incredible 80 percent. The nation's jobless rolls included millions who had earned good wages before 1929. These newly impoverished individuals experienced intense stress over their sudden decline in income and status. Some went to great lengths to maintain appearances, even when they had barely enough to eat. Advertisements promoting products ranging from mouthwash and deodorant to encyclopedias and correspondence courses capitalized on widespread feelings of shame. The ads played on people's fears of being found out, of having their failings and pretenses exposed.

Among those fortunate enough to work, many took jobs below their level of training: college alumni pumped gas, and business-school graduates sold furniture. Others eked out a few dollars by peddling products to neighbors as poor as themselves. "I'll never forget watching my mother trying to sell Two-in-One Shoe Polish door-to-door," a child of the depression recalled.

Nutritional deficiencies and people's inability to pay for medical and dental care laid the groundwork for later problems. "You have to have money to be sick—or [you] did then," novelist John Dos Passos said; "any dentistry also was out of the question, with the result that my teeth went badly to pieces. Without dough you couldn't have a tooth filled." The savings of older Americans evaporated. By the mid-thirties, 1 million Americans over age 65 were on relief.

Industrial Workers Unionize

The economic crisis and widespread hardship energized and transformed organized labor. Although the number of unskilled or semiskilled factory workers had doubled between 1900 and 1930, they remained almost completely unorganized at the start of the depression. Managers of major industries—steel, automobiles, textiles—had blocked all attempts at unionization, viewing it as a threat to their right to run their businesses. The prosperity and probusiness mood of the 1920s had further sapped the labor movement's energies.

Then in the 1930s, hard times and a favorable government climate led to labor militancy and a surge of unionization. When the National Labor Relations Act of 1935 guaranteed labor's right to organize and to bargain collectively, militant labor leaders such as John L. Lewis of the United Mine Workers (UMW) and Sidney Hillman of the Amalgamated Clothing Workers chafed at the American Federation of Labor's slowness in organizing factory workers. In November 1935 Lewis and Hillman founded the Committee for Industrial Organization (CIO) within the AFL. CIO activists preached unionization to workers in Pittsburgh's steel mills, Detroit's auto plants, and Akron's rubber factories. Unlike the restrictive, craft-based AFL, the CIO unions welcomed all workers in a particular industry, regardless of their race, gender, or degree of skill.

In 1936 the CIO-sponsored Steel Workers Organizing Committee (SWOC) geared up for a major strike to win union recognition from U.S. Steel, which John L. Lewis described as "the crouching lion in the path of labor." The crouching lion proved a pussycat. In March 1937 U.S. Steel recognized the union, granted a wage increase, and accepted a forty-hour workweek. Lewis had secretly negotiated the settlement with the head of U.S. Steel, Myron C. Taylor, who accepted unionization in the face of labor defiance and the strongly pro-labor atmosphere in Washington. Other steel companies followed, and by the year's end 400,000 steelworkers had signed their union cards.

Meanwhile, organizers for the United Auto Workers (UAW), led by the fiery young activist Walter Reuther, mapped a campaign to organize General Motors, a company deeply hostile to unions. In December 1936 thousands of workers at GM's two body plants in Flint, Michigan, stopped work and occupied the factories, paralyzing GM's production by their "sit-down strike." Keeping their action peaceful, however, the strikers protected the equipment and the cars on the assembly lines.

Women played a key part in the Flint strike. They picketed and paraded, opened a kitchen to feed the strikers, organized a speakers' bureau to present the union's side, and even produced a drama, *The Strike Goes On.* Women also figured prominently in the confrontation on January 11, 1937, between strikers and Flint police that led to the officers' opening fire on the unarmed strikers. Only when women joined the picketers did the police cease shooting. Fourteen strikers were injured; astonishingly, none died.

This episode resulted in the formation of the Women's Emergency Brigade, whose 400 members,

donning red berets and armbands, remained on twenty-four-hour alert for picket duty. Although the overall direction of the strike rested in male hands, the female participants discovered the exhilaration of working with others on a common cause. As one woman wrote in the UAW newspaper, "I only wish I'd gotten mad long ago . . . , but I didn't have time for anything outside of my own small circle. I'm living for the first time with a definite goal."

At first, GM fought unionization. Company officials called in the police to harass the strikers, sent spies to union meetings, and warned workers' families that strikers would be fired. The company also tried to persuade the Roosevelt administration to summon troops and to expel the strikers by force. Although FDR disapproved of the sit-down tactic, he refused to mobilize federal troops against the strikers. On February 11, seven weeks into the strike, GM signed a contract recognizing the UAW. Chrysler followed, and by the end of 1937, the UAW boasted more than 400,000 members.

In 1938 the Committee for Industrial Organization left the AFL to become the Congress of Industrial Organizations, a 2-million-member association of six major industrial unions. In response to the CIO challenge, the AFL became more vigorous and more flexible. Union membership shot up from under 3 million in 1933 to more than 8 million in 1941, with much of the increase after 1936.

These victories came hard as the heads of big corporations dug in their heels. Henry Ford, for example, hated unions, and his loyal lieutenant, a tough brawler named Harry Bennett, organized a squad of union-busting thugs to fight the UAW. In 1937, in a bloody encounter, Bennett's men beat Walter Reuther and other UAW officials outside Ford's River Rouge plant. Not until 1941 did Ford yield to union pressure. Another holdout was the Republic Steel Company, headed by union hater Tom Girdler. Even after U.S. Steel signed with the CIO in March 1937, Republic and other smaller companies known collectively as "Little Steel" adamantly refused.

In May 1937 workers in twenty-seven Little Steel plants, including Republic's factory in South

Chicago, walked off the job. Anticipating the strike, Girdler had assembled an arsenal of riot guns and tear gas. On May 30, Memorial Day, strikers approached the 264 police officers guarding the plant. Someone threw a large stick at the police, who opened fire, killing ten strikers and wounding more than eighty. A coroner's jury ruled the Memorial Day Massacre "justifiable homicide," but a Senate investigation concluded that it had been "clearly avoidable by the police." In 1941 Tom Girdler and the rest of Little Steel threw in the towel and finally signed union agreements with the CIO.

The union movement bypassed workers at the low end of the wage scale—domestics, farm workers, department-store clerks—who tended to be primarily female, black, or recent immigrants. Nonetheless, the unionization of vast sectors of the industrial work force represents one of the decade's most memorable achievements.

Why did powerful corporations cave in to unions after years of resistance? Workers' militancy and the tactical skills of a new generation of labor leaders played a central role. So, too, did management's fears of violence and sabotage. But above all, labor's successes after 1936 reflected the changed political climate. Where government officials had once helped to break strikes by force and legal intimidation, Roosevelt and key state officials refused to intervene on the side of management. (The willingness of the South Chicago police to act as a kind of private army for Tom Girdler represents a rare exception.) The Fair Labor Standards Act of 1938 and the role of the National Labor Relations Board in assuring fair union votes made clear that Washington would not line up with management in labor disputes. Once the chiefs of the nation's major industries realized this fact, most came to terms with the union leaders.

Mixed Blessings for Women

Senator Robert Wagner called the working woman in the depression years "the first orphan in the storm." Indeed, for the 25 percent of women gainfully employed in 1930, the depression brought hard times. The female jobless rate hovered above 20 percent through much of the decade. Women who continued working often had to take lower-paying, lower-status jobs. Many young women entering the job market had to settle for temporary or part-time work.

In the face of heavy competition from displaced male workers, the number of women in white-collar professions such as librarianship, social work, and public-school teaching declined. Women who did cling to their jobs encountered wage discrimination. In 1939 the average woman schoolteacher earned 20 percent less than her male counterpart with comparable experience. A number of NRA codes actually endorsed lower pay for women workers. The minimum-wage clause of the Fair Labor Standards Act of 1938 helped thousands of women whose hourly wage fell below the new minimum but did not cover many categories of working women.

Married women workers encountered enormous resentment. Most took jobs out of economic necessity but were commonly accused of seeking to earn "pin money." People complained that married women had no right to hold jobs with so many men out of work. Many cities refused to employ married women as schoolteachers and fired women teachers who married.

The unionization drive of the later 1930s had mixed results for women workers. Some benefited from the campaign to organize the mass-production industries; for example, female workers helped to plan and to carry out a "slowdown" strategy that forced a large GM parts factory in Detroit to sign a union contract. However, unionization made little headway in heavily female sectors of the labor force, including the textile industry and the clerical, sales, and service occupations. For instance, by the 1930s office work had been almost completely feminized, and most women office workers earned far less than male factory workers. Many secretaries responded with enthusiasm when the CIO chartered an office workers' union in 1937, and several strikes occurred. But the CIO drive to unionize clerical workers made little progress nationally.

The depression represented a low point for the women's movement. Battling the economic crisis, the nation had little patience for feminist issues or for the struggle to secure gender equality. Nonetheless, the proportion of women working for wages crept up slightly over the decade, from 25 percent to 26 percent. At the same time, the ratio of gainfully employed married women rose from 11.7 percent to 15.6 percent. Neither depression nor criticism could reverse the long-term movement of women into the workplace. Indeed, the depression may have accelerated that movement as married women worked to supplement the family income.

Blacks, Hispanic-Americans, and Native Americans Cope with Hard Times

The depression markedly slowed the urbanization of black Americans. Only 400,000 southern blacks moved to northern cities in the 1930s, far fewer than in the 1920s or the 1940s. In 1940, 77 percent of the nation's 12 million African-Americans still lived in the South.

Rural and urban blacks alike endured extreme hardships. New Deal agricultural policies often led to the eviction of black tenant farmers and sharecroppers. Among black industrial workers, persistent racism, discriminatory union policies, and fierce competition pushed the jobless rate far above that for whites.

Lynchings and miscarriages of justice continued for blacks as well, especially in the South. In the notorious "Scottsboro Boys" case, eight black youths were sentenced to death in 1931 by an all-white jury in Scottsboro, Alabama, on highly suspect charges of raping two white women. In 1935 the Supreme Court ordered a new trial because of the exclusion of blacks from the jury and the denial of legal counsel to the defendants. In 1936–1937 five of the defendants were again convicted, and they served lengthy prison terms.

Blacks did not accept racism and discrimination passively. The National Association for the Advancement of Colored People battled in courts and legislatures against lynching, racial segregation, and the denial of black voting rights. Urban blacks particularly resented the fact that whites owned most businesses in black neighborhoods and employed only whites. Under the banner "DON'T SHOP WHERE YOU CAN'T WORK," protesters boycotted such businesses in several cities. In March 1935 hostility against white-owned businesses in Harlem, intensified by generalized anger about racism and chronic unemployment, erupted into a riot that caused $200 million in property damage and left three blacks dead.

To some extent, the depression diverted attention from racial issues and from the desperate economic condition of black Americans. But the rising tempo of activism gave warning that blacks would not forever ignore blatant racial discrimination and inequality.

The 1930s likewise brought trying times for Hispanic-Americans. Recent arrivals from Mexico, Puerto Rico, Cuba, and elsewhere in Latin America and South America made up most of the nation's 2 million Spanish-speaking residents. Most were manual laborers, many of them migratory agricultural workers. As the depression deepened, Mexican-born farm workers of the Southwest, welcomed for years as cheap labor, faced mounting hostility. The influx of "Okies" fleeing the dust bowl worsened the job crisis, and by 1937 more than half the cotton workers in Arizona were out-of-staters who supplanted Mexican-American laborers.

With their access to migratory work disrupted, Mexican-Americans poured into southwestern cities and swelled the population of the Spanish-speaking neighborhoods (barrios). Discrimination pervaded the cities. Crude notices trumpeting such warnings as "NO NIGGERS, MEXICANS, OR DOGS ALLOWED" were not unknown. Finding themselves expendable, half a million Mexicans returned to their native land in the 1930s. Some did so voluntarily, but in 1932 immigration officials and local authorities expelled more than 200,000 Mexican aliens.

The Mexican-American agricultural workers who remained faced appalling labor conditions and near-starvation wages. In the mid-1930s they rose up in waves of protests and strikes across California. In 1933 cotton workers and strawberry, pea, and grape pickers struck for higher wages. A labor organization called the Confederación de Uniones de Campesinos y Obreros Mexicanos (Confederation

Los Angeles Barrio, c. 1930
The scene is of Chavez Ravine,
today the site of Dodger Stadium.

of Unions of Mexican Workers and Farm Laborers) emerged. Under the impetus of CUCOM, more strikes erupted in 1935–1936, from the celery fields and citrus groves of the Los Angeles area to the lettuce fields of the Salinas Valley.

Well-financed agribusiness organizations such as the Associated Farmers of California and the California Fruit Growers Exchange (which marketed citrus under the Sunkist brand name) fought the unions, sometimes resorting to violence in the process. Against heavy odds, the labor movement among Mexican-American farm workers did achieve some successes. Striking cotton pickers, for example, increased the rate for a hundred pounds of cotton from $.60 to $.75. Their strikes also awakened some Americans to the inhumane working conditions and shamefully low wages of one of the nation's most exploited groups.

The 1930s also revived attention to the nation's 170,000 Native Americans, most of whom existed in a world of poverty, scant education, poor health care, and bleak prospects. The Dawes Act of 1887 had dissolved the tribes as legal entities and tried to promote the Indians' assimilation into the American mainstream by allocating some tribal lands to individuals and selling the rest. By the early

1930s, whites owned about two-thirds of the land that Native Americans had possessed in 1887, including much of the most valuable acreage. Meanwhile, officials of the Bureau of Indian Affairs, including several Quaker humanitarians appointed by Herbert Hoover, had become convinced that the Dawes Act approach should be reversed. A leading advocate of reform was John Collier, who in 1923 had founded the American Indian Defense Association to preserve the spiritual beauty and harmony of traditional Indian life.

Appointed commissioner of Indian affairs in 1933, Collier translated his vision of renewed tribal life into policy. He secured funds from the CCC, the PWA, and the WPA to build schools, hospitals, and irrigation systems on Indian reservations—and to provide jobs for Native American workers. But Collier had larger goals. In 1934 he presented Congress with a bill halting the sale of tribal land to individuals, restoring the remaining unallocated lands to tribal control, creating new reservations, and expanding existing ones. The bill also would have set up tribal councils with broad powers of home rule and required Indian schools to focus on Native American history and traditional arts and crafts.

This visionary bill drew angry opposition in western states. Some Indian leaders criticized it as a plan to transform the reservations into living museums and treat Native Americans as an exotic minority. In fact, Collier's bill was widely thought to reflect the sentimental idealism of a benevolent outsider who believed that he understood what was best for the Indians; from the perspective of many observers, it did not express the actual views of the Native American population.

The law that finally emerged during the New Deal, the Indian Reorganization Act of 1934, represented a compromise between Collier and his critics. It ended the sale of tribal lands and enabled tribes to regain title to unallocated lands, but scaled back tribal self-government and dropped Collier's call for the renewal of traditional tribal culture.

Like the New Deal itself, Indian reform ebbed in the late 1930s. Collier resigned in 1945, his dream of revitalized tribal life unfulfilled. The tribes' special standing with the federal government had been largely terminated, and Native Americans were once more encouraged to abandon reservations and to give up traditional ways.

Family Life and Population Trends

For many parents in the 1930s, daily life was a constant uphill climb to make ends meet and to keep families together. They patched clothes, stretched food resources, and, when all else failed, turned to public assistance. Very poor families developed survival skills that more affluent families lacked.

Hard times disrupted marital patterns. Marriage rates tumbled in the early 1930s as people confronted harsh economic realities. The birthrate, too, dropped precipitously in the early depression years. Couples postponed families or limited their children to one or two. Family planning became easier with the spread and growing acceptance of birth-control devices such as the condom and diaphragm.

The declining birthrate and restrictions on immigration held population growth in the 1930s to a scant 7 percent, in contrast to an average of 20 percent in the three preceding decades. The economic crisis temporarily slowed urban growth, and many jobless young people returned home from the cities to their parents' farms. However, another long-term demographic trend, the westward movement, continued. Thousands of American families responded to hard times by seeking opportunities in the West, especially California. The proportion of the population living in the Pacific region rose steeply, and Los Angeles advanced from tenth to fifth among U.S. cities.

The depression inflicted deep psychological wounds on many families. In households with a tradition of male authority, the husband's loss of a job and erosion of self-confidence often had devastating consequences. One man expressed the depression's threat to his masculinity in extreme form when he admitted, "I would rather turn on the gas and put an end to the whole family than let my wife support me." Desertions increased, and the divorce rate reached a then all-time high by 1940.

Parents ruefully canceled vacation plans. Children found birthday presents never materializing and endured a home atmosphere tense with anxious discussions of family finances. Not all was bleak, however. People rediscovered skills such as painting their own houses and repairing their own cars. Home baking and canning thrived. Many later would look back at the depression as a time when adversity strengthened networks of sociability and support. One man recalled, "The feeling among people was beautiful. Supposing some guy was a hunter. He'd go out and get a hold of some ducks or some game, [and] they'd have their friends over and share it." But although sharing and making do could soften the depression's impact on family life, they could not eliminate the pain entirely, and the trials of the depression would long remain etched in the memories of those who lived through it.

The American Cultural Scene in the Thirties

The depression's cultural impact matched its broad social effects. Radio and movies provided diversion, and writers, artists, and social thinkers offered personal and probing views of American life. The mood shifted from critical pessimism to positive affirmation of the United States' history and traditions. This new tone reflected the renewed hope stimulated by the New Deal as well as the rallying of intellectuals against the rise of dictatorships abroad—regimes that made American democracy seem fragile and more worth preserving than some intellectuals had once appeared to think.

The Golden Age of Radio

As an antidote to hard times, radio proved enormously popular. Each evening millions of Americans gathered around their imposing Silvertone or Atwater Kent consoles to listen to their favorite news commentators, musical programs, and—above all—comedy shows. Radio humor reached its zenith in the 1930s, when the real world was hardly laughable. Comedians Jack Benny, Fred Allen, and George Burns and Gracie Allen won fiercely loyal audiences.

So, too, did the fifteen-minute afternoon dramas known as soap operas (because soap companies usually sponsored them), the favorites of housewives across the land. Listeners became so deeply involved with these daily dollops of idealized romance and melodrama that the line between fantasy and reality blurred. They even wrote earnest letters to soap-opera characters advising them how to handle their problems. Identifying with the ordeals and traumas of the radio heroines, listeners gained temporary escape from their own difficulties.

The standardization of mass culture continued. As successful radio shows spawned eager imitators, programming took on a monotonous, formulaic quality. One lament over the lost possibilities of the new medium came from Lee DeForest, commercial radio's inventor. "What have you done with my child?" he inquired plaintively.

The Silver Screen

In 1931 and 1932 the major movie studios tottered toward bankruptcy, but in true Hollywood fashion they staged a dramatic recovery in 1933 and prospered for the rest of the decade. Most people could still afford the quarter that it cost to see a movie at the local Orpheum or Bijou, and the introduction of double features (1931) and drive-in theaters (1933) also boosted attendance. In 1939, 65 percent of the population saw at least one movie a week.

A few movies dealt realistically with contemporary issues such as labor unrest in the coal industry (*Black Fury,* 1935) and sharecroppers (*Cabin in the Cotton,* 1932). Two documentaries made in 1936, *The River* and *The Plow That Broke the Plains,* evoked the human and emotional toll of a century of westward expansion. Casting off the bleak pessimism of the early thirties, Warner Brothers studio made a series of movies in 1934–1936 that portrayed the New Deal in glowing terms. And in *Mr. Deeds Goes to Town* (1936) and *Mr. Smith Goes to Washington* (1939), director Frank Capra, the son of Italian immigrants, offered a patriotic, idealistic message: that "the people" would always triumph over entrenched interests.

Gangster movies served up a stark style of film realism. Photographed in black and white and taking advantage of the advent of sound, such movies as *Little Caesar* (1930) and *The Public Enemy* (1931) grittily portrayed an urban America of giant skyscrapers, raw and rainswept streets, lonely bus depots and all-night diners, and the rat-tat-tat of machine guns as rival gangs battled it out. When civic groups protested that gangster movies glorified crime, Hollywood reversed the formula, making police and "G-men" (FBI agents) the heroes while maintaining the same level of violence. The lead characters, especially as played by actors Edgar G. Robinson and James Cagney, struck a responsive chord with depression-era moviegoers, for whom the odds seemed equally discouraging and the social environment equally threatening.

Above all, movies offered the chance to forget the depression for a couple of hours. Indeed, cinema's narcotic function in the thirties is clear. Lush musicals featured catchy tunes and cheerful plots involving the triumph of luck and pluck. Walt Disney's *Snow White and the Seven Dwarfs* (1937) brought animation to a new level of sophistication. *The Wizard of Oz* (1939) became a classic, beloved by generations of children and adults alike.

Light Moments in a Dark Decade
The Marx Brothers clown around in Animal Crackers *(1930).*

Comedies, too, provided cinematic escape and some of the decade's best movies. In films such as *Animal Crackers* (1930), *Monkey Business* (1931), *Duck Soup* (1933), and *A Night at the Opera* (1935), the Marx brothers, vaudeville troupers, created an anarchic world that satirized authority, fractured the English language, and demolished all rules of logic.

Filmmakers continued to stereotype blacks and women. The black actor Paul Robeson re-created his stage role in the movie *The Emperor Jones* (1933), but most African-American performers were confined to such parts as the weepy, scatter-brained maid played by Butterfly McQueen in *Gone with the Wind* (1939) or the indulgent house servant played by tap dancer Bill Robinson in the Shirley Temple feature *The Little Colonel* (1935). And Hollywood preached that women could find fulfillment only in marriage and domesticity, although a few films chipped away at the stereotype. In the comedy *Wedding Present* (1936), Joan Bennet played a strong-willed professional, and the tough, brassy, sexual, and fiercely independent Mae West, in *I'm No Angel* (1933) and other hits, cut her suitors down to size with a razor-sharp wit and made clear that she took orders from no one.

The Literature of the Early Thirties

American fiction of the early depression era exuded disillusionment, cynicism, and despair, challenging the fundamental premises of American ideology. James T. Farrell's *Studs Lonigan* trilogy (1932–1935) bleakly traced the hero's empty existence. The product of a chaotic working-class Irish-immigrant neighborhood, the young Lonigan stumbles through life, trying to piece together a coherent world view from the bits of mass culture that drift his way. Finally, not yet thirty, jobless, and alone, Lonigan dies of tuberculosis. John Dos Passos, in the innovative trilogy *U.S.A.* (1930–1936), drew a dark and intricate panorama of American history from 1900 through the early 1930s, painting a bloated, money-mad, exploitive society utterly lacking social or spiritual coherence. But the gloomiest view of the early thirties belonged to Nathaniel West. Drawing on his experiences as a night clerk in a seedy Manhattan hotel, West in *Miss Lonelyhearts* (1933) wove a nightmarish story of a newspaper advice columnist so oppressed by the stream of human misery flowing across his desk that he retreats first into apathy and then into insanity. In West's *A Cool Million* (1934), a parody of Horatio Alger, brave and virtuous young Lemuel Pitkin comes to New York seeking his fortune, only to be cheated, betrayed, beaten, imprisoned, and murdered.

Some radical novelists of the 1930s, encouraged by Communist party clubs, wrote explicitly of the decadence of capitalism, the exploitation of workers, and the approaching revolution. Jack Conroy's *The Disinherited* (1933), about exploitation and labor violence in the Missouri coal fields, gained force from the fact that Conroy's father and brother had died in a mine disaster. And radical playwrights brought the class struggle to the stage, including Clifford Odets, whose *Waiting for Lefty* (1933) offered cartoonlike stereotypes of noble workers and evil bosses and ended with the audience chanting "Strike! Strike! Strike!"

The Later Thirties: The Popular Front and Cultural Nationalism

In 1933–1934 the American Communist party vehemently attacked FDR and the New Deal. But after Soviet dictator Joseph Stalin, fearful of an attack on the Soviet Union by Nazi Germany under Adolf Hitler, in 1935 called for a worldwide "Popular Front" comprising opponents of fascism* and nazism, American communist leaders praised Roosevelt and recruited noncommunist intellectu-

---

*Fascism: a form of government involving one-party dictatorship, state control of production, extreme nationalism, and the forcible suppression of opposition.

als to the antifascist cause. For those who rallied to the Popular Front, few events aroused more passionate emotions than the Spanish Civil War (1936–1939). In July 1936 army units under fascist general Francisco Franco rebelled against Spain's legally elected government, a left-wing coalition. Spanish conservatives and monarchists, as well as landowners, industrialists, and the Roman Catholic hierarchy, supported Franco. His fellow fascists, Benito Mussolini of Italy and Hitler, provided military aid.

The anti-Franco loyalists, supporters of the elected government, won enthusiastic backing from many writers, artists, and intellectuals who sympathized with the Popular Front. Poet Archibald MacLeish pleaded eloquently for the loyalist cause. Ernest Hemingway, too, championed the loyalists' aims. His novel *For Whom the Bell Tolls* (1940) tells the story of a young American who joins a loyalist guerrilla band and eventually dies for the cause. Reflecting on his newfound capacity for political engagement, Hemingway wrote, "The Spanish Civil War offered something which you could believe in wholly and completely, and in which you felt an absolute brotherhood with the others who were engaged in it." (Franco's fascists gained control of Spain in 1939, and he ruled as a dictator, with American support, until his death in 1975.)

The Popular Front suffered a shattering blow on August 24, 1939, when the Soviet Union and Nazi Germany signed a pact agreeing not to make war on each other and dividing Poland between them. Stalin's cynical exercise in power politics shocked idealistic Americans allied with the Popular Front. Enthusiasm for cooperating with the communists under the banner of "antifascism" evaporated, and membership in the American Communist party dwindled. Although it was short-lived, the Popular Front significantly influenced U.S. politics and culture in the later 1930s and alerted Americans to the danger of fascism.

The emergence of fascism and the renewal of political faith summoned by the Popular Front combined with the achievements of the New Deal to stimulate a broad shift in America's cultural climate in the mid-1930s. The oppressiveness and cynicism of the early depression yielded to more hopeful views. Writers abandoned the satirical tone of the twenties and voiced admiration for the courage and solid virtue of ordinary Americans.

This mood found many expressions. In John Steinbeck's *The Grapes of Wrath* (1939), an uprooted dust-bowl family, the Joads, experience all kinds of misfortune as they make their way from Oklahoma to California. But they never give up and never refuse to help others. As Ma Joad says, "They ain't gonna wipe us out. Why, we're the people—we go on."

Another eloquent account of the new cultural experience dates from 1936, when writer James Agee and photographer Walker Evans spent weeks living with Alabama sharecroppers to research an article on rural poverty. It finally appeared in 1941 as *Let Us Now Praise Famous Men*. Enhanced by Evans's haunting photographs, Agee's beautifully written masterpiece evoked not only the precariousness of life at the bottom but also the strength and decency of Americans living at that level.

This positive assessment of American life reached the stage as well. Thornton Wilder's drama *Our Town* (1938) warmly portrayed a turn-of-the-century New England town where the deceptively ordinary routines of everyday life become, in memory, full of meaning. William Saroyan's *The Time of Your Life* (1939) celebrated the foibles and virtues of a colorful collection of American "types" assembled in a San Francisco waterfront bar.

American music also reflected this swell of cultural nationalism. In *Billy the Kid* (1938) and other compositions, Aaron Copland drew upon American legends and folk memories. George Gershwin turned to a popular 1920s play about black life for his opera *Porgy and Bess* (1935). And jazz flourished in the later thirties, thanks to the big bands of Benny Goodman, Count Basie, Glenn Miller, and others who developed a smoother, flowing style known as swing. For the next decade, swing dominated popular music.

Cultural nationalism also heightened interest in regional literature and art. In such fictional works as *Absalom, Absalom!* (1936) and *The Hamlet* (1940), William Faulkner of Mississippi continued the complex and often tragic saga of his mythic Yoknapatawpha County. Artists Thomas Hart Benton of Missouri, John Steuart Curry of Kansas, and Grant Wood of Iowa contributed a strongly regional note to painting.

Americans also began to recognize their rich folk-art heritage. Galleries mounted shows of Amish quilts, New Hampshire weathervanes, itinerant portraiture from the colonial era, and lovingly crafted children's toys. Eighty-year-old Anna "Grandma" Moses was only the best known of many folk artists "discovered" during this decade.

The patriotic absorption with all things American generated a fascination with the nation's past. Americans flocked to historical re-creations such as Henry Ford's Greenfield Village in Michigan and Colonial Williamsburg in Virginia. In 1936–1939 Texans restored the Alamo in San Antonio, the "Cradle of Texas Liberty." Americans made Margaret Mitchell's romantic epic of the Old South, *Gone with the Wind* (1936), a best-selling novel. Poet Carl Sandburg won a Pulitzer Prize for a four-volume biography of Abraham Lincoln that elevated the martyred Civil War president to near-mythic status.

As the 1930s ended, Americans viewed their society, their history, and their political system with a newly appreciative eye. The nation had overcome the economic crisis. Its social fabric had not disintegrated; revolution had not erupted. Other societies had collapsed into dictatorship, but American democracy seemed alive and well. Many intellectuals and writers who had appeared alienated in the 1920s now led the way in singing the praises of America and its people.

The Age of Streamlining

This restored confidence was captured in an exciting style of industrial design called streamlining, which by the mid-1930s had become a national vogue. Inspired by the romance of flight, industrial designers preached the elimination of all extraneous design features in favor of smoothly flowing surfaces. Graceful curves replaced clunky, square shapes. The goal, explained one designer, was to reduce products to their "utmost simplification in terms of function and form." Behind these aesthetic principles lay a social vision: that harmonious and functional consumer goods would produce a harmonious and functional society.

Streamlining appealed to American business. It also made products more attractive to consumers, a vital need during the economic stagnation. When Sears, Roebuck streamlined its Coldspot refrigerators, sales surged. Products ranging from stoves to toasters, alarm clocks, and cigarette lighters emerged in sleek new forms. Streamlining also helped business to rebuild its tattered reputation. By the mid-thirties, corporations were stressing the material benefits that business brought to society. Du Pont's "Better Things for Better Living Through Chemistry" summed up the new theme. Futuristic product designs fit perfectly with corporate America's effort to present itself as the benevolent shaper of the future.

The New York World's Fair of 1939 represented the high point of both the streamlining vogue and corporate America's public-relations counteroffensive. The hit of the fair was General Motors' Futurama, which gave visitors a vision of the United States in the distant year 1960—a nation of complex interstate highways complete with multiple lanes and stacked interchanges. For GM, Futurama represented a good public-relations investment that promoted GM vehicles and built public support for the costly highway system that the increasing number of cars and trucks would soon make essential.

Along with a first glimpse of such wonders as television and automatic dishwashers, the World's Fair offered its millions of visitors a memorable vision of "The World of Tomorrow"—a smoothly functioning technological utopia made possible by the nation's corporations. In one seductive, streamlined package, the fair epitomized capitalism's version of the cultural nationalism and reviving optimism that characterized the American mood as the thirties ended.

Undercurrents of Apprehension

But muted uneasiness and fear belied the surface appearance of reviving confidence. Although the economic crisis had eased, a dangerous situation was brewing overseas. The anxieties triggered by the menacing world situation flared at unexpected times and in unexpected ways. One such moment came on October 31, 1938, Halloween, when CBS radio aired a dramatic adaptation of H. G. Wells's *War of the Worlds*, directed by Orson Welles.

In realistic detail, the broadcast reported the landing of a spaceship near Princeton, New Jersey, the emergence of strange creatures with deadly ray guns, and their advance toward New York, destroying everything in their path. The vivid dramatization sparked a national panic as more than a million horrified listeners believed that aliens had landed, that New York had been obliterated, and that the end of the world was at hand. When word of the alarm reached the CBS studio, Welles inserted several announcements that the program was fictional. By then many people had already fled their homes, and not for several hours did the nation's heartbeat return to normal.

Beneath the panic about "Martians" lay a far more rational fear, that of an approaching war. For while the depression had preoccupied Americans, the international situation had deteriorated, and by October 1938 a global conflict seemed near. Radio news bulletins had warned for weeks of an impending war between Germany and England. Some listeners to *War of the Worlds* blurred the broadcast's details and concluded that a foreign nation had launched a surprise attack against the United States. The reaction was understandable, for by this time, the real world looked very scary indeed.

The United States in a Menacing World

Apart from efforts to improve Latin American relations, the early Roosevelt administration remained largely aloof from the rest of the world. As Italy, Germany, and Japan pursued aggressive and militaristic courses, American observers were torn between an impulse to resist fascism and an even stronger desire for peace. Determined not to bumble into war again, millions of Americans supported neutrality and peace. Others insisted that the United States should help embattled democracies abroad. All the while, Europe edged steadily closer to the precipice.

FDR's Nationalism and the Good Neighbor Policy

President Roosevelt at first put American economic interests above all else. Despite Secretary of State Cordell Hull's urging, FDR showed little interest in free trade or international economic cooperation.

In the summer of 1933, while Hull was representing the United States at an international conference on currency stabilization, FDR dispatched an adviser, Raymond Moley, to England with a blunt message: the president had no interest in any currency-stabilization plan that might undercut the New Deal recovery program. Hull was furious at being upstaged, and the conference broke up in angry frustration.

Roosevelt did, however, commit himself to an internationalist approach in Latin America, where bitterness over decades of "Yankee imperialism" ran high. In his 1933 inaugural, he had announced a "Good Neighbor" policy toward Latin America, and at a conference in Uruguay in 1933, the United States endorsed a statement of principles that declared, "No state has the right to intervene in the internal or external affairs of another." Under this policy Roosevelt withdrew the last U.S. troops from Haiti and the Dominican Republic, persuaded American bankers to loosen their grip on Haiti's central banking system, and reduced the U.S. role in Panamanian affairs. However, the United States remained closely identified with the repressive regimes of Raphael Trujillo in the Dominican Republic and Anastasio Somoza in Nicaragua.

Cuba and Mexico provided major tests of the Good Neighbor policy. In Cuba economic problems triggered by the highly protectionist Smoot-Hawley Tariff of 1930 brought to power a radical revolutionary government under Grau San Martín in 1933. American opposition to the San Martín administration found expression not in direct military intervention but in indirect action. Early in 1934, a conservative coalition enjoying U.S. support overthrew the San Martín regime. Strongman Fulgencio Batista gained power, aided by American manipulation of sugar quotas to aid the Cuban economy. He would retain power off and on until being overthrown by Fidel Castro in 1959.

In Mexico in 1936 a reform government came to power and nationalized several oil companies owned by U.S. and British corporations. The United States did not oppose nationalization but insisted on fair compensation. Economic pressure from Washington led to a compensation agreement that both the Mexican government and the oil companies accepted.

The Good Neighbor policy, in sum, did not terminate American interference in Latin America, but it did end heavy-handed intervention and military occupation.

The Rise of Fascism in Europe and Asia

Meanwhile, powerful forces raged across much of the world—forces that would once again pull the United States into war. As early as 1922, Italy's economic problems and social unrest had opened the way for Benito Mussolini and his Fascist party to seize power in Rome. The regime had swiftly suppressed dissent and imposed one-party rule.

More menacing events had unfolded in Germany with the rise of Adolf Hitler. An embittered war veteran, Hitler capitalized on the German people's resentment of the Versailles treaty and on the democratic government's inability to control runaway inflation. Briefly jailed after a 1923 grab for power failed, he had dictated his manifesto, *Mein Kampf* (My Struggle), filled with fanatic nationalism and anti-Semitism.

In 1929 an economic depression had struck Germany after a decade of runaway inflation and chronic recession. Hitler's National Socialist (Nazi) party had gained broad support as the economy deteriorated, and Hitler had become Germany's chancellor in January 1933. He promptly had crushed rivals within the Nazi party and fastened a brutal dictatorship on Germany. Young Nazis staged towering bonfires to burn the work of authors—many of them Jewish—whom they accused of "un-German" ideas. A racist who believed that he had to purify Germany of "inferior" taint, Hitler began driving out German Jews, whom he blamed for Germany's defeat in World War I.

In the mid-1930s Hitler pursued a militaristic, expansionist foreign policy that violated the Versailles treaty by rearming Germany and reoccupying

Adolf Hitler (1889–1945)

In this German magazine illustration from 1934, a belligerent Hitler is portrayed as his nation's savior.

European Aggression Before World War II

Less than twenty years after the end of World War I, war again loomed in Europe as Hitler launched Germany on a course of military and territorial expansion.

Japanese Expansion Before World War II

Dominated by militarists, Japan pursued an expansionist policy in Asia in the 1930s, extending its sphere of economic and political influence. In July 1937, having already occupied the Chinese province of Manchuria, Japan attacked China proper.

the Rhineland, the strip between the Rhine River and the French border specifically demilitarized at Versailles. Early in 1938 he proclaimed an *Anschluss* (union) between Austria and Germany. Meanwhile, Mussolini, intent on building an empire in Africa, had invaded Ethiopia in 1935. In London, Paris, Washington, and Geneva, the headquarters of the League of Nations, hand wringing but little firm action greeted these aggressive moves.

After Austria, Hitler turned to the Sudetenland, an area of Czechoslovakia containing 3 million ethnic Germans and 700,000 Czechs. Insisting that the Sudetenland was "racially" part of Germany, Hitler made clear his determination to take the area, by force if necessary. At a conference in Munich on September 29–30, 1938—which excluded the Czechs—British prime minister Neville Chamberlain and his French counterpart Edouard Daladier agreed to turn the Sudetenland over to

Germany. Stripped of a third of its population and territory, Czechoslovakia now faced Germany's massed tanks and troops. Viewing this appeasement of Germany a diplomatic victory, Chamberlain proclaimed "peace in our time." World War II was less than a year away.

In Tokyo, meanwhile, nationalistic militarists had gained control of Japan's government and begun a fateful course of expansion. In 1931–1933 Japanese troops had invaded the Chinese province of Manchuria, installed a puppet government, and forced China, with no outside support, to sign a treaty recognizing Japanese control of the province. In July 1937 Japan launched a full-scale war against China itself.

In 1936 Germany, Italy, and Japan signed treaties of political alliance and mutual defense. This alignment, called the Axis, would soon join forces in war.

The American Mood: No More War

The American response to these developments revealed a revulsion against war. By the mid-1930s millions of Americans believed that the United States' decision to enter World War I in April 1917 had been a ghastly mistake. In mid-decade a series of books reinforced this conclusion, arguing that banking and corporate interests had dragged the United States into World War I to protect their loans and weapons sales to England and France.

Public concern over the "merchants of death" issue led to the creation of a special congressional investigating committee under Senator Gerald Nye, a North Dakota Republican. In hearings from 1934 to 1936, the Nye committee compiled mountainous evidence of the heavy involvement of U.S. banks and corporations in financing World War I and supplying arms to the Allies. It documented these groups' lobbying and public-relations activities in support of U.S. intervention. In these hearings, Progressive Era suspicions of "Wall Street" and "big business" resurfaced powerfully. And in the midst of the depression, it was not hard to convince Americans that bankers were evil. A January 1937 poll showed that an astonishing 70 percent of the people believed that the United States should have stayed out of World War I.

Mistakenly equating Hitler with Kaiser Wilhelm, and the rise of fascism with the militaristic posturing of the pre-1914 European empires, many Americans concluded that the United States, protected by two oceans, could safely remain aloof from the upheavals convulsing other parts of the world. Reflecting this outlook, a peace movement spread across the nation's college and university campuses in 1935–1938. A peace strike in the spring of 1936 saw half a million students boycott classes to attend antiwar events.

In 1935–1937 a series of Neutrality Acts echoed the longing for peace. To prevent a repetition of the circumstances that had brought the United States into war in 1917, these measures outlawed arms sales and loans to nations at war and forbade Americans from traveling on the ships of belligerent powers. But the high point of peace legislation came early in 1938, when Indiana congressman Louis Ludlow proposed a constitutional amendment requiring a national referendum on any U.S. declaration of war except in cases of actual attack. Only after a direct appeal from FDR, and then by a narrow margin, did the House of Representatives reject the Ludlow Amendment.

Hesitant Response to the Fascist Challenge

The American people took alarm slowly at the fascist and militaristic regimes in Germany, Italy, and Japan. Indeed, many Americans initially praised Mussolini for imposing order and discipline, making trains run on time, and energizing Italy with a flurry of government activity, and even Hitler had American admirers. Some—including Joseph P. Kennedy, the ambassador to Great Britain (and father of a future president)—found the German chancellor tolerable because of his fanatic opposition to communism. And many Americans at first considered Hitler and Mussolini more ridiculous than menacing. From the beginning, however, others viewed fascism with grave apprehension. The Popular Front was one expression of this antifascist impulse. As early as 1933, Harvard literature professor Howard Mumford Jones warned that Nazi book burnings and suppression of free speech put freedom at risk everywhere.

FDR reacted ambivalently to the fascist onslaught. Fascinated by global politics, he advocated adequate national defense, and as early as 1933 he proposed naval expansion. At the same time, personalizing international affairs as he did domestic issues, Roosevelt communicated directly with world leaders, including Hitler and Mussolini, seeking avenues of accommodation. FDR recognized the strength of American antiwar sentiment and never pushed ahead of public opinion. After the Munich Pact, the president sent a terse telegram of praise ("Good Man") to Prime Minister Chamberlain and wrote that he was "not a bit upset" at the agreement to hand the Sudetenland over to Germany.

The administration responded more uneasily to Japanese aggression against China than to Hitler and Mussolini. Americans regarded China with special sympathy and interest. Christian missionaries saw the vast Eastern nation as a field ripe for harvest, and top government policy makers clung to the old dream of a boundless China market. The Open Door policy of the late nineteenth century reflected the American outlook on Asian nations, "the great potential markets of the world" as Secretary of State Hull termed them.

Now Japanese expansion into Manchuria, and then into China itself, threatened the Open Door. On an immediate level, the closing of China to U.S. trade meant the loss of $100 million in annual cotton sales. But long-term concern that Japanese goods, especially textiles, might someday flood the world market heightened Washington's uneasiness. As early as 1934, General William "Billy" Mitchell, an advocate of air power, declared, "Japan is our most dangerous enemy, and our planes should be designed to attack her." In cabinet meetings, FDR openly speculated about eventual war with Japan.

Publicly, Washington reacted to Japan's moves with symbolic gestures, refusing to recognize the Japanese puppet government in Manchuria, extending modest loans to China, and urging Americans to boycott Japanese silk. In October 1938 the U.S. ambassador to Japan protested Japan's violation of the Open Door principle. The Japanese responded that the Open Door was "inapplicable." Apart from these cautious steps, the United States did little as the Japanese tightened their grip on China.

1938–1939: The Gathering Storm

The interlude of reduced tension that followed the Munich Pact proved tragically brief. "Peace in our time" lasted a mere 5½ months. At 6:00 A.M. on March 15, 1939, Nazi troops thundered across the border into Czechoslovakia. By evening the Nazi flag flew over the ancient hall of kings in Prague. Five months later, the signing of the Nazi-Soviet Pact gave Hitler a green light to invade Poland.

In the United States the debate over the American role now intensified. Some almost desperately urged the nation to keep free of the approaching conflict. Opponents of intervention warned that

American involvement in a war could shatter New Deal reforms and spawn repression and reaction, as it had a generation earlier. But opinion was shifting rapidly. Pacifism and neutralism weakened, and the voices urging activism strengthened. In 1938, warning of the "malignant character and cancerous spread" of fascism, cultural critic Lewis Mumford issued "A Call to Arms" in the *New Republic*. Archibald MacLeish, having earlier championed the cause of Spain, exhorted his fellow citizens to mobilize against Hitler.

After the fall of Czechoslovakia and Albania early in 1939, FDR publicly called on Hitler and Mussolini not to invade thirty-one specific nations. A jeering Hitler read FDR's message before the German Reichstag (legislative assembly), and Nazis roared with laughter as he proclaimed, "Mr. President, I fully understand that the vastness of your nation and the immense wealth of your country allow you to feel responsible for the history of the whole world and for the history of all nations. I, sir, am placed in a much more modest and smaller sphere."

In October 1938 Roosevelt asked Congress for a $300 million military appropriation; in November he instructed the Army Air Corps to plan for an annual production of 20,000 planes; in January 1939, calling for actions against "aggressor nations . . . more effective than mere words," he submitted a $1.3 billion defense budget. Hitler and Mussolini, he said, were "two madmen" who "respect force and force alone."

America and the Jewish Refugees

Hitler and his followers had translated their hatred of Jews into official policy. The Nuremberg Laws of 1935 had denied German Jews citizenship and many legal rights. Then in 1938 the anti-Jewish campaign had become more brutal as the Nazis barred Jews from attending concerts and plays, expelled Jewish students from schools and universities, and required Jews to register their property. When a distraught Jewish youth assassinated a German official in Paris, Hitler levied a "fine" of $400 million on the entire Jewish population of Germany.

This remorseless campaign reached a crescendo of violence on November 9–10, 1938: *Kristallnacht,* the "Night of Broken Glass." Throughout Germany and Austria, Nazis vandalized Jewish homes, burned synagogues, and wrecked and looted thousands of Jewish-owned businesses. Not even Jewish hospitals, old people's homes, or children's boarding schools escaped the terror.

No longer could anyone mistake Hitler's malignant intent. This brutish repression foreshadowed the policy of outright extermination that would emerge during World War II, Hitler's "final solution" to the "Jewish problem." Jews, who had been leaving Germany since 1933, streamed out by the tens of thousands, seeking haven. Between 1933 and 1938, 60,000 had fled to the United States.

Among the victims of fascism who found refuge in America were several hundred distinguished scholars, writers, musicians, artists, and scientists. This remarkable company included pianist Rudolph Serkin, composer Béla Bartók, architect Walter Gropius, political theorist Hannah Arendt, and future secretary of state Henry Kissinger. Also among the refugees were three gifted physicists, Leo Szilard, James Franck, and Enrico Fermi, who would play key roles in building the atomic bomb. American cultural and intellectual life in the second half of the twentieth century would have been immeasurably diminished without these refugees.

While it welcomed famous and distinguished Jewish refugees, the United States proved far more reluctant to grant sanctuary to the mass of Hitler's Jewish victims. Congress consistently rejected all efforts to liberalize the immigration law, with its discriminatory quotas. FDR bears some responsibility. While deploring Hitler's persecution of the Jews and helping to establish the Inter-Governmental Committee on Refugees in 1938, he did little else to translate his generalized sympathy for the Jews into political efforts to relax restrictions on immigration.

Most Americans, according to public-opinion polls, condemned the Jews' persecution, but only a minority favored the admission of more refugees. In early 1938, when pollsters asked whether the immigration act should be amended to admit "a larger number of Jewish refugees from Germany," 75 percent responded no. Isolationism, anti-immigrant sentiment, and anti-Semitism sharply limited the American response to the tragedy of European Jewry.

The human result of such attitudes was graphically illustrated in June 1939 when the *St. Louis,* a German passenger ship jammed with 900 Jewish refugees, asked permission to put its passengers ashore at Fort Lauderdale, Florida. Not only did immigration officials refuse this request, but, according to the *New York Times,* a Coast Guard cutter stood by "to prevent possible attempts by refugees to jump off and swim ashore." The *St. Louis* turned slowly away from the lights of America and sailed back to Germany, where more than 700 of its passengers would die under Nazi brutality.

Conclusion

The ordeal of the *St. Louis* provides an appropriately somber conclusion to a decade that began with the stock-market plunge and ended with the nation teetering on the brink of war. Between these dismal developments, the 1930s brought bright moments of political creativity, social advance, and cultural achievement. American families showed sturdy resiliency, workers found solidarity in unions, and bold designs revolutionized consumer goods. Radio and movies provided standardized entertainment even as writers and others rediscovered the vitality of America's regional cultures. But by 1939 the world looked dark from the thunderheads of war gathering over Europe and Japan; it would soon look darker still.

Chronology

1930	*Little Caesar*, gangster movie starring Edward G. Robinson. *Animal Crackers*, classic Marx Brothers comedy.
1930– 1936	John Dos Passos, *U.S.A.* trilogy.
1931– 1932	Japan invades Manchuria and creates puppet government
1932– 1935	James T. Farrell, *Studs Lonigan* trilogy.
1933	Nathanael West, *Miss Lonelyhearts*. *She Done Him Wrong* and *I'm No Angel*, Mae West movie hits. Adolf Hitler becomes chancellor of Germany and assumes dictatorial powers.
1934	Indian Reorganization Act. Nathanael West, *A Cool Million*. United States plays role in rise of Cuban strongman Fulgencio Batista.
1934– 1936	Nye committee investigations. Strikes by Mexican-American agricultural workers in the West.
1935	Supreme Court reverses conviction of the "Scottsboro Boys." Clifford Odets, *Waiting for Lefty*.
1935– 1937	Neutrality Acts.
1935– 1938	Peace movement sweeps U.S. campuses.
1935– 1939	Era of the Popular Front.

1936	William Faulkner, *Absalom, Absalom!* *Mr. Deeds Goes to Town*, Frank Capra movie.
1936– 1937	Autoworkers' sit-down strike against General Motors (December 1936–February 1937).
1936– 1939	Spanish Civil War.
1937	U.S. Steel, General Motors, and Chrysler sign union contracts. "Memorial Day Massacre" at Republic Steel Company in South Chicago. Japan invades China.
1938	Formation of Congress of Industrial Organizations (CIO). Thornton Wilder, *Our Town*. *War of the Worlds* broadcast on CBS radio. Nazis occupy Austria. Munich Pact gives Sudetenland to Hitler. *Kristallnacht*, night of Nazi terror against German and Austrian Jews. United States protests Japanese violation of Open Door principle in China.
1939	John Steinbeck, *The Grapes of Wrath*. New York World's Fair. Nazis invade Czechoslovakia. Nazi-Soviet Pact. *St. Louis*, carrying Jewish refugees from Nazism, refused landing permission in Florida.
1940	Richard Wright, *Native Son*. Ernest Hemingway, *For Whom the Bell Tolls*.
1941	James Agee and Walker Evans, *Let Us Now Praise Famous Men*.

FOR FURTHER READING

Charles C. Alexander, *Nationalism in American Thought, 1930–1945* (1969). Illuminating overview of trends in American thought and culture in the depression years and World War II.

Irving Bernstein, *Turbulent Years: A History of the American Worker, 1933–1941* (1970). A thorough, well-researched account.

Caroline Bird, *The Invisible Scar* (1966). Moving look at the depression's human and psychological toll.

Robert Dallek, *Franklin D. Roosevelt and American Foreign Policy, 1932–1945* (1979). A fine study stressing FDR's responsiveness to domestic political currents.

Anthony Heilbut, *Exiled in Paradise: German Refugee Artists and Intellectuals in America from the 1930s to the Present* (1983). Good account of a refugee movement that profoundly influenced American culture.

Jeffrey Meikle, *Twentieth Century Limited: Industrial Design in America, 1925–1939* (1979). Fascinating study of the streamlining movement, with a good chapter on the New York World's Fair.

Arnold A. Offner, *American Appeasement: United States Foreign Policy and Germany, 1933–1938* (1969). A comprehensive and well-written study.

Susan Ware, *Holding Their Own: American Women in the 1930s* (1982). A good overview incorporating recent scholarly research.

Waging Global War, 1939–1945

*F*or most Americans, World War II was a "good war." Despite the deaths of more than 300,000 Americans on faraway islands or in small European towns, U.S. losses paled beside the millions of other casualties in Europe and Asia. Moreover, the United States escaped the physical devastation that engulfed Europe and Asia, and the booming wartime economy made America once again a land of opportunity and hope. Indeed, World War II lifted the nation out of the depression, led to a redistribution of income, and transformed the United States into a genuinely middle-class society. Women and blacks especially savored the independence and freedom conferred by the war. At the same time, the war profoundly changed national institutions and behavior. It reshaped the economy and the role and power of the government. It disrupted family relationships and traditional social values. And it ended American isolationism, pushing the United States to the forefront of world affairs in a new era of Cold War.

★ SILENCE MEANS SECURITY ★

(Right) Wartime security poster featuring a WAC, a member of the Women's Army Corps

Into the Storm, 1939–1941
America Mobilizes for War
War and American Society
The Battlefront, 1942–1944
Triumph and Tragedy, 1945

Into the Storm, 1939–1941

Twenty years after World War I ended, Germany and Japan unleashed international aggression that drew the United States into a second global conflict. After German victories in western Europe in the spring of 1940, President Franklin D. Roosevelt gave economic aid to nations resisting aggression by the so-called Rome-Berlin-Tokyo Axis. As the fascist menace grew, FDR accelerated rearmament and extended greater assistance to the Allies, principally Great Britain and France. Although reluctant to ask a divided Congress for a declaration of war, FDR understood that his uncompromising conduct toward Germany and Japan could cause the United States to be "pushed," as he said, into a worldwide war. Japan's attack in December 1941 on the U.S. fleet at Pearl Harbor would provide the push.

Storm in Europe

Adolf Hitler had precipitated the war by demanding that Poland return to Germany the city of Danzig (Gdansk), lost after World War I. When Poland refused, Nazi armies poured into Poland at dawn on September 1, 1939, and the *Luftwaffe* (German air force) devastated Polish cities. Two days later, Britain and France, honoring commitments to Poland, declared war on Germany. Although FDR invoked the Neutrality Acts (see Chapter 26), he refused to ask Americans to be impartial. Even a neutral, Roosevelt declared, "cannot be asked to close his mind or his conscience."

Determined to avoid an Allied defeat that would leave the United States alone to confront Germany, the president in September 1939 asked Congress to amend the Neutrality Acts to allow the Allies to purchase weapons on a "cash-and-carry" basis. But there would be no loans to the Allies, and they would transport the weapons on their own ships. FDR also requested authority to limit the places where American ships and passengers could travel. These cautious moves matched the public mood: polls taken in November showed that two-thirds of Americans favored aiding the Allies but

Hitler's *Blitzkrieg*
A Belgian mother and her children walk through rubble left by a German air attack.

that the same two-thirds considered staying out of war more important than saving England and France.

In April 1940 Hitler unleashed his *Blitzkrieg* (lightning war) on western Europe. After occupying Denmark and crushing Norway, Nazi panzer (armored) divisions sliced through the Low Countries (the Netherlands, Belgium, and Luxembourg) and drove the British Expeditionary Force back to the coast. In less than a week, May 28–June 4, using every vessel they could commandeer, the British evacuated their entire army, 338,000 troops, from the beaches of Dunkirk in northern France. Now only France remained on the Continent to face the German rampage. Moving virtually unimpeded through the Ardennes Forest, Germany outflanked the French army. With a German victory in sight, Italian dictator Benito Mussolini declared war on France and attacked in the south. On June 22 France capitulated. A jubilant Hitler dictated the armistice to the French in the same railway car in which a defeated Germany had accepted terms of surrender in 1918.

Hitler next took aim at Britain. In the Battle of Britain, in the summer and fall of 1940, the *Luftwaffe* tried to terror-bomb Britain into submission. Round-the-clock bombing wounded and killed thousands of civilians, destroyed the city of Coventry, and left parts of London in smoking rubble. With Nazi U-boats strangling Britain's lifelines, Prime Minister Winston Churchill pleaded for all possible American aid. Most Americans favored additional support for Britain, but a large minority opposed it as wasteful or as a ruse to involve Americans in a war not vital to U.S. interests.

The Election of 1940

As the war escalated, Americans wondered whether Roosevelt would run for an unprecedented third term. On the eve of the Democrats' July convention, the president revealed that, given the world crisis, he would consent to a "draft" from his party. The Nazi menace forced conservative anti–New Deal Democrats to accept both the third term and the nomination of Henry Wallace as vice president. The ultraliberal Wallace was disliked by many moderates.

German victories in Europe had an even greater impact on the Republican nomination. Dark-horse candidate Wendell Willkie, a former Democrat and a millionaire utility magnate,

championed internationalism and aid to Britain; his conservative opponents criticized Roosevelt's handling of foreign affairs. As his supporters deafened the delegates with a "We Want Willkie!" chant, Willkie won the GOP nomination on the sixth ballot. A formidable contender, he supported internationalism but denounced FDR's third-term bid.

Roosevelt adroitly played the role of a national leader too busy with defense and diplomacy to engage in partisan politics. To undercut GOP criticisms, he appointed Republicans to key cabinet positions: Henry L. Stimson as secretary of war and Frank Knox as secretary of the navy. With bipartisan support in Congress, Roosevelt endorsed a peacetime draft and a dramatic increase in defense funding. In September he engineered a "destroyers-for-bases" swap with England, sending fifty vintage American ships to Britain in exchange for leases on British air and naval bases in the Western Hemisphere. FDR claimed that the exchange was a way of averting American entry into the war.

Anti-interventionist critics condemned Roosevelt's "dictatorial" methods and accused him of scheming to entangle the United States in the European conflict. Isolationists organized the Committee to Defend America First to protest the drift toward war. Financed in large part by Henry Ford, the America First Committee featured Charles Lindbergh as its most popular speaker and proclaimed that "Fortress America" could stand alone. Although America First drew backers from every region, ideology, and ethnic group, most Americans supported Roosevelt's attempt to aid Britain while avoiding war.

As the election neared, with Willkie trailing, he accused FDR of secretly plotting war and

The Election of 1940				
Candidates	Parties	Electoral Vote	Popular Vote	Percentage of Popular Vote
FRANKLIN D. ROOSEVELT	Democratic	449	27,307,819	54.8
Wendell L. Willkie	Republican	82	22,321,018	44.8

promised that, if elected, "I will never send an American boy to fight in a European war." Roosevelt retorted, "Your president says this country is not going to war!" Voters gave FDR his third term by a 55–45 percent popular-vote margin and an electoral-college victory of 449 to 82.

From Isolation to Intervention

In December 1940 FDR declared that aiding Britain was the best way to defend the United States. Calling America the "great arsenal of democracy," he proposed the concept of lend-lease. Because England did not have the money to purchase essential materials, he asked Congress to rescind the "cash" provision of the cash-and-carry legislation and permit the president to lend or lease supplies to any country whose defense was vital to American security. The lend-lease bill amounted to a declaration of economic war against Hitler. Polls showed that nearly 80 percent of the public favored the measure. Congress approved lend-lease in March 1941 and appropriated $7 billion for supplies for Britain. After Hitler invaded the U.S.S.R. in June, the Soviet Union also received American war matériel. Despite American hostility to communism, FDR said that, to defeat Hitler, "I would hold hands with the Devil."

Most Americans remained determined to avoid war. However, the delivery of U.S. supplies to Great Britain edged the nation toward an undeclared naval war with Germany. In April, as Nazi submarines choked off the stream of aid to England, U.S. ships assisted the British in tracking U-boats. During the summer, with 10,000 tons of Allied shipping being sunk daily, the U.S. Navy started convoying British ships and carried orders to destroy enemy ships if necessary. U.S. forces also occupied Greenland and Iceland to keep them out of Nazi hands.

In mid-August Roosevelt met with Churchill aboard a warship off Newfoundland to discuss joint military objectives. They issued a document called the Atlantic Charter that contained their vision of a postwar world. Recalling Woodrow Wilson's Fourteen Points, the charter condemned aggression,

affirmed national self-determination, and endorsed the principles of collective security and disarmament. After a German submarine fired at an American destroyer in September, Roosevelt authorized naval patrols to shoot on sight all Axis vessels operating in the western Atlantic. On October 31, 1941, a U-boat torpedoed and sank the destroyer *Reuben James*, killing 115 American sailors.

Now on a collision course with Germany, Roosevelt in November asked Congress to permit the arming of merchant ships and to allow the transport of lend-lease supplies to belligerent ports in war zones. When Congress repealed the "carry" provision of cash-and-carry, virtually nothing remained of the Neutrality Acts. Unprepared for a major war, America was nevertheless fighting a limited one, and a full-scale war seemed imminent. Because the bill to extend the draft for another year had passed the House by only a single vote in August 1941, the president still feared that an attempt to secure a declaration of war would be defeated. Hitler also hesitated to take the final step toward declared belligerency, wanting no distractions from his life-and-death struggle with the Soviets.

Toward Pearl Harbor

Hitler's triumphs in western Europe encouraged Japan to expand its aggression from China to the resource-rich British, Dutch, and French colonial possessions in Southeast Asia. The United States opposed Japanese expansion virtually alone. But seeing Germany as America's primary threat, the Roosevelt administration tried to apply enough pressure to deter the Japanese without provoking Tokyo to war before the United States had built the "two-ocean navy" authorized by Congress in 1940. "It is terribly important for the control of the Atlantic for us to keep peace in the Pacific," Roosevelt told Harold Ickes, secretary of the interior, in mid-1941. "I simply have not got enough navy to go around—and every episode in the Pacific means fewer ships in the Atlantic." American military leaders agreed.

The Japanese, too, hoped to avoid war, but they would not compromise their goals. Japan's desire to create the Greater East Asia Co-Prosperity Sphere (an empire embracing much of China, Southeast Asia, and the western Pacific) matched America's insistence on the Open Door in China and the status quo in the rest of Asia. To the Japanese, American demands that they give up their Asian conquests seemed a smoke screen to thwart their legitimate national aspirations and to deny them essential raw materials and foodstuffs. Americans saw Japan as a militaristic predator, brutalizing Chinese peasants and bullying Europeans to rob them of their possessions in Asia.

Decades of "yellow-peril" propaganda, as well as Japan's invasion of China, prompted Washington's bellicosity. No American groups organized to prevent a clash with Japan, and isolationists were as virulently anti-Japanese as internationalists. Widely depicted as bowlegged little people with buckteeth and thick spectacles, the Japanese appeared pushovers for the American navy. With virtual unanimity, Americans applauded FDR's every step to thwart Japan.

The two nations became locked in a deadly dance, matching move for move. In the spring of 1940, the United States tried economic coercion against Japan, allowing the Treaty of Trade and Navigation (1911) with Japan to expire. In July 1940 Japan retaliated by initiating plans to implement its New Order in Asia. Roosevelt then embargoed the sale of aviation gasoline and scrap metal to Japan. Tokyo responded in September by occupying northern Indochina, a French colony in Asia, and signing the Tripartite Pact with the other Axis nations, Germany and Italy. Each Axis power pledged to help the others in the event of a U.S. attack. Washington answered by embargoing all metals as well as various chemicals and products vital to Japan.

In July 1941 the Japanese overran the rest of Indochina. Roosevelt then froze all Japanese assets in the United States and clamped a total embargo on trade with Japan. Tokyo had two choices: submit to the United States to gain a resumption of trade, or conquer new lands to obtain vital resources. In October the expansionist war minister Hideki Tojo became Japan's prime minister. Tojo, who opposed

compromise with the United States, set the first week in December as the deadline for Japanese forces to take the offensive if the United States did not yield. Watching their fuel meters drop toward empty, the Japanese believed that they had no option.

By late November U.S. intelligence's deciphering of Japan's top diplomatic code alerted the Roosevelt administration that war was imminent. The United States made no concessions during eleventh-hour negotiations under way in Washington, and Secretary of State Hull told Secretary of War Stimson, "I have washed my hands of it, and it is now in the hands of you and Knox—the Army and the Navy." War warnings went out to all U.S. commanders in the Pacific, advising that negotiations were deadlocked and that hostile Japanese action was possible. Most Americans expected Japan to continue southward, attacking Malaya or the Philippines. Instead, the Japanese would gamble on a knockout punch. They hoped that a surprise Japanese raid on the American naval base at Pearl Harbor would destroy the U.S. Pacific Fleet and compel Roosevelt, preoccupied with Germany, to seek accommodation with Japan.

Waves of Japanese dive-bombers and torpedo planes thundered across the Hawaiian island of Oahu on the morning of December 7, 1941, bombing ships at anchor in Pearl Harbor and strafing planes parked wingtip to wingtip at nearby air bases. American forces suffered their most devastating loss in history. In less than three hours, eight battleships, three light cruisers, and two destroyers had been sunk or crippled, and 360 aircraft destroyed or damaged. More than 2,000 Americans had died. Japan's spectacular victory opened the way for an advance to the threshold of Australia in April 1942. It also ensured an aroused and united America to avenge what President Roosevelt called a "date which will live in infamy."

On December 8, when Roosevelt asked Congress to declare war on Japan, only one dissenting vote was cast (by Montana's Jeannette Rankin, who had also voted against entry into World War I). But FDR still hesitated to request a declaration of war against Germany. Hitler resolved his dilemma.

Although his advisers begged him not to add the United States to the long list of anti-Nazi belligerents, Hitler went before a cheering Reichstag on December 11 to declare war on the "half Judaized and the other half Negrified" Americans. Mussolini chimed in with his declaration of war, and Congress reciprocated that same afternoon. America faced a global war that it was not yet ready to fight.

On the Defensive

After Pearl Harbor, U-boats wreaked havoc in the North Atlantic and prowled the Caribbean and the East Coast of the United States. Every twenty-four hours, five more Allied vessels went to the bottom. By the end of 1942, Hitler's submarines had destroyed more than 1,000 Allied ships, offsetting the pace of American ship production. The United States was losing the Battle of the Atlantic.

The war news from Europe and Africa was, as Roosevelt admitted, "all bad." Hitler's rule covered an enormous swath of territory, from the outskirts of Moscow, deep in Russia, to the Pyrenees on the French-Spanish border, and from northern Norway to the Libyan desert. In the spring of 1942, Nazi armies inflicted more than 250,000 casualties on the Soviet army in Crimea, and Hitler launched a powerful offensive to seize the Caucasian oil fields. German forces moved relentlessly eastward in North Africa, threatening the Suez Canal, Britain's oil lifeline.

Apparently as invincible as the Nazis, the Japanese inflicted defeat after defeat on Allied Pacific forces. Tojo followed Pearl Harbor with successful attacks on the Philippines, Malaya, and Thailand. By early 1942 the Japanese controlled Hong Kong, Guam, Wake Island, the Gilbert Islands, Manila, and Singapore, the key to Southeast Asia. In February Tojo's naval squadrons shattered Allied warships in the Java Sea, and in March Japan seized Java and the oil-rich Dutch East Indies and closed the Burma Road, the only mainland link to China. By mid-May, when the last American soldier in the Philippines surrendered, Japan's Rising Sun blazed over hundreds of islands in the central and western Pacific and over the entire eastern rim of the Asian mainland from the border of Siberia to the border of India.

America Mobilizes for War

The United States had begun to prepare actively for war after the fall of France in mid-1940. But many businesses, fearing a short-lived demand for war equipment, had hesitated. Constant bickering among the military, industry, and labor, combined with FDR's initial reluctance to speed mobilization, also hindered preparedness. In December 1941 American armed forces numbered only 1.6 million, and war production accounted for just 15 percent of U.S. industrial output. Moreover, Washington had not yet organized an efficient structure to direct mobilization.

Pearl Harbor changed everything. Within a week of the attack, Congress passed the War Powers Act, granting the president unprecedented authority. Hundreds of wartime agencies soon regulated American life. Volunteers and draftees swelled the army and navy. By the war's end 15 million men and nearly 350,000 women had served. To direct this military engine, Roosevelt formed the Joint Chiefs of Staff, made up of representatives of the army, navy, and army air force. The air force grew from a minor "corps" within the army to an autonomous, and vital, part of the military. The changing nature of modern warfare led to the creation of the Office of Strategic Services (OSS) to conduct espionage and to gather the information required for strategic planning. The far-reaching domestic changes under way would outlast the war and significantly alter the nation's attitudes, behavior, and institutions.

Organizing for Victory

After Pearl Harbor, Roosevelt called on Americans to produce an unprecedented quantity of supplies for the Allied fighting forces. He established the War Production Board (WPB) to allocate materials, to limit the production of civilian goods, and to distribute contracts. The newly created War Manpower Commission (WMC) supervised the mobilization of men and women for the military, war industry, and agriculture; the National War Labor Board (NWLB) mediated disputes between management and labor; and the Office of Price Administration (OPA) imposed strict price controls to check inflation.

In October 1942 FDR persuaded James F. Byrnes to leave the Supreme Court and take charge of America's domestic war effort. Byrnes was to increase coordination and cooperation among government agencies, industry, and the military. In May 1943 FDR appointed him to head the new Office of War Mobilization (OWM), which exercised control over the economy.

"The Americans can't build planes," a Nazi commander had jeered, "only electric iceboxes and razor blades." But in 1942 the United States achieved a miracle of war production. "It was not so much industrial conversion," one business leader remarked, "as industrial revolution, with months and years condensed into days." Car makers retooled to produce planes and tanks; a pinball-machine maker converted to armor-piercing shells. By late 1942, 33 percent of the economy was committed to war production. Whole new industries appeared virtually overnight. Ninety-seven percent of the nation's crude-rubber supply now lay in Japanese-controlled territory, but by 1944, 80 percent of the rubber consumed in the United States came from synthetic-rubber factories that had not existed two years earlier.

America also became the world's greatest weapons manufacturer, producing more war matériel by 1945 than its Axis enemies combined— 300,000 military aircraft, 86,000 tanks, 2.6 million machine guns, and 6 million tons of bombs. The United States also built 5,000 cargo ships and 86,000 warships. Henry J. Kaiser, who had supervised the construction of Boulder Dam, introduced prefabrication to cut the time needed to build ships. In 1941 the construction of a Liberty-class merchant ship took six months; in 1943, less than two weeks; by 1945, Kaiser and other shipbuilders completed a cargo ship every day.

Such breakneck production had costs. The size and powers of the government expanded as defense spending zoomed from 9 percent of GNP in 1940 to 46 percent in 1945; the federal budget soared from $9 billion to $98 billion. Federal civilian employees mushroomed from 1.1 million to 3.8 million. An alliance formed between the defense industry and the military. Because the government sought the maximum production in the shortest time, it encouraged corporate profits. "If you are going to try to go to war in a capitalist country," Secretary of War Stimson said, "you have to let business make money out of the process or business won't work."

To encourage business to convert to war production and expand its capacity, the government guaranteed profits, provided generous tax write-offs, and suspended antitrust prosecutions. Giant corporations benefited most from these actions. Two-thirds of all war-production dollars went to the hundred largest firms, and trends toward economic concentration accelerated.

A War Economy

The United States spent $250 million a day to defeat the Axis, ten times the cost of World War I. Wartime spending and the draft not only vanquished unemployment but also stimulated an industrial boom that made most Americans prosper. War expenditures doubled U.S. industrial output and nearly doubled the per capita GNP (to $1,074). By 1945 farm income had doubled from the 1940 level; net corporate profits had leaped 70 percent; and real wages, or purchasing power, had risen 50 percent.

Full employment, longer workweeks, larger paychecks, and the increased hiring of minorities, women, and the elderly brought a middle-class standard of living to millions of families. The war years produced the only significant shift in the distribution of income in the twentieth century. The fraction of total income going to the richest 5 percent shrank from 26 percent to 20 percent, whereas the share of the least affluent 40 percent climbed from 13 percent to 16 percent of all income. The middle class doubled in size.

The war reversed hard times for American farmers. With more than a million more new tractors in use in 1945 than in 1940, and with improved fertilizers and cultivation techniques, farmers harvested 477 million more bushels of corn, 324 million more bushels of wheat, and 500 million more pounds of rice. Higher prices, increased productivity, and a decline in the number of farmers raised the value of farm property by $20 billion. Radio comedians changed the words of a familiar nursery rhyme to "The farmer's in the dough." Mechanization and consolidation proceeded, farming became "agribusiness," and organized agriculture wielded power equal to organized labor, big government, and big business.

Organized labor expanded and grew wealthier. From 1940 to 1945, union membership rose from 9 million to 14.8 million workers, in part because of the expansion of the labor force. Although the National War Labor Board attempted to limit wage increases to restrain inflation, unions negotiated unprecedented fringe benefits for workers, including paid vacation time and health and pension plans. As most workers honored the "no-strike" pledge that they had given immediately after Pearl Harbor, less than one-tenth of 1 percent of wartime working time was lost to wildcat strikes. However, in 1943 United Mine Workers head John L. Lewis led more than half a million coal-field workers out of the pits and tunnels three times in two months. These strikes cost the union movement dearly as Congress passed the Smith-Connally War Labor Disputes Act in 1943, which limited workers' power to strike at a facility essential to the war effort.

Far more than strikes, inflation threatened the wartime economy. The Office of Price Administration (OPA) constantly battled inflation, which was fueled by greater spending power combined with a scarcity of goods. Throughout 1942 prices climbed at a 2-percent-a-month clip, but at the year's end Congress gave the president authority to freeze wages, prices, and rents. As the OPA clamped down, inflation slowed dramatically: consumer prices went up only 8 percent in the war's last two years.

The OPA also instituted rationing to combat inflation and to conserve scarce materials. Under the slogan "Use it up, wear it out, make it do or do without," the OPA rationed such products as gasoline, coffee, sugar, butter, cheese, and meat. Accepting rationing as a contribution to the security of loved ones fighting the war, most Americans cheerfully endured "meatless Tuesdays" and cuffless trousers, formed car pools, planted victory gardens, and recycled paper, fats, rubber, and scrap metal.

The sale of war bonds, like rationing, helped to limit inflation by draining consumer purchasing power. Bond buying gave civilians a sense of involvement in the war. Small investors bought $40 billion in "E" bonds, and wealthy individuals and corporations invested nearly twice that amount. Bond sales raised almost half the money needed to finance the war. FDR wanted to increase taxes to pay for the war, but Congress only grudgingly raised taxes. However, by the war's end the top income-tax rate had risen from 60 percent to 90 percent, and middle- and lower-income Americans were paying income taxes for the first time. The introduction of payroll deductions to withhold income taxes from wages facilitated tax collection.

Science and the War

Recognizing wartime scientific and technological developments, Winston Churchill dubbed World War II "a wizard war." In 1941 FDR created the Office of Scientific Research and Development (OSRD) for the development of new ordnance and medicines. OSRD spent more than $1 billion to produce improved radar and sonar, rocket weapons, and proximity fuses for mines and artillery shells. It also funded the development of jet aircraft, pressurized cabins, and high-altitude bombsights. Other OSRD research hastened the widespread use of insecticides, contributed to improved blood transfusions, and produced "miracle drugs" such as penicillin. The agency's medical advances saved thousands of lives during the war and would increase life expectancy in peacetime.

Scientists' most notable war-era undertaking was the development of the atomic bomb. In 1939 physicist Albert Einstein had warned Roosevelt that Nazi scientists were seeking to use atomic physics to construct an extraordinarily destructive weapon. In 1941 FDR launched a massive Anglo-American secret program—the Soviets were excluded—to construct an atomic bomb. The next year, the participating physicists, comprising both Americans and Europeans, achieved a controlled chain reaction and acquired the basic knowledge necessary to develop the bomb. In 1943–1944 the Manhattan Engineering District—the code name for the atomic project—stockpiled fissionable materials. By July 1945 the Manhattan Project had employed more than 120,000 people and spent nearly $2 billion.

Just before dawn on July 16, 1945, a blinding fireball with "the brightness of several suns at midday" rose over the desert at Alamogordo, New Mexico, followed by a billowing mushroom cloud. Equivalent to 20,000 tons of TNT, the blast from this first atomic explosion was felt 100 miles away. The awesome spectacle reminded J. Robert Oppenheimer, the scientific director of the Manhattan Project, of a line from Hindu scripture: "Now I am become death, the destroyer of worlds." The atomic age had begun.

Propaganda and Politics

People as well as science and machinery had to be mobilized. To sustain a spirit of unity, the Roosevelt administration carefully managed public opinion. The Office of Censorship, established in December 1941, examined all letters going overseas and worked with publishers and broadcasters to suppress information that might damage the war effort, such as details of troop movements. Much was concealed.

A year passed, for example, before the casualty and damage figures from Pearl Harbor were disclosed.

To shape public opinion, FDR created the Office of War Information (OWI) in June 1942. The OWI employed more than 4,000 writers, artists, and advertising specialists to explain the war and to counter enemy propaganda. Instead of stressing the U.S. commitment to the preservation of democratic values, the OWI focused on the Axis nations' barbarism and the need to crush them. Anti-Japanese propaganda contained a strong dose of racism.

While the Roosevelt administration concentrated on the war, Republican critics seized the initiative in domestic politics. Full employment and high wages undermined the Democrats' class appeal, and many of the urban and working-class voters essential to the Roosevelt coalition were serving in the armed forces and did not vote in the 1942 elections. As Republicans gained nine seats in the Senate and forty-six in the House, congressional politics shifted to the right. Conservative Republicans and southern Democrats held the power to make or break legislation. Resentful of the wartime expansion of executive authority, and determined to curb labor unions and welfare spending, the conservatives abolished the CCC and the WPA and turned back attempts to extend the New Deal.

Despite the strength of the conservative coalition, the war enormously expanded governmental and executive power as the federal government's budget, size, and powers ballooned. As never before, Washington managed the economy, molded public opinion, funded scientific research, and influenced people's daily lives.

With more than $300 billion expended on the war, economic despondency yielded to buoyant prosperity. Unemployment ended, organized labor and agriculture thrived, and millions entered the middle class. Big business also prospered and grew bigger, more highly concentrated, and increasingly intertwined with the military. The wartime "miracle of production" strengthened confidence in business leaders and in the government's fiscal role in maintaining a robust economy. The United States stood second to none in economic and military power. Its citizens' expectations of what the federal government could and should be were turned upside down.

War and American Society

Some 15 million Americans went to war. Most saw themselves as civilians in uniform and called themselves GIs, after the "Government Issue" stamp on their gear, to emphasize the temporary nature of their military service. Reluctant warriors, they accepted their duty so they could return home quickly.

But the war dragged on for almost four years, transforming its participants. Millions who had never been far from home traveled to unfamiliar cities and remote nations. Sharing tents and foxholes with fellow Americans of different religions, nationalities, and social backgrounds helped to erase deep-seated prejudices. Wartime service sowed the seeds of a more homogenized national culture. Many GIs acquired skills in jobs and professions that they had barely known existed. And under the Servicemen's Readjustment Act, the "GI Bill of Rights," several million veterans would be studying for a high-school diploma or enrolling in college in 1946. Countless second-generation immigrant veterans would acquire an education under the GI Bill, and it would provide the springboard for their entry into the expanding middle class.

Returning GIs would find that America had changed as much as they had. Sweeping wartime alterations in society challenged established values, redefined traditional relationships, and created new problems. Adjusting to this new world could be difficult and painful, and the transition sometimes proved impossible.

The New Mobility

Nothing transformed the social topography more than the vast internal migration of an already mobile people. Americans swarmed to the centers of war production, especially the Pacific coast states, which manufactured half the nation's wartime ships and airplanes. Six million people left farms to work

in cities, and several million southern whites and blacks migrated northward and westward. This mass uprooting made Americans both more cosmopolitan and tolerant of differences, and more lonely, alienated, and frustrated.

Life-styles became freewheeling as Americans moved far from their hometowns and traditional values. Housing shortages left millions living in converted garages, tent cities, trailer camps, or even their own cars. Overcrowding as well as wartime separations strained family and community life. High rates of divorce, family violence, and juvenile delinquency reflected the disruptions. Urban blight and conflicts between newcomers and oldtimers accelerated.

Education and Entertainment

The war production boom that created both overcrowded communities and ghost towns played havoc with the nation's school systems. More than 350,000 teachers joined the armed services or took on better-paying war work, leaving schools woefully understaffed. Students abandoned school in record numbers. High-school enrollments sank as full-time teenage employment rose from 900,000 in 1940 to 3 million in 1944.

The loss of students to the armed services and war production forced colleges to admit large numbers of women and to contract themselves out to the military. Military training programs sent nearly a million servicemen and women to college campuses to acquire skills in engineering, foreign languages, economics, and the sciences. Higher education became more dependent on the federal government, and universities competed for federal contracts and subsidies.

The war profoundly affected American culture. The media emphasized mass production and targeted mass audiences. Between 1941 and 1945 spending on books and theater entertainment more than doubled. Sixty million people attended movies weekly. Hollywood turned out a spate of war films that reinforced the image of Nazis and Japanese as fiends, portrayed GIs as freedom-loving heroes, and intensified Americans' appetites for unconditional victory. *Mission to Moscow* (1943), *Song of Russia* (1943), and other films glorified Soviet heroism. But as the war dragged on, people tired of propaganda, and Hollywood reemphasized romance and adventure.

Early in the war, popular music featured patriotic themes. "Goodbye, Mama, I'm Off to Yokohama" was the first hit of 1942. As the war continued, themes of lost love and loneliness dominated songs. By 1945 bitterness pervaded the lyrics of best-selling records, and such hits as "Saturday Night Is the Loneliest Night of the Week" revealed an impatience for the war's end.

Americans increasingly read nonfiction during the war. Few war novels appeared, but Marion Hargrove's *See Here, Private Hargrove*, a comic account of army life, and John Hersey's *A Bell for Adano* (1946), about the occupation of Sicily, became instant classics. Magazines such as *Life, Look, The Saturday Evening Post,* and *Time* filled American hunger for reports of battle actions and of the prospects for peace. Wendell Willkie's *One World* (1943) became the fastest-selling title in publishing history to that time, with 2 million copies snapped up in two years. A vision of a world without military alliances and spheres of influence, this brief volume expressed hope that an international organization would extend peace and democracy through the postwar world. The Government Printing Office published Armed Services Editions, paperback reprints of classics and new releases, and nearly 350 million copies were distributed free to soldiers.

Americans also stayed glued to their radios during the war. The quest for up-to-date information kept radio audiences at record levels. The voices of Edward R. Murrow and Eric Sevareid reporting from the battlefields became as familiar as those of Jack Benny and Eddie Cantor on their comedy shows.

Women and the Family

Millions of American women donned pants, put their hair in bandannas, and went to work in defense plants. Reversing a decade of efforts to exclude women from the labor force, the federal government in 1942 urged women into war production. Songs such as "We're the Janes Who Make the Planes" appealed to women to take up war work, and propaganda called on them to "help save lives" and to "release able-bodied men for fighting." More than 6 million women entered the labor force during the war, bringing the number of employed women to 19 million. Less than a quarter of the labor force in 1940, women constituted well over a third of all workers in 1945.

The characteristics of female wage earners changed. Before the war women workers were predominantly young and single, but 75 percent of the new female workers were married, 60 percent were over 35, and more than 33 percent had children under age fourteen. Women tended blast furnaces, operated cranes, drove taxis, welded hulls, and worked in shipyards. "Rosie the Riveter," in overalls and cap, assembling airplanes and tanks, became the symbol of the woman war worker, "making history working for victory."

Discrimination in employment continued, with women earning only 65 percent of what men did for the same work. Government propaganda portrayed women's war work as a temporary response to an emergency, and few women challenged traditional views of gender roles. "A woman is a substitute," asserted a War Department brochure, "like plastic instead of metal." Work was pictured as an extension of women's traditional roles as wives and mothers. A newspaperwoman wrote of the "deep satisfaction which a woman of today knows who has made a rubber boat which may save the life of her aviator husband, or helped fashion a bullet which may avenge her son!" Given the concern about jobs for veterans after the war, attitudes toward women's employment changed little; in 1945 only 18 percent of respondents in a poll approved of married women's working.

Traditional convictions about a woman's place also shaped government resistance to establishing child-care centers for women employed in defense. "A mother's primary duty is to her home and children," the Labor Department's Children's Bureau stated. New York Mayor Fiorello La Guardia proclaimed that the worst mother was better than the best nursery. Funds for federal child-care centers

Working for Victory
The federal government encouraged women to take on wartime defense work and pressured employers to hire them.

covered fewer than 10 percent of defense workers' children, and the young suffered. New terms such as *eight-hour orphans* and *latch-key children* described children forced to fend for themselves. Feeding the fears of those who believed that women's working outside the home would cause the family to disintegrate, juvenile delinquency increased fivefold, and the divorce rate nearly doubled.

The impact of war on women and children was multifaceted and even contradictory. Divorce rates soared, but so did marriage rates and birthrates. Although some women remained content to roll bandages for the Red Cross, more than 300,000 women joined the armed forces and for the first time served in positions there other than nurse. Female workers gained unprecedented employment opportunities and public recognition. Although many eagerly gave up their jobs at the end of the war, just as many did not relish losing their income and newfound independence. Overall, the war gave women a new sense of their potential. It allowed them to prove their capability and to participate in society outside the home, widening their world as nothing had before.

African-Americans and the War

The war also opened doors of opportunity for many blacks. The global conflict not only heightened blacks' aspirations but widened cracks in the wall of white racist attitudes and policies.

Realizing that the government needed the loyalty and work of a united people in order to win the war, black leaders saw new pathways to securing equal rights. In 1942 civil-rights spokesmen insisted that African-American support of the war hinged on the United States' commitment to racial justice. The battle against the Axis must destroy racism at home as well as Nazi racism, and victory must mean victory over racial discrimination as well as triumph on the battlefield, they said. Blacks responded with passionate commitment.

Membership in the NAACP multiplied nearly ten times, reaching half a million in 1945. The association pressed for anti–poll tax and antilynching legislation, decried discrimination in defense industries and the armed services, and sought to end black disfranchisement. The campaign for black voting rights gained momentum when the Supreme Court, in *Smith* v. *Allwright* (1944), ruled Texas's all-white primary unconstitutional. This decision eliminated a barrier that had existed in eight states, although these states promptly resorted to other devices to minimize black voting.

A new civil-rights organization, the Congress of Racial Equality (CORE), founded in 1942, advanced the strategy of nonviolent resistance to challenge Jim Crow. In 1942 CORE staged a sit-in in a Chicago restaurant that had refused to serve blacks, and its success inspired interracial groups in other cities to experiment with nonviolent direct action. Also in 1942, A. Philip Randolph, the president of the Brotherhood of Sleeping Car Porters, worked to build his March-on-Washington Committee into an all-black protest movement that would engage in civil disobedience.

In 1941 Randolph had called for a "thundering march" of 100,000 blacks on Washington "to wake up and shock white America." He had warned Roosevelt that if the president did not abolish discrimination in the armed services and the defense industry, African-Americans would besiege the nation's capital. FDR had agreed to compromise, in June 1941 issuing Executive Order 8802, the first presidential directive on race since Reconstruction. It prohibited discriminatory employment practices by federal agencies and all unions and companies engaged in war-related work, and established the

Fair Employment Practices Commission (FEPC) to enforce this policy. Although the FEPC did not apply to the armed forces and lacked effective enforcement powers, roaring war production and a shrinking labor pool resulted in the employment of 2 million blacks in industry and 200,000 in the federal civil service. Between 1942 and 1945, the proportion of blacks in war production shot up from 3 percent to 9 percent. Black membership in labor unions doubled, and the number of skilled and semiskilled black workers tripled. Average earnings for blacks increased from $457 to $1,976 a year, compared to $2,600 for whites.

About 1 million African-Americans served in the armed forces. Wartime needs forced the military to end policies of excluding blacks from combat units. The all-black 761st Tank Battalion gained distinction fighting in Germany, and the 99th Pursuit Squadron won eighty Distinguished Flying Crosses in combat against the *Luftwaffe*. Although the army and navy began experiments with integration in 1944, most blacks served in segregated units under white officers. Ironically, the Red Cross maintained separate black and white blood banks, even though a black physician, Dr. Charles Drew, had invented the process of storing blood plasma. The failure of military authorities to protect African-American servicemen off the post and the use of white military police to keep blacks "in their place" sparked conflict on many army bases. At least fifty black soldiers died in wartime racial encounters in the United States.

Violence within the military mirrored growing racial tensions at home. As blacks militantly protested against discrimination and rejected pleas to "go slow" in their campaign for first-class citizenship, many whites stiffened their resistance to raising blacks from their inferior economic and social positions. Numerous clashes occurred. In mid-1943 scores of cities reported pitched battles between whites and blacks. In June Detroit exploded in an orgy of racial beatings, shootings, burning, and looting. Fearing continued violence, African-American leaders concentrated on mitigating blacks' aggressive behavior. They realized that few Americans would tolerate a war against racism at home that impeded the war effort overseas.

These wartime developments would lead to eventual success in the drive for black civil rights. As more than 700,000 blacks migrated from the South, blacks' status in society became a national concern. Blacks were experiencing a new attitude of independence, and their greater educational and employment opportunities engendered hopefulness. With growing numbers of blacks voting in northern industrial cities, African-Americans held the balance of power in close elections. Consequently, politicians extended greater recognition to blacks and paid more attention to civil rights.

Blacks' optimism also flowed from the new prominence of the United States as a major power in a nonwhite world. As Japanese propaganda directed at Asians and Latin Americans emphasized lynchings of blacks and race riots in the United States, Americans confronted the peril that white racism posed to their national security. In addition, the horrors of Nazi racism made Americans sensitive to the harm caused by their own white-supremacist attitudes and practices. A former Alabama governor lamented that nazism had "wrecked the theories of the master race with which we were so contented so long."

In a massive study of race problems entitled *An American Dilemma* (1944), Swedish economist Gunnar Myrdal concluded that "not since Reconstruction had there been more reason to anticipate fundamental changes in American race relations." Returning black veterans and African-Americans who had served the nation on the home front alike faced the postwar era resolved to gain all the rights enjoyed by whites.

Native Americans, Mexican-Americans, and Jews in Wartime

Wartime winds of change brought new opportunities, and problems, to other American minorities. Twenty-five thousand Native Americans served in the armed forces, many in combat-communications teams using Indian languages to confuse enemy interceptors. Another 75,000 Indians left reservations to work in defense. For most, it was the first experience of living in a non-Indian world, and after the war many would remain in the cities. Continued discrimination, however, would force a majority back to their reservations, which suffered severely from budget cuts during the war and the immediate postwar years. Prodded by those who coveted Indian lands, lawmakers demanded that Indians be taken off the backs of taxpayers and "freed from the reservations" to make their own way like other Americans. To mobilize against the campaign to end all reservations and trust protections, Native Americans in 1944 organized the National Congress of American Indians.

In July 1942, to relieve labor shortages, the United States negotiated an agreement with Mexico to import *braceros*, or temporary workers. In exchange for seasonal employment in Arizona, California, and Texas, *braceros* were to be guaranteed adequate wages, medical care, and suitable living conditions. Large-scale growers frequently violated these terms, however, and encouraged the influx of illegal immigrants desperate for employment. Unable to complain without risking deportation, hundreds of thousands of Mexicans became illegal aliens, exploited by southwestern agribusinesses. At the same time, a large number of Chicanos left agricultural work for jobs in defense plants, shipbuilding yards, and garment factories in the Los Angeles area. Even as their occupational status and material conditions improved, most Mexican-Americans remained in communities segregated from the larger society.

In the military itself, Spanish-speaking Americans, like blacks, suffered discrimination. Nevertheless, nearly 350,000 Chicanos served in the armed forces, earning a disproportionate number of citations for distinguished service and Congressional Medals of Honor. And much like black and Indian veterans, Mexican-American veterans organized new groups to press for equal rights.

Despite the lip service paid to tolerance, American Jews also discovered that even a war against

The Holocaust

Entering Germany in 1945, American and Russian soldiers discovered the horrors that the Nazis had perpetrated on European Jews and others. One anonymous American GI wrote of the ghastly concentration-camp scenes, "I've seen what wasn't ever meant for human eyes to see."

nazism did not extinguish traditional prejudices. Anti-Semitism persisted in restrictive covenants to prevent the sale of homes to Jews, in employment ads stating that only Catholics or Protestants need apply, in rigid quota systems to limit the number of Jews in universities, and in "gentlemen's agreements" to exclude Jews from certain professions. Throughout the war, public-opinion polls revealed that a significant minority of Americans blamed either Wall Street Jews or Jewish communists for the war and thought Hitler justified in his treatment of Jews.

When reports of the Holocaust—the name later given to the Nazi effort to exterminate all European Jews—became known in the United States early in 1942, most Americans viewed it as a Jewish problem, of small concern to them. Most discounted the reports of Nazi massacres. Not until late November, with some 2.5 million Jews already dead, did the State Department admit knowledge of Hitler's genocide. Fourteen more months passed before Roosevelt established the War Refugee Board (WRB) to assist in the rescue and relocation of those condemned to the death camps. This tardy response reflected Britain's wishes to placate its Arab allies by keeping Jewish settlers out of Palestine; congressional and public fears of an influx of destitute Jews into the United States; and the hesitancy of many American Jewish leaders to press the matter and risk increasing anti-Semitism at home. Because of State Department obstruction of rescue efforts, the WRB saved the lives of only 200,000 Jews and 20,000 non-Jews. Six million other Jews were gassed and incinerated.

The Internment of Japanese-Americans

Only a tiny minority of Americans refused to support the war effort, and the nation generally avoided the mass assaults on aliens, repression of dissent, and strident "100 percent Americanism" that had marked World War I. The glaring exception was the internment of 112,000 Japanese-Americans, two-thirds of them native-born U.S. citizens, in relocation centers guarded by military police. The policy reflected forty years of anti-Japanese sentiment on the West Coast, rooted in racial prejudice and economic rivalry, as well as fears of Japanese saboteurs after Pearl Harbor. Self-serving politicians and farmers who wanted Japanese-American land had long decried the "yellow peril," and following the attack on Pearl Harbor they whipped up the rage and fears of many white Californians. In February 1942 Roosevelt gave in to the pressure and authorized the evacuation of all Japanese-Americans from the West Coast, despite the fact that not a single Japanese-American had been apprehended for espionage or sedition and neither the FBI nor military intelligence had uncovered any disloyal behavior by Japanese-Americans.

Forced to sell their lands and homes at whatever prices they could obtain, Japanese-Americans were herded into barbed-wire-encircled detention camps in desolate areas of the West. Stating that it would not question government claims of military necessity during the war, the Supreme Court, in *Korematsu v. U.S.* (1944), upheld the constitutionality of the evacuation. By then, however, the hysteria had subsided, and the government had begun a program of gradual release. In 1982 a special government commission would formally blame the Roosevelt administration's action on "race prejudice, war hysteria, and a failure of political leadership" and would apologize to Japanese-Americans for "a grave injustice." In 1988 Congress voted to compensate all Japanese-Americans interned during World War II in the amount of $20,000 each.

The Battlefront, 1942–1944

"No matter how long it may take us to overcome this premeditated invasion," President Roosevelt vowed in his war message on December 8, 1941, "the American people in their righteous might will win through to absolute victory." As the new year began, Britain, the Soviet Union, the United States, and twenty-three other countries signed the Declaration of the United Nations, creating a "Grand Alliance" pledged to devoting its full resources to victory. But in early 1942 the Allied outlook remained bleak. Nazi forces held much of Europe and threatened the Suez Canal; Japan controlled the western Pacific and a large part of Asia.

America's military might turned the tides of war. Diplomacy followed the fortunes of war, with Allied unity gradually diminishing as Germany and Japan weakened and as the United States, Britain, and the Soviet Union each sought wartime strategies and postwar arrangements best suited to its own national interest.

The Allied Drive in Europe

After Pearl Harbor, British and American officials agreed to concentrate first on defeating Germany and then on smashing Japan. But they differed on where to mount an attack. General George C. Marshall, army chief of staff, proposed an invasion of France to force Hitler to transfer troops west and thus to relieve pressure on the Russians, who faced the full fury of the Nazi armies. Prime Minister Churchill insisted on clearing the Mediterranean before invading France. He feared that a premature landing in France could mean slaughter, and he wanted American aid in North Africa to protect the Suez Canal, vital to the British. Over Soviet protests, Churchill persuaded Roosevelt to postpone the "second front" in western Europe and to invade North Africa instead. In November 1942, in Operation Torch, American and British troops under General Dwight D. Eisenhower landed in Morocco and Algeria. Pushing eastward, they trapped the German and Italian armies being pushed westward by the British, and in May 1943, some 260,000 German-Italian troops surrendered.

Left alone to face two-thirds of the Nazi force, the Soviet Union hung on and, in the turning point of the European war, defeated Germany in the protracted Battle of Stalingrad (August 1942–January 1943). After destroying an entire German army—more than 600,000 men—at Stalingrad, the Red Army went on the offensive along a thousand-mile front. Stalingrad cost the Soviet Union more battle deaths in four months than the United States suffered in the entire war.

Although Stalin renewed his plea for a second front, Churchill again objected, and Roosevelt again agreed to a British plan: the invasion of Sicily. In the summer of 1943, Anglo-American forces gained control of Sicily in less than a month. Italian military leaders deposed Mussolini and surrendered to the Allies on September 8. As Allied forces moved up the Italian peninsula, German troops poured into Italy. Facing elite Nazi divisions in splendid defensive positions, the Allies spent eight

0 500 Miles
0 500 Kilometers

NORWAY
FINLAND
SWEDEN
N. IRELAND
NORTH SEA
Leningrad besieged Sept. 1941 - Jan. 19, 1944
ESTONIA
LATVIA
Moscow
• Germans repulsed Dec. 1941
DENMARK
IRELAND
GREAT BRITAIN
Battle of the Bulge Dec. 16, 1944 - Jan. 31, 1945
LITHUANIA
Sept. 1944
BALTIC SEA
ATLANTIC OCEAN
London •
Berlin surrendered May 2, 1945
E. PRUSSIA (Ger.)
POLAND
July 1944
Aug. 1943
Stalingrad Aug. 21, 1942 - Jan. 31, 1943
D-Day June 6, 1944
Dunkirk BELG.
NETH.
April 1945
Elbe R.
Oder R.
Warsaw
Normandy
LUX.
Rhine R.
GERMANY
Mar. 1944
Don R.
Volga R.
Paris liberated Aug. 25, 1944
FRANCE
SLOVAKIA
UKRAINE
Aug. 1944
VICHY FRANCE occupied Nov. 1942
SWITZ.
HUNGARY
Dec. 1944
Aug. 1944
PORTUGAL
Aug. 1944
ROMANIA
Yalta
Caucasus
BLACK SEA
SPAIN
Corsica
ITALY
Adriatic Sea
Rome liberated June 4, 1944
YUGOSLAVIA
Danube R.
BULGARIA
Nov. 1942
Monte Cassino
Salerno
Sardinia
ALBANIA (It.)
GREECE
TURKEY
SP. MOROCCO
Sicily
Casablanca
Tunis
July 1943
MOROCCO
Kasserine Pass Feb. 14 - 22, 1943
TUNISIA
Crete (Greece)
Rhodes (It.)
Cyprus (Br.)
SYRIA (Fr.)
LEBANON
FRENCH NORTH AFRICA (Vichy France) joined Allies Nov. 1942
M E D I T E R R A N E A N   S E A
PALESTINE (Br.)
TRANS- JORDAN (Br.)
Alexandria
Suez Canal
Axis Powers and their allies
Neutral nations
Nov. 1942
El Alamein Oct. 23 - Nov. 5, 1942
Axis-held, early Nov. 1942
Allied advances
LIBYA (It.)
EGYPT (Br.)
Nile R.
RED SEA
Allied Powers and their allies
Major battles

World War II in Europe and Africa

The momentous German defeats at Stalingrad and in Tunisia early in 1943 marked the turning point in the war against the Axis. By 1945 the Allied conquest of Hitler's "thousand year" Reich was imminent.

months inching their way 150 miles to Rome and were still battling through the mud and snow of northern Italy when the war in Europe ended.

In 1943 and 1944, the United States and Britain turned the tide in the Atlantic and sent thousands of bombers over Germany. To the east, Soviet troops kept the Nazis in retreat.

American science and industry, as much as the American navy, won the Battle of the Atlantic. They developed not only sophisticated radar and

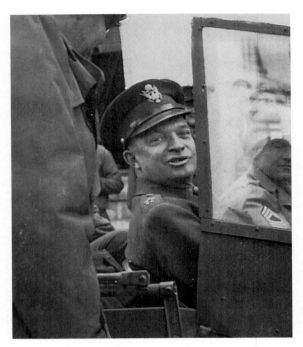

The Genial General
One American GI observed of Dwight Eisenhower, "He looks sort of like the guys you know at home."

sonar systems but also better torpedoes and depth charges, and produced ever-increasing quantities of aircraft and destroyers. In early 1943 British and American air forces began round-the-clock bombardment, raining thousands of tons of bombs on German cities. In raids on Hamburg in July 1943, Allied planes dropping incendiary bombs created terrible firestorms, killing at least 60,000 people and leveling the city, much as they had done earlier at Cologne.

Meanwhile, in 1943, as the Soviet offensive reclaimed Russian cities and towns from the Nazis, the German armies fell into perpetual retreat across the vast north European plain. Advancing swiftly, the Red Army drove the Germans out of Soviet territory by mid-1944 and plunged into Poland, where the Soviets set up a puppet government. Late summer and early fall saw Soviet troops seize Romania

and Bulgaria and aid communist guerrillas under Josip Broz Tito in liberating Yugoslavia. But the U.S.S.R. paid a terrible price for its victories: 24 million Soviet citizens, military and civilian, lay dead in the rubble of the western Soviet Union.

As eastern Europe fell under Soviet domination, Allied forces finally opened the long-delayed second front. On June 6, 1944—D-Day—150,000 Allied troops landed in Normandy in northwestern France, gaining a toehold on French soil. Within six weeks a million Allied troops had waded ashore. Under General Eisenhower, a man of superb administrative and diplomatic skills, the Allies liberated Paris in August and reached the German border by the end of summer. However, in the face of supply problems and stiffened German resistance, the Allied offensive ground to a halt.

In mid-December, as the Allies prepared for a full-scale assault on the German heartland, Hitler in a desperate gamble threw his last reserves against American positions. The Battle of the Bulge— named for the "bulge" eighty miles long and fifty miles wide that Hitler's troops drove into the Allies' line—raged for nearly a month, and when it ended American troops stood on the banks of the Rhine. Fifty-five thousand were killed or wounded, and 18,000 taken prisoner. But the way to Germany lay open, and the end of the European war was in sight.

The War in the Pacific

The day after the Philippines fell to Japan in mid-May 1942, U.S. and Japanese fleets confronted each other in the Coral Sea off northeastern Australia, the first time in history that a naval battle was fought entirely from aircraft carriers. Both sides took heavy losses, but the Battle of the Coral Sea stopped the Japanese advance on Australia. Less than a month later, a Japanese armada turned toward Midway Island, the crucial American outpost between Hawaii and Japan. Because the U.S. Signal Corps had broken the Japanese naval code, the plans and locations of Japan's ships became known. American carriers and their planes consequently won a decisive victory, sinking four Japanese carriers and

World War II in the Pacific

American ships and planes stemmed the Japanese offensive at the Battles of the Coral Sea and Midway Island. Thereafter, the Japanese were on the defensive against American amphibious assaults and air strikes.

destroying several hundred enemy planes. After the Battle of Midway, Japanese expansion turned into a defensive effort to hold what the Imperial Navy had already won.

Eight months after Pearl Harbor, on August 7, 1942, the United States assumed the offensive in the Pacific. Marines waded ashore at Guadalcanal in the Solomon Islands. Tropical diseases—malaria, fungus, dysentery—afflicted both sides, but in six

months of bloody fighting the United States drove the Japanese out of the Solomons. Japan left behind 25,000 dead, a gruesome preview of island battles to come.

In fall 1943 American forces began a two-pronged advance toward Japan. Under General Douglas MacArthur, who had commanded the heroic but futile defense of the Philippines, the army advanced north from Australia, "leapfrogging" from one strategic island to another. A second force under Admiral Chester Nimitz "island-hopped" across the central Pacific, isolating Japanese troops behind American lines and seizing key islands to serve as bases for American bombers sent against Japan itself.

Pacific operations remained secondary to the defeat of Germany, but the size of the conflict steadily increased. By late 1944 the United States had deployed 1.5 million marines and soldiers, along with the navy's fastest and largest aircraft carriers, in the Pacific. By the time MacArthur's troops liberated Manila in early 1945, they had lost 28,000 dead, fewer than the number killed in some individual battles in Europe. Under Nimitz, marines and naval forces seized strategic bases in the Gilbert Islands in November 1943 and the Marshall Islands in February 1944. Capture of the Marianas in the summer of 1944 put Tokyo within range of the new B-29 bombers, which by late 1944 were incinerating Japanese cities. In the fall of 1944, the American navy annihilated what remained of the imperial fleet at the battles of the Philippine Sea and Leyte Gulf. Japan's sea and air power were now totally shattered. Still, Japanese military leaders stymied attempts by civilians in the government to negotiate peace.

The Grand Alliance

Two primary goals underlay Roosevelt's wartime strategies: the total defeat of the Axis at the least possible cost in American lives, and the establishment of a world order strong enough to preserve peace, to open trade, and to ensure national self-determination in the postwar era. Aware that only a common enemy fused the Grand Alliance together, FDR tried to promote harmony by concentrating on military victory and postponing divisive postwar matters.

But Churchill and Stalin had other goals. Britain sought to retain its imperial possessions and a balance of power against the U.S.S.R. in Europe. The Soviet Union wanted a permanently weakened Germany and a sphere of influence in eastern Europe in order to protect itself against future attacks from the West. To hold together this uneasy alliance, FDR used personal diplomacy and met frequently with foreign leaders to plan strategy and to mediate conflicts.

In January 1943 Roosevelt and Churchill had met at Casablanca, Morocco's main port, where they had resolved to attack Italy before invading France and proclaimed that the war would continue until the Axis accepted "unconditional surrender." In this proclamation they sought to reduce Soviet mistrust of the West, which had deepened because of the postponement of the second front. Then in November 1943, at Cairo, Roosevelt had met with Churchill and Jiang Jieshi (Chiang Kai-shek), head of the Chinese government. To keep China in the war, FDR promised the return of Manchuria and Taiwan to China and guaranteed a free and independent Korea.

FDR and Churchill had continued on from Cairo to Tehran, Iran's capital, to confer with Stalin. Here they had set the invasion of France for June 1944 and agreed to divide Germany into zones of occupation and to impose reparations on the Reich. Most important to Roosevelt, at Tehran

The Election of 1944				
Candidates	Parties	Electoral Vote	Popular Vote	Percentage of Popular Vote
FRANKLIN D. ROOSEVELT	Democratic	432	25,606,585	53.5
Thomas E. Dewey	Republican	99	22,014,745	46.0

Stalin had also pledged to enter the Pacific war after Hitler's defeat.

The Election of 1944

As 1944 unfolded, Roosevelt turned his attention to domestic politics. Conservative gains in both the Republican and the Democratic party drove FDR toward the center. He dumped the liberal Henry A. Wallace from the ticket and chose Harry S Truman as his vice-presidential candidate. A moderate senator from Missouri, Truman had gained a national profile by chairing a subcommittee investigating waste in the defense effort. Not strongly opposed by any major Democratic faction, Truman, "the new Missouri Compromise," restored a semblance of unity to the party for the 1944 campaign. Hoping that unity would carry *them* to victory, the Republicans nominated moderate New York governor Thomas E. Dewey. The campaign focused more on personalities than issues, with the Republicans harping on FDR's failing health and FDR touting American military victories.

In November the American electorate handed FDR an unprecedented fourth term, but with his narrowest margin ever—only 53 percent of the popular vote. Roosevelt owed his triumph largely to the urban vote and the support of organized labor. The president now directed his waning energies toward defeating the Axis and constructing a new international order.

Triumph and Tragedy, 1945

The spring and summer of 1945 brought stunning changes. In Europe, the Yalta conference and the collapse of the Nazi Third Reich saw a new balance of power emerge. In Asia, continued Japanese resistance and reluctance to surrender led to the use of a terrible new weapon, the atomic bomb. And in the United States, a new president, Harry Truman, presided over the end of war with Germany and Japan and the beginning of a new, "cold" war.

The Yalta Conference

By the time Roosevelt, Churchill, and Stalin met at the Soviet city of Yalta in February 1945, the military situation favored the Soviet Union, for the Soviet offensive was nearly complete. The Red Army had overrun eastern Europe; driven the Nazis out of Yugoslavia; begun to organize Poland, Romania, and Bulgaria as communist states; penetrated Austria, Hungary, and Czechoslovakia; and now massed only fifty miles from Berlin. American forces, in contrast, were still recovering from the Battle of the Bulge and faced fanatical resistance on the route to Japan. The Joint Chiefs of Staff, predicting that an invasion of Japan would cost a million American casualties, insisted that obtaining Stalin's help in Asia was worth almost any price. For his part, Stalin was in a position to make demands. Roosevelt and Churchill could do little about Stalin's domination of eastern Europe but considered Soviet aid essential in Asia. The United States anticipated a long, bloody battle against Japan. Stalin, however, had the luxury of deciding whether or not to enter the Pacific war.

The Yalta agreements mirrored the new balance of power. Stalin again promised to declare war on Japan "two or three months" after Germany's surrender, and in return Roosevelt and Churchill reneged on their arrangement with Jiang Jieshi (made earlier at Cairo) and promised the Soviet Union concessions in Manchuria and the territories that it had lost in the Russo-Japanese War forty years before. Stalin then recognized Jiang as the ruler of China and promised to press Mao Zedong's (Mao Tse-tung's) Chinese communists to cooperate with Jiang. Stalin also accepted the temporary partitioning of Germany and the postponement of discussions about reparations. On the matter dearest to FDR's heart, Stalin approved plans for a United Nations conference to establish a permanent international organization for collective security.

Stalin, however, proved adamant about Soviet domination in eastern Europe, particularly Poland. Twice in the twentieth century, German troops had used Poland as a pathway for invading Russia. Stalin would not expose his land again, and after the Red Army had captured Warsaw in January 1945, he encouraged the Polish communists to subdue a noncommunist majority brutally. Roosevelt and Churchill refused to recognize the communist Lublin regime, but they accepted Stalin's pledge to include noncommunist Poles in the new government and to allow free elections. They could do little else. Short of going to war against the Soviet Union while battling Germany and Japan, FDR could only hope that Stalin would keep his promises.

The Defeat of Germany

Meanwhile, Allied armies closed the vise on Germany. In early March 1945 American troops captured Cologne and encircled Germany's industrial heartland. To counter the threat of Soviet power in postwar Europe, Churchill proposed a rapid thrust to Berlin, but Eisenhower, with Roosevelt's backing, overruled the British. Instead, to minimize their casualties and to reassure Stalin, the Americans advanced methodically on a broad front until they met the Russians at the Elbe River at the end of April. By then the Red Army had overrun Vienna and reached the suburbs of Berlin. On April 30 Hitler committed suicide in a bunker under the ruins of Berlin; the city fell to the Soviets on May 2. A hastily assembled German government surrendered unconditionally on May 8.

Jubilant Americans celebrated Victory in Europe (V-E) Day with ticker-tape parades and dancing in the streets. The rejoicing subsided as attention turned to the Pacific. Moreover, in the last weeks of the German war, Allied troops had liberated those still alive in the concentration camps, and Americans had viewed newsreels of the gas chambers at Auschwitz, the ovens at Dachau, and the corpses stacked like cordwood at Belsen. They learned with horror of the systematic murder of 6 million Jews and 1 million others in the Nazi death camps. And they mourned a death closer to home, the death of FDR. On April 12 the exhausted president, sitting for a portrait at his second home, in

Warm Springs, Georgia, died of a cerebral hemorrhage. His unprepared successor inherited leadership of the most powerful nation in history—as well as troubles with the Soviet Union that seemed more intractable every day.

A New President

"I don't know whether you fellows ever had a load of hay or a bull fall on you," Harry S Truman told reporters on his first day in office, "but last night the moon, the stars, and all the planets fell on me." Unpretentious, awed by his new responsibilities, Truman had little familiarity with world affairs. He distrusted the Soviets and counted on American military power to maintain the peace. In office less than two weeks, he lashed out at Soviet ambassador V. M. Molotov that the United States was tired of waiting for Moscow to allow free elections in Poland, and he threatened to cut off lend-lease aid if the Soviet Union did not cooperate. The Truman administration reduced U.S. economic assistance to the Soviets and stalled on their request for a $1 billion reconstruction loan. Stalin consequently broke his Yalta promises and strengthened his control of eastern Europe. The bluster of Stalin and Truman accelerated the dissolution of the Grand Alliance.

The United States would neither concede the Soviet sphere of influence in eastern Europe nor take decisive steps to terminate it. Truman still sought Stalin's cooperation in establishing the United Nations and in defeating Japan, but Soviet-American relations rapidly deteriorated. By June 1945, when the Allied countries framed the United Nations Charter in San Francisco, hopes for a new international order had dimmed, and the United Nations emerged as a diplomatic battleground. Truman, Churchill, and Stalin met at Potsdam, Germany, from July 16 to August 2, to complete the postwar arrangements begun at Yalta. But the allies could barely agree even to demilitarize Germany and to punish Nazi war criminals. All the major divisive issues were postponed. Given the diplomatic impasse, only military power remained to determine the contours of the postwar world.

The Atomic Bombs

The war with Japan ground on. Early in 1945 marines landed on the tiny island of Iwo Jima, 700 miles from Japan. Because Japanese soldiers had hidden in tunnels and behind concrete bunkers and pillboxes, it took six weeks and 26,000 marine casualties to secure the five-square-mile island. Then in June American troops waded ashore on Okinawa, 350 miles from Japan and a key staging area for the planned invasion of the Japanese home islands. They suffered nearly 50,000 casualties before taking the island.

If the capture of these small islands had been so bloody, what would the assault on Japan itself be like? Although a naval blockade and daily aerial pounding were exhausting Japan, the imperial government showed little disposition to surrender. Truman scheduled an invasion of Kyushu, the first of the home islands, for late 1945.

But the successful test of an atomic weapon at Alamogordo in mid-July presented an alternative. While at Potsdam, Truman, on July 25, secretly ordered that an atomic bomb be used if Japan did not surrender before August 3. He and Churchill publicly warned Japan to surrender unconditionally or face "prompt and utter destruction." When Japan rejected this Potsdam Declaration, Truman gave the military the go-ahead. On August 6 a B-29 named *Enola Gay* dropped an atomic bomb on the city of Hiroshima. Nearly 80,000 people died in the searing flash of heat and light, and thousands more died later of radiation poisoning. On August 8, as promised, Stalin declared war on Japan. The next day, an atomic bomb incinerated 40,000 people at Nagasaki and obliterated the city. Finally, on August 14 Japan surrendered, leaving the emperor on the throne but powerless. On September 2 General MacArthur, aboard the battleship *Missouri* in Tokyo Bay, formally accepted the Japanese surrender.

Many have questioned whether the war had to end with the atomic bombings. Some believe that racist American attitudes toward Japan motivated the decision to use the bombs. Yet from the beginning of the Manhattan Project, Germany had been the target; and considering the indiscriminate ferocity of the Allied bombings of Hamburg and Dresden, there is little reason to assume that the Allies would not have used atomic bombs against Germany had they been available. Others contend that demonstrating the bomb's destructiveness on an uninhabited island would have motivated the Japanese surrender. But American policy makers considered a demonstration too risky. Still others argue that Japan was ready to surrender and that an invasion of the home islands was unnecessary. We cannot know for sure. But we do know that as late as July 28, 1945, Japan rejected a demand for surrender, and that not until after the Hiroshima bombing did the Japanese government discuss acceptance of the Potsdam Declaration.

Rapidly worsening relations between the United States and the U.S.S.R. convinced some that Truman dropped the atomic bomb primarily to intimidate Stalin. The failure of the Americans and Soviets to resolve their differences had led Truman to seek an end to the Pacific war before Stalin could enter. He recognized that such an awesome weapon might give the United States leverage to oust the communists from eastern Europe. Just before the Alamogordo test, Truman had said, "If it explodes, as I think it will, I'll certainly have a hammer on [Stalin]." Truman's new secretary of state, James Byrnes, thought that the bomb would "put us in a position to dictate our own terms at the end of the war."

Although the president and his advisers believed that the atomic bomb would strengthen their hand against the Soviets, that was not the main reason that the bombs were dropped. Throughout the war Americans had relied on production and technology to win the war with a minimum loss of American life. Every new weapon had been used. No responsible official would counsel that the United States accept the deaths of thousands of Americans while not using a weapon developed with 2 billion taxpayer dollars. Indeed, to the vast majority of Americans, the atomic bomb was, in Churchill's words, "a miracle of deliverance" that shortened the war and saved lives.

Conclusion

The dropping of the atomic bombs ended the deadliest war in history. More than 14 million combatants, including 300,000 Americans, had died. Twenty-five million civilians had perished. Much of Europe and Asia was rubble.

Although physically unscathed, the United States had changed profoundly. Mobilization had altered the structure of the economy; accelerated trends toward bigness in business, agriculture, and labor; and enlarged the role of the military. World War II had also transformed the scope and authority of the federal government, especially the presidency, and catalyzed vital changes in racial and social relations.

Isolationism had all but vanished as the United States, the strongest nation in the world in 1945, assumed a role in global affairs inconceivable five years earlier. Many hoped that the United Nations would ensure future peace. But instead, the war spawned a new conflict, the Cold War. The mushroom clouds over Hiroshima and Nagasaki signaled a spiraling arms race that would threaten nuclear nightmare. Indeed, the advances in wartime science and technology had raised not only hopes for a healthier and better world but also fears of an end to life on earth. As Americans began a new era, the nation was both more powerful and less secure than ever before.

Chronology

1939   Germany invades Poland; World War II begins.
Soviet Union invades Poland.

1940   Germany conquers the Netherlands, Belgium, France, Denmark, Norway, and Luxembourg.
Germany, Italy, and Japan sign the Tripartite Pact.
Selective Service Act.
Franklin Roosevelt elected to a third term.

1941   Lend-Lease Act.
Roosevelt establishes the Fair Employment Practices Commission (FEPC).
Germany invades the Soviet Union.
Japan attacks Pearl Harbor; the United States enters World War II.
War Powers Act.

1942   Battle of Midway halts Japanese offensive.
Internment of Japanese-Americans.
Revenue Act expands graduated income-tax system.
Allies invade North Africa (Operation Torch).

First successful atomic chain reaction.
Congress of Racial Equality (CORE) founded.

1943   Soviet victory in Battle of Stalingrad.
Coal miners strike; Smith-Connally War Labor Disputes Act.
Detroit race riot.
Allied invasion of Italy.
Big Three meet in Tehran.

1944   Allied invasion of France (Operation Overlord).
GI Bill of Rights.
Roosevelt wins fourth term.
Battle of the Bulge.

1945   Big Three meet in Yalta.
Battles of Iwo Jima and Okinawa.
Roosevelt dies; Harry S Truman becomes president.
Germany surrenders.
Truman, Churchill, and Stalin meet in Potsdam.
United States drops atomic bombs on Hiroshima and Nagasaki; Japan surrenders.

FOR FURTHER READING

John Morton Blum, *V Was for Victory: Politics and American Culture During World War II* (1976). A critical analysis of American society during the war.

John Dower, *War Without Mercy* (1986). An insightful look at racism among the Americans and the Japanese.

Patrick Heardon, *Roosevelt Confronts Hitler: American Entry into World War II* (1987). An economic interpretation of U.S. foreign policy.

Warren Kimball, *The Juggler: Franklin Roosevelt as Wartime Statesman* (1991). A study of the president's war aims and postwar vision.

Gordon W. Prange, *At Dawn We Slept: The Untold Story of Pearl Harbor* (1981). A thoroughly researched, balanced examination of the controversies surrounding the Japanese attack.

Martin Sherwin, *A World Destroyed: The Atomic Bomb and the Grand Alliance* (1975). A cogent explanation of atomic diplomacy's rise and consequences.

Holly Cowan Shulman, *The Voice of America* (1991). An in-depth account of America's wartime propaganda policies and programs.

Cold War America, 1945–1952

Optimistic that there would not soon be another war, and confident that the nation could solve any problems, ordinary Americans of the postwar years rushed to grab a share of the good life. They married, had babies, made Dr. Benjamin Spock's child-care manual the hottest book since best-seller lists had begun, bought cars with automatic transmissions, and moved to new split-level houses in suburbs. However, the peace of mind that they yearned for eluded them, for World War II had wrought decisive and disturbing changes in society and in the global balance of power.

Disagreement over Eastern Europe's postwar fate sparked a confrontation in which the Soviet Union and the United States each sought to reshape the world to serve its own interests. An uncompromising Harry S Truman squared off against an obsessive Joseph Stalin, each intensifying the insecurities of the other. A new form of international conflict—the Cold War—emerged, in which the two superpowers avoided direct military clashes while using all their resources to thwart the other's objectives.

(Right) Slicing an "atomic cake" at the Pentagon, 1946

The Postwar Political Setting
Anticommunism and Containment
The Truman Administration at Home
The Politics of Anticommunism

The Cold War changed America. Abandoning its historical aloofness from events outside the Western Hemisphere, the United States now plunged into a global struggle to contain the Soviet Union and to stop communism. The nation that only a few years before had no military alliances, a small defense budget, and no troops on foreign soil built a giant military establishment, signed mutual-defense pacts with forty countries, directly intervened in the affairs of allies and enemies alike, built military bases on every continent, and embarked on a seemingly limitless nuclear-arms race. To oppose communist aggression in Asia, the United States dispatched thousands of Americans to fight in Korea.

The Cold War's political and social effects proved equally decisive. Preoccupation with the Soviet threat discredited the political Left and sapped liberalism's vitality. Conservatives remained convinced that the federal government's power should be strictly limited, but at the same time they applauded the growth of federal power when military expansion, sniffing out domestic disloyalty, and leading the world fight against communism were at issue. Socially, the free expression of ideas suffered during the Cold War, as popular fears of communist aggression and domestic subversion led to witch hunts against suspected communists that undermined civil liberties. In 1952 an anxious electorate turned hopefully to Dwight D. Eisenhower to deliver the stability for which they longed.

The Postwar Political Setting

In background and bearing, Harry S Truman could not have been more unlike FDR. The son of a Missouri horse and mule trader, Truman worked on his grandfather's farm until serving as an artillery captain in World War I. After returning from France, he operated a men's clothing store in Kansas City and dabbled in local politics until his business failed. Elected to the Senate in 1934, Truman was a diligent but colorless Democratic partisan, a supporter of FDR but not a committed New Dealer. Neither experienced in foreign policy nor supported

by any major group within the Democratic party, Truman won the vice-presidential nomination in 1944 because he was a safe alternative to the liberal Henry A. Wallace and the conservative James F. Byrnes.

After FDR's death, liberals voiced dismay at this "usurper" in the White House. Truman made it clear that he would rule in his own way, replacing cabinet New Dealers with moderates and appointing political cronies to key posts. Conservatives were unhappy when Truman urged Congress to adopt a major economic reform program and emphasized his role as the champion of the common people against special interests.

Deeply concerned for the public welfare, Truman displayed on his desk a framed motto of Mark Twain: "Always do right. This will gratify some people and astonish the rest." He wanted the government to do more to help people, but without altering the existing social and economic systems. "I don't want any experiments," he told an aide; "the American people have been through a lot of experiments and they want a rest." They would not get much of that. Despite his goal of moderate reform, Truman confronted an aggressively resurgent Republican party and a deeply divided Democratic party. Moreover, owing to congressional resentment of the enormous powers assumed by FDR during the war, Truman had to govern in an era of intense legislative suspicion of executive leadership.

Demobilization and Reconversion

When the war ended, GIs and civilians alike wanted all those who had served overseas "home alive in '45." Troops demanding transport ships barraged Congress with threats of "no boats, no votes." On a single day in December 1945, 60,000 postcards arrived at the White House with the message "Bring the Boys Home by Christmas." Truman bowed to popular demand, and by 1948 American military strength had dropped from 12 million at war's end to just 1.5 million.

Returning veterans faced readjustment problems intensified by a soaring divorce rate and a drastic housing shortage. As war plants closed, moreover, veterans and civilians feared the return of mass unemployment and economic depression. Defense spending plummeted from $76 billion in 1945 to under $20 billion in 1946, and more than a million defense jobs vanished. However, an economic boom began in 1946 as U.S. economic output leaped from $200 billion to $318 billion by 1950. Reconversion—the transition from wartime production to manufacturing consumer goods—ushered in a quarter-century of ever-expanding prosperity.

The Serviceman's Readjustment Act of 1944, the "GI Bill of Rights," stimulated economic growth by putting $15 billion into the hands of veterans to attend college, to receive medical treatment, and to purchase homes. A 1945 tax cut of $6 billion, coupled with huge wartime profits, enabled businesses to invest vigorously in new factories.

The Bretton Woods agreement (1944) among the Allies had set the stage for the United States to become economic leader of the noncommunist world. In addition to valuing ("pegging") other currencies in relation to the dollar, Bretton Woods created several institutions to oversee international trade and finance: the International Monetary Fund (IMF), the General Agreement on Tariffs and Trade (GATT), and the World Bank. The Bretton Woods system would function smoothly until the late 1960s.

The United States' favorable position in international trade and finance bolstered the idea that "the American century" of world peace and prosperity was at hand. Fears of depression faded into visions of limitless growth. With many nations in ruins, American firms could import cheap raw materials; with little competition from other industrial nations, they could increase their export sales to record levels. Wartime advances in science and technology, especially electronics and synthetic materials, led to the development of new industries and drove up productivity in others.

Wartime savings and a pent-up demand for consumer goods also kindled postwar growth and prosperity. The men and women who had endured the Great Depression and the Second World War craved the "good life," and by the end of 1945, they possessed $140 billion in bank accounts and government bonds. The rage to consume, and the ability to do so, more than compensated for the decline in defense spending. Advertisements promising "a Ford in your future" and an "all-electric kitchen-of-the-future" became reality as sales of homes, furniture, cars, appliances, and clothing skyrocketed. Scores of new products—televisions, filter cigarettes, electric clothes dryers, freezers, automatic transmissions, air conditioners, hi-fis—emerged as hallmarks of the middle-class life-style.

Truman's Troubles

Americans' hunger for the fruits of affluence left them little appetite for extension of the New Deal. Truman's only major legislative accomplishment in the Seventy-ninth Congress, the Employment Act of 1946, committed the federal government to assuring economic growth and established the Council of Economic Advisers to help to achieve "maximum employment, production, and purchasing power." Congress, however, had gutted from the proposed bill the goal of providing *full* employment, as well as the broad executive authority necessary to achieve that goal. Congress also blocked Truman's requests for public housing, a higher minimum wage, social-security expansion, a permanent Fair Employment Practices Commission, an anti–poll tax bill, federal aid to education, and government medical insurance.

Congressional eagerness to dismantle wartime controls, and inconsistent presidential leadership, hobbled the administration's ability to handle the major postwar economic problem: inflation. Consumer demand outran the supply of goods, putting intense pressure on prices. The Office of Price Administration (OPA) continued to set price controls after the war, but food producers, manufacturers, and retailers opposed controls strenuously. Many consumers favored preserving the OPA, but others saw the agency as a symbol of irksome wartime regulation. In June 1946, when Congress passed a bill that extended the OPA's life but removed its powers, Truman vetoed the bill. Within a week food costs rose 16 percent, and the price of beef doubled.

Congress passed, and Truman signed, a second bill extending price controls in weakened form. Protesting any price controls, however, farmers and meat producers threatened to withhold food from the market. Observing that "meatless voters are opposition voters," Truman lifted controls on food prices just before the November 1946 midterm elections. Democratic candidates fared badly at the polls anyhow. By the time Truman lifted all price controls, shortly after the election, the consumer price index had already jumped nearly 25 percent, and food prices had risen at an even faster rate.

These staggering price increases intensified organized labor's demand for higher wages. But inflation was not the only threat to workers' pay: wartime bonuses and overtime had ended, and employers were resisting higher wages. Worker dissatisfaction boiled over in a surge of strikes. In 1946 alone, more than 4.5 million men and women went on strike. After a United Mine Workers walkout paralyzed the economy for forty days, President Truman ordered government seizure of the mines. A week later, the miners returned to work, after Truman granted most of the demands. Six months later, the drama repeated itself.

In the spring of 1946, railway engineers and trainmen struck, shutting down the railway system. Truman exploded. "If you think I'm going to sit here and let you tie up this whole country," the president shouted at the heads of the two unions, "you're crazy as hell." In May Truman asked Congress for authority to draft workers who struck in vital industries. Only when the rail workers gave in did the Senate reject Truman's proposals. His threat alienated labor leaders, and his encouragement of inflationary wage-price agreements between powerful unions and industries forced consumers to pay the bill in the form of higher prices.

By autumn of 1946, having antagonized virtually every major political interest group, Truman appeared nearly unable to govern. An October poll found only 32 percent approval of his performance. Summing up public discontent, Republicans asked, "Had enough?" In the 1946 elections they captured twenty-five governorships and, for the first time since 1928, won control of Congress.

John L. Lewis (1880–1969; inset) and Illinois Coal Miners, 1946
The 1946 strikes called by Lewis, the head of the United Mine Workers, angered Truman and many other Americans, but the work stoppages led to a multimillion-dollar welfare fund for the powerful union.

Anticommunism and Containment

By the end of 1946, smoldering antagonisms between Moscow and Washington flared up. The U.S.S.R. and the United States had abandoned their wartime alliance of expedience and were struggling for advantage in the vacuum left by the defeat of Germany and Japan, the exhaustion and bankruptcy of Western Europe, and the crumbling of colonial empires in Asia and Africa. Misperception and misunderstanding proliferated as the two nations sought security, each feeding the other's fears. Fundamental ideological differences widened the chasm between the two powers.

Confrontation and Polarization

The destiny of Eastern Europe, especially Poland, remained at the heart of U.S.-Soviet contention. The Soviet Union wanted to end its vulnerability to invasions sweeping eastward across the plains of Poland. Stalin insisted on a demilitarized Germany and a buffer of nations friendly to the Soviet Union along its western flank. He considered a Soviet sphere of influence in Eastern Europe essential to national security, a just reward for the U.S.S.R.'s bearing the brunt of the war against Germany, and no different from the American spheres of influence in Western Europe, Japan, and Latin America. Stalin also believed that at Yalta, Roosevelt and Churchill had implicitly accepted a Soviet zone in Eastern Europe.

With the Red Army occupying half of Europe at the war's end, Stalin installed pro-Soviet governments in Bulgaria, Hungary, and Romania while communist governments independent of Moscow came to power in Albania and Yugoslavia. Ignoring the Yalta Declaration of Liberated Europe, the Soviet Union barred free elections in Poland and brutally suppressed Polish democratic parties.

Stalin's refusal to abandon dominance in Eastern Europe collided with Truman's unwillingness to concede Soviet supremacy beyond Russia's borders. What Stalin saw as critical to Russian security, the Truman administration viewed as a violation of the right of national self-determination, a betrayal of democratic principles, and a cover for communism's spread. Furthermore, Truman and his advisers believed that history taught that the appeasement of dictators only fed their appetites for expansion. The new administration thus determined to be tough with Moscow, because any "generous and considerate attitude" by the United States would be interpreted as weakness by Stalin and would lead to a "barbarian invasion of Europe." Moreover, many in Truman's inner circle believed that traditional European balance-of-power politics and spheres of influence had precipitated both world wars. Only a new world order, based on the self-determination of all nations working in good faith within the United Nations, could guarantee peace.

Truman also thought that accepting the "enforced sovietization" of Eastern Europe would betray American war aims and condemn nations rescued from Hitler's tyranny to another totalitarian dictatorship. Too, Truman worried, a Soviet stranglehold in Eastern Europe would imperil the health of an American economy dependent on exports and on access to raw materials in the countries that Stalin appeared resolute to control solely for Soviet economic betterment.

Domestic political considerations also shaped Truman's response to Stalin. The Democratic party contained 6 million Polish-Americans as well as millions of other Americans of Eastern European origin, all of whom remained keenly interested in the fates of their homelands. The president realized that the Democratic party courted disaster by reneging on the Yalta agreements. He also recognized the strength of anticommunism in American politics and was determined not to appear "soft on communism." Aligning his administration with growing American anti-Soviet sentiment would fortify it politically, Truman concluded.

Combativeness fit the temperament of the feisty Truman. Eager to demonstrate that he was in command, the president matched Stalin's intransigence on Polish elections with his own demands for reorganizing Poland's government along democratic lines. Emboldened by America's monopoly of atomic bombs and its undisputed position as the world's economic superpower, the president hoped that the United States could control the terms of postwar settlement.

The Cold War Begins

But Truman's assertiveness inflamed Stalin's mistrust of the West and deepened the Soviets' obsession with their own security. Stalin stepped up his confiscation of materials and factories from occupied territories and forced his satellite nations to close their doors to Anglo-American trade and influence. In February 1946 he warned that there could be no lasting peace with capitalism and vowed to make the Soviet Union secure against the Western challenge—and to overcome the American edge in weapons.

Two weeks later, a sixteen-page telegram from George F. Kennan, the American chargé d'affaires in Moscow, reached Washington. A leading student of Soviet politics, Kennan had long been at odds with the official policy of cooperation with the Soviet Union. His advocacy of toughness was well suited to Truman's mood. Indeed, the president had concluded that the time had come to "stop babying the Soviets."

Kennan's telegram asserted the inevitability of American conflict with the Soviet Union. Any attempt to negotiate an accommodation with the U.S.S.R. was foolish, Kennan insisted. Instead, America must base its foreign policy on the "long-term, patient, and vigilant containment of Russian expansive tendencies." Containment would force the Soviets to act prudently by reinforcing their tendency to pull back "when strong resistance is encountered at any point."

In later years, Kennan would apologize for his telegram, admitting that it read "exactly like one of those primers put out by the Daughters of the American Revolution, designed to arouse the citizenry to the dangers of a communist conspiracy." But in early 1946 Kennan's belief that only strong, sustained resistance could contain Russian aggression struck a deep chord with those who insisted on "no compromise" with the U.S.S.R. "Containment" consequently became unofficial Washington gospel. Republican leaders demanded that the United States "draw the line" with Moscow, and the Truman administration agreed.

In early March 1946 Truman accompanied Winston Churchill to Westminster College in Missouri, where the former British prime minister, in a famous speech, warned of a new threat to democracy, this time from Moscow. Stalin, he said, had drawn an iron curtain across the eastern half of Europe. Churchill called for an alliance of the English-speaking peoples against the Soviet Union and the maintenance of an Anglo-American monopoly on atomic weapons.

Convinced that American firmness could check Soviet expansionism, Truman in the spring of 1946 shifted his foreign policy in the direction prescribed by Kennan and Churchill. To force Stalin to keep an earlier promise to withdraw Soviet soldiers from the north of oil-rich Iran, Truman dispatched part of the Sixth Fleet to the Black Sea and threatened to send in American combat troops. In June Truman submitted to the United Nations an atomic-energy control plan requiring the Soviet Union to stop all work on nuclear weapons and to submit to a system of U.N. control and inspection before the United States would destroy its own atomic arsenal. As expected, the Soviets rejected the American proposal and offered an alternative plan equally unacceptable to the United States. As mutual hostility escalated, the Soviets and Americans rushed to develop doomsday weapons. In 1946 Congress established the Atomic Energy Commission (AEC) to regulate nuclear development. Although Congress specified that fissionable materials should be used for civilian purposes "so far as practicable," at least 90 percent of the AEC's effort focused on weapons.

Thus, less than a year after American and Soviet soldiers had jubilantly met at the Elbe River to celebrate nazism's defeat, the Cold War had begun. Economic pressure, nuclear intimidation, propaganda, and subversion rather than military confrontation characterized this conflict. Nonetheless, it would affect American life as decisively as any military engagement that the nation had fought.

European Crisis, American Commitment

In early 1947 America formally stated its commitment to combat Soviet power. On February 21 the British informed the United States that they could no longer afford to assist the governments of Greece and Turkey in their struggles against communist-supplied guerrilla insurgencies and against Soviet pressure for access to the Mediterranean. Britain asked the United States to assume the costs of thwarting communism in the eastern Mediterranean. The harsh European winter, the most severe in memory, heightened the sense of urgency in Washington. The economies of Western Europe had ground to a halt, famine and tuberculosis plagued the Continent, and colonies in Africa and Asia had risen in rebellion. Communist parties in France and Italy appeared ready to topple democratic coalition governments.

Truman resolved to meet the Soviet challenge. "Inaction, withdrawal, 'Fortress America' notions could only result in handing to the Russians vast areas of the globe now denied them," he later recalled. "This was the time to align the United States of America clearly on the side, and at the head, of the free world."

Truman first had to mobilize support for a radical departure from the American tradition of avoiding entangling alliances. In a tense White House meeting on February 27, the new secretary of state, former army chief of staff George C. Marshall, presented the case for massive aid to Greece and Turkey. Congressional leaders balked, more concerned about U.S. inflation than civil war in Greece. But Dean Acheson, the newly appointed undersecretary of state, seized the moment. The issue, he said, was not one of assisting the repressive Greek oligarchy and Turkey's military dictatorship—it was, rather, a universal struggle of freedom versus tyranny. "Like apples in a barrel infected by the corruption of one rotten one," he warned, the fall of Greece or Turkey would open Asia, Western Europe, and the oil fields of the Middle East to the Red menace. Shaken, the congressional leaders agreed to support the administration's request—if Truman could "scare hell out of the country."

Truman could and did. On March 12, 1947, addressing a joint session of Congress, he asked for $400 million in military assistance to Greece and Turkey. He depicted a world endangered by the spreading tentacles of communism. The United States, Truman said, must support free peoples everywhere who were "resisting attempted subjugation by armed minorities or by outside pressures." Called the Truman Doctrine, the president's declaration committed the United States to the role of global policeman facing an almost limitless confrontation with the Soviet Union and its allies. Endorsed by the Republican Congress, the Truman Doctrine laid the foundation for American Cold War policy that would endure for much of the next four decades.

A month later, the administration proposed massive U.S. assistance for European recovery. First proposed by the secretary of state and thus called the Marshall Plan, such aid, Truman thought, would be another weapon in the arsenal against the spread of communism. Truman wanted to end the economic devastation in Europe that he believed could readily be exploited by communist revolutionaries. Although the Marshall Plan ostensibly would help the hungry and homeless of *all* European countries, Truman calculated, correctly, that the U.S.S.R. and its communist allies would reject it because of the conditions and controls that were linked to the aid. The administration also accurately foresaw that Western European economic recovery would lead to an expansion in the sales of American goods abroad and thus promote domestic prosperity.

The Marshall Plan fulfilled its sponsors' hopes. Over a five-year period, Congress appropriated $17 billion for economic recovery in sixteen nations, and by 1952 the economic and social chaos that could have proved a fertile seedbed for communism had died down. Western Europe revived, prospered, and achieved an unprecedented unity. U.S. business, not coincidentally, boomed.

The Soviet Response

The Soviet Union reacted to the Truman Doctrine and the Marshall Plan by tightening its control in Eastern Europe. In mid-1947 Soviet-rigged elections in Hungary ensured a communist government, and in February 1948 the U.S.S.R. used a general strike

The Postwar Division of Europe

The wartime dispute between the Soviet Union and the Western Allies over Poland's future hardened after World War II into a Cold War that split Europe into competing American and Russian spheres of influence. Across an "iron curtain," NATO countries faced the Warsaw Pact nations.

and the threat of military intervention to fasten a communist-dominated government on Czechoslovakia—a regime that abolished other political parties and allowed the once-democratic Czechoslovak nation to be absorbed into the Soviet orbit.

Stalin then turned his sights on Germany. The Potsdam Agreement had divided Germany into four separate zones (administered by France, Great Britain, the Soviet Union, and the United States)

and created a joint four-power administration for Germany's capital, Berlin, which lay 110 miles inside the Soviet-occupied eastern zone. As the Cold War intensified, however, the Western nations denied Stalin a role in administering the Ruhr Valley, the industrial heart of western Germany. Angry, Stalin charged that the West was reneging on wartime promises. In April 1948 the Soviets began to impede the movement of supplies and people from the three Western-held zones of Germany into Berlin. On June 24, in reaction to Allied moves toward permanently uniting the three western zones into a pro-Western German state, the Russians blocked all rail and highway routes through the Soviet zone into Berlin. Stalin calculated that the Western powers, obstructed from feeding the 2 million pro-Western Berliners under their control, would either have to abandon plans to create an independent West Germany or to accept a communist Berlin.

Truman resolved neither to abandon Berlin nor to shoot his way into the city—and possibly trigger World War III. Instead, he ordered an elaborate, daring airlift to provide Berliners with the food and fuel necessary for survival. American cargo planes landed at West Berlin's Templehof Airport virtually every three minutes, around the clock, carrying a mountain of supplies. Then in July 1948 Truman hinted that he would use "the bomb" if necessary and sent a fleet of B29s, the only planes capable of delivering atomic bombs, to English bases. As tensions rose, Truman confided to his diary that "we are very close to war." The Berlin airlift continued for nearly a year.

In May 1949 the Soviets ended the blockade. Stalin's gamble had failed. The airlift highlighted American determination and technological prowess, revealed Stalin's willingness to use innocent citizens as pawns, and dramatically heightened anti-Soviet feeling in the West. In late 1948 U.S. public-opinion polls revealed an overwhelming demand for "firmness and increased 'toughness' in relations with Russia."

Continuing fears of a Soviet attack on Western Europe fostered support for a revitalized West German state and for an Atlantic collective-security alliance. Thus in May 1949 the United States, Britain, and France ended their occupation of Germany and approved the creation of the Federal Republic of Germany (West Germany). A month earlier, ten nations of Western Europe had adopted the North Atlantic Treaty, establishing a military alliance with the United States and Canada and declaring that an attack on any member would be considered an attack against all. For the first time in its history, the United States entered into a peacetime military alliance. After overwhelming Senate approval, the United States officially joined the North Atlantic Treaty Organization (NATO).

Two days after Senate ratification, Truman asked Congress to authorize $1.3 billion for military assistance to NATO countries. To underscore his determination to contain communism, Truman persuaded General Dwight D. Eisenhower to become supreme commander of the new mutual-defense force and authorized the stationing of four U.S. army divisions in Europe as the nucleus of the NATO armed force. The Soviet Union responded by creating the German Democratic Republic (East Germany) in 1949, by exploding its own atomic bomb that same year, and by forming an Eastern bloc military alliance, the Warsaw Pact, in 1955. The United States and Soviet Union had divided Europe into two armed camps.

The Cold War in Asia

Moscow-Washington hostility similarly carved Asia into contending military and economic camps. The Russians created a sphere of influence in Manchuria, the United States denied Moscow a role in postwar Japan, and the two superpowers partitioned a helpless Korea.

Under U.S. general Douglas MacArthur, Japan became a prosperous constitutional democracy firmly anchored in the American orbit by the late 1940s. In his capacity as commander of the occupational forces, MacArthur sanctioned the construction of American military bases near the Soviet Union's Asian rim and encouraged U.S. businesses to invest in Japan. Moreover, the United States assumed control of Japan's prewar island empire under a U.N. mandate and used the islands as air and naval bases and as atomic test sites. In 1949 MacArthur boasted that the Pacific had become "an Anglo-Saxon lake." To contain the Soviets in Asia and in Europe, the Truman administration also helped to crush a procommunist guerrilla movement in the Philippines and aided attempts by the

French to reestablish colonial rule in Indochina (Vietnam, Laos, and Cambodia), despite American declarations in favor of national self-determination and against imperialism.

In China, however, U.S. efforts to block communism failed. The Truman administration initially tried to mediate the civil war raging between Jiang Jieshi's Nationalist government and Mao Zedong's communist forces. Between 1945 and 1949 the United States sent nearly $3 billion to the Nationalists. But American dollars could not force Jiang's corrupt government to reform itself and to win the support of the Chinese people, whom it had widely alienated. As Mao's well-disciplined and motivated forces marched south, Jiang's soldiers mutinied and surrendered without a fight. Unable to stem revolutionary sentiment or to build loyalty among the peasants, Jiang's regime collapsed, and, he fled to exile on the island of Taiwan (Formosa).

Mao's establishment of the communist People's Republic of China shocked Americans. The most populous nation in the world, seen as a counterforce to Asian communism and a market for American trade, had become "Red China." Although the Truman administration insisted that it could have done little to alter the outcome and placed responsibility for Jiang's defeat on his failure to reform China, most Americans were unconvinced. China's fall to communism particularly embittered those conservatives who believed that America's future lay in Asia, not Europe. The former ambassador to China accused "pro-Communists in the State Department who . . . engineered the overthrow of our ally."

As the China debate raged, the president announced in September 1949 that the Soviet Union had exploded an atomic bomb. The loss of the nuclear monopoly shattered illusions of American invincibility. Combined with Mao's victory, this development would spawn an anticommunist hysteria and lead to irrational searches for scapegoats and subversives to explain American setbacks in world affairs.

A reeling Truman administration reassessed its strategy. In January 1950, stung by charges that he was soft on communism, the president ended a dispute among his scientific advisers by ordering the development of a fusion-based hydrogen bomb (H-bomb), hundreds of times more powerful than an atomic bomb. Leading scientists, including J. Robert Oppenheimer, argued that hydrogen bombs were too complex to construct and too immorally destructive to use. But in the fearful atmosphere pervading Washington in early 1950, Truman accepted the report of his secretaries of defense and state recommending a crash thermonuclear program. In November 1952 the United States exploded its first H-bomb in the Marshall Islands, projecting a radioactive cloud twenty-five miles into the atmosphere and blasting a canyon a mile long and 175 feet deep in the ocean floor. Nine months later, the Soviets detonated their own hydrogen bomb.

In April 1950 a presidentially appointed committee issued a top-secret review of defense policy. The report, NSC-68, emphasized the Soviet Union's aggressive intentions and military strength. To counter the U.S.S.R.'s "design for world domination"—the mortal challenge posed by the Soviet Union "not only to this Republic but to civilization itself"—NSC-68 called for a vast American military buildup. The nation must maintain a large standing army and drastically raise defense spending, and the American people must be persuaded to pay the taxes necessary for a 400 percent increase in military appropriations, the report asserted.

Truman hesitated to swallow his advisers' expensive medicine. An aide to Secretary of State Acheson recalled, "We were sweating over it, and then, with regard to NSC-68, thank God Korea came along." Indeed, on June 24, 1950, as Truman pondered NSC-68's implications, North Korean troops swept across the thirty-eighth parallel and invaded the Republic of Korea (South Korea). By the end of 1950, Truman would order the implementation of NSC-68 and triple the defense budget.

The Korean War

After Japan's defeat in World War II, the Soviet Union and United States had temporarily divided Korea at the thirty-eighth parallel for purposes of

Chaos in Korea
In this photograph taken in 1950, South Korean women and children flee from the communist invaders as U.S. infantrymen move in to hold the North Koreans from further advances.

military occupation. The dividing line had solidified into a political frontier between the Soviet-backed People's Democratic Republic in North Korea and the American-supported Republic of Korea. Each government hoped to unify Korea under its exclusive control.

Truman saw North Korea's invasion of South Korea not as an internal Korean matter, but as Soviet-directed aggression. Although the North Korean attack seemed to catch the Soviet Union off guard, and although the Soviets gave their ally little aid, Truman never doubted that Stalin was using Korea to test U.S. containment policy.

The president maintained, "If we are tough enough now, if we stand up to [the Soviets] like we did in Greece . . . they won't take any next steps. But if we just stand by, they'll . . . take over the whole Middle East." Mindful of the failure of appeasement at Munich in 1938, Truman later said

that "communism was acting in Korea just as Hitler, Mussolini, and the Japanese had acted ten, fifteen, and twenty years earlier." Failure to oppose aggression would embolden the communists "to override nations closer to our own shores" and would lead to a "third world war, just as similar incidents had brought on the second world war." Truman also had to prove to Republican critics that the Democrats would not allow another country to "fall" to the communists.

The president therefore decided to intervene in Korea. Without consulting Congress, he sought and gained United Nations backing to repel the North Korean attack in a "police action" to restore the borders of South Korea. On June 27 Truman ordered American air and sea forces to South Korea's aid and appointed General MacArthur to command the U.N. effort in Korea. Within three days, American soldiers were fighting in Korea. U.S. forces provided most of the air and navy support and half the troops fighting under the U.N. flag; South Korea supplied 43 percent of the forces, and fourteen other nations contributed less than 10 percent.

North Korea rapidly pushed the U.N. forces to the southeastern tip of the Korean peninsula. Then in mid-September a brilliant amphibious movement designed by MacArthur landed U.N. troops at Inchon, north of Seoul, and forced a North Korean retreat. Heartened, Truman permitted MacArthur to order U.N. armies across the thirty-eighth parallel toward the Yalu River, the boundary between Korea and China. The police action to restore the original border between the two Koreas was being transformed into a war of liberation to create "a unified, independent, and democratic" nation of Korea.

As U.N. troops approached the Yalu River, the Chinese warned that they would not "stand idly by" if their border was threatened. Ignoring this assertion, an overconfident MacArthur deployed his forces in a thin line below the river. On November 25 thirty-three Chinese divisions (about 300,000 men) counterattacked, driving stunned U.N. forces back below the thirty-eighth parallel. By March 1951 the fighting stabilized at roughly the original dividing line between the two Koreas.

The Korean War, 1950–1953

The experience of fighting an undeclared and limited war for the limited objective of containing communism confused the generation of Americans who had just fought an all-out war for the total defeat of the Axis. General MacArthur spoke for the many who were frustrated by the Korean conflict's mounting costs in blood and dollars: "There is no substitute for victory."

In the spring of 1951, Truman again reversed course and sought a negotiated peace based on the objective of restoring the integrity of South Korea. MacArthur rocked the boat, however, urging that he be allowed to bomb and blockade China, "unleash" Jiang Jieshi's troops against Mao's regime, and seek a total victory even at the risk of an all-out war with China. Truman rejected these ideas: "We are trying to prevent a world war—not to start one." Worried that the Soviet Union might take advantage of American involvement in Asia to pursue an aggressive course in Europe, he sought a limited war for a limited objective: to hold the line in Korea. But MacArthur would not accept a stalemate. "In war," he said, "there is no substitute for victory."

When MacArthur refused to stop criticizing administration policy, Truman relieved him of command, on April 10, 1951. Truman believed that MacArthur's insubordination seriously threatened the tradition of civilian control over the military. Public opinion, however, backed the general. The very idea of limited war baffled many Americans, and a mounting casualty list added anger to the mix. Radical Republican criticisms, such as Indiana senator William Jenner's charge that "this country today is in the hands of a secret coterie which is directed by agents of the Soviet Union," won support in some quarters.

The administration presented its case before Congress. General Omar Bradley, the chairman of the Joint Chiefs of Staff, testified that a showdown with China would lead to "a larger deadlock at greater expense." MacArthur's proposals, Bradley warned, "would involve us in the wrong war at the wrong place in the wrong time and with the wrong enemy." Talk of a total victory abated.

In July 1951 truce talks began, but they dragged on for two years as both sides continued their restricted but deadly war. By the time that wrangling over prisoner repatriation and the cease-fire line ended on July 26, 1953, the "limited war" had cost the United States almost 55,000 American lives, another 103,284 wounded or missing, and $54 billion. The conflict also accelerated implementation of NSC-68 and the expansion of containment into a global policy. From 1950 to 1953, defense spending zoomed from $13 billion to $60 billion—from one-third to two-thirds of the entire federal budget. The United States acquired new bases around the world, committed itself to rearm West Germany, and joined a mutual-defense pact with Australia and New Zealand. Increased military aid flowed to Jiang Jieshi's troops on Taiwan, and American dollars were extended to the French army fighting the communist Ho Chi Minh in Indochina (Vietnam). By 1954 the United States was paying about three-quarters of French war costs in Vietnam.

Truman's intervention in Korea preserved a precarious balance of power in Asia by preventing the South Korean regime from falling to its communist rival in the north. It also underscored the administration's commitment to the anticommunist struggle, as well as the shift of that struggle's focus from Europe to Asia. Containment, originally designed to justify U.S. aid to Greece and Turkey, served in the early 1950s as the ideological foundation for a major war in Korea and, ominously, for a deepening U.S. involvement with France's colonial war in Vietnam. By committing U.S. troops to battle with neither a declaration of war nor congressional approval, Truman set precedents for future undeclared wars and expanded presidential powers. Finally, the shock of China's fall and the frustrations of the inconclusive Korean War heightened conservatives' unhappiness with Democratic rule and set off domestic shock waves that would have broad political and cultural ramifications.

The Truman Administration at Home

When World War II ended, Americans wanted to bring the troops home and enjoy peace. Since 1929 the nation had known little but the sufferings and shortages of depression and war, and now it was time to enjoy life! Widespread postwar affluence let dreams become reality as Americans flocked to the suburbs, launched a "baby boom" of howling proportions, and rushed to buy stoves, refrigerators, televisions, and cars.

Not all Americans shared the good times. Poverty remained a stark fact of life for millions in the cities and on farms. Black Americans experienced the grim reality of racism. Many refused to yield, however, and from the early postwar period there emerged a civil-rights movement that in a few years would sweep the nation.

Family and career, not social issues, preoccupied most Americans, however, and New Deal reform energies subsided into a mood of complacency. Although Truman sought to extend reform, the times were against him. Congressional conservatives wanted to reduce, not expand, federal power. Anticommunism intensified the American tendency to identify social radicalism with disloyalty, and undercut efforts to alter the status quo.

After 1949 the Truman administration itself seemed to abandon reform, focusing primarily on anticommunism and rearmament. Fears of communism encircling the globe bred an atmosphere of domestic repression that stifled dissent and rewarded unquestioning conformity. When a senator from Wisconsin ran roughshod over principles of decency and fair play in the early 1950s, he was merely exploiting the paranoia that the White House itself had helped to create.

The Eightieth Congress

Many Republicans in the Eightieth Congress, which convened in January 1947, interpreted the 1946 elections as a mandate to reverse the New Deal. Republican-controlled, the Congress passed tax measures favoring the wealthy and defeated a proposal to raise the minimum wage. Determined "to meat-axe government frills," Republicans and conservative southern Democrats defeated Truman's requests for federal aid to education and a comprehensive housing program.

Truman and the conservatives waged their major battle, however, over the pro-union Wagner Act of 1935 (see Chapter 25). Postwar strikes had whipped up a national consensus for curbing union power. In 1947 Congress passed the Taft-Hartley Act (the Labor-Management Relations Act), which barred the closed shop and permitted the president to call a sixty-day cooling-off period to delay any strike that might endanger national safety or health. Unions termed the law a "slave labor bill" and demanded a presidential veto.

Truman did veto the measure, and he scolded Congress for "a shocking piece of legislation" biased against labor. Congress easily overrode the veto. But Truman had taken a major step toward regaining organized labor's support. This move reflected his recognition that his only hope for election in 1948 lay in reforging the New Deal coalition. To this end, he played the role of staunch New Dealer to the hilt, proposing a series of liberal reform bills— federal aid to education, housing, and health insurance; repeal of Taft-Hartley; and high farm-price supports. In his overall strategy, he was counting on the solid South to stay Democratic and was courting voters in the midwestern farm belt and the big cities.

Truman's foreign policy meshed with his domestic political strategy. Wooing Eastern European ethnic groups, Truman emphasized his opposition to communism's advance and supported laws to admit more wartime refugees. Shocked by the Holocaust, convinced that Israel was already an established fact, and needing Jewish votes, the president extended diplomatic recognition to the new state of Israel immediately after it proclaimed independence on May 14, 1948. In so doing, he overrode objections from those among his advisers who feared alienating the oil-producing Arab states.

The Politics of Civil Rights

Truman also made the federal protection of civil rights part of his agenda. Although he wished to retain the support of southern white Democrats and thus initially shied away from the race question, the accelerating civil-rights movement called for a response.

After the war, blacks who had served in the military and in the defense industry demanded the vote. Aggressive voter-registration drives raised the number of blacks registered to vote in the South from 2 percent in 1940 to 12 percent in 1947. Southern blacks risked intimidation, repression, and even murder in pursuing their right to vote, for white-supremacist politicians urged their followers to use any means to keep blacks from exercising that right.

Fearful of black assertiveness in seeking the vote and of other signs of a bold new spirit among African-Americans, some southern whites brutally asserted their dominance. In 1946 in rural Georgia, whites killed several black veterans who had voted that year, and in South Carolina blinded a black soldier for failing to sit in the rear of a bus. In Columbia, Tennessee, in 1946, whites rioted against blacks who insisted on their rights. Police arrested seventy blacks and looked the other way as a white mob broke into the jail to murder two African-American prisoners. Civil-rights leaders called for federal action.

In September 1946 Truman met with a delegation from some newly formed biracial groups to discuss racial terrorism in the South. Horrified by their accounts, he vowed to act. Truman believed that every American should enjoy the full rights of citizenship. He also understood the importance of the growing black vote, particularly in northern cities. The president realized, too, that white racism damaged U.S. relations with much of the world. The Soviet Union highlighted the mistreatment of American blacks, both to undercut U.S. appeals to racially diverse peoples in Africa, Asia, and Latin America and to counter U.S. condemnation of repression behind the Iron Curtain. After the 1946 elections, Truman established the President's Committee on Civil Rights to investigate race relations.

The committee's report, *To Secure These Rights*, dramatized the inequities of life in Jim Crow America. Underlining the compelling moral, economic, and international reasons why the government must act, it called for the eradication of racial discrimination and segregation. It also proposed antilynching and anti–poll tax legislation. Hailing the report as "an American charter of human freedom," Truman in February 1948 sent a special message to Congress, urging lawmakers to enact most of the committee's proposals.

Southern segregationists denounced Truman's "stab in the back." Many influential southern politicians warned of a boycott of the national Democratic ticket. Truman backtracked, flinching at the prospect of major southern defections. He dropped his plans, for example, to submit specific civil-rights bills to Congress and endorsed a weak civil-rights plank for the Democratic platform.

At the Democratic convention in July 1948, liberals and urban politicians who needed black votes rejected the watered-down civil-rights plank and committed the party to action on Truman's original proposals. Thirty-five delegates from Mississippi and Alabama responded by stalking out of the convention. They joined other southern segregationists to form the States' Rights Democratic party and nominated Governor Strom Thurmond of South Carolina for the presidency. The "Dixiecrats" hoped to win a hundred southern electoral votes, to restore their dominance in the Democratic party, and to preserve "the southern way of life" against an oppressive central government. They placed their electors on the ballot as the regular Democratic ticket in several states, effectively erecting a major roadblock to Truman's chances of victory.

The Election of 1948

Truman's electoral hopes faded when a band of left-wing Democrats joined with communists to launch a new Progressive party and nominated Henry A. Wallace for president. Truman had fired Wallace, his secretary of commerce and FDR's third-term vice president, for publicly questioning the administration's "get tough" stance toward the Soviet Union. The Wallace candidacy threatened Truman's chances in northern states, where many urban Democrats saw Wallace as the heir of New Deal liberalism.

To capitalize on Democratic divisions, Republicans bypassed conservative senator Robert A. Taft and nominated moderate governor Thomas E. Dewey of New York. Confident of victory and blandly appealing for national unity, Dewey ran a complacent campaign designed to offend the fewest people. The strategy made him seem aloof and smug.

Truman in contrast campaigned tirelessly, blasting the "no-good, do-nothing" Republican-controlled Eightieth Congress. To shouts of "Give 'em hell, Harry," the president hammered away at the GOP as the party of "privilege, pride, and

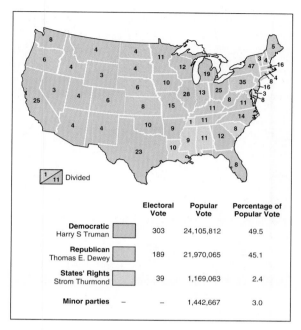

	Electoral Vote	Popular Vote	Percentage of Popular Vote
Democratic Harry S Truman	303	24,105,812	49.5
Republican Thomas E. Dewey	189	21,970,065	45.1
States' Rights Strom Thurmond	39	1,169,063	2.4
Minor parties	–	1,442,667	3.0

The Election of 1948

plunder" just waiting "to do a hatchet job on the New Deal." Pollsters applauded Truman's spunk but predicted a sure Dewey victory.

The experts failed to detect a late swing to Truman. A surprised nation awoke the day after the election to learn that the president had won in the biggest upset in U.S. history, 24.1 million votes to Dewey's 22 million. Ironically, the Progressives and Dixiecrats had helped Truman. Their radicalism had kept both moderate liberals and moderate conservatives safely in the Democratic fold. The attorney general of Virginia explained, "The only sane and constructive course to follow is to remain in the house of our fathers—even though the roof leaks, and there be bats in the belfry, rats in the pantry, cockroaches in the kitchen, and skunks in the parlor." Moreover, Dixiecrat defections had freed Truman to campaign as a proponent of civil rights.

In July 1948 Truman had issued executive orders barring discrimination in federal employment and creating a committee to ensure "equality of

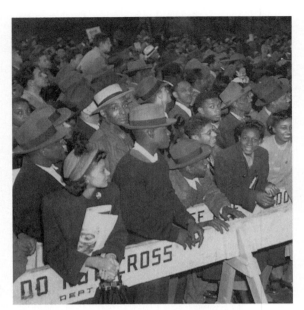

Harlem Residents Greet President Truman
Although stymied by Congress, Truman put forth un-precedented, sweeping civil-rights proposals that brought thousands of African-Americans out to see the president campaign in Harlem on October 29, 1948.

treatment and opportunity for all persons in the armed services without regard to race, color, religion or national origin." Truman had also benefited from two Supreme Court decisions. In 1946 the Court had declared segregation in interstate bus transportation unconstitutional, and in 1948 it had outlawed restrictive housing covenants that forbade the sale or rental of property to minorities. Blacks had taken heart from these changes and had voted accordingly. Truman won a higher percentage of black votes than FDR ever had.

Truman had succeeded in 1948 by re-creating the New Deal coalition. With the crisis in Berlin helping to rally Americans behind their president, he had seized every opportunity to remind farmers and laborers that the Republican "gluttons of privilege" planned to "turn the clock back" and strip away New Deal benefits.

The Fair Deal

Despite his narrow victory margin, Truman saw his election as a mandate for liberalism. In his 1949 State of the Union message, he proposed an ambitious social and economic program, the Fair Deal. He asked Congress to enlarge New Deal programs in economic security, conservation, and housing and to go beyond the New Deal in other areas.

The Eighty-first Congress complied with the extension of existing programs but rejected new measures. Lawmakers raised the minimum wage; increased social-security coverage and benefits; expanded appropriations for public power, conservation, and slum clearance; and authorized the construction of nearly a million low-income housing units. But they rejected federal aid to education, national health insurance, civil-rights legislation, larger farm subsidies, and the repeal of Taft-Hartley.

Congress's rejection of most Fair Deal proposals stemmed from Truman's own lessening commitment to domestic reform in favor of foreign policy, as well as from the strengthening of the congressional conservative coalition. And widespread prosperity sapped public enthusiasm for more reform. The postwar congresses mirrored the sense of well-being that most Americans enjoyed, and reflected the popular apprehensions over communism that doomed liberal hopes for social change.

The Politics of Anticommunism

As the Cold War evolved, some Americans concluded that the roots of the nation's foreign difficulties lay in domestic treason and subversion. How else could the communists have taken China and the Soviets have developed an atomic bomb? Millions of fearful Americans would eventually enlist in a crusade that would find scapegoats for the nation's problems and would equate dissent with disloyalty.

Since 1938 the House Committee on Un-American Activities (later called the House Un-American Activities Committee, HUAC) had served as a platform for conservatives' denunciation of the New Deal as a communist plot. At first only the extreme Right had embraced this viewpoint seriously, but after World War II mounting numbers of Democrats and Republicans climbed aboard the anti-Red bandwagon.

This so-called second Red Scare influenced both governmental and personal actions. Millions of Americans were subjected to loyalty oaths and security investigations after the war. The anticommunist hysteria would destroy the Left, discredit liberalism, and undermine labor militancy. The purge of controversial government officials, furthermore, would ensure foreign-policy rigidity and the postponement of domestic social change.

Loyalty and Security

The Cold War raised legitimate concerns about American security. The Communist party had claimed 80,000 members during World War II, and no one knew how many occupied sensitive government positions. In mid-1945 a raid of the offices of a procommunist magazine revealed that classified documents had been given to the periodical by two State Department employees and a naval intelligence officer. Ten months later, the Canadian government exposed a major spy network that had passed American military information and atomic secrets to the Soviets during the war.

Truman in late 1946 named a commission to study the loyalty problem and in March 1947 issued Executive Order 9835 establishing the Federal Employee Loyalty Program to provide a loyalty check on all government workers. The drive for absolute security soon overran concerns about rights, however, as civil servants suspected of disloyalty were allowed neither to face their accusers nor to require investigators to reveal sources. Instead of focusing on potential subversives in high-risk areas, the probe extended to the associations and beliefs of *every* government worker.

Mere criticism of American foreign policy could result in an accusation of disloyalty. People could lose their jobs if they liked foreign films, associated with radical friends or family members, or

were past members of organizations now declared disloyal. Between 1947 and 1951 loyalty boards forced nearly 3,000 government employees to resign and fired 300 on charges of disloyalty. The probe uncovered no evidence of subversion or espionage, but it did spread fear among government employees. "If communists like apple pie and I do," said one federal worker, "I see no reason why I should stop eating it. But I would."

The Anticommunist Crusade

The pall of conformity cast by Truman's loyalty inquest fed mounting anticommunist hysteria. The very existence of federal investigators promoted fears of communist infiltration and legitimized other efforts to expose subversives. Universities banned controversial speakers, and popular magazines ran articles like "Reds Are After Your Child." Even comic books joined the fray: "Beware, commies, spies, traitors, and foreign agents! Captain America, with all loyal, free men behind him, is looking for you." By the end of Truman's term, thirty-nine states had created loyalty programs, most with virtually no procedural safeguards. Schoolteachers, college professors, and state and city employees throughout the nation signed loyalty oaths or lost their jobs.

In 1947 the House Un-American Activities Committee began hearings to expose communist influence in American life. HUAC's probes blurred distinctions between dissent and disloyalty, between radicalism and subversion. People who refused to answer HUAC questions often lost their livelihoods. HUAC also frightened labor unions into expelling communist members and avoiding progressive causes. Fearing that to champion social justice would make them appear procommunist, unions concentrated on securing better pay and benefits and became bureaucratic special-interest pressure groups.

HUAC also left its mark on the entertainment industry. When certain prominent film directors and screenwriters refused to cooperate in 1947, HUAC had them cited for contempt and sent to federal prison. Blacklists in Hollywood and in radio broadcasting barred the employment of anyone with a slightly questionable past, thereby silencing many talented people.

The 1948 presidential campaign fed national anxieties. Truman ran as America's number-one anticommunist, lambasting Henry Wallace as a Stalinist dupe and accusing the Republicans of being "unwittingly the ally of the communists in this country." In turn, the GOP dubbed the Democrats "the party of treason." A rising Republican star, Richard M. Nixon of California, charged that Democrats bore responsibility for "the unimpeded growth of the communist conspiracy in the United States."

To blunt the force of such accusations, the Justice Department prosecuted eleven top leaders of the American Communist party under the Smith Act of 1940, which outlawed any conspiracy advocating the overthrow of the government. In some cases, U.S. citizens consequently were convicted and jailed, not for anything they had done but only for what they had said. In 1951 the Supreme Court upheld the prison terms and fines by ruling that, despite the First Amendment, Congress could curtail freedom of speech if national security demanded such restrictions.

Ironically, the Communist party was fading into obscurity at the very time that politicians were magnifying the threat it posed. By 1950 its membership had shrunk to less than 30,000. Yet Truman's attorney general warned that American Reds "are everywhere—in factories, offices, butcher stores, on street corners, in private businesses—and each carries in himself the germ of death for society."

Hiss and the Rosenbergs

Nothing set off more alarms about the diabolic Red conspiracy in the federal government than the case of Alger Hiss. Amidst the 1948 presidential campaign, HUAC conducted a sensational hearing in which Whittaker Chambers, a senior editor at *Time* and a former Soviet agent who had broken with the communists in 1938, identified Hiss as an underground party member in the 1930s.

Ethel and Julius Rosenberg
The couple is shown in 1951 leaving the New York City federal court after their arraignment on spy charges.

In the hearing, Chambers appeared a tortured soul crusading to save the West from the Red peril. The elegant and cultured Hiss, in contrast, seemed the very symbol of the liberal establishment; a Harvard Law School graduate, he had clerked for Justice Oliver Wendell Holmes, served as a presidential adviser on foreign affairs (including the Yalta conference), and headed the Carnegie Endowment for International Peace.

Hiss denied any communist affiliation and claimed not to know Chambers. Most liberals believed Hiss. They thought him the victim of conservatives bent on tarnishing New Deal liberalism. Rushing to Hiss's defense, Truman denounced Chambers's allegations as a "red herring" to deflect attention from the failures of the Eightieth Congress.

To those suspicious of the Rooseveltian liberal tradition, Chambers's persistence and Hiss's fumbling retreat intensified fears that the Democratic administration was teeming with communists. Under rigorous questioning by Richard Nixon, Hiss admitted that he had known Chambers, but denied having been a communist. Chambers broadened his accusation, claiming that Hiss had committed espionage in the 1930s by giving him secret State Department documents to be sent to the Soviet Union. Hiss protested his innocence, but a grand jury indicted him for perjury, or lying under oath. In January 1950 Hiss was convicted and received a five-year prison sentence. Emboldened congressional conservatives stalked other Hisses.

Just as the Hiss affair ended, another case shocked Americans. In early February 1950 the British arrested Klaus Fuchs, a German-born scientist involved in the Manhattan Project, for passing atomic secrets to the Soviets. Fuchs's confession led to the arrest of two Americans, Ethel and Julius Rosenberg, as coconspirators. The Rosenbergs insisted that they were victims of anti-Semitism and were being prosecuted for their leftist beliefs. But in March 1951 a jury found them guilty of conspiring to commit espionage, and on June 19, 1953, the husband and wife were executed, although they maintained their innocence to the end. "We are the first victims of American fascism," wrote Ethel Rosenberg shortly before her death.

At this point, some Americans could not separate fact from fantasy. For them, only conspiracy could explain American weakness and Soviet might. Frustrated by their unexpected failure in 1948, Republicans eagerly seized the theory. Doomed to four more years of exile from the White House, the GOP in 1949 abandoned restraint in leveling accusations that "Commiecrats" had sold out America.

McCarthyism

No individual would inflict so many wounds on the Democrats as Republican senator Joseph R. McCarthy of Wisconsin. Desperate for an issue to run on in 1952, McCarthy had noted the success of fellow Republicans who had labeled the Democrats "soft on communism." In February 1950 McCarthy boldly told a West Virginia audience that communists in the State Department had betrayed America. "I have here in my hand a list of 205," McCarthy reported as he waved a laundry list, "a list of names known to the Secretary of State as being members of the Communist party and who nevertheless are still working and shaping policy." Although he could produce no evidence to support his accusations, his senatorial stature and brazen style gave him a national forum. McCarthy soon repeated his charges, though lowering his numbers and reducing his indictment from "card-carrying communists" to "subversives" to "bad risks." A Senate committee found McCarthy's accusations "a fraud and a hoax," but he persisted. *McCarthyism* became synonymous with public charges of disloyalty without sufficient regard for evidence.

As the Korean War dragged on, McCarthy's efforts to "root out the skunks" escalated. He ridiculed Secretary of State Dean Acheson as the "Red Dean" and called Truman's dismissal of MacArthur "the greatest victory the communists have ever won." Buoyed by the partisan usefulness of McCarthy's onslaught, many Republicans encouraged him. McCarthyism especially appealed to midwestern party members indignant about the welfare state, restrictions on business, and the Europe-first emphasis of Truman's foreign policy. For them, anticommunism was a weapon of revenge against liberals and internationalists and a means to regain the controlling position that conservatism had once held. McCarthy also won a devoted following among blue-collar workers. His flag-waving patriotism appealed to traditionally Catholic ethnics, who wanted to gain acceptance as "100 percent Americans" through a show of anticommunist zeal. Countless Americans also shared McCarthy's scorn for privilege and gentility, for the "bright young men who are born with silver spoons in their mouths."

McCarthy's political power had two bases: the Republican establishment, and Democrats fearful of antagonizing him. The GOP support that McCarthy enjoyed made Democrats' condemnation look like mere partisan criticism. In the 1950 elections, when he helped Republicans to defeat Democrats who had denounced him, McCarthy appeared invincible. "Joe will go that extra mile to destroy you," warned the new Senate majority leader, Lyndon B. Johnson of Texas.

Over Truman's veto, Congress in 1950 adopted the McCarran Internal Security Act, which required organizations deemed communist by the attorney general to register with the Department of Justice and to provide membership lists and financial statements. It also barred communists from employment in defense plants, empowered the government to deny passports to communists, and authorized the arrest and detention during a national emergency of "any person as to whom there is reason to believe might engage in acts of espionage or sabotage." The McCarran-Walter Immigration and Nationality Act of 1952, also passed over a presidential veto, reaffirmed the quota system that severely restricted immigration from southern and eastern Europe. It also strengthened the attorney general's authority to exclude or deport aliens suspected of supporting communism.

The Election of 1952

By 1952 public apprehension about the loyalty of government employees combined with frustration over the Korean stalemate to sink Democratic presidential hopes to their lowest level since the 1920s. Both business and labor also resented Truman's freeze on wages and prices during the Korean conflict. In addition, revelations of bribery and influence peddling by some of Truman's old political associates gave Republicans ammunition for charging the Democrats with "plunder at home, and blunder abroad."

When Truman decided not to seek reelection, dispirited Democrats drafted Governor Adlai E. Stevenson of Illinois. But Stevenson could not separate himself from Truman, and his lofty speeches did not stir the average voter. Above all, he could not overcome the sentiment that twenty years of Democratic rule was enough.

The GOP once again bypassed conservative senator Robert A. Taft of Ohio, this time for the hugely popular war hero Dwight D. Eisenhower. Essentially apolitical, Eisenhower had once insisted that "lifelong professional soldiers should abstain from seeking higher political office," but he answered the call of the moderate wing of the Republican party and accepted the nomination. "Ike" chose as his running mate Richard M. Nixon, the former HUAC Red hunter.

Eisenhower and Nixon proved unbeatable. With his captivating grin and unimpeachable record of public service, Eisenhower projected both personal warmth and the vigorous authority associated with military command. His smile, wrote one commentator, "was a smile of infinite reassurance." Indeed, Eisenhower symbolized the stability for which Americans yearned. At the same time, Nixon kept public apprehensions at the boiling point. Accusing the Democrats of treason, he charged that a Democratic victory would bring "more Alger Hisses, more atomic spies."

The GOP ticket stumbled when newspapers revealed the existence of a "slush fund" that

The Election of 1952				
Candidates	Parties	Electoral Vote	Popular Vote	Percentage of Popular Vote
DWIGHT D. EISENHOWER	Republican	442	33,936,234	55.1
Adlai E. Stevenson	Democratic	89	27,314,992	44.4

California business leaders had created to keep Nixon in "financial comfort." But Nixon saved himself with a heart-tugging television defense. He explained the gifts, which included a cocker spaniel named Checkers given to his daughters, as intended to benefit his family. His appeal worked. The Republican ticket won 55 percent of the popular vote, cracked the solid South to carry thirty-nine states, and amassed 442 electoral votes. Enough Republicans rode Ike's coattails to give the GOP control of both houses of Congress by small margins.

Conclusion

The 1952 election closed the early postwar period. In many ways the years immediately following the war had confounded experts. The era had brought prosperity instead of renewed depression. America's costly triumph against fascism had led not to peace but to a new kind of dreadful conflict, the Cold War. Domestically, the era that was to have ushered in tranquillity instead saw bitter partisanship and an ugly mood of suspicion and repression.

This period laid the groundwork for trends that would mold the next half-century of American history. Cold War rhetoric would shape a generation's perception of the world. The anticommunist offensive would strengthen presidential power and fundamentally reorient the federal government. The first stirrings of civil-rights activism and of entanglement in Vietnam foreshadowed issues that would dominate the 1960s.

Among ordinary Americans, although some vaguely realized that the bright promise of August 1945 had slipped away, many looked with hope to their new president and to better times ahead.

Chronology

1945 Truman proposes economic reforms.

1946 Winston Churchill delivers his "iron curtain" speech.
Coal miners' strike.
More than a million GIs enroll in college.
Inflation soars to more than 18 percent.
Republicans win control of Congress.

1947 Truman Doctrine.
Federal Employee Loyalty Program.
Taft-Hartley Act.
Marshall Plan proposed to aid Europe.
President's Committee on Civil Rights issues *To Secure These Rights*.

1948 Communist coup in Czechoslovakia.
State of Israel founded.
Soviet Union blockades Berlin; United States begins airlift.
Congress approves Marshall Plan.
Truman orders an end to segregation in the armed forces.
Communist leaders put on trial under the Smith Act.
Truman elected president.

1949 North Atlantic Treaty Organization (NATO) established.
East and West Germany founded as separate nations.
Communist victory in China.
Soviet Union detonates an atomic bomb.

1950 Truman authorizes building a hydrogen bomb.
Soviet spy ring at Los Alamos uncovered.
Alger Hiss convicted of perjury.
Joseph McCarthy launches anticommunist crusade.

1950   Korean War begins.
Julius and Ethel Rosenberg arrested as atomic spies.
McCarran Internal Security Act.
Truman accepts NSC-68.
China enters the Korean War.

1951   Douglas MacArthur dismissed from his Korean command.
Supreme Court upholds Smith Act.
Rosenbergs convicted of espionage.

1952   First hydrogen bomb exploded.
Dwight D. Eisenhower elected president.

FOR FURTHER READING

John Diggins, *The Proud Decades, 1941–1960* (1989). A wide-ranging survey of U.S. culture and politics.

Richard M. Fried, *Nightmare in Red: The McCarthy Era in Perspective* (1990). A cogent account of McCarthyism's rise and fall.

John L. Gaddis, *The United States and the Cold War* (1992). A probing reexamination of the major issues.

Robert Griffith and Athan Theoharis, eds., *The Specter: Original Essays on the Cold War and the Origins of McCarthyism* (1974). A collection of revisionist interpretations.

Alonzo L. Hamby, *Beyond the New Deal: Harry S. Truman and American Liberalism* (1973). A positive assessment of Truman's efforts to preserve and extend the New Deal.

Melvyn Leffler, *A Preponderance of Power: National Security, the Truman Administration, and the Cold War* (1992). The most comprehensive and incisive history of the Cold War's early stages.

Athan Theoharis and John Stuart Cox, *The Boss: J. Edgar Hoover and the Great American Inquisition* (1988). A biographical analysis highlighting the FBI's role in the Red Scare of the 1950s.

Nostalgia has painted the 1950s as a decade of tranquillity, abundance, easy living, new homes in the suburbs, family togetherness, big cars, and cheap gasoline. Movies and television have captured the fifties as a sunny time when everybody liked Ike and loved Lucy. Teen-agers wore poodle skirts, pedal pushers, and white bucks, danced to "Sh-boom" and "Rock Around the Clock," and idolized Elvis Presley.

Behind these stereotypes lies a reality far more complex, and often far darker. Many Americans did enjoy the fruits of the decade's consumer culture. Having survived a depression and global war, they reveled in prosperity presided over by a popular president. They trusted Dwight D. Eisenhower and welcomed the thaw in the Cold War that came after the Korean War.

At the same time, the fifties saw the birth of the space age, of hydrogen bombs and intercontinental ballistic missiles, and of an automated, computerized industrial society, as well as a continuation of African-Americans' struggle for racial equality. Television transformed life, as did the "baby boom," mass suburbanization, and a remarkable internal

(Right) Family in Levittown, Long Island, 1949

America at Midcentury

The Eisenhower Presidency
The Cold War Continues
The Affluent Society
Consensus and Conservatism
The Other America
Seeds of Disquiet

migration. Mid-century America encompassed peace and a widening Cold War, prosperity and persistent poverty, civil-rights triumphs and rampant racism.

The Eisenhower Presidency

Rarely in U.S. history has a president better fit the national mood than Dwight David Eisenhower. Exhausted by a quarter-century of upheaval—the stock-market crash, the Great Depression, World War II, the Cold War—Americans craved stability and peace. And Eisenhower delivered. Most Americans overwhelmingly approved of his moderate policies. Eisenhower gave people weary of partisanship a sense of unity, and he inspired confidence.

Eisenhower epitomized the virtues and hopes of many Americans. The most distinguished general of World War II, he projected the image of a plain but good man. He expressed complicated issues in simple terms while governing a complex, urban, technological society and comforting an anxious people.

The General as Chief Executive

Dwight Eisenhower, born on October 14, 1890, in Denison, Texas, grew up in Abilene, Kansas, in a poor, strongly religious family. More athletic than studious, he graduated from the U.S. Military Academy at West Point in 1915. In directing the Allied invasion of North Africa in 1942, he revealed himself to be a brilliant war planner and organizer, and in 1944 he became Supreme Commander of Allied Forces on the Western Front. Respected for his managerial ability and talent for conciliation, Ike became a national hero.

Eisenhower's approach to the presidency reflected his wartime leadership style. He concentrated on major matters and worked to reconcile contending factions. His restrained view of presidential authority reflected his belief that FDR had concentrated too much power in his own hands and that Truman had demeaned the dignity of the Oval Office by feuding with Congress. Eisenhower rarely intervened publicly in the legislative process, shunned using his office as a "bully pulpit," and assured his cabinet members that he would "stay out of [their] hair." After establishing a chain of command, he delegated power to subordinates and conferred primarily with his top aides. This low-key style, combined with frequent fishing and golfing vacations, led Democrats to scoff at Eisenhower as a leader who "reigned but did not rule." In truth, Ike battled behind the scenes, his image of passivity masking an active and occasionally ruthless politician.

"Dynamic Conservatism"

Determined to govern the nation on sound business principles, Eisenhower staffed his administration with corporate executives. "Eight millionaires and a plumber," jested one journalist describing the new cabinet. In his first year Eisenhower worked with Congress to reduce farm-price subsidies, to cut the number of government employees, and to slash the federal budget. He also promoted the private development of hydroelectric and nuclear power and won congressional approval of a bill turning over to coastal states oil-rich "tidelands" that the Supreme Court had awarded to the federal government.

The Eisenhower administration followed a centrist course. More pragmatic than ideological, the president wished to reduce government spending and taxes, to contain inflation, and to govern efficiently. Instead of overturning the New Deal, he accommodated large-scale labor organizations and social-welfare policies. Milton Eisenhower, the president's brother and adviser, summed up Ike's views: "We should keep what we have, catch our breath for a while, and improve administration; it does not mean moving backward."

Eager to avoid a depression, Eisenhower relied heavily on the Council of Economic Advisers (CEA), despite conservative calls for its abolition. Arthur Burns, the head of the CEA, advocated a strong government effort to "fine-tune" the

The Election of 1956				
Candidates	Parties	Electoral Vote	Popular Vote	Percentage of Popular Vote
DWIGHT D. EISENHOWER	Republican	457	35,590,472	57.6
Adlai E. Stevenson	Democratic	73	26,022,752	42.1

economy. The president promised to use "any and all weapons in the federal arsenal, including changes in monetary and credit policy, modifications of the tax structure, and a speed-up in the construction of public works" to stimulate economic growth. When recessions struck in 1953 and 1957, Eisenhower abandoned a balanced budget and increased spending to restore prosperity.

Eisenhower labeled his ideas "dynamic conservatism" and "modern Republicanism." He described his approach as "conservative when it comes to money and liberal when it comes to human beings." He supported extending social-security benefits, raising the minimum wage to a dollar an hour, adding 4 million workers to those eligible for unemployment benefits, and providing federally financed public housing for low-income families. He also approved construction of the St. Lawrence Seaway, linking the Great Lakes and the Atlantic Ocean, and creation of the Department of Health, Education, and Welfare. In 1956 Eisenhower backed the largest and most expensive public-works program in American history: the Interstate Highway Act, authorizing construction of a 41,000-mile system of expressways. Freeways would soon snake across America, accelerating suburban growth, heightening dependence on cars and trucks, contributing to urban decay and air pollution, and drastically increasing gasoline consumption.

Republicans renominated Ike by acclamation in 1956, and voters gave him a landslide victory over Democrat Adlai Stevenson. With the GOP crowing "Everything's booming but the guns," the president won 36 million popular votes to Stevenson's 26 million and amassed 457 electoral votes.

The Downfall of Joseph McCarthy

Although he despised Joseph McCarthy, Eisenhower feared confronting the senator. Instead, he allowed McCarthy to grab plenty of rope in hopes that the demagogue would hang himself. In 1953 McCarthy forced the discharge of State Department employees whose views he opposed, although there was no evidence of subversion on their part. His demand that United States Information Agency libraries purge books by "communists, fellow travelers, et cetera" led to the banning and even burning of works by Ralph Waldo Emerson, Henry David Thoreau, and Mark Twain. In 1954 McCarthy accused the army of harboring communist spies, and the army charged McCarthy with using his influence to gain preferential treatment for a staff member who had been drafted.

Congress voted to investigate both charges, and on April 22, 1954, televised Army-McCarthy hearings began. A national audience witnessed McCarthy's boorish behavior. His dark scowl, raspy voice, endless interruptions, and disregard for the rights of others repelled many viewers. In June, when McCarthy smeared the reputation of a young lawyer assisting Joseph Welch, the army counsel, the mild-mannered Welch turned his wrath on McCarthy. "Until this moment, Senator, I think I really never gauged your cruelty or your recklessness. . . . Have you no sense of decency?" The gallery burst into applause.

The spell of the inquisitor broken, the Senate in December 1954 censured the Wisconsin senator for contemptuous behavior. This powerful rebuke demolished McCarthy as a political force.

McCarthy died in 1957, but the fears that he had exploited lingered. Congress continued to fund the House Un-American Activities Committee, and state and local governments continued to require loyalty oaths from teachers. Conservative groups, among them the John Birch Society, and self-proclaimed "new conservatives" such as William F. Buckley, warned that domestic communists posed a major subversive threat. Stressing victory over communism instead of containment, they bemoaned the "creeping socialism" of Eisenhower and Truman, advocated a return to older moral standards, and attacked the Supreme Court.

The Warren Court

Liberalized by the presence of a new chief justice, Earl Warren (1953), the Supreme Court drew conservatives' wrath for defending the rights of those accused of subversive beliefs. In a 1957 decision, the Court held that the accused had the right to inspect government files used by the prosecution, and that same year the justices overturned convictions of Communist party officials under the Smith Act (see Chapter 28). Right-wing opponents plastered "Impeach Earl Warren" posters on highway billboards.

These condemnations paled beside those of segregationists after the landmark *Brown* v. *Board of Education of Topeka* (May 1954) ruling. Unanimously reversing *Plessy* v. *Ferguson* (see Chapter 21), the Court held that separating schoolchildren "solely because of their race generates a feeling of inferiority as to their status in the community that may affect their hearts and minds in a way unlikely ever to be undone." Such segregation thus violated the equal-protection clause of the Fourteenth Amendment. The justices concluded that "separate educational facilities are inherently unequal." A year later, the Court ordered the states to desegregate their schools "with all deliberate speed."

The border states complied, but when white southerners rejected the court's ruling, Eisenhower refused to force them. "I don't believe you can change the hearts of men with laws or decisions," he observed. Although not a racist, he never publicly

endorsed the *Brown* decision, and privately he called his appointment of Earl Warren "the biggest damn fool mistake I ever made."

Encouraged by presidential inaction, southern white opposition stiffened. White Citizens Councils sprang up, and the Ku Klux Klan revived. Declaring the *Brown* decision "null, void, and of no effect," southern legislatures adopted "massive resistance" to thwart compliance with the law. They denied state aid to school systems that desegregated, and closed them down.

In 1955, 100 members of Congress signed the Southern Manifesto, denouncing *Brown* as "a clear abuse of judicial power." White southern politicians competed to "outnigger" each other in demonstrating unyielding opposition to integration. An Alabama candidate promised to go to jail to defend segregation, and his opponent promptly vowed to die for it. Segregationists also used violence and economic reprisals against blacks to maintain all-white schools. At the end of 1956, not a single black attended school with whites in the Deep South, and only a few did so in the Upper South.

The Laws of the Land

Southern resistance reached a climax in September 1957 when Arkansas governor Orval Faubus mobilized the state's National Guard to bar nine African-American students from entering Little Rock's Central High School under a federal court order. After another court order forced Faubus to withdraw the guardsmen, jeering whites blocked the black students' entry.

On national television Eisenhower decried this "disgraceful occurrence" and ordered those obstructing federal law "to disperse forthwith." When the mob defied him, the president federalized the Arkansas National Guard and dispatched federal troops to protect the blacks' rights. To ensure the blacks' safety, troops patrolled the high school for the rest of the year. Rather than accept integration, however, Faubus shut down Little Rock's public high schools for two years. When a federal court ruling reopened them, only three blacks attended

Central High School. As the fifties ended, fewer than 1 percent of African-American students in the Deep South attended integrated schools.

Nonetheless, *Brown* and Little Rock galvanized the federal government's power to mandate changes in the South. And TV broadcasts of events at Little Rock foreshadowed television's vital role in the eventual demise of Jim Crow. A 1957 public-opinion poll showed that 90 percent of whites outside the South approved the use of federal troops in Little Rock.

Most nonsouthern whites also favored legislation to enfranchise southern blacks, and during the 1956 presidential campaign Eisenhower proposed a voting-rights bill. The Civil Rights Act of 1957, the first civil-rights law since Reconstruction, established a permanent commission on civil rights with broad investigatory powers, but it did little to guarantee the ballot to blacks. The Civil Rights Act of 1960 only slightly strengthened the first measure's enforcement powers. Like the *Brown* decision, however, these laws revealed a changing attitude about race on the part of the federal government and encouraged blacks to fight on for their due.

The Cold War Continues

On the international front, the Eisenhower administration maintained Truman's containment policy. Joseph Stalin's death in 1953 and Eisenhower's resolve to reduce the risk of nuclear war did lead to a thaw in the Cold War, but ideological conflict still gripped the United States and the U.S.S.R. The Cold War did not end, nor did American determination to check communism waver.

Truce in Korea

Honoring his campaign pledge, Eisenhower visited Korea in December 1952, but he did not bring home a settlement. The fate of thousands of prisoners of war who did not want to return to communist rule remained the chief sticking point in negotiations. But the uncertainty in the communist world after

Stalin's death, and Eisenhower's veiled threat to use nuclear weapons, broke the stalemate. The armistice signed on July 23, 1953, set the boundary between North and South Korea close to the thirty-eighth parallel (the prewar demarcation line) and established a panel of neutral nations to oversee POW returns.

The end of the fighting relieved many Americans but left Korea divided and its political problems unresolved. Although Eisenhower maintained that the United States had vindicated the principle of collective security by checking aggression, his right-wing critics condemned the truce as peace without honor.

Ike and Dulles

Eager to ease Cold War hostilities, Eisenhower first had to placate the Republican Old Guard, which rejected containment and clamored for forceful efforts to roll back the Red tide. He enlisted the aid of his secretary of state, John Foster Dulles, a stiff, self-righteous anticommunist.

Dulles advocated a holy war against "atheistic communism." He called for "liberation" of the captive peoples of Eastern Europe and the unleashing of Jiang Jieshi against Communist China. Condemning neutralism on the part of other nations as "immoral," he threatened "an agonizing reappraisal" of American commitments if allies did not follow the U.S. lead. Believing that the Soviet Union understood only force, Dulles insisted on the necessity of "brinksmanship," the art of never backing down in a crisis, even if doing so meant risking war.

Such saber rattling pleased the Right, but Eisenhower preferred conciliation. Partly because he feared a nuclear war—the Soviet Union had tested its own hydrogen bomb in 1953—Eisenhower refused to translate Dulles's rhetoric into action. Too, the president understood the limits of American power. When the U.S.S.R. crushed insurrections in East Germany (1953) and Hungary (1956), the United States did not prevent the Soviet intervention. And despite talk of "unleashing" Jiang, a 1954 mutual-defense treaty with Taiwan specifically prohibited the Nationalists from any aggressive ventures without prior consultation with the United States.

Waging Peace

As multimegaton thermonuclear weapons replaced atomic bombs in American and Soviet arsenals, Eisenhower worked to reduce the possibility of mutual extinction. He proposed before the United Nations an "atoms for peace" plan whereby both superpowers would contribute fissionable materials to a new U.N. agency for use in industrial projects. Mounting fears about radioactive fallout from atomic tests, especially 1954 U.S. tests that spread strontium-90 over a wide area, heightened world concern about the nuclear-arms race.

In 1955 Eisenhower and Soviet leaders met in Geneva for the first East-West conference since World War II. Discussions produced no concrete results, but mutual talk of "peaceful coexistence" led reporters to hail the "spirit of Geneva." In March 1958 Moscow suspended atmospheric tests of nuclear weapons, and the United States followed suit.

But the Cold War continued. To "contain" the Soviet Union, the United States encircled it with military bases and alliances. Dulles negotiated mutual-defense pacts with any nation that opposed communism. His "pactomania" committed the United States to the defense of forty-three nations. However, the United States relied primarily on nuclear weapons to deter the Soviets. A "New Look" defense program guaranteed "more bang for the buck" by emphasizing nuclear weapons while cutting back the army and navy. This New Look stressed "massive retaliation" rather than the deployment of U.S. troops to fight "brushfire" wars in remote places—and it spurred the Soviets to seek "more rubble for the ruble" by enlarging their nuclear stockpile.

Meanwhile, the focus of the Cold War shifted from Europe to the Third World, comprising largely nonwhite, developing nations. There the two superpowers waged war by proxy, using local guerrillas and military juntas to battle in isolated deserts and steamy jungles. There, too, the Central Intelligence Agency (CIA) fought covert wars against those thought to imperil American interests.

The Clandestine CIA

To command the CIA, Eisenhower appointed Allen Dulles, a veteran of wartime OSS operations and the brother of the secretary of state. Established in 1947 to conduct espionage and to analyze information on foreign nations, the CIA during the 1950s ranged far beyond its original purpose and carried out undercover operations to topple foreign regimes believed hostile to the United States. In 1953 the agency plotted with Iranian army officers to overthrow a popularly elected government that had taken possession of rich oil resources long exploited by Britain. Fearing a precedent that might jeopardize Western oil interests in the Middle East, the CIA secretly returned the deposed shah of Iran to power and restored the oil wells to British firms. In return, the United States gained a loyal ally on the Soviet border, and American oil companies prospered from Iranian oil concessions. But the seeds of Iranian hatred of America had been sown—an enmity that would haunt the United States a quarter-century later.

In 1953 the CIA intervened in Philippine elections to ensure a pro-American government. In 1954 in Guatemala, it equipped and trained a Guatemalan force to destroy the incumbent regime, which had seized 225,000 acres from the American-owned United Fruit Company. The CIA's Guatemalan agents instituted a military dictatorship subservient to the United States, restored United Fruit's properties, and trampled political opposition, all with the approval of a handful of Washington officials.

In his second term Eisenhower allowed the CIA even greater leeway. By 1957 the agency was devoting half its personnel and 80 percent of its budget to "covert action," subverting governments, bribing foreign politicians, and subsidizing foreign newspapers and labor unions that hewed to a pro-American line. Unwilling to be drawn into long, costly military conflicts, Eisenhower relied on the CIA to help the United States' allies and to weaken its opponents.

Conflict in Vietnam

The most extensive CIA secret operations during the 1950s took place in Indochina (Vietnam). As a result of the Korean War and Mao Zedong's victory in China, the United States viewed Indochina as a Cold War arena. The Truman administration had provided the French, who were trying to reconquer their former colony of Vietnam, large-scale military assistance to fight the Vietminh, a broad-based Vietnamese nationalist coalition led by the communist Ho Chi Minh. By 1954 American aid accounted for 75 percent of French expenditures, but the French were losing. In early 1954 the Vietminh trapped and besieged 12,000 French troops in the valley of Dienbienphu.

France appealed for U.S. intervention, but the president demurred. Unwilling to commit American troops to a jungle war against a popular liberation front, people fighting to free their nation from colonialism, he voiced bitter opposition to American involvement: "I cannot conceive of a greater tragedy for America." On May 7, 1954, the French surrendered at Dienbienphu. In July an international peace conference in Geneva arranged a cease-fire and divided Vietnam at the seventeenth parallel, pending elections in 1956 to choose the government of a unified nation. The United States neither participated in the Geneva negotiations nor signed the final Geneva Accords.

Though opposed to committing the United States to an Asian land war, Eisenhower feared the consequences of a communist victory in Vietnam. If Vietnam fell, he warned, Thailand, Burma, Malaya, Indonesia, and ultimately all of America's Asian allies would follow. Because of his belief in this "domino theory," Eisenhower ignored the Geneva settlement.

In June 1954 the CIA Mission in Vietnam was established to help to install Ngo Dinh Diem, a fiercely anticommunist Catholic, as premier of France's puppet state. In 1955 Diem became president of an independent South Vietnam. CIA agents worked closely with him to train his armed forces and secret police, to eliminate political opposition, and to block the election to reunify Vietnam specified by the Geneva agreements. As Eisenhower later admitted, the United States opposed the election because "possibly 80 percent of the population would have voted for the communist Ho Chi Minh as their leader." Washington pinned its hopes on Diem to maintain a noncommunist South Vietnam.

But the autocratic Diem never rallied public support. His Catholicism alienated the predominantly Buddhist population, and his refusal to institute land reform and to end corruption raised widespread opposition. In 1957 former Vietminh guerrillas began sporadic antigovernment attacks, and in December 1960 opposition to Diem coalesced in the National Liberation Front (NLF). Organized by the Vietminh and backed by North Vietnam, the insurgency attracted broad support. Diem increasingly relied on the billions of dollars and growing corps of advisers that the Eisenhower administration supplied. When Diem spurned their requests for reform to undercut NLF appeal, American officials backed down. Diem had become their only hope in Vietnam.

Anti-Westernism in the Middle East

As troubles simmered in Vietnam, Eisenhower faced his greatest crisis in the Middle East. In 1954 Gamal Abdel Nasser came to power in Egypt. An Arab nationalist, he was determined to modernize Egypt and to buy arms from the Soviet bloc. To woo him, the United States offered financing for a dam at Aswan to harness the Nile River. But when Nasser declared neutrality in the Cold War, John Foster Dulles canceled the loan. In retaliation, on July 26, 1956, Nasser nationalized the foreign-owned Suez Canal, intending to use Suez revenues to finance the dam.

U.S. allies reacted strongly to Nasser's provocation. The British, viewing the canal as the lifeline of the British Empire, were outraged. The French, fearful of Arab nationalism in their Algerian colony, expressed alarm. And the Israelis were threatened by that same Arab nationalism. Tensions between Egypt and Israel peaked when Nasser in 1955 blockaded the Gulf of Aqaba, Israel's only Red Sea outlet. Israel, France, and Britain decided to fight Egypt in hopes of toppling Nasser. On October 29, 1956, war erupted when Israel attacked Egypt; two days later, British and French forces struck.

The Suez crisis infuriated Eisenhower. Not only had the attackers failed to consult him, but Moscow was threatening possible nuclear retaliation. Eisenhower condemned the expedition, at the same time ordering the Strategic Air Command on alert against the U.S.S.R. "If those fellows start something, we may have to hit 'em—and if necessary, with everything in the bucket," he warned. On November 6 Britain, France, and Israel promised to leave Egypt, and by March 1957 the last troops were gone.

The Suez crisis had momentous consequences. First, it intensified anti-Western sentiment in the Third World and enhanced Nasser's status. Second, it resulted in the United States' replacing Britain and France as the protector of Western interests in the Middle East. Anxious to guarantee the flow of oil to the West, the president issued, and Congress approved, the Eisenhower Doctrine, a proclamation that the United States would send military aid and, if necessary, troops to any Middle Eastern nation that asked for help against "international communism."

In July 1958 Eisenhower implemented the doctrine. A nationalist coup in Iraq brought to power an anti-Western regime, and the neighboring pro-Western Lebanese government requested U.S. support. Eisenhower ordered 14,000 marines into Lebanon. The marines soon left, but the United States continued to interpret Arab nationalism as communist inspired.

Frustration Abroad

Such interventions intensified the anti-American feelings of neutralists and nationalists in many small nations. In 1958 angry crowds in Peru and Venezuela spat at Vice President Nixon and stoned his car. In 1959 Fidel Castro overturned a dictatorial regime in Cuba and denounced "Yanqui imperialism." Anti-American riots in Japan in 1960 forced Eisenhower to cancel a trip to the United States' strongest Asian ally.

A tougher blow struck Eisenhower on May 1, 1960, two weeks before a scheduled summit conference with Soviet premier Nikita Khrushchev, when the Soviets shot down a U.S. spy plane 1,200 miles inside their border. Initially, Eisenhower announced that the downed plane was merely a weather reconnaissance aircraft that had strayed off course. An angry Khrushchev responded by displaying the captured CIA pilot, the U-2's spy cameras, and photos taken of Soviet missile sites. Although Eisenhower then admitted the spy mission, he refused to apologize, and the summit collapsed. Eisenhower—for whom defusing Soviet-American tensions had become a priority—dispiritedly told an aide that he "saw nothing worthwhile left for him to do now until the end of his presidency."

The Eisenhower Legacy

Three days before leaving office, Eisenhower offered Americans a farewell and a warning. The demands of national security, he stated, had produced the "conjunction of an immense military establishment and a large arms industry." Swollen Cold War defense budgets had tied American economic health to military expenditures, and military contracts had become a way of life for research scholars, for politicians, and for America's largest corporations. This intertwined combination of interests, Eisenhower believed, exerted enormous leverage and threatened the traditional subordination of the military in American life. He warned, "We must guard against the acquisition of unwarranted influence . . . by the military-industrial complex. The potential for the disastrous rise of misplaced power exists and will persist."

The president concluded by assessing his foreign policy. He admitted that he could not affirm that prolonged peace was in sight. Most scholars agreed. Eisenhower had ended the Korean War, maintained peace for more than seven years, avoided direct intervention in Vietnam, begun relaxing tensions with the Soviet Union, and suspended atmospheric nuclear testing. Yet he had also presided over an accelerating nuclear-arms race and expanded the Cold War; he had allowed the CIA to intervene around the globe; and he had committed U.S. power and prestige in Asia and the Middle East.

A moderate, Eisenhower had prevented crises from escalating into major armed conflicts. Similar balance and restraint had characterized his domestic policies. This middle-of-the-road strategy had pleased neither liberals nor conservatives. Conservatives had grumbled at his acceptance of New Deal social-welfare legislation; liberals had faulted him for passivity in the face of McCarthyism and racism. Nonetheless, Ike had given the majority of Americans what they most wanted—reassurance and a breathing spell in which to relish the comforts of life.

The Affluent Society

In 1958 economist John Kenneth Galbraith published *The Affluent Society*, a study of postwar America. The title reflected the broad-based prosperity that made the 1950s seem the fulfillment of the American dream. By the end of the decade, 60 percent of American families owned homes; 75 percent, cars; and 87 percent, at least one TV. Government spending, a large uptick in productivity, and steadily increasing consumer demand pushed the total gross national product from $318 billion to $488 billion during the decade.

Three brief recessions and a rising national debt, almost $290 billion by 1961, evoked concern but did little to halt economic growth. Indeed, the United States achieved the highest living standard ever during the 1950s. By 1960 the average worker's income, adjusted for inflation, was 35 percent higher than in 1945, and 200 percent higher than in the 1920s. With just 6 percent of the world's population, the United States produced and consumed nearly half of everything made and sold on earth.

The New Industrial Society

Federal spending constituted a major source of economic growth, nearly doubling in the 1950s to $180 billion. The outlays of state and local governments more than kept pace. Federal expenditures, composing just 1 percent of the GNP in 1929, reached 17 percent by the mid-1950s. These funds built roads and airports, financed home mortgages, supported farm prices, and provided stipends for education. But more than *half* the federal budget—10 percent of the GNP—went to defense spending. Continued superpower rivalry in atomic weapons, missile-delivery systems, and the space race kept the federal

General Electric Assembly Line
As Americans in the postwar years satisfied their pent-up demand for household conveniences like these washing machines, their consumption of dwindling natural resources increased dramatically, as did the amount of pollution they produced.

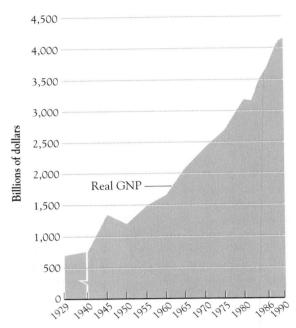

Gross National Product, 1929–1990

Following World War II, the United States achieved the highest living standard in world history. Between 1950 and 1970, the real GNP, which factors out inflation and reveals the actual amount of goods and services produced, steadily increased. However, in 1972, 1974–1975, 1980, and 1982 the real GNP declined.

NOTE: Data shown in 1982 dollars.
SOURCE: *Economic Report of the President, 1991.*

government the nation's chief sponsor of both scientific and technological research and development (R&D).

Breakthroughs in physics, electronics, and chemistry revolutionized industry. Chemicals surged from the fiftieth-largest prewar industry to the fourth-largest industry by 1960. Dacron suits, Orlon shirts, Acrilan socks, Teflon pots and pans, and scores of other synthetic-based goods transformed the nation into a plastic society. Electronics became the fifth-largest American industry, providing industrial equipment and consumer appliances. Electric consumption tripled in the 1950s as industry automated and consumers learned to "live better electrically," as commercials urged. Cheap petroleum fueled expansion in both the chemical and the electronics industries. Domestic oil production and the importation of foreign oil rose steeply; by 1960, oil replaced coal as the nation's main energy source.

Plentiful cheap gasoline fed the growth of the automobile and aircraft industries. Aircraft manufacture, the nation's third-largest industry in the 1950s, depended on massive defense spending, on commercial aviation's switch to jet propulsion, and on space research. The automobile industry, still the nation's largest, spent nearly one-fifth of its budget on R&D, using technology to fire up productivity. Just as machines had earlier replaced human workers in the automotive industry, automation now controlled the machines. Between 1945 and 1960 the number of hours and workers needed to produce a car both fell by 50 percent. Other industries followed, investing $10 billion a year throughout the fifties on labor-saving machinery.

The Age of Computers

The computer was a major key to technological revolution. In 1944 International Business Machines (IBM), cooperating with Harvard scientists, had produced the Mark I calculator, a slow, cumbersome maze of 500 miles of wiring and 3,000 electromechanical relays. Two years later, to improve artillery trajectory, the U.S. Army had developed ENIAC, the first electronic computer. Although still unwieldy, with tens of thousands of vacuum tubes and resistors, ENIAC could multiply two ten-place numbers in less than 3/1,000 of a second, compared to Mark I's three seconds. Then had come the development of operating instructions, or programs; the replacement of wires by printed circuits; and, in 1948, Bell Lab's invention of tiny, solid-state transistors that ended reliance on radio tubes.

Computers fundamentally changed the American economy and society. The federal government became a major client, and computers rose to a billion-dollar business. Computers were as indispensable to Pentagon strategists playing war games as to the Internal Revenue Service, as integral to Weather Bureau meteorologists as to aerospace scientists. By the mid-1960s more than 30,000 mainframe computers would be used by banks, insurance companies, stock brokerages, hospitals, and universities. With computers, fewer workers could produce more goods in less time than ever before.

Concentration and Consolidation in Industry and Agriculture

Rapid technological advances accelerated the growth and power of big business. In 1950 only twenty-two firms had assets of more than $1 billion; by 1960, fifty did. By then, one-half of 1 percent of corporations earned more than half the total corporate income in the United States. Wealthy firms, able to afford huge R&D outlays, swallowed weak competitors and became oligopolies. Three radio and television networks monopolized the nation's airwaves, and three automobile companies produced 90 percent of America's cars; large corporations controlled the lion's share of assets and sales in steel, petroleum, chemicals, and electrical machinery. Corporations formed conglomerates by merging companies in unrelated industries, and they acquired overseas facilities to become "multinational" enterprises.

Growth and consolidation meant greater bureaucratization. "Executives" continued to replace "capitalists"—by the mid-1950s American industry employed more than a quarter-million vice presidents. Divorced from the ownership of the corporations that they ran, professional managers oversaw R&D, production, advertising, sales, accounting, investments, and labor relations. Strong pressures for conformist behavior emerged, rewarding those who gave in to social pressure rather than adhering to personal values. Sociologist David Riesman contrasted managers' "other-directed" behavior—an obsession to fit in and to gain acceptance by following the dictates of a group or organization—

with the "inner-directed" orientation of small businesspeople and professionals of earlier years.

Changes in agriculture paralleled those in industry. Farming grew increasingly scientific and mechanized. Between 1945 and 1960, technology cut the work-hours necessary to grow crops by half. As productivity outpaced demand, prices declined and many farm families migrated to cities. In 1956 alone, one-eleventh of the farm population left the land. Meanwhile, heavily capitalized farm businesses prospered by using new machines and by saturating their acreage with chemical fertilizers, herbicides, and pesticides.

Although some scientists raised cautionary flags, most Americans remained unaware of how synthetic chemicals poisoned the environment until the publication of Rachel Carson's *Silent Spring* in 1962. A former researcher for the Fish and Wildlife Services, Carson demonstrated the problems created by the indiscriminate use of the insecticide DDT and its spread through the food chain. (The "silent spring" of her title referred to the death of robins from DDT toxicity.) States would gradually ban DDT use, and in 1972 the federal government followed suit.

Meanwhile, agribusinesses grew rich from the intensive use of chemicals and from $5 billion in federal farm subsidies. A 1956 soil-conservation program, paying farmers to take cropland out of production, benefited large farm businesses that could afford to allow tens of thousands of acres to lie fallow.

Blue-Collar Blues

Consolidation also transformed the labor movement. In 1955 the AFL and CIO merged, bringing 85 percent of union members into a single unit. Although leaders promised aggressive unionism, the movement's old militancy was gone.

Organized labor had fallen victim to its own success. Benefits hard earned at the bargaining table bred complacency. Higher wages, a workweek under forty hours, paid vacations, health-care coverage, and automatic wage hikes tied to the cost of living led most workers to view themselves as middle class, not an aggrieved proletariat. Labor turbulence quieted.

A decrease in the number of blue-collar workers also sapped labor's momentum. As automation replaced more and more workers in steel, coal, and automobiles, membership in these industries' once-mighty unions dropped by more than half. New jobs in the 1950s were concentrated in the white-collar and service sectors of the economy and in public employment. Organized labor saw its portion of the labor force drop from 36 percent in 1953 to 31 percent in 1960.

Prosperity, Suburbanization, and Mobility

As real income (adjusted for inflation) rose, Americans spent less of their income on necessities. They enthusiastically bought powered lawn mowers, air conditioners, and striped toothpaste and heaped their shopping carts with frozen, dehydrated, and fortified foods. When they lacked cash, they borrowed. In 1950 Diners' Club issued the first credit card, and American Express soon followed. Installment buying, home mortgages, and auto loans raised Americans' private indebtedness in the 1950s from $73 billion to $196 billion. Consumer culture dominated American life, and advertising expenditures nearly tripled.

Americans purchased 58 million new cars during the 1950s. Automobile registrations bounded, as did motor-vehicle miles traveled. Manufacturers enticed people to trade in and up by offering bigger and flashier models, more chrome, two-tone color schemes, tail fins, and more powerful engines, such as Pontiac's 1955 "Sensational Strato-Streak V-8" that could propel riders more than twice as fast as any existing speed limit. Hand in hand with these trends came rises in highway deaths, air pollution, oil consumption, and "autosclerosis"—clogged urban arteries.

Government policy as well as the proliferation of cars spurred white Americans' exodus to the suburbs. Federal spending on highways skyrocketed from $79 million in 1946 to $2.6 billion in 1960.

1957 Chevrolet Bel Air
Advertisements alliteratively described this classic car's automatic transmission as the Triple-Turbine Turbo-Glide.

Once-remote areas came within "commuting distance" for urban workers and became desirable places to live. The tax code further induced suburban home buying by allowing deductions for home-mortgage interest payments and for property taxes. The Federal Housing Administration (FHA) and Veterans Administration (VA) offered low-interest loans.

Eighty-five percent of the 13 million new homes built in the 1950s were in the suburbs. Affordable single-family housing drew many Americans there. Others fled the central cities' crime, grime, and newly urbanized minorities, who were still targets of racial prejudice. Young couples headed for suburbia in quest of communities oriented toward children and education.

Social critics complained about the suburbs' rows of cookie-cutter houses inhabited by bored housewives and harried husbands, but most suburbanites enjoyed their new life-style, tranquil surroundings, and like-minded neighbors. To a nation of immigrants, most from countries where only the elite owned property, taking title to a home of one's own was at the core of the American dream.

Whereas the urban population rose by 10 percent during the 1950s, the number of suburban dwellers nearly *doubled* as 18 million people moved to the suburbs. For the first time in the twentieth century, more Americans owned homes than lived in rented quarters. By 1960 the suburban population equaled that of the central cities, and by 1970 the suburbs contained two-thirds of the metropolitan-area population, and the cities only one-third.

Americans moved not only from city to suburb but also from North to South and from East to West. California's climate and industry lured millions—it would surpass New York as the most populous state in 1963. The Gulf Coast and the Pacific Northwest also attracted millions of Americans. The shift of masses of people from the frosty North and East to the balmy South and West had a major political and economic impact. Drawn to the Sun Belt by low taxes, low energy costs, and right-to-work laws, industrialists transferred not only their plants and corporate headquarters but also their conservative outlooks. By 1980 the population of the Sun Belt, which stretched from the Old Confederacy across Texas to southern California, would exceed that of the North and East. The political power of the Republican party would rise correspondingly.

Twenty years after the Great Depression, America had been transformed. Affluence had replaced financial worry for countless Americans, the suburbs had blossomed, and automation, computers, and new management techniques were modernizing industry at a breakneck pace.

Consensus and Conservatism

Not everyone embraced the fifties' materialism or sank unquestioningly into a deep cushion of contentedness. Disaffected intellectuals found American life shallow and despaired of the United States as a "packaged society" and its people as "all items in a national supermarket—categorized, processed, labeled, priced, and readied for merchandising." Such attacks, however, not only oversimplified reality but ignored social diversity as well as strong currents of dissent swirling beneath the surface. Nonetheless, critics correctly spotlighted the elevation of comfort over challenge, safety over risk, and private pleasures over public affairs. Anxious for a respite from the trials of preceding decades and hungry for security, Americans did indeed seek refuge in the good life.

Togetherness and the "Baby Boom"

In 1954 *McCall's* magazine coined the term *togetherness* to celebrate the ideal couple: the man and woman who married young, had a large family, and centered their lives on home and children. Americans of the 1950s wed at an earlier age than their parents and had more babies sooner. The fertility rate (the number of births per 1,000 women) peaked at 123 in 1957, when an American baby was born every seven seconds.

At the same time, medical science banished childhood diseases. Antibiotics virtually wiped out diphtheria and typhoid fever, while the Salk and Sabin vaccines eliminated polio. The plunge in childhood mortality helped to raise American life expectancy from 65.9 years in 1945 to 70.9 years in 1970. Coupled with the "baby boom," this decline led to a 19 percent population spurt. During the 1950s, a time of negligible immigration, the U.S. population jumped from 151 million to 180 million. By 1960 children under fourteen constituted one-third of the population.

The sheer size of the baby-boom generation guaranteed its importance, first as the Vietnam Generation and then as the Me Generation. The baby boom helped to fuel the economic boom and to expand the nation's educational system. It made child rearing a foremost concern and reinforced the idea that women's place was in the home. With Americans convinced of the psychological potency of early childhood experiences, motherhood became an increasingly vital, demanding calling.

No one did more to emphasize the presumed link between full-time mothers and healthy children than Dr. Benjamin Spock; only the Bible outsold his *Baby and Child Care* (1946) in the fifties. Spock urged mothers to create an atmosphere of warmth and intimacy for their children. Crying babies were to be comforted, breast-feeding came back into vogue, and specially designed slings allowed babies to be carried close to the heart. At best, Spock's advice meant less spanking and more "democratic" family discussions; at worst, it produced a "filiarchy" in which children's needs predominated. Spock even suggested that the government pay mothers so that they would not have to work outside the house.

Domesticity

"No job is more exacting, more necessary, or more rewarding than that of housewife and mother," a female writer proclaimed in a 1950 *Atlantic* article, and countless others agreed. Popular culture glorified marriage and parenthood, painting a woman's devotion to life in the home with her children as the most cherished goal. Television almost always pictured mother at home. Hollywood perpetuated the stereotype of career women as neurotic and of mothers and wives as happy. As Debbie Reynolds declared in *The Tender Trap* (1955), "A woman isn't a woman until she's been married and had children."

The educational system reinforced these ideas. Alongside academic subjects, girls studied typing, etiquette, and cooking. Guidance counselors cautioned young women not to miss out on marriage by pursuing higher education. "Men are not interested in college degrees, but in the warmth and humanness of the girls they marry," stressed a textbook on family living. In the 1950s women constituted a smaller percentage of college students than in the 1920s or 1930s. Only one-third of college women completed their degrees, and except at the most prestigious colleges these degrees were concentrated in such fields as home economics and primary education.

However, profound changes were under way. Despite the wave of layoffs of women workers when World War II ended, women had quickly returned to the work force. By 1960 nearly 40 percent of American women held full- or part-time jobs; 40 percent of working women had school-age children.

Most women worked to augment family income, not to challenge stereotypes, and took low-paying, low-prestige jobs. Organized feminism ebbed to its lowest point of the century during the fifties. Most women responded to prosperity and atomic jitters by concentrating on private satisfactions and by trying to make the home a haven in an uncertain world.

Religion and Education

The quest for security also stimulated renewed interest in religion. "Today in the U.S.," *Time* claimed in 1954, "the Christian faith is back in the center of things." Religious popularizers—fiery evangelist Billy Graham, riveting Roman Catholic bishop Fulton J. Sheen, and "positive-thinking" Protestant minister Norman Vincent Peale—had syndicated newspaper columns, best-selling books, and radio and television programs. Hollywood religious extravaganzas such as *The Robe* (1953) and *The Ten Commandments* (1956) became box-office hits, and TV commercials pronounced that "the family that prays together stays together."

Dial-a-Prayer offered telephone solutions for spiritual problems. Congress added "under God" to the Pledge of Allegiance and made "IN GOD WE TRUST" mandatory on all U.S. currency. Church attendance swelled from 64.5 million (48 percent of the population) in 1940 to 110 million (63 percent) in 1958.

Although millions embraced evangelical fundamentalism and became "born-again" Christians—a trend that would escalate—most Americans turned to religion mainly for reassurance in an anxious age. President Eisenhower declared, "Everybody should have a religious faith, and I don't care what it is." Despite the aura of religiosity in the fifties, the *intensity* of faith diminished for many people as mainstream churches downplayed sin and evil and preached Americanism and fellowship.

Similarly, education flourished in the 1950s, but seemed intellectually shallower than in prior decades. The baby boom inflated primary-school enrollment by 10 million. California opened a new school about every seven days throughout the decade and still faced a classroom shortage. The proportion of college-age Americans climbed from 15 percent in 1940 to more than 40 percent by the early 1960s. At every level, disciples of John Dewey promoted sociability and self-expression over science, math, and history. As community needs superseded intellectual rigor, the "well-rounded" student became more prized than the highly skilled or knowledgeable pupil.

Surveys of college students found them conservative, conformist, and careerist, a "silent generation" primarily seeking security and comfort. Business majors swamped majors in all other fields. Students' attitudes closely mirrored those of their elders in this decade of affluence and antiradicalism.

Affirmation and Anxiety: The Culture of the Fifties

American culture reflected the expansive spirit of a prosperous era and an undercurrent of discontent. With increasing leisure and fatter paychecks, Americans spent one-seventh of the GNP in 1950 on entertainment. Spectator sports boomed, new symphony halls opened, and books sales doubled in the 1950s.

In fiction, themes of doubt and alienation prevailed. Introspection and highly personal yearnings pervaded the era's novels, in contrast to the realism and political engagement that characterized fiction of the 1930s. Novels such as John Cheever's *The Wapshot Chronicles* (1957) and John Updike's *Rabbit Run* (1960) presented characters vaguely dissatisfied with jobs and home, longing for a more vital and authentic existence. Updike's "Rabbit" Angstrom finds his alcoholic wife and his job as demonstrator of the "MagiPeel" kitchen implement frustrating, especially compared to his glory days as a high-school basketball hero. J. D. Salinger's popular *The Catcher in the Rye* (1951) offered an adolescent version of the alienated, ineffectual protagonist. Young Holden Caulfield, expelled from prep school, is repelled by the "phoniness" of the adult world and considers a break for freedom. But he returns home, suffers a nervous collapse, and retreats into imagined heroism.

Southern, African-American, and Jewish-American writers turned out the decade's most vital fiction. William Faulkner continued his dense saga of a family in Yoknapatawpha County, Mississippi, in *The Town* (1957) and *The Mansion* (1960), while Eudora Welty evoked small-town Mississippi life in *The Ponder Heart* (1954). The black experience found memorable expression in James Baldwin's *Go Tell It on the Mountain* (1953), Lorraine Hansberry's *A Raisin in the Sun* (1959), and Ralph Ellison's *Invisible Man* (1951). Bernard Malamud's *The Assistant* (1957) depicted the Jewish immigrant world of New York's Lower East Side; Philip Roth's *Goodbye Columbus* (1959) wittily dissected the world of upwardly mobile Jews.

Hollywood reflected the diminished concern with social issues, churning out westerns, musicals, and costume spectacles. Movies about the 1950s portrayed Americans as one big, happy, white, middle-class family, exalting material success and romantic love. Career women were largely replaced by "dumb blondes," cute helpmates, and child-women. But as TV viewing soared, movie attendance plummeted by 50 percent and a fifth of the nation's theaters became bowling alleys and supermarkets.

The Message of the Medium

No cultural medium ever grew so huge so quickly, or so thoroughly reinforced the public mood, as American television in the 1950s. In 1946 several thousand households had TV sets; by 1950, 5 million did. By the early 1960s, 90 percent of all households owned at least one TV.

Business capitalized on the phenomenon. *TV Guide* soon outsold all other periodicals; by 1960, fifty-three separate editions went out to 7 million subscribers. First marketed in 1954, the TV dinner changed the nation's eating habits. By the mid-fifties the three major networks *each* had larger advertising revenues than any other communications medium in the world.

Early television showcased talent and creativity. High-quality shows appeared in prime time, including opera, documentaries such as Edward R. Murrow's "See It Now," and critically acclaimed original dramas on "Playhouse 90" and "Studio One." However, networks' drive for profits and McCarthy-era anxieties soon stunted innovation and transformed television into a cautious celebrator of conformity and consumerism. Corporations spent fortunes hawking their products—by 1960 they spent $2 billion on TV advertising—and networks competed for large audiences by appealing to the lowest common denominator of taste. Radio comedian Fred Allen observed, "They call television a medium because it's rare when it is well done."

Decrying TV's mediocrity in 1961, the head of the Federal Communications Commission dared broadcasters to watch their own shows for a day: "I can assure you that you will observe a vast wasteland." TV portrayed women as either zany madcaps ("I Love Lucy," "My Friend Irma") or saccharine-sweet housewives ("The Donna Reed Show," "Ozzie and Harriet"). "Father Knows Best," "Make Room for Daddy," and other popular programs celebrated the family's paternal protector and ignored the complexities of modern family life. An ongoing pageant of police dramas and westerns affirmed the value of violence in overcoming evil. Millions of children watched Howdy Doody, the Mouseketeers, and children's programs featuring mayhem and gunplay with equal enthusiasm.

Measuring television's impact on America is difficult. TV certainly nurtured consumerism and conformity. At best, it offered little to improve people; at worst, it reinforced racial and gender stereotypes and encouraged passivity. Television also profoundly influenced politics, elevating image over substance. Richard Nixon's televised "Checkers" speech in 1952 saved his political career. In 1960 John F. Kennedy's "telegenic" image would help him to win the presidency. And at another political level, TV's portrayal of contented citizens both reinforced complacency and obscured the existence of "the other America."

The Other America

"I am an invisible man," declared the African-American narrator of Ralph Ellison's *Invisible Man*; "I am invisible . . . because people refuse to see me." Indeed, few white middle-class Americans of the fifties perceived the extent of social inequality in the United States. Most ignored racism and never realized the pervasiveness of deprivation. "White flight" from cities to suburbs physically separated races and classes, while expressways walled off middle-class motorists from decaying urban ghettos and pockets of rural poverty. Popular culture focused on affluent Americans enjoying the "good life" and depicted minorities as servants, criminals, or figures of fun.

In the consensus of the Eisenhower era, many Americans believed that the nation had eliminated inequality. Historian Arthur Schlesinger observed: "The central problems of our times are no longer problems of want and poverty."

Poverty and Urban Blight

Economic realities belied such optimistic conclusions. In 1960 some 35 million Americans, one-fifth of the nation, fell below the "poverty line" (then defined as a family of four with a yearly income of less than $3,000) and remained victims of malnutrition, disease, and squalor. A Senate report in 1960 found that at least half of Americans sixty-five or older "cannot afford decent housing, proper nutrition, adequate medical care, or necessary recreation." Eight million of the aged had yearly incomes below $1,000, and a majority lacked medical and hospital insurance.

A third of the poor lived in depressed rural areas. The most abject poverty appeared among migrant farm workers. Observing a Texas migratory-labor camp in 1955, a journalist reported that 96 percent of the children had had no milk in the previous six months; eight out of ten adults had eaten no meat; and most slept "on the ground, in a cave, under a tree, or in a chicken house." In California's Imperial Valley, the infant death rate among migrant workers was more than seven times the statewide average.

The bulk of the poor huddled in decaying inner-city slums. Displaced deep South blacks and Appalachian whites, Native Americans forced off reservations, Puerto Ricans, and Mexican migrants strained cities' already inadequate schools and housing. Nearly 200,000 Mexican-Americans herded

The Other America
The quality of life for citizens like these poor white children and the black North Carolina grandmother substantiated Michael Harrington's claim that too much had been made of American affluence in the 1950s.

into San Antonio's Westside barrio; a local newspaper described them as living like cattle in a stockyard, "with roofed-over corrals for homes and chutes for streets." Trapped in a cycle of want and poverty, children of the poor started school at a disadvantage and rapidly fell behind; many dropped out. Living with neither hope nor skills, they bequeathed a similar legacy to their children.

Incubators of poverty, many cities became social-service wastelands. Affluent residents and business moved to the suburbs as the poor flooded in. City governments, their tax bases shrinking, watched helplessly as antiquated schools and mass-transit facilities deteriorated.

The pressing need for low-cost housing went unanswered. Slum-clearance and urban-renewal projects shunted the poor from one ghetto to another to make room for parking garages and cultural centers. The Los Angeles barrio of Chavez Ravine was bulldozed to permit the construction of Dodger Stadium. Landlords, realtors, and bankers deliberately excluded nonwhites from decent housing. Half of the housing in New York's heavily black Harlem predated 1900. There, a dozen people might share a tiny apartment with broken windows, faulty plumbing, and gaping holes in the walls. Harlem's rates of illegitimacy, infant deaths, narcotics use, and crime towered above city and national averages. "Where flies and maggots breed . . . where rats bite helpless children," a black social psychologist observed, "the conditions of life are brutal and inhumane."

Blacks' Struggle for Justice

The collision between the hopes raised by the 1954 *Brown* decision and the indignities of persistent discrimination and segregation sparked a new phase in the civil-rights movement. To sweep away the separate but rarely equal facilities of Jim Crow, African-Americans developed new tactics, founded new organizations, and followed new leaders. They also devised direct-action confrontations with local power structures, both to engage large numbers of African-Americans in their own freedom fight and to arouse white America's conscience.

Racism touched even the smallest details of daily life. In Montgomery, Alabama, black bus riders had to surrender their seats so that no white rider would stand. Although the city's blacks represented more than three-fourths of all passengers, they had to pay their fare at the front of the bus, leave and reenter through the back door, and sit only in the rear. In December 1955, when Rosa Parks, a strong-willed black woman, refused to get up so that a white man could sit, she was arrested. Montgomery's black leaders organized a massive boycott. "There comes a time when people get tired, tired of being segregated and humiliated, tired of being kicked about by the brutal feet of oppression," declared Martin Luther King, Jr., an eloquent twenty-seven-year-old minister who articulated the anger of Montgomery blacks. The time had come, he continued, to stop being patient "with anything less than freedom and justice." With this speech began what would be a year-long bus boycott by 50,000 black Montgomerians.

Both sides dug in for a protracted battle. African-Americans walked to work or organized car pools. Whites tried to crush the boycott by intimidation, but blacks stayed off the buses—and gained self-respect. "My soul has been tired for a long time," an old woman said; "now my feet are tired, and my soul is resting."

When city leaders refused blacks' repeated requests for first-come, first-served seating, with blacks in the rear and whites in the front, blacks filed suit, challenging bus segregation. In November 1956 the Supreme Court affirmed a lower-court decision outlawing such segregation. Thirteen months after the boycott had begun, African-Americans finally boarded unsegregated buses in Montgomery.

The bus boycott demonstrated black strength and determination. It shattered the myth that blacks liked segregation and that only outside agitators fought Jim Crow. It affirmed for blacks everywhere the possibility of social change. And it gave the nation a persuasive African-American leader, Dr. King, whose oratory simultaneously inspired black political activism and touched white consciences.

King's philosophy of civil disobedience fused the spirit of evangelical Christianity with the strategy of nonviolent resistance. His emphasis on direct action gave every African-American an opportunity for activism; and his insistence on nonviolence diminished the threat of bloodshed. Preaching that they must lay their bodies on the line to provoke crises that would force whites to confront their racism, he urged his followers to love their enemies. In this way, he believed, blacks would convert their oppressors and build a community of true brotherhood. In 1957 King and a network of black ministers formed the Southern Christian Leadership Conference (SCLC) to direct this new campaign against Jim Crow.

The Hispanic-American and Native American Predicament

Meanwhile, Mexican-Americans and Native Americans made little headway in ending discrimination against them. The newest minority group, Puerto Ricans (who are U.S. citizens), reached nearly a million by 1960. Crowded mainly into New York's East Harlem, they suffered from inadequate schools, sanitation services, and police protection and were denied access to middle-class jobs. Like countless earlier immigrants, they gained personal freedom in the United States while losing the security of a strong cultural tradition.

Family frictions flared in the transition from Puerto Rican to American ways. Parents felt upstaged by children who learned English and who obtained jobs that were closed to themselves. As Puerto Rican women found readier access to employment than men did, relations between husbands and wives changed, often becoming strained. Many Puerto Ricans who tried to embrace American ways encountered prejudice because of their skin color and Spanish language.

Mexican-Americans suffered the same indignities. Most of them were also underpaid, cheated and discriminated against, forced to attend segregated schools, and excluded from mainstream American life. The presence of countless "undocumented aliens" compounded their difficulties.

After World War II, the advent of new irrigation systems had added 7.5 million acres to the agricultural lands of the Southwest and stimulated demand for cheap Mexican labor. To stem the influx of illegal Mexican aliens, often called *mojados* or "wetbacks" because many had swum across the Rio Grande to reach the United States, the Eisenhower administration shipped more than 3 million allegedly illegal aliens back across the border. Periodic roundups, however, proved no substitution for a sound labor policy or an effective enforcement strategy, and millions of Mexicans continued to cross the poorly guarded border. Employers meanwhile persisted in exploiting Mexican-American citizens. Often arrested and detained while walking the streets, Mexican-Americans had to prove their legal right to be in the United States. Such civil-rights violations reinforced Mexican-Americans' mistrust of the government and intensified their alienation from Anglo society.

One-third of Mexican-Americans remained below the poverty line in the 1950s. The millions of *mojados* who escaped deportation contributed to the depression of wages for Chicanos in general, as did the continuation of the *bracero* program, which brought in nearly a half-million temporary Mexican agricultural workers a year. Whereas the newest arrivals worked in the fields, most Chicanos moved to urban *colonias* during the 1950s. By 1960 more than half a million Mexican-Americans resided in the Los Angeles metropolitan area. Denver, El Paso, Phoenix, and San Antonio also had large *colonias*.

Native Americans remained the poorest, most-ignored minority. Between 1900 and 1930 they had lost more than half their land. In 1953, pressured by agricultural, timber, and mining interests that coveted Indian lands, Congress adopted House Concurrent Resolution 108, which ended the Indians' status as wards of the United States, granted them citizenship, and called for the liquidation of the reservation system and the termination of special federal services to tribes. For the Menominees of Wisconsin and the Klamaths of Oregon, who owned valuable timberlands, the policy was disastrous. Further impoverishing the tribes, it transferred more than 500,000 acres of Native American lands to non-Indians. The federal Voluntary Relocation Program, designed to lure Indians off the reservations, provided Native Americans with moving costs, assistance in finding housing and jobs, and living expenses until they obtained work.

By 1960 more than 60,000 Indians had left their reservations. Some became middle class; some ended up in run-down urban shantytowns; and nearly a third eventually returned to their tribes. Their protests against termination and relocation ignored, Native Americans remained the most invisible of America's "invisible" men and women.

Seeds of Disquiet

For most white Americans, the Eisenhower years were a tranquil time. However, by the late 1950s, apprehensions rippled across the placid surface of life. Academic leaders spotlighted the shortcomings of American society. Harvard University's president warned that the United States was "adrift with little sense of purposeful direction, lacking deeply held conviction, wandering along with no more stirring thought in the minds of the people than the desire for diversion, personal comfort, and safety."

Periodic recessions, rising unemployment, and the ballooning national debt contributed to the uneasiness. Third World anticolonialism, especially Fidel Castro's takeover of Cuba, diminished Americans' sense of national pride and power. And adding to the disquiet were the growing alienation of American youth and a technological breakthrough by the Soviet Union.

Sputnik

On October 4, 1957, the Soviet Union launched the first artificial earth satellite, *Sputnik* ("Little

Traveler"). Weighing 184 pounds and only twenty-two inches in diameter, it circled the earth at 18,000 miles per hour. When *Sputnik II* went into a more distant orbit on November 3, critics indignantly said that Eisenhower had allowed a "technological Pearl Harbor." Democrats warned of a "missile gap" between the United States and the U.S.S.R.

Initially, the Eisenhower administration disparaged the Soviet achievement, quipping that the United States had no interest in an "outer-space basketball game." But behind the scenes, Eisenhower pushed to have the American Vanguard missile readied to launch a satellite. On December 6, with millions watching by TV, Vanguard rose six feet into the air and exploded. Newspapers mockingly wrote of America's "Flopnik."

The humor masked deep consternation. In 1958 Eisenhower doubled funding for missile development, and in 1959 he raised it to $5.3 billion. He also established the Science Advisory Committee, whose recommendations led to creation of the National Aeronautics and Space Administration (NASA) in July 1958. By decade's end, the United States had launched several space probes and successfully tested the Atlas intercontinental ballistic missile.

Sputnik also set off a feverish effort to reshape American education. Critics pointed out that the Soviet Union produced twice as many scientists and engineers as the United States and complained that Americans honored football stars more than outstanding students. Progressive education fell into disrepute. Americans embarked on a crash program to raise educational standards. Federal funding built new classrooms and laboratories, raised teachers' salaries, and installed instructional television systems in schools. In 1958 Congress passed the National Defense Education Act, which provided loans to college students and funds for teacher training and for the development of new instructional materials in science, mathematics, and foreign languages.

America now banked on higher education to ensure national security. The number of college students skyrocketed from 1.5 million in 1940 to 3.6 million by 1960. That year, the government funneled $1.5 billion to universities, a hundredfold increase over 1940.

Linked directly to the Cold War, this hike in educational spending raised unsettling questions. By 1960 nearly a third of scientists and engineers on university faculties worked full-time on government research, primarily defense projects. Some observers feared that a military-industrial-*educational* complex was emerging.

A Rebellion of Youth

The fifties also bred cultural restiveness and a search for self-definition among adolescents. Few adults considered the implications of widespread affluence or the consequences of having a generation of teenagers who could stay in school instead of working. Few thought about the effects of growing up in an age when traditional values such as thrift and self-denial seemed of declining relevance. And despite talk of togetherness, fathers were often too busy to give their children much attention, and mothers sometimes seemed to spend more time chauffeuring adolescents than listening to them. Much of what adults knew about teen mores they learned from Hollywood and the mass media, which focused on the sensational and the superficial.

Accounts of juvenile delinquency abounded. News stories painted high schools as war zones, streets as jungles ruled by gangs, and teenagers as gun-carrying hoodlums. In truth, the delinquency rate remained steady. Nonetheless, teenagers who sported tightly pegged pants, bandied street slang, and slicked their hair into "ducktails" aroused adult alarm and disapproval.

Equally dismaying to parents, young Americans embraced rock-and-roll. In 1952 Alan Freed, the former host of a classical-music program on a Cleveland radio station, started a new program, "Moondog's Rock and Roll Party," after observing teenagers dancing to and enthusiastically buying rhythm-and-blues records, traditionally recorded by and for blacks. The show caught on, and in 1954 Freed moved it to New York and made rock-and-roll a national craze.

White performers transformed black rhythm-and-blues, with its heavy beat and suggestive lyrics, into "Top Ten" rock-and-roll. In 1954 Bill Haley and the Comets dropped some of the sexual allusions from Joe Turner's version of "Shake, Rattle, and Roll," added country-and-western guitar riffs, and produced the first major rock-and-roll hit. In the mid-fifties, too, Mississippi-born Elvis Presley swaggered onto the rock music scene. From January 1956, with the release of "Heartbreak Hotel," to March 1958, when he was drafted, Elvis produced fourteen consecutive million-selling records. Girls screamed at his voice and swooned at his pouty-surly expression; boys wore their hair long and greasy in imitation of their idol.

Melding the pentecostal music of his boyhood with the hillbilly boogie that he heard on "Grand Ole Opry" radio shows, Presley possessed a raw energy and strutting sexuality that shocked middle-class white adults. But the more adults condemned Presley and other rock-and-roll stars, the more teenagers loved them. Record sales tripled from 1954 to 1960, and Dick Clark's "American Bandstand" became the decade's biggest TV hit.

Portents of Change

Nonconformist writers known as the Beats expressed a more fundamental revolt against middle-class society. In Allen Ginsberg's *Howl* (1956) and Jack Kerouac's *On the Road* (1957), the Beats scorned materialism and "square" America. Kerouac scoffed at the "rows of well-to-do houses with lawns and television sets in each living room with everybody looking at the same thing and thinking the same thing at the same time." Romanticizing society's outcasts, the Beats glorified uninhibited sexuality, spontaneity, and spirituality.

The educated college-age youth who were among the Beats' greatest admirers rejected the era's complacency and caution. They protested the ongoing HUAC investigations, decried the nuclear-arms race, and, in 1958 and 1959, staged Youth Marches for Integrated Schools. Together with the Beats and rock-and-roll, this vocal minority of the "silent generation" heralded the youth movement that would explode in the 1960s.

Conclusion

The disquiet of the late fifties underlined the paradox of midcentury America. The United States, mightier than any nation in history, basked in prosperity. At the same time, Americans felt uneasiness as the arms race heated up and as booming times brought unsettling social change.

Most Americans applauded President Eisenhower's moderation while ignoring his warnings about the military-industrial complex. They also closed their eyes to the persistent poverty within society and to the concentration of power in the economy. White middle-class Americans looked forward to continued affluence and peace. Indeed, few who followed the presidential campaign of 1960, in which the two major-party candidates promised to outdo each other in expanding prosperity and containing communism, imagined that Americans would soon be waging a war against poverty and a land war in Asia. Even fewer anticipated that the rock-and-roll generation would help to topple white supremacy, to challenge their elders' most-cherished values, and to usher in an era of confrontation.

Chronology

1944 Mark I calculator begins operation.

1946 Dr. Benjamin Spock, *Baby and Child Care*.
ENIAC, the first electronic computer, begins operation.

1947 Levittown, New York, development started.

1948 Bell Labs develops the transistor.

1950 Asociación Nacional México-Americana established.

1952 Dwight D. Eisenhower elected president.

1953 Korean War truce signed.
CIA-supported coup in Iran.
Earl Warren appointed U.S. chief justice.

1954 Army-McCarthy hearings.
Brown v. Board of Education of Topeka.
Fall of Dienbienphu; Geneva Conference.
CIA intervention in Guatemala.

1955 Salk polio vaccine developed.
AFL-CIO merger.
First postwar U.S.-Soviet summit meeting.
Montgomery bus boycott begins.

1956 Interstate Highway Act.
Suez crisis.
Soviet intervention in Poland and Hungary.
Allen Ginsberg, *Howl*.
Eisenhower reelected.

1957 Eisenhower Doctrine announced.
Civil Rights Act (first since Reconstruction).
Jack Kerouac, *On the Road*.
Little Rock school-desegregation crisis.
Soviet Union launches *Sputnik*.
Peak of "baby boom" (4.3 million births).

1958 U.S. troops sent to Lebanon.
National Defense Education Act.
United States and Soviet Union halt atomic tests.
National Aeronautics and Space Administration (NASA) founded.

1959 Fidel Castro comes to power in Cuba.
Khrushchev and Eisenhower meet at Camp David.

1960 National Liberation Front of South Vietnam (NLF) established.
U-2 incident.
Second Civil Rights Act.

1962 Rachel Carson, *Silent Spring*.

FOR FURTHER READING

Robert F. Burk, *Dwight D. Eisenhower* (1986). A balanced, analytical overview.

William H. Chafe, *The American Woman: Her Changing Social, Economic, and Political Roles, 1920–1970*, rev. ed. (1988). An incisive examination of discrimination against women and their efforts to overcome it.

David Garrow, *Bearing the Cross* (1986). A provocative, richly detailed biography of Martin Luther King, Jr.

Kenneth Jackson, *Crabgrass Frontier: The Suburbanization of the United States* (1985). An indispensable social history of suburban growth.

Jacqueline Jones, *The Dispossessed: America's Underclasses from the Civil War to the Present* (1992). A thorough analysis of the roots of modern poverty.

Walter A. McDougall, . . . *The Heavens and the Earth: A Political History of the Space Age* (1985). A probing investigation of the diplomatic and political factors affecting the space program.

Elaine Tyler May, *Homeward Bound: American Families in the Cold War Era* (1988). A social history of how the Cold War influenced gender roles, marriage, parenting, and family life.

Gary W. Reichard, *Politics as Usual* (1988). An incisive analysis of U.S. politics at midcentury.

The Turbulent Sixties

The complacency that characterized the 1950s was waning as the 1960s began. On February 1, 1960, four African-American students at North Carolina Agricultural and Technical College sat down at the lunch counter at the local Woolworth's and asked for coffee and doughnuts. When the waitress announced, "We don't serve colored here," the students remained seated, staying until the store closed. By the end of the week, hundreds of students had joined the sit-in. By April 1960 sit-ins had spread to 78 southern communities, and by September 1961 some 70,000 black students had targeted segregated restaurants, churches, beaches, libraries, and movie theaters.

The Greensboro "coffee party" was only one part of a sweeping series of changes stirring. Even as African-Americans throughout the nation were greeting the students' activism with hope and pride, other voices of protest were puncturing the apathy and self-satisfaction of the fifties. Socialist Michael Harrington was investigating the plight of the poor, Harvard Law School graduate Ralph Nader was sounding the alarm that many

(Right) Indian on Alcatraz Island, 1969

The New Frontier, 1960–1963
New Frontiers Abroad, 1960–1963
The Great Society
The Changing Struggle for Equality, 1964–1968
The Last Crusade in Vietnam, 1964–1968

American automobiles were "unsafe at any speed," and mother and writer Betty Friedan was working on what would be a pathbreaking critique of sexism, *The Feminine Mystique* (1963).

These endeavors symbolized a spirit of new beginnings. Impatience and idealism, especially among the young, would lead many young Americans to embrace John F. Kennedy's New Frontier and to rally behind Lyndon Johnson's Great Society. Both administrations' rhetorical emphasis on social change would generate fervent hopes and lofty expectations. But the assassinations of cherished leaders, ongoing racial strife, and a deepening quagmire in Vietnam would dampen optimism, and a reaction by the majority who opposed radical change would curtail reform. A decade that began with bright promise would end in discord and disillusionment.

The New Frontier, 1960–1963

Projecting an image of vigor and boldly proposing new approaches to old problems, John F. Kennedy personified the energy and self-confidence of American youth. His wealthy father, Joseph P. Kennedy, had held a series of appointive posts under Franklin D. Roosevelt. Joe Kennedy seethed with ambition, an ambition that he passed on to his sons, driving them to excel. Despite a severe back injury, John Kennedy had served in the navy during World War II. The elder Kennedy had arranged for a journalist to rework the Harvard-educated John's senior thesis into a book, *Why England Slept,* and persuaded a popular novelist to write articles lauding his heroism in rescuing his crew after their PT boat had been sunk in the South Pacific.

Esteemed as war hero and scholar, John Kennedy used his charm and his father's connections to win election in 1946 to the House of Representatives from a Boston district where he had never lived. Although Kennedy earned little distinction in Congress, Massachusetts voters sent him to the Senate in 1952 and overwhelmingly reelected him in 1958. By then he had a beautiful wife, Jacqueline, and a Pulitzer Prize for *Profiles in Courage* (1956), written largely by a staff member.

Despite the obstacle of his Roman Catholic faith, the popular Kennedy won a first-ballot victory at the 1960 Democratic convention, where, just forty-two years old, he sounded the theme of a "New Frontier." Issuing an urgent summons for reform at home and victory abroad, he called for "more sacrifice instead of more security" by Americans "on the frontier of unknown opportunities and perils."

The Election of 1960

Kennedy captured the imagination of youth. Recalled a University of Nebraska student, "All at once you had something exciting. . . . Kennedy was talking about pumping new life into the nation and steering it in new directions." But most voters, middle-aged and middle class, seemed to be looking for the stability, security, and continuation of Eisenhower's "middle way" that the Republican candidate, Vice President Richard M. Nixon, promised. Although scorned by liberals for his McCarthyism, Nixon was better known and more experienced than Kennedy. A Protestant, he also was closely identified with the still popular Ike.

Nixon fumbled his opportunity. Conceding that he and Kennedy disagreed more about means than goals, he spent much of his time defending the Eisenhower record. His greatest mistake, however, was agreeing to meet Kennedy in televised debates.

More than 70 million people tuned in to the nation's first televised debate between presidential candidates—a broadcast that secured the dominance of television in American politics. The tanned and dynamic Kennedy contrasted strikingly with his pale, haggard opponent. The telegenic Democrat radiated confidence; Nixon, sweating under his pasty facial makeup, appeared insecure. Radio listeners called the debates a draw, but television viewers declared Kennedy the clear victor. Kennedy shot up in the polls, and Nixon never regained the lead.

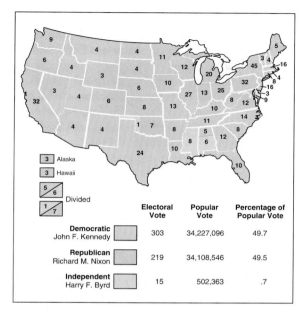

	Electoral Vote	Popular Vote	Percentage of Popular Vote
Democratic John F. Kennedy	303	34,227,096	49.7
Republican Richard M. Nixon	219	34,108,546	49.5
Independent Harry F. Byrd	15	502,363	.7

The Election of 1960

Kennedy also benefited from the embarrassing U-2 incident and an economic recession, as well as from his choice of a southerner, Senate majority leader Lyndon B. Johnson, as his running mate. Still, the 1960 election was the closest since 1888. Kennedy's tiny margin of victory reflected both lingering fears about a Catholic president and a widespread reluctance to change. In the end, Kennedy's religion cut both ways: it cost him millions of votes in the South, but Catholic voters in closely contested midwestern and northeastern states delivered crucial margins. Although Nixon carried more states than Kennedy, the Democrat's popularity with urban minorities helped to give Kennedy a slender triumph.

Kennedy's inauguration set the tone of a new era: "Let the word go forth from this time and place, to friend and foe alike, that the torch has been passed to a new generation of Americans." In sharp contrast to the Eisenhower administration's "eight millionaires and a plumber," Kennedy surrounded himself with young intellectuals. For attorney general he selected his brother Robert Kennedy; "I see nothing wrong with giving Robert some legal expertise before he goes out to practice law," JFK joked.

Kennedy's dynamic style played well on TV and underscored the president's charisma and determination "to get America moving again." Aided by his wife, he adorned his presidency with the trappings of culture and excellence, filling government posts with Rhodes scholars and studding his speeches with references to Emerson and Aristotle. Awed by his taste and grace, reporters extolled the first family's glamour and vitality.

Kennedy's Domestic Record

But media images would obscure Kennedy's lackluster domestic record. Indeed, the conservative coalition of Republicans and southern Democrats that had stifled Truman's Fair Deal doomed the New Frontier as well. Lacking the votes in Congress to overcome these barriers, Kennedy rarely pressed Congress for reform, maintaining that "there is no sense in raising hell and then not being successful."

Instead, JFK made economic growth his domestic priority. To stimulate the economy, he combined higher defense and space expenditures with investment incentives for private enterprise. In 1961 Kennedy persuaded Congress to boost the defense budget by 20 percent, vastly increasing America's nuclear stockpile of intercontinental ballistic missiles (ICBMs), medium-range missiles, and Polaris submarines. Abandoning the "bigger bang for the buck" strategy, moreover, he sought stronger conventional forces and enhanced U.S. capability of countering Third World insurgencies. JFK also persuaded Congress to finance a "race to the moon," an effort that would cost more than $25 billion to land astronauts Neil Armstrong and Buzz Aldrin on the lunar surface in 1969.

In addition, JFK proposed lower business taxes through investment credits and generous depreciation allowances. But the business community and

John Fitzgerald Kennedy (1917–1963)
The youthful, popular president throws out the first ball of the 1962 baseball season.

the Democratic president remained mutually suspicious. Business groups blamed the White House whenever stock prices tumbled. For his part, Kennedy reacted angrily when U.S. Steel raised prices immediately after the president, to curb inflation, had pressured the steelworkers' union to accept a noninflationary contract with minimal raises. JFK threatened the company with antitrust suits and mobilized the FBI and the Federal Trade Commission to investigate price agreements among steel producers. Although U.S. Steel backed down this time, JFK then ignored the corporation's subsequent price hikes. And in January 1963, when he announced his major initiative to catalyze economic growth, the president rejected proposals for increased social spending and advocated personal and corporate tax reduction to encourage private investment and consumption.

When the Kennedy presidency ended tragically in November 1963, the proposed tax cut was bottled up in Congress, but JFK's economic program had doubled the rate of economic growth, decreased unemployment, and held inflation at 1.3 percent a year. He had stimulated the longest uninterrupted era of economic expansion in American history. But liberals complained that the Kennedy administration was promoting military spending at the expense of social welfare and the public sector.

Meanwhile, environmental pollution had become a matter of deepening concern. Awareness of the ecosystem's fragility grew with the publication in 1962 of Rachel Carson's *Silent Spring* (see Chapter 29). JFK appointed an advisory committee on pesticides, and tough federal regulations followed. In 1963 the Clean Air Act regulated automotive and industrial emissions, and in 1966 Congress outlawed the dumping of wastes and pollutants into lakes and rivers. And an environmentally disastrous oil spill off Santa Barbara, California, led to the passage of a stronger water-quality control act in 1970. The nation was paying the environmental price of a modern industrial economy.

Kennedy and Civil Rights

JFK neither anticipated nor welcomed the crusade for civil rights that engulfed the South. Fearful that a struggle over civil rights would divide the nation, split the Democratic party, and entangle Congress in lengthy filibusters, he straddled the issue for two years.

To JFK, racial problems were a thorny thicket to tiptoe around, not a dominant issue requiring decisive leadership. He appointed an unprecedented number of African-Americans to high offices while naming some white racists to federal judgeships. Kennedy remained aloof from attempts by congressional liberals to enact civil-rights legislation and stalled for two years before issuing a weak executive order banning discrimination in federally financed housing.

But civil-rights agitators kept pressure on the president. In the spring of 1961, the Congress of Racial Equality (CORE) organized a "freedom ride" through the Deep South to dramatize widespread violation of a 1960 Supreme Court decision banning segregation in interstate transportation. The freedom riders' efforts to desegregate bus terminals aroused white wrath. In Anniston, Alabama, Ku Klux Klansmen savagely beat the freedom riders and burned their bus, while in Birmingham a white mob mauled a CORE group. When whites in Montgomery viciously assaulted the freedom riders, Kennedy finally dispatched federal marshals to end the violence. Scores more freedom rides and the arrest of hundreds of young protesters forced the president to press the Interstate Commerce Commission to enforce the Supreme Court's ruling.

In the fall of 1962, Kennedy again applied federal force to quell white racist violence. When a federal court ordered the University of Mississippi to enroll James Meredith, a black air-force veteran, angry whites rioted. Rallying behind Confederate flags, students and troublemakers attacked federal marshals escorting Meredith to "Ole Miss." The clash left two dead, hundreds injured, and the campus shrouded in tear gas. Federal troops finally restored order and upheld the right of a black American to attend the university of his home state.

The African-American Revolution

In Birmingham on Good Friday, 1963, Martin Luther King, Jr., determined to expose the violent extremism of southern white racism and to force the president's hand, organized a series of marches, sit-ins, and pray-ins. With each protest bringing more arrests, police commissioner Eugene "Bull" Connor scoffed that King would soon "run out of niggers." Resorting to force, Connor unleashed his men, armed with electric cattle prods, high-pressure water hoses, and snarling attack dogs, on the nonviolent demonstrators. The ferocity of the attack, chronicled on television news programs, filled the world with revulsion.

"The civil-rights movement should thank God for Bull Connor," JFK remarked. "He's helped it as much as Abraham Lincoln." Indeed, the combination of African-American activism and growing white support for equal rights had stimulated Kennedy to arrange a behind-the-scenes compromise ending the Birmingham demonstrations in return for desegregating stores and upgrading the status of black workers. By mid-1963 the rallying cry

Birmingham, 1963
Photographs of white brutality against African-American protesters, such as this horrific scene of blacks enduring the cannonlike force of water shot from high-pressure fire hoses, galvanized the nation's conscience and forced President Kennedy to submit a comprehensive civil-rights bill to Congress.

Martin Luther King, Jr. (1929–1968)

King warned of the "whirlwind of revolt" that would consume the nation if blacks' civil rights contin-ued to be denied.

"Freedom Now!" reverberated across the nation as the number and magnitude of similar protests grew. Increasingly concerned about America's image abroad and the "fires of frustration and discord" at home, Kennedy feared that if the federal govern-ment did not lead the way toward "peaceful and constructive" changes in race relations, blacks would turn to militancy. Accordingly, when Al-abama governor George Wallace in June 1963 re-fused to allow two black students to enter the University of Alabama, Kennedy forced Wallace—who had pledged "Segregation now! Segregation to-morrow! Segregation forever!"—to capitulate to a court desegregation order.

On June 11 JFK went on television to define civil rights as "a moral issue" and to assert that "race has no place in American life or law." Describing the plight of blacks in Jim Crow America, he asked, "Who among us would be content to have the color of his skin changed and stand in his place? Who among us would then be content with the counsels of patience and delay?" The president concluded, "It is time to act in the Congress, in your state and local legislative body, and, above all, in our daily lives." A week later, Kennedy proposed a comprehensive civil-rights measure—which most members of Con-gress ignored.

To compel Congress to act, nearly 250,000 Americans converged on the Capitol on August 28, 1963. There they heard the ringing words of Martin Luther King, Jr., proclaiming that he had a dream, a dream of brotherhood, of freedom and justice, a dream that "all of God's children, black men and white men, Jews and Gentiles, Protestants and Catholics, will be able to join hands and sing in the words of the old Negro spiritual, 'Free at last! Free at last! Thank God Almighty, we are free at last!'"

King's powerful oratory did not speed the civil-rights bill through Congress nor end racism, poverty, and despair. It prevented neither the ghetto riots that lay ahead nor the white backlash that smothered the civil-rights movement and

destroyed King himself. But King had turned a political rally into a historic event. In one of the great
speeches of history, he recalled America to the ideals of justice and equality.

Neither Kennedy's nor King's eloquence could
quell the anger of white racists. On the night of the
president's address, Medgar Evers, the head of the
Mississippi branch of the NAACP, was murdered by
a sniper in Jackson. In September the bombing of a
black church in Birmingham killed four girls. And
still, southern obstructionism kept the civil-rights
bill stymied in Congress, with little hope of passage.

New Frontiers Abroad,
1960–1963

In his inaugural, John F. Kennedy had declared,
"We shall pay any price, bear any burden, oppose
any foe to assure the survival and success of liberty."
He soon applied those ringing words to foreign policy, launching a major buildup of the nation's military arsenal and articulating a strategy of "flexible
response." To "deter all wars, . . . nuclear or conventional, large or small," JFK tripled America's
nuclear capabilities, augmented its conventional
military strength, and formed special forces units,
the "Green Berets," to meet the challenge of procommunist guerrillas in the Third World.

At the same time, Kennedy gained congressional backing for new programs of economic assistance to Third World countries. The Agency for
International Development coordinated foreign aid,
the Food for Peace program distributed surplus agricultural products, and the Alliance for Progress
worked for economic development and social reform in Latin America. The Peace Corps, created in
1961, exemplified the New Frontier blend of idealism and activism. By 1963, 5,000 Peace Corps volunteers were serving as teachers, crop specialists,
and health workers in more than forty Third World
nations. But despite these peaceful initiatives, containment and toughness remained central to American foreign policy.

Cold War Activism

Spring 1961 brought Kennedy's first foreign-policy
crisis. Concerned about the presence of a communist outpost on the United States' doorstep, the
president approved a CIA plan, drawn up under
Eisenhower, to invade Cuba. In mid-April 1961,
1,500 anti-Castro exiles landed at Cuba's Bay of
Pigs, assuming that their arrival would trigger a
general uprising to overthrow Fidel Castro. The
invasion was a fiasco.

Deprived of air cover by Kennedy's desire to
conceal U.S. involvement, the invaders never had a
chance against Castro's superior forces. The Cuban
people did not rise up, and in three days the island
militia either killed or captured the entire brigade.
Although Kennedy accepted blame for the failure, he neither apologized for nor ended attempts
to overthrow Castro. Determined to prove his
strength, he violated American treaty agreements
and aroused the resentment of Latin Americans by
supporting further raids on Cuba by exiles, and even
assassination plots against Castro.

In July 1961, on the heels of the Bay of Pigs
failure, Kennedy met in Vienna with Soviet premier
Nikita Khrushchev to try to resolve a number of issues involving a peace treaty with Germany. Com-
paring American troops in the divided city of Berlin
to "a bone stuck in the throat," Khrushchev threatened war unless the West retreated. Believing the
young president easily intimidated, Khrushchev
then announced that he would sign a separate German peace agreement with East Germany. A shaken
Kennedy returned to the United States and declared the defense of West Berlin essential to the
Free World. He mobilized 150,000 reservists and
National Guardsmen, sought higher defense spending, and, to prepare for a possible nuclear war, announced a crash program to build nuclear-fallout
shelters. The threat of thermonuclear war with the
U.S.S.R. escalated until mid-August, when the Soviets settled for a stalemate. Leaving the American
role in West Germany and Berlin unchanged,
Moscow constructed a wall of concrete and barbed

wire to seal off East Berlin, the Soviet-held sector, and later signed a peace treaty with East Germany. Designed to stop the flow of Germans from the communist zone—about 1,000 refugees a day by June 1961—the Berlin Wall ended the exodus of talent that had threatened East Germany's economic survival. "The Wall" became an enduring symbol of communisms' denial of personal freedom.

To the Brink of Nuclear War

In mid-October 1962, aerial photographs revealed that the Soviet Union had begun constructing missile bases and had placed intermediate-range nuclear missiles, capable of striking most U.S. soil, in Cuba. Smarting from the Bay of Pigs disaster, fearing unchecked Soviet interference in the Western Hemisphere, and insisting that national security was at stake, Kennedy responded strongly. On October 22 the president went on television to denounce "this clandestine, reckless, and provocative threat to world peace" and issued an ultimatum that the missiles be removed. The United States, he announced, would "quarantine" Cuba—impose a naval blockade—to prevent delivery of more missiles and would dismantle by force the missiles already in Cuba if the Soviet Union did not do so.

Kennedy's news rocked the world. The two superpowers appeared to be on a collision course toward nuclear war. As Khrushchev attacked the quarantine as "outright banditry," Soviet technicians worked feverishly to complete the missile launch pads, and Soviet missile-carrying ships steamed toward the blockade. Nearly 200 U.S. Navy ships in the Caribbean, meanwhile, prepared to confront the Soviet freighters; B-52s armed with atomic bombs took to the air; and nearly a quarter-million troops assembled in Florida to invade Cuba. On October 24 Secretary of State Dean Rusk reported, "We're eyeball to eyeball."

But Rusk continued, "I think the other fellow just blinked." Kennedy received a conciliatory message from Khrushchev guaranteeing to remove the missiles if the United States promised never to invade Cuba. As Kennedy prepared to respond positively, a second, far more belligerent message arrived from the Soviet leader. Hours later an American U-2 reconnaissance plane was shot down over Cuba. It was "the blackest hour of the crisis," according to a Kennedy aide. As the military urged an invasion, Robert Kennedy persuaded his brother to accept the first letter and simply to ignore the second one. In the early morning hours of October 27, Khrushchev pledged to remove the missiles in return for Kennedy's noninvasion promise.

Only recently have the full dimensions of the crisis been revealed. In January 1992 the Russian military disclosed that Soviet forces in Cuba had possessed thirty-six nuclear warheads and nine tactical nuclear weapons for battlefield use. Soviet field commanders had independent authority to use these weapons. Worst of all, no Washington decision maker had known about these weapons. Former secretary of defense Robert S. McNamara, speaking in 1992, recalled the pressure for an invasion in late October 1962. "We can predict the results with certainty. . . . U.S. troops could [not] have been attacked by tactical nuclear warheads without the U.S.'s responding with nuclear warheads. . . . Where would it have ended? In utter disaster."

Chastened by having stared over the brink of nuclear war, Kennedy and Khrushchev installed a telephone "hot line" so that the two sides could communicate instantly in future crises. In June 1963 JFK advocated a gradual relaxation of superpower tensions, and two months later the two nations agreed to a treaty outlawing atmospheric and undersea nuclear testing.

Expanding Eisenhower's peaceful-coexistence theme, Kennedy's efforts ushered in a new phase of the Cold War, *détente*, in which the superpowers tilted toward negotiation rather than confrontation. But the militarization of U.S.-Soviet relations continued. America remained committed to a gigantic arms buildup, and the Soviet Union embarked on an even more massive program to gain nuclear equality. Despite détente, the arms race escalated and the contest for power in the Third World widened.

Kennedy and Indochina

In early 1961 a crisis flared in Laos, a tiny, land-locked nation created by the Geneva agreement in 1954 (see Chapter 29). There a civil war between American-supported forces and procommunist rebels appeared headed for a communist triumph. Considering Laos strategically insignificant, Kennedy in July 1962 signed an accord restoring a neutralist government but leaving communist forces in the countryside. The Laotian settlement stiffened Kennedy's resolve not to allow further communist gains in Indochina, but it also confirmed North Vietnam's impression of American weakness.

Determined not to give further ground in Southeast Asia, Kennedy ordered large shipments of weapons to South Vietnam and increased the number of American "advisers" stationed there from about 700 in early 1961 to more than 16,000 by late 1963. He accepted Eisenhower's "domino theory" and viewed international communism as a monolithic force, a single global entity controlled by Moscow and Beijing. He was resolved to prove that the United States was not the "paper tiger" mocked by Mao Zedong.

To counter communist gains in South Vietnam, the United States uprooted Vietnamese peasants and moved them into fortified villages, or "strategic hamlets." Kennedy also pressured the autocratic Diem regime to win popular support by political and economic reforms. Instead, Diem brutally crushed demonstrations by students, the urban middle class, and Buddhists. By mid-1963 Buddhist monks were setting themselves on fire to protest Diem's repression, and Diem's own military leaders were plotting a coup.

Frustrated American policy makers concluded that only a new government could stave off a Vietcong victory, and secretly backed the coup efforts. On November 1, 1963, military leaders staged their coup, captured Diem and his brother, and shot them. Although the United States promptly recognized the new government, it made little headway against the Vietcong. JFK now faced two unpalatable alternatives: to use American combat forces or to withdraw and seek a negotiated settlement.

What Kennedy would have done remains unknown. Less than a month after Diem's death, John F. Kennedy himself fell to an assassin's bullet. His admirers contend that by late 1963 he was privately advocating the withdrawal of American forces after the 1964 election. JFK publicly proclaimed in the fall of 1963 that "it is their war. . . . In the final analysis it is their people and their government who have to win or lose the struggle." But skeptics note that the president followed this comment with a ringing restatement of the domino theory and a promise that the United States would not withdraw from the conflict. Virtually all of JFK's closest advisers believed that an American victory in Vietnam was essential to check the advance of communism in Asia.

The Thousand-Day Presidency

On November 22, 1963, during a trip to Texas to unite warring factions of the state Democratic party, a smiling JFK and Jackie rode in an open car along Dallas streets lined with cheering crowds. Suddenly gunshots rang out and the president slumped, his skull and throat shattered. While the driver sped the mortally wounded Kennedy to a nearby hospital, Secret Service agents rushed Lyndon B. Johnson to Air Force One to be sworn in as president.

Sorrow and disbelief paralyzed the nation. For the next four days, millions of Americans sat stunned in front of television sets and watched a steady stream of mourners file by the president's coffin in the Capitol rotunda; then the murder of the accused assassin, Lee Harvey Oswald; and then the somber state funeral. Few who watched would ever forget. TV's power to convey high national drama with incredible poignancy intensified the sense of personal and national loss and elevated the slain leader to heroic stature.

In hindsight, the justification for this heroic stature is less clear. Kennedy loyalists stress JFK's potential for greatness and his new directions on

Soviet relations and racial equality. His detractors, however, emphasize the gap between rhetoric and substance. For far from charting a New Frontier in foreign policy, Kennedy accepted basic Cold War assumptions. While he spoke of disarmament, he presided over a huge arms buildup, and he broadened American involvement in Vietnam. Nevertheless, in the thousand days of his presidency, Kennedy gradually changed from an unabashed Cold Warrior to a leader who questioned the necessity of conflict with the Soviets and appeared ready to take risks for peace.

The gap between rhetoric and reality was revealed, too, in the administration's domestic policy. Only one-third of Kennedy's legislative proposals became law. Although he helped to launch the longest sustained economic recovery in the nation's history, this upturn resulted from spending more on missiles than on people, more on the space race than on social welfare.

Yet JFK had fired the energies and imaginations of millions of Americans. He had given reformers new hope, touched the poor and powerless, and challenged youth to fight for what ought to be. His ideals had stimulated social criticism and activism. But along with a legacy of rising expectations at home, Kennedy bequeathed to his successor deep entanglements in Southeast Asia.

The Great Society

Distrusted by liberals as "a Machiavelli in a Stetson," regarded as a usurper by Kennedy loyalists, the new president, Lyndon Baines Johnson, had achieved his highest ambition—but only through the assassination of a popular president in Johnson's home state, Texas. Though just nine years older than Kennedy, he seemed a relic of the past, a back-room wheeler-dealer. When many Americans compared the crude and domineering LBJ to the martyred Kennedy, JFK in death appeared even more eloquent and gifted than he had in life.

Yet Johnson had substantial political assets. He had served in Washington almost continuously since 1932, accruing enormous experience. He

excelled at wooing allies, neutralizing enemies, forging compromise, and achieving legislative results. And he was a Protestant, a southerner, a moderate, and a close associate of Capitol Hill power brokers—all factors that would improve the chances for passage of the blocked Kennedy bills. LBJ set out to unite the American people and to win their devotion.

His first two years in office were extraordinarily successful. He deftly handled the transition of power, won a landslide electoral victory in 1964, and guided through Congress the greatest array of social-reform legislation in U.S. history. However, LBJ's swollen but fragile ego could not abide the sniping of the Kennedy loyalists, and he frequently complained that the media were not giving him "a fair shake." Wondering aloud, "Why don't people like me?" Johnson pressed on—to do more, to do it bigger and better, to vanquish all foes at home and abroad. Ironically, in seeking consensus and affection, Johnson would profoundly divide the nation.

Toward the Great Society

Calling for early passage of the tax-cut and civil-rights bills as a memorial to Kennedy, Johnson used his legislative skills to good effect. In February 1964 Congress passed a $10 billion tax-reduction bill that spurred economic growth and would shrink the budget deficit to $4 billion by 1966. In July lawmakers passed the Civil Rights Act of 1964, outlawing segregation in public accommodations, granting the federal government new powers to fight school segregation and black disfranchisement, and creating the Equal Employment Opportunity Commission (EEOC) to stop job discrimination because of race, religion, national origin, or gender.

In his boldest domestic initiative, LBJ also declared "unconditional war on poverty in America." Michael Harrington's *The Other America* (1962) had documented the persistence of widespread poverty in the larger affluent society. Some 40 million "invisible" people lived in substandard housing and subsisted on inadequate diets, Harrington had written. Unaided by social welfare, they lived with little hope, mired in a culture of poverty, deprived of the education, medical care, and employment opportunities that most people took for granted.

LBJ championed a $1 billion campaign to bring these "internal exiles" into the mainstream. Enacted in August 1964, the resulting Economic Opportunity Act established the Office of Economic Opportunity to fund and coordinate a Job Corps to train young people in marketable skills; VISTA (Volunteers in Service to America), a domestic peace corps; Project Head Start, to provide compensatory education for preschoolers from disadvantaged families; and an assortment of public-works and training programs. Black novelist Ralph Ellison hailed Johnson as "the greatest American president for the poor and the Negroes."

Summing up his goals in 1964, Johnson offered a cheering crowd in Ann Arbor, Michigan, his vision of the "Great Society." First must come "an end to poverty and racial injustice," LBJ said. But that would be just the beginning. The Great Society would also be a place where all children could enrich their minds and enlarge their talents, where humans could renew their contact with nature, and where people would be deeply concerned with the quality of their goals. A cornucopia of liberal programs targeting health, education, conservation, the environment, and racial equality appeared ready to flow from Washington if Johnson won election in November.

The Election of 1964

Johnson's Great Society unsettled conservatives, whose movement had remained strong. Leaders of the Right particularly scorned Kennedy-Johnson welfarism. Conservatives supported active government and high federal spending to defeat communism but objected to similar activism and spending when the enemies were poverty, injustice, and the lack of opportunity at home. To them, the lofty rhetoric of the Great Society only masked ever-greater government infringement on basic freedoms.

The Great Society's racial liberalism also frightened southern segregationists and a growing number of urban blue-collar workers who dreaded the integration of their neighborhoods and schools. Their support of Alabama's segregationist governor George Wallace in early 1964 presidential primaries heralded a "white backlash" against the civil-rights movement.

At the July 1964 Republican convention, these dissatisfied groups gained control of the GOP. They nominated the right-wing Arizona senator Barry Goldwater for the presidency, named conservative William Miller of New York as his running mate, and wrote a platform repudiating liberal republicanism. Determined to offer the nation "a choice, not an echo," Goldwater extolled his Senate votes against the civil-rights act and against the censure of Joseph McCarthy; suggested abolishing the graduated income tax; advocated eliminating "compulsory" social security; and hinted that he might use nuclear weapons against Cuba and North Vietnam if they did not give in to U.S. demands. Goldwater's stance appealed to Americans disturbed by the Cold War stalemate and the federal government's growing decision-making power.

Goldwater's conservative crusade let LBJ have the best of two worlds: he could run as a liberal reformer but still be the more moderate candidate. LBJ and his running mate, Senator Hubert Humphrey of Minnesota, painted Goldwater as an extremist not to be trusted with the nuclear trigger. When Goldwater charged that the Democrats had

The Election of 1964				
Candidates	Parties	Electoral Vote	Popular Vote	Percentage of Popular Vote
LYNDON B. JOHNSON	Democratic	486	43,126,506	61.1
Barry M. Goldwater	Republican	52	27,176,799	38.5

not pursued total victory in Vietnam, Johnson appeared the apostle of restraint: "We are not going to send American boys nine or ten thousand miles from home to do what Asian boys ought to be doing for themselves."

To no one's surprise, LBJ won a landslide victory, 43 million votes to Goldwater's 27 million. The GOP, moreover, lost 500 of the state legislative seats that it had held. Commentators proclaimed the death of conservatism. But Goldwater's coalition of white southerners and blue-collar workers presaged conservatism's future triumph. In fact, nearly 40 percent of the electorate had voted for Goldwater, an uncompromising conservative who had demanded total victory over communism and an end to the welfare state. In the short run, the Democrats secured huge majorities in both houses of Congress, nullifying the conservative coalition's power to block the presidential proposals. For the first time in a quarter-century, the liberals had a working majority.

Liberalism Triumphant

"Hurry, boys, hurry," LBJ urged his aides. "Get that legislation up to the hill and out. Eighteen months from now ol' Landslide Lyndon will be Lame-Duck Lyndon." With this imperative, Johnson established a host of task forces to flood Congress with Great Society proposals; he bombarded Congress with sixty-three separate messages calling for social legislation in 1965 alone. He got most of what he wanted.

The Eighty-ninth Congress enlarged the War on Poverty and passed another milestone civil-rights act. It also enacted a comprehensive plan of medical insurance for the elderly and medical care for the needy, established precedents for massive federal aid to education, and funded urban development, housing, and transit. Congress created new cabinet-level departments of transportation and housing and urban development and established the National Endowments for the Arts and the Humanities.

The Great Society also sought to reduce pollution and to protect and preserve nature. Secretary of the Interior Stewart Udall played a major role in establishing Redwood National Park and in defeating efforts to dam the Colorado River and flood the lower Grand Canyon. Congress strengthened the Clean Water and Clean Air acts, protected endangered species and wildlands, and preserved scenic rivers and millions of acres of wilderness.

Surveying the array of Great Society measures adopted by the Eighty-ninth Congress, Speaker of the House John McCormack exulted: "It is the Congress of accomplished hopes. It is the Congress of realized dreams." But for many Americans, the Great Society remained more a dream than a reality. In the words of Martin Luther King, Jr., Johnson's desire to end poverty and to provide equal opportunity for all was "shot down on the battlefields of Vietnam."

Indeed, by 1966 Johnson would spend twenty times more to wage war in Vietnam than to wage war on poverty. LBJ's shift of emphasis from welfare to warfare not only would destroy his drive for consensus but also would enrage those still mired in poverty. Resultant rising black militancy and urban riots would alienate "middle America." And growing bitterness about the Vietnam War would focus the wrath of liberals, particularly the young, on LBJ. The Democrats' loss of forty-seven House seats in 1966 would seal the Great Society's fate.

The Warren Court in the Sixties

By the mid-sixties the Supreme Court, headed by Chief Justice Earl Warren, was under siege. Its decisions from Brown v. Board of Education (1954) onward had incensed the far Right. "Impeach Earl Warren!" screamed billboards. In 1962 John F. Kennedy had appointed two liberals to the Court, replacing moderates, and LBJ appointed the even more liberal Abe Fortas and Thurgood Marshall, the Court's first black justice. During the 1960s the Warren court handed down a series of decisions that changed the tenor of American life.

In a series of landmark cases, the Court prohibited Bible reading and prayer in public schools, limited communities' power to censor books and films, and overturned state bans on contraceptives. In *Baker* v. *Carr* (1962) and related decisions, the Warren court ruled that "one man, one vote" must prevail in both state and national elections and that representation in all legislative bodies must be allocated on the basis of "people, not land or trees, or pastures." Especially unsettling to many was the Court's commitment to due process of law for everyone caught up in the criminal-justice system. Rulings that a poor defendant charged with a felony must be provided an attorney, and that the accused has the right to counsel during interrogation, appeared to handcuff law enforcement even as crime proliferated.

In 1966 criticism of the Warren court reached a crescendo when it ruled in *Miranda* v. *Arizona* that police must warn all suspects that anything they said could be used against them in court and that they therefore could choose to remain silent. Conservative candidates charged that the liberal Court had overstepped its bounds. In 1968 both Richard Nixon and George Wallace would promise to appoint judges who would emphasize "law and order" over individual rights and liberties.

The Changing Struggle for Equality, 1964–1968

Meanwhile, the drive for black equality crested and then receded in the two years following the 1963 March on Washington. The movement had brought the end of both legal discrimination and black disfranchisement and had gained improved educational and employment opportunities for blacks. But major problems remained: crime, drug addiction, family disorganization, and blacks' deep feelings of inadequacy. Persistent white racism, moreover, discouraged blacks, who increasingly questioned whether they would ever be seen as equals. For some, the movement had generated hopes that it could not fulfill, and kindled a racial pride that rejected integration as a desirable goal. "The paths of Negro-white unity that had been converging," wrote Martin Luther King, Jr., "crossed at Selma and like a giant X began to diverge."

The Civil Rights Act of 1965

In 1964 CORE and SNCC (Student Nonviolent Coordinating Committee) activists, believing that the ballot box held the key to real power for southern blacks, mounted a major campaign to register black voters. Focusing on the state most hostile to equal rights, field workers organized the Mississippi Freedom Summer Project of 1964. A thousand college-student volunteers assisted blacks in registering to vote and in organizing "Freedom Schools" that taught black history and emphasized African-American self-worth. Harassed by Mississippi law-enforcement officials and Ku Klux Klansmen, the volunteers endured the firebombing of black churches and civil-rights headquarters, arrests, beatings, kidnappings, and even murders.

Although they registered only 1,200 blacks to vote, the workers enrolled nearly 60,000 disfranchised blacks in the Mississippi Freedom Democratic party (MFDP) and took their case to the national Democratic convention in August 1964. The MFDP insisted that the convention seat MFDP delegates instead of the all-white delegation chosen by the Mississippi Democratic party. LBJ, trying to head off white southern walkouts, forged a compromise that granted two at-large seats to the MFDP and barred from all future conventions any delegations from states that discriminated against blacks. The compromise alienated militants in the civil-rights movement.

Undeterred, Martin Luther King, Jr., and the Southern Christian Leadership Council (SCLC), resolved to gain a voting-rights act, organized mass protests in Selma, Alabama, in March 1965. Blacks constituted half the voting-age population in Dallas County, where Selma was located, but only 1 percent were registered to vote. Selma's county sheriff

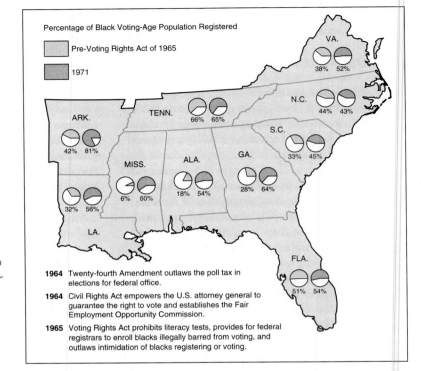

Percentage of Black Voting-Age Population Registered

Pre-Voting Rights Act of 1965

1971

VA. 38% 52%

N.C. 44% 43%

TENN. 66% 65%

ARK. 42% 81%

S.C. 33% 45%

MISS. 6% 60%

ALA. 18% 54%

GA. 28% 64%

32% 56%

LA.

FLA. 51% 54%

1964 Twenty-fourth Amendment outlaws the poll tax in elections for federal office.

1964 Civil Rights Act empowers the U.S. attorney general to guarantee the right to vote and establishes the Fair Employment Opportunity Commission.

1965 Voting Rights Act prohibits literacy tests, provides for federal registrars to enroll blacks illegally barred from voting, and outlaws intimidation of blacks registering or voting.

Voter Registration of African-Americans in the South, 1964–1971

As blacks overwhelmingly registered to vote as Democrats, some former segregationist politicians, among them George Wallace, started to court the black vote, and many southern whites began to cast their ballots for Republicans, inaugurating an era of real two-party competition in the South.

Jim Clark was every bit as ill tempered and violence prone as Birmingham's Bull Connor, and Clark's men attacked black protesters and bystanders indiscriminately and brutally. Showcased on television news, the vicious attacks provoked national outrage and fostered support for a voting-rights bill.

Signed by the president in August 1965, the resulting Voting Rights Act expanded black suffrage—and transformed southern politics. It authorized federal examiners to register voters and to suspend literacy tests in areas where fewer than half the minority residents of voting age were registered. Together with the Twenty-third Amendment, ratified in 1964, which outlawed the poll tax in federal elections, and a 1966 Supreme Court decision striking down the poll tax in *all* elections, the Voting Rights Act by 1968 had boosted the number of registered black voters in the South from 1 million to 3.1 million. For the first time since Reconstruction, African-Americans were a force to be reckoned with in southern politics.

The civil-rights movement altered rather than revolutionized race relations in the United States. Black voting power defeated some white supremacists while stirring other once ardent segregationists prudently to seek black support. Equal access to public accommodations gave African-Americans a new sense of dignity. "Now if we do want to go to McDonald's we can go to McDonald's," mused a black woman in Atlanta. "It's just knowing! It's a good feeling." But with discrimination lingering in many spheres and black unemployment still disproportionately high, the anger bubbling below the surface of the urban ghetto boiled over.

The Long, Hot Summers

On August 11, 1965, five days after the Voting Rights Act was signed, a confrontation between white police and young blacks in Watts, Los Angeles's largest black district, ignited the most destructive race riot in two decades. For six days nearly 50,000 blacks looted shops, firebombed white-owned businesses, and sniped at police officers, fire fighters, and National Guard troops. When the riot ended, 34 people had been killed, 900 injured, and 4,000 arrested, and $30 million worth of property had been devastated. In rapid succession blacks in Chicago and in Springfield, Massachusetts, took to the streets, looting, burning, and battling police.

In the summer of 1966, rioting erupted in more than a score of northern ghettos, forcing whites to heed the squalor of the slums, the savage behavior of police in the ghetto, and urban poverty—issues that the civil-rights movement had ignored. The following summer brought nearly 150 racial outbreaks and 40 riots, the most intense and destructive period of racial violence that the United States had ever witnessed. In 1968 riots again would flare in the ghettos of more than 100 cities after the assassination of Martin Luther King, Jr. (see Chapter 31). The 1964–1968 riot toll would include 200 dead, 7,000 injured, 40,000 arrested, and $200 million worth of property wrecked.

A frightened, bewildered nation asked why such widespread rioting was occurring just as blacks were beginning to achieve their goals. Explanations abounded. Militant blacks saw the uprisings as revolutionary violence directed at a racist, reactionary society. Conservatives described them as senseless outbursts by troublemakers. The National Advisory Commission on Civil Disorders (the Kerner Commission) indicted white racism for fostering "an explosive mixture" of poverty, slum housing, poor education, and police brutality. Warning that "our nation is moving toward two societies, one black, one white—separate and unequal," the commission recommended the creation of 2 million new jobs, the construction of 6 million units of public housing, an end to de facto school segregation in the North, and funding for a "national system of income supplementation." Aware of a swelling white backlash, LBJ ignored the commission's advice, and most whites approved of his inaction. Alarmed by demands for "Black Power" that had risen in recent riots, they preferred that their taxes be spent on strengthening local police forces instead of on improving ghetto conditions.

"Black Power"

The Black Power movement erupted in 1966. The calls for black power flowed from the same source as the riots: disappointment and bitterness over the slow pace of racial change, and white opposition to the most minimal black advances.

Black Power, less an ideology than a cry of fury and frustration, evolved from the teachings of Malcolm X. A former pimp, drug addict, and street hustler, Malcolm X had converted to the Nation of Islam, or Black Muslim faith, while in prison. Founded in Detroit in 1931 by Elijah Poole (who took the Islamic name Elijah Muhammed), the Nation of Islam insisted that blacks practice self-discipline and self-respect, and rejected integration. Malcolm X accordingly urged black Americans to separate themselves from the "white devil" and to take pride in their African roots and their blackness. Blacks, he claimed, must rely on armed self-defense and must seize their freedom "by any means necessary." In February 1965, after he broke with the Nation of Islam, Malcolm X was assassinated, but he was not silenced. *The Autobiography of Malcolm X* (1965) became the main text for the rising Black Power movement.

In the summer of 1966, Stokely Carmichael led SNCC away from its commitment to nonviolence and integration. "The only way we gonna stop them white men from whippin' us is to take over. We been saying freedom for six years and we ain't got nothin'. What we gonna start saying now is Black Power!" Carmichael's successor as SNCC head, H. Rap Brown, encouraged African-Americans "to get you some guns. . . . Don't be trying to love that honky [white man] to death. Shoot him to death." In 1966 two college students in Oakland, California, Huey Newton and Bobby Seale, organized the Black Panthers, who gained national publicity from a series of violent confrontations with the police and from Newton's repeated claim that "quoting from Chairman Mao, . . . political power comes through the barrel of a gun."

African-American leaders of every persuasion adopted the "Black Power" slogan. Revolutionaries used it to preach guerrilla warfare; liberals, to demand reform; conservatives, to emphasize self-help. A generation of black Americans was soon affirming that "black is beautiful." Young blacks donned dashikis, wore Afro hairstyles, enjoyed soul music and soul food, and established black-studies programs at colleges. Young SCLC leader Jesse Jackson asked students to repeat after him, "I may have lost hope, but I am . . . somebody. . . . I am . . . black . . . beautiful . . . proud. . . . I must be respected." Similar themes would reverberate through other social movements in the sixties.

Native American and Chicano Power

Activist Native Americans, whose peoples numbered nearly 800,000, also organized demonstrations to publicize their plight and to awaken self-respect and cultural pride. In 1961 representatives of sixty-seven tribes gathered in Chicago to draw up a Declaration of Purposes, and in 1964 hundreds of Indians assembled in Washington to lobby for recognition in the War on Poverty. Native Americans, they pointed out, suffered the worst poverty, the highest disease and death rates, and the poorest education and housing of any American group. President Johnson established the National Council on Indian Opportunity in 1965 and in 1968 sent Congress a special message seeking greater federal aid for the Indians.

By 1968 Indian activists were demanding "Red Power" and insisting on the name Native Americans. They agitated for preferential hiring, Native American studies programs, and reimbursement for lands taken from them in violation of federal laws and treaties. In 1968 Indians in Washington State tried to assert old treaty rights to fish in the Columbia River and Puget Sound, while Chippewa Indians in Minnesota inaugurated the American Indian Movement (AIM). Emphasizing Indians' rights to control their own affairs, AIM, like the Black Panthers, established armed patrols to protect Indians from police harassment.

Chicano Activism
The 1960s saw an intensified drive on the part of Mexican-Americans for equal rights and political power—"brown power." This photograph shows a Chicano farmworkers' protest.

Mexican-Americans also challenged whites' dominance. Their ethnic pride and solidarity were kindled by César Chávez, the founder of the United Farm Workers, who sought improved working conditions for farm laborers and used nonviolent resistance to fight for social change. Portraying the farm workers' struggle as part of the larger national movement for civil rights, Chávez in 1965 organized a California grape pickers' strike and a nationwide consumer boycott of grapes (and later, lettuce).

Young Mexican-American activists criticized Chávez's moderation and shunned mainstream American values. They demanded that other Americans call them *Chicanos*, battled for bilingual and bicultural education in Chicano schools and Chicano studies in universities, and insisted on Chicano-only organizations. Organizations like the Alianza in New Mexico, the Crusade for Justice in Colorado, and La Raza in Texas exemplified this new militancy. Young California Chicanos organized the Brown Berets and began to speak of "Chicano power." The issue, they insisted, was control: "control over our environment; control over our schools . . . ; control over the agencies which are supposed to be administering to the needs of our people; control over the police whose salaries we pay but who continually brutalize our people."

The Black Power, Red Power, and Brown Power movements could not sustain the fervent activism and media attention that they attracted in the late sixties. But by elevating the consciousness and nurturing the confidence of the younger generation, each contributed to the cultural pride of its respective group.

A Second Feminist Wave

Following the victory of the woman-suffrage campaign in 1920, the American feminist movement had lost virtually all momentum. In the 1950s feminist consciousness had hit a low point. But in the 1960s, the rising tempo of activism stirred a new spirit of self-awareness and dissatisfaction among middle-class women. A revived feminist movement emerged, profoundly altering women's view of themselves and their role in American life.

Several events fanned the embers of discontent into a flame. In 1961 John F. Kennedy had established the Presidential Commission on the Status of Women. Its 1963 report documented occupational inequities suffered by women that were comparable to those endured by minorities. Women received less pay than men for comparable or identical work and had far less chance than their male counterparts of moving into professional or managerial careers. Women composed 51 percent of the population but made up only 7 percent of the nation's doctors and less than 4 percent of its lawyers. The women who served on the presidential commission successfully urged that the Civil Rights Act of 1964 prohibit gender-based as well as racial discrimination in employment.

Dismayed, however, by the Equal Employment Opportunity Commission's handling of gender-based discrimination complaints, these women formed the National Organization for Women (NOW) in 1966. Defined as a civil-rights group for women, NOW lobbied for equal opportunity, filed lawsuits against gender discrimination, and mobilized public opinion.

NOW's popularity owed much to the publication in 1963 of Betty Friedan's *The Feminine Mystique*. Calling it "the problem that has no name," Friedan deplored the narrow view that women should only seek fulfillment as wives and mothers and "desire no greater destiny than to glory in their own femininity." Suburban domesticity—the "velvet ghetto"—left many women with feelings of emptiness, with no sense of accomplishment, and afraid to ask "the silent question—'Is this all?'" Friedan asserted that women must pursue careers and establish "goals that will permit them to find their own identity." *The Feminine Mystique* revealed to disillusioned women that they were not alone. Friedan's demand for "something more than my husband, my children, and my home" rang true to many educated middle-class women who found the creativity of homemaking and the joys of motherhood exaggerated.

Still another catalyst for feminism came from the involvement of young women in the civil-rights and anti–Vietnam War movements. Women activists in these causes gained confidence in their own potential, an ideology to describe oppression and to justify resolve, and experience in the strategy and tactics of protest.

In 1968 militant feminists adopted "consciousness raising" as a recruitment device and a means of transforming women's perceptions of themselves and society. Tens of thousands of women across the United States assembled in small groups to share their experiences and to air grievances. Individuals soon realized that they were hardly alone in dissatisfaction or frustration. "It makes you very sensitive—raw, even—this consciousness," wrote feminist Robin Morgan. "You begin to see how all-pervasive a thing is sexism—the definition of and discrimination against half the human species by the other half." This new consciousness brought a sense of "sisterhood" and a political commitment to eliminating sexism.

Women's liberation groups sprang up across the nation, employing a variety of publicity-generating and confrontational tactics to fight sexism. In 1968 radical feminists set up "freedom trash cans" into which women could discard high-heeled shoes, bras, curlers, and other items that they considered demeaning. "Women's libbers" established health collectives and day-care centers, founded abortion-counseling services, demonstrated against advertisements that portrayed women as sex objects, and protested the use of sexist words such as *chick* and *gal*.

In August 1970 various feminist factions put aside their differences to join the largest women's rights demonstration ever. Commemorating the fiftieth anniversary of woman suffrage, the Women's Strike for Equality brought out tens of thousands of women across the nation to parade for the right to equal employment and to safe, legal abortions. By then the women's movement had already pressured many financial institutions to issue credit to single women and to married women in their own name; ended newspapers' practice of listing employment opportunities under "Male" and "Female" headings; and gained guidelines that required corporations receiving federal funds to adopt nondiscriminatory hiring practices and equal pay scales. By 1970, moreover, more than 40 percent of all women held full-time jobs outside the home.

The changed consciousness of the feminist movement opened a larger world of choices and opportunities for American women. Domesticity remained an option, but it was no longer the *only* option. As never before, women were taking control of their own lives and defining their own goals.

The Lost Crusade in Vietnam, 1964–1968

Although the militancy of women, blacks, Indians, and Chicanos chipped away at the consensus that LBJ so desired, it was America's deepening involvement in Vietnam that most unraveled his hopes for a united society. Despite the president's desire to concentrate on domestic affairs, developments in South Vietnam sidetracked and ensnared his administration. Diem's successors had proved incompetent, and in 1964 Vietcong attacks on

noncommunist South Vietnam had become more damaging.

Johnson had to choose between intervening decisively or extricating the United States from Southeast Asia. While privately describing Vietnam as "a raggedy-ass fourth-rate country," LBJ feared that an all-out American military effort might lead to World War III. And he foresaw that a full-scale U.S. engagement in "that bitch of a war" would destroy "the woman I really loved—the Great Society." Yet Johnson did not want the United States to appear weak. Only American strength and resolve, he thought, would prevent a wider war. The president also worried that a pullout would leave him vulnerable to conservative attack. "I am not going to lose Vietnam," he insisted. "I am not going to be the president who saw Southeast Asia go the way China went."

Trapped between unacceptable alternatives, Johnson expanded the war, hoping that U.S. firepower would force Ho Chi Minh to the bargaining table. But the NLF and the North Vietnamese calculated that they could gain more by outlasting the United States than by negotiating. So the war ground on, devastating Southeast Asia and dividing the United States as nothing had since the Civil War.

The Gulf of Tonkin Resolution

In 1964 LBJ took bold steps to impress the North Vietnamese with American resolve and to block his vigorously anticommunist opponent, Barry Goldwater, from capitalizing on Vietnam in the presidential campaign. In February Johnson ordered the Pentagon to prepare for air strikes against North Vietnam. In May his advisers had drafted a congressional resolution authorizing an escalation of American military action, and in July LBJ appointed General Maxwell Taylor, an advocate of a greater American role in Vietnam, as ambassador to Saigon. In early August, North Vietnamese patrol boats reportedly clashed with two U.S. destroyers patrolling the Gulf of Tonkin (see map). Despite virtually no evidence of an attack, Johnson announced that Americans had been victims of "open

The Vietnam War, to 1968

Wishing to guarantee an independent, noncommunist government in South Vietnam, Lyndon Johnson remarked in 1965: "We fight because we must fight if we are to live in a world where every country can shape its own destiny. To withdraw from one battlefield means only to prepare for the next."

aggression on the high seas." Withholding the information that the U.S. destroyers had been aiding the South Vietnamese in clandestine raids against North Vietnam, the president condemned the alleged North Vietnamese attacks as unprovoked.

Johnson called on Congress to pass a resolution giving him the authority to "take all necessary measures to repel any armed attack against the forces of the United States and to prevent further aggression." Assured that this power would lead to no "extension of the present conflict," the Senate passed

the Gulf of Tonkin Resolution 88–2, and the House 416–0. Johnson called the resolution "grandma's nightshirt—it covered everything." The president, moreover, considered the resolution a mandate to commit U.S. forces to Vietnam as he saw fit. But the resolution would soon create a credibility problem for Johnson, allowing opponents of the war to charge that he had misled Congress and lied to the American people. By providing LBJ with a blank check, the resolution also made massive U.S. military intervention likely.

Americanization

Johnson quickly cashed his blank check. Early in 1965 he ordered "Operation Rolling Thunder," the sustained bombing of North Vietnam. Designed to inflict just enough damage to make Hanoi negotiate, to boost the morale of the Saigon government, and to stop the flow of soldiers and supplies southward from North Vietnam, the bombing accomplished none of these purposes. Further, for all of LBJ's concern about restraint, the United States dropped 800 tons of bombs daily on North Vietnam from 1965 to 1968, three times the tonnage used by all combatants in World War II.

Unable to turn the tide by bombing, Johnson made a fateful decision: he committed American combat troops to Vietnam. In March 1965 he ordered two marine battalions to South Vietnam to defend American airfields. Expanding their mission to include offensive operations, LBJ in July sent an additional 125,000 troops. By the end of the year, 184,000 Americans were fighting in Vietnam. The draft would soon summon millions more to arms.

LBJ did not stumble blindly into the quagmire; he saw no other course. "I feel like a hitchhiker caught in a hailstorm on a Texas highway," he moaned. "I can't run, I can't hide, and I can't make it stop." Each side continued to escalate. Prepared to fight until the United States lost its will, Hanoi infiltrated more and more troops into the South. Determined to prevent a North Vietnamese victory, Johnson had deployed 485,000 troops in Vietnam by the end of 1967, more men than the United States had deployed in Korea at the peak of the earlier Asian war.

Opposition to the War

At first on college campuses and then in the wider society, a growing number of Americans doubted the wisdom of the Vietnam War and vocally opposed it. A week after marines splashed ashore at Danang, South Vietnam, in March 1965, students and faculty at the University of Michigan staged the first teach-in to raise questions about U.S. involvement. Later that spring, 25,000 people, mainly students, rallied in Washington to applaud two senators for their votes against the Gulf of Tonkin Resolution. As new draft calls went out in 1966, large-scale campus antiwar protests erupted. Students demonstrated against the Pentagon and military research and began a draft-resistance movement.

Liberal intellectuals and clergy joined the chorus of opposition to the war. Some argued that the United States had no business meddling in a civil quarrel; others doubted that the nation could win at any reasonable cost. The expense of the war, $20 billion annually and rising, appalled many Americans, especially as Great Society programs shrank. In 1967 critics who included senators J. William Fulbright and Robert Kennedy, foreign-policy experts George Kennan and Walter Lippmann, and Martin Luther King, Jr., spurred hundreds of thousands to participate in antiwar protests.

Some opponents noted that the war fell especially hard on the poor. Owing to college deferments, the use of influence, and a military-assignment system that shunted the better educated to desk jobs, lower-class youths were twice as likely to be drafted and, if drafted, twice as likely to see combat duty as middle-class youths.

TV coverage of the war further eroded popular support. Scenes of shocking cruelty, of fleeing refugees, of children maimed by U.S. bombs, and of dying Americans, replayed in living rooms night after night, undercutting the official optimism of government press agents. Americans shuddered in horror as they watched napalm (a burning glue that adheres to skin and clothing) and defoliants lay waste Vietnam's countryside and leave thousands of civilians dead or mutilated. They saw American troops, who supposedly were winning the hearts and minds of the Vietnamese, uproot peasants, burn their villages, and desecrate their burial grounds.

Yet even at the height of the antiwar movement, most Americans either supported the war or remained undecided. As the war's costs rose and casualties surpassed those in the Korean War, however, the war's unpopularity deepened. The desire "to get out, but not give up" became a common sentiment. In mid-1967 Secretary of Defense McNamara admitted that "the picture of the world's

LBJ and Vietnam
The Vietnam War spelled President Lyndon Johnson's undoing. Here, young peace demonstrators express their feelings about the president's role in the war during a massive antiwar protest at the Pentagon in October 1967.

greatest superpower killing or seriously injuring a thousand noncombatants a week, while trying to pound a tiny backward country into submission on an issue whose merits are hotly disputed, is not a pretty one."

Equally disturbing was how polarized the nation had grown. "Hawks" would accept little short of quick and total victory, whereas "doves" insisted on negotiating, not fighting. The vast middle group of Americans, not opposed to the war on principle, was reaching the conclusion that the conflict was unwinnable. As Johnson lashed out at his critics and refused to de-escalate the conflict, demonstrators paraded past the White House and chanted, "Hey, hey, LBJ, how many kids did you kill today?" By 1968 the president had become a prisoner in the White House, unable to speak in public without drawing hecklers, and his Great Society lay in ruins.

Conclusion

Despite LBJ's woes in 1968, he had accomplished much. Under his predecessor, John F. Kennedy, idealistic young Americans had come to believe that it was time to rid the nation of racism and poverty. The civil-rights movement in the Kennedy years had vanquished legally enforced segregation, disfranchisement, and racial discrimination and nurtured blacks' self-respect. Other oppressed groups—women, Chicanos, Indians—had followed African-Americans' lead.

The reform impulse peaked during the first two years of the Johnson administration. Millions benefited from the Great Society as it made the United States a more caring and just nation. But the Great Society promised more than it could ultimately deliver. Despite LBJ's boast that the United States could fund a major war and still spend on social programs, the tremendous costs of the Vietnam War reduced the War on Poverty to a skirmish. By early 1966 the government was pouring $2 billion a month into Vietnam, more than it spent in an entire year to combat poverty. As U.S. involvement in Vietnam escalated, angry blacks and college-age youths turned to violence to hasten social change. Floundering in a futile war, Johnson and the Democratic party, like the American people as a whole, faced the election year 1968 in confusion and disarray.

Chronology

1960 Sit-ins to protest segregation begin.
John F. Kennedy elected president.

1961 Peace Corps and Alliance for Progress created.
Bay of Pigs invasion.
Freedom rides.
Berlin Wall erected.

1962 Michael Harrington, *The Other America*.
Cuban missile crisis.

1963 Civil-rights demonstrations in Birmingham.
March on Washington.
Test-Ban Treaty between the Soviet Union and
the United States.
Kennedy assassinated; Lyndon B. Johnson
becomes president.
Betty Friedan, *The Feminine Mystique*.

1964 "Freedom Summer" in Mississippi.
Civil Rights Act.

Gulf of Tonkin incident and resolution.
Economic Opportunity Act initiates War on
Poverty.
Johnson elected president.

1965 Bombing of North Vietnam and Americanization
of the war begin.
Assassination of Malcolm X.
Civil-rights march from Selma to Montgomery.
Voting Rights Act.
Watts riot in Los Angeles.

1966 Stokely Carmichael calls for Black Power.
Black Panthers formed.
National Organization for Women (NOW)
founded.

1967 Massive antiwar demonstrations.
Race riots in Newark, Detroit, and other cities.

FOR FURTHER READING

William Chafe, *The Unfinished Journey: America Since World War II*, rev. ed. (1991). An interpretive history of social change emphasizing issues of class, gender, and race.

Sara Evans, *Personal Politics* (1979). An analysis of the roots of modern feminism in the civil-rights movement and in the New Left.

Samuel Hays, *Beauty, Health, and Permanence: Environmental Politics in the United States, 1955–1985* (1987). A pathbreaking account of modern environmentalism.

George Herring, *America's Longest War*, rev. ed. (1985). A comprehensive account of the reasons for America's involvement and ultimate failure in Vietnam.

Allen Matusow, *The Unraveling of America: A History of Liberalism in the 1960s* (1984). A richly researched interpretation of liberal reform in the Kennedy-Johnson years.

Thomas Reeves, *A Question of Character: The Life of John F. Kennedy in Image and Reality* (1991). A compelling reexamination of the man and the myth.

Harvard Sitkoff, *The Struggle for Black Equality, 1954–1980* (1981). A dramatic account of the terror-laced struggle against white racism.

A Troubled Journey: From Port Huron to Watergate

The Free Speech movement . . . Students for a Democratic Society . . . "Make Love, Not War." . . . The baby boomers who deluged college campuses in the 1960s, espousing these and other outlooks and causes, spawned a student movement that gave the decade its distinctive cultural and political aura. In the short term, this movement, by assaulting traditional policies and values, produced vital changes. Ironically, in the longer run, it contributed to a conservative resurgence.

Both agent in and beneficiary of the era's realignment, Republican Richard M. Nixon won the presidency in 1968 and gained a stunning reelection victory in 1972. Winning high marks for his management of world affairs, Nixon ended U.S. involvement in Vietnam and inaugurated a period of reduced tensions with China and the Soviet Union. In 1974, however, having flouted the very law and order that he had pledged to uphold on the domestic front, Nixon resigned in disgrace to avoid impeachment. He left as his legacy a public disrespect for the political system unparalleled in U.S. history.

(Right) American GI in Vietnam, 1972

The Rise and Fall of the Youth Movement
1968: The Politics of Strife
Nixon and World Politics
Domestic Problems and Divisions
The Crisis of the Presidency

The Rise and Fall of the Youth Movement

In the 1950s the number of American students pursuing higher education rose from 1 million to 4 million, and in the 1960s the number doubled again, to 8 million. By then more than half the U.S. population was under age thirty. Their sheer numbers and their concentration in higher education gave the baby boomers a collective identity and guaranteed that their actions would have impact.

Most baby boomers followed conventional paths in the 1960s. If they went to college—and fewer than half did—they typically took business and other career-oriented degrees. Whether they attended college or entered the work force directly after high school, the vast majority had their eyes fixed on a good job, a new car, a family, and a pleasant home. They had little incentive to turn radical. In fact, many young Americans disdained the long-haired protesters and displayed the same bumper stickers as their elders: "My Country—Right or Wrong" or "America—Love It or Leave It."

Nevertheless, an insurgent minority of liberal-arts majors and graduate students at prestigious universities attracted considerable notice. The majority of them children of affluence, they could afford to be idealistic; economically secure, they could reject the idea that hard work, ambition, and self-denial were necessary. Reared by permissive parents in child-centered homes, they resented restrictions on their behavior and expected quick gratification.

Toward a New Left

This liberal-minded student minority welcomed the idealism of the civil-rights movement, the rousing call of John F. Kennedy for service to the nation, and the campaign against nuclear testing that had led to the 1963 test-ban treaty. Determined not to be a "silent generation," they admired the mavericks and outsiders of the 1950s: iconoclastic comedian Mort Sahl; Beat poet Allen Ginsberg; and pop-culture rebels like Elvis Presley and James Dean. Disillusionment and skepticism, however, mingled with their idealism. Kennedy's assassination had cut down an idolized leader. And Lyndon Johnson's coarse personal style, political wheeling and dealing, and above all his escalation of the war in Vietnam had alienated many of them.

The most alienated were the "red diaper" babies, the offspring of parents with roots in 1930s radicalism. It was they who provided the initial impetus for the campus awakening and for the rise of the radical movement that became known as the New Left in the 1960s. Indeed, Students for a Democratic Society (SDS), the embodiment of New Left campus radicalism, evolved from an old-time socialist organization.

In June 1962 an era of apathy ended when sixty students adopted the Port Huron (Michigan) Manifesto, a broad critique of American society and a call for more genuine human relationships. Written primarily by Tom Hayden, a twenty-two-year-old former editor of the University of Michigan student newspaper, the manifesto expressed SDS ideals: "We would replace power rooted in possession, privilege, or circumstances, with power rooted in love, reflectiveness, reason and creativity." Citing the success of civil-rights activists' sit-ins and freedom rides, SDS envisioned a nonviolent youth movement transforming the United States into a "participatory democracy" in which citizens would control the decisions on which their lives and well-being depended. Such a system, Hayden argued, would cure careerism, materialism, militarism, and racism.

SDS's early core consisted largely of red-diaper babies, altruistic youths typically raised in strongly religious homes that encouraged high ethics and political engagement. But many idealistic students never joined SDS and instead associated themselves with what they vaguely called the Movement. No matter what the label, a generation of activists found their agenda in the Port Huron Manifesto.

Thousands of students became radicalized in the sixties by what they saw as the impersonality and rigidity of campus administrators, the insensitivity of the nation's bureaucratic processes, and mainstream liberalism's inability to achieve deep, swift change. Only a radical rejection of compromise and consensus, they concluded, could restructure society along humane and democratic lines.

From Protest to Resistance

The first wave of student protest washed across the campus of the University of California, Berkeley. In the fall of 1964, civil-rights activists who were veterans of the Mississippi Freedom Summer Project tried to solicit funds and to recruit volunteers near the campus gate, a spot traditionally open to political activities. Prodded by local conservatives, however, the university suddenly banned such enterprises from the area. Organizing as the Berkeley Free Speech Movement, a coalition of student groups insisted on the right to campus political activity. The arrest of one student led to the occupation of the university administration building, more arrests, and a strike by nearly 70 percent of the student body. Mario Savio, a philosophy major, tried to place the Free Speech Movement in a broader context by claiming that the university not only greedily served the interests of corporate America but treated students like interchangeable robots. Likening the university to a giant machine, Savio insisted, "There is a time when the operation of the machine becomes so odious, makes you so sick to heart, that . . . you've got to make it stop."

As unrest spread to other campuses, the protests took many forms. Students held sit-ins to halt racial discrimination in fraternities and sororities, rallied to protest dress codes, marched to demand fewer required courses, and threatened to close down universities unless they admitted more minority students and stopped research for the military-industrial complex. The escalation of the Vietnam War in 1965 gave the New Left an opportunity to kindle a mass social movement. When the Johnson administration abolished automatic student deferments for the draft in January 1966, more than 200 new campus chapters of SDS appeared.

In 1966 SDS disrupted ROTC (Reserve Officer Training Corps) classes, organized draft-card burnings, and harassed campus recruiters for the military and for Dow Chemical Company, the chief producer of napalm and Agent Orange, chemicals used in Vietnam to burn villages and to defoliate forests. By 1967 SDS leaders encouraged more provocative acts of defiance, orchestrated civil disobedience at selective-service centers, and counseled students to flee to Canada or Sweden rather than be drafted. At the Spring Mobilization to End the War in Vietnam, which attracted nearly a half-million protesters to New York's Central Park, SDS members led chants of "Burn cards, not people" and "Hell, no, we won't go!"

The spring of 1968 saw at least 40,000 students on 100 campuses demonstrate against war and racism. Although the student movement was overwhelmingly peaceful, sometimes the confrontations turned violent. In April 1968, denouncing the university's proposed expansion into Harlem to construct a gymnasium, militant Columbia University students, shouting "Gym Crow must go," took over the administration building and held a dean captive. The protest expanded into a demonstration against the war and university military research. A thousand students occupied other campus buildings and made them "revolutionary communes." Galvanized by the brutality of the police who retook the buildings, the moderate majority of Columbia students joined a general boycott of classes that shut down the university. A pitched battle between police and antiwar demonstrators at the Democratic National Convention in Chicago that summer illustrated how the antiwar movement was pushing the nation into increasingly emotional confrontation.

August 1969 saw a high point of the movement with the New Mobilization, a series of huge antiwar demonstrations culminating in mid-November with the March Against Death in Washington, D.C. The 300,000 protesters who descended on the nation's capital formed a march that began at Arlington National Cemetery, snaked past the White House, and ended at the Capitol, where twelve wooden coffins were set up. For forty hours the marchers proceeded single-file through a cold drizzle, carrying candles and signs with the names of soldiers killed or villages destroyed in Vietnam.

The Waning of Student Radicalism

A crescendo of violence in the spring of 1970 marked the effective end of the student movement as a political force. On April 30, 1970, President Richard M. Nixon, Lyndon Johnson's successor, jolted a war-weary nation by announcing that he had ordered U.S. troops to invade Cambodia, a neutral Indochinese nation that the president claimed was a staging area for North Vietnamese forces. Nixon had decided to extricate the United States from Vietnam by "Vietnamizing" the ground conflict and intensifying bombing. The many students who had been lulled by periodic announcements of troop withdrawals from Vietnam now felt infuriated, frightened, and betrayed. They exploded in hatred for Nixon and the war.

At Kent State University in Ohio, as elsewhere, these frustrations unleashed new turmoil. A few radicals broke windows, pelted police cars with rocks and bottles, and tried to firebomb the ROTC building. Nixon lashed out at them as "bums." Ohio governor James Rhodes slapped martial law on the university and ordered 3,000 National Guardsmen to Kent. Donning full battle gear, the troops rolled onto the Kent State campus in armored personnel carriers.

On May 4, the day after the Guard's arrival, 600 Kent State students peacefully demonstrated against the Cambodian invasion. Suddenly a campus policeman boomed through a bullhorn, "This assembly is unlawful! This is an order—disperse immediately!" Students shouted back, "Pigs off campus!" Some threw stones. With bayonets fixed, the guardsmen moved toward the rally and laid down a blanket of tear gas. Hundreds of demonstrators and onlookers, choking and weeping, ran from the advancing troops. Guardsmen in Troop G, apparently panicking, raised their rifles and fired a volley into the retreating crowd. When the shooting stopped,

National Guardsmen at Kent State University, 1970

President Nixon's Commission on Campus Unrest concluded that "the [National Guard's] timing and manner of dispersal was disastrous. . . . The rally was peaceful and there was no impending violence."

eleven students lay wounded; four were dead. None was a campus radical; two had simply been passing by on their way to lunch.

The Guardsmen later alleged that they had fired to protect themselves from "a charging mob," but the FBI branded this claim a fabrication. A presidential commission investigating the Kent State incident denounced the shootings as "indiscriminate firing" and "unnecessary, unwarranted, and inexcusable."

Across the nation, students and others reacted with stunned disbelief followed by angry protest. Then on May 15 highway patrolmen looking into a campus demonstration fired into a women's dormitory at Jackson State College in Mississippi, killing two students and wounding eleven. Protests against such senseless violence, the war, and President Nixon thundered across campuses, and more than 400 colleges and universities shut down as students boycotted classes.

Popular reaction to these events demonstrated how polarized the nation had become. Although most college students blamed Nixon for widening the war and applauded the demonstrators' goals, far more Americans blamed the *victims* for the deaths at Kent State and criticized campus protesters for undermining U.S. foreign policy. Underlying these attitudes were a deep resentment of college students and impatience for an end to the social chaos. Symptomatically, Kent State students expressed profound alienation after the shootings, while a local merchant said that the National Guard "made only one mistake—they should have fired sooner and longer."

But the campus protests after Kent State and Jackson State represented the final spasm of a fragmenting, expiring movement. When a bomb planted by three antiwar radicals destroyed a science building at the University of Wisconsin in the summer of 1970, killing a graduate student, most students deplored the tactic. With the resumption of classes in the fall, the campus mood had changed dramatically. Frustrated by their failure to end the war, much less to revolutionize American society,

antiwar activists at Wisconsin and elsewhere turned to other causes or to communes, careers, or parenthood. SDS fell prey to hard-line disciples of Chinese communist Mao Zedong or Cuban revolutionary Che Guevara. A handful of frustrated radicals went underground, planning and sometimes carrying out terrorist acts that justified the government's repression of the remnants of the antiwar movement. The New Left had fallen victim to government harassment, to its own internal contradictions, and to Nixon's success in winding down the Vietnam War (see below).

The aftereffects of 1960s campus activism would linger long after the demise of the New Left. Festering resentment over the student revolt would stoke rising conservatism among middle-class and working-class Americans in the late sixties and early seventies. A right-wing backlash, fueled by opposition to the youth movement, would unite fundamentalist Protestants, white southerners, and blue-collar workers.

Early stirrings of this backlash propelled Ronald Reagan to prominence. In 1966 he won California's governorship, in part because of his opposition to demonstrators at the University of California's Berkeley campus. The actor-turned-politician won a resounding reelection victory by railing against radicals: "If it takes a bloodbath," he said, "let's get it over with. No more appeasement." Other conservatives gained office nationwide. And memories of student radicalism would weaken liberalism's appeal during the 1970s and 1980s.

At the same time, the New Left had incubated the growth of public opposition to the Vietnam War. The movement had elevated the campuses into a force that the government could not ignore, and it had made continued U.S. involvement in Indochina difficult. The New Left had also aided in liberalizing many facets of campus life and making university governance less authoritarian. Dress codes and curfews virtually disappeared; ROTC became an elective, not a requirement; schools now recruited minorities; and students sat on the committees that shaped their education.

Some New Left veterans would remain active in post-1970 causes, including environmentalism, consumer advocacy, and the antinuclear movement. Female students who had learned organizing skills while enduring blatant male chauvinism in the sixties' antiwar movement would form the backbone of a resurgent women's movement in the seventies.

These outcomes fell far short of the original New Left vision of remaking the social and political order. Masses of students could be mobilized in the short run against the Vietnam War, but only a few had made long-term commitments to radical politics.

The Youth Culture

The alienation that drew some youths into radical politics led others to cultural rebellion. Scorning their parents' materialism, these rebels discounted the economic ambitions of "the Establishment" and repudiated traditional notions of achievement. Some joined communes—group living arrangements whose members sought to cohabit in harmony and noncompetition—and many experimented with drugs and sex. Historian Theodore Roszak called them "a 'counter culture' . . . a culture so radically disaffiliated from the mainstream assumptions of our society that it scarcely looks to many as a culture at all, but takes on the alarming appearance of a barbarian intrusion."

The counterculture owed a debt to the Beats of the 1950s but went far beyond. Substituting the pleasure ethic for the work ethic, the "hippies" of the sixties scandalized the middle class with their sexual promiscuity and indulgence in drugs. Surveys estimated that least half the college students in the late sixties had tried marijuana and that a minority used mind-altering drugs, especially LSD and mescaline. Distancing themselves from middle-class respectability, many youths flaunted outrageous personal styles. They showed their disdain for consumerism by wearing surplus military clothing, torn jeans, and tie-dyed T-shirts. Especially galling to adults, young men sported shaggy beards and long hair, which became the badge of the counterculture.

Popular music both echoed and influenced the youth culture. In the early sixties, college students listened to folk music. Songs protesting racism and injustice mirrored the idealistic, nonviolent commitment of the civil-rights movement. Bob Dylan sang hopefully of changes "blowin' in the wind" that would transform society. Then in 1964 Beatlemania swept the United States. Moving beyond their early romantic songs, the Beatles gloried in the youth culture's drugs ("I'd love to turn you on"), sex ("why don't we do it in the road?"), and radicalism ("you say you want a revolution"). The Grateful Dead, Jefferson Airplane, and other bands launched "acid rock," which blended a heavy beat with lyrics extolling radical politics, drugs, and sex.

In August 1969, 400,000 young people gathered for the Woodstock festival in New York's Catskill Mountains to celebrate their vision of freedom and harmony. For three days and nights they reveled in the music of dozens of rock stars and openly shared drugs, sexual partners, and their contempt for the Establishment. The counterculture heralded Woodstock as the dawning of an era of love and peace, the Age of Aquarius.

In fact, the counterculture was disintegrating. Pilgrimages of "flower children" to San Francisco's Haight-Ashbury district and to New York's East Village in the mid-sixties had brought in their wake a train of muggers, rapists, and dope peddlers pushing hard drugs. With the decade's end came the shattering of the countercultural dream. In December 1969 the deranged Charles Manson and his "family" of runaways ritually murdered a pregnant movie actress and four of her friends. The tragedy revealed that something had gone profoundly wrong. Then a Rolling Stones concert at the Altamont Raceway near San Francisco deteriorated into a violent melee in which four concertgoers died. In July 1970 the Beatles disbanded. John Lennon sang, "The dream is over. What can I say?"

The Sexual Revolution

The counterculture practiced a "do your own thing" approach to sex that corresponded with an overall atmosphere of greater permissiveness. Indeed, many

Americans became more open than before in pursuing sexual activity. These shifts in attitude and behavior unleashed a sexual revolution that would flourish until the mid-1980s, when the AIDS epidemic and the "graying" of the youth movement chilled the ardor of open sexuality.

Most commentators linked the sexual revolution to waning fears of unwanted pregnancy. In 1960 oral contraceptives reached the market, and by 1970, 12 million women were taking "the Pill." Even more women used the intrauterine device (or IUD, later banned as unsafe) or the diaphragm for birth control. And states gradually legalized abortion. In 1970 in New York State, one fetus was legally aborted for every two babies born. The Supreme Court's *Roe* v. *Wade* decision (1973) struck down all remaining state laws infringing on a woman's right to abortion during the first three months of pregnancy.

Mass culture embraced the new sexuality. *Playboy* magazine featured ever-more-explicit erotica, and women's periodicals encouraged their readers to enjoy recreational sex. Barriers to public expression of sexuality fell as the Supreme Court extended First Amendment protection to books and films once banned as obscene and as Hollywood filled movie screens with scenes of explicit sex. Broadway presented plays featuring frontal nudity, mimed sex acts, and mock orgies, and even television presented frank discussions of once forbidden subjects.

The casual acceptance of sexuality influenced Americans' behavior. Many couples lived together without being married. Surveys showed that by the mid-1970s three-quarters of all college students had engaged in sexual intercourse before their senior year. The use of contraceptives (and to some extent, abortion) spread to women of all religious backgrounds—including Roman Catholics, despite the Catholic church's impassioned stand against "artificial" birth control. The national birthrate plunged steadily throughout the 1960s and 1970s, a drop that will significantly affect the American demographic profile well into the twenty-first century.

What some hailed as sexual liberation, others bemoaned as moral decay. Offended by "topless" bars, X-rated theaters, and "adult" bookstores, many Americans applauded politicians who promised a war on smut. The sexual revolution accentuated the "generation gap" that polarized the attitudes and behavior of many middle-class youths and their parents. Pubescent promiscuity, sex education in the schools, rising abortion rates, and homosexuals' "coming out of the closet" merged in many people's minds with pictures of student demonstrations and ghetto riots. In defense of embattled traditional morality, normally Democratic voters would swell the tide of conservatism as the sixties ended.

1968: The Politics of Strife

The social and cultural turmoil of the 1960s unfolded against a backdrop of frustration with the Vietnam War and an intensifying domestic political crisis. The stormy year 1968 brought these elements together explosively. The psychologically devastating Tet offensive was followed on the domestic scene by political assassinations, nominating conventions marred by violence, and new ghetto riots. Converging in the presidential campaign of 1968, the swirling currents of strife precipitated the first major realignment of American politics since the New Deal.

The Tet Offensive in Vietnam

In January 1968 liberal Democratic senator Eugene McCarthy of Minnesota, a Vietnam War critic, announced that he would challenge Lyndon B. Johnson for the presidential nomination. Pundits scoffed that McCarthy had no chance of unseating Johnson, who had won the presidency in 1964 by the largest margin in U.S. history. But McCarthy stuck to his course, determined that at least one Democrat would enter the primaries on an antiwar platform.

Shortly, America's hopes for victory in Vietnam sank, and with them LBJ's political fortunes. On January 31, the first day of Tet, the Vietnamese New Year, National Liberation Front (NLF) and North Vietnamese forces mounted a huge offensive, attacking more than 100 towns in South Vietnam and a dozen American bases. U.S. troops repulsed the offensive, regained the captured territory, and inflicted devastating casualties on the attackers. The U.S. commander in South Vietnam announced that "the enemy is on the ropes."

The media, however, emphasized the staggering number of American casualties and the scope of the offensive. Americans at home reacted sharply to the realization that no area of South Vietnam was secure from the enemy and that a foe whom the president had claimed was beaten could initiate such daring attacks. Many stopped believing reports of battlefield successes streaming from the White House and doubted that the United States could win the war at an acceptable cost.

After Tet, McCarthy's criticism of the war won new sympathizers. *Time, Newsweek,* and the *Wall Street Journal* published editorials urging a negotiated settlement. The nation's most respected newscaster, Walter Cronkite of CBS, observed that "it seems now more certain than ever that the bloody experience of Vietnam is to end in a stalemate." "If I've lost Walter," LBJ sighed, "then it's over. I've lost Mr. Average Citizen." Indeed, the president's approval rating dropped to a shocking 35 percent after Tet. The number of Americans who described themselves as prowar "hawks" slipped from 62 percent in January to 41 percent in March, while the antiwar "doves" jumped from 22 percent to 42 percent.

The Shaken President

Beleaguered, Johnson pondered a change in American policy. When the Joint Chiefs of Staff sought an additional 206,000 men for Vietnam, he consulted with advisers. Dean Acheson, the former secretary of state and a venerable Cold Warrior, told LBJ that "the Joint Chiefs of Staff don't know what they're talking about." Clark Clifford, the new secretary of defense, became convinced that the American course was hopeless. Johnson's foreign-policy experts urged the president to halt the bombing and to initiate negotiations.

Meanwhile, nearly 5,000 college students had swarmed to New Hampshire to stuff envelopes and ring doorbells for Eugene McCarthy. To be "Clean

for Gene," they cut their long hair and dressed conservatively. McCarthy astonished the experts by winning nearly half the popular vote and twenty of twenty-four nominating-convention delegates in the primary contest of a state usually regarded as conservative.

After this upset, twice as many students converged on Wisconsin to canvass its more liberal Democratic voters, anticipating a resounding McCarthy triumph in the nation's second primary. Hurriedly, on March 16 Senator Robert Kennedy entered the Democratic contest, also promising to end the war. Projecting the familiar Kennedy glamour and magnetism, Kennedy was the one candidate whom Johnson feared could deny him renomination. Indeed, millions viewed Kennedy as the rightful heir to the White House. Appealing to minorities, the poor, and working-class ethnic whites, Kennedy became, according to one columnist, "our first politician for the pariahs, our great national outsider." He also attracted support from mainstream Democrats responding to his charisma as well as his politics.

On March 31 LBJ informed a television audience that he was halting the bombing of North Vietnam. Saying that he wanted to devote all his efforts to the search for peace, Johnson then startlingly announced, "I shall not seek, and I will not accept, the nomination of my party for another term as your president." Embittered by the personal abuse that he had endured, and reluctant to polarize the nation further, the president called it quits. "The only difference between the Kennedy assassination and mine," he lamented, "is that I am alive and it has been more tortuous." Two days later, McCarthy trounced the president in the Wisconsin primary.

Assassinations and Turmoil

On April 4, three days after the Wisconsin primary, Martin Luther King, Jr., was killed in Memphis, Tennessee, where he had gone to support striking sanitation workers. The assassin was James Earl Ray, a white escaped convict. As the news spread, black ghettos burst into violence in 125 cities. Twenty blocks of Chicago's West Side went up in flames, and Mayor Richard Daley ordered police to shoot to kill arsonists. In Washington, D.C., under night skies illuminated by 700 fires, army units in combat gear set up machine-gun emplacements outside the Capitol and White House. The rioting left 46 dead and 3,000 injured. The violence stood in ironic contrast to King's message of reconciliation. As King was buried, Americans recalled the prophetic imagery of his speech to a Memphis audience the night before his death: "I've been to the mountaintop. . . . I may not get there with you, but I want you to know that we as a people will get to the promised land."

The Democratic contest for the presidential nomination became a three-cornered scramble as LBJ's vice president, Hubert Humphrey, entered the race as the standard-bearer of the New Deal coalition. But liberal antiwar activists who had once lionized him for his courageous stands on social justice now rejected Humphrey because of his support for the administration's Vietnam policy. Humphrey relied on labor chieftains, Johnson loyalists, and party bosses to line up delegates. McCarthy stood as the candidate of the "new politics"—a moral crusade against war and injustice directed to affluent and educated liberals. And Kennedy campaigned as the tribune of the less privileged, the only candidate who appealed to white ethnics and the minority poor. But on June 5, 1968, as he celebrated victory in the California primary at a Los Angeles hotel, the brother of the murdered president was himself assassinated. A Palestinian refugee, Sirhan Sirhan, who loathed Kennedy for his pro-Israel views, was apprehended on the spot.

The assassination crushed the dream of peace and racial justice, replacing it with despair. "I won't vote," one youth said. "Every good man we get they kill." Kennedy's death also dispirited the McCarthy forces and cleared the way for Humphrey, although some Democrats fumed that the party was about to nominate a prowar candidate who had not campaigned in a single primary.

Other Democrats turned to third-party candidate George Wallace or to Republican nominee Richard M. Nixon. Nixon took advantage of the sense of national disarray to emerge as the GOP frontrunner in 1968. Republicans hailed the "new Nixon" as a leader who would restore stability. In his acceptance speech at the Republican convention, Nixon promised to listen to "the voice of the great majority of Americans, the forgotten Americans, the non-shouters, the non-demonstrators, those who do not break the law, people who pay their taxes and go to work, who send their children to school, who go to their churches, . . . who love this country." George Wallace tapped into the same wellspring of angry reaction as Nixon. The Alabama governor's acrimonious speeches intensified working-class whites' animosity toward militant blacks, antiwar protesters, and welfare recipients. Wallace promised to crack down on rioters and "long-hair, pot-smoking, draft-card-burning youth."

In August 1968 violence outside the Democratic National Convention in Chicago reinforced the appeal of both Wallace and Nixon. Thousands descended on the city to protest the Vietnam War, hoping to pressure the convention to repudiate the administration's policy. Radicals among the protesters wanted to provoke a confrontation to discredit the Democrats, and a handful ridiculed the system by creating their own "Youth International Party." These anarchistic "Yippies" spoke of dumping LSD in the city's water system and releasing greased pigs in Chicago's crowded Loop area.

Remembering the rioting that had convulsed Chicago in the wake of King's assassination, law-and-order mayor Richard Daley turned the city into a war zone. On August 28, as a huge television audience tuned in, Daley's bluecoats clubbed protesters and bystanders alike and broke into Senator McCarthy's campaign headquarters. The brutality on the streets overshadowed Humphrey's nomination and tore the Democrats further apart, fixing Americans' image of them as the party of dissent and disorder.

Conservative Resurgence

Nixon capitalized on the tumult. His TV campaign commercials flashed images of campus and ghetto uprisings. He promised to appoint a tough attorney general, asserted that "our schools are for education—not integration," and claimed that "new leadership will end the war and win the peace" in Vietnam, without revealing his plans.

George Wallace, also appealing to the broad revulsion against radicalism, burned across the political landscape. He stoked the fury of the working class toward "those briefcase-totin' bureaucrats, ivory-tower guideline writers, bearded anarchists, smart-aleck editorial writers, and pointy-headed professors looking down their noses at us." He denounced school integrationists, welfare mothers, and radical professors alike. Promising to keep peace even if it took "30,000 troops armed with three-foot bayonets," he vowed that "if any demonstrator ever lays [sic] down in front of my car, it'll be the last car he'll ever lie down in front of."

By September Wallace had climbed to 21 percent in voter-preference polls. However, most voters were terrified by the suggestion of his running mate, retired air force general Curtis LeMay, that the United States should "drop nukes on Vietnam." Still, nearly 14 percent of the electorate voted for Wallace in November.

Nixon and Humphrey split the rest of the vote almost evenly, and Nixon squeaked to victory with 43.4 percent of the popular vote. He garnered only 301 electoral votes, the narrowest victory since Woodrow Wilson's slender triumph in 1916. A conservative majority had supplanted the New Deal coalition—Humphrey received just 38 percent of the white vote, not even half the skilled-labor vote, and only a third of the semiskilled-labor vote.

Most voters, including Democratic loyalists, had voted for law and order and respect for tradition and against expansion of Great Society programs. The 57 percent of the electorate who chose Nixon or Wallace would dominate American presidential politics into the 1990s. While the national Democratic party fractured into a welter of contending groups, the Republicans attracted a new majority who lived in the suburbs and the Sun Belt, regarded the federal government as wasteful, disdained student radicalism and the forced busing of schoolchildren, and objected to special efforts to assist minorities.

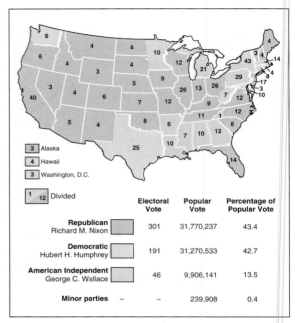

	Electoral Vote	Popular Vote	Percentage of Popular Vote
Republican Richard M. Nixon	301	31,770,237	43.4
Democratic Hubert H. Humphrey	191	31,270,533	42.7
American Independent George C. Wallace	46	9,906,141	13.5
Minor parties	–	–	239,908	0.4

The Election of 1968

The 1968 election rang down the curtain on one of the most tempestuous years in U.S. history. The Democrats' loss of some 12 million voters who had cast ballots for LBJ in 1964 but who opted for Nixon or Wallace in 1968 heralded a major electoral shift. The controversial, stalemated war in Vietnam had polarized society and shattered the liberal consensus that had supported domestic reform and global policing. A new majority now yearned for restraint abroad, for a reduction of government activism at home, and—most of all—for the restoration of domestic tranquillity and the end of the Vietnam War.

Nixon and World Politics

The new president, Richard M. Nixon, focused mainly on foreign affairs. Considering himself a master of realpolitik—a pragmatic approach stressing the advancement of the national interest rather than theoretical or ethical goals—he promoted a grand design to check Soviet expansionism and to promote global stability, to limit the nuclear-arms race, and to enhance the United States' economic well-being. Nixon recognized that the Vietnam War had eroded American support for similar armed interventions and that the Chinese-Soviet split had made the idea of monolithic communism obsolete. He planned to move the United States out of Vietnam and into an era of détente—an easing of tensions—with the communist world.

To manage diplomacy, Nixon chose Henry Kissinger, a refugee from Hitler's Germany and a Harvard professor of international relations who shared the president's realpolitik views. Kissinger served as national security adviser until 1973, when he became secretary of state. Nixon and Kissinger centralized foreign-policy decision making in the White House. Worrying that others in the government might leak sensitive material or obstruct their initiatives, they kept many of their actions hidden.

Vietnamization

The Nixon-Kissinger grand design meant ending the Vietnam War. The war was sapping American military strength, worsening inflation, and thwarting détente. In August 1969 the president unveiled what became known as the Nixon Doctrine, in which he redefined the United States' role in the Third World as that of a helpful partner rather than a military protector. In the future, Asian nations facing communist subversion could count on American financial and moral support, but they would have to defend themselves: "Asian hands must shape the Asian future."

The Nixon Doctrine reflected the president's understanding of the war weariness of both the electorate and the U.S. troops in Vietnam. Johnson's decision to negotiate rather than to escalate had left American troops with the sense that nothing mattered except survival. Morale had plummeted and discipline had collapsed. Army desertions rocketed from 27,000 in 1967 to 76,000 in 1970, and the desertion rate in the marines rose even faster. Racial conflict among American soldiers became commonplace and drug use soared.

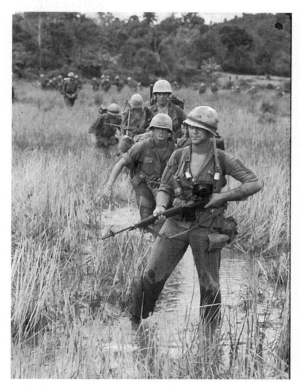

Bogged Down in Vietnam
Knee deep in a swamp, American soldiers prepare for an attack in the Hiep Duc district.

Instances of "fragging"—enlisted men's killing of officers—were reported.

American atrocities against the Vietnamese had also mounted. Especially after 1967, growing cases of Americans' dismembering enemy bodies, torturing captives, wantonly torching villages, and murdering civilians had come to light. In March 1968 an army unit led by an inexperienced lieutenant, William Calley, had massacred 347 defenseless women, children, and old men in the hamlet of My Lai. After stopping for lunch, the Americans had burned the village and slaughtered the livestock. Revelations of such incidents, and the rising number of returned soldiers who joined Vietnam Veterans Against the War, had undercut the already diminished support for the war.

Despite pressure to end the war, Nixon was determined to salvage America's prestige. Seeking "peace with honor," Nixon pursued three simultaneous courses. First, he implemented "Vietnamization," replacing American troops with South Vietnamese. By 1972 U.S. forces in Vietnam would shrink from 500,000 to 30,000. Second, Nixon bypassed South Vietnamese leaders by sending Kissinger to negotiate secretly with North Vietnam's foreign minister, Le Duc Tho. Finally, to force the communists to compromise despite U.S. withdrawal, the president radically escalated American bombing. To maximize the harm done to the enemy, Nixon in March 1969 secretly ordered the bombing of North Vietnamese supply routes in Cambodia and Laos and the intensification of bombing raids on North Vietnam. He told an aide, "We'll just slip the word to them that 'you know Nixon is obsessed about communism. We can't restrain him when he's angry—and he has his hand on the nuclear button'—and Ho Chi Minh . . . will be . . . begging for peace."

LBJ's War Becomes Nixon's War

But the secret B-52 raids against Cambodia neither made Hanoi beg for peace nor disrupted communist supply bases. They did, however, help to undermine the precarious stability of that tiny republic. In early 1970 North Vietnam increased its infiltration of troops into Cambodia, both to aid the Cambodian communists (the Khmer Rouge) and to facilitate the use of Cambodia as a staging area for attacks in South Vietnam. In turn, to demonstrate his toughness in what he saw as a contest of wills, Nixon ordered a joint U.S.–South Vietnamese incursion into Cambodia at the end of April 1970. It was successful; the invaders seized large caches of arms and bought time for Vietnamization. But the costs were high. The invasion ended Cambodia's neutrality, widened the war throughout Indochina, and provoked massive American protests against the war, culminating in the student deaths at Kent State and Jackson State universities.

In 1971 Nixon continued to combine American withdrawal with renewed blows against the enemy. In February, at the administration's initiative, the South Vietnamese army invaded Laos to destroy communist bases there and to interfere with the flow of supplies southward from North Vietnam. The South Vietnamese, however, were routed. Emboldened by this success, communist forces moved to occupy as much strategic territory as possible. In April 1972 the North Vietnamese mounted a major offensive throughout Cambodia and Vietnam. With fewer than 100,000 American troops still in Vietnam, Nixon retaliated by mining North Vietnamese harbors and ports and unleashing a rain of B-52s on Cambodia and on North Vietnamese cities.

American Retreat from the War

The bombing raids in the spring of 1972 broke the impasse in the Paris peace talks, stalemated since 1968. In October 1972 the North Vietnamese relented on their demand that a coalition government replace South Vietnam's President Thieu. Kissinger and Le Duc Tho negotiated a cease-fire that required the withdrawal of all American troops, provided for the return of U.S. prisoners of war, and allowed North Vietnamese troops to remain in South Vietnam. Shortly before the 1972 U.S. presidential election, Kissinger announced that "peace is at hand."

Nixon accordingly campaigned in 1972 as the architect of peace in Vietnam and announced that, if reelected, he would end the draft in mid-1973. But President Thieu refused to sign a cease-fire agreement permitting North Vietnamese troops to remain in the South. Angered by Thieu's rebuff, Le Duc Tho pressed for additional concessions. President Nixon again resorted to B-52 raids. The 1972 Christmas bombings of Hanoi and Haiphong, major North Vietnamese cities, aroused fierce opposition in Congress and the United Nations but accomplished their purpose. The deadlock was dissolved, and Nixon's secret reassurance to Thieu that the United States would "respond with full force should the settlement be violated by North Vietnam" ended Saigon's recalcitrance.

The Paris Accords, signed in late January 1973, essentially reiterated the terms of the October truce. The agreement ended hostilities between the United States and North Vietnam. But it left unresolved the differences between North and South Vietnam, guaranteeing that Vietnam's future would yet be settled on the battlefield.

The United States paused to assess its longest war. The conflict had exacerbated national problems and deepened social divisions. It had cost 58,000 American deaths, 300,000 wounded, and at least $150 billion. Twenty percent of those who had served, nearly 500,000, received less-than-honorable discharges, a measure of the desertion rate, drug usage, strength of antiwar sentiment in the military, and immaturity of the troops (the average U.S. soldier in Vietnam was just nineteen years old, seven years younger than the average GI in World War II).

Virtually all who survived, wrote one marine, returned "as immigrants to a new world. For the culture we had known dissolved while we were in Vietnam, and the culture of combat we lived in . . . made us aliens when we returned." Beyond occasional media attention to the psychological difficulties that they faced in adjusting to civilian life, the nation paid little heed to its Vietnam veterans.

Instead, relieved that the long nightmare had ended, most Americans tried to forget the war. The bitterness of many veterans moderated with time. Few Americans gave much thought to how the war had devastated Vietnam, inflicting 2 million casualties. Laos, too, had suffered, but Cambodia had paid the highest price. After the war engulfed this previously peaceful land, the fanatical Khmer Rouge emerged victorious in 1975. Three million Cambodians—40 percent of the nation's population—died in the killings and "relocations" that followed.

Détente

Disengagement from Vietnam helped Nixon to achieve a turnabout in Chinese-American relations and détente with the communist superpowers. These developments, the most significant shift in U.S. foreign policy since the start of the Cold War, created a new relationship among the United States, China, and the Soviet Union.

Presidents from Truman to Johnson had refused to recognize the People's Republic of China. The United States had vetoed the admission of "Red China" to the United Nations and pressured American allies to restrict trade with the communist giant. But by 1969 a widening Chinese-Soviet split made the prospect of improved relations attractive to both Nixon and Mao Zedong. That year, armed clashes between Soviet and Chinese troops along their mutual border prompted Beijing to seek better relations with Washington as security against the U.S.S.R.'s expansion. Playing one communist power off against another, Nixon and Kissinger calculated that cordiality toward China would constrain Soviet influence in Asia and push Moscow toward concessions in nuclear-arms limitations.

In the fall of 1970, Nixon opened what Kissinger called "the three-dimensional game" by calling China the People's Republic rather than Red China. In June 1971 Kissinger made a secret trip to China, and a month later Nixon announced that he would travel to the People's Republic "to seek the normalization of relations." In February 1972 the president's plane landed in China, beginning the first trip ever by a sitting American president to the largest nation in the world. Nixon toured the Great Wall and exchanged ceremonious toasts with Mao and Premier Zhou Enlai (Chou Enlai). Although differences between the two powers delayed official diplomatic relations until 1979, Nixon's visit signaled the end of more than twenty years of Chinese-American hostility.

Equally significantly, Nixon went to Moscow in May 1972. "There must be room in this world for two great nations with different systems to live together and work together," the president proclaimed. To that end, he concluded agreements with the Soviets on trade and technological cooperation (including the sale of $750 million in American grain) and, after the first Strategic Arms Limitation Talks (SALT I), signed two major arms-control pacts with Soviet leader Leonid Brezhnev. The SALT I agreements, overwhelmingly ratified by the Senate in October 1972, limited each nation to 200 antiballistic missiles (ABMs) and two ABM systems. SALT I reflected the belief that mutual

Nixon in China, 1972
American TV networks covered Nixon's dramatic visits to legendary landmarks such as the Great Wall, as well as his impromptu conversations with the Chinese people. One reporter remarked that "the White House was playing [the visit] as a pageant, not as a news story."

deterrence offered the surest guarantee against nuclear attack and that such mutuality could be preserved only if neither side built nationwide missile-defense systems. A separate agreement froze for five years the number of intercontinental ballistic missiles and submarine-launched missiles that each power could have. Like SALT I, it allowed both nations to monitor each other by photo-reconnaissance satellites. The limitations slowed the costly and dangerous nuclear-arms race, reduced Cold War tensions, and, in an election year, enhanced Nixon's stature as a proponent of peace.

American Self-Interest Abroad

The Middle East remained an arena of conflict. While trying to support Israel's security, the United States feared Soviet penetration of the area and hoped to gain or retain the friendship of anti-Israel Arab governments.

In 1967 Israel fought the Six-Day War with its Arab neighbors. The war erupted after Nasser's Egypt ejected U.N. peacekeeping forces, reoccupied

Sinai, and closed the Gulf of Aqaba. Egypt, Syria, and Jordan mobilized, and Israel responded by launching a preemptive strike against Egypt on June 5, 1967. When Jordan then attacked, Israel struck back against it, too. In less than a week, Israel had occupied the Gaza Strip (Egyptian-controlled Palestinian territory) and Sinai, Jordanian-ruled East Jerusalem and the West Bank, and Syria's Golan Heights.

A stalemate followed. Israel promised to give up most of the occupied lands in exchange for direct negotiations and peace, but the Arab states refused to negotiate with Israel or to recognize its right to exist. The Palestinian population turned to the Palestinian Liberation Organization (PLO), which had been founded in 1964, to defend its interests. The PLO sought international recognition of Palestinian rights and called for Israel's destruction. Competing PLO factions hijacked Western airliners, raided Israel, and murdered Israeli athletes at the 1972 Olympic games. To retaliate, Israel assassinated PLO agents abroad and bombed PLO bases and installations in refugee camps, especially in Lebanon.

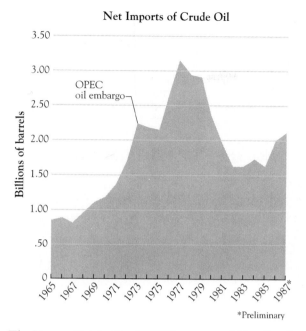

Net Imports of Crude Oil

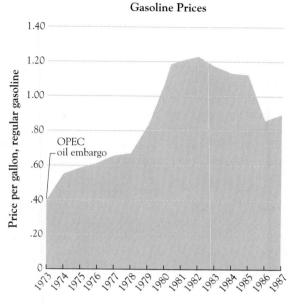

Gasoline Prices

*Preliminary

The Energy Crisis: Crude-Oil Imports and Gasoline Prices
Not until the 1980s, through the combination of a deep recession and fuel conservation, did U.S. petroleum imports finally begin dropping off (left). OPEC's ability to act as a supercartel in setting oil prices sent the cost of filling a car's gas tank skyrocketing in the 1970s (right).
SOURCE: Energy Information Administration, *Annual Energy Review*, 1987.

Nasser died in 1970, and his successor, Anwar el-Sadat, changed course. Through U.S. and U.N. intermediaries, Sadat made peace overtures to Israel, and in July 1972 he expelled Soviet military advisers. America's response consisted of vague assurances of a "peace initiative." But Nixon's preoccupation with Vietnam and Watergate precluded further U.S. interest. Hopes for negotiations dimmed; Moscow resumed shipping offensive weapons to Egypt and Syria.

War exploded again in 1973 when Egypt and Syria attacked Israel on October 6, Yom Kippur, the most sacred Jewish holy day. The United States and the Soviet Union airlifted tons of military equipment to their respective allies. Israel stopped the offensive and counterattacked. In retaliation, oil-

producing Arab states embargoed shipments of crude oil to the United States and its allies. The five-month embargo (October 1973–March 1974) spawned acute fuel shortages and sharply increased the cost of petroleum products in the United States, driving up inflation.

The Nixon administration, which had generally sided with Israel, now sought better relations with moderate Arab regimes in order to isolate Arab hard-liners. The dual shocks of the energy crisis at home and renewed Soviet influence among Arab hard-liners spurred Nixon and Kissinger to win Egypt for the pro-Western camp, to conciliate the oil-rich Arab rulers of the Persian Gulf, and to force Arab-Israeli peace talks. Beginning in October 1973, Kissinger pursued "shuttle diplomacy," flying from capital to capital to engineer disengagement accords between Israel and Egypt, and Israel and Syria. He also persuaded OPEC to end its oil embargo. Kissinger's diplomacy, designed to establish the United States as the sole Middle Eastern peacemaker, had limited but notable success. Splits among the Arabs widened, Egypt moved closer to Washington, and Syria broke with Egypt. The PLO itself split between moderate and hard-line factions, and some Palestinian insurgents struck all the harder against Israel and against U.S. citizens abroad.

Trying to shore up other American allies, the Nixon administration meanwhile liberally supplied arms to the shah of Iran, Reza Pahlavi; to President Ferdinand Marcos in the Philippines; and to the white-supremacist regime of South Africa. Nixon-Kissinger realpolitik based American aid on a nation's willingness to oppose the Soviet Union, not on the nature of its government. The administration also stepped up assistance to the repressive rulers of Argentina and South Korea, to military dictatorships in Brazil and oil-rich Nigeria, and to Portuguese colonial authorities in Angola.

When Chileans elected a Marxist, Salvador Allende, president in 1970, Nixon secretly funneled $10 million to the CIA to fund opponents of Allende's leftist regime. The United States also cut off economic aid to Chile, blocked private banks from granting loans, and successfully pressed the World Bank to drop Chile's credit rating. In September 1973 a military junta overthrew the Chilean government and killed Allende. Nixon quickly recognized the dictatorship, and economic aid and private investment again flowed to Chile.

The administration's active opposition to Allende reflected the extent to which American policy remained committed to containing communist influence. At the same time, Nixon understood the limits of U.S. power and the changed realities of world affairs. Discarding the vision of a bipolar world that had shaped American foreign policy since 1945, Nixon took advantage of the Chinese-Soviet split to improve American relations with both nations. The administration also ended American involvement in Vietnam and improved the U.S. position in the Middle East. Most significantly, the politician who had built his reputation as a staunch Cold Warrior initiated a new era of détente with the communist powers. The China opening and the arms-limitations agreements with the U.S.S.R. dramatically lowered Cold War tensions.

Domestic Problems and Divisions

Although Richard M. Nixon yearned to be remembered as an international statesman, domestic affairs kept intruding. In some ways, Nixon displayed domestic creativity, reforming welfare and abandoning traditional Republican hands-off conservatism to grapple with inflation and other complex economic problems. But another side of the Nixon administration appealed to the darker recesses of national character and intensified the fears and divisions among Americans. This underside was rooted in the complex character of Richard M. Nixon himself.

Richard Nixon: Man and Politician

Close observers of Nixon noted the multiple levels of his personality. Beneath the calculated public persona of the politician lurked a shadowy man who rarely revealed himself. Nixon the politician was highly intelligent, with phenomenal endurance and a capacity for total concentration. But the public Nixon also displayed the rigid self-control of a man monitoring his own every move. When the private Nixon did emerge, he was suspicious, insecure, and filled with anger. Nixon's conviction that enemies lurked on all sides, waiting to destroy him, verged on paranoia. He saw his life as a series of crises to be met and surmounted. A driven man, he sought to annihilate his partisan enemies, especially the "eastern liberal establishment" who had long opposed him.

Probing the source of his insecurities, some observers have viewed Nixon as the classic outsider: reared in pinched surroundings, physically awkward, unable to relate easily to others. It was hard work and self-discipline that had propelled him to the heights of national power. But even then, Nixon at some level remained the outsider, sensing that he was not fully accepted, suspicious that others laughed at his austere virtues, stern self-discipline, and public gaucheries. When he sneered at "the so-called best circles in America," it was with the resentment of one who recognized that many in that charmed circle held him in contempt. But whatever forces shaped Nixon's personality, many Americans identified with his outlook. Historian Garry Wills concluded that Nixon's strengths and deficiencies matched what was "best and weakest in America."

In the early Nixon years, the president's strengths were most apparent. Nixon spoke of national reconciliation, took bold initiatives internationally, and dealt with domestic problems responsibly. But the darker side would ultimately prevail and drive him from office in disgrace.

The Nixon Presidency

Nixon began his presidency with a moderation reminiscent of Eisenhower. His calm rhetoric and selection of a well-qualified cabinet of flexible conservatives promised the respite from unrest that most Americans desired. Symbolic of this positive start, the nation joined the new president in celebrating the first successful manned mission to the moon on July 20, 1969, as astronaut Neil Armstrong descended from the lunar lander *Eagle* to the surface of the Sea of Tranquillity, announcing to enthralled television audiences back on Earth, "That's one small step for man, one giant leap for mankind."

The first newly elected president since 1849 whose party controlled neither house of Congress, Nixon initially approved a moderate extension of Great Society programs. He signed bills to increase social-security benefits, to build subsidized housing, to expand the Job Corps, and to grant the vote to eighteen-year-olds. Although Nixon sided with corporate leaders who claimed that the cost of meeting stringent environmental standards would make U.S. industry uncompetitive with foreign enterprises, the Democrat-controlled Congress also enacted legisla-

tion targeting the adverse effects of material growth. New laws limited pesticide use, further protected endangered species, controlled strip-mining practices, safeguarded coastal lands, and established maximum levels for the emission of pollutants into the water and air. The National Environmental Policy Act (1970) required federal agencies to prepare environmental-impact analyses of all proposed projects and established the Environmental Protection Agency (EPA) to support the new statutes. In 1970 Congress also created the Occupational Safety and Health Administration (OSHA) to ensure workers' safety and well-being.

Growing environmental awareness culminated in the celebration of the first Earth Day in April 1970. Earth Day spotlighted such problems as thermal pollution, dying lakes, oil spills, and dwindling resources. The occasion also introduced Americans to the idea of "living lightly on the earth." Organic gardening, vegetarianism, solar power, recycling, and preventive health care became popular. Also in 1970, Nixon's Commission on Population Growth and the American Future promoted zero population growth, the idea that the birthrate should not exceed the death rate.

Annoyed that industry would have to absorb the costs of environmental objectives, angry Republican conservatives grew angrier in mid-1969 when Nixon unveiled his Family Assistance Plan (FAP). A bold effort to reform welfare, designed by Daniel Moynihan, a Democrat serving as Nixon's urban-affairs adviser, the FAP proposed to replace piecemeal handouts with a minimum annual income, $1,600 for a family of four. But conservatives criticized Nixon for sponsoring a measure that would jack up welfare costs, and liberals denounced FAP for its low payments and its requirement that heads of households on relief had to register for employment or job training. The plan passed the House but died in the Senate.

After the 1970 congressional elections, Nixon's conservatism clearly emerged. To cut federal spending, he vetoed more than a score of measures enacted by the Ninety-second Congress. When Congress overrode his vetoes, Nixon impounded (refused to spend) congressionally authorized funds. The president proclaimed that his policy, the "new federalism," would "reverse the flow of power and resources from the states and communities to Washington." To hasten that power shift from Washington to the states, Nixon proposed revenue sharing, or the allocation of some federal revenues to states and cities. The president hailed the new law, passed in October 1972, for its invigoration of local government, but the accompanying slashes in federal spending for social services left some financially pressed cities worse off than before.

A Troubled Economy

Nixon inherited the dire fiscal consequences of Lyndon B. Johnson's effort to wage the Vietnam War and finance the Great Society without raising

Inflation, 1920–1990

Inflation, which had been moderate during the two decades following the Second World War, began to soar with the escalation of the war in Vietnam in the mid-1960s. In 1979 and 1980 the nation experienced double-digit inflation in two consecutive years for the first time since World War I.

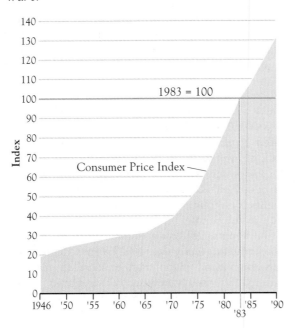

taxes. He faced what was then considered a whopping budget deficit, $25 billion, and an inflation rate of 5 percent. In 1969 the cost of living rose by 7 percent, and mounting prices for energy, food, and raw materials threatened worse inflation. Anxious to check inflation, Nixon cut government spending and encouraged the Federal Reserve Board to force up interest rates. Nixon's intent was to reduce inflation by slowing spending on the part of business and the consumer.

But despite rising unemployment and the first major recession since the Eisenhower era, inflation galloped upward. Democrats branded the alarming convergence of recession and inflation "Nixonomics." They complained, "All the things that should go up—the stock market, corporate profits, real spendable income, productivity—go down, and all the things that should go down—unemployment, prices, interest rates—go up."

Early in 1971 Nixon startled the nation by announcing, "I am now a Keynesian." Fearing the political consequences of the recession, he switched to the Keynesian tactic of reviving the economy through deficit spending and proposed an unbalanced federal budget to stimulate recovery. Nixon still refused to impose controls on wages and prices.

In August 1971 Nixon changed course again, introducing new measures to stabilize the economy and to deal with a major trade deficit. For the first time since 1890, the nation was importing more than it was exporting. He levied a 10 percent surcharge on imports and allowed the dollar to "float" against other currencies, abandoning the fixed relationships between the U.S. dollar and other currencies that was devised at Bretton Woods in 1944. Nixon then reversed himself further by decreeing a ninety-day freeze on wages, prices, and rents, to be followed by federal controls limiting maximum annual increases to 5.5 percent for wages and 2.5 percent for prices and rents.

The new policies perked up the economy, sent the Dow-Jones stock index above 1,000 for the first time in history, and reduced both inflation and the trade deficit. In January 1973, safely reelected, Nixon changed course again and replaced wage-and-price ceilings with "guidelines" and "voluntary" restraints. That year, inflation zoomed to 9 percent; it would remain a major headache throughout the 1970s.

Law and Order

Nixon hoped that federal suppression of domestic disorder, combined with his flexible economic policies, would forge an unbeatable coalition for the 1972 election. Seeking support among blue-color laborers, white southerners, and white ethnic minorities, he voiced his opposition to court-ordered busing and took every opportunity to spotlight his tough stand on law and order.

Nixon used full federal-government resources to target radicals. The Internal Revenue Service audited the tax returns of antiwar and civil-rights activists; the Small Business Administration denied them loans; and the FBI illegally wiretapped them. The FBI also infiltrated SDS and black radical groups with agents who, to discredit them, provoked violence within the movements. The Justice Department and the FBI worked with local officials to arrest Black Panthers on dubious charges. And the CIA illegally investigated and compiled dossiers on thousands of American dissidents. To focus the nation's fears on the radical threat, Nixon authorized the Department of Justice to prosecute antiwar activists and militant blacks in highly publicized trials.

Nixon also took steps to crush his opponents. Using unspent 1968 campaign funds, he created a secret task force in 1969 to spy on liberal columnists and congressional critics. Seeing political adversaries as personal enemies, Nixon compiled an "enemies list" of prominent Americans to be harassed by the government. "Anyone who opposes us, we'll destroy," warned a top White House official. "As a matter of fact, anyone who doesn't support us, we'll destroy."

In 1970 Nixon widened his offensive against the antiwar movement by approving the Huston Plan, which would use the CIA and FBI in various illegal missions. The plan called for extensive wiretapping and electronic surveillance, break-ins to find or plant evidence of illegal activity, and a new agency to centralize domestic covert operations under White House supervision. But FBI chief J. Edgar Hoover opposed the Huston Plan as a threat to the FBI's independence. Blocked, Nixon secretly created his own White House unit to discredit his opposition and to ensure executive security. Nicknamed the plumbers because of their assignment to plug government leaks, the team was headed by ex-FBI agent G. Gordon Liddy and former CIA operative E. Howard Hunt.

The plumbers first targeted Daniel Ellsberg, a former Defense Department analyst who had turned over to the press the secret Pentagon Papers, a documentary history of U.S. involvement in Vietnam. On June 13 the *New York Times* began publishing the Pentagon Papers, which revealed a long history of government lies to foreign leaders, Congress, and the American people. Although the papers contained nothing damaging about his administration, Nixon feared that they would undermine public trust in government and establish a precedent for publishing classified material. The Supreme Court ultimately ruled that the documents' publication was protected under the First Amendment. Livid, Nixon directed the Justice Department to indict Ellsberg for theft and ordered the plumbers to discredit him. In August 1971 Liddy and Hunt broke into the office of Ellsberg's psychiatrist in search of information against the man who had become an instant hero to the antiwar movement.

The Southern Strategy

While attacking radicalism, Nixon courted whites upset by the drive for racial equality, especially in the South. The administration testified before Congress against expanding the Voting Rights Act of 1965 and in favor of modifications to the Fair Housing Act of 1968 that would have crippled its enforcement. Moreover, it pleaded for the postponement of desegregation in Mississippi schools and argued against busing as a means to reduce segregation. In 1971, when the Supreme Court upheld busing as a constitutional and necessary tactic, Nixon condemned the ruling and asked Congress to enact a moratorium on busing.

The strategy of wooing white southerners dictated Nixon's Supreme Court nominations. To reverse the Warren court's liberalism, he named strict constructionists, judges who would not "meddle" in social issues or be "soft" on criminals. In 1969 he appointed conservative judge Warren Burger as chief justice. Later that year, he nominated Clement Haynesworth of South Carolina. Disturbed by Haynesworth's anti–civil rights rulings as a federal judge, however, seventeen Republicans joined most Democrats to reject the appointment.

Nixon, committed to appointing another conservative, chose G. Harrold Carswell of Florida. But Carswell's judicial record and vulnerability to charges of racism drew deep opposition. When the Senate rejected the president's newest nominee, Nixon again portrayed Democrats as contemptuous of the white South. By 1973 Nixon finally had succeeded in appointing three justices to the Supreme Court: Harry Blackmun of Minnesota, Lewis Powell of Virginia, and William Rehnquist of Arizona. The Nixon appointees would steer the court in a moderate direction. Although ruling liberally in cases involving abortion, desegregation, and the death penalty, the Burger court would shift to the right in rulings on civil liberties, community censorship, and police power.

The Silent Majority Speaks

To build a Republican majority, Nixon aimed to capture the backlash vote that had gravitated to George Wallace in 1968. Denouncing the Democrats as the party of New Left "hooligans, hippies, and radical liberals," the president blamed them for fostering drug use, supporting abortion, and cultivating social disorder. As the 1970 elections neared, Nixon encouraged his vice president, Spiro T. Agnew, to step up attacks on the liberal opposition. Crisscrossing the nation, Agnew assailed students as "parasites of passions," Democrats as "sniveling hand-wringers," intellectuals as "an effete corps of intellectual snobs," and the news media as "nattering nabobs of negativism." Although liberals deplored Agnew's alarming alliterative allegations, a number of Democratic candidates joined their Republican opponents in appealing for a restoration of law and order, patriotism, and family values. The 1970 elections were a draw, with the Democrats gaining nine House seats and the Republicans two Senate seats.

The Election of 1972

Nixon's reelection in 1972 appeared certain. He counted on his diplomatic successes and his winding down of the Vietnam War to win over moderate voters. He expected his southern strategy and law-and-order posture to attract Wallace voters. Continuing Democratic divisions boosted Nixon's optimism.

Nixon's only major worry, another third-party candidacy by George Wallace, vanished on May 15, 1972. During a campaign stop, Wallace was shot and paralyzed from the waist down. He withdrew from the race, leaving Nixon a monopoly on the white-backlash, law-and-order vote.

The Senate's most outspoken dove, George McGovern of South Dakota, capitalized on the support of antiwar activists to blitz the Democratic primaries. New party rules requiring state delegations to include minority, female, and youthful delegates in approximate proportion to their numbers aided the liberal McGovern. A disapproving labor leader complained about "too much hair and not enough cigars at this convention," but McGovern won the nomination on the first ballot.

Perceptions of McGovern as inept and radical drove away all but the most committed supporters. After pledging to stand behind his vice-presidential running mate, Thomas Eagleton, "1,000 percent" when it became known that Eagleton had received electric-shock therapy for depression, McGovern dumped Eagleton and suffered the embarrassment of having several prominent Democrats decline to run with him. McGovern's endorsement of income redistribution, the decriminalization of marijuana, immediate withdrawal from Vietnam, a $30 billion defense-budget cut, and pardons for those who had fled the United States to avoid the draft exposed him to GOP ridicule as the candidate of the radical fringe.

The Election of 1972				
Candidates	Parties	Electoral Vote	Popular Vote	Percentage of Popular Vote
RICHARD M. NIXON	Republican	520	47,169,911	60.7
George S. McGovern	Democratic	17	29,170,383	37.5

Meanwhile, Nixon, leaving no stone unturned, created the Committee to Re-Elect the President (CREEP) and appointed Attorney General John Mitchell as its head. The millions in contributions collected by CREEP financed a series of "dirty tricks" that spread dissension among Democrats and paid for a special internal espionage unit to spy on the opposition. Led by Liddy and Hunt of the White House plumbers, the Republican undercover team received Mitchell's approval to wiretap telephones at the Democratic National Committee headquarters in the Watergate apartment-office complex in Washington. Early one morning in June 1972, a security guard foiled the break-in to install the bugs. Arrested were James McCord, the security coordinator of CREEP, and several other Liddy and Hunt associates.

A White House cover-up began immediately. Nixon said "categorically" that "no one in the White House staff, no one in this administration, presently employed, was involved in this bizarre incident." Nixon ordered staff members to expunge Hunt's name from the White House telephone directory, to buy the silence of those arrested with $400,000 in hush money and hints of a presidential pardon, and to direct the CIA to halt the FBI's investigation of the Watergate break-in on the pretext that the probe would damage national security.

With the McGovern campaign a shambles and the Watergate incident seemingly contained, Nixon won the election overwhelmingly, amassing nearly 61 percent of the popular vote and 520 electoral votes. Strongly supported only by blacks, Chicanos, and low-income voters, McGovern carried just Massachusetts and the District of Columbia. The election solidified the 1968 realignment.

However, the GOP gained only twelve seats in the House, and the Democrats increased their Senate majority by two. The outcome demonstrated the growing difficulty of unseating incumbents, the prevalence of ticket splitting among voters, and the decline of party loyalty. Only 55.7 percent of eligible voters went to the polls, down from 63.8 percent in 1960. Whether indifferent to politics or disenchanted with the choices offered, a growing number of citizens no longer bothered to participate in the electoral process.

The Crisis of the Presidency

In his second inaugural, Nixon pledged to make the next four years "the best four years in American history." Ironically, they would rank among its sorriest. His vice president would resign in disgrace, his closest confidants would go to jail, and he would serve barely a year and a half of his second term before resigning to avoid impeachment.

The Watergate Cover-Up

The scheme to conceal links between the White House and the accused Watergate burglars had succeeded during the 1972 campaign. But after the election, federal judge John Sirica refused to accept the defendants' claim that they had acted on their own. Threatening severe prison sentences, Sirica coerced James McCord of CREEP into confessing that highly placed White House aides knew in advance of the break-in and that the defendants had committed perjury during the trial. McCord also stated that the White House had pressured him and his codefendants "to plead guilty and remain silent."

Two *Washington Post* reporters, Carl Bernstein and Bob Woodward, following clues furnished by "Deep Throat," an unnamed informant, wrote a succession of front-page stories tying the break-in to illegal contributions and "dirty tricks" by CREEP.

In February 1973 the Senate established the Special Committee on Presidential Campaign Activities to investigate. As the trail of revelations led closer to the Oval Office, Nixon fired his special counsel, John Dean, who refused to be a scapegoat. On April 30 the president announced the resignations of his principal aides, H. R. Haldeman and John Ehrlichman, and pledged to get to the bottom of the scandal. He appointed Secretary of Defense Elliott Richardson, a Boston patrician of unassailable integrity, as his new attorney general and, bowing to Senate demands, instructed Richardson to appoint a special Watergate prosecutor with broad powers of investigation and subpoena. Richardson selected Archibald Cox, a Harvard law professor and Democrat.

In May the special Senate committee began a televised investigation. Chaired by Sam Ervin of North Carolina, an expert on constitutional law, the hearings revealed a sordid tale of corruption. Witnesses testified to the existence of the "enemies list," to the president's use of governmental agencies to harass his opponents, and to administration favors in return for illegal campaign donations. Most damaging to Nixon, the hearings exposed the White House's active involvement in the Watergate cover-up. But the Senate still lacked concrete evidence of the president's criminality, the "smoking gun" that would prove Nixon's guilt. Because it was simply his word against that of John Dean, who testified that Nixon personally directed the cover-up, the president expected to survive the crisis.

Then another presidential aide shockingly revealed that Nixon had installed a secret taping system that recorded all conversations in the Oval Office. The Ervin committee and Cox insisted on access to the tapes, but Nixon refused, claiming executive privilege. In October, when Cox sought a court order to obtain the tapes, Nixon ordered Attorney General Richardson to fire him. Richardson

resigned in protest, as did the deputy attorney general. The third-ranking official in the Department of Justice, Solicitor General Robert Bork, dumped Cox. The furor raised by the "Saturday Night Massacre" sent Nixon's public-approval rating plunging downward. As Nixon named a new special prosecutor, Leon Jaworski, the House Judiciary Committee began impeachment proceedings.

A President Disgraced

Adding to Nixon's woes that October, Vice President Agnew, charged with income-tax evasion and accepting bribes, pleaded no contest—"the full equivalent of a plea of guilty," according to the trial judge. Agnew left office with a three-year suspended sentence and a $10,000 fine. Popular House minority leader Gerald R. Ford of Michigan replaced Agnew. Meanwhile, the unrelenting legal and political processes unfolding against Nixon made his continued presidency highly uncertain.

In March 1974 Jaworski and the House Judiciary Committee subpoenaed the president for the tape recordings of Oval Office conversations after the Watergate break-in. In April Nixon released edited transcripts of the tapes, filled with gaps and the phrase "expletive deleted." Despite the excisions, the president emerged as petty and vindictive. Senate Republican leader Hugh Scott of Pennsylvania referred to the tapes' revelations as "deplorable, disgusting, shabby, immoral." Although there was no smoking gun directly implicating the president, Nixon's standing was destroyed.

Nixon's sanitized version of the tapes satisfied neither Jaworski nor the House Judiciary Committee. Both pressed for unedited tapes. In late July the Supreme Court rebuffed the president's claim of executive privilege. Chief Justice Burger cited the president's obligation to provide evidence necessary for the due process of law and ordered Nixon to release the unexpurgated tapes.

On July 27 the House Judiciary Committee adopted the first article of impeachment, obstruction of justice for impeding the Watergate investigation. On July 29 the majority, including Republicans as well as Democrats, voted to condemn the president's abuse of power, especially his partisan use of the FBI and IRS. On July 30 the committee added as a third article of impeachment the president's contempt of Congress in refusing to obey a congressional subpoena for the tapes.

Nixon was checkmated. On August 5, 1974, he conceded in a televised address that he had withheld relevant evidence. He then surrendered the tapes, which contained the smoking gun proving that the president had ordered the cover-up, obstructed justice, subverted one government agency to prevent another from investigating a crime, and lied about his role for more than two years. Shocked Nixon loyalists on the Judiciary Committee rescinded their votes against impeachment. Nixon wavered, refusing to surrender, until Republican leaders informed him of the certainty of his impeachment and conviction. On August 9, 1974, Richard M. Nixon became the first American president to resign.

Conclusion

The conclusion of the Watergate scandal ended a period of extraordinary rancor. It capped a turbulent time in which one president elected by a record majority had feared to run for reelection, and his successor had won the next greatest percentage of the popular vote, only to resign in disgrace. Coming on the heels of the U.S. withdrawal from Vietnam, the energy crisis, and a deteriorating economy, Watergate intensified Americans' loss of confidence in their government.

American optimism is closely linked to the belief that Washington can govern effectively. In the 1940s and 1950s, people had faith in their government, which had decisively won World War II, ushered in unprecedented prosperity, provided social security, and built an impressive highway system. In the 1960s presidents Kennedy and Johnson had raised expectations about goals that they could not fulfill: better schooling, good health care at reasonable cost, reduced crime, and harmonious race relations. By the middle of the decade, the percentage of Americans who trusted Washington to do the right thing had dropped precipitously.

Capitalizing on anti-Washington, antiliberal sentiment, Richard M. Nixon fashioned a new majority coalition to replace FDR's New Deal coalition. Although Nixon masterfully reduced international tensions, he fell victim to the gulf between popular expectations and continued domestic problems. Promising to unite a divided people, he polarized them further. Stressing law and order, he employed illegal means to secure his goals and then tried to conceal the facts. Nearly fifty Nixon administration officials were indicted for fraud, extortion, perjury, obstruction of justice, and other crimes, and more than a score, including the attorney general, went to prison.

Nixon's successor, Gerald R. Ford, proclaimed, "Our long national nightmare is over." But as Americans in 1976 contemplated the bicentennial of the Declaration of Independence, most believed that recent events offered little reason for confidence in Washington or its leaders. Nixon's legacy would be a disquieting malaise and distrust in government that would further erode the nation's self-confidence and limit his successors' ability to lead effectively.

Chronology

1960 Birth-control pill marketed.

1964 Berkeley Free Speech Movement (FSM).

1967 March on the Pentagon.
Israeli-Arab Six-Day War.

1968 Tet offensive.
President Lyndon Johnson announces that he will not seek reelection.
Martin Luther King, Jr., assassinated; race riots sweep nation.
Student strike at Columbia University.
Robert F. Kennedy assassinated.
Violence mars Democratic convention in Chicago.
Vietnam peace talks open in Paris.
Richard Nixon elected president.

1969 *Apollo 11* lands first Americans on the moon.
Nixon begins withdrawal of U.S. troops from Vietnam.
Woodstock festival.
March Against Death in Washington, D.C.
My Lai massacre.

1970 United States invades Cambodia.
Students killed at Kent State University and Jackson State College.
Nixon proposes Huston Plan.
Environmental Protection Agency established.
Earth Day first celebrated.

1971 United States invades Laos.
New York Times publishes Pentagon Papers.
Nixon institutes wage-and-price freeze.
South Vietnam invades Laos.

1972 Nixon visits China and the Soviet Union.
SALT I agreement approved.
Watergate break-in.
Nixon reelected in landslide victory.
Christmas bombing of North Vietnam.

1973 Vietnam cease-fire agreement signed.
Trial of Watergate burglars.
Senate establishes Special Committee on Presidential Campaign Activities to investigate Watergate.
President Salvador Allende murdered in Chile.
Vice President Spiro Agnew resigns; Gerald Ford appointed vice president.
Roe v. *Wade*.
Yom Kippur War; OPEC begins embargo of oil to the West.

1974 Supreme Court orders Nixon to release Watergate tapes.
House Judiciary Committee votes to impeach Nixon.
Nixon resigns; Ford becomes president.

FOR FURTHER READING

David Harris, *Dreams Die Hard* (1983). The story of the antiwar and student movements as experienced by three participants.

Kim McQuaid, *The Anxious Years* (1989). A chronicle of national passions and struggles from 1968 to Nixon's resignation.

Herbert Parmet, *Richard Nixon and His America* (1990). A solid survey of the presidency and the era.

W. J. Rorabaugh, *Berkeley at War* (1989). A lively analysis of the events that rocked Berkeley in the 1960s.

Jonathan Schell, *The Time of Illusion* (1975). A thought-provoking analysis of the ties between Nixon's policies and the Watergate conspiracy.

Robert Schulzinger, *Henry Kissinger: Doctor of Diplomacy* (1989). A balanced examination of Kissinger-Nixon foreign policies.

Turning Inward: Society and Politics from Ford to Reagan

𝓘n the fifteen years after Watergate, personal preoccupations overshadowed public issues for many people, despite urgent national problems. Spiraling inflation gave rise to gnawing economic worries. The 1980 presidential election installed an administration committed to the free-enterprise system.

But however much Americans yearned to concentrate on private concerns, the world intruded. The later 1970s brought new crises in the Middle East and Central America even as American-Soviet relations deteriorated. This return to the bleakness of the early Cold War continued in the early 1980s. President Ronald Reagan, a long-time Cold Warrior as well as a free-market champion, pushed for big military-spending increases and indulged in anti-Soviet rhetoric, galvanizing a vigorous antinuclear movement in this otherwise passive political era.

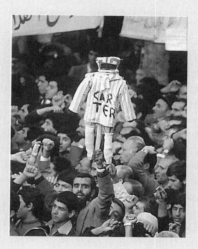

(Right) Hanging Jimmy Carter in effigy in Tehran, Iran

After Watergate: Changing Social and Cultural Contours

Politics After Watergate: The Limits of State Power, 1974–1984

From Détente to a Renewed Cold War, 1974–1984

After Watergate: Changing Social and Cultural Contours

Unlike its predecessors in the sixties, the generation that came of age in the seventies seemed intent on personal goals and financial success. Unprecedented numbers of women entered the work force, enrolled in professional schools, and launched careers. Black Americans joined the middle class in record numbers. Ethnic pride and a new sense of possibilities gave hope to the Indian population.

Although some people prospered, poverty stalked millions more. For many Americans, the emotional issue of abortion and the stark reality of AIDS forced revisions in sexual ideology and behavior. The era's strains and unsettling changes led to a search for spiritual solace that produced a resurgence of religion.

The Era of the Yuppie

In the 1970s social activism diminished in intensity and shifted in focus. But environmental consciousness remained high; Americans expressed concern about air and water pollution and endangered wildlife such as whales and certain species of owls and moths. In the late 1970s, concerns about nuclear power intensified, especially when a nearly catastrophic accident crippled the Three-Mile Island nuclear-power plant near Harrisburg, Pennsylvania.

For millions of young people, a sour political climate and a constricted economy acted against civic idealism. President Ronald Reagan's message of individualism, moreover, easily translated into self-centered materialism. Apart from calls for more military spending, Reagan offered no national agenda. The "campus radical" of the sixties became the "yuppie" (young urban professional), preoccupied with physical fitness, psychic harmony, and material consumption. But self-absorption too frequently became selfishness; writer Tom Wolfe christened yuppies the Me Generation.

A revolution in consumer electronics pulsed through the era as well. The TV set remained the living-room icon. Average daily viewing crept upward from six hours in 1970 to seven hours by 1990. Prime-time soap operas such as "Dallas" and "Falcon Crest" engrossed millions. Super Bowl extravaganzas also drew huge audiences. Cable television featured specialized programming for everything from the stock market to rock music, and first-run movies on HBO and other "premium" channels offered even more choices. The major networks meanwhile watched their market share shrink. Videocassette recorders (VCRs) allowed Americans to "time-shift" by taping TV shows for later viewing, and to rent movies on cassette. By the early 1990s, 70 percent of U.S. households had VCRs. Entertainment became privatized as families could "go to the movies" at home. Using laser beams to digitize sound waves, compact discs (CDs) offered remarkably high-quality sound. Americans cast aside their stereos and bought millions of CD players.

And the personal computer arrived. In the late 1970s two young Californians, Steven Jobs and Stephen Wozniak, reduced computers from room size to desk-top size and marketed the phenomenally successful Apple computer. As Apple sales shot up, computer manufacturers multiplied, especially in California's "Silicon Valley," named after the silicon computer chip. In 1981 IBM launched its PC (personal computer) and quickly grabbed 40 percent of the market, but computer entrepreneurs continued to proliferate. By 1991, 60 million personal computers were in use in American offices, schools, and homes.

By the late 1980s self-absorbed materialism had ebbed but had hardly vanished. In a 1987 survey of college students, 76 percent identified "being very well off financially" as a top personal objective—nearly double the percentage that had embraced this goal in 1970.

The Women's Movement: Gains and Uncertainties

The 1960s had revitalized the women's movement and led to basic changes in the status of women. Betty Friedan's *The Feminine Mystique* (1963) had heralded a new feminist activism. Millions of young, middle-class women had begun to re-examine their subordinate status in society. This rejuvenated feminism represented a rare source of social involvement in the generally quiescent 1970s. The 50,000 members of NOW (the National Organization for Women), feminist support groups, and *Ms.* and other magazines spread the message.

Activism meant political clout—exemplified by the National Women's Political Caucus (1971), which promoted a feminist agenda. By 1972 many states had liberalized their abortion laws and outlawed gender discrimination in hiring. That same year, Congress passed the Equal Rights Amendment (ERA) to the Constitution, asserting that "equality of rights under the law shall not be denied or abridged by the United States or any State on the basis of sex." Twenty-eight states quickly ratified it, and adoption seemed sure. In the landmark case of *Roe v. Wade* (1973), the Supreme Court proclaimed women's constitutional right to abortion.

By the early 1980s, however, the women's movement had splintered into moderate and radical camps. Although both espoused gender equality, moderates deplored the radicals' sometimes strident rhetoric. Betty Friedan's *The Second Stage* (1981) urged those feminists who had (controversially) downgraded family values to incorporate family issues into their campaign rather than leave this potent agenda to their opponents.

As the women's movement gained visibility, its opposition hardened. In 1972 President Nixon had vetoed a bill to establish a national network of day-care centers on the basis that it would weaken the family. Ratification of the ERA bogged down. Although polls showed that three-fourths of Americans supported the ERA, fiery opposition surfaced, and the amendment died in 1982, three states short of the required three-fourths.

Abortion became the most controversial issue relating to women. After the *Roe v. Wade* ruling, conservative Protestants and Roman Catholics organized the "Right-to-Life" movement and pressed for a constitutional amendment outlawing abortion.

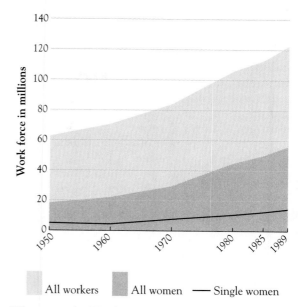

All workers   All women   — Single women

Women in the Work Force, 1950–1989

Since 1960 the proportion of American women who are gainfully employed has surged upward. As a result, young women coming of age in the 1990s have far different expectations about their lives than did their grandmothers or even their mothers.

SOURCES: Statistical Abstract of the United States, 1988 (Washington, D.C.: U.S. Government Printing Office, 1987), 373; *World Almanac and Book of Facts, 1989* (New York: Pharos Books, 1988), 152; *Statistical Abstract of the United States, 1991* (Washington, D.C., U.S. Government Printing Office, 1991), 387, 390.

They charged that abortion undermined respect for human life and amounted to the murder of the unborn. Although the constitutional amendment failed, Congress in 1976 halted Medicaid funding for most abortions, thus putting abortion out of the reach of the poor. Most feminists, however, took a "pro-choice" stance and argued that individual women and their doctors, not laws, should dictate the decision. Polls showed that a majority of Americans agreed. Between 1973 and 1980 the number of women seeking abortions doubled, reaching 1.5 million, but then leveled off.

The baby boom yielded to the baby bust as birthrates reached a low in 1976. Couples were marrying later and having fewer children. By 1980 the statistically average American family had 1.6 children. The number of unmarried couples living together rose steadily, reaching 2.8 million by 1990, and the divorce rate catapulted to 480 per 1,000 marriages, up from 258 per 1,000 in 1960.

By 1990, 58 percent of women worked outside the home, up from 35 percent in 1960, as a through-the-roof cost of living sent women into the work force to supplement family income. Many women workers remained at the low end of the wage scale. Increasing numbers, however, entered corporate management and professions such as law and medicine. Working women juggled careers and family life—and coped with new kinds of stress. "Superwomen" pushed themselves to be successful professionals, attentive mothers, superb cooks, efficient housekeepers, and seductive wives. Conservatives increasingly voiced fears about the breakdown of the family.

Older feminists worried that young women had lost sight of the movement's original goals. They questioned whether women could function as equals in the male world without absorbing its competitiveness and careerism. But they recognized, too, that a long road lay ahead in overcoming ingrained gender discrimination. Working women's wages still lagged behind those of men. Gender segregation of the workplace largely persisted. Nursing and secretarial work remained overwhelmingly female, and, despite inroads by women, men still dominated high-prestige professions, especially at the upper ranks.

The eighties was not a favorable decade for confronting these inequities. The Reagan administration, suspicious of government activism on social issues, opposed many feminists' and other minorities' goals. Reagan appointees to the Civil Rights Commission hesitated to act. Reagan budgets cut social-welfare programs that benefited women and children. As women heading single-parent families swelled the welfare rolls, observers

spoke of the "feminization of poverty." By 1990 feminist leaders and women would recognize that major challenges still loomed and complex problems remained unresolved.

The Two Worlds of Black America

The story of African-Americans in the seventies and eighties was really two very different stories. Millions of blacks moved upward as the civil-rights movement opened long-closed doors. In 1965 black students had accounted for only 5 percent of college enrollment; by 1990, however, the figure reached 12 percent. And by 1990 some 46 percent of black workers held white-collar jobs.

But outside this circle lay a second, much grimmer realm of inner-city slums where blacks who had missed the "up" escalator were trapped. A third of all African-Americans inhabited this world, in which half the young people never finished high school and the jobless rate hovered around 60 percent.

Economic trends as well as racism contributed to their desperate situation. Structural changes in the American economy had eliminated many unskilled jobs once held by the urban poor. Recessions in the 1970s and early 1980s, moreover, battered the already struggling black underclass, and job cuts in steel, automaking, and other basic industries hit skilled black workers. Demands for a well-educated work force further shut out the poor and uneducated, and welfare payments lagged behind the rising cost of living.

Cocaine, especially the potent "crack," flooded urban ghettos in the 1980s. In some cases, eight- and nine-year-old black children earned up to $100 a day as lookouts for drug dealers; dealers in their early teens earned in two days as much as they would in a year at McDonald's. The cocaine plague stretched across the American landscape to include "yuppies," athletes, and entertainment figures.

Drugs and poverty in turn escalated urban violence. In the 1980s a young black male was six times as likely to be murdered as a young white male. In

1987 sixty black children under age seventeen were slain in Detroit. That same year, two major youth gangs, the Bloods and the Crips, accounted for more than 400 killings in Los Angeles. One observer summed up the situation in 1988: "Young black males in America's inner cities are an endangered species. . . . They are [the] rejects of our affluent society."

Meanwhile, among young, unmarried black women in the slums, the pregnancy rate soared. Single women, most of them young, poor, and uneducated, accounted for 63 percent of all black births in 1988. Millions of them, scarcely more than children, depended on welfare payments for survival. Caught in a deep rut of dependence, they raised the specter of a permanent American underclass.

Unemployment, drug use, illegitimacy, and welfare dependency affected all racial and ethnic groups, but they emerged most starkly among inner-city black and Hispanic populations. Buffeted by complex economic and social forces, the predominantly nonwhite inner cities posed major social challenges.

New Patterns of Immigration

America's recent population growth—from 204 million in 1970 to 250 million in 1990—reflects a steady influx of both legal and illegal immigrants. Whereas most former immigrants came from Europe, 45 percent of the new immigrants hailed from the Western Hemisphere, and 30 percent from Asia.

Immigration and a high birthrate made Hispanics the nation's fastest-growing ethnic group. In 1990 the Hispanic population stood at 20 million, up from 9 million in 1970. Mexican-Americans concentrated in the Southwest, while Cubans, Puerto Ricans, and other West Indians lived mainly in New York, Florida, Illinois, and New Jersey.

Desperate economic conditions had driven these newcomers to America. The collapse of world oil prices intensified unemployment and chronic poverty in Mexico during the 1980s, spurring many to seek opportunity in the north. These recent immigrants often faced hardship and poverty in their adopted land. In 1990 nearly 20 percent of

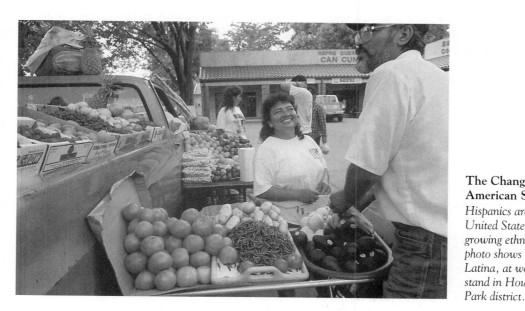

The Changing Face of American Society
Hispanics are today the United States' fastest-growing ethnic group. This photo shows Estella Ortiz, a Latina, at work at her fruit stand in Houston's Magnolia Park district.

Mexican-Americans and 30 percent of Puerto Ricans lived below the poverty line.

Proud of their language and traditions, these Hispanic newcomers strongly influenced U.S. culture. In some areas of Los Angeles, home to nearly a million Mexican-Americans, one could drive for miles in the 1980s and see only Spanish business signs and movie marquees. Large parts of Miami seemed wholly Latino.

By 1990 estimates of the number of illegal aliens in the United States ranged as high as 12 million. Working long hours under harsh conditions with few legal protections, these impoverished immigrants, primarily Mexican and Haitian, performed hard manual labor, sweated in the garment trades, cleaned homes and cared for children, and bent their backs in agricultural fields. The Immigration Reform Control Act of 1986 outlawed the hiring of illegal aliens and strengthened immigration controls at the border. The law also offered legal status to aliens who could prove that they had lived in the United States since January 1, 1982.

At the same time, immigration from Asia rose. Newcomers from Korea, Vietnam, and the Philippines joined well-established Chinese and Japanese communities in California, and many migrated eastward. These newest Americans worked hard, sought higher education, and moved up rapidly. All these trends made the United States of the 1980s a far more diverse and vibrant place than it had been a generation earlier.

Brightening Prospects for Native Americans

The status of American Indians had reached a new low in the 1950s as the federal government had promoted Indians' relocation to cities, where, it was tacitly hoped, they would disappear as a distinct ethnic group. Aroused by this destructive and ill-conceived policy, and influenced by the social-protest climate of the sixties, members of the militant American Indian Movement (AIM) had dramatized their cause by occupying Alcatraz Island in San Francisco Bay in 1969, the Bureau of Indian Affairs in Washington in 1972, and a trading post at Wounded Knee, South Dakota (the site of the 1890 massacre) in 1973.

Indians' militancy worked. In 1970 President Nixon rejected the "termination" approach and the federal government's traditional paternalism toward Indians and called for greater autonomy for Native Americans. The Indian Self-Determination Act of 1974 granted tribes control of federal-aid programs on reservations and oversight of their schools.

Indian peoples also felt heightened pride in their heritage. By 1990 more than 1.7 million persons identified themselves as Native Americans, up from 800,000 in 1970. Natural increase—in which the number of births surpasses the number of deaths—could not account for this growth, and census analysts concluded simply that more people than before chose to identify themselves as Indians.

Ethnic pride inspired economic development on Indian reservations. Tribal ventures ranged from resorts to mining and logging enterprises. Food-processors, electronics firms, and other businesses built factories that created much-needed jobs on tribal lands.

Indian tribes also reasserted long-ignored treaty rights. In 1971 native peoples in Alaska won 40 million acres of land and $1 billion in settlement of long-standing claims. In 1980 the Sioux received $107 million for South Dakota land taken from them illegally a century earlier, and the Penobscots of Maine won claims based on a 1790 law. In 1988 the tiny Puyallup tribe of Washington State was given $162 million to settle claims that the city of Tacoma occupied land granted them by treaty in the 1850s. The Puyallups announced plans to restore the salmon runs of the Puyallup River and to construct a deep-water port on Puget Sound.

It is true that high rates of unemployment, alcoholism, and disease persisted for Native Americans. But the renewal of tribal life, the new direction of federal policy, and the larger society's willingness to honor ancient treaties represented an advance.

Sexuality in the Era of AIDS

The sexual revolution of the 1960s had a particular impact on the homosexual community. Beginning in the early 1970s, many gay men and women "came out of the closet" to acknowledge their sexual preference openly. They rallied, paraded, and organized to fight job discrimination and other forms of harassment. As one leader observed, "We are 20 million strong in this nation. We are moving from gay pride to gay politics."

Religious conservatives deplored this trend as evidence of society's moral disintegration. Evangelist Jerry Falwell proclaimed, "Homosexuality is . . . so abominable in the sight of God that he destroyed the cities of Sodom and Gomorrah because of this terrible sin."

The loosening of traditional sexual mores received a jolting setback in the 1980s with the proliferation of sexually transmitted diseases, including AIDS (acquired immune deficiency syndrome), first diagnosed in the United States in 1981. By 1991 more than 106,000 Americans had died of AIDS, and perhaps a million carried HIV, the causative virus. Public-health officials warned that a vaccine lay far in the future. Although confined largely to sexually active homosexuals and bisexuals, intravenous drug users, and those having intercourse with these high-risk groups, AIDS appeared in the general population, too, and medical authorities warned of the need for caution and the use of condoms. This somber message was driven home in 1991 when basketball superstar Earvin "Magic" Johnson announced that he had tested positive for the HIV virus and retired from the Los Angeles Lakers to devote himself to AIDS education. Young AIDS victims like Ryan White and Kimberly Bergalis also heightened popular awareness of the disease.

The AIDS scare provided some Americans with an excuse to express their hatred of homosexuality. Others responded more sympathetically. Research on the mysterious disease received massive funding. Hospices opened to provide care and support for patients; a quilt bearing the names of AIDS victims toured the nation, and grew steadily larger; candlelight marches memorialized the dead.

Fearful of exposure to AIDS, herpes, and other sexually transmitted diseases, Americans grew more cautious in their sexual behavior. Condom use increased markedly, and the exuberant 1960s slogan "Make Love, Not War" gave way to "Safer Sex."

The Evangelical Renaissance

Religion became highly visible in the post-1970 United States as many Americans sought beliefs that gave meaning to life and resolved ethical dilemmas. Religious faith played a larger role after 1970 than it had for years.

This intensified religious interest took varied forms. Cults such as the Reverend Sun Myung Moon's Unification Church and the International Society for Krishna Consciousness prospered. A most significant development was the rapid growth of evangelical Protestant denominations, including the 2-million-member Assemblies of God and the 14-million-strong Southern Baptist Convention. All these groups believed in the Bible's literal truth, in "born-again" religious experience, and in an earthly life governed by personal piety and strict morality.

Evangelical Christians had pursued social reform before the Civil War, and many twentieth-century evangelicals also turned to political activism. In 1980 and 1984 Jerry Falwell's pro-Reagan Moral Majority registered nearly 2 million new voters. While targeting specific issues—abortion, pornography, and public-school prayer—evangelicals embraced a strongly conservative, anticommunist world view.

Fueling this rejuvenation was a network of religious bookstores, radio stations featuring religious programming, and, above all, television evangelists. Jerry Falwell, Pat Robertson, Jim and Tammy Bakker, Oral Roberts, and Jimmy Swaggart among others accounted for countless hours of broadcasting. Robertson's Christian Broadcasting Network

(CBN) became the nation's fourth-largest cable network. Televangelists repelled many Americans with their endless pleas for money, but millions of others found their spiritual message reassuring.

The "electronic church" suffered severe jolts after 1987. Jim Bakker resigned after acknowledging a sexual encounter with a church secretary and pay-offs to buy her silence. The fiercely moralistic Jimmy Swaggart fell from grace when his repeated trysts with prostitutes were revealed. But the TV preachers' tribulations could not obscure the growing influence of evangelical religion. Confronting change on all sides, evangelicals found comfort in their faith and profoundly influenced American life in the late twentieth century.

Politics After Watergate: The Limits of Power, 1974–1984

Social change and public discontent shaped the politics of the 1970s and 1980s. With Richard Nixon's graceless exit from the presidency, the nation lost spirit and direction. His successors, Republican Gerald R. Ford and Democrat Jimmy Carter, grappled with a tangle of domestic and foreign problems—inflation, unemployment, and recession—and a foreboding sense of limits gripped many Americans.

In 1980 voters turned to a presidential candidate who promised to break with the recent past, Ronald Reagan. Reagan's unabashed patriotism appealed to a nation still traumatized by Vietnam, and his denunciation of "tax and spend" policies seemed to strike at the root of "stagflation," the dismal combination of business stagnation and inflation. His attacks on liberal ideology reflected an international anti-statist trend, a current that had carried Margaret Thatcher to power in England in 1979 and that would wash over the communist world as well.

As president, Reagan revived national pride and confidence. His economic policies lowered inflation and triggered a consumer buying spree and a surge of speculative investment. They also laid the groundwork, however, for serious economic difficulties after his departure.

The Caretaker Presidency of Gerald Ford

Gerald Ford became president on August 9, 1974, after Richard M. Nixon's resignation. A former Michigan congressman who had served as Republican minority leader before becoming vice president, Ford displayed human decency, if little evidence of brilliance. While comedians poked fun at his verbal gaffes ("If Lincoln were alive today, he'd roll over in his grave"), most Americans found him a welcome relief after Nixon. Only a month into his term, however, Ford strained his popularity by pardoning Nixon for "any and all crimes" committed while in office, thus shielding the ex-president from prosecution for his Watergate role. Ford insisted that the pardon would help the nation to forget the scandal, but many Americans were outraged.

Ford, more conservative than Nixon on domestic issues, vetoed environmental, social-welfare, and public-interest measures, but the heavily Democratic Congress overrode most of the vetoes. Economic problems especially bedeviled Ford. Oil

"The Summer of '73"
Cartoonist Paul Szep used the stark image of a thirsty gasoline tanker to convey the gravity of the economic crisis spawned by the Arab oil embargo.

The Election of 1976				
Candidates	Parties	Electoral Vote	Popular Vote	Percentage of Popular Vote
JIMMY CARTER	Democratic	297	40,827,394	49.9
Gerald R. Ford	Republican	240	39,145,977	47.9

prices had shot up in 1973 as a result of the Arab oil embargo and OPEC (Organization of Petroleum Exporting Countries) price hikes. These blows fell hard on the United States, which imported one-third of its oil. The soaring cost of gasoline, home heating oil, and other petroleum-based products worsened already serious inflation. Consumer prices rose 12 percent in 1974 and 11 percent in 1975.

In October 1974 Ford initiated a program of voluntary restraint called Whip Inflation Now (WIN). Although the president gamely wore his big "WIN" button, prices continued to rise. Ford also cut federal spending and endorsed the Federal Reserve's attempt to cool the economy by raising the discount rate. However, a severe recession resulted in 1974–1975. Unemployment climbed to nearly 11 percent in 1975, tax receipts dropped as business stagnated, and the federal deficit spurted to record levels. Although Ford proposed a tax cut and measures to coax consumer spending, economic headaches persisted.

The oil crisis battered the U.S. auto industry. Americans stopped buying gas-guzzlers and turned to smaller, more fuel-efficient imports. General Motors, Ford, and Chrysler laid off 225,000 workers in 1974, and imports doubled their share of the U.S. market, reaching 33 percent by 1980.

Problems overseas compounded domestic economic woes. Americans found little to cheer as the nation entered 1976, an election year and the bicentennial of the Declaration of Independence.

The Man from Georgia: Jimmy Carter in the White House

President Ford won the Republican nomination in 1976. The Democratic nomination went to a little-known Georgia politician and peanut farmer, Jimmy Carter, who carried out a brilliant primary campaign. The folksy, toothy-grinned Carter made a virtue of his status as an outsider to Washington, pledged never to lie to the American people, and freely avowed his "born-again" Christianity. Carter and his running mate, Senator Walter Mondale of Minnesota, drew support by attacking the Ford administration's high inflation and unemployment rates.

The Democrats won by a narrow margin—49.9 percent of the popular vote to Ford's 47.9, and 297 electoral votes to the Republican's 240. The vote broke sharply along class lines: the well-to-do voted heavily for Ford; the disadvantaged, overwhelmingly for Carter. The Georgian swept the South and received 90 percent of the black vote.

As president, Carter rejected the trappings of what some in Nixon's day had called the imperial presidency. On inauguration day, he walked from the Capitol to the White House. In an attempt to echo FDR's radio chats, he later delivered some televised speeches from an easy chair by a fireplace.

But such symbolism could not ensure a successful presidency. Because Carter had entered the White House without a clear political philosophy, liberals and conservatives alike claimed him. Moreover, the intensely private Carter relied on a circle of young, inexperienced staff members from Georgia and took little pleasure in socializing with politicians. "Carter couldn't get the Pledge of Allegiance through Congress," groused one legislator. Disciplined and intelligent, Carter focused well on specific problems but lacked a larger political vision.

In his first year Carter used a tax cut and public-works programs to fight the recession. The unemployment rate dropped to 5 percent by late 1978.

However, Carter showed little sympathy for social-welfare measures involving federal spending. Carter also introduced administrative reforms in civil service and the executive branch early in his presidency. But poor relations with Congress frustrated his attempts to promote national health insurance, to overhaul the welfare system, and to reform loophole-ridden income-tax laws. He did leave one notable domestic legacy, however, by appointing a substantial number of women and members of minority groups to federal judgeships.

A Sea of Troubles as Carter's Term Ends

Inflation reached horrendous levels as Carter's term wore on. Prices vaulted by more than 13 percent in both 1979 and 1980, driven by staggering energy costs. In 1979 a second oil crisis hit as a revolution in Iran led to a diminished world oil reserve and as oil-guzzling nations, including the United States, waged a bidding war for the reduced supply. In response, OPEC boosted oil prices to above $30 a barrel. Americans who were used to paying $.30 for a gallon of gasoline saw prices edge toward $1 a gallon. As oil stopped flowing freely into the pipeline for international commerce, shortages arose and long lines formed at gas stations. In 1979 alone, Americans paid $16.4 billion in added costs related to oil-price increases. Carter relied on voluntarism to curb the inflationary spiral; his Council on Wage and Price Stability urged workers and manufacturers to hold the line. But repeated hikes in oil prices thwarted his efforts.

As the Federal Reserve Board pushed the discount rate higher and higher, bank interest rates reached an unheard-of 20 percent by 1980. Mortgages and business loans consequently dried up, and economic activity remained in the doldrums. Government borrowing to compensate for slumping tax revenues drove up interest rates still more.

Carter had drawn a larger lesson from the oil crisis: that the nation's wasteful consumption of dwindling fossil fuels must yield to conservation. He recognized that two key factors underlying a generation of economic growth—cheap, unlimited energy,

and the lack of foreign competition—were about to disappear. Americans must learn to survive in a "zero-sum" society that could no longer anticipate endless expansion, the president believed. In 1975 Congress had set fuel-efficiency standards for cars and mandated a national speed limit of fifty-five miles per hour. Convinced that more must be done, Carter in 1977 had created the Department of Energy and proposed taxes on oil and gasoline consumption, tax credits for conservation measures, and research on alternative energy resources. In 1978 Congress had passed a watered-down energy bill.

But with the oil crises and attendant economic jitters, Americans turned against the remote figure in the White House. Carter's approval rating plummeted to 26 percent in the summer of 1979. The president delivered a televised address discussing "national malaise" and "loss of confidence," but the speech only deepened the spreading suspicion that Carter himself was a large part of the problem. Frustration over the seizure of a group of U.S. hostages in Iran deepened Carter's problems, and by mid-1980 his approval rating had sunk to 23 percent.

Carter remains a fascinating but controversial political figure. His sudden emergence vividly illustrates the power of television, which permitted an unknown candidate to bypass the laborious process of amassing support among power brokers and interest groups. Pursuing the presidency at a moment when Americans longed to see integrity and competency restored to that office, Carter seemed to fill the bill precisely.

Carter's limitations, initially less evident than his strengths, undid him. He identified fundamental issues that would dominate the national agenda in the future: energy policy; tax, welfare, and health-care reform; and the need to redefine America's world role. But he lacked the political skills to work well with Congress and to inspire the nation to confront its problems. By the end of his term, a victim of his own flaws and of large-scale forces that might have overwhelmed even the ablest president, Carter was lonely and discredited. In time, Americans would reach a more appreciative assessment, but few were sorry to see him go when he left office in

January 1981. As his successor, voters chose a high-spirited, seemingly uncomplicated candidate who appeared the opposite of the gloomy, introspective Carter.

Background of the Reagan Revolution

Several economic, ideological, and social trends underlay Ronald Reagan's presidential victory. First, the prospect of endless stagflation frightened and angered voters, and Carter's orthodox economic policies offered little hope for relief. Reagan's simplistic "supply-side" proposals—the idea that sharp tax cuts would increase people's incentive to work, save, and invest, leading to greater productivity in the economy and ultimately to more tax revenues for the government—impressed many voters as an idea worth trying. Moreover, a belief in self-help and private enterprise had remained entrenched despite the New Deal–Great Society ideology of government activism. Simultaneously, decades of Cold War rhetoric had imprinted deeply on the American consciousness a determination to remain ahead of the Soviets militarily. Carter struck many voters as vacillating in his dealings with Moscow.

To these conservative themes, the 1970s added the ideology of the "New Right," a cultural conservatism stressing social and moral issues. Upset by social turmoil, the sexual revolution, the women's movement, and rising rates of divorce and abortion, millions of Americans called for a restoration of morality and "traditional values." TV evangelist Jerry Falwell's Moral Majority was one of many groups eager to translate public concerns into political action.

Population shifts in the 1970s also played a role in Reagan's success. New York, Chicago, and the other cities of the Northeast and upper Midwest had lost population as Texas, Florida, California, and the Sun Belt had grown rapidly. These areas were historically conservative and suspicious of Washington. Westerners had organized the "Sagebrush Revolution" to demand less government control and the return of federal lands to state control.

The economic setbacks of the seventies and the feeling that the United States had lost its way in a dangerous world contributed to the shifting political climate. Waiting in the wings, ready to translate the nation's mood into a powerful force at the polls, was Ronald Wilson Reagan.

The Man Behind the Movement

Reagan grew up in Dixon, Illinois, the son of an alcoholic father and a pious mother involved in the Disciples of Christ church. After graduating from Eureka College, he worked as a sports announcer before striking out for Hollywood in 1937. His fifty-four films enjoyed only moderate success, but after 1954 he made a name for himself as a spokesperson for General Electric. A former New Dealer, Reagan moved to the right in the 1950s and won prominence through a TV speech for Barry Goldwater in 1964, praising individualism and free enterprise.

Recognizing Reagan's flair for politics, a group of California millionaires engineered his election as governor in 1966. In Sacramento he popularized conservative ideas while demonstrating an ability to compromise. After nearly winning the Republican presidential nomination in 1976, Reagan in 1980 had little trouble disposing of his principal opponent, George Bush, whom he then made his running mate.

Capitalizing on frustrations building since the 1960s, Reagan promised Americans a new deal. Unlike FDR's New Deal, however, Reagan's version offered diminished government activity, reduced taxes and spending, and the unleashing of the free-enterprise system. Internationally, Reagan called for the restoration of American leadership and pride.

The Democrats glumly renominated Jimmy Carter, but double-digit inflation, 20 percent interest rates, 8 percent unemployment, and the Iranian hostage crisis gave him no chance. Asking "Are you better off now than you were four years ago?" Reagan captured 51 percent of the popular vote to Carter's 41 percent. (An independent candidate, liberal Republican congressman John Anderson, collected most of the balance.) Reaping the benefits of Nixon's southern strategy, Reagan carried every southern state except Carter's own Georgia and every state west of the Mississippi. More than half

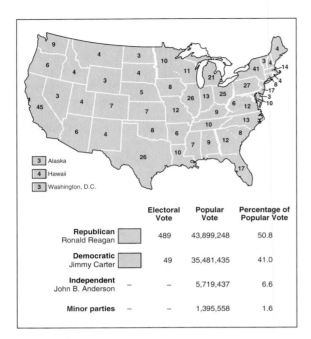

	Electoral Vote	Popular Vote	Percentage of Popular Vote
Republican Ronald Reagan	489	43,899,248	50.8
Democratic Jimmy Carter	49	35,481,435	41.0
Independent John B. Anderson	–	5,719,437	6.6
Minor parties	–	1,395,558	1.6

Map legend:
3 Alaska
4 Hawaii
3 Washington, D.C.

The Election of 1980

the nation's blue-collar workers voted Republican. Only black voters remained firmly Democratic. Republicans also gained eleven Senate seats and, for the first time since 1955, a majority. These Senate victories reflected the power of conservative political-action committees (PACs) using computerized mass-mailings to focus on such "hot-button" issues as abortion and gun control.

Reagan's term began auspiciously. On inauguration day, January 20, 1981, the Iranian hostages boarded planes heading home. With this trauma past, the nation sized up its new leader. Although nearing his seventieth birthday, Reagan seemed fit and vigorous. Few had a clear notion of his program beyond his rhetorical commitment to patriotism, military strength, the free market, and traditional values, but Reagan soon gave concrete substance to these generalities.

Reaganomics

"Reaganomics," the new president's economic program, boiled down to the belief that American

capitalism, freed of heavy taxes and government regulation, would surge to great heights of productivity. Reagan's first budget message proposed a five-year, $750 billion tax cut built around a 30 percent reduction in federal income taxes over three years. Trimming the proposal slightly, Congress in May 1981 voted a 25 percent income-tax cut over three years. Middle- and working-class Americans applauded.

To compensate for the lost revenues, Reagan proposed severe spending reductions for school lunches, student loans, job training, and urban mass transit. In all, Congress slashed more than $40 billion from domestic spending in 1981. Conserva-

Ronald Reagan, Outdoorsman
Though President Reagan was often photographed in natural settings, his administration gave little support to the cause of environmental protection.

tive Democrats supported the reductions. Although mainstream economists warned that the tax cut would produce catastrophic federal deficits, Reagan remained convinced that lower tax rates would stimulate economic growth and raise total tax revenues. He was wrong.

Appointees to key agencies implemented another component of Reaganomics, radical cutbacks in the federal regulation of business. Reagan insisted that "government is not the solution to our problems; government *is* the problem." Deregulation, begun under Carter, was extended to banking, the savings-and-loan industry, transportation, and communications. The head of the Federal Communications Commission gutted federal rules governing the broadcast industry, and the secretary of transportation trimmed regulations reducing air pollution and increasing efficiency and safety in cars and trucks. Secretary of the Interior James Watt, a leader in the Sagebrush Rebellion, opened public lands in the West to commercial developers. But despite the administration's success in deregulation, Reagan's attack on "big government" had little effect on checking the growth of the federal budget and of the federal bureaucracy.

While implementing Reaganomics, the White House also had to cope with the immediate problem of inflation. The Federal Reserve Board led the charge against inflation, pushing the discount rate ever higher. This harsh medicine, coupled with a sharp downturn in world oil prices, worked. Inflation dropped to 4 percent in 1983 and held steady thereafter. But the high interest rates necessary to curb inflation spawned another severe recession, one that exceeded those of the Ford and Carter years. By late 1982 one of every ten Americans was jobless.

Falling exports added to the Reagan recession. As high U.S. interest rates lured foreign investors, the dollar rose in value vis-à-vis foreign currencies, making American goods more expensive abroad. The decline in U.S. exports—accompanied by enormous increases in imported TVs, stereos, and cars—propelled the U.S. trade deficit (the gap between exports and imports) from $31 billion in 1981 to $111 billion in 1984. The trade gap with Japan alone widened to a towering $33 billion in 1984.

Meanwhile, the United States' industrial heartland reeled under the triple blow of slumping exports, stiff foreign competition, and technological obsolescence. The aging steel mills, machinery plants, automobile companies, and other smokestack industries of the Midwest and Great Lakes laid off hordes of workers. Some plants closed. From 1979 through 1983, 11.5 million Americans lost jobs as a result of plant shutdowns or slack work.

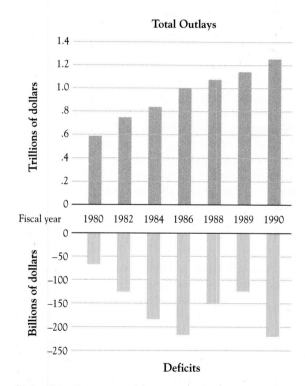

Federal Budget Expenditures and Deficits, Fiscal Years 1980–1990

After mounting to more than $200 billion in 1986, the federal deficit declined somewhat and then surged again in 1990. Driven by mushrooming health-care costs, it could surpass $400 billion by 2002.

SOURCES: U.S. Department of the Treasury; Office of Management and Budget; *New York Times*, 1 March 1992, p. 1.

The drop in exports hurt farmers as well. From 1980 to 1985 wheat exports fell 38 percent, and corn exports 49 percent. Some lost farms that their families had run for generations.

Spiraling federal deficits compounded the economic muddle. Reagan's tax cuts reduced federal revenues without immediately stimulating business, and increases in military spending more than offset domestic spending cuts. With the economy in crisis, the government awash in red ink, and critics denouncing him as callous, Reagan urged patience and insisted that his program would soon take effect. At the same time, he accepted a reduced rate of military spending, slower funding cuts in social programs, emergency job programs, and tax increases euphemistically described as "revenue-enhancement measures."

As recession's grip remained tight through 1982, the Democrats gained twenty-six House seats in the fall elections. The Reagan presidency appeared headed toward failure until early 1983, when the economy rebounded. Encouraged by tax cuts, declining interest rates, and evidence that inflation had been licked, consumers went on a buying binge. The stock market surged, unemployment dropped, and the gross national product shot up by almost 10 percent.

The Great Bull Market

Revived consumer spending unleashed a wave of stock-market speculation reminiscent of the 1920s. The great bull market began on August 12, 1982, and lasted five years. Entrepreneurs such as Manhattan real-estate tycoon Donald Trump, "junk-bond king" Michael Milken, and stock analyst Ivan Boesky became celebrities. The 1984 autobiography of Lee Iacocca, who had rescued Chrysler from near bankruptcy, was a best-seller. Corporate mergers burgeoned. Chevron bought Gulf for $13 billion; GE acquired RCA for $6.3 billion. Meanwhile, the stock market steadily roared on. Banks and savings-and-loan companies, newly deregulated, loaned billions to developers for the construction of shopping malls, luxury apartments, retirement villages, and office buildings.

In the mid-1980s the dark side of this feeding frenzy emerged. The E. F. Hutton brokerage firm pleaded guilty to manipulating funds and defrauding hundreds of banks. Ivan Boesky went to prison after his 1986 conviction for insider trading. Michael Milken received a ten-year federal prison sentence for violating securities laws. On October 19, 1987, "Black Monday," the Dow Jones plunged 508 points as one-fifth of the paper value of the nation's stocks evaporated. The downslide was eerily similar to the 1929 crash that precipitated the Great Depression, but prompt government action prevented another collapse.

Even at the height of the bull market, serious economic problems remained. The trade gap persisted, the deficit surpassed $200 billion in 1986, and farmers, the poor, and former industrial workers did not share in the renewed prosperity. The United States had been transformed from the world's largest creditor to the world's largest debtor. But—just in time to brighten Reagan's reelection prospects—the overall economic picture looked more hopeful than it had in years.

From Détente to a Renewed Cold War, 1974–1984

From the final throes of the Vietnam debacle through Reagan's first term, three American presidents, Gerald Ford, Jimmy Carter, and Ronald Reagan, pursued different Cold War strategies while tackling complex Third World problems. Détente faltered in the early 1980s as President Reagan revived the belligerent rhetoric of the early Cold War, raised the stakes in the arms race with the Soviets, and supplied money and weapons to anticommunist forces in Latin America. But Reagan soon found himself enmeshed in foreign problems that did not easily fit into his highly ideological and bipolar world view.

Ford, Carter, and the Cold War

President Ford retained Henry Kissinger as secretary of state and supported détente with China and the U.S.S.R. In 1974, the president and Soviet leader Leonid Brezhnev moved toward a new arms-control treaty, SALT I, limiting each side to 2,400 nuclear missiles. The following year, Ford and Brezhnev joined thirty-one European nations in adopting the Helsinki Accords, formalizing Europe's post-1945 boundaries and vowing respect for human rights. The Helsinki Accords boosted the forces of change in the Soviet bloc and may well represent Ford's most important accomplishment.

In April 1975 battered American morale suffered a further blow when the South Vietnamese government fell. The triumphant northerners swiftly changed the name of Saigon to Ho Chi Minh City. TV chronicled desperate helicopter evacuations from the roof of the U.S. embassy. A few weeks later, the new communist government in Cambodia seized an American merchant ship, the *Mayagüez*. Ford ordered a military rescue that freed the thirty-nine *Mayagüez* crewmen but cost the lives of forty-one U.S. servicemen.

The foreign-affairs achievements of Ford's successor, Jimmy Carter, outshone his domestic record. Carter and his secretary of state, Cyrus Vance, worked vigorously to inject human rights into foreign policy and to combat abuses in Chile, Argentina, Ethiopia, South Africa, and other nations. Human-rights violations by American allies such as South Korea and the Philippines received far more gingerly treatment. Trying to adapt U.S. policy to a multipolar world, Carter also sought better relations with the new black nations of Africa. A State Department official summed up the administration's view: "It is not a sign of weakness to recognize that we alone cannot dictate events elsewhere. It is rather a sign of maturity in a complex world."

In some areas Carter, like Ford, pursued initiatives launched by his predecessors. Earlier administrations had begun negotiating a more equitable treaty relationship with Panama. The Carter administration completed negotiations on two treaties transferring the Panama Canal and the Canal Zone to the Panamanians by 1999. Although the agreements protected U.S. interests, conservatives attacked them as proof of the United States' post-Vietnam loss of nerve. Why should the nation give up the canal, asked Ronald Reagan; "we stole it fair and square." In 1977 the Senate ratified both treaties.

The strengthening of ties with China accelerated after Mao Zedong's death in 1976. Carter opened full diplomatic relations with the People's Republic of China on January 1, 1979, opening the door to scientific, cultural, academic, and commercial exchanges. And toward the world's other communist superpower, the Soviet Union, Carter showed both toughness and conciliation. In 1979 Carter and Brezhnev signed SALT II. Critics, however, charged that the agreement favored the Soviets, and after the U.S.S.R. invaded neighboring Afghanistan in January 1980, Carter withdrew the treaty from the Senate. He also took a series of hard-line measures against the Soviet Union, including a boycott of the 1980 Moscow Olympics. This get-tough policy reflected the views of Carter's national-security adviser, Zbigniew Brzezinski, a Polish immigrant political scientist who harbored hostility toward the Soviet Union and viewed détente with suspicion.

The Middle East: Peace Accords and Hostages

Jimmy Carter's proudest achievement—and harshest setback—came in the Middle East. A state of war prevailed between Israel and Egypt when Carter took office. After Egyptian leader Anwar el-Sadat surprised the world by flying to Israel in November 1977 to negotiate personally with Israeli prime minister Menachem Begin, Carter invited the two leaders to Washington. In September 1978 at Camp David, the presidential retreat in Maryland, they hammered out the framework of a peace treaty, which was signed in March 1979.

At the heart of the Camp David Accords lay a timetable for a transition to autonomy for West Bank and Gaza Strip Palestinians. But hopes for a comprehensive Middle East settlement evaporated when Israel continued building settlements in the Jewish-occupied territories and when Islamic fundamentalists assassinated Sadat in 1981, in part because he had negotiated with Israel. Tensions among Israel, the Palestinians, and hard-line Arab "rejectionists" (led by Syria) remained electric. Limited though it was, Camp David constituted the high point of Carter's presidency.

A fresh Middle East crisis that erupted in Iran in 1979 overshadowed Camp David. For years, Iran had been ruled by a staunch U.S. ally, Shah Mohammed Reza Pahlavi, who had been restored to power with CIA help in 1953 and erected a repressive regime. The spiritual head of Iran's Shiite Islamic population, Ayatollah Ruhollah Khomeini, rallied opposition forces from his exile in Paris. In January 1979 the Shiite revolution toppled the shah, who fled Iran. Khomeini returned to impose strict Islamic rule and to rail against "the Great Satan," the United States.

In early November Carter allowed the shah to enter the United States for cancer treatment. Shortly after, militant Iranian students stormed the U.S. embassy in Iran's capital, Tehran, and seized more than fifty American hostages. For 444 days the hostage crisis paralyzed the Carter administration. A failed U.S. rescue attempt in April 1980 added to the perception of Oval Office ineptitude. And to Carter's bitter chagrin, the hostage crisis persisted through the 1980 presidential campaign. Not until January 20, 1981, Ronald Reagan's inaugural day, did authorities release the hostages.

Reagan Confronts the "Evil Empire"

With the fading of détente in the late seventies, anti-Soviet rhetoric escalated when Ronald Reagan took office. The president blasted the Soviet Union as an "evil empire" and "the focus of evil in the modern world." Anti-Soviet sentiment crested in September 1983 when the Soviets shot down a Korean passenger aircraft that had strayed into their airspace, killing 269. Moscow claimed that the plane had been spying, but most Americans rejected this explanation.

Obsession with the Soviets also influenced Reagan policy in El Salvador and Nicaragua, two poor Central American nations caught up in revolutionary turmoil. In El Salvador the administration supported the ruling military junta in its ruthless suppression of a leftist insurgency backed by Cuba and Nicaragua. Even after the more moderate José Napoleon Duarte won the 1984 presidential election with U.S. support, death squads continued to operate. In Nicaragua Carter had at first aided the Sandinista revolutionaries who overthrew dictator Anastasio Somoza in 1979. Reagan reversed this policy, claiming that the Sandinistas were creating another Cuba and a staging area for Soviet expansion. Under director William Casey, the CIA in 1982 organized and financed a 10,000-man guerrilla army, the contras, based in Honduras and Costa Rica. The contras, many of them linked to the Somoza regime, conducted raids, planted mines, and carried out sabotage inside Nicaragua.

Fearing another Vietnam, Americans grew alarmed as details of this "covert" war leaked out. Congress imposed a series of bans on military aid to the contras, but Reagan's enthusiasm for the contras, whom he labeled "the moral equivalent of our Founding Fathers," held steady. Secret contra aid, organized within the White House by a National Security Council aide named Oliver North and others, continued despite congressional prohibitions. In 1988 Reagan, still hoping for a contra victory, grudgingly supported a truce between the Sandinistas and the contras.

Reagan's militarization of American policy fell heavily on the West Indian island of Grenada, ruled by a radical leftist regime. In October 1983, 2,000 U.S. Marines invaded Grenada, overthrew the government, and installed one friendly to the United States. The Reagan administration maintained that American strategic interests had justified the action. Most Grenadians expressed their approval.

Tragedy and Frustration in the Middle East

At first the Reagan White House paid little attention to the Middle East. Hoping to stem Islamic fundamentalism, the United States tilted toward Saddam Hussein's Iraq in its long war with Iran. Attempts to court "moderates" in Iran culminated in a morass of arms-for-hostages deals, which would be exposed in 1985 as the Iran-contra scandal unfolded (see Chapter 33). Cold War policies dictated other U.S. actions in the Middle East.

In August 1981 Israel and the Palestine Liberation Organization (PLO) concluded a cease-fire, but the PLO continued building up its forces and carved out a sanctuary in southern Lebanon from which it could threaten Israel and defend itself against Syrian and Lebanese government hostility. In June 1982, when PLO extremists critically wounded the Israeli ambassador to Great Britain, Prime Minister Begin ordered Israeli troops to invade Lebanon and destroy the PLO. The incursion defeated the PLO militarily and forced its leaders to leave Lebanon. It also intensified civil war among Lebanese Christian and Islamic factions. A Christian militia took the opportunity to massacre Palestinians in a refugee camp near Beirut, Lebanon's capital.

Initially sympathetic to the Israeli invasion, the Reagan administration deployed 2,000 U.S. Marines to Beirut as part of a multinational peace-keeping force. The Muslim militias saw the Americans as favoring Israel and the Christian side and began firing on the marines. The U.S. Navy shelled the Lebanese coast in retaliation. Then tragically, in October 1983, a Shiite Muslim crashed a truck laden with explosives into poorly guarded barracks, killing 239 marines. Because Reagan had never defined American interests in Lebanon, the disaster underscored the failure of his Lebanese policy. By early 1984 the marines withdrew, leaving Lebanon to its warring factions and to the Syrians.

Disappointment also dogged Reagan's attempt to promote a wider Middle East settlement. In September 1982 the president announced the "Reagan Plan" to restart Arab-Israeli peace talks along the lines envisioned by the Camp David Accords. Over the next four years, the administration tried to bring PLO leader Yasir Arafat and Jordan's King Hussein together for a "Jordanian solution" to the Palestinian question in the West Bank. But his efforts were scuttled by Syria's opposition, stemming from that nation's exclusion from the process; by PLO reluctance; and by Israel's fears for its future military security—and its resultant hesitation to relinquish large amounts of land.

Military Buildup and Antinuclear Protest

Convinced that the United States had grown dangerously weak militarily, Reagan launched the most massive military expansion in American peacetime history. From 1981 to 1985, the Pentagon's budget swelled from $171 billion to more than $300 billion. Nuclear weapons were a key element of the U.S. buildup. In 1983 the administration deployed 572 cruise and Pershing II missiles in Western Europe, counterbalancing Soviet missiles in Eastern Europe. Reagan's supporters would later claim that the U.S.S.R.'s collapse in the late 1980s came from its efforts to match this American stockpiling. Others, however, would see the collapse as the result of internal events largely unaffected by American policy. There are no definitive answers yet.

On the domestic front, the Federal Emergency Management Agency responded to the nuclear buildup by designing an elaborate civil-defense plan whereby city residents would flee to remote "host communities" if nuclear war threatened. A Defense Department official averred that backyard shelters would save millions of people in a nuclear holocaust. "If there are enough shovels to go around," he asserted, "everybody's going to make it." Such talk, coupled with the military buildup and the breakdown of arms control, sparked a grass-roots reaction as millions of Americans felt a growing threat of nuclear war. Concerned citizens campaigned for a freeze on the manufacture and deployment of nuclear weapons. In June 1982, 800,000 antinuclear protesters, the largest political demonstration in

The Election of 1984

Candidates	Parties	Electoral Vote	Popular Vote	Percentage of Popular Vote
RONALD REAGAN	Republican	525	54,451,521	58.8
Walter Mondale	Democratic	13	37,565,334	40.5

U.S. history, rallied in New York's Central Park. Nine states passed freeze resolutions in the following fall elections.

Responding to the "No nukes!" clamor, the administration in June 1982 proposed the total removal of medium-range nuclear missiles from Europe and commenced talks with the Soviets on strategic-arms reductions. In March 1983 Reagan proposed the Strategic Defense Initiative (SDI), a vast space-based defense system against nuclear missiles. Nicknamed Star Wars after the popular 1977 movie, SDI reflected America's deep faith in technology. But even as the Pentagon launched an SDI research program, critics pointed out not only the project's prohibitive cost and technological implausibility but also the likelihood that it would further escalate the arms race.

Reagan Reelected

As the 1984 election approached, liberal Democrats and independents found much to criticize in the Reagan presidency: runaway military spending, worsening Cold War tensions, yawning budget deficits, a cavernous foreign-trade gap, sharp cuts in social programs, and the assault on regulatory functions. To critics, Reaganism meant jingoism abroad and selfishness at home.

But the American people widely supported Reagan's attacks on government waste and inefficiency, as well as his get-tough policy toward the Soviets. Rhetoric aside, the administration had ended inflation and created a booming economy. Reagan's popularity remained high; some dubbed him the Teflon president because nothing bad seemed to stick to him. By 1984 many Americans believed that Reagan had revitalized the free-enterprise system, rebuilt U.S. military might, and made the nation "stand tall" in the world. Buoyed by evidence of broad support, Reagan confidently prepared to campaign for a second term. The 1984 Republican convention, scripted for TV, accentuated patriotism, prosperity, and the personality of Ronald Reagan.

Democratic hopefuls included Jesse Jackson, a black Chicago minister and one-time associate of Martin Luther King, Jr. Jackson attempted to build a broad "rainbow coalition" of African-Americans, Hispanic-Americans, displaced workers, and other outsiders in Reagan's America. Former vice president Walter Mondale, however, won the Democratic nomination. He ignited little enthusiasm, despite his choice of a woman, New York representative Geraldine Ferraro, as his running mate.

Reagan and Bush collected 59 percent of the popular vote and carried every state but Minnesota and the District of Columbia. Reagan's popular ideology and mastery of television teamed with a booming economy to secure his solid victory. Democrats remained in control of Congress, but Republican dominance of presidential politics, broken only by Carter's single term, held firm.

Conclusion

The United States of the 1970s and 1980s seemed two separate societies that barely recognized each other's existence. Yuppies abandoned social activism to enjoy the Me Decade and celebrated the successes of Michael Milken, Donald Trump, and Ivan Boesky, whose materialistic obsessions represented a grotesque intensification of widely shared values. The other America, the world of the poor, centered primarily in the inner cities, was a realm of crime, drugs, decaying housing projects, and a failing educational system, and it augured dire consequences. The middle and elite classes showed little concern for problems outside their own charmed circles.

Presidents Gerald Ford and Jimmy Carter tackled complex foreign and domestic problems with little success. In 1980 voters sent to the White House a man who had pledged radical changes in the government's role. The "Reagan Revolution," however, promised far more than it delivered, and its most enduring legacy may well be the crushing public debt that the nation is struggling with today.

Internationally, Reagan's first-term bellicosity heightened Cold War tensions and convinced many Americans that a full-scale nuclear war was no longer unthinkable. But in Reagan's second term, seismic shifts would rock the Soviet Union, transforming the Cold War and altering the world balance of power in ways that few could have dreamed in 1984.

Chronology

1963   Betty Friedan, *The Feminine Mystique*.

1966   Founding of National Organization for Women (NOW).

1972   Equal Rights Amendment passed by Congress.

1973   Major rise in OPEC prices; Arab oil boycott.
        Roe v. *Wade*.

1974   Richard Nixon resigns presidency; Gerald Ford sworn in.
        Whip Inflation Now (WIN) program.
        Indian Self-Determination Act.
        Ford-Brezhnev meeting.

1975   South Vietnamese government falls.
        Mayagüez incident.

1976   Jimmy Carter elected president.

1977   Panama Canal treaties ratified.

1978–   Double-digit inflation and soaring interest rates.
1980

1979   Menachem Begin and Anwar el-Sadat sign peace treaty at White House.
        Second round of OPEC price increases.
        Accident at Three Mile Island nuclear plant.

        Carter and Leonid Brezhnev sign SALT II.
        Carter restores full diplomatic relations with the People's Republic of China.

1980   Carter withdraws SALT II agreement from Senate after Soviet invasion of Afghanistan.
        Iran hostage crisis preoccupies nation.
        Ronald Reagan elected president.

1981   Major cuts in taxes and domestic spending, coupled with large increases in military budget.

1981–   Severe recession (late 1981–early 1983).
1983

1982   Equal Rights Amendment dies.
        CIA organizes contra war against Nicaragua's Sandinista government.
        Nuclear-freeze rally in Central Park.
        Stock-market boom begins.

1983   239 U.S. Marines die in Beirut terrorist attack.
        U.S. invasion of Grenada.
        Reagan proposes Strategic Defense Initiative.

1984   Reagan defeats Walter Mondale in landslide.

1986   Immigration Reform and Control Act.
        Federal deficit rises to $221 billion.

FOR FURTHER READING

Ken Auletta, *The Underclass* (1981). Well-written exploration of the culture of poverty in urban America.

Paul Boyer, ed., *Reagan as President: Contemporary Views of the Man, His Politics, and His Policies* (1990). Contemporary speeches, articles, and editorials commenting on President Reagan and his program.

Peter Carroll, *It Seemed Like Nothing Happened* (1983). A perceptive, readable overview history of the 1970s.

John Crewden, *The Tarnished Door: The New Immigrants and the Transformation of America* (1983). A review of recent immigration trends and their effects on American life.

Robert Heilbroner and Lester Thurow, *Five Economic Challenges* (1983). An incisive look at the major economic changes affecting modern America.

Haynes Johnson, *Sleepwalking Through History: America in the Reagan Years* (1991). A highly readable account of American politics and culture in the 1980s.

Gaddis Smith, *Morality, Reason, and Power* (1986). Evaluation of Jimmy Carter's foreign policy by an able diplomatic historian.

Theodore White, *America in Search of Itself* (1982). A reflective look at the Reagan phenomenon, focusing on the 1980 presidential campaign.

Garry Wills, *Reagan's America: Innocents at Home* (1987). A stimulating, wide-ranging work by a distinguished political writer.

Daniel Yankelovich, *New Rules: Search for Self-Fulfillment in a World Turned Upside Down* (1981). An assessment of the American mood on the basis of public-opinion interviews and surveys.

The Cold War Ends

*O*ptimism about foreign affairs dominated Ronald Reagan's second administration as new Soviet leadership under Mikhail Gorbachev edged away from the totalitarian repression of the old Stalinist system and toward a new openness, *glasnost*. At the same time, U.S. domestic politics soured owing to rocketing budget deficits and revelations of wrongdoing by Reagan administration officials. Reagan's successor, George Bush, closed out the Cold War and reasserted American leadership in the Persian Gulf War, but he ignored thorny domestic problems, particularly a seemingly endless recession. Freed of Cold War concerns, Americans voted Bush out of office in 1992 in favor of Governor Bill Clinton of Arkansas, who pledged to focus on jobs and deficit reduction.

(Right) Soldier after failed coup attempt in Moscow, August 1991

Problems and Opportunities in Reagan's Second Term

Beyond the Cold War

The Aftermath of Reaganism: The Domestic Scene Since 1989

Problems and Opportunities in Reagan's Second Term

In his first term, Ronald Reagan had set a political agenda of tax cuts, deregulation, and expanded military spending. In his second term, a growing budget deficit and trade gap, and the Iran-contra scandal, overtook him. Foreign affairs temporarily eclipsed domestic issues, however, as a new era of Soviet-American cooperation and friendship replaced the "evil empire" confrontation of Reagan's first term. Despite chronic economic problems and misconduct at the highest levels of government, Reagan left office in 1989 with very favorable approval ratings, the first president since Dwight Eisenhower to complete two terms.

Tax Reform, Budget Deficits, and Trade Gaps

Reagan achieved significant legislative victories in his second term, including a new immigration law and tax reform. To make the system fairer, the tax-reform law eliminated many deductions, established uniform rates for people at comparable income levels, and removed 6 million low-income Americans from the tax rolls.

But sky-high federal deficits, the legacy of Reaganomics, persisted. In 1985 and 1986, the budget deficit reached $200 billion before settling at $150 billion in 1987 and 1988. Enormous federal debts and an escalating trade gap, which hit $154 billion in 1987, represented long-term economic problems bequeathed by Reagan to his successor.

The Iran-Contra Scandal

On November 3, 1986, a Beirut newspaper reported that in 1985 the United States had shipped 508 antitank missiles to the violently anti-American Iranian government. Thus began the worst scandal of the Reagan administration. Acknowledging the sale, Reagan declared that his goal had been to encourage "moderate elements" in Iran and to secure the release of American hostages held in Lebanon by pro-Iranian radicals. In February 1987 a presidential investigative panel placed heavy blame on the administration, prompting the resignation of Chief of Staff Donald Regan.

Soon more details surfaced. It was learned that national-security adviser Robert McFarlane had accompanied the second arms shipment to Iran and had carried a chocolate cake and a Bible autographed by President Reagan for Ayatollah Khomeini. The most explosive revelation was that Lieutenant Colonel Oliver North had diverted millions in profits from the arms sales to the Nicaraguan contras (see Chapter 32) at a time when Congress had made such aid illegal. In November 1986 North and his secretary had held a "shredding party" to destroy incriminating documents.

In the summer of 1987, a joint House-Senate investigative committee on the Iran-contra affair heard 250 hours of testimony from twenty-eight witnesses. A fascinated nation watched "Ollie" North, resplendent in his military uniform, portray himself as a true patriot. Former national-security adviser John Poindexter testified that he had deliberately concealed the diversion of funds from Reagan.

The committee found no evidence that President Reagan personally knew of illegalities, but severely criticized the casual management style and disregard for the law that had fed the scandal. In early 1988 a court-appointed special prosecutor, Lawrence Walsh, won criminal indictments against Poindexter, North, and others. In 1989 a federal jury convicted North of obstructing a congressional inquiry, destroying and falsifying Security Council documents, and accepting an illegal gratuity, but the conviction was later reversed because North had been promised immunity before testifying before the joint committee. Proclaiming himself vindicated, North began a public-speaking career and published memoirs claiming that Reagan had been fully aware of his activities. The Iran-contra scandal dogged the Reagan administration's final years. Questions about his role in the Iran-contra mess, moreover, would later embarrass President George Bush in his 1992 reelection attempt.

More Scandals and Embarrassments

Other disturbing revelations, some of them involving the president's closest associates, plagued Reagan's second term. His old friend Attorney General Edward Meese was accused of influence peddling and resigned in July 1988. That same year, former chief of staff Donald Regan's *For the Record* painted Reagan as little more than an automaton: "Every moment of every public appearance, every word was scripted, every place where Reagan was expected to stand was chalked with toe marks." Regan also revealed that first lady Nancy Reagan regularly consulted an astrologer about the president's schedule and pending decisions. News broke of bribery and conspiracy involving some of the Pentagon's largest suppliers. In 1989 still other revelations came, this time about former interior secretary James Watt's and other prominent Republicans' acceptance of hundreds of thousands of dollars for interceding with the Department of Housing and Urban Development on behalf of developers seeking federal subsidies.

But the dirty linen did not sully Reagan's own popularity. His admirers did not look to him for administrative brilliance or conventional political skills. The sources of his popularity lay far deeper, in his uncanny ability to articulate the beliefs, fears, and hopes of millions of Americans. For that, they forgave him almost any lapse.

Reagan's Mission to Moscow

The Cold War thawed dramatically in Reagan's second term. Meeting at Geneva, Switzerland, in 1985 and Reykjavík, Iceland, in 1986, Reagan and Soviet leader Mikhail Gorbachev explored large-scale weapons cuts. Beset by economic crisis at home, Gorbachev sought an easing of superpower tensions to gain a breathing space for reform and crafted a policy of *glasnost,* or openness, to begin *perestroika,* the restructuring of Soviet society.

In December 1987 Gorbachev came to Washington to sign the Intermediate Nuclear Forces (INF) Treaty. Providing for the removal of 2,500

Ronald Reagan's Mission to Moscow
As the Cold War eased, President Reagan visited Moscow in 1988 to sign a nuclear-arms reduction treaty with Soviet premier Mikhail Gorbachev.

American and Soviet missiles from Europe, this treaty revived the arms-control process and for the first time eliminated an entire class of nuclear weapons. INF also provided on-site inspections to verify compliance.

This agreement led to Reagan's historic visit to Moscow in May 1988. The two leaders not only signed the INF Treaty but also established a cordial personal relationship. Asked about the "evil empire," Reagan replied that he had been talking about an earlier era. Gorbachev announced Soviet withdrawal from Afghanistan, resolving another major sticking point.

Détente, derailed in the 1970s, was back on track and barreling ahead at a rate unimaginable a few years earlier. Even critics of Reagan's domestic policies applauded the turnabout. The ardent Cold Warrior, denouncer of earlier arms-control treaties and champion of mammoth military spending, seemed destined to be remembered for bettering superpower relations, signing an important arms agreement, and reducing the risk of global war.

The Election of 1988

As the Reagan era ended, Vice President George Bush nailed down the Republican nomination for the presidency. A seven-way battle among Democrats narrowed into a contest between Jesse Jackson and Massachusetts governor Michael Dukakis. Preaching concern for the poor and urging a full-scale war on drugs, Jackson drew impressive numbers of white as well as black votes. However, Dukakis victories in major primary states, including New York and California, proved decisive. He chose Texas senator Lloyd Bentsen as his running mate.

On the Republican side, the only surprise came in the vice-presidential selection. Bush chose a little-known conservative senator from Indiana, J. Danforth ("Dan") Quayle III. Bush apparently hoped that Quayle's boyish good looks would appeal to the younger generation and to women voters and that Quayle's conservative credentials would strengthen his own standing with the Republican Right. The press soon learned that in 1969 Quayle had pulled strings to avoid service in Vietnam, but the issue faded.

Bush called for a "kinder, gentler America" and promised no new taxes. He emphasized peace and prosperity, pointing to better superpower relations, low inflation, and the 14 million new jobs created during the eighties. While Bush personally took the high road, some of his commercials took the low road. One campaign ad, playing on latent racist stereotypes, featured a black man who had committed rape and murder after his release under a Massachusetts prisoner-furlough program. In his most demagogic attack, Bush assailed Dukakis's veto of a bill requiring Massachusetts schoolchildren to recite the Pledge of Allegiance, although the Supreme Court had already declared such a law unconstitutional. For his part, Dukakis declined to attack Bush and stressed that "this election is not about ideology, it's about competence." Boasting his accomplishments as governor, he hammered at the failures of the "Swiss-cheese" Reagan economy. But Dukakis seemed edgy and defensive, and his dismissal of ideology made it difficult for him to define his vision of America.

Both candidates avoided serious issues in favor of TV-oriented "photo opportunities" and "sound bites." Bush visited flag factories and military plants; Dukakis looked spectacularly out of place posing in a tank. Editorial writers grumbled about the "junk-food" campaign, but in an era when fleeting impressions counted for everything, the image, the catchy phrase, and the twenty-second spot on the evening news were the essence of presidential politics.

Bush's negative campaign, coupled with Americans' generally upbeat mood and Dukakis's weak-

The Election of 1988

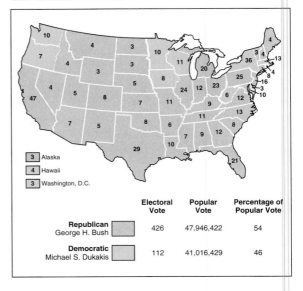

	Electoral Vote	Popular Vote	Percentage of Popular Vote
Republican George H. Bush	426	47,946,422	54
Democratic Michael S. Dukakis	112	41,016,429	46

nesses, carried the day. Bush gained 54 percent of the vote, won 40 states, and emerged with a lopsided 426–112 electoral margin. The Democrats retained control of both houses of Congress.

The departing president could look back on foreign policy triumphs, having had the good fortune to serve as the Cold War and the Soviet menace had ended. Reagan had also restored national pride; but his domestic record was mixed. Luxuriating in apparent prosperity, the administration—and the American people—had ignored serious social issues and structural weaknesses in the economy. Some Reagan policies, in fact, laid the groundwork for later problems. And despite his popularity, Reagan's image dimmed quickly. From the perspective of the early 1900s, his presidency seemed more an interlude of nostalgia and drift than one of positive achievement, and a time when individual gain took precedence over the public good.

Beyond the Cold War

At first few Americans grasped the magnitude of the changes overtaking the Soviet Union. By the early 1990s, however, radical reformers had elbowed aside Mikhail Gorbachev, repudiated communism, embraced free-market ideas, and dismantled the Soviet Union itself in a rush of ethnic and nationalist fervor. Americans watched the end of the Cold War with a mixture of elation, fascination, and apprehension.

But many global challenges remained, both in the former Soviet domain and in the still turbulent Middle East. Iraq's invasion of Kuwait in August 1990 presented President Bush with a major foreign crisis. He responded shrewdly, building international support for a war that pushed the Iraqis back into their own territory.

Gorbachev Loses Control

Soviet power collapsed with breathtaking speed. When Gorbachev refused to use Soviet troops to prop up Eastern Europe's unpopular communist regimes, they swiftly fell. New capitalist governments sprang up behind what had been the Iron Curtain. In November 1989 exuberant Germans tore down the Berlin Wall, and within a year Germany was reunited for the first time since 1945. The Baltic republics—Latvia, Lithuania, and Estonia—forcibly annexed by the Soviet Union on the eve of World War II, declared their independence. Other Soviet republics followed.

The Cold War was suddenly over; the enemy that had dominated American foreign policy for forty years was no more. The arms race, the Cold War's evil twin, seemed to wind down as well. In August 1991 President Bush and Gorbachev signed a treaty reducing their strategic arsenals by 25 percent. Secretary of Defense Dick Cheney called for a 25 percent reduction in U.S. military forces over five years. With the Warsaw Pact gone, NATO planned a 50 percent troop reduction.

In August 1991, as the Soviet Union inched toward a market economy, increasing economic chaos led hard-line Communist party leaders to stage a coup against Gorbachev. But a wall of opposition blocked the attempt. Rallied by Boris Yeltsin, the president of the Russian Republic, the Russian people protectively surrounded the Russian parliament to defy the plotters and their tanks. Gorbachev returned to power, but Yeltsin assumed a dominant role.

The failed coup accelerated the death of the Soviet Communist party and of the Soviet Union itself. Exultant crowds toppled statues of Lenin and other communist leaders across the nation, and Leningrad reverted to its tsarist name, St. Petersburg. As the Soviet republics rushed to independence, Gorbachev was overwhelmed by the forces that he had released. Seeking to reform the Soviet economic and political system, he had also tried to preserve a unified Soviet Union, to retain a role for the Communist party, and to remain in charge of the reform process. In these latter goals he failed. The August 1991 coup stripped the last shred of legitimacy from the Soviet Communist party. Later that year, led by Yeltsin, most of the Soviet republics proclaimed the end of the U.S.S.R. and formed the vaguely defined Commonwealth of Independent States. On Christmas Day 1991,

**The End of the
Cold War**

Communist regimes overthrown since 1989

Soviet Union, dissolved in 1991

Yugoslavia, dissolved in civil war, 1991–

★ Hot spot

Soviet war in Afghanistan, 1979–1989.

Armenian-Azerbaijan conflict, 1990–.

Iran-Iraq War, 1980–1989.

Kurdish uprising, 1991–.

Gulf War, 1991

Persian Gulf crisis, 1990.

Palestinian Intifada begins, 1987; Israel-Palestinian agreement, 1993.

Gorbachev assumes power, 1985; Moscow coup fails, and U.S.S.R. dissolved, 1991.

Rise of Solidarity, 1980.

Fall of Berlin Wall, 1989; Germany unified, 1990.

Yugoslavia dissolves in civil war, 1991–.

The Breakup of Yugoslavia

enthralled American TV viewers watched as the hammer and sickle were lowered over the Kremlin for the last time. Bowing to the inevitable, Gorbachev resigned.

The Post–Cold War World

Contemplating world changes, the *New York Times* observed: "Everything—keeping track of nuclear weapons, providing economic aid, negotiating treaties, even training diplomats—will be much more complicated now." Secretary of State James Baker and President Bush proceeded cautiously as the Soviet empire disintegrated. American influence was limited, in any event, as nationalism and ethnic issues exploded in Eastern Europe and the former Soviet Union. Economic chaos and social upheaval especially threatened the Russian Republic. Some economists and political leaders argued for massive Western aid, but others warned that a flood of outside relief could swamp Russia's transition to a free-market economy and slow the shift of resources from the military to the civilian sector.

The future of the Soviet arsenal, 27,000 nuclear weapons, remained a particularly vital concern. Baker worked, with limited success, to assure the security and orderly dismantling of these weapons and to prevent the flow of nuclear technology to Third World nations and to nonnuclear European nations. Early in 1992, as strategic talks progressed, Bush announced major reductions in the American nuclear arsenal.

The situation in the Middle East remained volatile. In December 1987 the Intifada, a Palestinian uprising against Israeli occupation, began in Gaza and spread to the West Bank. Reagan's secretary of state, George Shultz, attempted in 1988 to bring Jordan and the Palestinians into negotiations with Israel over an accelerated Palestinian

The Mideast Crises, 1980–Present
The Bush administration, like its predecessors, had trouble formulating a coherent and effective policy toward the Middle East, a region torn by ethnic, religious, and national conflicts.

autonomy plan. But the Israeli government rejected the "land for peace" formula and refused to negotiate until the Intifada ended; and the Palestinians rejected Shultz's proposals for not going far enough toward establishing a Palestinian state. Israel meanwhile continued to build Jewish settlements on the West Bank.

In the late 1980s the Middle East conflict generated a deadly by-product: kidnappings, airplane hijackings, airport attacks, and other terrorist acts.

The United States in Latin America and the Caribbean

Plagued by poverty, population pressures, repressive regimes, and drug trafficking, Latin America saw turmoil and conflict—but also some hopeful developments—in the 1980s and 1990s. In the long tradition of Yanqui *intervention, U.S. forces invaded Grenada in 1983 and Panama in 1989.*

In April 1986, after terrorists bombed a Berlin nightclub popular with American GIs, President Reagan ordered a retaliatory air attack on Libya, which had been implicated in the bombing. In the worst of the terrorist incidents, a bomb exploded aboard a Pan Am jet over Scotland in December 1988, killing all 259 aboard, many of them Americans. In 1991 the U.S. and British governments formally charged Libya with complicity in the bombing. Colonel Muammar el-Qaddafi, Libya's ruler, denied the charges and refused to extradite the accused officials.

Capitalizing on the favorable diplomatic climate created by the outcome of the Gulf War (see below), Bush called for a renewed Middle Eastern peace effort. Secretary of State Baker orchestrated the diplomacy, which culminated in the opening of talks involving Israel, the Palestinians, and various

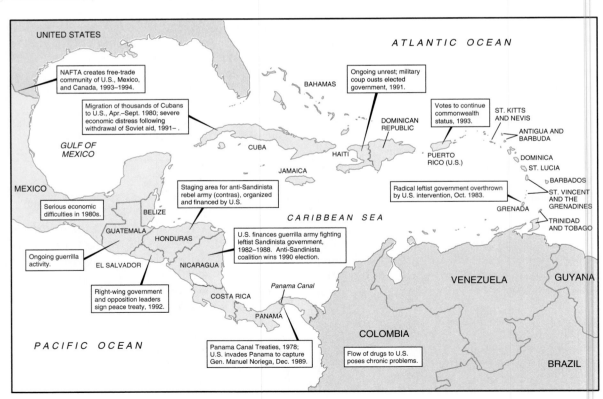

Arab states in November 1991. Polls showed that 80 percent of Israelis favored a settlement, but whether the longtime enemies could reach agreement remained unclear.

The Cold War's end also offered opportunities for the resolution of regional conflicts elsewhere in the world. For decades, the superpowers had aided allies, client states, and rebel forces throughout the Third World. But with the Cold War over and only one superpower left, the prospects for resolving local disputes brightened.

Asia and Latin America offered vivid evidence of the change. North and South Korea, after forty years of hostility, moved cautiously toward friendly relations. In Latin America, the bloody civil wars of the Cold War era wound down. The Bush administration abandoned its predecessors' financing of the Nicaraguan contras and worked at reintegrating them into Nicaragua's life and politics. In 1989 the Sandinistas and contras agreed to elections the next year, greater press freedom, and an end to their war. Victory in the elections went to newspaper publisher Violetta Chamorro, the leader of an anti-Sandinista coalition. In tiny El Salvador, where the United States had spent more than $1 billion to keep leftist guerrillas from power, the right-wing government and the guerrillas signed a treaty in 1992, ending a twelve-year civil war that had left 75,000 dead.

But enormous problems linked to poverty, ignorance, and economic exploitation still plagued Latin America. Open guerrilla warfare continued in Peru. Cocaine and heroin flowed from South and Central America to U.S. cities. In December 1989 concern over the drug traffic led to a U.S. invasion of Panama to capture General Manuel Noriega, Panama's leader and an unsavory thug with ties to the CIA. Noriega was brought to the United States and put on trial in 1991 for drug trafficking.

America's relations with the Philippines, a former colony and longtime ally, shifted as well. Resistance to the corrupt government of President Ferdinand Marcos intensified after the 1983 assassination of Benigno Aquino, a popular opposition leader. After a fraud-ridden election in 1986,

Aquino's widow, Corazon, proclaimed herself victor, and the United States recognized her government. Marcos accepted exile in Hawaii. But the Philippines remained turbulent. In 1991 the Philippines legislature ended long-term American leases on two military bases, spurring a U.S. reassessment of its needs in the post–Cold War world.

South Africa became a focus of debate in Reagan's second term. Anglican bishop Desmond Tutu, a leader of South Africa's blacks, appealed for U.S. support against apartheid, the white government's policy of racial segregation. The Reagan administration condemned apartheid but opposed economic sanctions. In 1986 Congress overrode Reagan's veto and imposed stiff sanctions, banning South African products and prohibiting U.S. investments there.

Worldwide sanctions helped to bring extraordinary changes to South Africa. In 1990 President F. W. de Klerk released black leader Nelson Mandela after twenty-seven years in prison and opened negotiations with his African National Congress. The South African parliament scrapped most apartheid laws in 1991, and Bush lifted some U.S. sanctions. In 1992 a strong majority of the nation's whites voted to continue dismantling apartheid and to extend political rights to South Africa's black majority.

China proved a major exception to the world trend toward democracy. In 1989 U.S. relations with China suffered a serious setback when the Chinese army brutally crushed a prodemocracy demonstration by thousands of unarmed students in Beijing's Tiananmen Square. As many as 1,000 students died, and repression, arrests, and public executions followed. The Bush administration protested but neither broke diplomatic relations nor canceled trade agreements with China. Americans watched anxiously to see what the future would bring to China, a nation ruled by aging leaders and torn between hard-liners and advocates of liberalization.

As Cold War worries waned, international trade issues took on growing significance. The towering U.S. trade deficit with Japan, which ranged from $40 billion to $55 billion in the late 1980s, aroused particular concern. In early 1992 President

Bush led a high-level trade mission to Japan, accompanied by the heads of the "big three" U.S. auto companies. But efforts to open Japanese markets proved futile. When Bush collapsed from the flu during a state dinner in Tokyo, the mishap seemed unhappily symbolic. Some Americans began "Japan bashing," blaming the Japanese for U.S. economic problems. The fiftieth anniversary of Pearl Harbor, December 7, 1991, provided an occasion for reflection on relations between the two nations whose recent histories were so closely, and sometimes so tragically, intertwined.

The United States also faced the challenge of redefining its relationship with a resurgent Europe dominated by a reunified, prosperous, and confident Germany. When the European Community—the agency for full European economic union—began to coalesce in 1992, Americans watched nervously. The Soviet menace had held together the NATO coalition, and the end of that threat called for a re-definition of American ties to Western Europe.

Along with uncertainty, the end of the Cold War ushered in encouraging developments, most importantly the breakdown of totalitarian ideology in a major region of the world and the vastly diminished possibility of nuclear war. The United Nations, long a pawn in superpower conflict, seemed ready to play the positive role envisioned by idealists in 1945. The U.N. figured prominently in a series of positive developments in 1991–1992: the negotiation of the El Salvador peace treaty; the release of the last American hostages in Lebanon; and efforts to mediate a vicious civil war in a disintegrating Yugoslavia. By 1992, sixty thousand U.N. peacekeeping troops were in place or planned for eleven global hot spots.

In the early 1990s the United States remained a major world power, but it was no longer the colossus of the early post–World War II years. The nation's share of the world's total output of goods and services had tumbled from one-third in 1950 to one-fifth in 1990. A nagging sense of eroding power and narrowing possibilities troubled many Americans. In the early 1990s, too, the nation was still adjusting to a new historical age in which tangled international problems would have to be addressed on their

own terms rather than reduced to the simplistic slogans of the Cold War. In 1992 political analyst Richard J. Barnet tartly observed, "Ever since the Cold War ended, there has been a good deal of talk about a new world order, but, for all the talk, the nightly news is a kaleidoscope of disorder."

Operation Desert Storm

On August 2, 1990, the Middle Eastern nation of Iraq invaded its oil-rich neighbor, Kuwait. Iraq's dictator, Saddam Hussein, had dismissed Kuwait's nation-state status as a creation of Western imperialists and asserted Iraq's claim to the area.

Under Saddam, Iraq had for years threatened not only its Arab neighbors but Israel as well. Iraq's military buildup, including chemical- and nuclear-weapons programs, had worried many governments in the 1980s. However, during the Iraq-Iran war (1980–1988), the United States had tilted toward Iraq because of Iran's rabid anti-Americanism. But lessened Iranian hostility after Ayatollah Khomeini's death in 1989 had removed the United States' incentive to placate Iraq. Thus when Iraq invaded Kuwait, Washington denounced the aggression.

Determined to avoid the mistakes of the Vietnam era, Bush carefully built a consensus for anti-Iraqi action in Congress, in the United Nations, and among the American people. He also articulated a clear military objective—Iraqi withdrawal from Kuwait—and provided the necessary military force. More than 400,000 troops were shuttled to Saudi Arabia.

The United Nations imposed economic sanctions on Iraq and insisted that Saddam withdraw from Kuwait by January 15, 1991. On January 12, after somber debate, both houses of Congress endorsed military action against Iraq. Most Democrats, however, voted against war, favoring continued economic sanctions.

On January 16 a massive, sustained air assault opened the war. For nearly six weeks both American and allied land- and carrier-based planes pounded troops, supply depots, and command and communications targets in Iraq's capital, Baghdad. They flew up to 3,000 sorties daily. Iraq offered little direct resistance to the air attacks. But Saddam ordered Soviet-made Scud missiles fired against Israeli and Saudi Arabian cities. Americans watched transfixed as the Cable News Network carried live coverage of U.S. Patriot missiles streaking off to intercept incoming Scuds. Carefully edited for its mass television viewers, the war often seemed a glorified video game. The reality of an estimated 100,000 Iraqi deaths, both military and civilian, hardly impinged on Americans' consciousness.

On February 23, 200,000 U.N. forces, comprising U.S. troops and their allies under General H. Norman Schwarzkopf, advanced across the desert toward Kuwait. Within three days Iraqi soldiers were in full flight or surrendering en masse. U.N. forces destroyed 3,700 Iraqi tanks while losing only three. One hundred hours after the ground war had begun, with Iraqi resistance crushed and Kuwait City liberated, President Bush declared a cease-fire. American casualties numbered 148 dead, including 35 killed by "friendly fire," and 467 wounded.

When victory celebrations back in the United States played out, the war's political aftermath came into focus. Kuwait created a refugee nightmare by expelling thousands of Palestinian workers who had supported Iraq. Within Iraq, amid widespread civilian hardship and malnutrition, Saddam clung to power. His army brutally suppressed rebellions by Shiite Muslims in the south and by a large Kurdish ethnic minority in the north. U.N. inspectors found convincing evidence of an advanced nuclear-weapons project under way in Iraq, and its discontinuance brought general relief. Nevertheless, by early 1992 the Gulf War seemed more distant, and feelings about it more mixed, than anyone would have predicted a year before.

The Aftermath of Reaganism: The Domestic Scene Since 1989

Ronald Reagan had become president knowing exactly what he wanted: a bigger military budget, reduced social spending, lower taxes, less federal regulation, a less activist judiciary, and an unshackling of the engine of free enterprise. Public issues requiring government leadership, such as health care, consumer protection, education, and urban poverty, were shunted aside. The "Reagan revolution" unleashed entrepreneurial energies, powered a stock-market surge and a wave of corporate takeovers, and set off an economic boom that gave the 1980s a patina of prosperity. But in the 1990s the longer-term effects of Reaganism began to be felt. As the economy slowed, the go-go eighties seemed remote. Under George Bush, Americans, especially the middle class, bristled with economic discontent.

Economic Strains

The son of a powerful Connecticut senator, George Bush had fought in World War II and attended Yale before entering the Texas oil business. He had served in Congress, lost a Senate race, directed the CIA, and fought for the 1980 Republican nomination before being tapped as Ronald Reagan's running mate in 1980.

As president, Bush confronted—or evaded—a morass of economic problems directly related to Reagan policies. First came the collapse of the savings-and-loan (S&L) industry, long a source of home loans to borrowers and of a secure return to depositors. In the late seventies, S&Ls had paid high interest rates to attract depositors, even though their assets were tied up in fixed-rate mortgages. In the early eighties, capital freed up by the Reagan tax cuts had flowed to S&Ls just as they were deregulated. Caught up in the high-flying economic mood of the eighties, S&Ls across the nation had made risky loans on speculative real-estate ventures. As the economy cooled, many such investments went bad. In the period 1988–1990, nearly 600 S&Ls failed, wiping out thousands of depositors' savings.

Because the federal government insures S&L deposits, the Bush administration in 1989 set up a program to repay depositors and to sell millions of dollars' worth of foreclosed office towers and apartment buildings in a depressed real-estate market. Estimates of the cost of the bailout topped $400 billion. In 1991 a chain of bank failures, for similar causes, intensified the crisis. Federal banking officials predicted that up to 440 banks might go under, at a cost of billions of dollars.

Meanwhile, the federal deficit, already worsened by the Reagan tax cuts and runaway military spending, mounted. In the fall of 1990, Congress and Bush agreed on a five-year deficit-reduction package that clipped government spending and increased taxes. Controversially, Bush had abandoned his 1988 campaign pledge, "Read my lips: no new taxes." But the red ink flowed on; a $350 billion deficit was forecast for 1992. Total federal debt neared $4 trillion, with monstrous deficits predicted for years to come. The Gulf War, the S&L bailout, and soaring welfare and Medicare-Medicaid payments shattered the budget-balancing effort.

Making matters worse, a recession struck in the summer of 1990. Retail sales slumped, housing starts declined, and unemployment rose. Troubled times continued into 1992, with a jobless rate of more than 7 percent. Hard-pressed states gutted social-welfare funding. Michigan cut AFDC (Aid to Families with Dependent Children) payments by 17 percent, and New Jersey and California planned to follow suit. As the number of Americans below the poverty line rose by 2.1 million, the plight of the poor roused more resentment than sympathy. Ohio's governor declared, "Most Ohioans have had enough welfare, enough poverty, enough drugs, enough crime." The middle class, political strategists discovered, were suffering from "compassion fatigue."

Recessions were hardly new, but economists warned of structural problems in the economy as comparatively low-paying service jobs replaced higher-paying manufacturing jobs. Important manufacturing sectors continued to decline. Battered by Japanese imports, the U.S. auto industry fared disastrously in 1991. A week before Christmas, GM unveiled plans to close twenty-one plants and cut its work force by more than 70,000. Even the service sector of the economy, a success story in the 1980s, faltered as employers coped with overexpansion, runaway costs, and rising competition. In 1992 the *New York Times* reported, "Most economists expect the great American job machine, even after it gets going again, to run at just half speed through much of the 1990s. . . . They expect job growth in the nineties to be the slowest since the 1950s."

Economic jitters made many Americans look back on Reagan's policies skeptically. If 1984 was "morning in America," wrote a columnist, quoting a Reagan campaign slogan, 1989–1990 was the "morning after." For most middle-class Americans, the situation produced more anxiety than desperation, but the gloomy economic picture clouded much of Bush's presidency.

Domestic Dilemmas

The hobbled economy intensified deep-seated social problems. Middle- and working-class Americans, although relatively prosperous, felt that they were on a treadmill. From 1970 to 1990 average family income, adjusted for inflation, rose less than 7 percent. Factory workers' earnings, adjusted for inflation, fell. With health-care costs accelerating 20 percent a year, a medical crisis or extended retirement expenses could quickly erase a person's life savings. Thus real income declined. Americans at the bottom of the ladder made sheer survival their top priority. Many of the 37 million Americans without health insurance were in the ranks of the poor.

Throughout America, racism lived on. Its tenacity was starkly revealed in 1992 with the release of videotapes of white California police officers beating an African-American motorist, Rodney King, who seemed to be trying to escape. When an all-white jury acquitted the four officers, the predominantly black south-central section of Los Angeles exploded into riots that took a terrible toll in both life and property.

Among black Americans, the gulf between the middle class and the inner-city poor widened. By 1990 one-third of black high school graduates went on to college, up from one-quarter in 1985. More than 7,300 blacks held public office in America in 1990, up from 1,300 in 1970. Most visible were New York City's first black mayor, David Dinkins, and the nation's first black governor, Virginia's Douglas Wilder. Bush appointed African-Americans Colin Powell chairman of the Joint Chiefs of Staff, Louis

Sullivan secretary of health and human services, and Clarence Thomas Supreme Court justice. But the record of black achievement could not obscure the harsh realities for the one-third of African-Americans below the poverty level.

Similar patterns emerged in the Hispanic-American population. By 1991 more than 4,000 Latinos held public office in California alone. At the same time, more than a quarter of all Hispanics remained poor, eking out a living in urban barrios or on the exhausting migrant-labor circuit.

Reflecting middle-class white and business priorities, the Bush administration did little to address these issues. In 1990 Bush vetoed a bill broadening federal protection against job discrimination, claiming that it would encourage "racial quotas." In 1991 he signed a similar bill. When Bush showed up in Atlanta in 1992 to sing "We Shall Overcome" on the birthday of Martin Luther King, Jr., King's daughter, the Reverend Bernice King, asked bitterly, "How dare we celebrate in the midst of a recession, when nobody is sure whether their jobs are secure?"

An inrushing stream of immigrants from many nations raised concerns about whether the country could absorb so many newcomers, the vast majority of them from Latin America and Asia. Debate focused on the issue of whether the United States should become a "salad bowl" of multiple cultures, a society not only tolerating but even encouraging diverse ethnic groups and languages. In the academic world, similar concerns led to attacks upon, and fervent defense of, the "canon" of traditional Western literature. Critics argued that this canon drew almost exclusively from "dead white males" and demanded the inclusion of non-European literature and philosophy.

In the realm of public education, the recession stung school budgets at a moment of much hand-wringing over shortcomings in the American educational system. Remedies proved elusive. Bush ballyhooed himself as the "education president" but addressed the issue only fitfully. His first budget requested $3 million less for education than Ronald Reagan had proposed in his last budget. Bush called for standardized national testing of schoolchildren,

Cleaning Up After the *Exxon Valdez* Disaster
Volunteers on Green Island in Alaska's Prince William Sound collect and bag sea otters killed in the Exxon Valdez *oil spill of March 1989, a catastrophe that focused attention on the mounting ecological toll of industrialization.*

supported a voucher system by which parents could withdraw their children from public schools and enroll them in private or church schools, and urged corporate America to support a fund for experimental schools. These proposals hardly matched the magnitude of the problem.

Ongoing environmental dangers were spotlighted in March 1989 when a 987-foot oil tanker, the *Exxon Valdez*, ran aground in Alaska's beautiful Prince William Sound and spilled more than 10 million gallons of crude oil. The accident fouled 600 acres of coastal and marine habitats, killed thousands of sea otters and shore birds, and jeopardized vital salmon and herring industries. Then in the summer of 1989, the Environmental Protection Agency (EPA) reported that air pollution exceeded federal standards in more than one hundred cities. In Louisiana alone, industry pumped 2 million pounds of pollutants into the air daily. In 1991 the EPA reported that pollutants were depleting the ozone shield—the layer that protects humans from cancer-causing solar radiation—over the United States at twice the rate that scientists had predicted.

Caught between public pressure for change and corporate calls for a go-slow policy, the Bush administration compiled a mixed environmental record. Bush called the *Exxon Valdez* spill a "major tragedy" but supported offshore oil exploration and drilling. In a rare bipartisan effort, the White House and the Democratic Congress passed a tough Federal Clean Air Act in 1990. The government also began the multibillion-dollar task of disposing of radioactive waste and cleaning up nuclear-weapons facilities and nuclear-power plants that had been contaminating soil and ground water for years.

But the Bush administration, like the Reagan government, generally dismissed environmental concerns. Vice President Dan Quayle ridiculed environmentalists; the administration scuttled international treaties on global warming and mining in Antarctica, recommended oil exploration in the Alaskan wilderness, and proposed opening vast tracts of protected wetlands to development.

The Supreme Court Moves Right

Like all presidents, Reagan and Bush sought to perpetuate their political ideology through Supreme Court appointments. In addition to nominating Sandra Day O'Connor, Reagan in 1986 elevated William Rehnquist to chief justice and chose judicial conservative Antonin Scalia to fill the vacant seat. Then in 1987 Reagan named Robert Bork, a judge and legal scholar whose intellectual rigidity, doctrinaire opposition to judicial activism, and scant regard for the Supreme Court's role in protecting individual liberties led the Senate to reject him. Reagan's next nominee withdrew after admitting

that he had smoked marijuana, but Reagan's third choice, Anthony Kennedy, also very conservative, won speedy confirmation.

President Bush solidified the Court's new conservative majority with nominations in 1990 and 1991: David Souter and Clarence Thomas. Souter, a New Hampshire judge, gained easy confirmation, but the Thomas nomination proved controversial. Bush nominated him to fill the seat vacated by Thurgood Marshall, a black who had fought segregation as an NAACP lawyer. Thomas, also an African-American, espoused a conservative political ideology, praised Oliver North as a maligned hero, and opposed affirmative-action programs designed to enhance minority opportunities. The head of the Equal Employment Opportunity Commission (EEOC) under Reagan, Thomas saw individual effort, not government programs, as the avenue for black progress. Noting Thomas's right-wing ideology and his thin record as a federal judge, critics charged Bush with cynically playing racial politics.

The nomination drew even more challenges when a former Thomas associate at EEOC, law professor Anita Hill, charged him with sexual harassment years before. For several days, the Senate Judiciary Committee's hearings on Hill's accusations filled the nation's TV screens. Thomas narrowly won confirmation, 52–48.

These Reagan-Bush appointments seemed to ensure that a conservative majority would rule the Court into the twenty-first century. The liberal social activism that had characterized the Court from the New Deal through the Earl Warren years was blunted. Hints of the Court's new conservatism came early. In a series of 5–4 rulings in 1989, the Court upheld a Missouri law limiting women's right to abortion and imposed confining new definitions on widely used civil-rights laws aimed at protecting the employment rights of women and minorities and at remedying past inequities. In its 1990–1991 term, the Court narrowed the rights of an arrested person and upheld regulations barring physicians in federally funded family-planning clinics from discussing abortion with their patients. Then in a 5–4 decision in June 1992, the Supreme Court upheld a Pennsylvania law placing various restrictions on abortion. The majority, however, led by Souter, O'Connor, and Kennedy, affirmed *Roe* v. *Wade* (1973), the decision that had upheld women's constitutional right to abortion.

The Politics of Frustration

Bush's shifting political fortunes were a barometer of the public mood. In the afterglow of Operation Desert Storm, his approval ratings shot up to 88 percent, only to plummet below 50 percent as the recession eroded national confidence. In a 1991 election to fill a Senate vacancy in Pennsylvania, Bush's weakened influence showed when his attorney general, Richard Thornburgh, lost to a political novice who articulated middle-class concerns about high taxes and ever-escalating health-care costs.

Heeding such warning signals, Bush proclaimed that "getting the economy back on track is my Number 1 priority." Yet in late 1991, a damning *New York Times* editorial commented, "Nearly three years into his term, George Bush remains mystifyingly incomplete: shrewd and energetic in foreign policy and just the opposite—clumsy and irresolute—at home. . . . The domestic Bush flops like a fish, leaving the impression that he doesn't know what he thinks or doesn't much care, apart from the political gains to be extracted from an issue." Democrats meanwhile attacked Bush for his preoccupation with foreign affairs. Declared Senate majority leader George Mitchell, "The president seeks a new world order. We ask him to join us in putting our own house in order."

Bush's 1992 State of the Union message contained a recession-fighting package, including middle-class tax relief, tax breaks for first-time home buyers, and tax credits to help Americans buy health insurance. Refurbishing traditional Republican formulas, Bush also asked for lower taxes on capital gains, tax incentives for business investment, and an end to the luxury tax on yachts and private planes. He additionally proposed a $50 billion cut in military spending by 1997. Democrats dismissed Bush's belated attention to domestic issues as politically motivated and inadequate.

In the 1992 race for the White House, the Bush-Quayle ticket coasted to renomination. But the Republican right dominated the convention and platform, while moderates deplored this rightward turn. Undaunted by Bush's apparent invulnerability after Desert Storm, Governor William ("Bill") Clinton of Arkansas withstood doubts about his character and accusations of marital infidelities to defeat his opponents in the primaries and sew up the Democratic presidential nomination in early summer 1992. Choosing Senator Albert Gore of Tennessee, an eloquent advocate for the environment, as his running mate, Clinton pledged an activist government and oriented the Democratic party toward middle-class concerns.

Folksy billionaire H. Ross Perot presented a political challenge to politics-as-usual. His insistence that the nation's economic problems were simple, and that only party politics stood in the way of their solution, carried Perot to a nearly 40 percent peak in the polls. However, the Texan's autocratic ways and thin-skinned response to criticism turned off many supporters. In July 1992 he left the race for poorly explained reasons, but he returned in October 1992, spent millions of his own dollars on television advertising, and participated in televised presidential debates.

Bush ran a negative campaign, attacking Clinton's character and charging that the Arkansas governor had been a draft dodger during the Vietnam War. Toward the campaign's end, Bush ridiculed Clinton and Gore as "crazies" and "bozos." Clinton called for an industrial policy that would give Washington an active role in promoting economic recovery and innovative technologies, and put health-care reform high on his agenda.

The voters spoke on November 3, when 43 percent chose Clinton. Bush trailed with 38 percent, and Perot amassed 19 percent—the largest share for a third party since Teddy Roosevelt's 1912 Bull Moose party. In the electoral tally, Clinton carried 370 votes to Bush's 168.

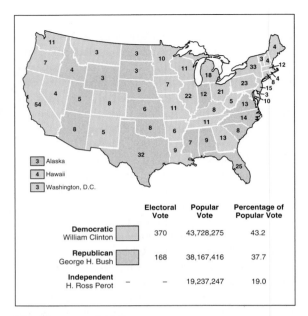

		Electoral Vote	Popular Vote	Percentage of Popular Vote
Democratic William Clinton		370	43,728,275	43.2
Republican George H. Bush		168	38,167,416	37.7
Independent H. Ross Perot		–	19,237,247	19.0

The Election of 1992

Clinton's electoral success rested largely on his ability to resurrect the Democratic coalition, luring blue-collar and "Reagan Democrat" voters as well as reclaiming parts of the South. With the presidency and both houses of Congress in Democratic hands, Americans hoped for the end of legislative gridlock. The new Congress itself was becoming more representative of U.S. society as a whole as thirty-eight African-American and seventeen Hispanics won election to the 1993–1994 session, up from twenty-five and ten, respectively. And the new Congress included fifty-three women: six in the Senate and forty-seven in the House. This outcome, combined with the advent of Hillary Rodham Clinton, the first presidential spouse to have a career in her own right, buoyed those who had declared 1992 the "Year of the Woman."

Clinton in Command

Clinton's first year yielded mixed results. The new chief executive clearly relished formulating the details of policy. His hands-on involvement as a "pol-icy wonk" represented a pronounced change from the detached styles of Reagan and Bush and underscored the fact that Clinton was a product of the activist 1960s. But the White House's often frenetic policy-making initiatives in 1993 led to charges of executive disorganization. Public perceptions of confusion at the top, combined with the slow pace of economic expansion and job creation, kept the new president's poll ratings at historically low levels during his first year.

Politically, Clinton tried to balance between the more conservative "new Democrats" with whom he had associated before his election, and the liberal Democratic constituencies that had given him an important share of his winning margin. Thus he ran into early trouble by insisting that homosexuals be permitted to serve in the military without facing automatic expulsion, and he tried but failed to persuade Congress to add $30 billion in spending initiatives to "jump-start" the economy. In the end his budget, shorn of its "stimulus package," passed Congress by paper-thin margins, with no Republican support. After winning wide popular backing when he announced his health-care initiative in February and put Hillary Rodham Clinton in charge of shaping it, the president saw public consensus behind the program dissolve as word leaked out of the complexities and costs that it would entail. Liberals continued to press for a Canadian-style health program that would make the government the ultimate employer of the nation's health-care professionals, and conservatives gained ground in their demand that health-care reform rely less on price controls and regulations and more on market forces.

In June 1993 the new president demonstrated his centrism and his political finesse with the appointment of Ruth Bader Ginsburg to the Supreme Court. A pioneer in the movement for women's legal equality, Ginsburg became the second woman, after Justice Sandra Day O'Connor, on the Supreme Court and the first justice appointed by a Democrat in twenty-six years, since the presidency of Lyndon Johnson. The new justice's quick confirmation reflected both senatorial and national approval of Clinton's choice.

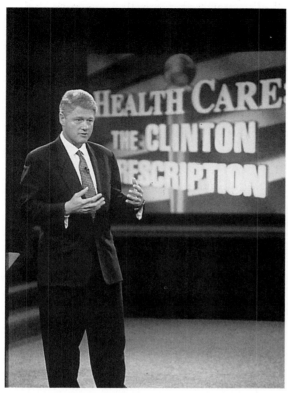

The Clinton Prescription
In this 1993 photograph, President Bill Clinton presents his proposed health-care plan, which aims to provide health insurance to all Americans.

Clinton's greatest test as a centrist came in the crucial area of international trade. Not long before Clinton took office, the Bush administration concluded years of negotiation on a free-trade pact with Canada and Mexico, known as NAFTA (the North American Free Trade Agreement). Labor unions, many liberals, and most environmental groups charged that NAFTA would promote environmental degradation (especially along the U.S.-Mexican border) and cause investors and employers to kill American jobs by shifting to cheap Mexican labor. A disparate anti-NAFTA coalition arose, proving the old adage that politics makes strange bedfellows. Joining the veteran public figures who attacked NAFTA—Ralph Nader, Jesse Jackson, and the leaders of most unions—were the raucous voices of H. Ross Perot and Patrick Buchanan, who took an essentially isolationist line laden with anti-Mexican prejudice. Ranged on the other side were almost all of the nation's economists, many prominent business leaders, and most Republicans in Congress. The public's feelings on NAFTA divided along lines of class and race: most blue-collar workers and blacks opposed the pact, but support for it ran higher as income and educational attainment rose. Clinton's initial waffling—he insisted that "side agreements" to protect American jobs and the environment be negotiated before he submitted the treaty to Congress—encouraged opponents. For a long time the anti-NAFTA forces seemed to have the upper hand. Only in the fall of 1993, after the president belatedly announced his enthusiastic support for an amended NAFTA treaty and began twisting congressional arms, did the agreement win passage. The decisive moment came just a week before the November 1993 congressional vote when Vice President Gore outshone Perot in a nationally televised debate. With a majority of Republicans—but only a minority of Democrats—in the House voting to implement NAFTA, the president's position won by the unexpectedly comfortable margin of 234–200.

By ensuring NAFTA's ratification, which he called a victory for hope over fear, Clinton had salvaged a critical victory. Moreover, he had gained the momentum he needed to conclude the even more important GATT agreement, aimed at lowering trade barriers worldwide, in December 1993. Ever since the end of World War II, liberalizing international trade had been a key objective of American foreign policy and one of the foundations of the postwar Western economic recovery. The fact that under Clinton's leadership the United States had held to this position signaled that the new administration did not intend to return to prewar isolationism and protectionism. But the fight over NAFTA opened deep divisions in the Democratic party and pitted the president against a majority of his liberal supporters. How he would repair this rift remained a difficult challenge. And whether

American liberalism would embrace inward-looking protectionism or maintain its association with free trade—one of its hallmarks since the Progressive Era and the New Deal—posed a question of even larger historical significance.

Clinton had won the election in large part because voters liked his promise to concentrate on improving the nation's economy rather than on conducting its foreign policy, George Bush's area of primary interest. In his first year Clinton tried to respond to the voters' yearning to put domestic affairs first. For example, he did not once visit Europe, to which every Cold War era president from Truman to Bush had felt impelled to travel soon after taking office. Yet foreign affairs kept intruding, often causing Clinton acute embarrassment by underscoring America's limited ability to solve the world's problems. The civil war in Bosnia-Herzegovina ground on relentlessly, offering American television audiences heart-wrenching images nightly of starvation and war atrocities. Clinton's attempts in the spring of 1993 to galvanize armed intervention by NATO in the conflict foundered when Western European governments refused to put their ground forces at risk. The United States clearly was not prepared for a solo plunge into a bloody quarrel between age-old Balkan enemies. In the rather parallel case of Somalia, where organized government had collapsed in 1992, the modest humanitarian intervention that Bush had begun in the last days of his outgoing administration turned into a major dilemma for the new president. Events there took an ominous turn as one of the worst of the Somali warlords found that he could attack American and other U.N. forces without effective counterstrokes, a "no-win" situation that unavoidably made Clinton look inept. Meanwhile, in Haiti, the military forces that had driven elected president Jean-Bertrand Aristide into exile in 1991 stubbornly clung to power as Clinton and the U.N. unsuccessfully tried to remove them by blandishments and threats.

But despite these uncomfortable reminders of Jimmy Carter's troubles in the 1970s, when difficult foreign problems not wholly of this nation's making had also combined to make it seem impotent, the worst did not happen. In Russia, Boris Yeltsin crushed political opponents who, if successful, might well have led the West's Cold War adversary back into a confrontational stance. In South Africa, the demolition of apartheid continued, perhaps preventing that tortured land from collapsing into a race war. In the Middle East, Muslim fundamentalists failed to take power in such crucial states as Egypt and Jordan. And in an especially hopeful development, Israel, the PLO, and Syria initiated serious steps toward mutual accommodation. The Clinton administration did what it could to encourage all these signs that a more peaceful world would emerge with the impending dawn of a new millennium in the twenty-first century.

Conclusion

The closing years of the twentieth century brought profound changes. The economic problems that dogged the 1980s boom surfaced alarmingly in the early 1990s. The recession's crunch deepened fears of a population permanently divided between an educated and relatively well-off middle class and an underclass mired in poverty and hopelessness.

Women poured into the workplace, and African-Americans, Asian-Americans, and Hispanics assumed an increasingly visible role in national life. Although these changes sparked contention—charges of reverse discrimination, worries about family breakdown, controversies over "Eurocentric" textbooks—the tensions forced Americans to explore anew the meaning of democracy and equality.

Politically, the early post-Reagan era seemed a time of drift rather than direction. President George Bush's popularity hit a high point after the Gulf War, but as Americans dealt with nagging problems at home, many viewed him as an opportunist with poor leadership qualities, little grasp of the depth of national discontent, and few ideas of what to do. Combined with the recession, these perceptions were enough to cost him the presidency. With the election of Bill Clinton in 1992, the nation said farewell to the generation of political leaders shaped by the Great Depression and World War II and welcomed a new generation formed during the tumultuous sixties.

Globally, the late 1980s and early 1990s produced incredible changes: the end of the Cold War, the dissolution of the Soviet Union, the fall of communism in Eastern Europe. The bipolar world that had emerged from the wreckage of World War II receded, and with it the struggle that had shaped America's foreign policy, budgetary decisions, and home-front policies for forty years. With victory in the Cold War came a sense of long effort rewarded and an occasion to reaffirm the principles of America's enduring vision—such as democracy, individual rights, and freedom of expression—that had proved more powerful than totalitarianism. The Cold War's end also brought disorientation and uneasiness. As familiar global power arrangements dissolved, Americans watched anxiously to see the shape of the new order and to discover what their nation's place in it would be.

Chronology

1984–1986 Congress bars military aid to contras.

1985 Palestinian airline hijackings and other terrorism.

1986 Congress passes South African sanctions.
U.S. air raid on Libya.

1987 Congressional hearings on Iran-contra scandal.
Stock-market crash.
Trade deficit reaches $170 billion.

1988 U.S. warship *Vincennes*, in Persian Gulf, shoots down Iranian passenger plane, killing 290.
Oliver North, John Poindexter, and other Iran-contra figures indicted.
Reagan signs INF Treaty in Moscow.
George Bush elected president.

1989 Oliver North convicted for Iran-contra role.
Massive Alaskan oil spill by *Exxon Valdez*.
Supreme Court limits access to abortion.
Supreme Court restricts civil-rights laws.
U.S. invasion of Panama; Manuel Noriega overthrown.
China's rulers crush prodemocracy movement.
Berlin Wall is opened.

1990   Federal Clean Air Act passed.
President Bush and Congress agree on five-year budget-deficit reduction package.
Iraq invades Kuwait.
Recession begins.
Germany reunified; Soviet troops start withdrawal from East Germany and rest of Eastern Europe.

1991   Gulf War (Operation Desert Storm).
United States and U.S.S.R. sign treaty reducing strategic nuclear arms by 25 percent.
Political and economic upheavals in Soviet Union after Gorbachev survives coup attempt.

Clarence Thomas seated on Supreme Court amid controversy.
Soviet Union collapses.

1992   Supreme Court upholds *Roe* v. *Wade*.
Arkansas governor Bill Clinton elected president.
American troops deployed in Somalia.

1993   North American Free Trade Agreement approved.
General Agreement on Tariffs and Trade renegotiated.
Israel, Palestinians reach peace agreement.
Clinton health plan developed, revealed.

For Further Reading

Robert Bellah et al., *The Good Society* (1991). Thoughtful reflections on the sources of community in the American historical experience.

Thomas Byrne Edsall with Mary D. Edsall, *Chain Reaction: The Impact of Race, Rights, and Taxes on American Politics* (1991). A perceptive analysis of the shifting American political landscape.

Al Gore, *Earth in the Balance: Ecology and the Human Spirit* (1992). A sobering assessment of the environmental challenges facing humankind.

Patricia Albjerg Graham, *S.O.S.: Sustain Our Schools* (1992). Compassionate and sensible probing of the dilemmas facing U.S. public education.

David Halberstam, *The Next Century* (1991). A noted journalist's reflections on what may lie ahead and prescriptions for radical changes in conventional ways of thinking.

Joseph S. Nye, *Bound to Lead: The Changing Nature of American Power* (1990). A hopeful view of the United States' continued potential for leadership.

Robert Reich, *The Work of Nations: Preparing Ourselves for 21st Century Capitalism* (1991). A fresh examination of the nation's economic and social situation and its future prospects.

Arthur M. Schlesinger, Jr., *The Disuniting of America* (1991). A historian's concerns about the centrifugal tendencies in contemporary U.S. society and education, and pleas for new efforts to define what it is to be an American.

U.S. News and World Report, *Triumph Without Victory: The Unreported History of the Persian Gulf War* (1992). The most complete early history of Operation Desert Storm.

Appendix

Declaration of Independence

IN CONGRESS, JULY 4, 1776

The Unanimous Declaration of the Thirteen United States of America

When, in the course of human events, it becomes necessary for one people to dissolve the political bands which have connected them with another, and to assume, among the powers of the earth, the separate and equal station to which the laws of nature and of nature's God entitle them, a decent respect to the opinions of mankind requires that they should declare the causes which impel them to the separation.

We hold these truths to be self-evident: That all men are created equal; that they are endowed by their Creator with certain unalienable rights; that among these are life, liberty, and the pursuit of happiness; that, to secure these rights, governments are instituted among men, deriving their just powers from the consent of the governed; that whenever any form of government becomes destructive of these ends, it is the right of the people to alter or to abolish it, and to institute new government, laying its foundation on such principles, and organizing its powers in such form, as to them shall seem most likely to effect their safety and happiness. Prudence, indeed, will dictate that governments long established should not be changed for light and transient causes; and accordingly all experience hath shown that mankind are more disposed to suffer, while evils are sufferable, than to right themselves by abolishing the forms to which they are accustomed. But when a long train of abuses and usurpations, pursuing invariably the same object, evinces a design to reduce them under absolute despotism, it is their right, it is their duty, to throw off such government, and to provide new guards for their future security. Such has been the patient sufferance of these colonies; and such is now the necessity which constrains them to alter their former systems of government. The history of the present King of Great Britain is a history of repeated injuries and usurpations, all having in direct object the establishment of an absolute tyranny over these states. To prove this, let facts be submitted to a candid world.

He has refused his assent to laws, the most wholesome and necessary for the public good.

He has forbidden his governors to pass laws of immediate and pressing importance, unless suspended in their operation till his assent should be obtained; and, when so suspended, he has utterly neglected to attend to them.

He has refused to pass other laws for the accommodation of large districts of people, unless those people would relinquish the right of representation in the legislature, a right inestimable to them, and formidable to tyrants only.

He has called together legislative bodies at places unusual, uncomfortable, and distant from the depository of their public records, for the sole purpose of fatiguing them into compliance with his measures.

He has dissolved representative houses repeatedly, for opposing, with manly firmness, his invasions on the rights of the people.

He has refused for a long time, after such dissolutions, to cause others to be elected; whereby the legislative powers, incapable of annihilation, have returned to the people at large for their exercise; the state remaining, in the mean time, exposed to all the dangers of invasions from without and convulsions within.

He has endeavored to prevent the population of these states; for that purpose obstructing the laws of naturalization of foreigners; refusing to pass others to encourage their migration hither, and raising the conditions of new appropriation of lands.

He has obstructed the administration of justice, by refusing his assent to laws for establishing judiciary powers.

He has made judges dependent on his will alone, for the tenure of their offices, and the amount and payment of their salaries.

He has erected a multitude of new offices, and sent hither swarms of officers to harass our people and eat out their substance.

He has kept among us, in times of peace, standing armies, without the consent of our legislatures.

He has affected to render the military independent of, and superior to, the civil power.

He has combined with others to subject us to a jurisdiction foreign to our constitution, and unacknowledged by our laws, giving his assent to their acts of pretended legislation:

For quartering large bodies of armed troops among us;

For protecting them, by a mock trial, from punishment for any murders which they should commit on the inhabitants of these states;

For cutting off our trade with all parts of the world;

For imposing taxes on us without our consent;

For depriving us, in many cases, of the benefits of trial by jury;

For transporting us beyond seas, to be tried for pretended offenses;

For abolishing the free system of English laws in a neighboring province, establishing therein an arbitrary government, and enlarging its boundaries, so as to render it at once an example and fit instrument for introducing the same absolute rule into these colonies;

For taking away our charters, abolishing our most valuable laws, and altering fundamentally the forms of our governments;

For suspending our own legislatures, and declaring themselves invested with power to legislate for us in all cases whatsoever.

He has abdicated government here, by declaring us out of his protection and waging war against us.

He has plundered our seas, ravaged our coasts, burned our towns, and destroyed the lives of our people.

He is at this time transporting large armies of foreign mercenaries to complete the works of death, desolation, and tyranny already begun with circumstances of cruelty and perfidy scarcely paralleled in the most barbarous ages, and totally unworthy of the head of a civilized nation.

He has constrained our fellow-citizens, taken captive on the high seas, to bear arms against their country, to become the executioners of their friends and brethren, or to fall themselves by their hands.

He has excited domestic insurrection among us, and has endeavored to bring on the inhabitants of our frontiers the merciless Indian savages, whose known rule of warfare is an undistinguished destruction of all ages, sexes, and conditions.

In every stage of these oppressions we have petitioned for redress in the most humble terms; our repeated petitions have been answered only by repeated injury. A prince, whose character is thus marked by every act which may define a tyrant, is unfit to be the ruler of a free people.

Nor have we been wanting in our attentions to our British brethren. We have warned them, from time to time, of attempts by their legislature to extend an unwarrantable jurisdiction over us. We have reminded them of the circumstances of our emigration and settlement here. We have appealed to their native justice and magnanimity; and we have conjured them by the ties of our common kindred, to disavow these usurpations, which would inevitably interrupt our connections and correspondence. They, too, have been deaf to the voice of justice and of consanguinity. We must, therefore, acquiesce in the necessity which denounces our separation, and hold them, as we hold the rest of mankind, enemies in war, in peace friends.

We, therefore, the representatives of the United States of America, in General Congress assembled, appealing to the Supreme Judge of the world for the rectitude of our intentions, do, in the name and by the authority of the good people of these colonies, solemnly publish and declare, that these United Colonies are, and of right ought to be, FREE AND INDEPENDENT STATES; that they are absolved from all allegiance to the British crown, and that all political connection between them and the state of Great Britain is, and ought to be, totally dissolved; and that, as free and independent states, they have full power to levy war, conclude peace, contract alliances, establish commerce, and do all other acts and things which independent states may of right do. And for the support of this declaration, with a firm reliance on the protection of Divine Providence, we mutually pledge to each other our lives, our fortunes, and our sacred honor.

JOHN HANCOCK [*President*]
[*and fifty-five others*]

Constitution of the United States of America

PREAMBLE

We the people of the United States, in order to form a more perfect union, establish justice, insure domestic tranquility, provide for the common defense, promote the general welfare, and secure the blessings of liberty to ourselves and our posterity, do ordain and establish this CONSTITUTION for the United States of America.

ARTICLE I

Section 1.   All legislative powers herein granted shall be vested in a Congress of the United States, which shall consist of a Senate and a House of Representatives.

Section 2.   The House of Representatives shall be composed of members chosen every second year by the people of the several States, and the electors in each State shall have the qualifications requisite for electors of the most numerous branch of the State Legislature.

No person shall be a Representative who shall not have attained to the age of twenty-five years, and been seven years a citizen of the United States, and who shall not, when elected, be an inhabitant of that State in which he shall be chosen.

Representatives and direct taxes shall be apportioned among the several States which may be included within this Union, according to their respective numbers, *which shall be determined by adding to the whole number of free persons, including those bound to service for a term of years and excluding Indians not taxed, three-fifths of all other persons.* The actual enumeration shall be made within three years after the first meeting of the Congress of the United States, and within every subsequent term of ten years, in such manner as they shall by law direct. The number of Representatives shall not exceed one for every thirty thousand, but each State shall have at least one Representative; *and until such enumeration shall be made, the State of New Hampshire shall be entitled to choose three, Massachusetts eight, Rhode Island and Providence Plantations one, Connecticut five, New York six, New Jersey four, Pennsylvania eight, Delaware one, Maryland six, Virginia ten, North Carolina five, South Carolina five, and Georgia three.*

When vacancies happen in the representation from any State, the Executive authority thereof shall issue writs of election to fill such vacancies.

The House of Representatives shall choose their Speaker and other officers; and shall have the sole power of impeachment.

Section 3.   The Senate of the United States shall be composed of two Senators from each State, *chosen by the legislature thereof,* for six years; and each Senator shall have one vote.

Immediately after they shall be assembled in consequence of the first election, they shall be divided as equally as may be into three classes. The seats of the Senators of the first class shall be vacated at the expiration of the second year, of the second class at the expiration of the fourth year, and of the third class at the expiration of the sixth year, so that one-third may be chosen every second year; *and if vacancies happen by resignation or otherwise, during the recess of the legislature of any State, the Executive thereof may make*

NOTE: Passages no longer in effect are printed in italic type.

temporary appointments until the next meeting of the legislature, which shall then fill such vacancies.

No person shall be a Senator who shall not have attained to the age of thirty years, and been nine years a citizen of the United States, and who shall not, when elected, be an inhabitant of that State for which he shall be chosen.

The Vice President of the United States shall be President of the Senate, but shall have no vote, unless they be equally divided.

The Senate shall choose their other officers, and also a President *pro tempore*, in the absence of the Vice President, or when he shall exercise the office of the President of the United States.

The Senate shall have the sole power to try all impeachments. When sitting for that purpose, they shall be on oath or affirmation. When the President of the United States is tried, the Chief Justice shall preside: and no person shall be convicted without the concurrence of two-thirds of the members present.

Judgment in cases of impeachment shall not extend further than to removal from the office, and disqualification to hold and enjoy any office of honor, trust or profit under the United States; but the party convicted shall nevertheless be liable and subject to indictment, trial, judgment and punishment, according to law.

Section 4. The times, places and manner of holding elections for Senators and Representatives shall be prescribed in each State by the legislature thereof; but the Congress may at any time by law make or alter such regulations, except as to the places of choosing Senators.

The Congress shall assemble at least once in every year, and such meeting *shall be on the first Monday in December, unless they shall by law appoint a different day.*

Section 5. Each house shall be the judge of the elections, returns and qualifications of its own members, and a majority of each shall constitute a quorum to do business; but a smaller number may adjourn from day to day, and may be authorized to compel the attendance of absent members, in such manner, and under such penalties, as each house may provide.

Each house may determine the rules of its proceedings, punish its members for disorderly behavior, and with the concurrence of two-thirds, expel a member.

Each house shall keep a journal of its proceedings, and from time to time publish the same, excepting such parts as may in their judgment require secrecy; and the yeas and nays of the members of either house on any question shall, at the desire of one-fifth of those present, be entered on the journal.

Neither house, during the session of Congress, shall, without the consent of the other, adjourn for more than three days, nor to any other place than that in which the two houses shall be sitting.

Section 6. The Senators and Representatives shall receive a compensation for their services, to be ascertained by law and paid out of the treasury of the United States. They shall in all cases except treason, felony and breach of the peace, be privileged from arrest during their attendance at the session of their respective houses, and in going to and returning from the same; and for any speech or debate in either house, they shall not be questioned in any other place.

No Senator or Representative shall, during the time for which he was elected, be appointed to any civil office under the authority of the United States, which shall have been created, or the emoluments whereof shall have been increased, during such time; and no person holding any office under the United States shall be a member of either house during his continuance in office.

Section 7. All bills for raising revenue shall originate in the House of Representatives; but the Senate may propose or concur with amendments as on other bills.

Every bill which shall have passed the House of Representatives and the Senate, shall, before it become a law, be presented to the President of the United States; if he approve he shall sign it, but if not he shall return it with objections to that house in which it originated, who shall enter the objections at large on their journal, and proceed to reconsider it. If after such reconsideration two-thirds of that house shall agree to pass the bill, it shall be sent, together with the objections, to the other house, by which it shall likewise be reconsidered, and, if approved by two-thirds of that house, it shall become a law. But in all such cases the votes of both houses shall be determined by yeas and nays, and the names of the persons voting for and against the bill shall be entered on the journal of each house respectively. If any bill shall not be returned by the President within ten days (Sundays excepted) after it shall have been presented to him, the same shall be a law, in like manner as if he had signed it, unless the Congress by their adjournment prevent its return, in which case it shall not be a law.

Every order, resolution, or vote to which the concurrence of the Senate and House of Representatives may be necessary (except on a question of adjournment) shall be presented to the President of the United States; and before the same shall take effect, shall be approved by him, or being disapproved by him, shall be repassed by two-thirds of the Senate and House of Representatives, according to the rules and limitations prescribed in the case of a bill.

Section 8.   The Congress shall have power

To lay and collect taxes, duties, imposts, and excises, to pay the debts and provide for the common defense and general welfare of the United States; but all duties, imposts and excises shall be uniform throughout the United States;

To borrow money on the credit of the United States;

To regulate commerce with foreign nations, and among the several States, and with the Indian tribes;

To establish an uniform rule of naturalization, and uniform laws on the subject of bankruptcies throughout the United States;

To coin money, regulate the value thereof, and of foreign coin, and fix the standard of weights and measures;

To provide for the punishment of counterfeiting the securities and current coin of the United States;

To establish post offices and post roads;

To promote the progress of science and useful arts by securing for limited times to authors and inventors the exclusive right to their respective writings and discoveries;

To constitute tribunals inferior to the Supreme Court;

To define and punish piracies and felonies committed on the high seas and offenses against the law of nations;

To declare war, grant letters of marque and reprisal, and make rules concerning captures on land and water;

To raise and support armies, but no appropriation of money to that use shall be for a longer term than two years;

To provide and maintain a navy;

To make rules for the government and regulation of the land and naval forces;

To provide for calling forth the militia to execute the laws of the Union, suppress insurrections, and repel invasions;

To provide for organizing, arming, and disciplining the militia, and for governing such part of them as may be employed in the service of the United States, reserving to the States respectively the appointment of the officers, and the authority of training the militia according to the discipline prescribed by Congress;

To exercise exclusive legislation in all cases whatsoever, over such district (not exceeding ten miles square) as may, by cession of particular States, and the acceptance of Congress, become the seat of government of the United States, and to exercise like authority over all places purchased by the consent of the legislature of the State, in which the same shall be, for erection of forts, magazines, arsenals, dock-yards, and other needful buildings;—and

To make all laws which shall be necessary and proper for carrying into execution the foregoing powers, and all other powers vested by this Constitution in the government of the United States, or in any department or officer thereof.

Section 9. *The migration or importation of such persons as any of the States now existing shall think proper to admit shall not be prohibited by the Congress prior to the year 1808; but a tax or duty may be imposed on such importation, not exceeding $10 for each person.*

The privilege of the writ of habeas corpus shall not be suspended, unless when in cases of rebellion or invasion the public safety may require it.

No bill of attainder or ex post facto law shall be passed.

No capitation, or other direct, tax shall be laid, unless in proportion to the census or enumeration herein before directed to be taken.

No tax or duty shall be laid on articles exported from any State.

No preference shall be given by any regulation of commerce or revenue to the ports of one State over those of another; nor shall vessels bound to, or from, one State, be obliged to enter, clear, or pay duties in another.

No money shall be drawn from the treasury, but in consequence of appropriations made by law; and a regular statement and account of the receipts and expenditures of all public money shall be published from time to time.

No title of nobility shall be granted by the United States: and no person holding any office of profit or trust under them, shall, without the consent of the Congress, accept of any present, emolument, office, or title, of any kind whatever, from any king, prince, or foreign state.

Section 10. No State shall enter into any treaty, alliance, or confederation; grant letters of marque and reprisal; coin money; emit bills of credit; make anything but gold and silver coin a tender in payment of debts; pass any bill of attainder, ex post facto law, or law impairing the obligation of contracts, or grant any title of nobility.

No State shall, without the consent of Congress, lay any imposts or duties on imports or exports, except what may be absolutely necessary for executing its inspection laws: and the net produce of all duties and imposts, laid by any State on imports or exports, shall be for the use of the treasury of the United States; and all such laws shall be subject to the revision and control of the Congress.

No State shall, without the consent of Congress, lay any duty of tonnage, keep troops or ships of war in time of peace, enter into any agreement or compact with another State, or with a foreign power, or engage in war, unless actually invaded, or in such imminent danger as will not admit of delay.

ARTICLE II

Section 1. The executive power shall be vested in a President of the United States of America. He shall hold his office during the term of four years, and, together with the Vice President, chosen for the same term, be elected as follows:

Each state shall appoint, in such manner as the legislature thereof may direct, a number of electors, equal to the whole number of Senators and Representatives to which the State may be entitled in the Congress; but no Senator or Representative, or person holding an office of trust or profit under the United States, shall be appointed an elector.

The electors shall meet in their respective States, and vote by ballot for two persons, of whom one at least shall not be an inhabitant of the same State with themselves. And they shall make a list of all the persons voted for, and of the number of votes for each; which list they shall sign and certify, and transmit sealed to the seat of government of the United States, directed to the President of the Senate. The President of the Senate shall, in the presence of the Senate and the House of Representatives, open all the certificates, and the votes shall then be counted. The person having the greatest number of votes shall be the President, if such number be a majority of the whole number of electors appointed; and if there be more than one who have such majority, and have an equal number of votes, then the House of Representatives shall immediately choose by ballot one of them for President; and if no person have a majority, then from the five highest on the list said house shall in like manner choose the President. But in choosing the President the votes shall be taken by States, the representation from each State having one vote; a quorum for this purpose shall consist of a member or members from two-thirds of the States, and a majority of all the States shall be necessary to a choice. In every case, after the choice of the President, the person having the greatest number of votes of the electors shall be the Vice President. But if there should remain two or more who have equal votes, the Senate shall choose from them by ballot the Vice President.

The Congress may determine the time of choosing the electors and the day on which they shall give their votes; which day shall be the same throughout the United States.

No person except a natural-born citizen, *or a citizen of the United States at the time of the adoption of this Constitution,* shall be eligible to the office of President; neither shall any person be eligible to that office who shall not have attained to the age of thirty-five years, and been fourteen years a resident within the United States.

In case of the removal of the President from office or of his death, resignation, or inability to discharge the powers and duties of the said office, the same shall devolve on the Vice President, and the Congress may by law provide for the case of removal, death, resignation, or inability, both of the President and Vice President, declaring what officer shall then act as President, and such officer shall act accordingly, until the disability be removed, or a President shall be elected.

The President shall, at stated times, receive for his services a compensation, which shall neither be increased nor diminished during the period for which he shall have been elected, and he shall not receive within that period any other emolument from the United States, or any of them.

Before he enter on the execution of his office, he shall take the following oath or affirmation:—"I do solemnly swear (or affirm) that I will faithfully execute the office of the President of the United States, and will to the best of my ability preserve, protect and defend the Constitution of the United States."

Section 2.   The President shall be commander in chief of the army and navy of the United States, and of the militia of the several States, when called into the actual service of the United States; he may require the opinion, in writing, of the principal officer in each of the executive departments, upon any subject relating to the duties of their respective offices, and he shall have power to grant reprieves and pardons for offenses against the United States, except in cases of impeachment.

He shall have power, by and with the advice and consent of the Senate, to make treaties, provided two-thirds of the Senators present concur; and he shall nominate, and by and with the advice and consent of the Senate, shall appoint ambassadors, other public ministers and consuls, judges of the Supreme Court, and all other officers of the United States, whose appointments are not herein otherwise provided for, and which shall be established by law: but Congress may by law vest the appointment of such inferior officers, as they think proper, in the President alone, in the courts of law, or in the heads of departments.

The President shall have power to fill up all vacancies that may happen during the recess of the Senate, by granting commissions which shall expire at the end of their next session.

Section 3.   He shall from time to time give to the Congress information of the state of the Union, and recommend to their consideration such measures as he shall judge necessary and expedient; he may, on extraordinary occasions, convene both houses, or either of them, and in case of disagreement between them, with respect to the time of adjournment, he may adjourn them to such time as he shall think proper; he shall receive ambassadors and other public ministers; he shall take care that the laws be faithfully executed, and shall commission all the officers of the United States.

Section 4. The President, Vice President and all civil officers of the United States shall be removed from office on impeachment for, and on conviction of, treason, bribery, or other high crimes and misdemeanors.

ARTICLE III

Section 1. The judicial power of the United States shall be vested in one Supreme Court, and in such inferior courts as the Congress may from time to time ordain and establish. The judges, both of the Supreme and inferior courts, shall hold their offices during good behavior, and shall, at stated times, receive for their services a compensation which shall not be diminished during their continuance in office.

Section 2. The judicial power shall extend to all cases, in law and equity, arising under this Constitution, the laws of the United States, and treaties made, or which shall be made, under their authority;—to all cases affecting ambassadors, other public ministers and consuls;—to all cases of admiralty and maritime jurisdiction;—to controversies to which the United States shall be a party;—to controversies between two or more States;—*between a State and citizens of another State;*—between citizens of different States;—between citizens of the same State claiming lands under grants of different States, and between a State, or the citizens thereof, and foreign states, citizens or subjects.

In all cases affecting ambassadors, other public ministers and consuls, and those in which a State shall be party, the Supreme Court shall have original jurisdiction. In all the other cases before mentioned, the Supreme Court shall have appellate jurisdiction, both as to law and fact, with such exceptions, and under such regulations, as the Congress shall make.

The trial of all crimes, except in cases of impeachment, shall be by jury; and such trial shall be held in the State where said crimes shall have been committed; but when not committed within any State, the trial shall be at such place or places as the Congress may by law have directed.

Section 3. Treason against the United States shall consist only in levying war against them, or in adhering to their enemies, giving them aid and comfort. No person shall be convicted of treason unless on the testimony of two witnesses to the same overt act, or on confession in open court.

The Congress shall have power to declare the punishment of treason, but no attainder of treason shall work corruption of blood, or forfeiture except during the life of the person attainted.

ARTICLE IV

Section 1. Full faith and credit shall be given in each State to the public acts, records, and judicial proceedings of every other State. And the Congress may by general laws prescribe the manner in which such acts, records, and proceedings shall be proved, and the effect thereof.

Section 2. The citizens of each State shall be entitled to all privileges and immunities of citizens in the several States.

A person charged in any State with treason, felony, or other crime, who shall flee from justice, and be found in another State, shall on demand of the executive authority of the State from which he fled, be delivered up, to be removed to the State having jurisdiction of the crime.

No person held to service or labor in one State, under the laws thereof, escaping into another, shall, in consequence of any law or regulation therein, be discharged from such service or labor, but shall be delivered up on claim of the party to whom such service or labor may be due.

Section 3.   New States may be admitted by the Congress into this Union; but no new State shall be formed or erected within the jurisdiction of any other State; nor any State be formed by the junction of two or more States, or parts of States, without the consent of the legislatures of the States concerned as well as of the Congress.

The Congress shall have power to dispose of and make all needful rules and regulations respecting the territory or other property belonging to the United States; and nothing in this Constitution shall be so construed as to prejudice any claims of the United States, or of any particular State.

Section 4.   The United States shall guarantee to every State in this Union a republican form of government, and shall protect each of them against invasion; and on application of the legislature, or of the executive (when the legislature cannot be convened), against domestic violence.

ARTICLE V

The Congress, whenever two-thirds of both houses shall deem it necessary, shall propose amendments to this Constitution, or, on the application of the legislatures of two-thirds of the several States, shall call a convention for proposing amendments, which, in either case, shall be valid to all intents and purposes, as part of this Constitution, when ratified by the legislatures of three-fourths of the several States, or by conventions in three-fourths thereof, as the one or the other mode of ratification may be proposed by the Congress; provided *that no amendments which may be made prior to the year one thousand eight hundred and eight shall in any manner affect the first and fourth clauses in the ninth section of the first article;* and that no State, without its consent, shall be deprived of its equal suffrage in the Senate.

ARTICLE VI

All debts contracted and engagements entered into, before the adoption of this Constitution, shall be as valid against the United States under this Constitution, as under the Confederation.

This Constitution, and the laws of the United States which shall be made in pursuance thereof; and all treaties made, or which shall be made, under the authority of the United States, shall be the supreme law of the land; and the judges in every State shall be bound thereby, anything in the Constitution or laws of any State to the contrary notwithstanding.

The Senators and Representatives before mentioned, and the members of the several State legislatures, and all executive and judicial officers, both of the United States and of the several States, shall be bound by oath or affirmation to support this Constitution; but no religious test shall ever be required as a qualification to any office or public trust under the United States.

ARTICLE VII

The ratification of the conventions of nine States shall be sufficient for the establishment of this Constitution between the States so ratifying the same.

Done in Convention by the unanimous consent of the States present, the seventeenth day of September in the year of our Lord one thousand seven hundred and eighty-seven and of the Independence of the United States of America the twelfth. In witness whereof we have hereunto subscribed our names.

[Signed by]
G° WASHINGTON
Presidt and Deputy from Virginia
[and thirty-eight others]

Amendments to the Constitution

ARTICLE I*

Congress shall make no law respecting an establishment of religion, or prohibiting the free exercise thereof; or abridging the freedom of speech, or of the press; or the right of the people peaceably to assemble, and to petition the government for a redress of grievances.

ARTICLE II

A well-regulated militia being necessary to the security of a free State, the right of the people to keep and bear arms shall not be infringed.

ARTICLE III

No soldier shall, in time of peace, be quartered in any house without the consent of the owner, nor in time of war, but in a manner to be prescribed by law.

ARTICLE IV

The right of the people to be secure in their persons, houses, papers, and effects, against unreasonable searches and seizures, shall not be violated, and no warrants shall issue but upon probable cause, supported by oath or affirmation, and particularly describing the place to be searched, and the persons or things to be seized.

ARTICLE V

No person shall be held to answer for a capital, or otherwise infamous crime, unless on a presentment or indictment of a grand jury, except in cases arising in the land or naval forces, or in the militia, when in actual service in time of war or public danger; nor shall any person be subject for the same offense to

be twice put in jeopardy of life or limb; nor shall be compelled in any criminal case to be a witness against himself, nor be deprived of life, liberty, or property, without due process of law; nor shall private property be taken for public use without just compensation.

ARTICLE VI

In all criminal prosecutions, the accused shall enjoy the right to a speedy and public trial, by an impartial jury of the State and district wherein the crime shall have been committed, which district shall have been previously ascertained by law, and to be informed of the nature and cause of the accusation; to be confronted with the witnesses against him; to have compulsory process for obtaining witnesses in his favor, and to have the assistance of counsel for his defense.

ARTICLE VII

In suits at common law, where the value in controversy shall exceed twenty dollars, the right of trial by jury shall be preserved, and no fact tried by a jury shall be otherwise reexamined in any court of the United States, than according to the rules of the common law.

ARTICLE VIII

Excessive bail shall not be required, nor excessive fines imposed, nor cruel and unusual punishments inflicted.

ARTICLE IX

The enumeration in the Constitution, of certain rights, shall not be construed to deny or disparage others retained by the people.

*The first ten Amendments (Bill of Rights) were adopted in 1791.

ARTICLE X

The powers not delegated to the United States by the Constitution, not prohibited by it to the States, are reserved to the States respectively, or to the people.

ARTICLE XI   [*Adopted 1798*]

The judicial power of the United States shall not be construed to extend to any suit in law or equity, commenced or prosecuted against one of the United States by citizens of another State, or by citizens or subjects of any foreign state.

ARTICLE XII   [*Adopted 1804*]

The electors shall meet in their respective States, and vote by ballot for President and Vice President, one of whom, at least, shall not be an inhabitant of the same State with themselves; they shall name in their ballots the person voted for as President, and in distinct ballots the person voted for as Vice President, and they shall make distinct lists of all persons voted for as President, and of all persons voted for as Vice President, and of the number of votes for each, which lists they shall sign and certify, and transmit sealed to the seat of government of the United States, directed to the President of the Senate;—the President of the Senate shall, in the presence of the Senate and House of Representatives, open all the certificates and the votes shall then be counted;— the person having the greatest number of votes for President shall be the President, if such number be a majority of the whole number of electors appointed; and if no person have such majority, then from the persons having the highest numbers not exceeding three on the list of those voted for as President, the House of Representatives shall choose immediately, by ballot, the President. But in choosing the President, the votes shall be taken by States, the representation from each State having one vote; a quorum for this purpose shall consist of a member or members from two-thirds of the States, and a majority of all the States shall be necessary to a choice.

And if the House of Representatives shall not choose a President whenever the right of choice shall devolve upon them, before *the fourth day of March* next following, then the Vice President shall act as President, as in the case of the death or other constitutional disability of the President.

The person having the greatest number of votes as Vice President shall be the Vice President, if such a number be a majority of the whole number of electors appointed; and if no person have a majority, then from the two highest numbers on the list the Senate shall choose the Vice President; a quorum for the purpose shall consist of two-thirds of the whole number of Senators, and a majority of the whole number shall be necessary to a choice. But no person constitutionally ineligible to the office of President shall be eligible to that of Vice President of the United States.

ARTICLE XIII   [*Adopted 1865*]

Section 1. Neither slavery nor involuntary servitude, except as a punishment for crime whereof the party shall have been duly convicted, shall exist within the United States, or any place subject to their jurisdiction.

Section 2. Congress shall have power to enforce this article by appropriate legislation.

ARTICLE XIV   [*Adopted 1868*]

Section 1. All persons born or naturalized in the United States, and subject to the jurisdiction thereof, are citizens of the United States and of the State wherein they reside. No State shall make or enforce any law which shall abridge the privileges or immunities of citizens of the United States; nor shall any State deprive any person of life, liberty, or property, without due process of law; nor deny to any person within its jurisdiction the equal protection of the laws.

Section 2. Representatives shall be apportioned among the several States according to their respective numbers, counting the whole number of persons in each State, excluding Indians not taxed. But when the right to vote at any election for the choice of Electors for President and Vice President of the United States, Representatives in Congress, the executive and judicial officers of a State, or the members of the legislature thereof, is denied to any of the male inhabitants of such State, being twenty-one years of age and citizens of the United States, or in any way abridged, except for participation in rebellion, or other crime, the basis of representation therein shall be reduced in the proportion which the number of such male citizens shall bear to the whole number of male citizens twenty-one years of age in such State.

Section 3. No person shall be a Senator or Representative in Congress or Elector of President and Vice President, or hold any office, civil or military, under the United States, or under any State, who, having previously taken an oath, as a member of Congress, or as an officer of the United States, or as a member of any State legislature, or as an executive or judicial officer of any State, to support the Constitution of the United States, shall have engaged in insurrection or rebellion against the same, or given aid and comfort to the enemies thereof. Congress may, by a vote of two-thirds of each house, remove such disability.

Section 4. The validity of the public debt of the United States, authorized by law, including debts incurred for payment of pensions and bounties for services in suppressing insurrection or rebellion, shall not be questioned. But neither the United States nor any State shall assume or pay any debt or obligation incurred in aid of insurrection or rebellion against the United States, or any claim for the loss or emancipation of any slave; but all such debts, obligations, and claims shall be held illegal and void.

Section 5. The Congress shall have the power to enforce, by appropriate legislation, the provisions of this article.

ARTICLE XV [*Adopted 1870*]

Section 1. The right of citizens of the United States to vote shall not be denied or abridged by the United States or by any State on account of race, color, or previous condition of servitude.

Section 2. The Congress shall have power to enforce this article by appropriate legislation.

ARTICLE XVI [*Adopted 1913*]

The Congress shall have power to lay and collect taxes on incomes, from whatever source derived, without apportionment among the several States, and without regard to any census or enumeration.

ARTICLE XVII [*Adopted 1913*]

Section 1. The Senate of the United States shall be composed of two Senators from each State, elected by the people thereof, for six years; and each Senator shall have one vote. The electors in each State shall have the qualifications requisite for electors of [voters for] the most numerous branch of the State legislatures.

Section 2. When vacancies happen in the representation of any State in the Senate, the executive authority of such State shall issue writs of election to fill such vacancies: Provided, that the Legislature of any State may empower the executive thereof to make temporary appointments until the people fill the vacancies by election as the Legislature may direct.

Section 3. This amendment shall not be so construed as to affect the election or term of any Senator chosen before it becomes valid as part of the Constitution.

ARTICLE XVIII [*Adopted 1919; repealed 1933*]

Section 1. *After one year from the ratification of this article the manufacture, sale, or transportation of intoxicating liquors within, the importation thereof into,* *or the exportation thereof from the United States and all territory subject to the jurisdiction thereof, for beverage purposes, is hereby prohibited.*

Section 2.   *The Congress and the several States shall have concurrent power to enforce this article by appropriate legislation.*

Section 3.   *This article shall be inoperative unless it shall have been ratified as an amendment to the Constitution by the legislatures of the several States, as provided by the Constitution, within seven years from the date of the submission thereof to the States by the Congress.*

ARTICLE XIX   [Adopted 1920]

Section 1.   The right of citizens of the United States to vote shall not be denied or abridged by the United States or by any State on account of sex.

Section 2.   The Congress shall have the power to enforce this article by appropriate legislation.

ARTICLE XX   [Adopted 1933]

Section 1.   The terms of the President and Vice President shall end at noon on the 20th day of January, and the terms of Senators and Representatives at noon on the 3d day of January, of the years in which such terms would have ended if this article had not been ratified; and the terms of their successors shall then begin.

Section 2.   The Congress shall assemble at least once in every year, and such meeting shall begin at noon on the 3d day of January, unless they shall by law appoint a different day.

Section 3.   If, at the time fixed for the beginning of the term of the President, the President-elect shall have died, the Vice President-elect shall become President. If a President shall not have been chosen before the time fixed for the beginning of his term, or if the President-elect shall have failed to qualify, then the Vice President-elect shall act as President until a President shall have qualified; and the Congress may by law provide for the case wherein neither a President-elect nor a Vice President-elect shall have qualified, declaring who shall then act as President, or the manner in which one who is to act shall be selected, and such persons shall act accordingly until a President or Vice President shall have qualified.

Section 4.   The Congress may by law provide for the case of the death of any of the persons from whom the House of Representatives may choose a President whenever the right of choice shall have devolved upon them, and for the case of the death of any of the persons from whom the Senate may choose a Vice President whenever the right of choice shall have devolved upon them.

Section 5.   Sections 1 and 2 shall take effect on the 15th day of October following the ratification of this article.

Section 6.   This article shall be inoperative unless it shall have been ratified as an amendment to the Constitution by the Legislatures of three-fourths of the several States within seven years from the date of its submission.

ARTICLE XXI   [Adopted 1933]

Section 1.   The eighteenth article of amendment to the Constitution of the United States is hereby repealed.

Section 2.   The transportation or importation into any State, Territory, or Possession of the United States for delivery or use therein of intoxicating liquors, in violation of the laws thereof, is hereby prohibited.

Section 3.   This article shall be inoperative unless it shall have been ratified as an amendment to the Constitution by conventions in the several States, as provided in the Constitution, within seven years from the date of submission thereof to the States by the Congress.

ARTICLE XXII   [*Adopted 1951*]

Section 1.   No person shall be elected to the office of President more than twice, and no person who has held the office of President, or acted as President, for more than two years of a term to which some other person was elected President shall be elected to the office of President more than once. But this article shall not apply to any person holding the office of President when this article was proposed by the Congress, and shall not prevent any person who may be holding the office of President, or acting as President, during the term within which this article becomes operative from holding the office of President or acting as President during the remainder of such term.

Section 2.   This article shall be inoperative unless it shall have been ratified as an amendment to the Constitution by the legislatures of three-fourths of the several States within seven years from the date of its submission to the States by the Congress.

ARTICLE XXIII   [*Adopted 1961*]

Section 1.   The District constituting the seat of Government of the United States shall appoint in such manner as the Congress may direct:

A number of electors of President and Vice President equal to the whole number of Senators and Representatives in Congress to which the District would be entitled if it were a State, but in no event more than the least populous State; they shall be in addition to those appointed by the States, but they shall be considered for the purposes of the election of President and Vice President, to be electors appointed by a State; and they shall meet in the District and perform such duties as provided by the twelfth article of amendment.

Section 2.   The Congress shall have the power to enforce this article by appropriate legislation.

ARTICLE XXIV   [*Adopted 1964*]

Section 1.   The right of citizens of the United States to vote in any primary or other election for President or Vice President, for electors for President or Vice President, or for Senator or Representative in Congress, shall not be denied or abridged by the United States or any State by reason of failure to pay any poll tax or other tax.

Section 2.   The Congress shall have the power to enforce this article by appropriate legislation.

ARTICLE XXV   [*Adopted 1967*]

Section 1.   In case of the removal of the President from office or of his death or resignation, the Vice President shall become President.

Section 2.   Whenever there is a vacancy in the office of the Vice President, the President shall nominate a Vice President who shall take office upon confirmation by a majority vote of both Houses of Congress.

Section 3.   Whenever the President transmits to the President pro tempore of the Senate and the Speaker of the House of Representatives his written declaration that he is unable to discharge the powers and duties of his office, and until he transmits to them a written declaration to the contrary, such powers and duties shall be discharged by the Vice President as Acting President.

Section 4.   Whenever the Vice President and a majority of either the principal officers of the executive departments or of such other body as Congress may by law provide, transmit to the President pro tempore of the Senate and the Speaker of the House of Representatives their written declaration that the President is unable to discharge the powers and duties of his office, the Vice President shall immediately assume the powers and duties of the office as Acting President.

Thereafter, when the President transmits to the President pro tempore of the Senate and the

Speaker of the House of Representatives his written declaration that no inability exists, he shall resume the powers and duties of his office unless the Vice President and a majority of either the principal officers of the executive department[s] or of such other body as Congress may by law provide, transmit within four days to the President pro tempore of the Senate and the Speaker of the House of Representatives their written declaration that the President is unable to discharge the powers and duties of his office. Thereupon Congress shall decide the issue, assembling within forty-eight hours for that purpose if not in session. If the Congress, within twenty-one days after receipt of the latter written declaration, or, if Congress is not in session, within twenty-one days after Congress is required to assemble, determines by two-thirds vote of both Houses that the President is unable to discharge the powers and duties of his office, the Vice President shall continue to discharge the same as Acting President; otherwise, the President shall resume the powers and duties of his office.

ARTICLE XXVI   [Adopted 1971]

Section 1.   The right of citizens of the United States, who are eighteen years of age or older, to vote shall not be denied or abridged by the United States or by any State on account of age.

Section 2.   The Congress shall have power to enforce this article by appropriate legislation.

ARTICLE XXVII*   [Adopted 1992]

No law, varying the compensation for services of the Senators and Representatives, shall take effect, until an election of Representatives shall have intervened.

---

*Originally proposed in 1789 by James Madison, this amendment failed to win ratification along with the other parts of what became the Bill of Rights. However, the proposed amendment contained no deadline for ratification, and over the years other state legislatures voted to add it to the Constitution; many such ratifications occurred during the 1980s and early 1990s as public frustration with Congress's performance mounted. In May 1992 the Archivist of the United States certified that, with the Michigan legislature's ratification, the article had been approved by three-fourths of the states and thus automatically became part of the Constitution. But congressional leaders and constitutional specialists questioned whether an amendment that took 202 years to win ratification was valid, and the issue had not been resolved by the time this book went to press.

Presidential Elections, 1789–1992

Year	States in the Union	Candidates	Parties	Electoral Vote	Popular Vote	Percentage of Popular Vote
1789	11	GEORGE WASHINGTON	No party designations	69		
		John Adams		34		
		Minor candidates		35		
1792	15	GEORGE WASHINGTON	No party designations	132		
		John Adams		77		
		George Clinton		50		
		Minor candidates		5		
1796	16	JOHN ADAMS	Federalist	71		
		Thomas Jefferson	Democratic-Republican	68		
		Thomas Pinckney	Federalist	59		
		Aaron Burr	Democratic-Republican	30		
		Minor candidates		48		
1800	16	THOMAS JEFFERSON	Democratic-Republican	73		
		Aaron Burr	Democratic-Republican	73		
		John Adams	Federalist	65		
		Charles C. Pinckney	Federalist	64		
		John Jay	Federalist	1		
1804	17	THOMAS JEFFERSON	Democratic-Republican	162		
		Charles C. Pinckney	Federalist	14		
1808	17	JAMES MADISON	Democratic-Republican	122		
		Charles C. Pinckney	Federalist	47		
		George Clinton	Democratic-Republican	6		
1812	18	JAMES MADISON	Democratic-Republican	128		
		DeWitt Clinton	Federalist	89		
1816	19	JAMES MONROE	Democratic-Republican	183		
		Rufus King	Federalist	34		
1820	24	JAMES MONROE	Democratic-Republican	231		
		John Quincy Adams	Independent Republican	1		
1824	24	JOHN QUINCY ADAMS	Democratic-Republican	84	108,740	30.5
		Andrew Jackson	Democratic-Republican	99	153,544	43.1
		William H. Crawford	Democratic-Republican	41	46,618	13.1
		Henry Clay	Democratic-Republican	37	47,136	13.2
1828	24	ANDREW JACKSON	Democratic	178	642,553	56.0
		John Quincy Adams	National Republican	83	500,897	44.0
1832	24	ANDREW JACKSON	Democratic	219	687,502	55.0
		Henry Clay	National Republican	49	530,189	42.4
		William Wirt	Anti-Masonic	7 ⎫	33,108	2.6
		John Floyd	National Republican	11 ⎭		

Because candidates receiving less than 1 percent of the popular vote are omitted, the percentage of popular vote may not total 100 percent.

Before the Twelfth Amendment was passed in 1804, the electoral college voted for two presidential candidates; the runner-up became vice president.

Year	States in the Union	Candidates	Parties	Electoral Vote	Popular Vote	Percentage of Popular Vote
1836	26	MARTIN VAN BUREN	Democratic	170	765,483	50.9
		William H. Harrison	Whig	73		
		Hugh L. White	Whig	26		
		Daniel Webster	Whig	14	739,795	49.1
		W. P. Mangum	Whig	11		
1840	26	WILLIAM H. HARRISON	Whig	234	1,274,624	53.1
		Martin Van Buren	Democratic	60	1,127,781	46.9
1844	26	JAMES K. POLK	Democratic	170	1,338,464	49.6
		Henry Clay	Whig	105	1,300,097	48.1
		James G. Birney	Liberty		62,300	2.3
1848	30	ZACHARY TAYLOR	Whig	163	1,360,967	47.4
		Lewis Cass	Democratic	127	1,222,342	42.5
		Martin Van Buren	Free Soil		291,263	10.1
1852	31	FRANKLIN PIERCE	Democratic	254	1,601,117	50.9
		Winfield Scott	Whig	42	1,385,453	44.1
		John P. Hale	Free Soil		155,825	5.0
1856	31	JAMES BUCHANAN	Democratic	174	1,832,955	45.3
		John C. Frémont	Republican	114	1,339,932	33.1
		Millard Fillmore	American	8	871,731	21.6
1860	33	ABRAHAM LINCOLN	Republican	180	1,865,593	39.8
		Stephen A. Douglas	Democratic	12	1,382,713	29.5
		John C. Breckinridge	Democratic	72	848,356	18.1
		John Bell	Constitutional Union	39	592,906	12.6
1864	36	ABRAHAM LINCOLN	Republican	212	2,206,938	55.0
		George B. McClellan	Democratic	21	1,803,787	45.0
1868	37	ULYSSES S. GRANT	Republican	214	3,013,421	52.7
		Horatio Seymour	Democratic	80	2,706,829	47.3
1872	37	ULYSSES S. GRANT	Republican	286	3,596,745	55.6
		Horace Greeley	Democratic	*	2,843,446	43.9
1876	38	RUTHERFORD B. HAYES	Republican	185	4,034,311	48.0
		Samuel J. Tilden	Democratic	184	4,288,546	51.0
		Peter Cooper	Greenback		75,973	1.0
1880	38	JAMES A. GARFIELD	Republican	214	4,453,295	48.5
		Winfield S. Hancock	Democratic	155	4,414,082	48.1
		James B. Weaver	Greenback-Labor		308,578	3.4
1884	38	GROVER CLEVELAND	Democratic	219	4,879,507	48.5
		James G. Blaine	Republican	182	4,850,293	48.2
		Benjamin F. Butler	Greenback-Labor		175,370	1.8
		John P. St. John	Prohibition		150,369	1.5

*When Greeley died shortly after the election, his supporters divided their votes among the minor candidates. Because candidates receiving less than 1 percent of the popular vote are omitted, the percentage of popular vote may not total 100 percent.

Year	States in the Union	Candidates	Parties	Electoral Vote	Popular Vote	Percentage of Popular Vote
1888	38	BENJAMIN HARRISON	Republican	233	5,477,129	47.9
		Grover Cleveland	Democratic	168	5,537,857	48.6
		Clinton B. Fisk	Prohibition		249,506	2.2
		Anson J. Streeter	Union Labor		146,935	1.3
1892	44	GROVER CLEVELAND	Democratic	277	5,555,426	46.1
		Benjamin Harrison	Republican	145	5,182,690	43.0
		James B. Weaver	People's	22	1,029,846	8.5
		John Bidwell	Prohibition		264,133	2.2
1896	45	WILLIAM McKINLEY	Republican	271	7,102,246	51.1
		William J. Bryan	Democratic	176	6,492,559	47.7
1900	45	WILLIAM McKINLEY	Republican	292	7,218,491	51.7
		William J. Bryan	Democratic; Populist	155	6,356,734	45.5
		John C. Wooley	Prohibition		208,914	1.5
1904	45	THEODORE ROOSEVELT	Republican	336	7,628,461	57.4
		Alton B. Parker	Democratic	140	5,084,223	37.6
		Eugene V. Debs	Socialist		402,283	3.0
		Silas C. Swallow	Prohibition		258,536	1.9
1908	46	WILLIAM H. TAFT	Republican	321	7,675,320	51.6
		William J. Bryan	Democratic	162	6,412,294	43.1
		Eugene V. Debs	Socialist		420,793	2.8
		Eugene W. Chafin	Prohibition		253,840	1.7
1912	48	WOODROW WILSON	Democratic	435	6,296,547	41.9
		Theodore Roosevelt	Progressive	88	4,118,571	27.4
		William H. Taft	Republican	8	3,486,720	23.2
		Eugene V. Debs	Socialist		900,672	6.0
		Eugene W. Chafin	Prohibition		206,275	1.4
1916	48	WOODROW WILSON	Democratic	277	9,127,695	49.4
		Charles E. Hughes	Republican	254	8,533,507	46.2
		A. L. Benson	Socialist		585,113	3.2
		J. Frank Hanly	Prohibition		220,506	1.2
1920	48	WARREN G. HARDING	Republican	404	16,143,407	60.4
		James N. Cox	Democratic	127	9,130,328	34.2
		Eugene V. Debs	Socialist		919,799	3.4
		P. P. Christensen	Farmer-Labor		265,411	1.0
1924	48	CALVIN COOLIDGE	Republican	382	15,718,211	54.0
		John W. Davis	Democratic	136	8,385,283	28.8
		Robert M. La Follette	Progressive	13	4,831,289	16.6
1928	48	HERBERT C. HOOVER	Republican	444	21,391,993	58.2
		Alfred E. Smith	Democratic	87	15,016,169	40.9

Because candidates receiving less than 1 percent of the popular vote are omitted, the percentage of popular vote may not total 100 percent.

Year	States in the Union	Candidates	Parties	Electoral Vote	Popular Vote	Percentage of Popular Vote
1932	48	FRANKLIN D. ROOSEVELT	Democratic	472	22,809,638	57.4
		Herbert C. Hoover	Republican	59	15,758,901	39.7
		Norman Thomas	Socialist		881,951	2.2
1936	48	FRANKLIN D. ROOSEVELT	Democratic	523	27,752,869	60.8
		Alfred M. Landon	Republican	8	16,674,665	36.5
		William Lemke	Union		882,479	1.9
1940	48	FRANKLIN D. ROOSEVELT	Democratic	449	27,307,819	54.8
		Wendell L. Willkie	Republican	82	22,321,018	44.8
1944	48	FRANKLIN D. ROOSEVELT	Democratic	432	25,606,585	53.5
		Thomas E. Dewey	Republican	99	22,014,745	46.0
1948	48	HARRY S TRUMAN	Democratic	303	24,105,812	49.5
		Thomas E. Dewey	Republican	189	21,970,065	45.1
		Strom Thurmond	States' Rights	39	1,169,063	2.4
		Henry A. Wallace	Progressive		1,157,172	2.4
1952	48	DWIGHT D. EISENHOWER	Republican	442	33,936,234	55.1
		Adlai E. Stevenson	Democratic	89	27,314,992	44.4
1956	48	DWIGHT D. EISENHOWER	Republican	457	35,590,472	57.6
		Adlai E. Stevenson	Democratic	73	26,022,752	42.1
1960	50	JOHN F. KENNEDY	Democratic	303	34,227,096	49.7
		Richard M. Nixon	Republican	219	34,108,546	49.5
		Harry F. Byrd	Independent	15	502,363	.7
1964	50	LYNDON B. JOHNSON	Democratic	486	43,126,506	61.1
		Barry M. Goldwater	Republican	52	27,176,799	38.5
1968	50	RICHARD M. NIXON	Republican	301	31,770,237	43.4
		Hubert H. Humphrey	Democratic	191	31,270,533	42.7
		George C. Wallace	American Independent	46	9,906,141	13.5
1972	50	RICHARD M. NIXON	Republican	520	47,169,911	60.7
		George S. McGovern	Democratic	17	29,170,383	37.5
1976	50	JIMMY CARTER	Democratic	297	40,827,394	49.9
		Gerald R. Ford	Republican	240	39,145,977	47.9
1980	50	RONALD W. REAGAN	Republican	489	43,899,248	50.8
		Jimmy Carter	Democratic	49	35,481,435	41.0
		John B. Anderson	Independent		5,719,437	6.6
		Ed Clark	Libertarian		920,859	1.0
1984	50	RONALD W. REAGAN	Republican	525	54,451,521	58.8
		Walter F. Mondale	Democratic	13	37,565,334	40.5
1988	50	GEORGE H. W. BUSH	Republican	426	47,946,422	54.0
		Michael S. Dukakis	Democratic	112	41,016,429	46.0
1992	50	WILLIAM J. CLINTON	Democratic	370	43,728,275	43.2
		George H. W. Bush	Republican	168	38,167,416	37.7
		H. Ross Perot	Independent		19,237,247	19.0

Because candidates receiving less than 1 percent of the popular vote are omitted, the percentage of popular vote may not total 100 percent.

Supreme Court Justices

Name	Terms of Service	Appointed By
JOHN JAY	1789–1795	Washington
James Wilson	1789–1798	Washington
John Rutledge	1790–1791	Washington
William Cushing	1790–1810	Washington
John Blair	1790–1796	Washington
James Iredell	1790–1799	Washington
Thomas Johnson	1792–1793	Washington
William Paterson	1793–1806	Washington
JOHN RUTLEDGE*	1795	Washington
Samuel Chase	1796–1811	Washington
OLIVER ELLSWORTH	1796–1800	Washington
Bushrod Washington	1799–1829	J. Adams
Alfred Moore	1800–1804	J. Adams
JOHN MARSHALL	1801–1835	J. Adams
William Johnson	1804–1834	Jefferson
Brockholst Livingston	1807–1823	Jefferson
Thomas Todd	1807–1826	Jefferson
Gabriel Duvall	1811–1835	Madison
Joseph Story	1812–1845	Madison
Smith Thompson	1823–1843	Monroe
Robert Trimble	1826–1828	J. Q. Adams
John McLean	1830–1861	Jackson
Henry Baldwin	1830–1844	Jackson
James M. Wayne	1835–1867	Jackson
ROGER B. TANEY	1836–1864	Jackson
Philip P. Barbour	1836–1841	Jackson
John Cartron	1837–1865	Van Buren
John McKinley	1838–1852	Van Buren
Peter V. Daniel	1842–1860	Van Buren
Samuel Nelson	1845–1872	Tyler
Levi Woodbury	1845–1851	Polk
Robert C. Grier	1846–1870	Polk
Benjamin R. Curtis	1851–1857	Fillmore
John A. Campbell	1853–1861	Pierce
Nathan Clifford	1858–1881	Buchanan
Noah H. Swayne	1862–1881	Lincoln
Samuel F. Miller	1862–1890	Lincoln
David Davis	1862–1877	Lincoln
Stephen J. Field	1863–1897	Lincoln
SALMON P. CHASE	1864–1873	Lincoln

NOTE: The names of Chief Justices are printed in capital letters.

*Although Rutledge acted as Chief Justice, the Senate refused to confirm his appointment.

Name	Terms of Service	Appointed By
William Strong	1870–1880	Grant
Joseph P. Bradley	1870–1892	Grant
Ward Hunt	1873–1882	Grant
MORRISON R. WAITE	1874–1888	Grant
John M. Harlan	1877–1911	Hayes
William B. Woods	1881–1887	Hayes
Stanley Matthews	1881–1889	Garfield
Horace Gray	1882–1902	Arthur
Samuel Blatchford	1882–1893	Arthur
Lucious Q. C. Lamar	1888–1893	Cleveland
MELVILLE W. FULLER	1888–1910	Cleveland
David J. Brewer	1890–1910	B. Harrison
Henry B. Brown	1891–1906	B. Harrison
George Shiras, Jr.	1892–1903	B. Harrison
Howell E. Jackson	1893–1895	B. Harrison
Edward D. White	1894–1910	Cleveland
Rufus W. Peckham	1896–1909	Cleveland
Joseph McKenna	1898–1925	McKinley
Oliver W. Holmes	1902–1932	T. Roosevelt
William R. Day	1903–1922	T. Roosevelt
William H. Moody	1906–1910	T. Roosevelt
Horace H. Lurton	1910–1914	Taft
Charles E. Hughes	1910–1916	Taft
EDWARD D. WHITE	1910–1921	Taft
Willis Van Devanter	1911–1937	Taft
Joseph R. Lamar	1911–1916	Taft
Mahlon Pitney	1912–1922	Taft
James C. McReynolds	1914–1941	Wilson
Louis D. Brandeis	1916–1939	Wilson
John H. Clarke	1916–1922	Wilson
WILLIAM H. TAFT	1921–1930	Harding
George Sutherland	1922–1938	Harding
Pierce Butler	1923–1939	Harding
Edward T. Sanford	1923–1930	Harding
Harlan F. Stone	1925–1941	Coolidge
CHARLES E. HUGHES	1930–1941	Hoover
Owen J. Roberts	1930–1945	Hoover
Benjamin N. Cardozo	1932–1938	Hoover
Hugo L. Black	1937–1971	F. Roosevelt
Stanley F. Reed	1938–1957	F. Roosevelt
Felix Frankfurter	1939–1962	F. Roosevelt
William O. Douglas	1939–1975	F. Roosevelt
Frank Murphy	1940–1949	F. Roosevelt
HARLAN F. STONE	1941–1946	F. Roosevelt

Name	Terms of Service	Appointed By
James F. Byrnes	1941–1942	F. Roosevelt
Robert H. Jackson	1941–1954	F. Roosevelt
Wiley B. Rutledge	1943–1949	F. Roosevelt
Harold H. Burton	1945–1958	Truman
FREDERICK M. VINSON	1946–1953	Truman
Tom C. Clark	1949–1967	Truman
Sherman Minton	1949–1956	Truman
EARL WARREN	1953–1969	Eisenhower
John Marshall Harlan	1955–1971	Eisenhower
William J. Brennan, Jr.	1956–1990	Eisenhower
Charles E. Whittaker	1957–1962	Eisenhower
Potter Stewart	1958–1981	Eisenhower
Byron R. White	1962–1993	Kennedy
Arthur J. Goldberg	1962–1965	Kennedy
Abe Fortas	1965–1970	L. Johnson
Thurgood Marshall	1967–1991	L. Johnson
WARREN E. BURGER	1969–1986	Nixon
Harry A. Blackmun	1970–1994	Nixon
Lewis F. Powell, Jr.	1971–1987	Nixon
William H. Rehnquist	1971–1986	Nixon
John Paul Stevens	1975–	Ford
Sandra Day O'Connor	1981–	Reagan
WILLIAM H. REHNQUIST	1986–	Reagan
Antonin Scalia	1986–	Reagan
Anthony Kennedy	1988–	Reagan
David Souter	1990–	Bush
Clarence Thomas	1991–	Bush
Ruth Bader Ginsburg	1993–	Clinton

Growth of U.S. Population and Area

| Census | Population of United States | Increase over the Preceding Census | | Land Area (Sq. Mi.) | Pop. Per. Sq. Mi. | Percentage of Pop. in Urban and Rural Territory | |
		Number	Percentage			Urban	Rural
1790	3,929,214			867,980	4.5	5.1	94.9
1800	5,308,483	1,379,269	35.1	867,980	6.1	6.1	93.9
1810	7,239,881	1,931,398	36.4	1,685,865	4.3	7.2	92.8
1820	9,638,453	2,398,572	33.1	1,753,588	5.5	7.2	92.8
1830	12,866,020	3,227,567	33.5	1,753,588	7.3	8.8	91.2
1840	17,069,453	4,203,433	32.7	1,753,588	9.7	10.8	89.2
1850	23,191,876	6,122,423	35.9	2,944,337	7.9	15.3	84.7
1860	31,433,321	8,251,445	35.6	2,973,965	10.6	19.8	80.2
1870	39,818,449	8,375,128	26.6	2,973,965	13.4	24.9	75.1
1880	50,155,783	10,337,334	26.0	2,973,965	16.9	28.2	71.8
1890	62,947,714	12,791,931	25.5	2,973,965	21.2	35.1	64.9
1900	75,994,575	13,046,861	20.7	2,974,159	25.6	39.7	60.3
1910	91,972,266	15,997,691	21.0	2,973,890	30.9	45.7	54.3
1920	105,710,620	13,738,354	14.9	2,973,776	35.5	51.2	48.8
1930	122,775,046	17,064,426	16.1	2,977,128	41.2	56.2	43.8
1940	131,669,275	8,894,229	7.2	2,977,128	44.2	56.5	43.5
1950	150,697,361	19,028,086	14.5	2,974,726*	50.7	64.0	36.0
1960†	179,323,175	28,625,814	19.0	3,540,911	50.6	69.9	30.1
1970	203,235,298	23,912,123	13.3	3,536,855	57.5	73.5	26.5
1980	226,504,825	23,269,527	11.4	3,536,855	64.0	73.7	26.3
1990	249,975,000	22,164,068	9.8	3,536,855	70.3	N.A.	N.A.

*As measured in 1940; shrinkage offset by increase in water area.
†First year for which figures include Alaska and Hawaii.

SOURCE: Census Bureau, *Historical Statistics of the United States*, updated by relevant *Statistical Abstract of the United States*.

Admission of States into the Union

State	Date of Admission	State	Date of Admission
1. Delaware	December 7, 1787	26. Michigan	January 26, 1837
2. Pennsylvania	December 12, 1787	27. Florida	March 3, 1845
3. New Jersey	December 18, 1787	28. Texas	December 29, 1845
4. Georgia	January 2, 1788	29. Iowa	December 28, 1846
5. Connecticut	January 9, 1788	30. Wisconsin	May 29, 1848
6. Massachusetts	February 6, 1788	31. California	September 9, 1850
7. Maryland	April 28, 1788	32. Minnesota	May 11, 1858
8. South Carolina	May 23, 1788	33. Oregon	February 14, 1859
9. New Hampshire	June 21, 1788	34. Kansas	January 29, 1861
10. Virginia	June 25, 1788	35. West Virginia	June 20, 1863
11. New York	July 26, 1788	36. Nevada	October 31, 1864
12. North Carolina	November 21, 1789	37. Nebraska	March 1, 1867
13. Rhode Island	May 29, 1790	38. Colorado	August 1, 1876
14. Vermont	March 4, 1791	39. North Dakota	November 2, 1889
15. Kentucky	June 1, 1792	40. South Dakota	November 2, 1889
16. Tennessee	June 1, 1796	41. Montana	November 8, 1889
17. Ohio	March 1, 1803	42. Washington	November 11, 1889
18. Louisiana	April 30, 1812	43. Idaho	July 3, 1890
19. Indiana	December 11, 1816	44. Wyoming	July 10, 1890
20. Mississippi	December 10, 1817	45. Utah	January 4, 1896
21. Illinois	December 3, 1818	46. Oklahoma	November 16, 1907
22. Alabama	December 14, 1819	47. New Mexico	January 6, 1912
23. Maine	March 15, 1820	48. Arizona	February 14, 1912
24. Missouri	August 10, 1821	49. Alaska	January 3, 1959
25. Arkansas	June 15, 1836	50. Hawaii	August 21, 1959

Profile of the U.S. Population

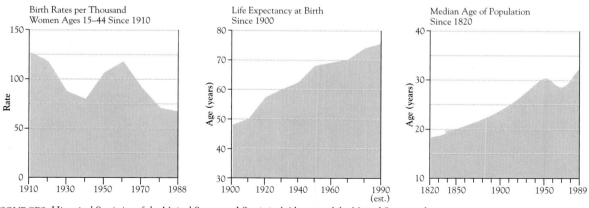

SOURCES: *Historical Statistics of the United States* and *Statistical Abstract of the United States*, relevant years.

Political and Physical Map of the United States

Puget Sound

WASH.

Olympia ★

Mt. Rainier ▲

CASCADE MTS.

COLUMBIA

Columbia R.

PLATEAU

Salem ★

OREGON

IDAHO

★ Boise

Snake R.

ROCKY

MOUNTAINS

HIGH PLAINS

MONTANA

Helena ★

GREAT PLAINS

Red River of the North

N. DAKOTA

Bismarck ★

MINN.

Pierre ★

S. DAKOTA

WYOMING

FRONT RANGE

NEBRASKA

Cheyenne ★

Platte R.

IOWA

M

Lincoln ★

COASTAL RANGES

SIERRA NEVADA

Central Valley

GREAT BASIN

Great Salt Lake

Salt Lake City ★

NEVADA

UTAH

Carson City ★

Sacramento ★

Mt. Whitney ▲

CALIFORNIA

Colorado R.

Grand Canyon

ARIZONA

Phoenix ★

Gila R.

Mesa Verde ▲

COLO.

Denver ★

Santa Fe ★

NEW MEXICO

Arkansas R.

KANSAS

Topeka ★

OKLA.

Oklahoma City ★

Red R.

Rio Grande

TEXAS

Austin ★

S

PACIFIC OCEAN

Extent of Continental Shelf

MEXICO

Arctic Circle

Bering Strait

ARCTIC OCEAN

BROOKS RANGE

Yukon R.

Mt. McKinley (Denali) ▲

ALASKA RANGE

Ancient Alaska-Siberia land bridge

Juneau ★

ALASKA

N. PACIFIC OCEAN

Niihau

Kauai

Oahu

Honolulu ★

Molokai

Lanai

Maui

Mauna Kea ▲

PACIFIC OCEAN

HAWAII

Hawaii

CANADA

L. Superior

L. Michigan

L. Huron

L. Ontario

L. Erie

WIS.

Paul

Madison ★

MICH.

Lansing ★

AIRIE
AINS

O.

ferson
City

uri R.

Springfield ★

Wabash R.

Indianapolis ★

ILL.

IND.

OHIO

Columbus ★

Ohio R.

Frankfort ★

KY.

ARK
TEAU

Little
Rock ★

K.

Nashville ★

TENN.

Tennessee R.

A.

MISS.

Jackson ★

ALA.

Montgomery ★

Mississippi R.

H

aton Rouge ★

sippi Delta

Gulf of Mexico

W.VA.

Charleston ★

APPALACHIAN   MTS.

PIEDMONT

PA.

Harrisburg ★

Susquehanna R.

Trenton ★

N.J.

Dover ★

Delaware R.

Delaware Bay

MD.

Annapolis ★

DEL.

VA.

Potomac R.

Richmond ★

Chesapeake Bay

N.C.

Raleigh ★

TIDEWATER

S.C.

Columbia ★

Savannah R.

Atlanta ★

GA.

COASTAL   PLAIN

Tallahassee ★

FLA.

Everglades

Adirondack
Mts.

N.Y.

Albany ★

Niagara
Falls

Hudson R.

ME.

Augusta ★

VT.

Montpelier ★

Concord ★

N.H.

MASS.

Boston ★

Cape Cod

Hartford ★

R.I.

Providence ★

Long I.

CONN.

St. Lawrence R.

Grand
Banks

ATLANTIC
OCEAN

GULF STREAM

Cape Hatteras

Extent of
Continental Shelf

0   500 Miles

0   500 Kilometers

ATLANTIC OCEAN

San Juan ★

PUERTO RICO

San Salvador
(Watling I.)

Over 10,000 feet

1,000 – 10,000 feet

500 – 1,000 feet

Sea level – 500 feet

Photograph Credits

Chapter 16   p. 335: Library of Congress; p. 345: Granger Collection; p. 346: Cook Collection/Valentine Museum.

Chapter 17   p. 361: DeGolyer Library/Southern Methodist University; p. 367: National Anthropological Archives/NMNH/Smithsonian Institution; p. 374: Rose Collection, Western History Collections/University of Oklahoma; p. 375: Library of Congress.

Chapter 18   p. 383: Library of Congress; p. 384: Library of Congress; p. 390: U.S. Dept. of the Interior, National Park Service, Edison National Historic Site; p. 393: Library of Congress; p. 399: Library of Congress.

Chapter 19   p. 405: Bettmann Archive; p. 409: Statue of Liberty National Monument, National Park Service; p. 415: Harper's Weekly; p. 418: Jane Adams Memorial Collection, University of Illinois at Chicago Circle.

Chapter 20   p. 425: The Strong Museum, Rochester, New York c. 1885; p. 428: AT&T Archives; p. 435: Henry Ford Museum & Greenfield Village; p. 438: North Wind Picture Archives; p. 441: Ticor Collection, San Diego Historical Society.

Chapter 21   p. 445: Library of Congress; p. 447: Watertown Historical Society; p. 458: Division of Political History, Smithsonian Institution; p. 465: California Museum of Photography, University of California, Riverside.

Chapter 22   p. 469: Museum of American Textile History; p. 470: California Historical Society; p. 479: Bettmann Archive; p. 483: Bettmann Archive; p. 487: Library of Congress.

Chapter 23   p. 495: Collection of Picture Research Consultants; p. 504: National Archives; p. 511: Granger Collection.

Chapter 24   p. 517: Library of Congress; p. 519: Bettmann Archive; p. 527: Bettmann Archive; p. 529: Chicago Historical Society; p. 532: Bettmann Archive.

Chapter 25   p. 539: FDR Library; p. 542: Ivan E. Prall; p. 557: Library of Congress.

Chapter 26   p. 561: Wide World Photos; p. 566: Dick Whittington; p. 569: Bettmann Archive; p. 574: Granger Collection.

Chapter 27   p. 581: National Archives; p. 582: Bettmann/UPI Newsphotos; p. 592: FPG International; p. 595: US Army; p. 598: Bettmann/UPI Newsphotos.

Chapter 28   p. 607: Historical Pictures Collection/Stock Montage, Inc.; p. 610: Wide World Photos; p. 610 (inset): Bettmann/UPI Newsphotos; p. 617: UPI/Bettmann; p. 622: UPI/Bettmann; p. 624: UPI/Bettmann.

Chapter 29   p. 629: Bernard Hoffman/Life Picture Service; p. 637: UPI/Bettmann; p. 640: Bruce Wrighton ©/Laurence Miller Gallery; p. 645 (left): Magnum Photos; p. 645 (right): Magnum Photos.

Chapter 30   p. 651: Wide World Photos; p. 654: Fred Ward/Black Star; p. 655: Charles Moore/Black Star; p. 656: Magnum Photos; p. 666: Fusco/Magnum Photos; p. 671: UPI/Bettmann.

Chapter 31   p. 673: Larry Burrows/Life Picture Service; p. 676: Wide World Photos; p. 683: C. Simonpietri/Sygma; p. 686: Sygma.

Chapter 32   p. 697: Henri Bureau/Sygma; p. 701: Paul Howell; p. 704: Paul Szep/Boston Globe; p. 708: Ronald Reagan Presidential Library.

Chapter 33   p. 717: Sygma; p. 719: Ronald Reagan Presidential Library; p. 729: UPI/Bettmann Newsphotos; p. 733: Wally McNamee/Sygma.

Index

A&P, 427, 520

A & W Root Beer, 525

Abilene (Kansas), 376, 377

Abortion: during 1960–1970, 679; during 1970–1980, 699; during 1990–1992, 730–731; legalization of, 679, 699; Supreme Court and, 679, 699, 730–731

Absalom, Absalom! (Faulkner), 571

Acheson, Dean, 613, 625, 680

Adamson Act (1916), 491

Addams, Jane, 418–419, 465, 475, 500, 507, 524

Adventures of Huckleberry Finn (Twain), 379, 437

Advertising: during 1920–1929, 520; during 1930–1940, 562; during 1950–1960, 609, 643, 644; by the flour industry, 391; product merchandising and use of, 427, 520; World War I and, 501, 505–506

Affluent Society, The (Galbraith), 637

Afghanistan, Soviets and, 711, 720

AFL. *See* American Federation of Labor

Africa, World War II and fighting in North, 596

African Methodist Episcopal Church, 347, 472

African National Congress, 725

Afro-American Council, 481

Agee, James, 571

Agency for International Development, 657

Age of Aquarius, 678

Agnew, Spiro, 692, 694

Agricultural Adjustment Act (1933), 546, 552, 558

Agricultural Adjustment Act (1938), 551, 558

Agricultural Adjustment Administration (AAA) (1933), 546, 548

Agriculture: alliance movement, 452–453; depression of 1893–1897 and, 457; depression of 1929 and, 541; dry farming, 371; during 1860–1900, 348, 378, 452–453; during 1920–1929, 521, 525, 541; during 1930–1940, 546, 548, 551–552, 555, 557, 558; during 1940–1945, 588; during 1950–1960, 639; during 1980–1990, 710; dust bowl of 1930–1935, 548; farm aid during 1900–1920, 491; Farmers' Holiday Association, 543; Grange, 372–373; impact of railroads on, 370; impact of technology on, 370, 525; New Deal and, 546, 548, 551–552, 555, 557, 558; Reconstruction and land, labor, and sharecropping, 347–348; strikes by agricultural workers, 565–566, 666; white racism and agrarian protest, 454; World War I and, 508. *See also under type of crop*

Aguinaldo, Emilio, 465

AIDS (acquired immune deficiency syndrome), 703

Airforce, World War II and U.S., 585, 586

Airplanes, World War I, 503

Air pollution, 654, 730

Alabama (Confederate ship), 351

Alamo, 571

Alaska, purchase of, 351

Albania, Nazi invasion of, 577

Alcatraz Island, Native American takeover of, 702

Alcohol: Native Americans and, 367. *See also* Temperance

Aldrin, Buzz, 653

Alger, Horatio, 397, 412

Alianza, 666

Allen, Fred, 568, 644

Allen, Gracie, 568

Allende, Salvador, 688

Alliance for Progress, 657

Alliance movement, 452–453

Altgeld, John Peter, 401

"American Bandstand," 649

American Civil Liberties Union (ACLU), 534

American Dilemma, An (Myrdal), 594

American Expeditionary Force (AEF), 502–505

American Express, 640

American Federation of Labor (AFL): blacks in, 455, 520; creation of, 398, 400; during 1900–1920, 473; during 1930–1940, 563; merged with the CIO, 639; World War I and, 508

American Future, 689